D1258829

ALSO BY LOU CANNON

President Reagan: The Role of a Lifetime
Reagan
Reporting: An Inside View
The McCloskey Challenge
Ronnie and Jesse: A Political Odyssey

OFFICIAL
NEGLIGENCE

OFFICIAL NEGLIGENCE

How Rodney King
and the Riots
Changed Los Angeles
and the LAPD

LOU CANNON

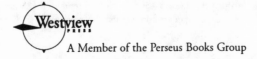

Westview
PRESS

A Member of the Perseus Books Group

All rights reserved. Printed in the United States of America. No part of this publication
may be reproduced or transmitted in any form or by any means, electronic or mechanical,
including photocopy, recording, or any information storage and retrieval system, without
permission in writing from the publisher.

Copyright © 1999 by Lou Cannon

Published in 1999 in the United States of America by Westview Press, 5500 Central
Avenue, Boulder, Colorado 80301-2877, and in the United Kingdom by Westview Press,
12 Hid's Copse Road, Cumnor Hill, Oxford OX2 9JJ.

First published by Times Books, a division of Random House, Inc., New York.

A CIP record for this book is available from the Library of Congress.
ISBN 0-8133-3725-9

The paper used in this publication meets the requirements of the American National
Standard for Permanence of Paper for Printed Library Materials Z39.48-1984.

10 9 8 7 6 5 4 3 2 1

To Mary Shinkwin Cannon,
my wife, collaborator, and bulwark,
and to
Jaxon Van Derbeken,
reporter and friend,
with appreciation

"It was the city that failed. . . . It was police management, past and present, that has failed. This has to be taken into account to reflect a just and fair sentence. . . . There simply has to be some allowance for the official negligence of the city which allowed this to take place and which will take place again."

—Attorney Ira Salzman at the sentencing of
Sergeant Stacey Koon, August 4, 1993

Acknowledgments

WRITERS ARE IN PERPETUAL DEBT, AND MY DEBTS FOR THIS BOOK are enormous. What began as a two-year project took five years and would never have been completed except for the dedication and contributions of my wife, Mary Shinkwin Cannon, and Jaxon Van Derbeken, a fine reporter who covered the Los Angeles Police Department with distinction for the Los Angeles *Daily News* and now works for the *San Francisco Chronicle*. Mary did the research, transcribed the interviews, prepared the chapter notes and the bibliography, and served as editor, critic, and friend. Jaxon conducted more than eighty interviews, mainly of LAPD officers, and shared his extensive knowledge of police issues.

I am also indebted to Jim Newton of the *Los Angeles Times*, whose excellent coverage of the LAPD and the federal trial of the so-called Rodney King officers set a high journalistic standard. Jim generously shared his insights into the LAPD and encouraged me to do this book.

Several friends read the manuscript, caught mistakes, and gave counsel. The acclaimed historian William Lee Miller, who read three of my previous books in manuscript, again struggled to salvage my grammar and add clarity. Jud Clark, who long ago helped on the manuscript of my first book, also improved this one. My eldest son, Carl Cannon of *The Sun* of Baltimore, made helpful suggestions.

When this book began, I was Los Angeles bureau chief for *The Washington Post*, for which I covered the two criminal trials resulting from the 1991 Rodney King incident and the 1992 riots. Leonard Downie, executive editor of *The Post*, and Karen DeYoung, assistant managing editor of the national staff, were consistently supportive, even when the book took much longer than anticipated. So were Alan Shearer, editorial director of The Washington Post Writers Group, which syndicated my column for many years, and Anna Karavangelos, the associate editor.

Two former news aides in the Los Angeles bureau of *The Post*, good reporters and friends, deserve special thanks. Leef Smith, who made valuable contributions to the riot coverage, interviewed jurors after the state trial of the LAPD officers. Jessica Crosby Young interviewed jurors after the trial resulting from the Reginald Denny beating and interviewed LAPD officers for a story we did together. I drew upon these interviews.

Many staff members at *The Washington Post*, which has been my professional home since 1972, helped in various ways, especially Joan Biskupic, Bill Claiborne, Bill Elsen, Bill Hamilton, Robert Kaiser, Jay Mathews, Tom Wilkinson, and Bob Woodward.

Thanks also to Kim Arrington, Jennifer Belton, Michael duCille, Sheryl Rosenthal, and Joe Weatherford of *The Washington Post* for assistance in obtaining photographs. For photographs obtained from the Los Angeles *Daily News*, my thanks to Edna Trunnell and Dean Musgrove. For photographs obtained from the *Los Angeles Times*, my thanks to Carol Stogsdill.

Bill Boyarsky, an eminent columnist for the *Los Angeles Times*, shared his insights into the LAPD. I also appreciate the assistance of Barbara Murphy, who with Dawn Webber covered the first King trial for the *Daily News*. Warren Cereghino explained why KTLA used the videotape of the King beating as it did. Ed Turner and David Farmer of CNN, John Siegenthaler of the Freedom Forum, and Daniel Amundson and Robert Lichter of the Center for Media and Public Affairs provided additional information on videotape use. Ken Reich of the *Los Angeles Times*, a biographer of Peter Ueberroth, shared his insights. Thanks also to Bart Bartholomew, a free-lance photographer for *The New York Times*; Warren Olney of KCRW; Jim Tranquada, formerly of the *Daily News*, and Lyle Gregory, producer of the *Michael Jackson Show* on KABC radio.

Many lawyers were involved in the four criminal trials examined in this book, and most of them were cooperative. Three gave special assistance. Harland Braun, a premier Los Angeles defense attorney who represented Ted Briseno in the federal civil rights trial, helped on many legal and political issues. Former Assistant U.S. Attorney Steven Clymer, an exceptional prosecutor, explained the case from the government's perspective. Former Los Angeles County District Attorney Ira Reiner analyzed key issues in the state prosecution of the officers. I am also indebted to Braun's secretary, January King.

Two chapters examine *People v. Soon Ja Du*, in which a Korean woman was tried for killing a black teenager. Reiner also helped analyze this case. I appreciate Judge Joyce Karlin's candor in explaining the reasons for her sentence, and the assistance of the competing attorneys: Deputy District Attorney Roxane Carvajal and defense attorneys Charles Lloyd and Richard Leonard. Leon Jenkins, civil attorney for the Harlins family and Gina Rae, a family friend, helped. So did Glenn Britton, the deputy district attorney who prepared the appeal of the sentence, and Andrea Ford, who covered the trial for the *Los Angeles Times*.

Prosecutors and defense attorneys in the state trial of the King officers, *People v. Powell*, shared their analyses. They were Terry White and Alan Yochelson, Los Angeles County deputy district attorneys, and defense lawyers Michael Stone, Darryl Mounger, Paul DePasquale and John Barnett. Stone also represented Officer Laurence Powell in the federal trial and was again helpful. Roger Gunson, then chief deputy of the Special Investigations Division of the Los Angeles District Attorney's Office, gave an especially valuable interview.

Superior Court Judge Stanley Weisberg, who presided at the state trial, declined to be interviewed but responded by letter to some of my questions. Joan Dempsey Klein, presiding justice of the Second District of the California Court of Appeal, gave a candid interview explaining why she granted a change of venue. Attorney Patrick Thistle, who sought the venue change, was helpful.

In the federal trial of the officers, *United States v. Koon*, attorneys for both sides assisted. In addition to Clymer the prosecutors included Barry Kowalski and Alan Tieger of the Department of Justice, and Lawrence Middleton of the U.S. attorney's office in Los Angeles. Kowalski, well-known for his prosecution of civil rights cases, provided a broad historical perspective. For the defense, Ira Salzman replaced Mounger as attorney for Stacey Koon and gave much assistance, as did his aide, Kelly Hart. Attorney William Kopeny was especially helpful on matters relating to appeal of this case. I appreciate the insights of Dan Caplis, a Denver lawyer and television commentator, and of Laurie Levenson, a Loyola Law School professor and former federal prosecutor who monitored the federal criminal and the federal civil trial arising from a lawsuit filed by Rodney King.

Three federal judges helped me better understand the issues of the criminal trial. My thanks especially to U.S. District Court Judge John G. Davies, who presided over this sensitive trial with skill and fairness. Judge Betty Binns Fletcher of the U.S. Court of Appeals for the Ninth Circuit discussed her reasoning in the appeal of this case. Judge Stephen Reinhardt, also of the Ninth Circuit, explained his disagreement. Reinhardt, a former president of the Los Angeles Police Commission, also shared his historical knowledge of the LAPD.

Jurors in the two King criminal trials and the state trial of the defendants charged with assaulting Reginald Denny and others gave revealing accounts of their deliberations. I am particularly indebted to jury forewoman Dorothy Bailey and juror Anna Charmaine Whiting in the state trial of the officers, to jury foreman Bob Almond and juror Maria Escobel in the federal trial, and to jury forewoman Carolyn Walters in the trial of the Reginald Denny defendants. In the state trial of the officers, I also drew upon "Reaching for Doubt" by D. M. Osborne in the September 1992 issue of *The American Lawyer*, and upon an interview with Osborne.

Assistant City Attorney Don Vincent provided information about Rodney King's civil lawsuit, as did attorney Federico Sayre, who helped represent King in this proceeding.

Rodney King provided information about his post-trial experiences. I interviewed King in the office of his attorney, Edi Faal, who also represented Damian Williams, the principal defendant in the assault of Denny. Faal and Deputy District Attorney Janet Moore, a key prosecutor, helped analyze the Denny trial. Steven Lerman, the attorney who represented King after the beating, gave an important interview. So did Tom Owens, a former LAPD officer who investigated the beating for Lerman. King's parole officer, Tim Fowler, helped in my understanding of King, as did King's aunt, Angela King, and Stryker McGuire of *Newsweek*.

The four police officers accused of using excessive force against Rodney King candidly discussed their cases during the trials. Stacey Koon, Tim Wind, and Ted Briseno also gave extensive interviews away from the courtroom. I appreciate the help of Edwin Powell, father of Laurence Powell.

I consulted many analyses of the King incident. Particularly helpful were the assessments of Taky Tzimeas, the detective who directed the Internal Affairs Division investigation for the LAPD, and Cliff Ruff, a detective and longtime board member of the Los Angeles Police Protective League.

As jury consultant for the LAPD officers and later for the so-called Reginald Denny defendants, the perceptive Jo-Ellan Dimitrius had a unique perspective, which she was kind enough to share.

Warren Christopher, who chaired the commission that investigated the LAPD after the King incident, contributed to my understanding of the LAPD. Two members of the Christopher Commission, Leo Estrada and Andrea Ordin, helped explain the workings of that important panel, as did John Spiegel, its chief counsel, and Bryce Nelson, a journalism professor at the University of Southern California who served as the commission's director of information.

Members of the Los Angeles Police Commission helped, especially Stanley Sheinbaum, who was president of the commission during a tumultuous period, and Ray Fisher, a subsequent commission president now with the Justice Department. Thanks also to Commissioner Edith Perez, who succeeded Fisher as president, and to Commissioner T. Warren Jackson and former commissioner Gary Greenebaum.

Many members of the LAPD provided significant assistance. The late Jesse Brewer, who became a police commissioner after retiring as assistant chief, was a reliable guide to LAPD history and culture. Lieutenant John Dunkin, a valued homicide detective who has held many positions within the LAPD and is known for his fair-mindedess, was a reality check on police issues. Sergeant Charles Duke of the Metropolitan Division, commonly called Metro, a witness for the defense in both King trials, was responsive and informed.

Three former LAPD chiefs—Ed Davis, Daryl Gates, and Willie Williams—gave useful interviews. So did many officers involved in the clash at Florence and Normandie Avenues, the epicenter of the 1992 riots. I conducted interviews with two of the key figures in this action—former Lieutenant Michael Moulin and former Captain Paul Jefferson, now police chief in Modesto, California. Many others were interviewed by Jaxon Van Derbeken. Lieutenant Michael Hillmann of Metro thoughtfully analyzed LAPD preparations for the riots.

Two scholarly analyses of the riots were helpful. They were "Riot Control and the Los Angeles Riot of 1992" by Dr. Bert Useem and Commander David J. Gascon of the LAPD and "A Riot of Color: The Demographic Setting of Civil Disturbance in Los Angeles" by Peter A. Morrison and Ira S. Lowry of RAND. Useem, Gascon, and Morrison also gave useful interviews.

On LAPD use-of-force and training issues, I relied on Sergeant Scott Landsman, Sergeant Duke, and Officer Ted Hunt, a longtime instructor at the Los Angeles Police Academy. I also drew on an interview with Lieutenant Greg Meyer and on Meyer's writings on these issues. LAPD personnel who gave informative interviews include former Assistant Chief David Dotson, Deputy Chiefs Ronald Frankle, Mark Kroeker, and Bernard Parks (now chief), Captain Tim McBride, and Officers Greg Baltad, Gregory Dust, John Sheriff, and David Zeigler. Joe Gunn, a former LAPD commander who is Mayor Richard Riordan's aide on police matters helped on several issues, as did Katherine Mader, the LAPD inspector general. Bayan Lewis, interim LAPD chief in 1997, was also helpful.

William Webster, a former FBI and CIA director, and Hubert Williams a former Newark, New Jersey, police chief who heads the Police Foundation, directed the formal inquiry into the 1992 riots. Both gave valuable interviews.

Members of the Bush administration explained the process that led to federal prosecution of the LAPD officers. Thanks especially to former Attorney General William Barr, former White House press secretary Marlin Fitzwater, and William Kristol, who was chief of staff for Vice President Dan Quayle.

My knowledge of local governance was enriched by Robin Kramer, deputy mayor of Los Angeles and Mayor Riordan's chief of staff, and by Leo Estrada, Jane Pisano, and Mark Pisano. Noelia Rodriguez, the mayor's press secretary, was consistently helpful. Felicia Bragg, born and raised in Watts, helped me better understand the 1965 Watts riot and the experiences of African Americans in South Central, as did Larry Aubrey and Earl Ofari Hutchinson. Leo Estrada, Gregory Rodriguez, David Hayes-Bautista, County Supervisor Gloria Molina, and pollster Sergio Bendixen explained Latino perspectives. Angela Oh performed this service for the Korean community. David Joo and the late Richard Rhee gave interviews on the Korean experience during the riots that I conducted with Jessica Crosby

Young. Scott Carrier, spokesman for the Los Angeles County Coroner's Office, carefully updated the information on riot fatalities.

Mayor Riordan and former Mayor Tom Bradley gave important interviews, as did Councilman Mark Ridley-Thomas and Councilwoman Laura Chick. Eric Rose, a reserve LAPD officer and aide to Chick, helped on police matters. Former city councilman and now Los Angeles County Supervisor Zev Yaroslavsky explained why the city responded as it did to Rodney King's civil suit. My thanks also to Linda Griego, a deputy mayor under Tom Bradley and later head of RLA, and to Professor Gene Grigsby of UCLA.

Governor Pete Wilson of California explained his role in the state response to the riots. His former communications director, Dan Schnur, was helpful. So were Los Angeles County Sheriff Sherman Block and Captain Dan Burt of his department.

The political insights of Sherry Bebitch Jeffe and her husband, Doug, have long contributed to my understanding of Los Angeles. Mary and I thank the Jeffes and our friend, Sally Stewart, for opening their homes to us after the Northridge earthquake, and our Summerland neighbors and friends, David and Pat Van Every, for providing us a place to edit this manuscript.

Others who helped in various ways include Colin Powell, Johnnie Cochran Jr., Steve Chawkins, Ed Cray, Mary Drake, Joel Dreyer, Blythe Egan, Mark Fabiani, Sandi Gibbons, Phil Gollner, Jerry Guzzetta, Joseph McNamara, Diane Marchant, Calvin Naito, Arnold Steinberg, Jack White, and James Q. Wilson. I appreciate the counsel of John Diamond and Ed Guthman at critical moments in the final stages of the manuscript.

My superb agent, Kristine Dahl of ICM, represented me with her customary skill and dedication. Thanks also to her assistant, Sean Desmond.

And thanks to Peter Osnos, the former publisher of Times Books, for commissioning this book, and Peter Bernstein, the present publisher, for seeing it through to completion. I also thank Harold Evans, the publisher of Random House; John Newton and Salma Abdelnour for careful attention to matters relating to the book's production; Darrel Jonas, for her many courtesies; and Lesley Oelsner, for assistance on legal issues.

My special thanks to Nancy Land and Publications Development Company for the professionalism of their typesetting and for careful attention to important details.

I also thank Westview Press for the paperback edition of this book, especially publisher Marcus Boggs and Andrew Day, my editor at Westview.

Last but far from least, my deepest thanks to Merrill McLoughlin for her deft and sensitive editing of a manuscript that she improved in many ways and for being a joy to work with.

Any mistakes or misjudgments are entirely my responsibility and not in any way the fault of those who helped.

—Lou Cannon
Summerland, California, October 1997

Contents

Prologue

TWO STARK AND BRUTAL VIDEOTAPES SYMBOLIZE THE RODNEY King beating and the deadly riots that broke out in South Central Los Angeles in the spring of 1992. The first videotape, taken on March 3, 1991, by an amateur cameraman who had been awakened after midnight by sirens and the noise from a police helicopter, is of the King incident. It shows uniformed officers swarming around a large man who writhes on the ground and attempts to rise, but is clubbed and kicked into submission while other policemen watch with folded arms. The second video, shot from a news helicopter hovering over the intersection of Florence and Normandie Avenues during the riots a year later, shows the driver of a cement truck, Reginald Denny, being dragged from his cab by neighborhood toughs, then kicked and smashed in the head with a brick until he lies near death while one of his assailants does a jig.

Because King is black and the police officers are white and Denny is white and his attackers are black, these two videotapes convey a powerful message of racism and brutality. The symbolism was reinforced by several trials in which the videotapes were used as evidence. In April 1992, in suburban Simi Valley, a jury with no black members exonerated three of the police officers of using excessive force against King and acquitted another officer of all but one charge. The Simi Valley verdicts triggered the riots, in which fifty-four people died,[1] more than two thousand were injured, and more than eight hundred buildings burned. Then, in 1993, in a second trial, a federal jury with two black members convicted two of the police officers and acquitted two others of violating King's civil rights. Later that year a state jury on which there were four blacks, four Latinos, two Asians, and two whites acquitted Reginald Denny's black assailants of attempted murder and other charges and found the principal defendant guilty of a lesser felony.

I covered the trials of the officers and the riots for *The Washington Post*. Along with most journalists and the public, I at first assumed that the videotape of the King beating would assure conviction of the police defendants. I didn't know that the tape shown repeatedly on television was a partial, edited record. While the videotape is brutal in any version, the larger record is vital to an understanding of why the Simi Valley jurors acted as they did.

In time I learned that the mythology of the King case concealed a complex story of official negligence that was even more appalling than the videotape. It involved official negligence in which local governments and the police department were implicated. For example, the political leaders of Los Angeles had insisted on equipping LAPD officers with bone-breaking metal batons even though they knew that use of these crude weapons was producing a mounting toll of serious injuries. Meanwhile, the police department had failed to train some officers—including the officer who delivered most of the blows to Rodney King—in the basic techniques of using this baton and taking a resistant suspect into custody without hurting him. Official negligence extended to a judicial system that in the days before the trial of O. J. Simpson was considered one of the best in the land. Judges who traditionally had refused to grant a change of venue even in the most notorious murder cases moved the trial of the officers accused of assaulting King to a community that is one of the most pro-police in America.

The riots exposed other mythologies. The LAPD has been the nation's best known and most glamorized police department since the days of *Dragnet* in the 1950s. The LAPD's critics sometimes accused it of harsh treatment of criminal suspects and minorities, but few of them questioned its competence and professionalism. Police Chief Daryl F. Gates, a field commander during the 1965 Watts riot, had vowed that the department never again would be surprised by civil disorders, and most of the public believed him. After Watts the LAPD acquired helicopters and armored personnel carriers and developed a mobile strike force, all conspicuous by their absence during the 1992 riots. The officers whom Joseph Wambaugh had celebrated as "new centurions" proved to be knights in rusty armor, poorly equipped and badly led. It was widely believed in South Central that the LAPD did not want to protect the city's poor, minority neighborhoods. The shocking reality was that the LAPD was unable to provide such protection.

The circle of negligence widened after the riots. President Bush on national television expressed a "deep sense of personal frustration and anguish" about the Simi Valley verdicts. His words set in motion the machinery that led to the second trial, in a federal court, before a jury fearful of more riots. Politics also affected the trial of the Denny defendants in which community activists openly tried to influence jurors who were fearful of another riot.

Los Angeles is a diverse and dynamic city that rarely looks back. After a brief corporate fling at rebuilding the riot-torn area, announced with great fanfare and then quietly abandoned, city leaders did their best to forget the trials and the riots. By the time Rodney King's civil lawsuit for damages was tried in 1994, the attention of journalists had faded. King's continuing brushes with the law, mostly for driving under the influence of alcohol, were barely mentioned by the media. Reginald Denny faded into obscurity. The leaders who had occupied center stage—Mayor Tom Bradley, Chief Gates, and District Attorney Ira Reiner—retired under pressure.

But the problems remained. A new white mayor could not ease the tensions of a multicultural community. A new black police chief could not win the support of a department traumatized by the legacy of the King case and the riots. A new district attorney found it difficult to separate politics from the administration of justice.

The significance of the Rodney King story and the Los Angeles riots extends beyond Southern California's borders. Racial tensions are commonplace in America. Many urban communities contain blighted or neglected areas, often at the core, where police protection, justice, and decent living standards are in short supply. By understanding the causes of the King case and the riots, we may improve our chances of avoiding another descent into the chaos that gripped Los Angeles during five terrifying spring days in 1992. That is the purpose of this book.

OFFICIAL
NEGLIGENCE

1

DREAM CITY

"Imagine Los Angeles in the first decade of the 21st century. . . . More different races, religions, cultures, languages and people mingle here than in any city in the world."

—"LA 2000: A City for the Future,"
a report of the LA 2000 Committee.

THE LAST THING THE LEADERS OF LOS ANGELES EXPECTED IN THE early 1990s was that their city would become the scene of the nation's deadliest urban race riot since the Civil War. To the contrary, Mayor Tom Bradley was confident that the city he had led since 1973 was "at the brink of a great destiny," poised to become the multicultural crossroads of the world. His optimism was shared by the downtown financiers who had bankrolled his political campaigns and were his enduring allies. Together they had transformed a sprawling municipality once disparaged as forty suburbs in search of a city into a metropolis of chrome-and-steel skyscrapers, a magnet for investment from Canada, Japan, and other nations of the Pacific Rim.

Bradley and his backers as well as political leaders in Sacramento, the state capital, believed that California was essentially recession-proof. They foresaw neither an end to the cornucopia of defense spending which had funneled federal dollars into the state since World War II nor the collapse of what seemed a perpetual real estate boom. After five decades of steadily increasing values, even nondescript tract houses were selling for fifteen to twenty-five times their original price, and homes were considered better investments than certificates of deposit or mutual funds. Despite air pollution and crowded freeways, Southern Californians were convinced they lived in one of the best places on earth. In a 1943 article, *Life* magazine had described Southern California as "irresistibly attractive to hordes of people." The state's entire population was then just under 7 million, 2 million less than the 1990 population of Los Angeles County alone. But people continued to pour into Southern California in pursuit of the American dream that William Faulkner had defined "as a sanctuary on earth for individual man." As *Life* had put it, "Mister, this is dreamland."

Bradley was a visionary black man in a city that had come to reflect all the colors of the rainbow. When Bradley was a boy, Los Angeles had been the most white, Anglo-Saxon, and Protestant big city in the nation. By 1990, however, it had become a salad bowl of cultures in which 106 languages were spoken, a fifth of the residents had been born in a foreign country, nearly half the public-school children conversed in Spanish at home, and the Roman Catholic Church was the city's most influential religious institution.

The Los Angeles electorate did not reflect the rainbow composition of the population. Latinos, mostly of Mexican origin or descent, made up 40 percent of the city's population and Asians another 9 percent. But since many Latinos and Asians were ineligible to vote, they comprised only one-eighth of an electorate that in the early 1990s remained two-thirds non-Hispanic white and nearly one-fifth black. It was this older Los Angeles that had elected Bradley mayor five times, even though it was the newer city that captured his imagination. Economic forecasts assured him that Los Angeles was an engine of diversity propelling California into the leadership of a brave new world where goods and workers would flow freely among nations of the Pacific Rim. If demographics were destiny, then Los Angeles was the harbinger of a multicultural democracy without a racial or an ethnic majority. By the middle of the twenty-first century, or so demographers said, the entire United States would resemble the Los Angeles of 1990.

The mayor thought of Los Angeles as a harmonious city where Latinos, blacks, Asians, and whites worked together to enrich a region that would increasingly resemble the world with which it traded. A civic leadership often more attuned to what occurred in Tokyo or Mexico City than to what was happening in Watts shared this shining vision, which seemed real enough from the gleaming downtown skyscrapers that were the monuments of the Bradley era. But at ground level, Los Angeles looked squalid. In South Central and in the neighborhoods of Pico-Union and Westlake, west of downtown, ethnic diversity and growing population density produced unruly competition for the most low-paying and menial jobs. Poverty and discord rippled through forty square miles of mean streets. This Los Angeles was the city of which mystery writer Walter Mosley said, "It's a land that on the surface is of dreams, and then there's a kind of slimy underlayer."[1]

But what Bradley called a "world city" was a concept more compelling than any ground-level reality. The mayor and his business allies commanded a city built by dreams. In this respect they were true to the promoters who had lured 1.5 million people to Southern California in the 1920s. "Los Angeles has touched the imagination of America," proclaimed a brochure of the period. "She has become an idea . . . . a longing in men's breasts. She is the symbol of a new civilization, a new hope, another try."

THE BELIEF THAT PEOPLE COULD ACHIEVE IN LOS ANGELES WHAT they had been unable to accomplish elsewhere held resonance for Tom Bradley, who was an overachieving son of Texas sharecroppers. Lee and Crenner Bradley had quit school in the fifth grade and picked cotton for pennies in the sun-baked fields of Calvert, Texas. They came to Los Angeles in 1924 when Tom was seven years old, and it took Lee Bradley more than a year to win "another try" as a porter for the Santa Fe Railroad. This nomadic work and similar jobs that followed left the burden of raising a family to Crenner, who took in ironing and worked long hours as a maid to support five children. Even in the depths of the Depression, she never went on welfare.

The Bradleys were part of the largest wave of black immigration to reach California before World War II. The black population of Los Angeles doubled in the twenties, reaching 30,000 by 1930. The Bradleys lived on the East Side, an area now almost entirely Latino, and moved frequently. "Although I never asked why, I am sure some of our moves had to do with our not being able to pay the rent," Tom Bradley later recalled.[2] He was ten when a white friend told him that his parents had forbidden him to play with colored children. Much later, after he was an adult, white homeowners tried to prevent Bradley and his family from moving into a neighborhood where no blacks lived.

Bradley was a tall and handsome young man who read widely and was fortunate to have teachers who encouraged him to ignore the standard counseling that black students should take vocational training and work with their hands. His idol was Jesse Owens, the black track star who had upstaged Adolf Hitler at the 1936 Olympic Games in Berlin. Bradley won a track scholarship to the University of California at Los Angeles, becoming one of a hundred blacks in a student body of 7,000. But in 1940, with California still in the grips of the Depression, Bradley took the police entrance examination, scored 97 percent, and was invited to become a police officer. Being a cop meant having job security, something his parents had never known, and Bradley quit UCLA in his junior year to join the mostly white and strictly segregated Los Angeles Police Department. The LAPD provided a pathway to success for Bradley, who attended law school at night, passed the bar, and entered politics after retiring from the department in 1961.

Bradley started out in public life as a "Negro politician" involved in black causes and representing a city council district with a black plurality. But he was from the beginning an apostle of diversity who reached out to people of all ethnic groups and political affiliations, a prerequisite for political success in a white-run city where the local offices, as elsewhere in California, are nonpartisan.

It was the 1965 Watts riot and the damage it inflicted on the city's reputation that gave Bradley a chance to become mayor. After the riot, the business community was anxious to project a more progressive image of Los Angeles and more willing to take a chance on a black man whose dignified personality and police background made him relatively reassuring to whites. Still, when Bradley first ran for mayor in 1969, he narrowly lost to the incumbent Sam Yorty, a durable demagogue who conducted a race-baiting campaign and suggested that Bradley would clamp down on the LAPD in retaliation for the humiliation he had suffered while working in a segregated police department. Yorty had started out in the 1930s as a far-left Democrat and moved right across the political spectrum without changing party registration. He was a classic California lone-wolf anti-politician who had mastered the art of appealing to white resentment and knew how to stir a crowd. Yorty did particularly well in the San Fernando Valley, where conservative homeowners were not quite ready to elect a black.

By 1973, however, even conservatives had become disillusioned with Yorty. Bradley defeated him in a rematch and presided over the creation of modern Los Angeles. His commitment to downtown development guaranteed him the backing of a financial elite alarmed by the loss of business to suburbia, while his race and mild liberalism made him an ideal advertisement for a city that had begun to promote diversity. Until his image was tarnished by conflict-of-interest charges late in his fourth term, Bradley remained popular with blacks, Jews, Latinos, and moderates of all races.

Bradley's greatest political triumph was bringing the 1984 Olympic Games to Los Angeles. At fifteen, he had peeked through the fence around the Los Angeles Coliseum to watch the 1932 Olympic Games, and later he ran the 440 on the Coliseum track then used by UCLA. As mayor, he pressured a divided city council to ratify a contract with the International Olympic Committee that it had initially rejected.[3] Bradley went down to the Pacific Coast Highway on July 21, 1984, to watch football hero O. J. Simpson, the pride of the University of Southern California, carry the Olympic torch into Santa Monica. When Bradley saw an onlooker climb a cactus, oblivious of the thorns, to get a better view of Simpson, he knew the games would be a huge success.

Fortune smiled on Los Angeles during the summer of 1984 in the form of exceptionally mild and smog-free weather. Despite a boycott by the Soviet Union and its eastern European dependencies, a record number of 140 nations participated in the Los Angeles Olympics, the first such international competition to be privately financed. Spectators also turned out in record numbers, ignoring terrorism scares. From the moment that Rafer Johnson sprinted up the steps of the Coliseum to light the Olympic torch and Vickie McClure sang "Reach Out and Touch Somebody's Hand," the games were a public relations triumph for Bradley, who was cheered by a crowd of 55,000 when he was introduced for the first Olympic baseball game. When the Games ended on August 12 in the glow of $500,000 worth of fireworks and the landing of a fake spaceship, Los Angeles was reluctant to see them go.[4] The United States had won a record eighty-four gold medals, and most Americans did not seem to mind that the gold had been devalued by the Soviet boycott. The Olympics had brought $3.3 billion into Los Angeles, created 74,000 temporary jobs, and produced a surplus of $222 million. It had been the most profitable sporting event in world history. But to the mayor, the real story of the Olympics was diversity, not dollars. In the fierce but peaceful competition of the athletes from many nations, Bradley saw an advertisement for his world city.

In 1985, during his fourth mayoralty campaign, Bradley proposed developing a "strategic vision" for Los Angeles. The mayor's critics, of whom there then were few, called the idea a political stunt, but after he was re-elected, Bradley asked eighty-five leading citizens, the LA 2000 Committee, to prepare a blueprint for the future. In 1988, they produced a plan, "LA 2000: A City for the Future," which optimistically discussed issues of growth management, education, housing, transportation, and environmental quality.

"Just as New York, London and Paris stood as symbols of past centuries, Los Angeles will be THE city of the 21st century," the report declared in a particularly exuberant paragraph.

> The potential for Los Angeles as a prosperous international center for communications, trade, investment and culture is immense. It will be a leading hub of world trade, especially as the United States gateway to the Pacific Rim nations, where the combined economies are expanding at the rate of $3 billion a week toward a projected 27 percent share of the world's gross product before the end of the century. Los Angeles can be a leading financial center and a communications axis where major business enterprises from all over the world will want to have a headquarters, a branch office or a manufacturing facility. Los Angeles can continue to be a magnet that attracts people from every nation as a place of opportunity as well as a pacesetter that shapes cultures worldwide through its leadership in science, technology and education as well as in the arts and entertainment industry.

THE BELIEF THAT A DREAM OR AN IDEALIZED VISION CAN BE imagined or proclaimed into existence is part of the essence of Southern

California. It was the secret of Ronald Reagan's popular appeal and the key to the "magic" of Hollywood. In an epilogue to the LA 2000 report, historian Kevin Starr suggested that the very existence of Los Angeles represents a triumph of vision and will over material circumstances. "Los Angeles did not just happen or arise like so many other American cities out of existing circumstances," Starr wrote. "Indeed, for a long time it had none of these. Los Angeles envisioned itself, then externalized that vision through sheer force of will, springing from a platonic conception of itself, the Great Gatsby of American cities."

Since Los Angeles lacked the raw materials of a city and since most of the region was a desert, it was able to grow only by imposing its visions on others. Water was imported from northern California at a heavy cost to once-wild rivers and the magnificent estuary known as the San Francisco Bay Delta. The Owens Valley was also sacrificed. Los Angeles created a deepwater port, developed a flourishing citrus agriculture that it then displaced with subdivisions, and built a splendid rail transit system that was removed to accommodate freeways and the automobile culture.

One of the downsides of a society created by a triumph of will is that its members, having persuaded themselves that anything is possible, are susceptible to self-deception. The LA 2000 report itself was clouded by miscalculation. "Every economist I talked to had said that California's economy was so broad-based and had such a critical mass that it would resist a recession," said Jane Pisano, president of the Los Angeles 2000 Committee. "Then the report was published and the bottom fell out of the economy. That was not supposed to happen."[5]

In fact, "every economist" had underestimated California's dependence on military spending, a mainstay of the state's economy since the defense plants and shipyards of World War II had ended the Depression.[6] California had become prosperous, said Richard Riordan, Bradley's successor as mayor, because it had been "subsidized by people around the world to build things to kill people."[7] During much of the Cold War the state routinely received $80 billion to $100 billion a year in federal defense dollars. Even as late as 1992, when military spending in California had declined to $51 billion, the state was still absorbing 21 percent of the national defense budget. "The California economy was on steroids," said Kevin Starr.[8]

It was an apt metaphor. California had become economically muscular by injections of federal defense spending, and the state suffered withdrawal symptoms when the dosage was reduced as the Cold War wound down. From 1988 to 1993, California lost 140,000 aerospace jobs at a time when the state was growing so rapidly that it needed to create 200,000 new jobs a year just to stay even. The aerospace collapse sent an enormous ripple through the economy, as housing construction nose-dived and the thinly stretched real estate bubble burst. Subdivisions were festooned with "for sale" signs in front of homes that often sold, if at all, at prices far below the listed values. While relatively few poor blacks or Latinos were directly employed by aerospace companies, they held jobs in the markets, shops, restaurants, and service stations along the Los Angeles County coast and into Orange County. Many of these jobs vanished. One economist put the California employment loss over seven years at 300,000, including jobs from military-base closings.[9]

The severity of the downturn robbed Californians of their optimism. By 1992, the year of the Los Angeles riots, 93 percent of those surveyed by California pollster Mervin Field, said the state was undergoing "bad times"—up from 24 percent in 1989. Field, who had been sampling California public opinion for nearly a half century, had never before found such high levels of pessimism. What seemed most significant to him was that many Californians doubted that their state would ever recover its former luster.

The effect of the aerospace collapse rippled through South Central, mingling with other currents to create the economic context of the 1992 riots. Los Angeles had been a center of traditional manufacturing for three decades after World War II, but ten of the twelve largest non-aerospace plants had closed between 1978 and 1982 in the face of foreign competition and rising production costs in Southern California. One of the plants that shut down was a General Motors assembly line in South Gate, a blue-collar community east of South Central that employed substantial numbers of blacks. The exodus of the automobile industry from Southern California was completed in 1992, when GM shut down a Van Nuys plant that had produced more than six million vehicles over forty-five years, shifting production of its Chevrolet Camaros and Pontiac Firebirds to a plant in Canada.

The point was sometimes made that thousands of automotive jobs were created in places like Irvine, La Jolla, and Newport Beach to offset the job losses in South Gate, Van Nuys, and Pico Rivera, where Ford had closed a plant in the early 1980s. But the new jobs were research, design, and sales positions for foreign-car makers in relatively remote and sanitized suburban communities. There were few new jobs for blue-collar workers. South Central, the historic industrial core of Los Angeles, lost 70,000 jobs in the 1978–82 plant closures and continued to hemorrhage through the rest of the decade while most of California prospered.

By 1990, apparel manufacturing was the only substantial industry within easy driving distance of South Central. Apparel was also the only manufacturing industry that continued to grow as the California economy declined, and its growth was greatest in Los Angeles County, which in 1991 employed 99,400 of the state's 141,000 garment workers. The downtown garment district on the northern rim of South Central is home to the California Mart, a three-million-square-foot complex that boasts of being the world's biggest apparel market. It also harbors over-heated sweat shops where garment workers produce ready-to-wear clothing at piece rates.

Ironically, the "world city" celebrated by Mayor Bradley was one of reduced wages and expectations. While almost as many apparel jobs were created in Los Angeles County during 1990–91 as were lost in the aerospace industry, the median annual wage was $17,000 in garment work compared to $45,000 in aerospace. Since it took 2.5 garment jobs to equal the purchasing power of a single aerospace job, consumer spending declined, as did government revenues from sales and income taxes. Nor were the new, low-paying jobs available to everyone. Latino and Asian immigrants held two-thirds of the jobs at the garment factories, and blacks held very few.[10] This intensified racial and ethnic friction within South Central, where immigrants also competed with African Americans for living space. By 1990, the Latino and black populations of South Central were nearly equal in a community that had been two-thirds black in 1980.

The aerospace collapse came at a time when social services in California, especially in poor communities, were strained. The Reagan administration had eliminated the Comprehensive Employment and Training Act (CETA) and virtually dismantled the Job Corps. California had also paid a heavy, if delayed, price for Proposition 13, the 1978 initiative pushed by populist Howard Jarvis at a time when the state legislature was hoarding budget surpluses and property taxes were sky-rocketing. The measure had been opposed by almost every public official, including then-governor Edmund G. (Jerry) Brown and then-San Diego mayor Pete Wilson, but it was approved overwhelmingly by tax-weary California voters.

Proposition 13 was cheered by homeowners because it fixed property taxes at a low level. But it also undermined the ability of local governments to pay for public services and had the radical effect of taking fiscal authority away from local governments and placing it in the hands of the state. After the initiative passed, these local governments sought help from Sacramento, and a chastened legislature distributed the accumulated surpluses to cities and counties. This delayed the negative impact of Proposition 13, but over time, the view that local governments could provide the same services with a shrunken tax base proved as much of an illusion as the myth of permanent California prosperity. As the aerospace and real estate collapse reduced state revenues, the state reduced aid to local governments and cities and counties in turn cut services. In Los Angeles County, this forced closure of medical trauma centers and libraries and deferred purchases of police cars and emergency communications equipment. When the riots came, the LAPD responded to emergencies in cars that had been driven 100,000 miles and tried to answer calls over radios that often didn't work.

Since blacks made up more than 22 percent of the Los Angeles municipal workforce, they were disproportionately affected by the budget squeeze. Mayor Bradley had made a point of hiring minorities and promoting them. But Los Angeles had only 2,600 more municipal jobs in 1991 than it had in 1973, the year Bradley became mayor. This was a 6 percent growth rate in city jobs while the population was increasing by 670,000, or 24 percent. Only a thousand more blacks held city jobs in 1991 than when Bradley took office.[11]

The combination of disappearing jobs and reduced services was devastating in South Central, where blacks suffered, as in other inner cities, from a terrifying trend of family breakdown. But the national stereotype of a black underclass in which fatherless families lived on welfare checks did not accurately describe the poor in South Central. Poverty in Los Angeles was "notable for its diversity," as one study put it.[12] Men comprised 43 percent of the poor. Only 25 percent of the adult poor in Los Angeles collected any form of public assistance.

What may have hurt South Central as much as family breakdown was the exodus of the growing black middle class during the 1980s. Middle-class people of any race tend to move out of South Central as soon as they are financially able to do so, and blacks are no exception. The black population of South Central in 1990 was down 122,000 from a decade before, a 17 percent decrease. Meanwhile, the black population grew by 50 percent or more in 60 Los Angeles County communities, including many in which blacks were a tiny minority. Felicia Bragg, a teenager in Watts at the time of the 1965 riot who retains familial ties with the community, notes that the increased mobility of blacks deprived Watts and much of South Central of middle-class role models close to home. "Racism had a good effect on us because even middle-class blacks had to live with us . . . they couldn't move," said Bragg, who moved to Pasadena.[13] Most of the people who couldn't move were desperately poor, however, and many were unemployed. A year before the 1992 riots, 40,000 South Central black teenagers between the ages of sixteen and nineteen were out of school and out of work.

Latinos in South Central were also poor. While they were more likely to be employed and have intact families than African Americans, they worked for such low wages that their poverty rate was nearly identical with that of blacks. Most Latinos who had lived in Southern California for a decade or longer were from Mexico, and they frequently found themselves in competition with new arrivals from Central America as well as with blacks. One study based on census data showed that the poverty rate in Los Angeles increased 50 percent from 1969 through 1989, while remaining nearly static in the nation. Of South Central's 630,000 residents, 92 percent were black or Latino, and 230,000 of them lived below the poverty line. The poor included 40 percent of the children.

GEORGE DEUKMEJIAN, THE REPUBLICAN GOVERNOR OF CALIFORNIA during most of the 1980s, was isolated in Sacramento, nearly four hundred miles away, and knew even less than the Los Angeles elite about what was happening in South Central. Deukmejian, cautious and conservative, had been a state legislator from Long Beach before becoming attorney general. He won the Republican gubernatorial nomination in 1982 and faced Tom Bradley, the Democratic nominee, in the general election. That same year, gun-control advocates qualified a handgun-registration initiative for the statewide ballot. The measure spurred a heavy turnout of white, conservative voters who defeated the initiative and in the process helped Deukmejian win a narrow victory.

Deukmejian was an unassuming and unimaginative governor with a passion for prison building. He easily won reelection in 1986, with Bradley again his opponent. In 1989, after a crazed gunman killed several children with an assault rifle in a Stockton school yard, he courageously defied the gun lobby and signed a bill banning various assault weapons.

Deukmejian was the Calvin Coolidge of California. Like Coolidge, he was a decent man devoted to family and friends. Also like Coolidge, he was oblivious to portents of economic catastrophe. In 1990, the year he retired as governor, he agreed to a state budget that was balanced on the breathtaking assumption that California's economic growth would continue unabated after the end of the Cold War. After the election, Deukmejian casually told governor-elect Pete Wilson that state revenue collections had been below estimates since July, the first month of the new fiscal year. As they talked, a Deukmejian aide arrived with news that revenues had taken an especially precipitous downturn in October. In fact, Deukmejian had left his Republican successor a $7 billion deficit which would grow to more than $10 billion and cast Wilson as the Herbert Hoover of the California economic decline.[14]

It would later be said in defense of Deukmejian that the world changed too abruptly for him to foresee the aerospace decline. Certainly, he had no warning of either the collapse of communism or the subsequent worldwide recession. But the reduction of defense spending had been in the offing since late 1987, when President Reagan and Mikhail Gorbachev signed a treaty to reduce U.S. and Soviet intermediate-range nuclear weapon arsenals. Aerospace companies had not waited until the Berlin Wall fell to begin laying off workers. At Hughes Aircraft Company, the largest industrial employer in California during the 1980s, chief executive officer Malcolm Currie, early in

1989, began a 25 percent "downsizing," as he called the mass layoffs that became endemic in the industry. Lockheed and other aerospace giants followed suit.

Small businesses in California were also quicker than political leaders to read the tea leaves of decline. Business start-ups began falling in 1987. They continued to fall for the next five years. This information was available to the Deukmejian administration, if anyone had sought it, at a state agency down the street from the Capitol. While there was no comparable data on the exodus of established businesses, organizations led by the California Chamber of Commerce were complaining that the state suffered from overlapping federal, state, county, and local regulations that made obtaining even the simplest permit agonizing and time-consuming.[15] Peter Ueberroth, a Bradley ally who had organized the 1984 Olympics and was named by Governor Wilson to head a Council on California Competitiveness, described the regulatory system as a "well-oiled, job-killing machine."[16] A 1991 survey of executives by the California Business Roundtable found that 25 percent of them had plans to relocate their businesses outside of California.

MOST RESIDENTS OF SOUTH CENTRAL DID NOT HAVE THE LUXURY of packing up and leaving for an industrial park in Utah or Nevada. The comment of one black gang member accurately reflected the outlook of many African-American males. "It's like we're animals left in a cage, and you're feeding us nothing but poison," said Freddie (FM) Jelks. "Hunger is going to make me eat it." Jelks at twenty-eight was the father of four and, like one in six black males over the age of sixteen, an ex-convict. He had frequently applied for work but never held a job.[17]

Alicia Aguilar, thirty-two, immigrated to Los Angeles from Toluca, Mexico, and sewed blouses in an overheated factory run by Koreans in the garment district. She worked from 7:00 A.M. until 6:00 P.M. six days a week on piece rates, receiving the equivalent of the minimum wage only if she completed 10 blouses an hour, 110 blouses a day, 660 blouses a week. She lived in a one-bedroom South Central apartment with her husband and their three boys, aged ten to thirteen, who slept together in the living room. "There was more room in Mexico," she said. Aguilar's dream was that her boys would study and have careers so she could return to Mexico. Since her husband also worked, there was no one to supervise her young children, who were cared for by a neighbor when they arrived home from school.[18]

What happened to the children of Jelks and Aguilar had more to do with the future of Los Angeles than all the visionary gush in the LA 2000 report. But the prospects of the poor did not engage the leaders of Los Angeles as South Central became the breeding ground for a riot that would dwarf Watts, and they ignored a perceptive report that pointed out the problems while there was still time to solve them.

Unlike the expansively funded LA 2000 Committee, the Los Angeles County Commission on Human Relations had a small budget and a tiny staff. But in 1985, the year Mayor Bradley proposed a "strategic vision" for Los Angeles, the commission and the even smaller Los Angeles City Commission on Human Relations worked together to analyze conditions in South Central twenty years after the Watts riot. The two commissions took testimony from eighteen analysts and community leaders and issued a report called "McCone Revisited: A Focus on Solutions to Continuing Problems in South Central Los Angeles." The title referred to John McCone, a former Central Intelligence Agency director who had headed the inquiry into the 1965 Watts riot. "McCone Revisited" was issued on plain paper, written in uninspired prose, and had no illustrations. It lacked the artiness and optimism of the lavishly designed LA 2000 report, offering only a somber and dispassionate assessment of what had happened in South Central since the 1965 riot. Improvements in transportation and health services were duly noted, but "critical problems" in employment and social services had not improved since Watts, while other "critical problems" of education and housing had become worse.

"McCone Revisited" gathered dust for seven years. It was not mentioned by the LA 2000 Committee report in 1988 or, as far as I am aware, in any other of the many surveys of Southern California life that proliferated in the 1980s. Nor did the report or the deteriorating conditions for African Americans attract attention from national or local media. "Latinos and diversity were the new media fashion in the eighties," recalled Jay Mathews, then the Los Angeles bureau chief of The Washington Post. "Blacks were the old minority, on the way out. Racial tension was unfashionable as a media story. Black frustration and the reaction of blacks to the police was a twenty-year-old story. It was old hat."[19]

The frustrated complaints of the jobless poor were drowned out by happy talk about the region's future. Many reports that purported to discuss "Los Angeles" were actually broad-brush examinations of regional attitudes. For example, RAND, a Santa Monica–based think tank, conducted telephone interviews with 1,230 people for the LA 2000 Committee. Only 187 of those interviewed were South Central residents and only 46 of these respondents were black. Anyone too poor to own a telephone—and the 1990 census found 11,111 such residents in South Central—was automatically eliminated.

South Central and its poor black and Latino population was invisible to most non-Hispanic whites in Southern California before the 1992 riots. Blacks made up 47.6 percent of South Central's population in the 1990 census, but only 13 percent of the city population, 10.5 percent of the county population, and 6 to 9 percent of the regional population, depending on how the region was defined.

There is no universally accepted definition of Southern California. Social historian Carey McWilliams used the traditional "south of Tehachapi," a reference to the mountain range that reaches the Pacific Coast north of Santa Barbara. This included Santa Barbara County south of these mountains, all of Ventura, Los Angeles and Orange counties, and western Riverside, San Bernardino and San Diego counties, which were also divided by mountain ranges from the inland desert. RAND surveyed residents of "the larger Los Angeles region" of Los Angeles County, northern Orange County and, curiously, eastern Riverside and San Bernardino counties. Dan Walters in *The New California* referred to an "uninterrupted, sprawling megalopolis" extending from Riverside County on the south and east to Ventura County on the north and west. "They are, in effect, the boroughs of one continuous city that's nearly 100 miles long and 75 miles wide, even though their residents try to separate themselves from Los Angeles by postal designation or city limit lines," Walters wrote.

South Central lies at the heart of this "continuous city," surrounded by elevated freeways that enable millions of passersby to avoid this poorest section of Southern California.[20] Within the area bounded by these freeways, South Central occupies nearly forty square miles in a city of 479 square miles and a county of 4,079 square miles. South Central had a population of 630,000 in 1990. The city of Los Angeles had a population of 3,485,398 and Los Angeles County, which contains 88 separate cities and 163 identifiable communities, had a population of 8,863,154. These official figures are, in fact, probably low because they don't take into account the illegal immigrants, called "undocumented workers" by Latinos. These immigrants are a source of cheap labor for businesses and Anglo homeowners, but increase the competition for scarce jobs and living space in South Central and other poor areas. Blacks felt particularly threatened by the immigrant influx, which helped keep wages down.[21]

IN SPITE OF THE BOOSTERISM OF MANY SOUTHERN CALIFORNIA leaders in the 1980s, there was a vague but growing sense of foreboding that all was not well. This was reflected in the 1988 RAND survey, whose respondents were wealthier and better educated than the overall population. Of those responding, 83 percent said life was good, but 43 percent were pessimistic about the future. Even the hyper-optimistic LA 2000 report sounded an uneasy note in a paragraph sandwiched between passages that discussed the "impressive strengths" of the region. "Los Angeles is rapidly becoming a bimodal society as the number of mid-level jobs fails to keep up, widening the disparity between high-skill, high-paying jobs and low-skill, low-paying jobs," the report said.

A few months after the LA 2000 report was submitted to Mayor Bradley the *Los Angeles Times* published in its April 2, 1989, Sunday magazine the results of a survey on "The Quality of L.A. Life." Based on a poll of 2,046 Los Angeles County residents, this survey produced the then-surprising statistic that 48 percent were considering moving, a majority outside the region and many to another state.

The survey was accompanied by an article on the lives of six families that catalogued horror stories of congestion, traffic problems, and crime. Laura Bowen's Volkswagen convertible had been stolen three times during her first year in Los Angeles, and budget cuts had eliminated the music program at her daughter's elementary school in affluent Toluca Lake. Pam Herbert, a college student, had been harassed by leather-clad high school students known as "mall rats." Salvador Mariscal, a farmer, had moved from Mexico to join his children in Los Angeles. He detested the food, was frightened by the freeways, and had bought a cow to remind him of home. Melinda Garcia, a psychologist, was dismayed by cross-burnings and vandalism of synagogues that received little attention from the media. "There's a mystique that this city is tolerant, and it's not true," she said.

Both the RAND and the *Los Angeles Times* surveys found that crime was overwhelmingly cited as the worst feature of life in Southern California. Fear of crime was greatest among blacks, who were most apt to live in high-crime areas and were statistically the most frequent victims as well as the most frequent perpetrators of crime. The *Times* recounted the experiences of Maurice and Paulette Bennett, who lived with their three children in Inglewood, a stable city with a black majority that is home to the Forum, where the Los Angeles professional basketball and hockey teams play, and the Hollywood Park racetrack. Life had been good for the Bennetts until their working-class neighborhood was invaded by youthful cocaine dealers. "This is no place to raise kids," Paulette Bennett had decided. "I'm afraid one will get jumped."

The fears of the Bennetts reflected an attitude of the 1980s that at first glance seemed to be disputed by the facts. Personal and household crimes in the United States declined from a peak of 41 million in 1981 to 34 million in 1990, while surveys were showing increasing public concern about crime. This apparent contradiction was partly because such usually non-violent crimes as burglary and auto theft declined sharply while violent crime fell only slightly. Citizens were understandably less concerned about the inconvenience of burglary than with the possibility they might be mugged, robbed, raped, assaulted, or killed.

In addition, the comforting statistics concealed a trend within a trend. All categories of crime decreased early in the decade, but the crime rate turned upward again in the mid-1980s, spurred by an epidemic of crack cocaine. Within Los Angeles County the rate of violent crime rose steadily from a decade low of 1,179 incidents per 100,000 inhabitants in 1984 to 1,601 in 1989.[22] The increase in violent crime fed the public's fears and put pressure on Southern California law enforcement agencies to "do something" at a time when police forces were feeling the impact of cumulative budget cuts.

What Los Angeles Police Chief Daryl F. Gates decided to do was launch Operation Hammer, a series of street sweeps of gang-infested areas in South Central. Starting in April 1988, as many as a thousand police officers moved from neighborhood to neighborhood, arresting hundreds of suspected gang members and drug dealers. Gates believed that such "proactive" policing was necessary to bring the gangs to heel. But while the sweeps inconvenienced drug dealers, gang killings and assaults continued to rise steadily.

Then on August 1, 1988, eighty Los Angeles police officers, acting on a tip, descended on four apartments near Thirty-ninth Street and Dalton Avenue that they believed were gang-controlled crack cocaine houses. They smashed toilets, destroyed furniture, broke windows, and wrote pro-police graffiti on an outside wall. Thirty-three African Americans were arrested, and some said they were cuffed around by police. Although this accusation was never proved in court, the raid became a costly embarrassment to the Los Angeles Police Department. The tip had been wrong. The raid yielded less than an ounce of cocaine and six ounces of marijuana and resulted in a single successful prosecution on a minor charge. Dozens of officer participants were disciplined, and three were prosecuted on felony vandalism and other charges. While the officers were eventually acquitted by a racially mixed jury, the city paid out $3.7 million in civil damages. Police Commander Chet Spencer, who presided over a disciplinary hearing of the one officer to admit wrongdoing, concluded that the incident was "an extremely dark day in the history of the Los Angeles Police Department."

South Central wanted, needed, and deserved police protection. While some activists described the LAPD as an occupying army, polls showed that a majority of blacks and Latinos were supportive of the police.[23] One objective measure of the community's attitude was the consistent support given by South Central voters, especially blacks, to ballot measures that would have raised taxes to pay for additional officers or better police equipment. Such measures usually failed to win the two-thirds margin required by Proposition 13 (which itself had not received the support of two-thirds of the state's voters) because white, conservative voters in well-off areas were unwilling to tax themselves to pay for extra police.[24] Poor, law-abiding citizens in South Central could not afford the luxuries of gated communities or private security forces. They wanted more police protection than they were receiving.

What the people of South Central did not want was to be treated with contempt or prejudice. Operation Hammer removed hundreds of gang members from the streets, but also resulted in the rounding up, and sometimes the roughing up, of teenagers whose crime was being in the wrong place at the wrong time. The Thirty-ninth and Dalton raid strained fragile ties between citizens and a police force that under Chief Gates resisted "community policing," in which neighborhoods are enlisted as allies of the police. But neither South Central nor the LAPD was a monolith, and individual officers in high-crime precincts often developed ties with citizens who favored a crackdown on the gangs. These ties were most apt to be with Latinos. The Latino fear of black gangs was an unpublicized element of the Thirty-ninth and Dalton raid, which was partially provoked by threats made to a Latino family living in a house between the four apartments that were ransacked by police. An instructive poll showed that Latinos critical of the LAPD were most apt to fault police for slow response to emergency calls, while blacks were more apt to cite racism or harassment.[25]

Blacks, particularly young males, complained that they were often stopped by police and "proned out"—made to lie face down with legs and arms spread and palms up—for minor traffic violations or for no reason at all. Such indignities had been a prelude to the Watts riot. After Watts the LAPD instituted race-relations training, and a steady influx of black and Latino officers had changed the composition of the once white police department. The proportion of blacks within the LAPD became roughly equivalent to the proportion of blacks within the city population. Nevertheless, many blacks were convinced that they were persistently mistreated by police officers of all races.

The neglected "McCone Revisited" report had addressed this issue in 1985. While the report took note of programs designed to improve community relations and the recruitment of minority police officers, it found that "the issue of equitable law enforcement continues to be one of the contentious and serious problems for residents of South Central Los Angeles." The report urged Mayor Bradley and the city council to ask police commissioners and Chief Gates to develop a plan "to improve police-community relations, police-community communication and the current allocation or deployment formula [of police] in South Central Los Angeles." Its bureaucratic language notwithstanding, "McCone Revisited" was a valuable and distant warning of the troubled situation in South Central, had anyone in authority chose to heed it.

But no one was paying attention. Nothing was done to make law enforcement more equitable, nor was action taken on the report's recommendations to reduce infant mortality and improve housing and education in South Central. No notice was taken by Chief Gates, who often dismissed concerns about police-community relations by saying that he was greeted in a friendly fashion whenever he visited South Central. No notice was taken by Mayor Bradley, who was too absorbed in downtown development and his vision of a world city to focus on the growing poverty and violence in his own backyard.

"McCone Revisited" was issued when Bradley and Los Angeles were basking in an Olympics afterglow and Southern California was still a place of dreams. The mayor had no inkling that his visionary dream would become a nightmare.

2

TRIAL BY VIDEOTAPE

"This is great! They got it on tape! Now we'll have a live, in-the-field film to show police recruits. It can be a real-life example of how to use escalating force properly."

—Sergeant Stacey Koon.[1]

RODNEY KING REMEMBERED THE PAIN OF THE BEATING AND OF feeling like "a crushed can" when it was over. Officer Laurence Powell remembered that he was "scared to death" when King charged at him and that he became exhausted from hitting King with his metal police baton. Officer Timothy Wind recalled that "King's arms were as big as my thighs" and that he behaved the way suspects were supposed to act when under the influence of the drug phencyclidine, or PCP. "Shit, I got to get out of here," Wind thought. Officer Theodore Briseno remembered that nothing went right. He recalled King's iron strength and the ease with which King threw him from his back when he tried to bring his arms together to handcuff him. He remembered the charge and a wild swing by Officer Powell with his baton which clipped King in the head and knocked him down. He remembered that Powell continued to flail away, "out of control."

Sergeant Stacey Koon, the supervising officer, remembered that he had directed officers to swarm King before a blow was struck and that King tossed them off his back like so many rag dolls. He remembered firing two volleys into King from his electric stun gun without stopping him and telling Powell and Wind to hit King in his joints with their batons to keep him on the ground. Koon was convinced that he had abided by Los Angles Police Department policy and very possibly saved King from being shot, but he knew that what had happened had not been pretty to watch. "I have seen uses of force of considerable violence, but I have not seen anything that is as violent as this in my fourteen and a half years [as a Los Angeles police officer]," Koon subsequently testified.[2]

The incident was recalled in so many conflicting variations by those involved that their stories resembled the classic Japanese film, *Rashomon*, in which every witness sees a murder and a rape from a different perspective. But what King and the officers remembered would have little to do with public perceptions. The vivid and emotional recollections of the participants were overshadowed by the graphic observations of an uncompromising and emotionless witness, the famous videotape of the beating.

The man who made the videotape, George William Holliday, then the thirty-one-year-old manager of the Hollywood office of a national plumbing company, was not out to expose police brutality or make a name for himself. He was a quiet man with a new Sony camcorder who had planned to arise at 6:00 A.M. that Sunday so he could videotape an employee who was running in the Los Angeles Marathon. But at about 12:45 A.M., he was awakened by the noise of a helicopter and the sound of sirens, and his attention was drawn across Foothill Boulevard, just past its intersection with Osborne Street. Groggy from sleep, Holliday peered out the bedroom window of his second-floor apartment in Lake View Terrace. From a distance of ninety feet, he could see police cars and a man, his hands on the roof of a car, surrounded by police. Holliday asked his wife, Maria, to videotape what was happening. "No," she said sleepily. Holliday decided to do the videotaping himself. He put on his trousers, walked into the living room, and grabbed the camcorder. Out on the balcony, he began taping. By this time, Holliday recalled later, "they were hitting him."[3]

Video cameras are commonplace in Los Angeles. Two other residents of Holliday's apartment complex who were awakened by the noise that night also tried taping the arrest scene, but lacked second-floor vantage points or reacted too slowly to obtain footage of King being beaten. Holliday was quicker on the draw. When he began taping, Rodney King was charging toward Officer Powell, who had his baton drawn in a vertical position. Holliday then moved the camera slightly and shot the entire sequence of events.

Holliday taped his fateful video on the day Iraq accepted the terms of the United States and its allies for ending the Persian Gulf War, a conflict that Americans had seen first and often on Cable News Network. CNN had become a fixture in American homes during the war, and within a few days the battle scenes would be replaced by excerpts of the Rodney King beating. "Television used the tape like wallpaper," said Ed Turner, executive vice president for CNN.[4] The Holliday videotape made Rodney King a household name around the world.

SERGEANT KOON REPORTED KING'S ARREST AT 12:56 A.M. ON Sunday, March 3, 1991, on the portable computer in his police car: "U just had a big time use of force. Tased and beat the suspect of CHP [California Highway Patrol] pursuit. Big Time."[5] Neither Koon nor anyone else at the scene knew that this big-time use of force had been taped, and Holliday was in no particular hurry to spread the news. He went back to bed, arose on schedule, drove downtown to tape the marathon, and used his camcorder again at a wedding later in the day.

But Holliday wondered why the officers had hit and kicked the unknown black man so many times. He thought about what he had seen and decided to tell the police about his videotape. Whoever answered his call at the Foothill Police Station—and no one at Foothill ever acknowledged taking it—wasn't interested. Disappointed that the police had "pretty much hung up" on him, Holliday decided to tell CNN's Los Angeles bureau about his tape. This proved another disappointment, for no one was at CNN to take the call.[6] By now Holliday was convinced that the world should see what he had taped from his balcony. On Monday morning he took the tape to KTLA, the Los Angeles station on which he watched local news. It made a strong and immediate impact. "We were all shocked by it and realized from the first that it was important," said Warren Cereghino, then KTLA news director.[7] A copy of the tape was taken downtown to LAPD headquarters in Parker Center, where senior officers watched in disbelief. Lieutenant Fred Nixon, the LAPD deputy spokesman, promised that the department would investigate. "Anybody who would look at it . . . would want to do an investigation," Captain Tim McBride said later.[8]

Chief Daryl Gates was out of town, and Assistant Chief Robert Vernon was in charge. He moved swiftly, ordering Internal Affairs investigators who were on their way home to return to their posts. At 8:30 P.M., he ordered Captain McBride to return to Foothill Station to assist in the inquiry. McBride commanded the Foothill Division, which polices an area that sprawls for sixty square miles across the eastern San Fernando Valley into the surrounding foothills. It includes all or part of eight communities, among them Lake View Terrace.

The investigators were still trying to identify the officers on the Holliday videotape when the first story of the King beating ran, at 10:15 P.M. on KTLA, leading the second section of the evening news. It was seen simultaneously at 1:15 A.M. EST Tuesday, March 5, at the Atlanta headquarters of CNN, which has an affiliation agreement with KTLA. The tape made as strong an impression on CNN producers as it had on Cereghino and LAPD officials. CNN immediately obtained a microwave feed of the KTLA tape and began to use it early that morning. KNBC, the NBC affiliate in Los Angeles, obtained a copy of the tape later in the day, and Cereghino made it available to other local stations and their networks.

By Wednesday, March 6, the tape that would transform the Rodney King beating into an international symbol of police brutality was receiving more attention in the Los Angeles media market than the just concluded war. The tape would be shown hundreds of times on local television in the year to come and in widely watched segments of CNN Headline News. KTLA would win a Peabody Award for showing it. The tape was also seen recurrently on network television, sometimes as a background for voice-over narration of developments in the story. In the ensuing thirteen months, the NBC, CBS, and ABC networks would do eighty-seven stories on the evening news alone.[9]

The scene that was burned into the brains of television viewers differed in a small but significant way from the original Holliday videotape. Holliday's video starts with three minutes and twenty-five seconds of family pictures followed by nine minutes and twenty seconds of tape from the incident at Foothill and Osborne. The first event of the incident as it was recorded by Holliday is King's charge toward Powell, who responds with a swift baton blow that knocks King to the ground. Eighty-one seconds elapse between this initial blow and the final baton strike, after which King was taken into custody. But the tape that shaped the opinion of the world had been edited at KTLA from eighty-one seconds to sixty-eight seconds. This eliminated a blurry ten-second segment caused by Holliday's movement of the camera soon after he began taping. Removed with the blurry ten seconds was the crucial three-second segment just preceding it that showed King's charge at Powell. The charge was part of the story because it showed King's resistance to being taken into custody, but millions of viewers who saw the incident on television never knew it existed, nor, indeed, did many of the producers at other stations who were responsible for showing the tape. The decision to remove this segment, a decision that defined the incident for the world, was the act of editors at a single local station. Although this editing went unnoticed in the furor that followed, the missing three seconds would return to haunt the prosecution when the police officers accused of beating King were tried in Simi Valley.

Some of Sergeant Koon's supporters (and for a time Koon himself) would become convinced that the editing was an act of political bias. But it more probably reflected the mindless but no less harmful bias of an industry that demands picture quality even at the cost of comprehension. "We edit tape so we get the most dramatic footage that tells the story," Cereghino said. "We do it all the time."[10] Cereghino was an experienced and respected news director and no liberal ideologue. Later he would say that the rarity of Holliday-type tapes in a city awash with video cameras argues in favor of Chief Gates' contention that the King beating was an "aberration." Indeed, KTLA had a reputation for giving the police the benefit of the doubt, and the station management gave the LAPD advance warning by delivering a copy of the full tape to Parker Center hours before it was broadcast. But the KTLA editing was nonetheless prejudicial to the LAPD, and all the more so because other stations that began using the tape did not know the editing had occurred.

David Farmer, CNN's Los Angeles bureau chief, subsequently had qualms about the editing of the Holliday tape. He told me that it reflected a "built-in aversion to showing out-of-focus and inexplicable footage."[11] But the three-second segment of King's charge that comes before the blurry section is only slightly out of focus and hardly inexplicable. On the contrary, this deleted opening section and the events that occurred before Holliday began filming are crucial to understanding what happened. This was eventually recognized at CNN, which obtained a copy of the full Holliday tape from Cereghino several weeks after the incident. When the omission of the section showing King's charge became an issue nearly a year later, Ed Turner directed that CNN use the full eighty-one-second tape whenever it was shown. But the tape wasn't being shown very often at this point because CNN had belatedly heeded Turner's sensible admonition against using it as "wallpaper." Other networks, and most importantly the local stations in Los Angeles, continued to use the abbreviated version of the videotape.

Even if the missing three seconds are included and the context explained in a light favorable to the police, the videotape depicts a brutal incident. The beating appalled not only citizens who are squeamish about the realities of police work but LAPD officers who suspected that there was more to the incident than the tape revealed. Captain Paul Jefferson, an African American who would play a critical role in the initial stages of the riots in 1992, saw the tape for the first time when it was televised in the coffee room of the Van Nuys Police Station. "It was unreal," Jefferson said. "When the officers saw the tape, there wasn't a word said. They just turned around and walked out with their heads down. Nobody said a word. They were in shock."[12]

The shock was shared by Chief Gates, who had returned from Washington, D.C., to Los Angeles around midnight on March 4, after participating in a conference on violence sponsored by the Bush administration. The chief's security aide told him about the incident when he picked him up at the airport, but Gates was not prepared for what he saw when he watched the tape the following morning. Staring at the screen in disbelief, he played the tape twenty-five times. "To see my officers engaged in what appeared to be excessive use of force, possibly criminally excessive, to see them beat a man with their batons *fifty-six times*, to see a sergeant on scene who did nothing to seize control, was something I never dreamed I would witness," Gates wrote later. "It was a very, *very* extreme use of force—extreme for any police department in America. But for the LAPD, considered by many to be perhaps the finest, most professional police department in the world, it was more than extreme. It was impossible."[13]

THE INCIDENT THAT LEFT GATES "SICK TO MY STOMACH, SICK AT heart" began at 12:30 A.M. on March 3 as the California Highway Patrol husband-and-wife team of Tim and Melanie Singer was patrolling Interstate 210, the Foothill Freeway, north of Los Angeles in a marked car. Melanie Singer was driving, heading west in the direction of Simi Valley. As she completed a long descent near the Sunland Boulevard off-ramp, she glanced in her rear-view mirror and saw the headlights of a car approaching at high speed. She exited at the off-ramp and returned to the freeway behind the speeding car. It was the beginning of a 7.8-mile pursuit during which Singer clocked the speed of the car she was following, a white 1988 two-door Hyundai Excel, at 110 to 115 miles an hour on the freeway and up to 85 miles an hour on residential streets after it exited the freeway at Paxton Street. The driver of the Hyundai ignored the flashing lights and screaming sirens of the highway patrol car, prompting Tim Singer to radio for help.

After the Hyundai left the freeway, Melanie Singer activated the spot lamp on the left side of her car, illuminating the interior of the car that was being pursued. She saw "three black male occupants," one of them in the backseat. A car from the Los Angeles Unified School District, which then had its own police department, joined the pursuit as the driver of the Hyundai sped on, committing what the Singers later said were numerous traffic violations. The Hyundai ran a red light at Van Nuys and Foothill Boulevards, nearly causing a collision. By the time it finally stopped, just beyond the intersection of Osborne Street and Foothill Boulevard, LAPD units were participating in the chase, and an LAPD helicopter was hovering overhead, its spotlight focused on the scene below. King had pulled to a stop near a darkened entrance to Hansen Dam Park, just beyond The Corral, the saloon where Arnold Schwarzenegger in *Terminator 2* beats up a pool-playing customer who will not relinquish his motorcycle.

King would give various explanations of why he stopped where he did, but the truth seems to be that he had no choice. His path was blocked by a red pickup truck whose driver had pulled over after hearing the sirens but was still partially blocking the road. The cornered King stopped so abruptly that the highway patrol car behind him nearly struck the rear bumper of the Hyundai. Melanie Singer swerved, putting her car abreast of the Hyundai, which meant that Tim Singer was staring directly at Rodney King. Realizing that her husband might be in danger if the driver was armed, Melanie Singer slammed the patrol car into reverse and wound up a few feet behind King's car. Using a hand-held microphone, Tim Singer then barked orders, asking the occupants of the Hyundai to exit and surrender.

Noise and confusion dominated the scene. The siren of the Los Angeles school district vehicle was still blaring, and the highway patrol car was so close to the Hyundai that Tim Singer's commands were lost in the feedback of the car's public address system. The roar of the helicopter added to the din. Three Los Angeles Police Department cars arrived, and the officers drew their guns and took cover behind car doors. Officers Laurence Powell and Timothy Wind were in one car and Officers Theodore Briseno and Rolando Solano in another. Sergeant Stacey Koon had arrived by himself in the third car. He parked at a 45-degree angle about twenty feet away from the Hyundai.

Tim Singer realized that his commands could not be heard, and he dropped the microphone and stepped out of the patrol car, yelling at the driver of the Hyundai to exit. King stayed put, but his passengers obeyed Singer's commands, left the vehicle, and lay face down on the ground. Tim Singer turned his attention to the two passengers while Melanie Singer yelled again at the driver to leave the car. King finally tried to climb out but was pulled back by his seat belt. He unsnapped the belt and exited. King was smiling and looked "almost happy" to Melanie Singer. King then put his hands on the roof of the car, looked up at the helicopter, waved, and did a little dance. As he looked up, King started talking gibberish. Watching him in the light from the helicopter, Tim Wind noticed that King was glistening with sweat although he was wearing only a thin cotton shirt and the night was cold. Then King put one hand into his pants pocket, a move Koon thought "dangerous" and that caused Officer Wind to bring his gun up and sight it on King. "Oh, my God, he has a gun," Wind thought.[14] But King put his hand back on top of the car, and Wind saw he held nothing in it. King then meandered away from the Hyundai, talking to himself and smiling, and went to his knees in front of the car occupied by Powell and Wind. "He got on all fours like a dog," Wind said. "And he turned around and he continued to mutter and giggle and smile. At one point he patted the ground."[15]

Officers were shouting commands at King to lie on his stomach and put his hands behind his back. Instead, he moved to what Wind later described as a push-up position and Koon thought was a runner's crouch. King looked directly at Koon, who realized that he was probably drunk and began to suspect that he was also on PCP. Koon reached into the front seat of his car for an electric stun gun known as a Taser, a weapon he had often used when assigned to the Los Angeles County Jail, where officers are not allowed to carry firearms.

"Taser" is an acronym for "Thomas A. Swift Electric Rifle." The weapon fires two cassette cartridges which connect to skin or clothing with small darts. Each cartridge is supposed to deliver fifty thousand volts of low-amperage electricity, instantly felling a suspect. The weapon was normally used by a sergeant, who was frequently a supervising officer at an arrest. Koon had used the Taser many times and swore by it, but its infallibility was not universally accepted. An analysis by the LAPD of Taser use during the first six months of 1989 showed that the weapon had an 86 percent success rate and that it caused virtually no injuries beyond minor irritation.[16] But sometimes the Taser failed to work because its voltage was low or the darts failed to "get a good spread," the phrase used to describe proper separation of the darts on the suspect's body or clothing. And while the study didn't mention it, some command officers also were concerned that sergeants sometimes became too preoccupied with the Taser to supervise an arrest.

While Koon was unholstering the Taser, Melanie Singer was shouting at King to show his hands. King ignored her. "He was laughing like a smirk, smirking," she later told a grand jury. It was at this point that King made a movement that later became significant to those who believed he was beaten for racial reasons but that in any event was critical because it prompted Koon to take control of King's arrest. King put his hands on his buttocks, briefly causing Melanie Singer and other officers to wonder if he were reaching for a gun. He then shook his buttocks at Singer, an action later described by Koon in this way: "He grabbed his butt with both hands and began to shake and gyrate his fanny in a sexually suggestive fashion. As King sexually gyrated, a mixture of fear and offense overcame Melanie. The fear was of a Mandingo sexual encounter."[17]

Singer, who told grand jurors that she had "never come into contact with something like this," drew her weapon and directed King to "get your hands away from your butt" and lie down. When King finally complied, Singer told him to turn his head away. Singer felt the situation was then safe enough to approach King, gun in hand. But as she drew within five or six feet, she heard a voice yell, "Stand back. Stand back. We'll handle this." Singer looked toward the voice and saw a jut-jawed LAPD officer with sergeant's stripes. Melanie Singer yielded to rank, relinquishing the arrest to Stacey Koon.

THE SERGEANT SINGER OBEYED WAS ACCUSTOMED TO THE PERILS of street command. Stacey Cornell Koon, then forty-one, was a well-educated and experienced officer who took pride in being in control of himself and dangerous situations. During fourteen and a half years on the LAPD he had earned more than ninety commendations and only three reprimands and had a reputation for bravery and stiff-necked rectitude. Working in the tough 77th Street Division, in the heart of South Central, Koon had once shot and wounded a gang member who was about to shoot another officer with an assault rifle. The shooting was found to be justified, and the officer targeted by the gang member believed that Koon had saved his life.

Subsequently, Koon became a living legend in the 77th Division for his response to a situation that he remembered as far more frightening than the shooting incident. Koon was on duty when a black transvestite prostitute with bleeding, open sores about his lips and mouth was brought into the station. Fearing that the prostitute had AIDS, officers gave him a wide berth. But suddenly, while waiting to be booked, the prostitute collapsed from an apparent heart attack. No one moved toward him except Koon, who dropped to his knees and administered mouth-to-mouth resuscitation. "His face was pale, he was scared, but he did it anyway," said Officer Greg Baltad, the arresting officer. The prostitute died, but Baltad thought Koon's futile attempt to save him was the greatest act of heroism he had ever seen. When an autopsy revealed that the prostitute indeed had AIDS, the 77th Street Division cops were in awe of Koon and paid tribute with the gallows humor typical of police. "Stacey, you're losing weight," they would say in the weeks after the incident. "Stacey, you look pale."[18]

On the night he took over the arrest of Rodney King, Koon was more angry than scared. As Koon saw it, Melanie Singer was injecting a gun into a situation that didn't require a lethal weapon. LAPD officers are taught not to approach a suspect with a drawn gun, and Singer's "lousy tactic" offended Koon. "Had she proceeded, either she was going to shoot Rodney King, or he was going to take her gun away and shoot her," Koon said in *Presumed Guilty*, a book he wrote about the incident. Koon's apprehension was shared by Theodore Briseno, the most experienced of the officers Koon would call on to take King into custody. "Oh shit, he's going to reach up there and take that gun from her hand, and we'll have a big shooting and a dead cop," Briseno thought.[19] Before this could happen, Koon ordered the police officers who were watching King to holster their weapons. He then told four LAPD officers—Powell, Wind, Briseno and Solano—to surround King and "swarm" him by jumping on his back. Koon would later say he did not ask the highway patrol officers or the school district officers to assist because they were needed to take the Hyundai passengers into custody. But Koon also questioned the training of these officers. He trusted only members of the LAPD.

Hindsight and the videotape suggest that Koon had more than four LAPD officers available, although not everyone who was present at the end of the incident was on the scene when Koon took over from Melanie Singer. But several officers stood by as King was beaten, which on the videotape conveyed the impression that they were watching the imposition of street justice on a hapless suspect who had no hope of resistance or escape. Their passivity seemed to undermine the claims of those involved in the arrest that they were in fear for their lives. But Koon lacked the perspective of television viewers. Standing within a cone of light shining from the police helicopter overhead, he did not realize that a total of twenty-five law enforcement officers were at the scene, including fourteen LAPD "bystander officers," as they became known.[20] Koon told Internal Affairs investigators that he knew of only nine officers on hand, including the highway patrol and school district officers. Other participants in the arrest were also largely unaware of the bystander officers. "It pissed me off," Briseno said later, to learn that there were so "many officers out there and nobody wanted to do anything."[21]

Indeed, after Melanie Singer stepped back, Koon was for a time the only officer who was doing anything. Hoping he could "de-escalate" the tense situation, Koon ordered everyone else to "shut up," and he tried to talk King into complying with him. "Get your face down," he shouted repeatedly. Wind remembered that Koon also may have yelled, "Get your fuckin' face down."[22] But King paid no attention.

King's behavior increased Koon's suspicions that King was "dusted," as police call suspects who have been using PCP. His initial perception was based on King's sweatiness on this cold night, his gibbering, and the bizarre behavior he had exhibited toward Melanie Singer. The perception was reinforced when Koon established eye contact with King from a distance of fifteen feet. King stared back with a "glazed . . . spaced-out" look. "It's like he's looking at me, doesn't see me, he's just kind of looking right through me," Koon told Internal Affairs investigators. None of these symptoms are inconsistent with intoxication, and King did not exhibit a classical symptom of PCP use called nystagmus, a rapid, involuntary oscillation of the eyeballs. Nevertheless, Koon jumped to the conclusion that King was a PCP user. Wind also thought that King was different from any drunk he had ever seen. He remembered that other officers, one of whom he identified as Powell, yelled, "He's dusted," after King ignored Melanie Singer's commands and crawled around like a dog.

The belief that King was on PCP is crucial to understanding Koon's behavior. Police stations abound in horror stories about the exploits of PCP users, who are feared by cops because of their reputed imperviousness to pain. Four years earlier Koon had given a Taser to an inexperienced officer in the 77th Street Division during the arrest of a man suspected of using PCP. The officer fired the Taser and hit the suspect, who instead of collapsing leaped through a living room window and menaced an elderly woman. He was finally subdued, but Koon resolved that he would never again let a PCP suspect get the upper hand. He thought about this as he watched King, a muscular man Koon estimated to be six feet two inches tall and to weigh 250 pounds. Koon saw that King was "buffed out"; that is, he had a highly developed upper body. To Koon, that meant King had lifted weights in prison. He concluded that King was an ex-convict, as he proved to be.

As Koon later told the story in his book and on the witness stand in three trials, he immediately formulated a "tactical plan" for taking King into custody. More probably, other officers have told me, Koon reacted instinctively and relied on techniques that had worked for him in other situations. But whatever the degree of planning, Koon's actions show that he intended to take King into custody without harming him. Swarming King was the least violent tactic that could be used against a suspect who ignored verbal commands.

Koon later told investigators that he relied on "a young group of officers" with less experience than he would have liked. Laurence Michael Powell, twenty-eight, chosen as the lead officer in the attempt to subdue King, had served three and a half years on the LAPD and led the Foothill Division in arrests. Some of Powell's fellow officers considered him more cocky than competent, however, and he had by coincidence been singled out less than two hours earlier for inefficient use of the baton. As part of their ongoing training, LAPD officers are sometimes called upon at roll calls to demonstrate a particular police technique. When he went on duty that night at Foothill Station, Powell had been told to demonstrate "power strokes" with his side-handled metal baton, known by police as the "Monadnock," after the name of the manufacturer. The "power stroke" is a forceful blow, using the entire weight of an officer's body. Powell had failed the test and was told by his supervisors to practice.

Powell was nearly six feet, weighed 193 pounds and was slightly pudgy. He was also tired because he had recently moved to the midnight-to-eight shift—known as "morning watch"—and found it difficult to sleep during the day. "I can't sleep, that's the problem," he had said in a computer message to another officer eleven minutes before joining the King pursuit. "I need to get worn out." Powell was serving as a training officer because the LAPD was expanding and Foothill needed twenty-three new training officers to accommodate a large class that had recently graduated from the Police Academy. Foothill's Captain McBride didn't like the situation. "You're selecting too many people in too short a period of time with too little research . . ." he said later. Powell was one of those people.[23]

Powell was the training officer for Timothy Wind, a quiet thirty-year-old rookie who was older and more experienced than the officer instructing him. Wind was a former Green Beret who had served seven years on the fifty-six-member police force in Shawnee, Kansas, before moving to Los Angeles to advance his career. After Powell was cited for inefficient power strokes at roll call, Wind had demonstrated the proper use of the baton. Despite his proficiency, Wind had used the baton only in training. He had been paired with Powell for three days and seems to have had a premonition about his partner. "All I care about is I don't get any 181s," Wind told Powell on the first night they were together, referring to the Los Angeles Police Department Manual number [1.81.0] for a personnel complaint. "Why are you saying that?" asked Powell, who then inaccurately declared that he had not been the subject of previous complaints.[24]

Thirty-eight-year-old Theodore Briseno, the smallest of the officers involved in the King arrest, was a wiry, hard-working nine-year veteran of the LAPD who was at most five feet seven and weighed only 135 pounds. Briseno had participated in violent arrests and won several commendations but had also been suspended in 1987 for using force on a handcuffed suspect accused of child abuse. He was the training officer for twenty-seven-year-old Rolando Solano, a rookie barely five months out of the Police Academy.

At Powell's direction, Wind cautiously inspected the Hyundai to make certain no one else was inside. Then, at Koon's command, the four officers jumped on King. Powell and Briseno grabbed his arms while Wind and Solano took his legs. Powell kept his knee on King's back, trying to force his left arm back to handcuff it. King was drenched in sweat. "His arm was rigid, and it wasn't moving at all," Powell told investigators. "I couldn't move it." Then, with a quick motion, King tossed the two officers off his back. "And all of a sudden, when he cut loose, he hit me in the chest and I see Powell flying off his [other] side," Briseno said. "I don't know what's going on . . . but I'm thinking, man, this sucker is on something. This is a bad ass."[25]

After King tossed off Powell and Briseno, Koon ordered Wind and Solano to stand back. They were only too eager to comply. "I didn't want to get near this man," Wind said later.[26] But Wind stayed and obediently followed Koon's subsequent commands, while Solano retreated and virtually became a bystander. As far as Koon was concerned, King's actions in throwing off Powell and Briseno had confirmed his suspicions. King had exhibited the "superhuman strength" of the typical PCP user, becoming the "hulk" of his nightmares. "I know if he gets hold of me and he grabs me in [the] neck . . . it's going to be like a death grip, and you can have all 8,300 members of this police department pull this guy off and it's not going to work," Koon told Internal Affairs investigators.

When King still paid no attention to Koon's shouted commands to lie face down on the ground, the sergeant fired the Taser, hitting him in the back with the darts. King groaned and fell to his knees, then rose and turned toward Koon. Koon, who had shut off the Taser, reactivated it and fired again, this time hitting King's chest from a distance of about nine feet.

King once more groaned and collapsed but braced himself on his right elbow and again began to come to his feet. From Powell's perspective, King did a 180 degree turn and stared at him and Wind from a distance of six feet. "Does anyone else have a Taser?" Koon asked. No one did.

THIS WAS THE MOMENT, AS KING STRUGGLED TO REGAIN HIS balance, when George Holliday began videotaping on the balcony of his apartment across the street. It was also the moment, or very close to it, when the frustrated Koon ordered Powell and Wind to deliver power strokes with their batons, telling them not to hit the suspect in the head. And it was the moment before the moment when King charged wildly in Powell's direction looking "like he was trying to imitate a mean dog," as Wind put it. Internal Affairs investigators realized that Powell and Wind had been terrified. "The Taser wasn't working," Powell told them. ". . . I drew my baton to defend myself." He also said he was "fighting for my life."

The belief that he had been engaged in a potential death struggle with someone on PCP would overshadow all of Powell's memories of the incident. He had flailed away with his baton as King charged, not with the controlled "power strokes" that Koon had ordered, but with wild swings. King was so close to Powell that Koon mistakenly thought they had collided. One of Powell's swings, probably the first one, knocked King down. Koon thought this crucial blow had landed on King's collarbone, while Powell told investigators that it had hit King's left arm. Melanie Singer saw it differently. "Officer Powell came up to the right side of the driver with his baton out, and he struck the right side of the driver's face . . ." Singer said. "I saw the blood come out of his face. I heard the driver scream." Recalling the event two years later, she said tearfully, "There is no doubt in my mind that he hit Mr. King repeatedly in the face. I will never forget it to the day I die."[27]

Singer testified later that Powell followed up the first blow by delivering an additional four to six blows to King's head or face, some to the left side. But her testimony is supported neither by the videotape, which appears to show a single head blow, nor by the fact that doctors found virtually no injuries on the left side of King's head. No one doubted the sincerity of Singer's recollections, but her vivid account was clearly affected by the stress of the moment.

Koon and Powell were under at least as much stress as Singer, and the accuracy of their recollections is similarly disputed by the videotape and by medical evidence brought out in the subsequent trials. King suffered a broken cheekbone and multiple fractures on the right side of his face, lacerations on the forehead, a fracture of the distal fibula in the right leg, and various bruises, contusions, and abrasions.

Powell and Koon never conceded that King was hit in the head and maintained that his head injuries were the result of falls to the ground. When Powell testified thirteen months after the event, he said King had "collided" with his baton and taken the first blow on the chest rather than on his left arm. He seems sincerely to have struggled with the problem of reconciling his recollections with a videotape that depicts events quite differently from the way he remembered them. While the tape is not entirely conclusive on the issue of the head blow, it was evident to Powell as he watched it more than fifty times that the blow had at least landed high on King's body. Try as he might, Powell could not remember this. "It has confused my memory because it is not my perspective," he said of the videotape.[28] He finally decided that his first baton blow had landed on King's chest.

The truth is that Powell remembered so little except his fear that he could not have reconstructed the beating without the videotape. When he talked to Internal Affairs investigators after the incident, Powell was only vaguely aware of Melanie Singer's presence. He did not know that Koon had used a second Taser. He did not realize that his partner Wind had also used his baton to keep King down. When Powell first viewed the videotape, he was so surprised at what he saw that he had trouble recognizing himself as the officer who kept hitting Rodney King.

Koon's memory was better, and he was more polemical than Powell in resisting the evidence of a head blow. Like Singer, Koon was reluctant to modify his recollections to conform them to the videotape. But in his efforts to convince others that his perceptions were accurate, Koon ignored any information that contradicted his theory of events. Koon wrote in his book that "most of us at the scene" believed King shattered his cheekbone when he fell to the pavement after being hit on the collarbone by Powell, implying that other officers agreed that King was not struck in the face. This is inaccurate and misleading. The three other LAPD officers close to the action believed that Powell had struck King in the head or the face with his baton. Solano, from a distance he estimated at three feet, saw four blows by Powell, two of which bounced off King's shoulders and struck King on each side of the face. "I didn't like the sound that [Powell's baton] made," said Solano, who testified that he looked away. Briseno, from roughly the same distance, thought Powell's first blow clipped King in the head. Wind, standing next to Powell, saw two blows to the arm as King lunged at his partner. Then he saw King's "head came up and his body came up. And he moved enough that Powell hit him in the face."[29]

Wind was positive about the facial hit but convinced that it was the result of King's movement rather than Powell's intent. Wind was nearest to Powell, and his account is the most compatible with the videotape and was given immediately after the incident to Internal Affairs investigators. His

version of events, substantially reinforced by the testimony of Solano and
Briseno, conclusively establishes that Powell hit King in the face.

This one baton strike to the right side of King's face did more damage
than all the subsequent baton blows combined, and the obstinate refusal of
either Powell or Koon to acknowledge it ultimately would prove as legally
damaging to the officers as it was physically harmful to King. Intentional
head blows except in self-defense are a violation of policy in the LAPD, as
in most police departments, and such blows can constitute powerful evidence of criminal misconduct. The key word is "intentional." The most sensible course of action for Koon and Powell would have been to concede the
head blow and say, accurately, that it was unintentional. But Koon had not
seen the head blow. He was stubbornly unwilling to concede that it had occurred, perhaps because it undermined his argument that King was subdued
by controlled and proper use of force.

Koon was even unwilling to use the valid alibi that the stress of a difficult arrest may have altered his perceptions. Taky Tzimeas, the experienced
Internal Affairs Division detective who interrogated Koon, Powell, and
Wind separately soon after the incident, realized that all the officers had
been afflicted to some degree by "tunnel vision," a common phenomenon
in which police officers become so fixated on events in front of them that
their peripheral vision is severely limited. During his interrogation, Tzimeas
suggested to Powell and Wind that tunnel vision had affected their perceptions. They agreed. But Koon was unwilling to relinquish his view that he
had taken control of a potentially dangerous incident, conceived a sound
tactical plan, and followed policy in using steadily escalating force to subdue a combatant suspect.[30]

After King was knocked down by Powell's baton blow to the right side
of his face, he spent most of the next eighty seconds on the ground, sometimes half-rising or getting to his knees or haunches but never again reaching his feet. No matter how often he was hit, King was unwilling or unable
to comply with Koon's command to assume the "felony prone" position—
face down with legs spread out and arms outstretched. Instead, he moved
around in what prosecutors would say was a natural reaction of a drunken
man to incessant blows and numerous kicks. But as King rolled around on
the ground, Koon saw not a hapless drunk trying to escape the pain of a severe beating but a wily ex-convict doing "the Folsom roll." This is a technique supposedly learned by convicts at Folsom Prison in which a suspect
rolls into an officer, throws him off balance, and grabs his gun belt. Koon
believed that King was trying to make contact with Wind, who easily evaded
him by stepping back and delivering a series of baton blows.

Shocked viewers of the videotape would find Koon's analysis ludicrous.
Most viewers believed that the tape showed the vicious beating of a

defenseless man who was surrounded by police officers. But even analyses of the tape that took the harshest possible views of the officers' conduct showed that the force used against King was not continuous. An undetermined number of blows—Koon thought at least a dozen—are delivered during the ten seconds of blurred videotape. When the blurry section clears, King is on his stomach with his torso raised and no blows are being struck. Briseno's arm is seen coming up to restrain Powell, who stands over King with upraised baton.

Wind told investigators that Briseno was at this moment warning him and Powell that they could be shocked if they made contact with the Taser wires which were still attached to King. Briseno, however, always maintained that he raised his hand to stop the beating, not the electric shock of his fellow officers.[31] Whatever Briseno intended, his action momentarily halted the rain of baton blows fifteen to seventeen seconds after they had begun. But Powell then saw King starting to rise again, and he resumed swinging his baton. Briseno could not see King's movement from where he stood, but he saw the baton come up and he stepped back, fearing that he might be struck by one of Powell's uncontrolled swings.

Powell's next blows hit King in the upper torso while he was sitting on his calves. King toppled over, rising to his hands and knees. Powell and Wind continued to strike him, and Wind to kick him in an effort to keep King on the ground. Both officers told police investigators that they were amazed that their baton blows had little apparent effect on King, who kept trying to get to his feet. Koon barked out futile commands to King, and he lost track of the number of baton blows struck by Powell and Wind. Thirty-five seconds into the tape, Powell shifts his baton attack to the lower extremities of King's body, apparently in response to Koon's commands to strike at the leg and elbow joints. A blow delivered by Powell at the forty-third second of the tape appears to have been the one that shattered the fibula of King's right leg. Koon knew and acknowledged that these blows had the potential to cause serious injury, but he believed this was preferable to the deadly force that might have been used if King had succeeded in reaching his feet.

Koon's subsequent contention that the force used to subdue King was reasonable depended heavily on his interpretation of the slight pauses by Powell and Wind as "evaluations" of the use of force. Brief pauses occur at twenty and thirty-five seconds into the videotape, when the officers are supposedly conducting these evaluations. Wind, at least, certainly seems to be evaluating, for he steps back in an apparent effort to assess the impact of the blows. But the pauses in Powell's actions are so brief that they are barely noticeable when the tape is played at normal speed. He pauses a second and a half to two seconds at the twenty-second point and a single second at the thirty-five second point. From the thirty-fifth to the fifty-fifth second of the tape, Powell hits King repeatedly, mostly on the lower extremities but also once in the upper torso. At this point King rolls over onto his back, and Powell's next blow strikes him in the chest. That blow might well have been the last one of the incident. Eight seconds after delivering it Powell reaches for the handcuffs that dangle from his right rear trousers pocket, a sign that he thinks King is ready to comply with the officers.

The pause is ended two seconds later by Briseno, who rushes in and delivers a swift downward movement of his left foot to the upper back of the inert King. King starts to rise in response, but Powell and Wind have no way of knowing that the movement was caused by the force applied by Briseno. What Powell sees is an unsearched felony suspect once more attempting to reach his feet. He delivers five to seven additional baton blows, and Wind delivers four more and six kicks. "Please stop," King cried out in his first words that Koon could understand. King had been beaten and kicked for eighty-one seconds. Koon then ordered all the officers in the vicinity to jump him and they responded in what Koon called one of the "sloppiest swarms I have ever seen." Powell handed his handcuffs to Briseno, who knelt down and clamped them on an unresisting King.

Why did Briseno stomp King? The federal government's explanation, when Briseno was charged with violating King's civil rights, was that Briseno was being "one of the boys" and showing solidarity with Powell and Wind. Government lawyers said that such conduct was in character for Briseno, who in 1987 had been suspended for hitting a handcuffed suspect with his baton and then kicking him in the neck area while he was face down on a carpeted floor. The suspect, accused of savagely beating two children, was only slightly injured and said he had relieved the pain of his stiff neck with two aspirin. But there was no doubt about Briseno's misconduct, which was witnessed by two other officers. According to testimony at a Board of Rights hearing, Briseno had been enraged and abusive to the suspect. The board recommended a sixty-six day suspension, an action routinely approved by Chief Gates.[32]

Still, any similarities between Briseno's conduct in this incident and the King arrest are outweighed by the differences. In contrast to the 1987 incident, when he arrived after the other officers were in control of the situation, Briseno was involved in the King arrest almost from the moment it was taken over by Koon. He participated in the first unsuccessful swarm and was hurled off King's back. He then tried to stop the beating, whether or not he used the Taser wires as an excuse, an action that was praised by state and federal prosecutors even while they were trying to convict him. Briseno's assertion that he stepped back when the beating continued because he wanted to avoid being hit by one of Powell's wild swings is uncontradicted by other testimony. Briseno subsequently yelled at King to stay flat on the ground, which made sense because Briseno could see that King was being hit and kicked whenever he moved. As Briseno remembered the events, he took advantage of the first significant lull in the beating to put his foot on King in an attempt to keep him down. This "stomp," as prosecutors subsequently called it, was the only use of force administered by Briseno throughout the entire incident. The tape shows that Briseno was not in a position to see Powell reaching for his handcuffs any more than Powell or Wind could see that Briseno's stomp caused King to move again.

After the incident, Briseno did not brag about it, as Powell did, or portray it as a textbook example of arrest procedure, as Koon did. Of the twenty-five officers at the scene, Briseno is the only one known to have criticized the arrest before learning of the existence of the videotape. Rolando Solano, the rookie cop who rode in Briseno's patrol car, supported Briseno's recollection that he was aghast at Powell's wild behavior. Briseno also recalled yelling at Koon during the incident, although the busy sergeant did not remember that Briseno had said anything to him. What is undisputed is that Briseno, usually respectful of authority, criticized Koon to Solano. "Sarge really fucked up out there tonight," he told him. Briseno could not wait to leave the scene.

RODNEY KING DID NOT HAVE THE OPTION OF LEAVING. AFTER HE was subdued by the swarm, he was double-handcuffed—a common precaution with PCP suspects—and cord-cuffed so that his legs were tied to his hands behind his back. This practice, known as hog-tying and then routinely used by the LAPD, would become controversial within the next two years after separate incidents in which two people died after being cord-cuffed and placed on their stomachs. King was not hurt by the hog-tying, but he suffered other indignities. Officer Louis Turriaga, later suspended for forty-four days by the LAPD, stepped on King's face during the cuffing and then dragged him face down to the roadside. Solano saw what was happening and rushed to aid Turriaga by lifting King's body so that it cleared the ground. This act did not go unnoticed by the LAPD high command. Originally facing termination because he was a probationary officer participating in a questionable incident, Solano was instead suspended for twenty-two days.

Medical help was promptly sought for King, but the way in which Powell and Koon went about it would be used as evidence against them. Powell made a call requesting an "RA [rescue ambulance] at Foothill and Osborne." When he was asked why, he said, "A victim of ah, ah" and then paused. "Beating," Koon shouted from the background. Powell gave a high-pitched laugh, almost a giggle, and said, "Yeah . . . numerous head wounds." The laughter was interpreted by prosecutors as a sign of gloating, while Powell would say it was a symptom of relief. There is no doubt that Powell, who was breathing hard and pacing after he holstered his baton, was relieved. "I was scared," he told Officer Susan Clemmer, who had been directing traffic at the scene. "The guy threw me off his back. I thought I was going to have to shoot him."

Koon also reported on the incident, issuing his message on the "big time use of force" and receiving a reply from Leslie Wiley, the area command dispatcher at Foothill Station, "Oh well, I'm sure the lizard didn't deserve it. Ha, ha. I'll let them know, OK?" Koon was matter-of-fact, following up on his report by asking that a fresh Taser and darts be readied for him when he returned to the station. But Powell, with the tension dissipated, began to brag about his exploits to Officer Corina Smith, who was in another patrol car miles from the scene. "Oops," he said in a message to Smith from his in-car computer, known as a Mobile Digital Terminal (MDT). "Oops what?" Smith asked.

"I haven't beaten anyone this bad in a long time," Powell messaged back.

"Oh, not again," Smith said.* "Why for you do that? I thought you agreed to chill out for awhile. What did he do?"

Powell replied: "I think he was dusted . . . many broken bones later."

Powell later made light of these remarks, and his lawyer dismissed this exchange as an attempt to impress an attractive female officer.[33]

As for King himself, he would be unable to explain much about what happened to him that fateful night because he was simply too intoxicated—and, arguably, too badly beaten—to remember. During the next three years, King gave fragmentary and contradictory testimony about what had occurred. The most significant contradiction involved the issue of alleged racist conduct by the police officers. King said after the beating that none of the officers expressed racial hostility. Later he changed his story and said the officers called him "nigger" as they beat him. Still later, at the federal criminal trial, King said he was not sure whether they had used this offensive word.

Other significant elements of King's account also changed with time and trials. He initially denied that he was intoxicated but subsequently told

* Smith apparently was referring to an unpublicized incident of October 3, 1990, in which she and Powell were accused of using excessive force against a handcuffed prisoner. LAPD personnel records show that Smith was accused of striking the prisoner with a baton and Powell of hitting him with a flashlight. Sergeant Koon investigated the complaints and found them without merit, apparently because the prisoner withdrew the accusations. An Internal Affairs inquiry into this incident after the King beating cleared Smith, sustained the complaint against Powell, and found the question of whether Koon had properly investigated unresolved.

a police investigator that he had consumed two forty-ounce bottles of malt liquor and another twelve-ounce bottle of malt liquor in a five-and-a-half-hour period before the incident. A blood-alcohol test taken more than five hours after King's arrest showed a level of 0.079 percent, just below the 0.08 percent blood-alcohol level that in California is presumptive evidence of intoxication. Extrapolating from this figure, state prosecutors and defense attorneys stipulated that King's blood-alcohol level at the time of arrest had been 0.19 percent, nearly two and a half times the legal limit. They also stipulated that a urine specimen taken from King at the time of the blood test showed no trace of PCP.

But the lack of evidence does not resolve the question of whether King ingested something more than beer in the hours before the incident. It is an enduring mystery. King's urine was highly alkaline, and doctors testified at the criminal trials of the officers that an alkaline urine can mask the presence of PCP. Detective Tzimeas of Internal Affairs knew that officers sometimes cried "PCP" as an alibi for excessive force, and he initially treated the contention that King had been using PCP with skepticism. As he plunged deeper into the investigation, however, Tzimeas concluded that these particular officers were telling the truth when they said they thought King had been using PCP. Particularly telltale in the detective's view was a moment after the beating when Koon had called upon any officer involved in the use of force to raise his hand. Powell and Wind raised their hands, and each was surprised to find that the other had been involved. Tzimeas did not consider this an excuse for the beating, but it convinced him that the officers had been "terrified" of King and fixated on him to the exclusion of anything else.

"Here you have a group of officers who are beating the snot out of this guy and it's not working," said Tzimeas. "Why isn't it working? They believed he was on something." Tzimeas found "very revealing" a statement by Wind, whom the detective believed to be especially truthful. "He said he started kicking [King] because his arms were tired. Put aside the victimization of King for a moment. It was wrong to kick him. But this is a statement of an officer who doesn't understand what is happening. He doesn't believe he was doing anything wrong."[34]

Tzimeas wanted to know more about what King was "on" the night of his arrest. Because he lacked confidence in the LAPD laboratory, he persuaded his superiors to send King's urine specimen to a private laboratory in Bakersfield that used more sophisticated testing procedures.[35] While these tests also did not produce evidence of PCP, they detected traces of an analogue of marijuana that had gone undetected by the LAPD laboratory. Could some other combination of drugs and liquor have accounted for King's behavior and his ability to absorb as many blows as he did? Tzimeas didn't know, and King wasn't telling. After his arrest King denied using marijuana, PCP, or any other drugs. But this story, like King's other accounts, also changed with time.

WHATEVER DRUGS KING MAY HAVE USED, THERE IS NO DOUBT that excessive drinking was his principal problem, as it had been for his father, Ronald, who died in 1987 at the age of forty-two after a life of heavy drinking. Rodney, known to his family and friends by his middle name, "Glen," was heading in the same direction. Friends and relatives agree that he was usually gentle and friendly when sober but temperamental when drinking. "He was a basically decent guy, with borderline intelligence but [who] could function in society," said his parole officer, Tim Fowler, a tall and muscular African American who developed an empathetic relationship with King. "His problem was alcoholism. He had been drinking from an early age."[36]

Rodney Glen King was born in Sacramento on April 4, 1965, four months before the Watts riot. His father was the son of a frequently absent Air Force sergeant from Kentucky and a mother who had abandoned Ronald and his sister, Angela, when they were toddlers. She eventually returned with two babies by another father, who were given to the older children to raise. Ronald King went to high school in Sacramento, which Angela remembers as more accepting of blacks than Southern California, and married Angela's best friend, Odessa. Lured by the promise of jobs in Southern California, the extended family moved south to Altadena, a Los Angeles community north of Pasadena. Ronald worked in construction when work was available and he was sober, and as a janitor at other times. Construction work was scarcer than he had been led to believe and so, sometimes, was food. Young Rodney's greatest fault in Aunt Angela's eyes was that he was a "big eater" who was "greedy" at the dinner table.[37]

Angela played a large role in raising Rodney. She thought of him as "the meek one" in a family of four boys and one girl but knew that the meekness concealed a stubborn streak. The biggest difference between Rodney King and his father, said Angela, was that the son would defend himself when provoked and would not back down from a fight, as Ronald often had done. This observation would unknowingly be echoed by Stacey Koon, who knew something about stubbornness. "The only thing that made Rodney King different [from other resisting suspects] was his will," Koon told me. "I've never seen anyone with a will like that."[38]

King had strength and coordination to go with his will. He was good at sports, especially baseball, and played outfield and third base on school and pickup teams. While not fast afoot, he could hit for distance and fielded well. But Rodney King's enduring passion, and his principal bond with his father, was fishing. Rodney King could happily fish at any time, and he seemed surprised when asked by a lawyer if he knew that Hansen Dam Park, where the high-speed chase ended on March 3, 1991, was closed at night. "My dad and I used to fish there all night long," he said.

In time, however, his father's drinking made a deeper impression on Rodney than their fishing trips. Ronald King worked less and less. His wife, Odessa, distraught about the drinking, joined the Jehovah's Witnesses. After Ronald's death in 1987, a sister moved into the home with her husband, who beat her until Rodney intervened. Another sister disappeared and was never heard from again. Rodney King's younger brother Juan was involved in the beating of a police officer and spent a year in jail.[39]

Rodney King had worked with his father from an early age. "When I was a kid, I went to work with my dad from the fourth and fifth and sixth grade," King told me. His father had a contract to clean buildings at night, and Rodney remembers working with him from 5:00 P.M. until 2:00 A.M., then getting four hours of sleep and going back to school. "So my concentration was really whacked, you know, as far as staying focused and in school," King recalled.[40] By the time he reached junior high school, he had his own contracts to do janitorial work at night.

Teachers and classmates at the racially mixed John Muir High School in Pasadena, which Jackie Robinson had attended nearly a half century earlier, thought that Glen King was easygoing. Jeanne Dea, a math teacher, remembered him as "a good-looking kid . . . kind of cute and sweet." King excelled in shop classes, where he learned to use welding equipment and other machinery and made wire rims for his first car.[41] But his memory was shaky, and he could barely read. King's teachers realized that he suffered from a learning disability and assigned him to special classes, but he made little progress. Six months before he would have graduated, King dropped out of John Muir and took a construction job.

Construction work suited King, who joined the Plasterers and Laborers Union and later enrolled in a building-construction class at Pasadena City College. "I get a real thrill out of building skyscrapers, getting up early in the morning, being on top of a bridge," King recalled years later. "I love that type of work."[42]

Rodney King fathered a daughter out of wedlock in 1982, when he was 17.[43] In 1984, he married another woman, his high school sweetheart, Dennetta. They also had a daughter but soon separated. On July 27, 1987, according to a legal complaint filed by Dennetta, King went to her home, beat her while she was sleeping, demanded her car keys, then dragged her outside the house and beat her some more. King did not contest a charge of battery. On March 28, 1988, he was placed on a mild form of probation, known as "diversion" and ordered to obtain counseling, which he never did. He and Dennetta divorced, and he married a neighborhood girl named Crystal Waters, who had two children by an earlier relationship.

Stacey Koon had been right in guessing that King was an ex-convict. Returning from a fishing trip without money, King stopped at a convenience store in Monterey Park, just east of Los Angeles, on November 3, 1989. He picked up a package of bubble gum and handed the grocer, Tae Suck Baik, a dollar's worth of food stamps. According to King, he had already stopped in two other stores that had refused to accept food stamps. When Baik also refused to take them, King pulled a two-foot-long tire iron from his jacket. "Open the cash register," he said.[44]

Baik, at five feet eight inches and 175 pounds, was at a significant physical disadvantage in relation to the hefty King. He was willing to surrender his cash but became enraged when King tried to take two checks from the open register. "You don't need the checks," said Baik, who grabbed the tire iron. King lost his balance, fell behind the counter, and knocked over a display case of pies and doughnuts, which flew in all directions. He picked up a piece of the pie rack and swung it at Baik, who swung back with the tire iron. Both men missed. Baik then fled toward the back of the store while King ran out the front door and drove away in his Hyundai with $200. Baik took down the license plate number.

King was quickly arrested and charged with second-degree robbery, assault with a deadly weapon, and intent to commit great bodily injury. He pleaded guilty to the robbery charge in an agreement in which the assault charges were dropped. But after pleading guilty on February 8, 1990, he told his probation officer, Barry Nidorf, that he had not committed the robbery and did not know how the checks had come to be found in his car. Nidorf knew King was lying, but he also realized he was not dealing with a career criminal. Even Baik had told the probation officer that he did not think King had tried to hurt him. Nidorf decided that King had committed the robbery as a "secondary act" after losing his temper. "The problem [that] this defendant may present to the community is not that he steals and robs but that he may have an explosive temper," Nidorf wrote perceptively. He recommended that King serve a year in county jail, receive intensive counseling, and be given five years' probation. Instead, Superior Court Judge Lillian Stevens sentenced King to two years in a state prison.

King was a model prisoner at the minimum-security California Correctional Center at Susanville. Good conduct earned him an assignment to an unfenced work camp near Mount Shasta, where he cleaned roadways and ditches, cut fire breaks, and helped battle a forest fire. In October 1990, he was sent to a work-furlough center in Hollywood, which enabled him to resume ties with his wife Crystal and her two children. The "buffed out" look that made such an impression on Koon was enhanced during this period by thrice-weekly workouts at a nearby health spa. "He was liked by staff and peers," said Geri Conley, who directed the furlough center. "He was a good resident here." King was paroled on December 27, 1990, and found work on a construction job at Dodger Stadium, where he was also popular. "You could set your watch by his timeliness," said his superintendent, Scott Dalgleish.

But King continued to drink even though refraining from alcohol was a condition of his parole. His favorite drink was a forty-ounce bottle of Olde English 800, known in his Altadena neighborhood as an "eightball." And it was eightballs that King said he had been drinking on the evening of March 2, 1991, while watching a basketball game at the home of Bryant Allen, known as "Pooh." Allen, in King's words, was "a friend of mine—my brother has a kid by his sister." It was after the game that King decided to go on his fateful drive, taking Allen, who rode in the back of the Hyundai, and Freddie Helms, who was the front-seat passenger.

Helms was a friend of Allen. King had not met him until that night and would never know him well, for Helms was killed in an automobile accident on June 29, 1991, when he was again a passenger in a car whose driver was intoxicated. On the night of March 2, Helms had been drinking so heavily that he fell asleep in the front seat as King drove down the 210 freeway, singing along to loud music from the radio. King sped on into the night, driving at a speed he later estimated at 80 miles an hour, although he had not looked at his speedometer. He was never able to explain why he had driven west on the freeway. He would vaguely remember heading for Hansen Dam, where he had fished with his father, when he saw the lights of the highway patrol cruiser that he later learned was driven by Melanie Singer.

King habitually displayed bad judgment when drinking. On the night of March 2, he continued his high-speed freeway drive in defiance of the highway patrol's lights and sirens. Allen was yelling at him to pull over, but King ignored him. He said later that he knew that driving under the influence—DUI or "deuce," in police jargon—could lead to the revocation of his parole. "I was scared of going back to prison," King testified, "and I just kind of thought the problem would just go away."[45]

King remembered that when he finally pulled over, he heard commands to put his hands where police could see them. He remembered trying to get out of the car and being yanked back by the seat belt and being told to put his hands on the car. He remembered that a "police lady" ordered him to get down and then advanced on him with her gun drawn while he was on the ground, saying over and over again, "I mean it, I mean it, I mean it." King turned his head away and made a clicking sound that is a prison noise of disrespect. King said later that he feared he would be shot. "They want[ed] to blow my fucking brains out, man," he said.[46]

OVER THE NEXT TWO YEARS, KING GAVE SEVERAL CONFLICTING accounts of the beating. His story changed nearly every time he told it, often substantially, and at times he denied that he had been either drinking or speeding. He told a federal grand jury that he tried to escape because of the pain he suffered from the Taser shots. He said he ran in Powell's direction with his hands up so that officers could see he had no gun and would not shoot him. This statement has the ring of truth. King had seen Melanie Singer's gun, and Koon also feared that the incident would end in a shooting, which is why he ordered the officers to holster their weapons. The validity of King's fear and Koon's concern is underscored at one point on the audio track of the Holliday tape when a male voice can clearly be heard shouting above the helicopter noise, "You're gonna' get shot, you're gonna' get shot."[47]

King was never able to explain satisfactorily in any testimony or interview why he ran directly at Powell instead of to his right if he was trying to escape into the darkened park area surrounding Hansen Dam. But King was drunk, and it is possible that the combined effects of the malt liquor and the two Taser shots hampered his sense of direction. There is no doubt he suffered from the Taser. Witnesses, including Melanie Singer and Tim Wind, described him as writhing when he was struck by the darts, and King graphically described the "very painful" effects to the grand jury. "It's currents running all through your body, like a bunch of little needles sticking into you," he said. After the second Taser shot, King said he decided to get to his feet and "run toward the hills, the park area." In a recollection again consistent with the videotape but in conflict with other accounts he gave, King told the grand jurors that an officer struck him with something "on the side of my head area" as he ran. He pointed to the right side of his head where Powell's first baton blow had landed.

King's recollections of what happened during the next eighty seconds were confused and fragmentary. "My whole body went numb after the first blow to the head," he said. While he had difficulty remembering with any precision what happened after the first blow, he knew that he was in agony from being hit and kicked so many times.

King passed out from the beating. He awakened in an ambulance on the way to Pacifica Hospital in Sun Valley with a sheet over his head. "I have claustrophobia, and I felt real closed in by being up under the sheet like that and not being able to breathe," he told grand jurors. King would have nightmares about the beating and the ambulance ride to the hospital and the next ride in a police car to Foothill Station and then another ride to Los Angeles County–USC Medical Center. As he tried to piece together what had happened to him, with his swollen head bandaged and his broken leg in a cast, King was at first amazed and then angered that the officers who had beaten him so badly also blamed him for the incident. "I just felt horrible," he said. "I felt beat up and like a crushed can. That's what I felt like, like a crushed can all over, and my spirits were down real low . . . I was in so much pain. It's hard to explain. To wake up [and be told] that I attacked some officers. I felt real bad."[48]

King had no idea how many times he had been struck by police batons, and it soon became apparent that no one else did either. Powell initially told police investigators that he had hit King fourteen or fifteen times after the initial flurry of blows, but he had no estimate of the total number of baton strikes. Koon estimated twenty to thirty total strikes when he was interviewed by Detective Tzimeas of Internal Affairs but increased the number to thirty-three by the time he wrote *Presumed Guilty*. Neither Wind nor Briseno had any idea how many blows had been delivered. High-ranking LAPD officers finally settled on an official figure of fifty-six blows, which became the number used by Chief Gates, state prosecutors, and King's civil lawyer, Steven Lerman, who at one point sought $56 million in damages, "one for each blow." The truth was that any count involved some guessing because it was impossible to know how many baton blows were delivered during the ten-second blurry section of the videotape, even after an FBI enhancement partially cleared up this segment.

Of more significance than the number of swings is the issue of how many baton blows actually connected with Rodney King. Captain Robert Gale, then patrol commanding officer at Foothill Station, conducted an unusually thorough administrative hearing on the excessive-force charges against Wind, reviewing sixty-nine interviews and carefully studying the videotape at regular speed and in slow motion. He determined that Wind had swung his baton sixteen times, hitting King with eleven of these blows. Sergeant Charles Duke, a twenty-one-year veteran of the LAPD who had been in charge of training at the Police Academy in the 1980s and was noted for his exploits with the Special Weapons and Tactics (SWAT) team, estimated that at least half of Powell's baton blows, and perhaps as many as 60 percent of them, missed King. By this estimate, if Powell swung forty of the fifty-six blows, he would have struck King at most twenty times. Counting the blows struck by both Powell and Wind, this means that King was actually hit thirty-one times. Sergeant Scott Landsman, a nineteen-year LAPD veteran who had taught baton training and martial arts at the Police Academy, said that only two or three of these blows were "power strokes" delivered with the proper force.[49]

Those who watched the videotape at home without the benefit of slow motion or seeing King's charge at any speed were understandably shocked at what seemed to be a motiveless and excessive beating. Police trainers and martial arts experts who viewed the full tape were shocked, too, but for a different reason. What appalled Sergeant Duke, who testified for the defense

in the trials of the police officers, was not the brutality of the beating but
its ineffectiveness. If the officers who hit King "knew what they were doing
with the baton," Duke said, they would have broken his arm or his leg with
the first four or five blows and immobilized him.[50]

Sergeant Landsman was similarly appalled. Even before he learned that
Powell had been singled out at roll call for improper use of the side-handled
baton, Landsman believed that many Los Angeles police officers did not
know how to use the weapon, and he suspected that Powell's training was
deficient. Like many younger LAPD officers, Powell had practiced only
against stationary targets, which at Foothill Station meant using an ax handle covered with rubber firehose against a stack of tires. He did not swing
the baton with proper force even against a stationary object. When Landsman analyzed the tape, he concluded that many of Powell's blows had missed
and that most of the later blows had landed on well-padded areas of the
body. These blows bruised King without immobilizing him and also reinforced the officers' perception that King was a PCP user impervious to pain.
Landsman believed that a well-directed first blow might have stopped King
in his tracks.

Neither the prosecution nor the defense in the subsequent trials wanted
to dwell on the awful possibility that LAPD officers are simply too poorly
trained and ill-equipped to take physically powerful and combative drunks
into custody without beating them into submission. Such an explanation
was unpalatable to prosecutors because it let the officers off the hook. It
was unpalatable to Sergeant Koon because it demolished his argument that
the arrest was a managed and controlled use of force. And it was unpalatable to Chief Gates because it undermined the LAPD's long cultivated myth
that the department was a highly trained "thin blue line" that could do more
with less than other police departments. Instead of using the King beating
as an opportunity for departmental self-examination, Gates described it as
an "aberration" and bridled at any suggestion that such use of force might
be widespread.

In fact, every investigation of the incident revealed appalling deficiencies in the skills, training, and judgment of the officers who arrested Rodney King. The panicky and immature Powell, a training officer himself in
need of training, was an accident waiting to happen. Wind, while a promising professional, was conscious of the LAPD mandate that required probationers to support their training officers. Briseno was small and ineffective.
Solano was new on the job. Koon, while dedicated and experienced, had
concluded that King was on PCP, and saw all of King's actions through the
lens of this perception.

King was certainly powerful, but (in Landsman's view) he gained the
leverage needed to hurl Powell and Briseno off his back largely because

Solano and Wind were holding his legs down. Koon interpreted this feat as a sign of superhuman strength. The Taser's failure to stop King in his tracks further reinforced Koon's belief that he was dealing with a "duster," even though the 1989 study on Taser effectiveness showed that the stun gun had worked on thirteen of sixteen PCP users.[51] While Koon prided himself on keeping up with police-training literature, he was either unaware of this study or rejected its conclusion because of the single incident in his own experience in which a Taser had proved ineffective on a PCP suspect. All of King's actions after the Taser failed were interpreted by Koon as the response of a "duster" who felt no pain. Since LAPD policy discourages grappling with PCP suspects, Koon believed he was justified in allowing King to be beaten and kicked until he pleaded for mercy.

The notion that LAPD policy required such a beating to make an arrest seemed preposterous to Taky Tzimeas, the Internal Affairs investigator. Tzimeas, of Prussian descent, was known within the LAPD as "TZ" and had the reputation of being honest, thorough, and cold. In fact, he agonized over whether he was being fair. "I was hoping and praying that one witness would say something that would justify what would happen," he said long afterward. "I turned over every rock, and it just wasn't there." Tzimeas believed the officers were mostly telling the truth but thought Koon was fooling himself when he said he "directed this or that." Watching the tape with the sound on, Tzimeas concluded that Koon was mostly telling King to get down. If he was giving directions to the officers, Powell and Wind did not hear him. "Powell thinks that what he's doing he's doing on his own," Tzimeas said.[52]

Koon was at once the most admirable and the most exasperating of the LAPD officers involved in the Rodney King affair. On the one hand, he displayed a breathtaking sense of accountability in a department where senior officers often used subordinates as scapegoats. He took responsibility for every blow and kick, even Powell's first damaging baton strike to King's face, which was almost certainly a defensive reaction rather than a response to an order. It was also obvious to Sergeant Landsman that Koon did not see some of Powell's subsequent blows. But the other side of Koon's unflinching acceptance of responsibility was a stubborn unwillingness to reconsider his actions or those of other participants in light of the videotape or the observations of witnesses. While he did concede that he might not have seen every blow or kick, he never acknowledged that some of them may have been delivered after King was no longer a threat.

Sergeants are taught to respond to pursuits because the LAPD has learned from experience that excessive force is most likely when the passions of the chase and the adrenaline of officers and suspects are running high. What amazed Jack White, a twenty-seven-year veteran of the LAPD who investigated the incident for the district attorney, was not the extent of the force used against King but the fact that it had been used with a supervisor on the scene. The city of Los Angeles in 1990 paid $3.5 million to settle claims arising from alleged police misconduct, but none of the claims involved repeated use of force in the presence of a supervisor. White knew that a supervisor was present at the King beating only because someone wearing a sergeant's stripes was visible on the videotape.

Why did Koon, who was experienced and respected, abdicate his supervisory role? This question preoccupied the officers who sought to reconstruct the events of March 3, 1991. Some officers, including Captain Tim McBride, thought that Koon's first mistake was impulsively taking the arrest away from Melanie Singer. This was also the opinion of both Jack White and Cliff Ruff, a burly detective and twenty-nine-year LAPD veteran who had investigated the 1987 Briseno use-of-force incident for the department. Ruff had become a director of the Los Angeles Police Protective League, the police union, by the time of the King beating, and he was responsible for obtaining legal representation for the officers involved. He knew that the beating had created a crisis for the LAPD, and he thought it was a crisis of Koon's making. "It was a highway patrol situation," Ruff said. "They were still in control."[53]

Ruff believed that once Koon took over the arrest, he immediately became too involved to supervise it. "He was too close to the trees to see the forest," he said. Koon was preoccupied with the Taser, a weapon in which he had almost blind faith. When the first Taser volley failed to stop King, Koon moved even closer to King. McBride was also critical of Koon for becoming so engrossed in operating the Taser that he failed to "clearly assess the situation and see other officers arriving at the scene."

Whether Koon would have used these officers if he had seen them remains an open question. What Koon saw when he looked at King was not a strong and uncooperative drunk but a "duster" who felt no pain and possessed a "death grip" that made a second try at a swarm potentially dangerous. Koon may have been in a funk after the Taser failed to stop King. Officers who knew Koon suspected that he put such great store in his weaponry that he really did not know what to do when it did not perform as advertised.

"Koon relied more on mechanical devices than I do," said Sergeant Nick Titiriga, who at six feet four inches is one of the few LAPD officers taller than Rodney King. Titiriga had served with Koon in 77th Street Division and considered him highly capable but believed he "might have gotten blown away" when the Taser shots failed to stop King. "He has tunnel vision," Titiriga said. "He has Powell and Wind giving baton shots, but they're not very effective shots. So the Tasers aren't working, and the batons aren't working. Rather than just do the old-fashioned thing of wrestling this sonofabitch to the ground, they hesitated. But I'd like to see the critics stop this guy, the media included. I'd give them guns and badges, too."[54]

This was a prevalent view within the LAPD, where it was widely believed that the arrest was conducted in good faith. But even some of Koon's staunchest partisans found his behavior inexplicable. He had taken over an arrest that he then failed to supervise. After the attempts to swarm King and after the Taser shots, Koon had allowed the beating to continue when he was literally surrounded by officers who could have helped him. Ruff watched the tape over and over without ever being able to understand Koon's conduct. "I have much more respect for Koon than I do for Powell, but I think that Powell's conduct was more comprehensible and explainable in some ways than Koon's," Ruff said.[55]

Tzimeas agreed. "Koon is a puzzle," said the detective. "I think possibly he was overwhelmed by this situation where nothing seemed to work. I think he went brain-dead. When you panic, you sometimes run amok. Other times you freeze. He looked around and saw a bunch of rookies. He tunneled in."[56]

But such reflective assessments could not be heard above the roar of the political firestorm that swept over Los Angeles in the aftermath of the King beating. It was almost impossible to turn on a television set without seeing a clip from the Holliday tape or an outraged public official demanding prosecution of the "white officers who had beaten a black motorist," as they were usually called. On March 5, the day after the Holliday tape was first shown, the FBI opened an investigation, Chief Gates pledged an inquiry but warned against making a premature judgment, and Mayor Bradley promised "appropriate action" against the officers. "This is something that we cannot and will not tolerate," he said. On March 6, Rodney King was released from Los Angeles County Men's Central Jail after District Attorney Ira Reiner found insufficient evidence to prosecute him. On March 7, Gates said that the officers involved in the beating would be prosecuted. On March 8, Reiner announced that he would seek indictments from the grand jury. Fifteen officers who were at the scene were suspended. A *Los Angeles Times* poll on March 10 found that 86 percent of those surveyed had seen the videotape and that 92 percent of those who had seen it thought excessive force had been used. On March 12, the American Civil Liberties Union, launching a campaign to fire Gates, ran a full-page ad in the *Los Angeles Times* that asked, "Who do you call when the gang wears blue uniforms?"

A variant of this question echoed within the grand jury room in downtown Los Angeles, where Deputy District Attorney Terry White sought indictments against Koon, Powell, Wind, and Briseno. Beginning on March 11, the grand jury heard testimony for four days and watched the videotape. White's first witness was George Holliday, who told how he had been awakened in the middle of the night by the helicopter noise and sirens and began to videotape the beating.

"Why didn't you call the police while you were viewing this?" White asked.

"They were there," Holliday replied.

On March 14, the grand jury returned indictments against the four officers. It was, said District Attorney Reiner, a most "terrible moment" when officers sworn to uphold the law were charged with taking it into their own hands.

3

THE *DRAGNET* LEGACY

"The future of America may well rest in the hands of the police."
—LAPD Chief William Parker, 1957[1]

TIMOTHY EDWARD WIND DROVE HIS BLUE-AND-SILVER FORD pickup truck from Kansas to California in May 1990, eager to join what he was certain was the finest police department in the world. He had dreamed of faraway adventures since his boyhood in Lake of the Forest, a secluded community in the rolling hills of east Kansas near Bonner Springs. Wind had joined a nearby fire department while still in high school, and he enlisted in the Army after he graduated, becoming a paratrooper and a Green Beret. The Army had given him a taste of the world, but he intended to spend his life as a police officer, not a soldier. When he applied to the LAPD, he had worked seven years in the police department of Shawnee, Kansas, where the crime rate was low and promotions came slowly. "I wanted to be with the best," Wind said.

Wind was a handsome thirty-year-old who looked younger than his age when he entered the Los Angeles Police Academy. His wife, Lorna, and their infant son soon joined him in Los Angeles, and they found a home in Santa Clarita, north of the city, where many police officers live. At the Academy, Wind was evaluated as being "highly motivated, eager to learn, and extremely safety conscious."[2] On the night of March 3, 1991, he had served exactly four months as a probationary officer in Foothill Division, where his supervisors considered him a promising officer who used "good judgment and patience even in dealing with violent suspects."[3] Joseph Napolitano, one of the bystander officers at Rodney King's arrest, saw Wind eating breakfast in a restaurant a few hours later and told him there would be times when he would have to use force as a police officer but that he should never enjoy it. "I didn't enjoy it," Wind replied.

Neither Wind nor Napolitano knew of the existence of the Holliday videotape when they had this conversation. Wind was told about it by other officers in the locker room of Foothill Station when he arrived for roll call on the night of March 4. The tape didn't seem of consequence to him because he could not imagine that he had done anything wrong. Then he was summoned from roll call and interrogated for four hours by Internal Affairs investigators. Even then, Wind had no real idea that he was in trouble. "Son, if you do the right thing for the right reasons, you'll be all right," his mother had often told him, and Tim Wind believed her.

Los Angeles police officers sign a statement when they are employed agreeing to answer questions from their superiors on pain of dismissal. Because of the constitutional protection against self-incrimination, these statements cannot be used in a criminal prosecution unless the officer waives his rights. Wind was on the verge of doing just this when Internal Affairs investigators gently suggested that he protect himself. The investigators, led by Detective Taky Tzimeas, were under pressure to find an explanation for the beating that Chief Gates could use to defend himself against the accusation that the LAPD condoned brutality, but they were touched by Wind's naive belief that all would go well if only he told the truth. While other officers would not remember the events depicted on the tape or would deny that anything had gone wrong, Wind remembered everything, denied nothing, and answered every question put to him without evasion. He was a lamb, leading himself to the slaughter.

Long after his codefendants knew better, Wind clung to his starry-eyed belief that the LAPD would not abandon him. It would take the emotional burdens of successive prosecutions, three stress-induced surgeries, joblessness, and the prospect of bankruptcy for Wind to question his faith in the values and quality of the police department he had assumed was the nation's best. But years later, as he replayed the events of March 3, 1991, in his mind, he wondered why his training officer had not known how to use the side-handled baton and why the bystander officers had not come forward to help subdue Rodney King. "Lately I've been wondering how is it they came to be number one," Wind said of the LAPD. "Then it came to me. The LAPD made the list."[4]

While intended partly as a joke, Wind's comment was on the mark. Although the LAPD may not literally have drawn up a list on which it ranked itself as the nation's best police department, it had made a professional virtue of aggressive, "proactive" policing and defined or developed many of the standards by which law enforcement agencies are judged. One reason the King case sent shock waves through the law enforcement community, as Chief Gates accurately noted after watching the videotape, was that the incident had occurred not in some rural backwater but in a modern, urban department that was considered a citadel of police professionalism.

The LAPD was established late in the nineteenth century and from its inception reflected the exigencies of a mostly lawless land afflicted with ethnic animosities. Los Angeles, founded by a Spanish garrison sent from Mexico in 1781, was a quiet and insignificant pueblo until gold was discovered in northern California in 1848. Thousands of gold seekers trekking north from Sonora after the Mexican War with the United States came into conflict with the Anglo adventurers who had wrested California from the Mexican gentry. California's admission to the Union in 1850 was followed by a period of so-called "Mexican banditry," really a resumption of the Mexican War in guerrilla form on California soil. "The practice of lynching Mexicans soon became an outdoor sport in Southern California," wrote Carey McWilliams.[5] Another historian noted that Los Angeles after the gold rush "became a way-station for desperadoes, gamblers and drifters of every type. For two boisterous and bloody decades it was the 'toughest' town in the entire West."[6]

County sheriffs and city marshals were powerless to deal with this violence. Several were killed in gun battles, and replacements were hard to come by. Ranger and volunteer companies were often little more than vigilante groups. When more than a score of innocent Chinese were lynched in Los Angeles in 1871 and some of the city's peace officers were implicated, the city council increased the number of marshals and paid them regular wages. But the marshals proved incompetent, and in 1876 the council replaced them with the Los Angeles Police Department, patterned after eastern police forces that depended on political patronage. The job of police chief lacked prestige and rotated so frequently that Los Angeles had thirteen chiefs between 1877 and 1889. But reformers rewrote the city charter in 1889, creating a police commission and putting Los Angeles on the path to professional government and law enforcement.

These reformers, first a movement and then a political party, were known as the Progressives. They were the great moralizing political force in Southern California for the next three decades, and their ideas and values remain embedded in the governing structures of the region. Almost without exception, the Progressives were white, Protestant, nativist, and middle-class "do-gooders" who believed in education, good government, "scientific" business management, modern technology, and nonpartisan municipal elections, which became the law throughout California. They opposed prostitution, gambling, and, usually, alcoholic beverages. They distrusted political parties and bosses. Because of an absence of strong, ethnic-based political machines of the kind that existed in eastern cities, the Progressives experienced unusual success in Southern California, where their influence was more long lasting than anywhere else, with the possible exceptions of Wisconsin and Minnesota.

The Progressives shaped the distinctive nature of the LAPD. The Police Commission created by the 1889 charter appointed the first notable Los Angeles police chief, John M. Glass, who in an eleven-year tenure established professionalism as the department's goal. Glass created a detective bureau and a system that required daily reports by every police officer. He emphasized professional appearance and prohibited drinking, smoking, and card playing on duty—exceptional requirements in what was still largely a frontier police force. As historian Joseph G. Woods noted, Glass also "established a tradition yet to be broken by a Los Angeles chief, requesting significant increases in men, plant and equipment."[7]

Anticipating the path that would be taken in the 1950s by William Parker, the LAPD's most famous chief, Glass put his faith in machines as much as in manpower. While seeking a 20 percent increase in personnel, he also requested two new substations and the installation of a Gamewell communications system which would enable police officers to call a centralized switchboard. More than seven decades before Proposition 13, Los Angeles politicians were campaigning on antitax platforms, and the city council viewed the recommendations as a way to save money on personnel, which even then accounted for 90 percent of the police budget. Gamewell was state-of-the-art technology at the time, and the fifty-box system was quickly approved and installed in 1899, at a cost of $50,000. But many of the requests for more policemen were rejected, much as a city council more than a half century later would reject Chief Parker's plea for more officers while approving the purchase of an LAPD helicopter. As Woods observed, the council substituted telephones, call boxes, substations, bicycles, motorcycles, and automobiles for manpower and kept taxes low while satisfying their police chief's need for efficient professional equipment.

But the Progressives, despite their achievements, could not maintain control of Los Angeles. Reform administrations came and went, often supplanted by corrupt regimes that disgusted the public and led to other waves of reformers. This cycle reflected a failure of the reformers to finance their candidates. As a result, even reform politicians often accepted campaign contributions from those with a vested interest in maintaining the downtown vice district that flourished in Los Angeles from 1915 to 1938. The vice lords also paid off the police, as their counterparts did in eastern cities. Nevertheless, the idea of a professional police force had been implanted in the culture of Los Angeles, never to be uprooted. A popular Progressive-backed chief, Charles Sebastian, was elected mayor in 1915 largely because he advocated closing the city to vice. Unfortunately for the causes of reform and police professionalism, Sebastian was soon enmeshed in scandal and forced to resign. The standards of conduct within the LAPD declined, reaching a low point during the 1922–23 reign of Chief Louis Oaks, a secret member of the

Ku Klux Klan who presided over a department that was heavily involved in gambling, bootlegging, and the large-scale fixing of traffic tickets.

The return to near frontier vice conditions spurred a particularly vigorous surge of the reform movement, which proposed to correct police corruption with a typical Progressive remedy. A city charter amendment on the 1923 ballot, supported by an incumbent mayor who was trying to distance himself from Chief Oaks, made the police chief's job a civil service position. The amendment passed overwhelmingly as voters responded to the reform argument that civil service protection would insulate chiefs from political influence and guarantee impartial law enforcement. Reformers expected that Oaks would fail the civil service examination, but he was fired because of his scandalous activities before he had a chance to take it. A reform-minded Board of Police Commissioners (hereafter called the "Police Commission," as it is popularly known) then brought in the renowned August Vollmer, the nation's most noted police scientist, to head the LAPD.

At the time of his appointment, the self-educated Vollmer was a professor of criminology at the University of California at Berkeley and chief of that community's small police force. He was well-known and admired for his writings on crime prevention and police administration and seems to have accepted the LAPD appointment because he recognized a need to put his theories into practice in a big-city department. Stacey Koon, in his 1978 master's thesis, accurately called Vollmer "the father of professionalism in American law enforcement," but Vollmer's mission went beyond upgrading the police. Joseph Woods described him as "a utopian progressive whose ultimate theory engrossed the moral reform of mankind and the creation of a society in which crime would not occur . . ."[8] Vollmer was a true Progressive who believed in the perfectibility of mankind and thought that police officers needed to be educated and enlightened in order to be effective. He was convinced that criminal behavior was caused by environmental influences and that crime could be deterred by education and early counseling. As LAPD chief, Vollmer created a Police Crime Prevention Division, in which social workers developed programs to aid delinquent youths. He introduced psychological and educational tests to eliminate unfit police applicants. These became permanent features of LAPD entrance examinations, although it would take the arrival of Chief Parker in 1950 for the tests to be fully utilized.

Vollmer's persistence in weeding out police officers he regarded as unfit inevitably made enemies. He was forced out by a political dispute after only a year, but it was a year that permanently changed the LAPD. Vollmer's scientific methods of crime detection and his ideas about administration and personnel training were adopted. A complete police laboratory replaced a single chemist. New jails and police stations were built and equipped with telephone, teletype, and signal systems. He reorganized the

LAPD into divisions and proved, as Woods put it, "that when the chief is under civil service a rather small group of honest policemen could defeat organized criminals." To demonstrate his integrity, Vollmer led a secret raid against gamblers who had been protected by crooked politicians and ordered another raid against bootleggers protected by federal officials.

Despite his short tenure, Vollmer did more than any other Los Angeles police chief before William Parker to professionalize the LAPD and to establish its independence. His success won the approval of the public, if not that of the politicians, and enshrined the concept of civil service protection for police chiefs even though Vollmer himself did not take advantage of it. This unique system protected bad chiefs as well as good ones and would in time enable a Los Angeles police chief to thumb his nose at the mayor and the city council with virtual impunity.

The nadir of political and police corruption in Los Angeles was reached during the administration of Mayor Frank Shaw (1933–38), who presided over one of the most venal municipal governments in the nation's history. Shaw was white and Protestant, a Mason, and a registered Republican. He called himself a "friend of business" because as a councilman he had eliminated the occupational tax and blocked an ordinance requiring landlords to ratproof their dwellings, but his only real interest was self-enrichment. "I go where the money goes," he said, anticipating the reason Willie Sutton would one day give for robbing banks.

Shaw systematically looted the city of Los Angeles, taking immense payoffs to protect thriving prostitution and gambling operations and smaller payoffs from police officers and other city officials in return for promotions. He debased the Police Commission and the Board of Civil Service Commissioners and bought off grand juries that attempted to investigate his operations. When Clifford Clinton, a brave cafeteria owner, instigated a grand jury investigation of the mayor, his home was firebombed. The car of a former LAPD officer who was investigating corruption for a civic reform group was destroyed by another bomb. This was the final straw for a shocked city. A police captain was indicted and sent to prison for attempted murder. In September 1938, after a radio campaign by Clinton, Shaw was recalled and replaced by reform candidate Fletcher Bowron. It was the first successful recall of a U.S. mayor.

Bowron served sixteen years, longer than any other mayor of Los Angeles until the twenty-year reign of Tom Bradley. He struggled to restore professionalism in the LAPD but was unable to cope with the strain placed on the department by World War II. The war changed Los Angeles from a white Protestant bastion to a multicultural city. People of all races and ethnic groups poured into Southern California to work in the burgeoning aircraft industries and in the Port of Los Angeles, which became a principal embarkation point for troops heading to the Pacific. Hundreds of Los Angeles police officers joined the armed services, and others retired, depleting the LAPD in numbers and competence. The city council, typically tax conscious and shortsighted, refused to enlarge the department and filled vacancies by waiving intellectual and physical standards. Many of the new police officers were "badge happy," and police brutality replaced corruption as a focus of the department's critics. In 1943, in the notorious "Zoot Suit" riots, sailors and soldiers on liberty beat and stripped Mexican youths known as "Pachucos" while the police declined to intervene.

It took still another police scandal to force change. On June 1, 1949, the day after Bowron won his final term as mayor, a grand jury began an investigation into police corruption. The issue this time was the alleged protection by the LAPD's Gangster Squad of a call-girl and brothel operation with ties to mobster Mickey Cohen. Both the head of the Gangster Squad and the police chief resigned after a contentious investigation. In the belief that an outsider was needed to reform the department, Bowron brought in U.S. Marine Major General William Worton as the new chief.

Worton, who became chief when the city charter did not allow outside appointments of more than sixty days, is an important and neglected figure in LAPD history. Mayor Bowron used various technicalities to keep him as chief for thirteen months, and Worton used this time to put his stamp on the department. He is best remembered for creating the Internal Affairs Division (then bureau) and choosing William Parker to direct it. Internal Affairs had rank-and-file police support because it allowed the department to block the creation of a full-time civilian board to review complaints against the police, a reform proposed by Edward Roybal, who had just been elected as the first Mexican-American member of the city council.

Transitional chief though he was, Worton instituted a military plan of organization that placed a premium on obedience and enormously affected the officers' attitudes. "General Worton created a military paradigm," observed Ted Hunt, a nineteen-year veteran of the LAPD and an instructor at the Los Angeles Police Academy. "What other model did he know? That was great in 1950, but it didn't work in the mid-sixties or after, when no military organization could do well in a social setting. It was a paradigm for an occupying army or at least a military force, not for a modern police department."[9]

Worton's other significant contribution to the LAPD was his role in choosing William Parker his successor. There was no doubt about Parker's qualifications. He had twenty-three years of unblemished service in the LAPD, a law degree, and had placed first on the civil service examination for chief. As a captain in the U.S. Army, Parker had been awarded a Purple

Heart for a shrapnel wound he received during the Normandy invasion, and he had set up police systems in Munich and Frankfurt after the war. But he had been given little chance to succeed Worton because he was a Roman Catholic in a city in which the thirty-nine previous police chiefs had been Protestant. His principal opponent was Thaddeus Brown, a personable chief of detectives who possessed the requisite Protestant and Masonic qualifications. Three of the five police commissioners favored Brown, but one of them died the day before the vote. Mayor Bowron named Worton as the replacement on the commission, and Parker was approved by a 3–2 vote in an historical accident that some would see as an act of fate.

ON AUGUST 9, 1950, WILLIAM HENRY PARKER WAS INSTALLED AS chief of the LAPD, a position for which he had been preparing for much of his life. Parker was born June 21, 1902, in Lead, South Dakota. His grandfather had been a well-known frontier lawman in the Badlands and later was a congressman. An uncle was a prosecuting attorney. Parker became a hotel detective while still in high school, expelling prostitutes from Deadwood hotels. He arrived in Los Angeles in 1922, two years before Tom Bradley's family, and worked as a cab driver while attending classes at the Los Angeles College of Law. Parker continued his studies after joining the LAPD in 1927 and passed the bar in 1930. He would later say he considered opening a law practice but because of the city's bleak economic conditions during the Depression decided in the interests of job security to stay with the LAPD.

While advancing through the ranks during the most violent and corrupt period in the department's history, Parker was never touched by any scandal. But for a long time he was refused advancement beyond the rank of captain despite placing first on many promotions lists. "I was the most passed-up officer in the history of the Los Angeles Police Department," he told the actor Jack Webb.[10] It was this frustration that led Parker to join the Army. When he returned, he was promoted to inspector (the equivalent rank of what is now commander) but placed in charge of the traffic division, the LAPD's least prestigious unit. Even there Parker made an impression, for he eliminated the practice of favoritism in traffic tickets by making acceptance of bribes or payoffs a firing offense. His fortunes changed permanently when Worton recognized that his reputation for integrity made him the ideal person to head Internal Affairs.

After he became chief, Parker made it his mission to extend this reputation to the entire Los Angeles Police Department. His situation was similar to that of Glass in 1899 and Vollmer in 1923. "The city was still growing rapidly, but the crime rate was rising even faster," Joseph Woods wrote.

This placed a relentless strain on the police, and required the chief to lobby continually for more men, money and machines. Vice, both as a matter of civic hygiene and as an exploitable issue, continued to excite churchmen, newspaper reporters and political opportunists. A minority of brutal, corrupt officers abused their authority, casting doubt on the integrity of the entire department. The best men still avoided the service, in part due to the small salary and in part because of the policeman's low social status.[11]

Parker determined to change the status and performance of the LAPD. Taking a page from Vollmer's book—quite literally, in all probability, since he had studied Vollmer's writings—he devoted his initial efforts to improving police administration and reorganizing the bureaucracy. He introduced a planning and research division to streamline the booking procedure, improved training manuals, freed officers for street duty, and increased arrests. Traffic patterns in the city were improved and traffic enforcement strengthened. The death rate from automobile accidents fell from 32.9 to 13.7 per 1,000 inhabitants. Los Angeles went from having the highest mortality rate for such accidents among cities with a population of 1 million or more to having the lowest rate.

Like Vollmer, Parker was intent on recruiting officers who were mentally and emotionally capable as well as physically strong. The intelligence and psychiatric tests introduced by Vollmer had remained on the books but had not been honored during wartime because of the shortage of able recruits. Parker again made these tests prerequisites for employment. Strict standards of scholastic achievement, intelligence, age, height, and weight were enforced. Much to the delight of Worton, training at the Los Angeles Police Academy was patterned after a Marine boot camp with thirteen (later twelve) weeks of "spit and polish" training.[12]

Under Parker, LAPD officers were disciplined and blocked from promotion for any conduct hinting of dishonesty. They were prohibited from accepting meals, gifts, or favors and were required to maintain a good personal appearance and keep themselves in physical shape. Parker described what he looked for in a police officer in an interview in 1962: "He must have a high sense of integrity. He must have a deep, sympathetic interest in people. He cannot be self-centered. The man with a high paranoid factor is a problem; if you give him authority he is likely to use it unwisely. He must be a man who will devote himself completely to his task and who has the physical and mental energies to perform it. He must have a high sense of vocation and be free from a desire to gain great wealth."[13]

Parker's approach differed from Vollmer's in one important respect. While Vollmer had cared nothing for politics, Parker was determined to achieve a long tenure and recognized that he needed political support to accomplish this goal. "You have to build a power base," Parker told his young driver, Daryl Gates, in 1950. "If you don't, the chief can be swept out of here in no time at all."[14]

Parker set out to build such a base from the moment of his installation as chief. His acceptance speech was broadcast on radio and contained a potent if somewhat mixed message. He expressed alarm about postwar increases in the crime rate but pointed with pride to Los Angeles as "the white spot of America" when compared with other major cities. This was not a racial reference, at least not in any conscious sense, but simply the rhetoric of civic boosterism that had long presented Southern California as an idyllic land free of the crime and turmoil of the East. The other theme of Parker's speech was a promise that the people of Los Angeles would be able to take pride in the integrity and competence of their police department.

The new chief gave a dozen or more speeches a week, presenting police work as a struggle of good versus evil and pledging to keep the LAPD free of corruption. "With all the fiber of my being I will see to it that crooked rats who would change the City of Angels into the City of Diablos will not do so," Parker said.[15] Within the department, he "served warning on his subordinates that the LAPD would not be a haven for thieves, as it had been in the past . . ."[16] But Parker also gained the loyalty of a department in which he had not been particularly popular—Gates said he had "a reputation as a bully"—by using the LAPD's restored prestige to win pay raises and pension benefits from a usually parsimonious city council. Parker quickly became so popular that on the anniversary of his first year in office the Chamber of Commerce presented him with an award for outstanding work in reorganizing the department and restoring public confidence in the police.

No other law enforcement officer in U.S. history, with the possible exception of J. Edgar Hoover, was as skilled in publicizing the achievements of his agency and minimizing its deficiencies. Parker replaced the department's dreary, statistics-laden annual report with a brightly colored, illustrated brochure that described the LAPD's history, organizational divisions, current problems, and Parker's plans for improvements. He created a public-information division that prepared news releases and "story ideas" which were snapped up by local newspapers and radio stations. Public information officers with access to the chief provided reporters with information on breaking stories. They presented the "police side" of controversies and planted "good stories" representing the LAPD point of view, which in practice meant Parker's point of view. Parker usually had the editorial support of the powerful *Los Angeles Times* and other newspapers, but he benefited as much from the positive coverage that he cultivated among rank-and-file reporters.

More than any of his contemporaries in law enforcement, Parker realized the potential of television. He appeared for a time on his own program, *The*

Thin Blue Line, named after his frequent and famous description of the LAPD. But by far his greatest asset in the selling of the LAPD was *Dragnet*, a popular radio program created by Jack Webb, who took it to television in 1952.

Webb was born in Santa Monica in 1920 and served in the Army Air Corps as a bomber pilot in the Pacific during World War II. After the war he moved to San Francisco and produced a weekly radio program, *One Out of Seven*, for ABC that focused on racial injustice. He returned to Los Angeles in 1947, creating and portraying a series of hard-boiled detectives in programs on the ABC, Mutual, and CBS radio networks. Although Webb was a successful movie actor, notably in *Sunset Boulevard* (1950), his film work was overshadowed by *Dragnet*, a show that he wrote, directed, produced, and starred in as the now legendary LAPD Sergeant Joe Friday whose clipped speech and demand for "just the facts" epitomized Parker's idea of how a detective should conduct himself. Webb founded his own production company and sold the show to NBC in 1949.

Chief Parker formed a symbiotic relationship with Webb, who received virtually unlimited access and useful advice and cooperation from the police. Parker received the benefits of a program that captured the public imagination and glorified the LAPD. "The story you are about to see is true," every *Dragnet* episode began. "The names have been changed to protect the innocent." The stories were taken from LAPD files. Each episode ended with the disposition of the case; all defendants were found guilty, although one significant case was overturned on appeal.

Dragnet was an immense hit, finishing among the ten most watched programs during its first four seasons and successfully resurrected in the 1960s. As Parker saw it,

> Dragnet was one of the great instruments to give the people of the United States a picture of the policeman as he really is. It was most authentic. We participated in the editing of the scripts and in their filming. If we had any objections on technical grounds, our objectives were met. This program showed the true portrait of the policeman as a hard-working, selfless man, willing to go out and brave all sorts of hazards and work long hours to protect the community.[17]

Webb was similarly effusive about Parker. "He has fought the newspapers and politicians, harassed gangsters and Communists, opposed racial pressures on the police, and tangled with his own district attorney," Webb wrote in a 1958 book. "Recently, he has broadened his target range to include the California State Supreme Court and the California State Legislature. Whether his views are asked or not, he expresses them bluntly on any controversial subject involving law enforcement . . ."[18]

In the late 1950s, *Dragnet* increasingly advanced Parker's conservative political views. The *Dragnet* episode ending with an overturned conviction, for example, was based on the case of Charles Cahan, who was found guilty of bookmaking with evidence obtained by microphones secretly installed by the LAPD. In 1955, in a 4–3 decision that came as a shock to police officers, the California Supreme Court overturned the conviction on grounds that the evidence had been obtained in violation of the Fourth Amendment's guarantee of "the right of people to be secure in their persons, houses, papers, and effects against unreasonable searches and seizures." The decision reversed a 1922 ruling exempting municipal peace officers in California from Fourth Amendment restrictions and anticipated similar action by the U.S. Supreme Court. Parker found the new ruling "terrifying" and accused the courts of conducting "a civil war on police departments." He also linked such liberal court decisions to Communist purposes. "The bloody revolution, long the dream of the Comintern, cannot be accomplished in the face of a resolute police," he said.[19]

Parker's concerns about restrictive court decisions and the Communist menace were familiar within the law enforcement community. But as he became entrenched in his position, Parker showed an increasing intolerance for contrary views. He also possessed a fiery temper that may have been aggravated by alcoholism. Daryl Gates said he "too often . . . [would] drive him home drunk" and that Parker was privately known as "Whiskey Bill" to cops and police-beat reporters.[20] In Parker's day, however, such failings were unreported even by those journalists otherwise willing to criticize the chief.

WHAT ULTIMATELY DAMAGED PARKER'S REPUTATION WAS NEITHER his political views nor his drinking but insensitivity to the demographic transformation of Los Angeles. The black population more than doubled from 1940 to 1950, and in the next decade, the *Dragnet* decade, it doubled again. In 1960, the city's black population was 334,915, or 13.5 percent of the total. The Mexican-American population also increased significantly during this period, although the precise numbers are unavailable because "Hispanics" were not then separately classified by the Census Bureau.

Mexican Americans had always been shabbily treated in Southern California. People of Mexican origin who had been unable to prove U.S. citizenship had been deported in railroad boxcars during the Depression, often with no regard for legal formalities, then welcomed back during World War II because of labor shortages. After the war, returning Mexican-American veterans began to assert their rights. Ed Roybal often called Mexican Americans "the sleeping giant" of California, and Roybal's 1949 election to the Los Angeles city council, with the support of a multiracial coalition of Mexican

Americans, blacks, and liberal Jews, was a portent of the giant's awakening. It was a turning point that went unrecognized by Chief Parker.

Racism was embedded in the California culture in ways that differed from the national experience. The animosities of mid-nineteenth century white settlers had been directed less toward black people than toward Mexicans or the remnants of the few Native American tribes that had survived successive disastrous encounters with the Spanish and Mexican cultures. Later in the century, anti-Chinese agitation, known as "the bloody shirt," became the rallying issue for nativist demagogues who resented the importation of cheap Chinese labor. A notorious 1854 decision by the California Supreme Court denied legal protection to Chinese and helped create the conditions for the infamous 1871 mass lynching of Chinese in Los Angeles, the event that indirectly brought the LAPD into being.[21]

As Raphael Sonenshein has observed, Los Angeles in its early years was more hospitable to blacks than to people of Mexican, Chinese, or Japanese origin. Antiblack prejudices "were overwhelmed by the consuming desire to build a great city."[22] Developers often pitted blacks against Asians, much as they had previously imported Asians to depress the wages of whites. In 1933, for instance, a strike of Japanese workers who were building a Los Angeles County interurban rail system was broken by 1,400 black laborers, some imported from Texas.

Blacks had first come to Los Angeles in the Southern California land boom of the 1880s. Although their numbers were small, they did well enough in real estate to create a black middle class and a 34 percent rate of home ownership at the turn of the century—"a remarkable figure for the time."[23] While blacks were a negligible political force because of their low numbers and because citywide elections kept the council lily-white, they had sufficient status to prod city officials into hiring a token number of blacks.

In 1886, the LAPD became the first police department in the nation to hire a full-time black peace officer. The city soon afterward hired a black firefighter and, in 1919, the nation's first black policewoman. For decades afterward, between 2 and 4 percent of LAPD officers were black. Black officers were usually assigned to the downtown vice district or black residential neighborhoods and were rarely promoted. The exception was the detective bureau, which limited the number of blacks employed at any given time, usually to half a dozen, but tended to treat them on merit. In 1924, August Vollmer made Detective William Glenn an acting captain in the detective bureau, the highest rank a Los Angeles black police officer was allowed to attain until 1969.

In 1922, the year that William Parker arrived in Los Angeles, the Ku Klux Klan had become so strong in Southern California that it was conducting vigilante raids against bootleggers and prostitutes. One such raid on an alleged bootlegger in the then suburban town of Inglewood resulted in a shootout in which a Klansman was killed and several wounded. When the dead Klansman was identified as a police constable, Los Angeles Police Chief Louis Oaks ordered KKK members in the department to quit either the Klan or the LAPD. It was then revealed that Oaks himself, as well as the county sheriff and the U.S. attorney, were members of the Klan. Hostile attitudes toward blacks had become commonplace in Los Angeles, partly because of a large influx of southern whites. When thousands of blacks moved into Watts in 1926, Los Angeles quickly annexed the small community to prevent the creation of a town with a black government. Soon afterward, in a successful effort to encourage housing segregation and force blacks out of neighborhoods where they had lived for decades, restrictive housing covenants were widely adopted in Los Angeles.

The racist practices of the LAPD reflected the attitudes of the society it served. Earl Broady and Roscoe Washington were promoted to lieutenant on Christmas Eve of 1940, becoming the department's first black line officers. This would have put them in command of white officers, violating an unwritten LAPD rule. To prevent this, the LAPD established a segregated Black Watch composed entirely of black officers. The new unit required only a single lieutenant, and the position was given to Washington. Two days before completing his probation as lieutenant, Broady read in a newspaper that he had been demoted to the ranks. When he complained, he was told to accept the demotion or resign. Broady became a sergeant in 1943, took the lieutenant examination again, and placed within the top ten. Nonetheless, he was passed over for additional promotion eighteen times before he retired from the LAPD in 1945 after sixteen years of service. Broady went on to become a lawyer and Superior Court judge.

Tom Bradley began his twenty-one year career on the LAPD a few months before the Black Watch was formed. His 1940 Police Academy class, which graduated in the grim months when Nazi Germany was occupying much of Europe, was close-knit and idealistic. It voted unanimously to hold its graduation party at the Police Academy after a downtown hotel made it clear that Negro police officers were not welcome.[24] But the war dispersed Bradley's class, and it was difficult for blacks to remain idealistic on a police force where segregation held an iron grip. Black patrol car officers were required to have black partners. "If you were on patrol and your partner went home, you did too, because they wouldn't let a white work with you," said Jesse Brewer, a highly decorated World War II Army combat officer who joined the LAPD in 1952 at Bradley's urging.[25]

Although barriers to promotion were not as stiff for Mexican Americans as for blacks, obstacles to recruitment were greater. Chief Parker's insistence on maintaining a minimum height of five feet nine inches for police officers hampered the recruiting of Mexican Americans in the 1950s, when the city's growing Mexican-American population was unrepresented on the LAPD. During this period, alleged mistreatment of Mexican Americans in East Los Angeles by the LAPD and the Los Angeles County Sheriff's Department received more public attention than did complaints of brutality against blacks, who were unrepresented on the city council.

The most serious incident of police brutality during the early Parker years occurred in 1951, when drunken police officers from Wilshire Station reacted to a false rumor that seven young Mexican Americans had maimed a police officer while they were being taken into custody at a Christmas Eve party. The officers went to the cell in the Lincoln Heights Jail where the prisoners were being held and beat them with gloved fists and wet towels until the cell walls were covered with blood. The incident, known as "Bloody Christmas," outraged Councilman Roybal, who accused the LAPD of systematic brutality and cited fifty specific instances of misconduct to make his point. A Municipal Court judge urged a grand jury inquiry, and the FBI launched an investigation. Eight officers were indicted on state charges. Two of them were eventually convicted of assault and a third was convicted of a lesser charge. The grand jury also issued a report criticizing weaknesses in the command structure of the LAPD and deploring "a lack of military discipline." Parker, who had firm support from the press, dismissed the grand jury criticism as "nebulous" and rejected Mayor Bowron's suggestion that the police chief had delayed the internal police probe until outside investigations forced him to act. But act Parker did. Six officers were dismissed after trial board proceedings and three dozen others were disciplined. Parker contended, as Gates would after the Rodney King affair, that the department's actions showed that the LAPD could deal firmly with misconduct.

Parker's hesitant initial response gave the impression that he condoned police brutality and cost the LAPD control of the inquiry. The chief would not make this mistake again. His unwavering objective was an independent, professional police department that was not accountable to civilian (Parker said "political") authority. To accomplish this, he was willing to dismiss, discipline, or reassign any officer who embarrassed the LAPD. His principal weapon was the Internal Affairs Division, which became a powerful investigative body that served the dual purpose of rooting out misconduct and providing public justification for Parker's assertion that the police could police themselves. Internal Affairs became feared and distrusted within the LAPD for its arbitrariness. That was fine with Parker, who wanted a department that answered to no one but its chief. He achieved this goal and in the process became a chief who answered to no one.

The cornerstone of Parker's independence was the civil service protection provided Los Angeles police chiefs in the 1923 city charter amendment, but he built on this cornerstone by successfully establishing a political base that made him more popular than any mayor. Before Parker, mayors had controlled the police department by appointing compliant police commissioners, who named the chief. This indirect control had proved so effective that no Los Angeles police chief had ever survived a change in municipal administrations. But Parker changed the equation. While a mayor might indirectly name the police chief by controlling the Police Commission, he could remove a chief only for cause and only after written charges and public hearings before the Board of Civil Service Commissioners, whose decision was subject to judicial review. Parker realized early on that a police chief who enjoyed a political base and civil service protection would become virtually unaccountable to elected officials.

Parker also had at his disposal the intelligence section of the LAPD, which he referred to by the military nomenclature of "G2." Police spying on suspected subversives, trade unionists, mobsters, and political opponents had been accepted LAPD practice at least since the bombing of the *Los Angeles Times* by labor radicals in 1910. Until the Cahan decision in 1955, telephonic eavesdropping and wiretapping were an integral part of the police culture throughout California.

The intelligence section of the LAPD was expanded under Parker, and it was often asserted that the department compiled elaborate dossiers on political figures or anyone suspected of radicalism. The extent of these dossiers remains a matter of dispute, but there is no doubt that politicians believed the LAPD to be well-informed. This was of concern to Sam Yorty, who had been allied with Communists early in his political career before becoming a prominent Red hunter. When Yorty ran for mayor in 1961, he tried to put Parker on the defensive, accusing the LAPD of spying on his campaign staff and friends. After Yorty defeated incumbent Mayor Norris Poulson, he met with Parker, who brought with him a briefcase that supposedly included damaging files on the new mayor. While the story that Parker emptied his briefcase of documents incriminating to Yorty may be apocryphal, the two men left their meeting amiably expressing mutual confidence. Yorty became one of Parker's principal defenders. When James Roosevelt opposed Yorty in the mayoral election of 1965, Parker spoke at Yorty rallies and praised the mayor for interfering less with the LAPD than any previous mayor.

This freedom from interference allowed Parker to ignore minority politicians' claims that Negroes and Mexican Americans were mistreated by the LAPD. Poulson had sought minority votes in 1953, and Yorty did the same eight years later, by mildly criticizing the police on this issue and promising to integrate the LAPD if elected. But Parker treated all such criticisms as campaign talk, and his gift for public relations did not extend to mollifying minority politicians. He was sharply criticized by Roybal for a reference to people "not far removed from the wild tribes of Mexico," a remark Parker made in 1960 while testifying before the U.S. Civil Rights Commission that referred to Parker's experiences as a patrol officer thirty years earlier. Liberals and civil rights groups were often infuriated by Parker's insistence that accusations of police misconduct were attempts to divert attention from high crime rates in Negro and Mexican-American communities. But Parker did not approve of police brutality, and each complaint of misconduct that came to his attention was investigated by Internal Affairs. Daryl Gates remembered an incident in 1966 where Parker became emotional as he denounced the shooting of a black man by a white officer in South Central Los Angeles as "murder." A department investigation found that the shooting—of a man named Leonard Deadwyler who was rushing his pregnant wife to the hospital—was accidental, and a coroner's jury agreed.[26]

Nevertheless, the racial even-handedness of LAPD law enforcement under Parker was open to question. It had been challenged in 1959 by Judge David Williams, who released twenty-five black defendants arrested on gambling charges and cited statistics provided by Parker which showed that nearly 12,000 blacks—and only 1,200 whites—had been arrested for gambling during a two-year period. Williams, a black, wanted to know why the LAPD made few gambling arrests in predominantly white West Los Angeles or the San Fernando Valley. Parker, backed by a majority of the Police Commission, blandly replied that blacks accounted for 73 percent of gambling arrests nationally, exclusive of bookmaking. As the chief saw it, the higher percentage of blacks arrested in Los Angeles (where blacks were only about 13 percent of the population) was evidence not of discrimination but of superior law enforcement. The one black member of the five-member Police Commission resigned in disgust.[27]

PARKER REFLECTED VIEWS THAT WERE COMMONPLACE IN A CITY that often seemed more southern than western in its racial attitudes. Los Angeles was one of the last big cities in the West to accept blacks as customers in restaurants or as guests in hotels. It clung to restrictive housing covenants long after they were outlawed by the Supreme Court in 1948. The municipal fire department remained segregated until 1955. Parker inherited a police department steeped in racism. *Dragnet*, with its white cops and white criminals, was a mirror of the LAPD.

It was also a mirror of the Los Angeles political culture and the Los Angeles press. The powerful *Los Angeles Times*, the most reactionary of the nation's major newspapers until it embarked on a progressive course under Otis Chandler in the mid-1960s, was unfriendly to the civil rights movement. The city council had no minority members until Roybal was elected in 1949 and no blacks until the breakthrough election of 1963 when three blacks—Tom Bradley, Gilbert Lindsay, and Billy Mills—won council seats. By then, Parker was accustomed to dealing with a white city government. He shared the white majority's sanguine view that the local Negro population was satisfied with its lot, an attitude undergirded by a 1964 National Urban League study ranking Los Angeles first among sixty-eight cities surveyed in living conditions for Negroes. When racially based civil disorders erupted in seven eastern cities during the summer of 1964, Parker said, "It can't happen here."[28]

Tom Bradley knew better. In his early years in office, he was an outspoken council member who realized that police behavior toward blacks had the potential to ignite a riot, but he and other black council members were unsuccessful in persuading Parker of this. When Councilman Mills complained that police had stopped his car more than a dozen times for no reason except his race, the chief refused to believe it. In fact, black male drivers were often pulled over and searched if they were in a predominantly white neighborhood on the ostensible grounds that they fit a criminal "profile."

Such searches were an inevitable by-product of Parker's emphasis on aggressive (later "proactive") policing which encouraged officers to prevent crimes by questioning people they believed were acting suspiciously or were in the wrong place at the wrong time. While the policy itself was not necessarily racist, it gave latitude to officers who were. Parker never faced this issue. He believed that politicians who complained of aggressive police behavior were unwisely trying to tie the hands of the police at a time when resistance to authority was increasing. Because some of this resistance was fomented by the civil rights movement, which Parker believed was infiltrated by Communists, the chief tended to be hostile even to middle-class, law-abiding civil rights organizations such as the National Association for the Advancement of Colored People.

Parker failed to heed several warnings that Los Angeles was headed for a racial collision. On May 30, 1961, four LAPD officers were injured and twenty-two persons arrested when the attempt to arrest a black teenager in Griffith Park turned into a riot. On April 28, 1962, Los Angeles police accosted two Black Muslims at a mosque on South Broadway, touching off a gun battle in which a Muslim was killed and six others, along with three police officers, were injured. On April 11, 1964, the arrest of a black teenager at a Jefferson High School track meet ignited another riot at which a police officer was knocked unconscious. On April 25, 1964, blacks who had gathered at the scene of a traffic accident followed injured police officers to Central Hospital, where a melee resulted in nine arrests.

The civil disorder that became known as the Watts riot began on August 11, 1965, during a torrid heat wave. A passing black motorist told Lee Minikus, a white California Highway Patrol motorcycle officer, that he had seen another black man driving recklessly. Minikus chased the offender, pulling him over at 116th Street and Avalon Boulevard, near but not in Watts. The driver was a twenty-one-year-old named Marquette Frye. After Frye failed a roadside sobriety test, Minikus arrested him and called for a police car to take him to jail and a tow truck to impound his car.

Meanwhile, Frye's brother, the lone passenger in the car, had gone to his home two blocks away to tell his mother what had happened. The mother arrived at the scene of the arrest and berated Marquette for drinking. He became obstreperous, and a crowd that had been peaceably watching the arrest grew steadily in size and belligerency. Other officers arrived and two of them went into the crowd to arrest a woman dressed in a barber's smock who was said to have spit at them. A rumor spread that the officers were abusing a pregnant woman. Police cars were stoned, and the riot erupted. Before it ended six days later, 34 persons had died and another 1,032 had been injured. The central business district of Watts was burned to the ground, much of it never to be rebuilt.

Chief Parker bears some responsibility for the riot, if only because he ignored so many warnings of impending trouble. As a conservative political figure, he was imprisoned by a narrow ideological view of the civil rights movement and an unwillingness to recognize that police conduct had contributed to the steady decline of race relations in Los Angeles. Parker embodied the dilemma famously described by Gunnar Myrdal in which the "American creed" of equality clashes with racial prejudice. But Parker was a professional police officer who recognized that black officers had legitimate grievances about being passed over for promotion, as he himself had been passed over so many times.

This professionalism was Parker's saving grace. When an officer named Vivian Strange scored well on a merit examination in 1950, Parker made her the LAPD's first black female sergeant over what Gates said were "the strenuous objections of many among the departmental brass."[29] A few other black officers who did well on their merit examinations were also promoted to sergeant, but it was difficult for them to advance to higher ranks in a department in which whites continued to resist being commanded by black officers. Since the Black Watch was no longer a politically acceptable option, blacks who did well on written examinations were blocked from advancement to the rank of lieutenant by the practice of giving them low marks on oral tests, which were scored subjectively by white officers.

One casualty of this racist practice was Jesse Brewer, who became a sergeant in 1958 and periodically was given a low mark on the oral section of the lieutenant examination despite high marks on the written test. Several of the LAPD's twenty-five black sergeants in the early 1960s had similar experiences. Frustrated by the lack of opportunities for advancement, they began studying law, and at least nine became practicing attorneys. "How interesting," observed a black LAPD historian, that black officers could serve fifteen to twenty years on the LAPD, become sergeants, graduate from law school, pass the bar, and succeed as lawyers yet consistently fail the oral examinations for police lieutenant.[30] Whites with no education beyond a high school degree were often promoted to lieutenant or captain during this period.

The exception was Tom Bradley, the only black promoted to lieutenant during the fifteen years between Parker's appointment as chief and the Watts riot. Bradley, a sergeant since 1946, had caught Parker's eye in 1950 for cracking a bookmaking operation. The chief realized that Bradley, who was already politically active in his off-duty hours, was respected in the black community and had public relations value to the LAPD. In 1955, Parker granted Bradley's request to be transferred from the Vice Squad to the LAPD's new community relations detail. He started sending Bradley to address liberal groups who were critical of the LAPD. According to Gates, Parker lost confidence in Bradley because of an intelligence report that said Bradley bad-mouthed the department and the chief in these speeches. But it seems unlikely that the circumspect Bradley, who was aware of the pervasiveness of LAPD intelligence, would have given his adversaries such an easy opening.

Whatever the proximate cause of his dissatisfaction, it is clear that Parker decided Bradley was more interested in advancing his political career than in making the LAPD look good. In 1958, Bradley was promoted to lieutenant, a revolutionary step from Parker's perspective, but he was never again a confidant of the chief. Soon after his promotion Bradley attempted to integrate radio patrol cars in the Wilshire Division. When white officers undermined the order by calling in sick, Parker refused to support the integration effort. Bradley resigned from the LAPD in 1961. Later that year, Parker himself ordered integration of the radio cars, prodded by Sam Yorty's campaign promise to integrate the LAPD. Yorty was elected on May 31, and the chief issued the desegregation order before the new mayor took office a month later. "He wanted to beat Yorty to the punch," said Jesse Brewer. "He didn't want to be ordered to do it."[31]

Even with Parker's sanction and Yorty's political mandate, integration did not come easily to the LAPD. "After years of working together, of sharing locker rooms with us, of solving cases together, whites still didn't want to integrate," said Brewer, then a detective. "I couldn't believe that."[32] Brewer stayed the course and rose to the then unprecedented rank of assistant chief under Daryl Gates. But he remembered the early 1960s as a difficult period for black members of the LAPD. Two black lieutenants who were holdovers from the pre-Parker years joined Bradley in retirement, beginning what a historian called a "dark era" in which no black held a rank above sergeant.[33] While a few black police officers were promoted in the years after the Watts riot, only about 5 percent of the LAPD was black in 1972. It took the election of Tom Bradley as mayor in 1973 to make the LAPD fully accept integration and begin recruiting large numbers of black officers. "Bradley made it known that he remembered how he had been treated," recalled Brewer. "Affirmative action became a policy. Those who resisted it began to become concerned about their jobs."[34]

In Brewer's view, Parker's go-slow approach to integration reflected the concern that he might hurt LAPD morale if he pushed too hard to change ingrained racist behavior. "As an administrator, he was always very concerned about morale," Brewer said.[35] Parker also thought of integration as a distraction from his goal: making the LAPD a tough and mobile police force that compensated for shorthandedness with aggressive police work and the highest ratio of arrests per officer in any big-city department. Other police departments might answer nearly every call for help, but the LAPD responded only to calls with the highest "potential for trouble."[36] Parker wanted action-oriented police officers, not social workers. He discontinued youth-oriented crime-prevention programs in minority areas, a legacy of the Vollmer days, and distrusted anything that smacked of what later became known as "community policing."

Even Tom Bradley lauded Parker's model of a police force kept "lean and mean,"[37] but this approach may have been Parker's way of making a virtue of necessity. He inherited an understaffed department, and his efforts to expand it were thwarted by a political culture that emphasized low taxes and believed technology could compensate for manpower shortages. In some respects, Parker was defeated by his own propaganda about Los Angeles being the best-policed city in the nation. The city council seized on this claim to reject Parker's plea for more police officers to deal with a rising crime rate and a rapidly increasing multicultural population. Instead of additional officers, the council gave Parker more patrol cars and a helicopter.

While he made the best of it, the chief never suffered from the illusion that an undermanned police force was an advantage. After his requests for more personnel were rejected, he shrewdly maneuvered to increase the effective strength of the LAPD by creating police programs that he subsequently staffed with civilians, releasing officers for police duty. He forced the Los Angeles County Sheriff's Department to assume its neglected responsibility for housing city prisoners, which released more than 200 LAPD officers from jail duty, and prodded the California Highway Patrol to take responsibility for freeway traffic patrol within the city limits. But none of this was enough. "We are the most under-policed of all the large cities in the world," Parker said.[38] He claimed that the LAPD had been able to "hold the

line" only because there was "a great desire on the part of the individual officers to accomplish their task efficiently and professionally."

In the view of Los Angeles Police Academy instructor Ted Hunt, the
LAPD over time became the functional equivalent of the U.S. Marine
Corps, an elite force that was first to fight in the war against crime. LAPD
officers were taught that they were the last line of defense against what
Parker called "a world-wide revolution against constituted authority" in
which the police officer was the "living, physical symbol of authority."[39] An
us-against-them attitude naturally flourishes in police cultures, but Parker
promoted it as essential to the esprit de corps of his elite and overworked department. The idea that Los Angeles police officers were outnumbered war-
riors who battled to save an indifferent world was an underlying theme of
Dragnet and, later, of the gut-wrenching novels of Joseph Wambaugh, himself a former LAPD officer. The titles of these novels, *The New Centurions*
and *The Blue Knight*, are revealing. Wambaugh's LAPD officers are violent,
profane, and cynical but stand between civilization and the forces of evil
that would destroy it.

Stacey Koon, among others, would come to believe that the LAPD was
captive of its own propaganda. "From the moment you enter the LAPD
academy, you're taught that you are the elite of the law enforcement community," Koon wrote. "You're the best of the best."[40] Certainly, Parker believed this. He was so convinced that the LAPD was the nation's best police
force that he became irate when a police expert ranked it fifth, behind Milwaukee, Detroit, St. Louis, and Cincinnati. In reaction, Parker cited the
opinion of the respected Orlando Wilson, who put the LAPD first.[41] Only
the number-one ranking satisfied Parker, and he and his successors cease-
lessly promoted the notion that the LAPD deserved this honor. Tim Wind
had been right in perceiving that the LAPD had become the nation's most
highly rated police department by drawing up the list itself.

But there were drawbacks to the "lean-and-mean" approach. In the
1960s, as racial minorities became more militant and resistance to authority more evident, many police chiefs realized that law enforcement agencies
needed to establish deeper roots and better relationships within minority
communities. This was not the path Parker had chosen for the LAPD. When
he reviewed the Watts riot, he rejected the idea that community involvement
or better treatment of blacks by police officers could have prevented the disorders. Instead, Parker became convinced that a more iron-fisted approach
during the original arrests would have made the difference. Had the arrests
been made by the LAPD instead of the California Highway Patrol, Parker insisted, the riot never would have started in the first place.

But the problems that triggered the Watts riot were more fundamental
than those involving the tactics of any particular arrest, and the LAPD was

resented within the Watts community to a much greater extent than was the CHP. Once the Watts riot flared out of control, its leaders were angry, young black males who had frequently been stopped and harassed by the LAPD. The McCone Commission found that the riot was caused by "10,000 Negroes [who] took to the streets in marauding bands" and were "caught up in an insensate rage of destruction." The Commission said only 2 percent of the Negro population of Los Angeles County had engaged in lawless behavior and suggested that the riot did not have widespread support within Watts.

A public opinion survey taken in the riot area disputed the McCone Commission's conclusion, which became known as the "riffraff" theory of the riot. The survey showed widespread community support for the rioters, based in no small measure on a deep resentment of the police. Even arrest records of the riot cast doubt on the McCone Commission's view that the disorder was essentially the work of thugs. Police arrested 3,431 adults and 547 juveniles on various charges. One third of the adults and half the juveniles had never been taken into custody previously, and another one third of the adults had only minor criminal records. Among the juveniles, only 43 had previous records of significant criminal offenses.

After the National Guard was called in and the riot suppressed, black leaders renewed their criticisms of the LAPD, saying that the police had been unnecessarily heavy-handed. The McCone Commission received seventy specific complaints of police brutality, mostly by the LAPD and the Los Angeles County Sheriff's Department. "Chief Parker appears to be the focal point of the criticism within the Negro community," the Commission found.

> He is a man distrusted by most Negroes and they carefully analyze for possibly anti-Negro meaning almost every action he takes and every statement he makes. Many Negroes feel that he carries a deep hatred of the Negro community. However, Chief Parker's statements to us and collateral evidence such as his record of fairness to Negro officers are inconsistent with his having such an attitude. Despite the depth of the feeling against Chief Parker expressed to us by so many witnesses, he is recognized, even by many of his vocal critics, as a capable Chief who directs an efficient police force that serves well this entire community.

Although the McCone Commission included Judge Earl Broady, the black former LAPD officer who had been forced to give up his promotion to lieutenant in 1940, it was predominantly white in composition and conventional in its views. Unlike Daryl Gates after the riots of 1992, Parker remained immensely popular with the city's white majority, perhaps even more popular than before the Watts riot. But his health was failing. He underwent heart surgery at the Mayo Clinic in October. His recovery was slow, and he took sick leave again the following March. Still, he refused to retire, telling subordinates that the LAPD needed him.

In the summer of 1966, a riot erupted on Chicago's West Side, confirming Parker's fears that the nation faced a long siege of civil unrest. National Guard troops were patrolling Chicago's streets with shoot-to-kill orders on July 16 when Parker and his wife attended a banquet in the chief's honor sponsored by the Second Marine Division Association at the Statler Hilton Hotel in Los Angeles. Parker had just received an award in recognition of "the services he had extended to the men of our armed forces" and returned to his table with the applause of a thousand veterans ringing in his ears when he was stricken by another heart attack. He died thirty-five minutes later.

Los Angeles mourned the loss of its great, flawed chief who had remade the city's police department in his own incorruptible image. Parker's body lay in state in the City Hall rotunda as tributes poured in from friends and foes. Thomas Kuchel, Republican senator from California, hailed Parker as a man who had "feared God and nothing else." Governor Edmund G. (Pat) Brown, an old foe, said "the chief literally gave his life to the law." A requiem mass at St. Vibiana's Cathedral was broadcast over loudspeakers to thousands of mourners who lined the downtown streets outside. Police officers wept. "He was," said former Mayor Fletcher Bowron, "the outstanding police chief of the United States."

Parker's achievements were in fact considerable. He had transformed a corrupt and inefficient department into an honest and elite force, numbering more than 5,000 at his death, that specialized in rapid deployment and vigorous investigation. He had demonstrated, with a commanding sense of public relations and the assistance of *Dragnet*, that it was possible to develop public support and even admiration for the police during a time when officers in many cities were denounced as "pigs" and long-standing premises of law enforcement were being struck down by the courts. But Parker's most singular achievement was that he had made the Los Angeles Police Department virtually autonomous and free from political control.

If establishing the LAPD's independence was Parker's supreme accomplishment, it was also his most dubious contribution to the city he loved so much. While the LAPD under Parker was an effective crime-fighting force, the dash and swagger of its officers and their frequent racial insensitivity made them seem like an "occupying army" in minority communities, as LAPD Officer Ted Hunt had feared. Other police departments aroused similar feelings, but many of them were more responsive to civil authority. The LAPD could not be brought to heel.

Autonomy had value in the short run, for it helped Parker improve professional and disciplinary standards without the delays required by political consultation. Over time, however, the LAPD's independence fostered arrogance and contempt of civilian authority among officers who feared only their chief and Internal Affairs. While other departments developed closer ties within minority communities, the LAPD resisted the trend. Parker equated closeness to a community with corruption, which he always believed was a greater danger than isolation. When Parker addressed graduation classes at the Police Academy, he invariably warned new officers to stay away from people who said they liked policemen or wanted to do something special for them. "The conscientious officer who has received a favor from someone feels he is obligated to return that favor," Parker said.[42]

Los Angeles paid a high price for the stubborn isolation of its police department. This was recognized by political leaders such as Roybal and Bradley and by career police officers such as Jesse Brewer, all of whom tried persistently to communicate with Parker or his successors. It was recognized at the Police Academy by instructors such as Ted Hunt and on the streets by sergeants like Stacey Koon, who were disillusioned by the increasing lack of responsiveness of the LAPD leadership. It was recognized by informed outsiders such as Hubert Williams, a former Newark police chief who became president of the Police Foundation. Long before Williams served as cochairman of the commission that investigated the LAPD's breakdown in the 1992 riots, he had learned from experience that it was perilous for police departments to became estranged from the communities they were supposed to protect and serve or from the civil authorities to whom they were presumed to be accountable.

"You cannot create autonomy in the police leadership despite the problems of corruption they once had in Los Angeles," Hubert Williams said. "There has to be accountability. You can't have a private police force."[43]

4

OFFICIAL NEGLIGENCE

"Police officers are not raised on police farms where they are born and bred to be police officers. They come out of all walks of society with all the prejudices and problems of everyone else."
—Sergeant Scott Landsman,
Los Angeles Police Department.[1]

WITH HIS BLACKENED RIGHT EYE SWOLLEN HALF-SHUT AND HIS right leg in a cast, Rodney King was wheeled out of the Los Angeles County Jail on March 6, 1991, three days after he was beaten. Answering questions from reporters, King denied having led police on a high-speed freeway pursuit. "There was no chase," he said. According to King, he had been pulled over because he "may have been speeding just a little bit," maybe driving 40 to 45 miles an hour. Then he was handcuffed and beaten. He said he did not think he had been beaten because he was black nor did he remember the officers making racial comments. "They beat me so bad I didn't pay any attention to what they were saying," King said.

King's attorney, Steven Lerman, agreed that race was not an issue. Lerman had not been the first choice of King's family, who had sought the services of Johnnie L. Cochran Jr., the city's premier black defense lawyer. But Cochran's receptionist said he was involved in a trial.[2] Desperate, King's mother, Odessa, made inquiries of friends and came up with Lerman, a white lawyer with a Beverly Hills office who had represented a black defendant in a police brutality case. Deputy District Attorney Terry White, an African American, suspected that race might have been a motive for the King beating. But he was dissuaded by Lerman. "Very early on, Lerman told me he didn't think race was an issue," White said.[3]

Daryl Gates had his own suspicions, and he was relieved when LAPD investigators suggested only that the incident was an extreme example of a police tendency to use excessive force after a high-speed chase. That was comprehensible, if not defensible. Gates had been around a long time and knew the old LAPD maxim, "If you run, you get beat."[4]

But Gates was not relieved for long.

Six days after King's news conference at the jail, Internal Affairs investigators at Parker Center handed the chief a transcript of comments made the night of the King arrest on the Mobile Digital Terminal (MDT) in the patrol car assigned to Laurence Powell and Timothy Wind. The MDT is a portable computer that LAPD officers have used since 1983 to communicate with other police cars and dispatchers. Digital transmission is faster than radio transmission, and the system exemplified the LAPD's commitment to technological innovation. While MDT messages were rarely monitored, they were stored in the department's main computer, where authorship could be identified by patrol-car designation. The car assigned to Powell and Wind was numbered 16A23. Detectives had searched the records of MDT messages sent from this car and every other patrol vehicle present at the King arrest.

The transcript handed to Gates contained Powell's message to Officer Corina Smith saying that he hadn't "beaten anyone this bad in a long time." But what caught the chief's eye was another message from Powell to Smith sent from 16A23 less than half an hour before the King incident. Smith had been waiting out an anticipated narcotics arrest in the foothill community of Tujunga.

"Sounds almost exciting as our last call," Powell's message said. "It was right out of gorillas in the mist."

"Hahahaha. Let me guess who be the parties," Smith replied.

Gates had never seen the movie *Gorillas in the Mist*, but when the reference was explained to him, he understood that Powell's message equated black people with gorillas, and he ordered an investigation of the "last call" mentioned in the transmission. It proved to be a disturbance at a Saturday night party at which Powell and Wind had calmed an inflammatory situation. The partygoers, all African Americans, told police investigators that the officers had behaved courteously and professionally.[5] Reassuring as this was to Gates, he knew that Powell's MDT message had made the King affair a racial case. He telephoned Mayor Bradley and members of the Police Commission to tell them about the message. On March 18, after the officers were indicted, the LAPD released the MDT transcripts.[6]

No one was more surprised by the "gorillas" message than Tim Wind. He had been paired with Powell for only three days and, as he later recalled, had been writing a traffic ticket when Powell sent the message. Wind had glanced at Powell and noticed that he was grinning as he typed a message into the MDT, but he had not asked about its contents. As a probationary officer, Wind had a subservient role. He drove the patrol car and wrote police reports—except for the report on the King beating, which Powell insisted on doing himself.

Wind learned about the "gorillas" message while watching television on the evening of March 18. A CNN story said the message had been sent from the Powell-Wind patrol car before the King beating but did not identify the officer who sent it. Detectives had interviewed Corina Smith, who had told them about the conversation with Powell, but in relaying the story, LAPD representatives had failed to say that Powell was the author of the "gorillas" message. The two officers were blanketed together, and Wind was thus branded a racist. He was stunned and spent hours on the telephone trying to reassure bewildered family members in Kansas that he had not sent any messages ridiculing black people.

Wind had been raised to believe that racial prejudice was morally wrong. His mother, Angela, who died from cancer in 1983, had taught disadvantaged black students to read and write and had kept pictures of John F. Kennedy and Martin Luther King Jr. on her desk at the high school where she worked. "She preached against racism," Wind remembered.[7] Wind's boss in the Green Berets, whom he respected, was black. As far as investigators could determine, no one had ever heard Wind make a derogatory reference about any racial or ethnic group. Wind was so embarrassed by the "gorillas" message that he barely spoke to Powell afterward, even though they sat near each other through two trials. "It was immature, irresponsible and unprofessional," Wind said. "It tarred us all."[8]

Stacey Koon was also bothered, if less surprised, by Powell's message. Koon's commitment to racial equality may simply have been a manifestation of his devout Catholicism, but whatever the source of his views, he was liked and respected by black officers. When he worked out of the tough 77th Street Division in South Central Los Angeles, Koon befriended a black officer who had been injured in a traffic accident and then cashiered by the LAPD, helping him win pension and other benefits. John Sheriff, a black patrol officer and twenty-year veteran of the LAPD, said that "Stacey is a guy you can walk up to and he'll give you the shirt off his back." Sheriff, who had been present at the 77th Street Station the night Koon gave mouth-to-mouth resuscitation to the black transvestite, said Koon was "a good man" who was never racist.[9]

While Koon was popular with rank-and-file officers of all races at the 77th Street Division, he had angered veteran white officers at Foothill for vigorously pursuing an allegation of police brutality that may have had racial undertones. As a desk sergeant at Foothill, Koon had investigated the accusations of two black transients, Theresa Carney and William Gable, who complained that a white officer had struck them several times with his baton when they ignored his order to leave a street corner. Allegations by homeless people are often brushed aside by the LAPD, as they are by many other departments, but Koon investigated this complaint on his own time, persuaded the officer's rookie partner to tell him what had happened, and ordered a police lineup at which the transients identified the officer who had abused them.

The offending officer was Lance Braun, a twenty-one-year LAPD veteran who had a reputation for using excessive force but had never been held to account for it. White officers at Foothill, however, were more offended by Koon than by Braun. They complained to Captain Tim McBride, the Foothill Division commander, who issued a memorandum that prohibited calling in officers from the field to participate in lineups. But Koon's tactics brought results. Braun retired after he was identified by the transients. He was subsequently prosecuted and found guilty of two counts of using excessive force "under color of authority."*[10]

After disclosure of the "gorillas" transcript, the LAPD and the district attorney's office examined all MDT transmissions known to have been sent by Powell, Wind, Koon, and Ted Briseno. No other racially offensive messages were found. Briseno's record was blemished by his previous suspension for excessive use of force, but racial bias had not been a factor in that incident. As far as any investigator could determine, no one had ever complained about racial derogation or discrimination by Koon, Wind, or Briseno.

From a race-relations standpoint—indeed, from almost any standpoint—the problem officer among the four defendants was Laurence Powell, who was then twenty-eight. Powell had led Foothill Division in arrests during the eight months before the King affair, but he also had been accused of using excessive force and unprofessional conduct.

Powell, who shared with Rodney King a fondness for fishing, had been raised in an affluent section of La Crescenta, a middle-class community in the eastern San Fernando Valley. He was the youngest of four children and the only boy. His father, Edwin Powell, who served twenty-seven years with the Los Angeles County Marshal's Office and rose to the rank of lieutenant, had talked often to his son about the value of a career in law enforcement. When Larry Powell was twenty-two, his mother had converted their house into a foster home, providing care for children, many of them

---

* During his fourteen and a half years on the LAPD prior to the King incident, Koon was the recipient of only one known excessive force complaint. This was the result of a September 30, 1986, confrontation with an eighteen-year-old robbery suspect who appeared in an alleyway as Koon and two other officers were pursuing him. The suspect reached toward his waistband, Koon kicked him, and the officers jumped him and arrested him. An Internal Affairs inquiry did not sustain the excessive-force complaint, but Koon was suspended for five days for failing to report the incident. Koon said he became involved in a murder case and several pursuits the following day and forgot to report it. He said he did not think it worthwhile to contest the suspension.

black or Latino, who had been abused or born with drug addictions. The senior Powells had won praise from the county for the quality of their foster care, and family members and friends cited this as a defense against the charge that Larry Powell was racially prejudiced. He "wasn't taught to look down at minorities," said Jerry Guzzetta, a friend and private investigator.[11]

After graduating as an honor student at predominantly white Crescenta Valley High School, Powell took courses for three semesters at California State University-Northridge, where he did well in math and physics and showed an aptitude for computers. He joined the Los Angeles police reserves and worked part-time as a Municipal Court clerk. Edwin Powell told me during the federal trial that his son had joined the reserves because he wanted to be a cop. But jury consultant Jo-Ellan Dimitrius, who sympathized with Powell, was convinced that he was "living in the footsteps of what his father expected of him." Dimitrius thought that Powell had appealing qualities but that law enforcement was the wrong profession for him.[12]

Powell's advancement through the ranks of the LAPD was rapid—too rapid in the belated opinion of his division commander, Captain McBride. Powell graduated near the top of his class at the Los Angeles Police Academy in June 1987. Because he had worked four shifts a week without pay as a reserve officer, his customary one-year probation was reduced to six months. Soon after Powell became a full-time officer, he was one of twenty-three current or former reservists honored by the city's Human Relations Commission for "outstanding service." The citation said that he had "received nine commendations for productivity and devotion to duty and was recognized as Van Nuys area's officer of the month. His move to a full-time officer is an immediate loss to the reserve program but a definite gain to the City and to the Police Department."

Indeed, Powell seemed a promising officer in his early days on the LAPD, where he was a member of the prestigious CRASH (Community Resources Against Street Hoodlums) unit that suppressed gangs in Hollywood, Wilshire, and West Los Angeles. "He was a hard worker, always had a smile on his face . . . a real positive attitude," said then-Lieutenant Brad Merritt, who was in charge of the unit.[13] Merritt said that Powell had left to become a field-training officer at Foothill in the summer of 1989 because promotional opportunities in the CRASH unit were limited. "You could have knocked me over with a feather when I heard he was involved in [the King incident]," Merritt added.[14]

Powell's involvement was less surprising to his peers, who considered him enthusiastic but lacking in good judgment. At Municipal Court, where female co-workers complained that Powell told jokes belittling women, his boss James Switzer described him as "immature." This word was also used to characterize Powell by Wind, who didn't like him, and by Dimitrius, who did.

Some of Powell's LAPD colleagues thought Powell worse than immature. When Janine Bouey, a black LAPD officer arrived at Foothill Station
one day in 1990 and saw that she was scheduled to ride with Powell, she
surreptitiously rearranged the names on the assignment board so that she
was paired with another officer. "If I could get out of working with Powell,
I would," she said. "He treated everybody like crap. He always had his hand
on his gun. We could be ordering a soda, talking to the lady at the register,
and he would have his hand on his gun. We call it badge-heavy."[15] Bouey
said she had seen Powell stop and curse a black motorist because he was
driving in a white neighborhood.

Powell could also be brutal. While arresting Salvador Castaneda, who
had chased a drinking companion with a machete, Powell struck him repeatedly with his baton, breaking an elbow. Castaneda filed an excessive-
force lawsuit and received $70,000 from the city in an out-of-court
settlement. Five months before the King beating, Powell struck a handcuffed
prisoner, Danny Ramos, with his flashlight, an incident for which he was
eventually reprimanded and in which Corina Smith was also involved but
cleared of wrongdoing.[16] Two weeks before the King arrest, Powell was involved in a controversy with three black San Fernando Valley College students who had engaged in a shouting match with a white couple. As the
students related the story to the community newspaper, *The Wave*, Powell
and an unidentified officer had forced them to lie on the ground, handcuffed them and made racially derogatory remarks. John Bray, the only male
in the trio, said Powell refused to hear the students' side of the story. When
Bray protested that he was handcuffed too tightly, Powell laughed and said,
"You complain more than the bitches."

The students filed a complaint against Powell, but nothing was done
about it, and Captain McBride acknowledged that the sergeant who was
supposed to investigate the case had "dropped the ball."[17] It was a costly
error. Had disciplinary proceedings been instituted, Powell might not have
been working on the night of March 3, 1991.

On balance, Powell was a uniformed accident in waiting and an example of official negligence at its worst. That he was not only on patrol
but also serving as a trainer is a sad comment on the professionalism of
the LAPD. What kind of police force would send an officer into the field
on the same night that he demonstrated his incompetence with the
baton? The Castaneda arrest and the two other incidents had sent danger signals that Powell's superiors ignored. "Powell [was] an overaggressive
and slightly sadistic police officer of questionable judgment," said Jack
White, who investigated the King case for the district attorney. "He's not
really a bad guy unless something ignites him."[18] What most easily ignited Powell was resistance to arrest, especially if the person who resisted

was black or Latino. Racism and incompetence are a particularly incendiary combination.

THE PUBLIC WAS LARGELY UNAWARE THAT POWELL WAS AN exception among the four defendants in his racial attitudes. Chief Gates was so determined to distance the LAPD from all four officers that he was uninterested in providing information that might have helped any one of them. Gates would later deplore the blanket portrayal of the defendants as racists, but he contributed to the stereotyping. The LAPD brass was particularly remiss in concealing Koon's efforts in behalf of the black transients in Foothill Division, where racism ran deep.

Mayor Bradley was also uninterested in drawing distinctions among the officers. He remembered his own humiliating experiences on the then-segregated LAPD, and he saw the King beating as an opportunity to mobilize public opinion against Chief Gates, who had become a political foe. Bradley responded to the disclosure of the MDT messages by issuing a statement from Hawaii, where he was lobbying to bring the 1993 Super Bowl to Los Angeles. In it, he deplored the "casual and cavalier attitude" of the officers "toward this horrific beating." The mayor deliberately painted all the defendants and, by inference, the LAPD with the brush of Powell's racist remarks.

"It is no longer possible for any objective person to regard the King beating as an aberration," Bradley's statement declared in a contemptuous reference to Gates' description of the incident. "We must face the fact that there appears to be a dangerous trend of racially motivated incidents running through at least some segments of the Police Department." Other prominent blacks thought much the same. John Mack, the president of the Los Angeles Urban League, said the MDT messages provided "clear evidence of the savage, racist brutality that was inflicted on Rodney King." Pamela Roberts, an LAPD sergeant, recalled thinking, when she first saw the tape, "Look at those fools in South Africa."[19]

The computer messages notably affected the tone of the media coverage. "Officers in Los Angeles Joked About Beating Black," said the headline over The New York Times story about the MDT disclosures. Stories about the case, my own dispatches to The Washington Post included, routinely described the incident as the beating of "a black motorist" by four white officers, as if King had been out for a quiet Sunday drive. The white officers would have preferred a contrary but no less prejudicial journalistic shorthand that identified King as a paroled robber or an ex-convict. But generally the media coverage after the transcripts were released drew a group portrait of white officers who had brutally beaten an innocent black man without provocation and then joked about what they had done.

By mid-April, six weeks after the first showing of the truncated Holliday tape, a survey of registered voters in Los Angeles County showed that 81 percent believed the defendants guilty. Of the remaining voters, 16 percent were uncertain (although their responses suggested that most of them leaned toward guilty verdicts) and only 3 percent believed the defendants not guilty. There was virtually no difference in the responses of whites and blacks. Even a voter who was legally blind said he had been able to see enough on television to be convinced that the officers were guilty.[20] This widespread public prejudgment became the wedge argument in the attempts of the defense to move the trial out of Los Angeles County.

In view of the saturation use of the edited videotape on local television, it seems unlikely that more balanced print coverage would have affected public opinion. Still, an investigation by newspapers into the backgrounds of the officers might have helped the public draw distinctions among them. As far as I have been able to determine, Koon's pivotal role in securing justice for the black transients at Foothill went unreported before the first criminal trial. The Los Angeles Times and the Daily News ran informative stories early in February 1992 that examined the lives of the defendants and described the episode in which Koon had administered mouth-to-mouth resuscitation to the AIDS-stricken black transvestite.[21] But these stories came too late. The trial had long since been moved to Simi Valley, where it would be the prosecutors and Rodney King who were in need of balanced judgments.

The computer messages affected the strategy of King's attorney, Steven Lerman, who contradicted his earlier statements and took the position that his client had been beaten because of his race. Whether King himself readily reached the same conclusion remains a matter of conjecture. On March 19, 1991, after the MDT messages had been released, Lerman said that he had asked King if he now thought he was beaten because of his color. "I'm scared to say that," Lerman quoted King as saying. "I don't want to start a riot."[22] Deputy District Attorney Terry White, who was busily assembling information for the prosecution's case, suspected that Lerman took a militant position because he feared losing his valuable client to a black lawyer, which is what eventually happened. "Lerman was constantly aware that he could lose this case, and he wanted to keep people away from Rodney King," White said. "And that includes the prosecution, because every time I met with him, Lerman was always present. And the funny thing was whenever I met with [King] and would ask him questions, it wasn't so much that he would talk as Lerman would talk. It was like, 'Rodney, remember you told me this, Rodney, remember you told me that.' And I never knew what Rodney King knew or did not know." Lerman said that King remembered different details of the beating as time passed.[23]

Over time a revised version of the King arrest developed in the Lerman camp. Tom Owens, Lerman's investigator, said that King had told him that Briseno had called him "nigger" when he ordered him to put his hands behind his back. Owens said that on another occasion King explained that what appears to be a charge at Officer Powell in the first few seconds of the Holliday videotape was in fact an attempt to flee the scene because Koon had said to him, "You better run now, nigger, 'cause we're going to kill you." The new allegation about Briseno's conduct, although not Koon's, was buttressed by the opinion of George Papcun, a University of New Mexico audiologist. Papcun told KCET-TV that when the audio tape was enhanced, he could hear the words, "Nigger, put your hands behind your back."[24]

But neither state nor federal prosecutors, despite the extensive technology available to the FBI, could hear any such language on enhanced versions of the audiotape. Two officials at the Department of Justice, listening repeatedly to the audiotape, wound up in a furious argument. One was certain he heard the word "asshole," a familiar LAPD term for criminal suspects. The other could not hear "asshole" but was positive he heard "motherfucker." Neither official heard the word "nigger."[25]

None of the prosecutors believed that Koon had called King a racial name and told him to run for his life—even though they were not charitable in their judgment of Koon's conduct. The Singers, who resented the way Koon had taken over their arrest, also did not believe this allegation. Apart from the fact that King's revised account contradicted his original story, in which he denied that he had led the police on a chase and falsely claimed he had been beaten after being handcuffed, the accusation concerning Koon made no sense on its face. Koon had tried in three different ways to take King into custody—verbal commands, a swarm by four officers, and the Taser shots—before the first baton blow was struck. Had he desired to administer street justice for any reason, he had plenty of opportunity to do so early in the incident and well before the videotape began. But it is inconceivable that Koon would have used derogatory language in the presence of officers from another law enforcement agency that he did not trust. Prosecutors were reluctantly forced to conclude that King's revised story was cut from whole cloth.

What is more difficult to determine is whether subliminal attitudes on the part of the arresting officers affected their perceptions. State prosecutors suspected that the "gorillas" message reflected a racial bias that might have unconsciously influenced Powell during the beating. Later, federal prosecutors would be similarly suspicious of Koon's written description of King's confrontation with Melanie Singer as a "Mandingo sexual encounter." An LAPD survey of racial attitudes within the department after the King beating found that more than one fourth of the officers (27.6

percent) agreed with the statement that "an officer's prejudice toward the suspect's race may lead to the use of excessive force." Another 15 percent had no opinion.[26]

Veteran black officers familiar with LAPD history were candid in discussing the department's ingrained racism. Joseph Rouzan, who joined the LAPD in 1955 and became police chief in two Southern California cities and executive director of the Los Angeles Police Commission, believes that racial prejudice is endemic to police cultures and that it comes to the fore when white officers brought up in middle-class surroundings are assigned to crime-ridden black communities. "If you work in Watts or Newton Division and you walk into a family dispute and they've five kids in one room and it's not as clean as your home is and the guy uses language in front of the kids, you start saying, God, what a low life," Rouzan said. "I've had many white officers tell me this." Stereotypes are reinforced because white officers see that "all the whores are black, all the pimps are black, all the dope pushers are black, . . . sixty percent of the people in jail are black."[27]

Rouzan rose to high positions in the LAPD. More typically for a black officer, John Sheriff, who counted Koon as a friend, remained in the ranks. Sheriff joined the LAPD in the mid-1970s after serving as an Air Force mechanic and has spent most of his career as a patrol officer in the 77th Street Division. He vividly recalls his indoctrination to LAPD racial attitudes when he was a young officer. "[They would say] don't get upset if I say 'nigger' because I'm not talking about you. You see, there's different types of people of color. You got niggers, you got Negroes, you got blacks and you got coloreds. And they would break these down. A nigger is the guy who's yelling on the corner, screaming and jumping up and down, ready to kill you, hurt you, beat you, shoot you. Coloreds are the older black folks who did their time and generally want to be left alone. Blacks are the militant types. . . . And you, you're the Negro."[28]

Sheriff had moved his family from South Central to suburban Walnut, a mixed-race community where police took a common-sense approach to juvenile crime. If a young person hurled a rock through a window, an officer would typically settle the issue with the parents, who would pay for the window and promise it wouldn't happen again. "In 77th, it's solved by me going out, putting a set of cuffs on this kid, and bringing him to the station. And let the court order this kid to buy the window," said Sheriff. "That's not right."[29]

As Rouzan and Sheriff observed and the LAPD survey suggests, many police officers tend to treat black suspects more harshly than white suspects. This is especially true if the suspect is a black male, and even more so if he is fleeing the police. Officers are often required to make split-second assessments of the danger posed by a suspect who confronts them, and race is an inevitable factor in decision making. A well-informed white officer observed in 1994 that blacks, who then made up 13 percent of the population of Los Angeles, account for more than 45 percent of the felony arrests. "We know this, but aren't allowed to say it," the officer told me, as if saying it would be prima facie admission of racism.

Nevertheless, the overwhelming view of both black and white officers in the LAPD is that Rodney King was beaten because of his conduct and his size rather than his race. That is also still the opinion of Daryl Gates, who believes that race had "absolutely" nothing to do with the King beating. "Bigness had something to do with it," Gates said. "Bigness and the belief that he was under PCP."[30]

There is considerable anecdotal evidence to support the prevailing police view. It is highly probable that King would never have been harmed if he had complied with police orders and allowed himself to be handcuffed. But it is also possible that ingrained racial attitudes contributed to the perceptions that defined King as dangerous. "I don't think Rodney King was beaten because of his race," said Cliff Ruff of the Police Protective League, who helped obtain legal representation for the officers. "But I also don't think what happened to King would have happened to a white man from Encino."[31]

THE WIDESPREAD STEREOTYPING OF THE POLICE DEFENDANTS AS white racists after disclosure of the Powell computer messages was unfair to Koon, Wind, and Briseno, but it was not drawn in a vacuum. Blacks had been shot, strangled, or beaten in encounters with the LAPD for years. They were also humiliated in circumstances where whites would have been more apt to receive courteous treatment. State Senator Nate Holden, later a city councilman and a defender of Chief Gates, was held at gunpoint outside his Crenshaw Boulevard office in 1977 by two LAPD officers who mistook him for a bank-robbery suspect. In 1983, a black off-duty Santa Monica police officer, John Henry, was taking his father, mother, and eight-year-old son to visit a sick relative when his car was stopped for a traffic violation by two white LAPD officers. Henry was insulted, pushed with a baton, handcuffed, and taken to jail. "It was overwhelming, to put it mildly," said Henry many years later. "I had taught my son to respect law enforcement, and for him to be trying to get out of the car to come and help me, that was bad."[32] In 1988, Hall of Fame baseball player Joe Morgan was mistaken for a drug courier by an LAPD detective and roughed up at Los Angeles International Airport. In 1990, a car driven by former Los Angeles Laker basketball player Jamaal Wilkes was pulled over by white officers who did not recognize him.

Wilkes was placed in handcuffs, told that his registration was about to expire, and cited because his license plate light was burned out.

Holden received a formal apology from the Police Commission. Henry won a civil suit against the city and settled for $22,500 in damages after a new trial was ordered for technical reasons. Morgan won $461,000 from a federal jury in 1991, and the city council settled a claim of punitive damages two years later by boosting the payout to $796,000. In 1990, the year before the King beating, the city paid out more than $11.3 million in lawsuits and settlements arising from LAPD-related litigation. This was slightly more than the payouts for police-related cases in New York City, which had three times as many officers, and more than the police-related payouts in any other city in the nation except Detroit. But many ordinary citizens who were mistreated by the LAPD never gained redress, particularly if they were young blacks or Latinos. On a cold February night in 1990, two dozen black and Latino youths were forced to lie face down on the Will Rogers Memorial Park polo field while LAPD officers abused and taunted them. These victims received no compensatory damages or apologies.

Every post-Parker police chief had tried to improve the image of the LAPD within the black community. Thomas H. Reddin, who took over the department in 1967, increased the community relations staff from four people to more than one hundred. "He ordered the police to fraternize with minority citizens, and to wear nametags for easy identification," Joseph Woods wrote. "He himself met in frequently acrimonious debate with militants and radicals as well as moderate blacks. He increased the training period to five months and included 'sensitivity' classes. He returned some officers to foot patrol, used black ex-convicts in police-community liaison work, and reinstituted a broad variety of youth-related programs."[33]

After the assassination of Martin Luther King Jr., Reddin required his officers to drive with their headlights on as a mark of respect. He tried to recruit more black and Mexican-American officers. He adopted a recommendation of the McCone Commission to establish a position of inspector general, and he put this officer in charge of Internal Affairs and had him report directly to the chief. But Reddin's changes were unpopular with the LAPD rank and file, and he was not chief long enough to put his stamp on the department. In 1969, he abruptly resigned to become a television news commentator.

From a reform standpoint, Reddin's timing could not have been worse. His resignation left the LAPD leaderless during the 1969 mayoral campaign and gave credence to Mayor Yorty's contention that police officers would resign en masse if Tom Bradley were elected. Yorty was re-elected, and on

August 29, after a five-month interim, Reddin was succeeded by the formidable Edward M. Davis.

At the time of his appointment, Ed Davis had spent twenty-nine of his
fifty-three years in the LAPD, where he was viewed as a tough-minded administrator cut from the Parker mold. He had been raised as a Roman
Catholic and had attended Catholic schools, leaving the church to become an
Episcopalian when he was twenty-four because of what he called "a basic
disagreement" on birth control. "When I belong to an outfit, I've got to be a
full-fledged member," Davis said many years later.[34] He joined the LAPD in
1940, graduating from the Police Academy in the same class as Tom Bradley.
Unlike Parker at the time of his selection as chief, Davis was popular with
the LAPD rank and file. As head of the LAPD union, the Police Protective
League, during the 1950s, he had worked to improve police salaries.

The new chief was a study in contrasts. He was a careful administrator
who surrounded himself with competent subordinates and capably deployed
the LAPD; he was also a bombastic public figure who delighted even more
than Parker in extreme denunciations of the courts, legislatures, governors,
presidents, the media, and the women's liberation movement. Davis derided
wealthy liberals as "swimming-pool communists," called homosexuals
"fairies" and "fruits," and said the way to deal with airplane hijackers was
to "hang them at the airport."[35]

Davis was an innovator who strived for what he called "ethnic balance"
in the police leadership and was one of the first big-city chiefs to appoint a
black as his executive officer. He was particularly appalled by the LAPD's
terrible reputation in the black community. "It was Ed Davis who made dramatic changes," said Jesse Brewer, whose promotions were no longer blocked
by white officers who gave him low scores on oral tests. "He was no right-
wing zealot, despite the statements he liked to make. He was a true leader.
And he promoted blacks, although he had a blind spot toward women."[36]

Davis was an advocate of community service policing, which is variously
known as team policing, the beat commander project, or the neighborhood
police team, and has been tried in Syracuse, Cincinnati, Detroit, San Diego,
and elsewhere. What all these plans have in common is that they make officers or a group of officers responsible for a particular neighborhood or area
instead of dispersing them throughout the city. As James Q. Wilson has observed, "The immediate objective is to develop among the officers a strong
sense of territoriality—their beats are 'their turf'—out of which will arise,
it is hoped, a stronger sense of identification with the community and the
fostering of reciprocity in information and service."[37]

Davis had read Robert Ardrey's *Territorial Imperative*, and was fascinated
by the idea that living organisms will fiercely defend their turf. In his own

book, *Staff One: A Perspective on Police Management*, published in 1978, Davis related "territoriality" to world events and to police work.

The Los Angeles variant of team policing introduced by Davis was called the "basic car plan." Officers were deployed in patrol cars (instead of on the foot beats common in eastern cities) within a relatively small area. Davis gradually extended team policing throughout the LAPD, starting with a team in Venice, then adding a team in Watts. Officers were taught that residents of their territory were "their people." As Davis explained in *Staff One:*

> If the policeman is white and the people he serves are black, he may think at first, "I don't like black people very much," and the black people may think at first, "We don't like white cops very much." Yet he's their protector, and he knows that they are depending on him; and if they sit down and rap together about how to protect the area, pretty soon the whiteness and the blackness disappear, and it becomes *Us*, a feeling of unity. We, the police and the people of Watts, against the criminal army.[38]

The basic car plan was extended to the entire city in 1970, and there is no doubt that it produced results, especially when combined with the Neighborhood Watch plan that Davis also promoted. Crime declined, along with random violence by LAPD officers against minorities and accompanying complaints that the LAPD was an occupying army. No riots blemished the Los Angeles landscape in the eight years Davis served as chief. Unfortunately, the Davis reforms were overshadowed by the chief's loose talk. "I think in terms of administrative ability he has been one of the outstanding chiefs in the country," Tom Bradley said in 1977. "But I've said to him more than once that his rhetoric and inflammatory language have distorted and detracted from the effective things he's done."[39]

Although Bradley liked Davis, he also worried that the chief could become a political threat. The mayor remembered that the LAPD high command and the police union had played a major role in his defeat at the hands of Sam Yorty in 1969 and that many LAPD officers had again supported Yorty when Bradley won their rematch election in 1973. Bradley feared that the lieutenants Davis had designated "community relations officers" (known as CROs, or "Crows") and put in charge of the community policing teams would become the basis of a political machine loyal to Davis. In dismissing these officers as "public relations people [who] didn't do any police work," Bradley ironically made common cause with reactionary and racist elements of the LAPD who sneered at community policing as coddling the black community.[40]

Davis's open display of political ambition did little to allay Bradley's suspicions. The chief's predecessor, Tom Reddin, had run for mayor in 1973, although he failed to make it into the runoff, and Davis, who had more of a following, also flirted with the idea of becoming a candidate. He eventually discarded the idea. "I do not want to be mayor of this city," Davis told the *Los Angeles Times* in 1977. "That position has no power. I have more power than the mayor." Instead of running for mayor, Davis left the LAPD in January 1978 to seek the Republican nomination for governor. He lost, but in 1980 was elected state senator from a San Fernando Valley district which he represented capably for a dozen years, surprising conservatives with his support for gay rights and other social causes that he had scorned as police chief. Although his rhetoric often belied it, Davis believed in treating people fairly. "He was gruff but had a good heart," Bradley said.[41]

Community-service policing in Los Angeles might over time have changed the "occupying army" outlook of the LAPD in South Central and put the department in a better position to avert or contain the 1992 riots. Sadly, the concept did not survive the departure of Davis. While less liberal mayors in other cities were supporting variants of team policing as a way to bridge the gap between the police and minority communities, Bradley, in an odd alliance with the new police chief, Daryl Gates, killed the program.

Davis believes that Gates went along with Bradley in abolishing community policing because he wanted "to make a hit with the detectives" who resented being under control of the community officers.[42] The new chief may also have seen an opportunity to cement his relations with an LAPD old guard that hated team policing in any form. He encountered no opposition from liberals such as Stephen Reinhardt, a Democratic activist who was then vice president of the Police Commission.[43] In another city, Reinhardt might have been an advocate of the concept, but Los Angeles liberals feared LAPD political activity too much to appreciate the long-term advantages of community policing. The issues-oriented Reinhardt thought it a "very dangerous system" because the CROs might influence people to oppose court decisions restricting the power of the police.[44]

Only in a city where local elections are nonpartisan and political organizations primitive could seventeen LAPD lieutenants have been perceived as potential ward bosses in the vanguard of a police political machine. Bradley's reflexive opposition to community policing was based upon his resentment of police support for Sam Yorty but also reflected a limitation of vision that would eventually undo his administration. And the mayor was not alone. The city council also feared LAPD political activity. Another blow to the program was delivered by the passage of Proposition 13 in 1978. It was easy for the council to eliminate a few police positions that neither the mayor nor the police chief cared to save.

It might have been less easy for the council to abolish team policing if the concept had captured the hearts and minds of the LAPD rank and file. It never did. "One of the biggest things that police fear is that they'll become social workers with guns," said Ted Hunt, a team-policing advocate who joined the LAPD in the Davis years.[45] The idea of serving punch and cookies at neighborhood meetings has limited appeal to rough-and-tumble cops anywhere, and it was anathema to a police force raised on the *Dragnet* legacy.

Even if community-service policing had won acceptance from the politicians and rank-and-file police officers, it would have been difficult to implement on a large scale in Los Angeles. Community policing by its nature requires additional officers, and the LAPD was too small and thinly spread, with fewer than two officers for each thousand persons, less than half the ratio of many other cities. The lack of officers placed a premium on productivity and encouraged LAPD commanders to use arrests as the prime measure of officer effectiveness. It was a one-dimensional measurement deplored by Officer Sheriff in South Central because it encouraged dubious arrests for minor offenses and decried by Joseph Rouzan because it failed to reward officers who excel at crime prevention but make few arrests. The danger of equating arrests with effective performance is demonstrated by the overvaluing of Officer Laurence Powell, who was tolerated at Foothill despite the complaints against him because he led the division in arrests. "Too many police officers would rather kick ass," said Ed Davis in deploring the low repute of team policing. "There is a time for that, but that's not the essence of police work."[46]

DARYL GATES WAS SWORN IN AS POLICE CHIEF OF LOS ANGELES on March 28, 1978, four days after his selection by a Police Commission that was not happy with its choice. City charter provisions gave preference to LAPD experience. Gates, who was assistant chief under Davis, placed second on the civil service examination behind an outside candidate but moved up to first place when credited for his twenty-nine years of service with the department. Under the arcane rules by which the commission was then bound, the outsider was eliminated. The commission had the choice of Gates or two LAPD deputy chiefs, Robert Vernon and Charles Reese. The commissioners had no doubt that Gates was the best of the three but wanted him to show deference to the commission and promise to keep the LAPD out of politics. Instead, he was defiant during his interview, displaying a stubborn independence that endeared him to the LAPD rank and file and foreshadowed the intractability he would display in future political confrontations.

"I kind of liked Gates," Commissioner Stephen Reinhardt recalled. "I had breakfast with him and told him that it's hard for you to lose this, but after your interview you may do it. He still wouldn't bend much, and that's because he knew it would be difficult to choose the other two."[47] When

Gates was named, Reinhardt used the occasion to make a speech in which he criticized the process of choosing a chief and called for "depoliticization of this department." But Gates had no intention of kowtowing to a part-time civilian commission that had selected him only because it liked the other candidates even less. He pointedly told reporters that he disagreed with Reinhardt. Gates had become chief without any strings attached.

Like William Parker and Ed Davis before him, Gates was a career LAPD cop who had never worked in any other department. His childhood was hard. He was born in Glendale on August 30, 1926, the second and middle child of Paul and Arvilla Gates. The family was then a reasonably well-off middle-class family, but his father lost his plumbing business in the Depression. When Daryl was four, they moved to a poor section of town where Daryl shared a bed with his older brother Lowell and their mother went to work as a seamstress in a dress factory. She left for work early in the morning while her sons were asleep and returned late at night.

Paul Gates was an alcoholic whose frequent drunken behavior made him a target of the law. When there was a knock on the door, the Gates boys never knew if marshals had come to serve papers on their parents for their debts or the Glendale police had arrived to take their father to jail. Gates wrote in his autobiography that he awoke one morning when he was seven with a swollen face and complained to his father, who drunkenly shrugged off his son's condition. As soon as his mother saw him when she came home, she called a doctor. Daryl Gates had an acute kidney condition which left him bed-ridden for three months. "It took me a long, long time to forgive my father for his neglect," he wrote.[48] In fact, he never forgave him, although Paul Gates eventually stopped drinking and resumed work as a plumber.

It is not surprising that Gates gravitated to his Mormon mother and away from his Roman Catholic father. He developed a revulsion toward drunkenness, typical of children of alcoholics, which doubtless accounts for his horror when he discovered that Chief Parker had a drinking problem. Gates left home after finishing high school, joined the Navy at seventeen, and manned an antiaircraft gun on a destroyer in several Pacific naval battles during the final year of World War II. After his discharge he attended the University of Southern California on the GI Bill of Rights, married, fathered a child and was hard-pressed to pay his bills. Gates was on the verge of quitting college when a friend told him that the LAPD paid recruits to complete their education. As Gates tells the story, he joined the LAPD for the money, then the munificent sum of $290 a month.

Gates became a cop on September 16, 1949, less than a year before Parker was named chief. He was bright, hard-working, and a good test taker who rose with exceptional speed through the ranks: sergeant in 1955, lieutenant in 1959, captain in 1963, commander in 1965, deputy chief in 1968, and one of three assistant chiefs to Davis in 1969. As he climbed the LAPD ladder, Gates showed a flair for innovation, notably in developing the Special Weapons and Tactics (SWAT) team, a heavily armed, quasi-military unit designed to respond to street militants and hostage situations.

SWAT was the polar opposite of community policing. Gates first employed the unit as assistant chief (while Davis was in Mexico) during a raid on a Black Panthers headquarters in 1969. Six Panthers were arrested, three after being wounded. In 1974, SWAT was involved in a televised shootout with the Symbionese Liberation Army. It ended when six members of the group burned to death in the house from which they exchanged fire with the police. But SWAT also saved lives in bloodless hostage rescues that were less publicized, and police forces across the nation copied the idea. Gates was proud of SWAT, which he saw as epitomizing LAPD aggressiveness. He remained personally combative as chief, once chasing down a drunken driver in his unmarked car on the Pasadena Freeway as he and his chauffeur returned from a black-tie dinner in Beverly Hills. "There is a side of me that is clearly part of the cowboys and very aggressive, and I believe in very aggressive police work," Gates told Bill Boyarsky in 1988. "I preach it all the time."[49]

While calmer in manner and metaphor than Davis, Gates had an equal talent for creating controversy. He was named chief on March 24, a Friday. On Saturday, Boyarsky interviewed him at his home in a gated community south of Laguna Beach. Boyarsky, a respected reporter who had covered politics for the Associated Press and the Los Angeles Times, liked Gates and was impressed by his "tough but enlightened" approach.[50] Gates said that "the department has to reflect the character of the city that it serves" and needed more black and Latino officers. Expanding on this theme, Gates added that the LAPD was not doing well in promoting Latinos and said it was partly the department's fault. "Blacks are far better organized, far more committed to advancing themselves and working much harder than Latino officers, and we're going to have to do something about that," Gates said. "We've got to get some enthusiasm in our Latin officers."[51]

The interview appeared in the Los Angeles Times on Monday, the day before Gates became chief. It caused a storm among Latinos and was frequently shorthanded in subsequent press accounts to say that Gates had accused Latino officers of being "lazy." Actually, Gates had praised the job Latinos were doing as police investigators and confined his criticism to saying that they weren't interested in advancement. It was an honest, if undiplomatic, assessment that set the pattern for many self-inflicted verbal wounds.

What is rarely quoted from the same interview is Gates' partial embrace of a revised and improved LAPD shooting policy. Davis had resisted changes in the traditional policy allowing officers to shoot at a fleeing suspect or escapee. The Police Commission wanted to limit shootings to circumstances in which a police officer had reason to believe a suspect was dangerous. In the Boyarsky interview, Gates signaled a willingness to accept such a policy, provided it was amended to allow officers to fire at fleeing felons. This compromise became the outline of a policy change that Stephen Reinhardt considered the Police Commission's most substantive accomplishment during the five years he was a member. As so often happened, however, the change was forced on the LAPD by events on the streets.

Eulia Love was a thirty-nine-year-old African-American widow whose husband had died of sickle-cell anemia. She lived in South Central under a mound of debt, paying the mortgage and supporting her three daughters with a monthly $680 Social Security check. Her debts included an overdue $69 gas bill. On the morning of January 3, 1979, a gas company employee told Love that he would turn off the gas to her house unless she paid at least $22 of the bill. She said she had no money to pay the bill. When he then tried to turn off the gas, Love struck him on the arm with a shovel. Two gas-company employees returned in the afternoon but said they were threatened by Love, who was now brandishing a kitchen knife.

Police were called. Two officers, one African American and one white, confronted Love outside her house and asked her to drop the knife. After a five-minute standoff, the white officer struck Love on the right hand with his baton, knocking the knife from her grasp. But Love retrieved it before he did and, from a distance of six to eight feet, threw it in the direction of one of the officers. They emptied their service revolvers into Eulia Love, firing twelve times and hitting her with eight bullets. She was dead when the ambulance arrived. "Any way you viewed it, it was a bad shooting," Gates acknowledged.[52]

This "bad shooting" proved a watershed for Gates, who had maintained good relations with the Bradley administration during his first nine months as chief. But they were not strong enough to withstand the sensational accounts of the Love shooting by the *Los Angeles Herald-Examiner*, then struggling to compete with the dominant *Los Angeles Times*. As the *Herald-Examiner* described the story, Love had been killed by the police for non-payment of a $22 gas bill. The *Herald-Examiner* prodded local television and eventually the *Times* into competing coverage, and the Love shooting was soon viewed as a racial case within the black community, even though one of the officers who killed her was black. Gates was on the spot. He knew that harshly disciplining the officers who shot Love would send a welcome signal to blacks and to the Bradley administration, which was also feeling the political heat.

No one in the LAPD pretended that the officers who shot Love had used good judgment. The issue was whether the shooting was acceptable under

LAPD procedures—"in policy," "in police jargon. A review board of deputy chiefs decided the question affirmatively on a 4–1 vote, ruling that the officers had fired in self-defense. Gates thought the officers had been tactically wrong to confront Love at close quarters but also believed that they had abided by LAPD guidelines in firing their weapons. Upholding the review board, he declared the shooting of Love to be in policy.

It was a decision that he might have made differently later in his tenure as chief. Long before the Rodney King case, Gates had learned to distance himself from politically unpopular police mistakes and crack down on misconduct, although he was usually more severe in dealing with corruption than in dealing with excessive force. Still, by the time of the Thirty-ninth and Dalton raid in 1988, Gates had become intolerant of actions justified only by a narrow reading of permitted procedures: Thirty-eight officers were cited for violating department rules after that incident, which helped victims of the raid win substantial legal judgments against the city. But in 1979, Gates was new to his job and felt the need to show support for his deputy chiefs when they were under political attack.

After the killing of Eulia Love, the Police Commission adopted a compromise version of the shooting policy change that Reinhardt had sought. One of its provisions, which required officers to assess the impact of initial shots before firing again, directly reflected the Love incident and was endorsed by Gates. But the chief's decision upholding the shooting confirmed the suspicions of LAPD critics that Gates was a strongman in the Parker mold who would defend even the most outrageous actions of his officers. This view of Gates carried over into the next police controversy, a furor over the deaths of suspects who were subdued by upper-body control holds, commonly called "choke holds."

THE LAPD HAD A DEPLORABLE RECORD ON CHOKE-HOLD USE. Although there were quibbles over the data, tabulations up to April 1982 appeared to show that fifteen persons arrested by the LAPD had been killed by choke holds during a seven-year period, with most of the deaths occurring after Gates had become chief. Since eleven of the fifteen choke-hold victims were black, it is not surprising that blacks wanted choke holds banned. The deaths were not the only reason. Choke holds were sometimes used to humiliate blacks by causing them to "do the chicken"—flop around from a loss of oxygen.[53]

Most of the choke-hold deaths were blamed on improper use of the bar-arm control hold, in which an officer places a forearm against a suspect's trachea and applies pressure. In some cases this resulted in a broken neck and instant death. Davis and Gates preferred a modified and less dangerous hold, in which pressure is applied to the carotid arteries on each side of the neck, interrupting the flow of oxygen to the brain and causing a quick blackout. Both holds were taught at the Police Academy and widely used by LAPD officers.

As the clamor for banning the choke hold increased, the LAPD fought back on two fronts. First, the department contended that many of the deaths attributed to the choke hold were actually the result of drug overdoses. Second, and more persuasively, Gates argued that restricting the choke hold was no panacea. The Monadnock PR-24 side-handled aluminum baton, then almost always used as a defensive weapon, had been introduced in 1980 into the LAPD, where it had gradually replaced the wooden billy club. Gates said that if officers were denied the use of the choke hold in making arrests, they would use the metal baton and karate kicks instead, with harmful consequences. "If used, these would result in injury in almost every case, a result which does not occur from employment of upper body control holds," Gates wrote the Police Commission. "Abandonment of these valuable tools would only provide less protection for the citizens of Los Angeles and would be a callous disregard for police officers who must face an increasing tide of physical violence."[54]

Such arguments did not impress the black community or the Bradley administration. Nor did they impress U.S. District Court Judge Robert Takasugi of Los Angeles, who in December 1980 issued a preliminary injunction limiting use of the holds to situations in which police officers were threatened with serious injury.* The LAPD was in an untenable position when its deadly record of choke-hold use was compared with that of other cities. Some cities that allowed the use of the holds, such as San Diego, had never had a choke-hold death. In New York City (which subsequently banned the holds) only one choke-hold death had occurred in a decade. Closer to home, in the Los Angeles County Sheriff's Department, choke-hold deaths were unknown even though that department was no stranger to accusations of brutality. Sheriff's officers had used the Monadnock PR-24 baton since 1974. What was apparent to critics of the choke

---

* The lawsuit that resulted in the injunction was filed by a black man, Adolph Lyons, who was stopped in Watts in 1976 for a traffic violation and subjected to a choke hold that caused him to lose consciousness and spit blood. Lyons sought to prevent the LAPD from continuing to use the choke hold, an issue that became moot after the city itself restricted the holds to situations involving deadly force. But when the injunction was argued before the Supreme Court, before the choke hold had been restricted, the city defended the LAPD's right to use choke holds. Frederick Merkin, a senior assistant city attorney, argued that officers used such holds only in rare situations when needed to "gain control" over a resistant suspect. This comment provoked an angry outburst from Justice Thurgood Marshall, who asked: "Doesn't a loaded gun gain control? Why do you have to choke them to death?"

hold, if not to Gates, was that LAPD officers were using the holds in ways that should have been unacceptable in a civilized society.

When such arguments failed to sway either Gates or conservatives on the city council, critics of the choke hold shifted to economic grounds. City Councilman Robert Farrell, who had served as black community coordinator in Bradley's first two mayoralty campaigns and owed his seat largely to the mayor's support, asserted late in 1981 that it would be more "cost-effective for the city to settle claims for broken bones of combative suspects who are hit with batons rather than to pay settlements" arising from the choke-hold deaths.[55]

The incident that made it impossible for Gates to preserve even the modified carotid hold as an approved technique in some ways foreshadowed the Rodney King affair. James Thomas Mincey Jr. was a twenty-year-old teaching assistant in the Los Angeles Unified School District. He was a black man with a criminal record who led police on a high-speed car chase through residential areas of Lake View Terrace and resisted arrest when he finally stopped. Like King he was subdued by a number of officers while others watched and an LAPD helicopter hovered overhead.

Mincey had been in trouble with the law since committing a strong-arm robbery at the age of thirteen. He was a gifted football player who had been expelled from high school for repeated incidents of drug use. During a robbery attempt when he was fifteen, he hit a youth so hard he broke his jaw. At sixteen he committed three batteries. When he was nineteen, after committing another strong-arm robbery, he grabbed the pistol of an officer who was trying to arrest him. The officer finally subdued him by striking him in the head with the weapon.

On the night of March 22, 1982, two LAPD officers stopped Mincey after a short pursuit and ticketed him for speeding and having a shattered front windshield. Thirty minutes later, near the Foothill and Osborne intersection where the King pursuit would end nine years later, Mincey passed another LAPD squad car. One of the officers in the car noticed Mincey's shattered windshield. The officers turned on their lights and siren, but Mincey refused to stop. Instead, he led the police on a chase at speeds of up to 65 miles an hour that ended in the driveway of his Lake View Terrace home. When officers approached, Mincey began a fight that police would finish and that forever changed LAPD policy.

Officer Robert Simpach was present at both the Mincey and King arrests. At the King arrest he was a bystander and the most experienced officer on the scene. In the Mincey incident, he launched the pursuit and tried to take Mincey into custody in the driveway of his home. Mincey told police officers he would "kick your asses" if they tried to handcuff him. He shoved Simpach away. Simpach responded by spraying Mincey with tear gas which also splashed over his partner, Officer Frank Bonnette. As Mincey scuffled with the officers, his stepfather, Alfred Fowler, and then his mother, Rozella Fowler, came out of the house to urge him to cooperate with the police.

Simpach recalled many years later that Mincey was "wet and slippery" and that he was unable to get a grip on him, much as Ted Briseno would find it difficult to hold on to Rodney King. The tear gas seemed to have no more impact on Mincey than the Taser would have on King. After their initial struggle, Simpach sprayed it again, this time into Mincey's eyes. To Simpach's amazement, it still seemed to have no effect. Simpach knew that tear gas sometimes failed to work on PCP suspects, and he wondered if Mincey had been using the drug. By then Simpach himself was half-blinded by the tear gas. He tried to apply the carotid hold to Mincey but couldn't get a good grip. Mincey was yelling at Simpach that he had already stopped him once and given him a ticket. "I don't know what you're talking about, . . . but you didn't stop, and you're under arrest," Simpach said. But Mincey wouldn't submit. While Simpach was trying to wrestle Mincey to the ground in a rose garden, Bonnette radioed for help. Simpach wondered why it was so slow in coming. "Where are the cops?" he thought. "They should have been here a long time ago."[56]

The backup officers eventually arrived, and before the arrest was completed, ten LAPD officers were at the scene with a helicopter hovering overhead. By the time the other officers reached the driveway, Simpach and Bonnette had managed to handcuff Mincey with his hands in front of him. Mincey had refused to put his hands behind him because of a previous injury to his right arm.

With Mincey in custody, even though improperly handcuffed, the incident should have been over. But Mincey, as Simpach would remember it, was "acting like a wild man." The officers decided they could not put him into a squad car with his hands in front of him. They took Mincey to a grassy area between the sidewalk and the street, telling him they were going to rehandcuff him with his hands behind his back and take him to Foothill Station. Officer Rolland Cannon used what he subsequently called "a right hip-throw movement" to force Mincey face down on the ground, where officers held each of his limbs. As soon as Officer Cannon removed the right cuff, Mincey sat up. Cannon was a burly officer and Mincey was lithe—six feet-two and 170 pounds. His sudden movement surprised the officers, knocking Simpach off and sending Cannon flying, much as Rodney King would throw cops off his back when they swarmed him. Simpach thought Mincey displayed "superhuman strength" and district attorney's investigators would later refer to his "maniacal behavior." But officers piled on Mincey, forcing him down on the grass again. His forehead struck the curb and began to bleed. Cannon applied the carotid hold, but all the officers together could not force Mincey's arms behind him so that they could be locked together with a single set of handcuffs. They finally made a chain of four sets of handcuffs, each end of which held one of Mincey's wrists.

Still, Mincey struggled. He knocked an officer away and kicked loose the restraints two other officers were trying to fasten to his legs. With two officers holding Mincey's head, Cannon continued, at the direction of Lieutenant Maurice Rubio, to apply the carotid hold until the leg restraints had been secured. Cannon estimated he applied the hold for twenty to thirty seconds and said that Mincey was conscious when he was bundled into Simpach's squad car for a four-block ride to Pacoima Memorial Hospital.

Later, Simpach would time the drive from the Mincey home to the hospital over and over again, always making it in a minute and twenty seconds or less. He believes he must have driven it even more quickly that night, for it was close to midnight and there was no traffic. When Simpach's squad car arrived at the hospital, a gurney was waiting. Mincey was placed on it and rolled into the emergency room. "Code Blue, Code Blue," said an attendant, meaning that the patient's vital life signs were failing. Simpach did not know what "Code Blue" meant. "Get these fucking handcuffs off of him," the attendant said.[57] Somebody removed the cuffs. That was the last that Simpach saw of Mincey.

No one had recorded the Mincey arrest in this pre-camcorder age, but witnesses who were subsequently interviewed by the police told conflicting stories.[58] Three witnesses said police had beaten Mincey repeatedly while he was face down on the ground. A neighbor, Leon Townsell, said that Mincey had not been offering resistance at the time he was thrown down and that the choke hold had been applied for at least a minute, until Mincey became unconscious. Investigators from the district attorney's office did not believe these witnesses, in part because a statement by Alfred Fowler supported the police account that his stepson had not been beaten. Since there was no medical evidence of a beating, the district attorney concluded that no criminal charges should be filed.

But there was more to the Mincey affair. When Mincey's mother called Foothill Station to find out what had happened to her son, she was told there was no record of his arrest. Later, a police investigator came to her home and said that her son was in the hospital but was doing "all right."[59] By this time, Mincey had lapsed into a coma. Mincey's mother, seeing blood spurt from her son's mouth after he was choked, had said to the officers, "You killed him." And that was the medical determination when Mincey died on April 5, two weeks after his arrest. Coroner Ronald Kornblum said the cause of death was blunt-force trauma to the neck. "In layman's terms, Dr. Kornblum said Mincey had suffered brain death as the result of being deprived of oxygen . . ." the district attorney's investigators concluded. Toxicological tests found no trace of PCP, but Mincey had phenobarbitals, other drugs, and "a substance resembling steroids" in his body fluids. Because of the time that elapsed between Mincey's fatal injury and his death, doctors could not determine if he had used PCP the night of his arrest.

Mincey's death set off a new clamor for a choke-hold ban, and the LAPD responded, as it usually did, by blaming the victim. The department issued a statement declaring that a white powdery substance believed to be cocaine had been found in Mincey's car. Six days after Mincey's death, however, an LAPD spokesman acknowledged that the substance was not cocaine but a legal nonprescription drug known as tetracaine. He said that tetracaine was sometimes used in the cutting and selling of cocaine, as if this somehow excused or mitigated the killing of Mincey.

THE VICTIM BLAMING BY THE OFFICERS INVOLVED IN THE MINCEY death tells more about what was wrong with the LAPD than any technical assessment of the merits or deficiencies of upper body control holds. Evaluating the incident a decade later, Gates observed that LAPD officers had used choke holds 137 times in the first quarter of 1982 on almost equal numbers of non-Hispanic whites, Latinos, and blacks. "The only serious injury was Mincey's," said Gates.[60] It does not seem to have occurred to him, either at the time of the incident or later, that Mincey's death was unnecessary. Mincey was unarmed and was not considered dangerous by the officers who had pursued him on a minor traffic charge. He had no way to escape. Even if the police version of the arrest is accurate and the most charitable interpretations are placed on the motivations of the officers, Mincey was killed while in custody after he had been handcuffed. Alfred Fowler would be reminded of his helplessness when he saw the tape of the Rodney King beating nearly nine years later. "It gives me chills," he said. "It's just like opening up a wound and . . . I can't bear to look at it anymore."[61]

After Mincey's death, Gates fought a stubborn uphill battle to find a compromise that would save the choke hold. Late in April he proposed a revised policy restricting the circumstances under which upper-body control holds could be used. When this failed to impress the Police Commission, Gates unilaterally banned the bar-arm hold in a last-ditch effort to keep the modified carotid hold. "I think it's insane to suggest we cannot use the modified carotid," he said. "It's a super hold."[62] It was this "super hold" that had killed Mincey. Gates then ruined whatever chance he had of a compromise solution with an unwitting remark. On May 8, two days after Gates banned the bar-arm hold, a story in the *Los Angeles Times* quoted him as saying: "We may be finding that in some blacks when it [the choke hold] is applied the veins or arteries do not open up as fast as they do in normal people. There may be something arresting the ability of the blood to flow again (after the hold is applied). We're going to look at that very carefully."*

The comment was typical of Daryl Gates, who often displayed an ill-timed flair for inflammatory statements that played into the hands of his critics. When Americans were taken hostage in Iran in 1979, Gates suggested they could be rescued by LAPD's SWAT team. During the 1984 Olympics, Gates created a needless controversy by suggesting that immigrant Russian Jews were Soviet agents who were being sent to Los Angeles for purposes of espionage. He described a local television anchorwoman in 1980 as an "Aryan broad," and the killer of a female police officer in 1991 as "an El Salvadoran drunk—a drunk who doesn't belong here."

Such comments were in the tradition of Chief Parker, to whom expression of outlandish opinion was a way of showing solidarity with rank-and-file cops against outsiders and politicians who dared to denigrate the LAPD. What distinguished Gates from his predecessors, observed Bill Boyarsky, was his capacity for making bombastic comments in "a remarkably calm tone, as if he were discussing his department's budget or the purchase of a new computer."[63] When his comments landed him in hot water, Gates usually complained that he had been quoted out of context. In this case, he said he had picked up the phrase "normal people" from a reporter's question.

Gates was no racist, and even some of his critics recognized that his awkward answer had not meant to suggest that it was abnormal to be black. Martha Fleetwood, director of an NAACP committee on police violence, called Gates' remark "outrageous" and "laughable" but said "there is nothing to indicate any racial connection." Nevertheless, the black community was seething when the Police Commission convened a hearing at Parker Center on May 12, four days after the story appeared. Speaker after speaker denounced Gates, who stoically faced his critics and made a last attempt to preserve the choke hold. He did not succeed. Police Commissioner Sam Williams, a distinguished attorney (and an African American) who had served on the McCone Commission staff, proposed a six-month moratorium on choke-hold use, saying the LAPD should use the Taser and the Monadnock PR-24 baton instead. One of the signs of the way the political winds were blowing came from Councilman Zev Yaroslavsky, a key member

---

* There may have been something to what Gates said, if not the way he said it. In 1991, the rate of stroke deaths among black males was 55 for every 100,000 persons compared to 27 among white males. Medical researchers at the University of Texas' Houston Medical School associated stroke risk with a thickening in the carotid arteries. In a study reported in 1995 they blamed the higher death rate among blacks on a genetic mutation that produced growth of muscle cells in artery walls, causing them to thicken.

of the black-Jewish alliance that was the cornerstone of the Bradley coalition. Yaroslavsky had been quoted the previous August as saying that substituting the baton for the choke hold posed "the specter of billy-club confrontations."[64] But at the May 12 hearing, he said that the moratorium did not go far enough.

The moratorium passed by unanimous vote, was ratified by the city council, and remains LAPD policy to this day. It was a posthumous victory for James Mincey, who is remembered less in Los Angeles then Eulia Love or Rodney King but whose death accomplished the most significant policy change ever imposed on the LAPD. The department's use-of-force policy guidelines lay out a continuum of alternatives available to officers ranging from verbal commands that are appropriate in almost any circumstances to lethal force. Choke holds had been an intermediate level of force, appropriate in situations where billy clubs, tear gas, and swarms could also be used to take suspects into custody. The commission's action moved choke holds to the level of deadly force, putting them into the same category as shootings. Given the choice of choke holds or their revolvers in life-threatening situations, most officers opted to use their guns.

The Police Commission moratorium resolved the choke-hold debate without immediately ending use of the choke hold. Two days after the moratorium was imposed, a black singer who was stopped by LAPD officers for having an unregistered car was choked unconscious. Then, just before dawn on July 21, a nude black man in a car with two children was spotted in the median strip of a South Central intersection. He was handcuffed and leg-shackled and placed in the back of a squad car, where police said he began scuffling on the way to the station. A rookie officer applied the carotid hold. The nude man, Donald Ray Wilson, died in a hospital emergency room. His death ignited an emotional demonstration outside the 77th Street Police Station by a group called United Against Black Genocide. This time, however, blood tests substantiated the familiar police claim of PCP use, and the coroner found that Wilson had suffered from a weakened heart, which also may have been caused by drug use.

The killing of Wilson brought the LAPD choke-hold death toll to seventeen in six years, including thirteen blacks. Although Gates continued to campaign for the carotid hold, he bowed to civil authority with more grace than Parker had ever displayed. Three weeks after Donald Ray Wilson's death, Gates issued a directive requiring that every officer in the LAPD receive a copy of the Police Commission order banning the choke hold and sign a statement acknowledging that he or she had read it. This ended routine use of upper-body control holds by the LAPD.

A few LAPD old-timers continued to run the risk of disciplinary action for choking out suspects, fearing that the alternatives were worse. Officer

David Zeigler told me in 1993, when he was president of the Los Angeles Police Protective League, that he had continued to use the choke hold on his foot beat in MacArthur Park because it was less provocative and less harmful to suspects than the PR-24 baton. Zeigler is a beefy officer, six feet one inch tall, who lifts weights and weighs 230 pounds. Typically, he arrested Latino suspects who were much smaller. "And on a Saturday or Sunday, there's probably a thousand people watching what I do," Zeigler said. "So if I'm going to arrest a robber or a drunk and those people see me standing there and [beating] him into submission with a baton, it's going to look real bad for me. It's almost like I'm inciting a riot."[65] Zeigler thought it far preferable in such situations to apply the choke hold and quickly take the suspect into custody.

Zeigler said he had applied the carotid hold hundreds of times without ever causing injury or prompting a complaint of excessive force. He believes the choke hold should have been used to subdue Rodney King and that Sergeant Koon would have been a "hero" had he done so. But Zeigler strictly timed his choke holds. He said he never applied the carotid hold for more than nine seconds and that this was always sufficient to cause unconsciousness. In police accounts of the Mincey and Wilson deaths, it was estimated that a choke hold was used for twenty to thirty seconds.

While use of PCP may have contributed to the choke-hold death toll, LAPD Lieutenant Greg Meyer, a well-known police tactics consultant, believes that many deaths attributed to choke-hold use actually resulted from a phenomenon known as "positional asphyxia." This occurs when suspects are placed on their stomachs after being hog-tied with wrists and ankles behind their backs.[66] The technique, used on Rodney King, can interfere with breathing and is especially dangerous to suspects who are obese or drug users. It has since been banned by the LAPD.

A Los Angeles County coroner's investigation determined that Rodney King's barber, Michael Bryant, was killed by "cocaine intoxication and asphyxiation from restraint procedures" when he was hog-tied and put on his stomach on March 9, 1993, in violation of department regulations, after a chase in which Los Angeles, Pasadena, and San Marino police cars participated. Meyer maintains that an investigation of the choke-hold deaths of the late 1970s and the early 1980s would show that most victims were similarly hog-tied or suffering from "drug-induced delirium." Lieutenant Meyer's informed speculation deserves to be taken seriously, but it does not explain why the death toll was higher in Los Angeles than in other cities where hog-tying was used. Assessing the impact of the choke-hold ban in September 1993, when the city finally settled the last of a long string of lawsuits arising from Mincey's death, Councilman Yaroslavsky said, "I think the moratorium on the hold in the last decade has not only saved money, but saved lives."[67]

But supporters of the ban were too sanguine about the dangers of the "new, broad spectrum of control techniques," as Police Commission president Reva Tooley blandly referred to the PR-24 baton the day before the choke-hold moratorium was imposed.[68] Injuries to suspects arrested by the LAPD increased immediately, as had been predicted by police training experts. By January 1984, when Chief Gates reported on the LAPD's first fifteen months without the choke hold, injuries to suspects during arrests had climbed from three per week to twenty-three. Even if allowance is made for the possibility of more zealous police reporting of injuries after the choke-hold ban, this was a frightening increase that reflected negatively on the PR-24 baton or the way in which it was being used or both. What's more, police injuries during arrests nearly doubled during the same time frame.

"The moratorium left us with a great big hole in how to deal with dangerous behavior," Gates told NAACP representatives a month after the ban was imposed, and neither the chief nor the Police Commission had any good idea of how to fill it.[69] The ban caused particular problems at the Police Academy, where instructors struggled to find a new doctrine to match the new policy. "We had nothing to address the loss of the choke hold," said Sergeant Scott Landsman, then a physical training instructor.[70] Instead of teaching recruits to subdue combative suspects with the choke hold, "the emphasis shifted to not tying up with the suspect and using the baton." Landsman and other officers trained in the martial arts found the change disturbing. As Greg Meyer put it, "We had adopted the inhumane policy of beating suspects with a metal pipe."[71]

The new policy was accepted without protest by political leaders. Neither Bradley nor the city council nor the Police Commission took any action before the King beating to limit use of the metal baton despite the soaring injury rates and increased lawsuits. Matthew Hunt, the LAPD commander in charge of training at the time of the ban, worked with an aerospace company, Jet Propulsion Laboratory, in an attempt to develop alternatives to the baton, such as capture nets and leg grabbers, that could be used to arrest combative suspects without hurting them. When JPL sought a modest $60,000 to continue its research, Hunt was told that the city had no money available.[72]

While Hunt followed the lead of the LAPD high command in accepting the choke-hold ban, the Policy Academy, over which he had jurisdiction, became a center of resistance to the new policy. Sergeant Ken Dionne, a rough-and-ready cop in charge of physical training, didn't get along with Hunt, who had previously commanded the Equal Opportunity Employment Division and prided himself on a progressive approach to police work. They clashed on training issues, including an attempt by Dionne to give officers alternatives to baton strikes and choke holds by making them more adept in martial arts. When Hunt showed no interest, Dionne transferred out of the Academy. Ten of the eleven physical training officers who worked for him, including Landsman, followed suit. Their departure left a huge gap in training continuity at a time when the LAPD could least afford it.

Sergeant Charles Duke, another tough-minded LAPD veteran, replaced Dionne as the lead physical training instructor. He was outspoken, opinionated, and as appalled as Dionne had been by the steadily mounting toll of baton injuries. As Duke remembers it, Hunt wasn't interested in his protests. Duke told me that Hunt once stuck his finger in his ear when he started to complain and ordered him to teach the use of the metal baton, regardless of the consequences. Hunt, who is now retired, is a humane cop who didn't want to hurt anyone. But Dionne and Duke believe that he accepted a bad policy that resulted in suspects sometimes being beaten into submission.

Chief Gates himself seems to have lost track of what was happening. After the King beating, when he was trying to distance himself from the officers involved, the chief and his high command engaged in what Sergeant Duke called a "monumental cover-up" to conceal the reality of baton injuries.[73] But the truth was there to see, if the politicians or the media had paid as much attention to the consequences of baton use as they had to the choke hold.

The number of complaints about LAPD use of excessive force doubled between 1983 and 1988. Payouts in settlements and awards for LAPD-related litigation soared from $891,000 in 1980 to $11.3 million in 1990. The LAPD reported 3,781 incidents of baton use in the four-year period from 1987 to 1990, more than nine hundred a year.[74] The King beating, as bad as it looked, was not an isolated event. It can better be described as the inevitable outcome of a flawed policy that was ignored until the Holliday videotape made Rodney King a household symbol of police brutality.*

THE DEMISE OF THE CHOKE HOLD AND THE WIDESPREAD USE OF the PR-24 coincided with other changes that had a profound impact on police training. The 1980s were a time of ferment within the LAPD as minorities and women struggled to join a police force that had long been predominantly white and male. Like Ed Davis before him, Daryl Gates

* David Shaw, media critic for the Los Angeles Times, reported in a May 26, 1992 article that his newspaper rarely published LAPD statistics before the King incident. He quoted a former city editor as saying that such data were "very suspect" and "notorious for being unreliable." Shaw noted, however, that after the Christopher Commission cited LAPD statistics in its report, the Times and other newspapers made them page-one news. Shaw's May 1992 series on media coverage of the LAPD, of which this article was a part, is an excellent account of how police abuses were largely ignored by the mainstream media in Los Angeles until the King case.

believed in recruiting and promoting minority officers. Unlike Davis, he recognized that the department no longer could resist the admission of women. In 1981, the LAPD signed a consent decree requiring that nearly three-fourths of new hires be women or minorities. (The required percentages were 25 percent female, 22.5 percent black, and 22.5 percent Hispanic.) This emphasis on affirmative action, particularly the admission of women, required a change in LAPD physical requirements. The minimum height of five-feet-nine inches in the Parker years had been reduced to five-eight under Davis. It was dropped to five-four in 1982 and then to five feet in 1984.

Many male LAPD officers resented the influx of women, a prejudice commonly expressed in the belief that women are not strong enough to perform the street duties expected of police officers. When women started being admitted to the LAPD in large numbers in the mid-1980s, their presence created training problems in a department that tried to balance the requirements of the new quota with its traditionally high physical standards. Elimination of the choke hold complicated things. As Gates has accurately observed, some women officers (and some shorter men) liked the option of the choke hold, which can be an equalizer when a small officer is facing a large, combative suspect. Scott Landsman believes that reduction of the height minimums made an especially strong case for teaching martial arts. "But martial arts was associated in the public mind with karate and violence, and Hunt wanted no part of it," Landsman said.[75]

Replacement of the choke hold by the PR-24, laxity in pursuing use-of-force alternatives, training conflicts, and the turnover of instructors at the Police Academy, plus the angst over affirmative action, combined to create a training crisis that went unrecognized by the public and largely unaddressed by the department. The LAPD remained a stable force of 7,000 officers while the city's population, crime rate, and calls for service increased. In 1987, when the LAPD began its first expansion in eight years after a period of budget cutting caused largely by Proposition 13, its training facilities were stretched to the limit. This was when Larry Powell was becoming a full-fledged LAPD officer. In many ways, Powell epitomized the crisis in the LAPD. His training at the Police Academy was abbreviated because he was a reservist, and the understaffed department was eager to get officers with even limited experience into the field. He was never taught the choke hold. He never learned the "swarm technique" that prosecutors contended should have been used to take Rodney King into custody. He became a training officer in Foothill Division because of a shortage of qualified trainers.

The most pertinent criticism of Powell and the training that put him into an ineffective and brutal confrontation with King was made by Sergeant Duke, who in extended testimony at both criminal trials of the officers involved in the King beating defended every one of Powell's baton blows. Duke believed that Powell was a "one hundred eighty pound powder puff," no match for King in size or strength and unprepared by his training to take him into custody. "First of all, Powell should never have been out in the field," Duke said. "Because after he got out of roll call and they found out that he was defective in his [baton] tactics and needed training, why put him back out in the field?"[76]

But the once exacting LAPD no longer applied such common-sense standards—for batons or for other weapons. As Duke observed, officers who flunked marksmanship tests could stay on the range, pay a few dollars to retake the test, and continue to fire their revolvers until they qualified. "What they should have done to Powell was say 'You need some remedial training and you need to be out of the field.' And they should have assigned him to the desk that night," Duke said. "But that's what happens because the quality of training on the police department is poor, and you don't have quality instructors."[77]

Gates was incensed by such criticism, which undermined his "aberration" defense of the King beating. The LAPD tried unsuccessfully to muzzle Duke, a valued member of the SWAT team who had won many commendations, and refused to allow him to appear in uniform when he testified. But what set Duke apart from his peers was less the nature of his critique than the bluntness with which he delivered it. Had Gates been more self-critical or less distanced, he might have realized that the LAPD's once vaunted training standards had slipped.

Far from being an aberration, the Rodney King incident was an inevitability—indeed, variants of it had happened many times before but had not been recorded on videotape. Many police officers in the field recognized that it could have been them on the Holliday videotape, which was no doubt one of the reasons that the LAPD rank and file, in contrast to the department's leadership, was sympathetic to the four police defendants.

The King beating was a systems failure, the result of a breakdown in which political leaders, the police chief, and senior officers ignored what was happening in the field. "The most important need is better training," David Zeigler told me in 1993 when he was president of the Los Angeles Police Protective League. "It's our view that another Rodney King incident could happen this evening."[78]

5

LATASHA'S SHIELD

*"The most important thing to me is that my family is always pro-
tected by a shield so that they won't be harmed by dangerous, ruthless, uncaring people."*

—Latasha Harlins

ON A PEACEFUL SATURDAY MORNING IN MARCH 1991, THIRTEEN
days after the beating of Rodney King, a fifteen-year-old high school
freshman named Latasha Harlins who had spent the night with a friend was
walking home on Figueroa Street when she made an innocent decision with
deadly consequences. Harlins decided that she wanted some orange juice.
Her route took her by the Empire Liquor Market Deli, a white stucco convenience store owned by a Korean family in a mostly black neighborhood of
South Central Los Angeles. It was not a popular store. People in the neighborhood complained that its prices were too high and said the Korean owners were rude to customers. But it was the nearest store with groceries in a
neighborhood of few choices, and Harlins had not eaten breakfast. At
9:40 A.M. on March 16, she entered Empire Liquor, strolled to the refriger-
ator, and extracted a $1.79 plastic container of orange juice. Shoving the
container halfway into her backpack, she headed toward the counter with
two dollars in her left hand.

Soon Ja Du, a forty-nine-year-old Korean woman, was behind the
counter, waiting on two black children, a twelve-year-old girl and her nine-
year-old brother, who were buying hair gel for their mother. She watched
fearfully as Harlins put the orange juice into her backpack and came toward
the counter. Harlins was five feet six inches tall and weighed 150 pounds.
She was an imposing figure to the diminutive Du, who distrusted black people, disliked South Central, and hated working behind the counter at Empire Liquor. Du lived in the faraway San Fernando Valley, where blacks were
few and she felt safer and among friends, as she had once felt safe in Korea.
South Central was another country. Blacks had robbed Empire Liquor the

previous Saturday when her husband, Hung Ki, known to Americans as Billy, was in charge. Black gang members had robbed the store the previous December when her oldest son, Joseph, who was thirty, was behind the counter. They had threatened to kill him. These terrible memories flashed through Soon Ja Du's mind as Harlins approached. Shoplifting was commonplace at Empire Liquor. Her husband and her son had warned Soon Ja that blacks stole items by hiding them in their clothing. Du expected the worst from the black girl, whom she took to be a woman in her mid-twenties.

"Are you trying to steal my orange juice?" Du asked Harlins.

"No, I'm not," Harlins replied with an edge in her voice. "I'm trying to pay for it."

Harlins turned, as if to show Du the plastic container protruding from the backpack, but Du was incensed. Reaching across the counter, she grabbed Harlins by her sweater.

"Bitch, let go," Harlins said angrily. "I'm trying to pay for it."

Du did not believe her. "Bitch, you are trying to steal my orange juice," she screamed and called repeatedly for her husband, who was sleeping in a van parked outside the back of the store. He did not hear his wife's cries for help. Harlins said again that she was trying to pay for the orange juice.

They were struggling now, with Du tugging frantically on Harlins' sweater. The backpack swung free and fell to the counter. Du pulled it away. Then Harlins punched Du three times in the face, hard blows that knocked her to the floor.[1] Du came back up with a chair, which she hurled at Harlins, who moved closer. With a quick movement the shopkeeper reached underneath the counter and pulled a revolver from a brown holster. Harlins bent over and picked up the orange juice container, which had dropped to the floor in the struggle, and placed it on the counter. Du knocked the container behind the counter with a swipe of the gun.

Harlins knew what guns could do. When she saw the gun in Du's hand, she turned and began to walk away. Bracing herself on the counter and using two hands on the gun, Du fired a single shot at the retreating girl. The bullet, fired from a distance of less than four feet, struck Harlins in the back of the head exiting from her forehead. She died instantly, her brain matter mingling with blood on the market floor.

After Du fired, she peered repeatedly over the counter, as if trying to find Harlins. Billy Du had heard the shot and rushed into the store, dressed in the clothes he had slept in. He saw the body on the floor and his wife at the counter. "Where is the girl who was just here?" she said to him. Soon Ja told her husband there had been a robbery. He telephoned 911. "We got a holdup," he said. The dispatcher kept Billy Du on the phone, getting location and details, and he said his wife had shot the "robber lady."

"Did you shoot?" asked the dispatcher.

"No, my wife shot," Billy Du said.

"Is your wife okay?"

"Yes, my wife is okay."

When the police arrived, Soon Ja Du was slumped in a chair behind the counter. Billy Du was still standing at the telephone. Harlins was beyond help, and Soon Ja Du appeared unconscious. Uncertain about her condition, Officer Ralph Spinello walked over to Du and lifted an eyelid. He discerned movement, which he knew meant that she was conscious. Spinello thought the woman was feigning unconsciousness, but he did not have time to reflect on it. Before he could do anything, Billy Du began slapping his wife repeatedly, hitting her with such force that Spinello pulled him away. Paramedics arrived and cut open Harlins' jacket and upper clothing as they vainly searched for signs of life. They left the body in a spreading pool of blood on the floor, where it awaited the arrival of detectives. Soon Ja was bundled into an ambulance and taken to Martin Luther King Jr. Hospital/Drew Medical Center, a modern medical facility that is South Central's most tangible benefit of the Watts riot. Spinello began taking statements from the two children who had been customers in the store.

EMPIRE LIQUOR, AT 9127 SOUTH FIGUEROA STREET, IS THIRTY-SIX miles southeast and a light year away from the suburban neighborhood where the pursuit of Rodney King ended. But for African Americans in Los Angeles, these two unrelated incidents would become intertwined, reinforcing the perception that blacks could not obtain justice even when irrefutable evidence showed they had been victimized.

The shooting of Harlins had been recorded by an in-store security camera. Unlike the Holliday videotape, however, this video was solely in the hands of the authorities—first the police and then the district attorney—who withheld it from the media. As a result, the killing on Figueroa Street did not at first cause much of a stir. The media were preoccupied with Rodney King. The day after Harlins was shot, the *Los Angeles Times* reported the incident in a six-paragraph story on the fifth page of the metro section without mentioning the names of those involved. On the section's first page, the *Times* published a profile of King, depicting him as a lost soul who was rarely violent.

Although the *Los Angeles Times* ultimately gave extensive and balanced coverage to the Latasha Harlins story, the incident never attracted much media attention outside Los Angeles. But the shooting stirred anger and compassion in South Central, where the daily risks faced by children make their lives dear to the women who raise them under perilous circumstances. Latasha Harlins was a promise of the future, the bright hope of the aunt and grandmother with whom she lived. While gunfire and violent death are commonplace in South Central, the Harlins killing seemed especially senseless. Harlins had no record of criminal behavior. Du told officers after her arrest that she thought the girl had a weapon in her backpack, but there appeared to be no rational basis for this assertion. Police found a few items of clothing and toiletries in the backpack and nothing that had been stolen or could be used as a weapon.

Du was promptly charged with murder. Because Harlins had been shot in the back of the head and the shooting had been recorded on videotape, even blacks who were skeptical about the fairness of the legal system assumed Du would be convicted and sent to prison. Based on what was known of the killing, the outcome seemed as inevitable as the conviction of the police officers who had beaten Rodney King. The officers who beat King had used unnecessary force. Du had shot to death an unarmed girl who was walking away after a quarrel over a bottle of orange juice. It was all there on videotape for jurors to see.

But justice was not automatic. Even authorities who deplored the killing understood that there was a broader context in which to view the incident. When Deputy District Attorney Roxane Carvajal addressed the grand jury on April 24, seeking indictment of Soon Ja Du, she said, "There has been a lot of tension in the black community, racial tension between Korean shopkeepers and customers. The Korean shopkeepers are constantly accusing the black customers of shoplifting and terrorism. The black customers are constantly accusing the Korean shopkeepers of being disrespectful and rude to blacks. This may be something to explain why [Mrs. Du] acted as she did."

Racial tension and crime were particularly prevalent in the corridor occupied by Empire Liquor. Figueroa, one of Los Angeles' best-known streets, is at its shabbiest and most dangerous in this desolate stretch of single-story stucco homes, fleabag motels, storefront churches, and isolated businesses two blocks west of the Harbor Freeway and south of Manchester Boulevard. In 1990 the thirty-two blocks surrounding Empire Liquor at Ninety-first Street and Figueroa had one of the city's highest crime rates: 936 reported felonies that included 5 murders, 9 rapes, 184 robberies, and 254 assaults. The real crime rate was almost certainly higher than the statistics revealed. Nationally, 40 percent of serious crimes go unreported, mostly because victims think it unlikely that stolen property will be recovered or the crime solved.[2] Since the LAPD responds only to serious emergencies, reporting a minor crime can be especially futile in Los Angeles. Joseph Du would testify at his mother's trial that Empire had been burglarized more than thirty times and that shoplifting was frequent. Although the family often did not bother to report shoplifting, they had called police on December 19, 1990, when Joseph Du was robbed and terrorized at the store by ten to fourteen members of the Main Street Crips.

At the time of the Harlins killing, three of these gang members were awaiting trial for assaulting Joseph Du, and the family had closed the market for two weeks in February because Joseph had been told that his life would be in danger if he testified. When Empire Liquor reopened, Joseph was afraid to work there. Soon Ja, who usually tended counter at a more peaceful Du family store in suburban Saugus, substituted for her son on weekends. She was afraid too, especially after the March 9 robbery, although no one had been threatened or harmed in this incident.

And Billy Du was exhausted. Beginning at midday Friday, March 15, he had worked a fourteen-hour shift that did not end until the store closed in the early hours of Saturday morning. Soon Ja knew her husband badly needed rest. Despite her qualms and the robbery the previous Saturday, she volunteered to reopen at 9:00 A.M., knowing that Saturday mornings were usually quiet times. This Saturday morning had started quiet, too.

After the trial Soon Ja Du acknowledged her fear and dislike of African Americans. She confided to a white probation officer that blacks were lazy and used welfare money to buy liquor instead of feeding their children.[3] As Carvajal had told the grand jury, Du's attitude was shared by many Korean-American merchants. Some Koreans tried to hide their feelings, but many did not. Richard Rhee, one of the city's most successful Korean-American grocers, became a hero to his compatriots in Koreatown during the 1992 riots when he organized an armed and successful defense of his market. Unlike the Du family, Rhee was in control of his fears. But his view of black people was similar to Soon Ja Du's. "Black people don't like to work; that's the problem to me," he said.[4]

Koreans have been a focus of racial conflict in California since they first began arriving shortly after the turn of the century. Nearly 10,000 Koreans had been admitted before the 1924 Immigration Act blocked most Asian immigration. Many of these early immigrants were young, single, uneducated male laborers who aroused resentment among native Californians because they worked for low wages and were sometimes used as strikebreakers. Another 20,000 Koreans came to the United States during and immediately after the Korean War. More than half were war brides, but the Korean immigrants also included exchange students, diplomats, and orphans.

The third and largest wave of Korean immigration, one still breaking on American shores, began after enactment of the liberalizing 1965 Immigration Act. This wave included a disproportionate number of educated middle-class urban professionals and entrepreneurs who brought families with them. Because of language and cultural barriers, many of the later immigrants were unable to find work in the professional or managerial occupations for which they had been trained and became self-employed. Typically, they lived in urban areas with high concentrations of Koreans, especially New York City, Washington, D.C., and Los Angeles. The 1990 census counted just under 800,000 Korean Americans, more than double the population of a decade earlier, including 145,000 in Los Angeles County, which Korean activist Angela Oh calls "the gateway to Korea." Many Koreans believe they were undercounted in the census. But there is no disputing that Los Angeles is home to more Koreans than any city except Seoul.

Typically, Koreans are attached to both their new country and their old. As the scholar Edward Taehan Chang explains it, they are motivated by two concepts, *han* and *jung*, that have no precise English equivalents.[5] *Han* relates to accumulated experiences of oppression, like that suffered under Korea's long occupation by the Japanese, and to rage and frustration. Koreans attempt to release *han* by working hard to make the American dream come true. *Jung* encompasses feelings of love, compassion, sympathy, and sentiment. It drives Koreans to work together and to bring even distant relatives from Korea to live with them in the United States. Korean immigrants sometimes pool their resources under an ancient system known as *kae*, in which a group of families and friends contribute to a rotating pool of money that is maintained without written record. Every member of a *kae* is able to draw upon it in turn, for purposes ranging from pleasure trips to the buying of businesses.

Utilizing *kae*s as venture capital and borrowing from Korean banks, Korean immigrants operated 3,300 convenience and liquor stores in the Los Angeles area at the time of the Harlins killing—including the Monterey Park store robbed by Rodney King. Such robberies were frequent, although they often went unreported in the English-language press. But Korean-language newspapers kept track. According to one compilation of Korean-language press reports, thirteen Korean-operated stores in the Los Angeles area were the scenes of armed assaults in 1990, and nine Korean Americans were killed. In the same year the National Korean American Grocers Association found that nineteen Korean grocers had been killed in Los Angeles County in the past decade.[6] As Korean merchants saw it, they were under systematic attack, most often by African Americans.

In South Central, blacks were equally certain that they were victimized by Korean merchants. "The Koreans are in our community, taking money, and giving blacks nothing," said Gina Rae, an African American who would become a close friend of the Harlins family and a leader of efforts to obtain justice for Latasha. "They won't let you use the restroom, they never smile or say thank you and they overcharge."[7]

In fact, James Q. Wilson observed, shopkeepers of any race charge more in poor neighborhoods because the cost of doing business in these neighborhoods is higher. Koreans owned some 350 stores in South Central, many of them businesses abandoned by Jewish merchants after the Watts riot. Black resentment of the Koreans reminded Wilson of black rage against Jewish merchants in Chicago, where he had been a graduate student in the 1950s. Du's lawyer, Charles Lloyd, an African American, also compared resentment of Korean merchants with resentment of Jews but thought that the black-Korean situation was worse because the cultural gulf was wider. Cultural differences often exacerbate racial tensions. Black and white Americans, for instance, are taught to look people directly in the eye, but this familiar American sign of trustworthiness is bad manners among Koreans. Still, the Du family seems to have been rude by any cultural standard. "One day I came up to the counter to pay for a bottle of wine and the guy says to me, 'Oh, you didn't steal anything today,'" said a thirty-eight-year-old black man who lived around the corner from Empire Liquor. "I stopped going in there right then."[8]

SOON JA DU WAS BORN IN 1941 IN JAPANESE-OCCUPIED KOREA, the daughter of the only doctor in a farming village. Her mother was a nurse. Soon Ja went to college in Seoul, where she majored in literature and met Hung Ki, a colonel in the Korean Army and an instructor in the martial arts. They married, and Soon Ja dropped out of college in her third year. They had two sons and a daughter, whom Soon Ja cared for at home. "She had a good life in Korea," said her daughter Sandy Du. "She never had to work outside the house."[9]

The family's life changed in 1976, when the Dus came to the United States to provide their children greater educational opportunities. They followed a time-honored immigrant prescription for getting ahead: Work hard, save money, buy your own business. Hung Ki, now Billy, was resourceful. He became an electrical repairman, fixing radios and television sets. Soon Ja found work as a couch assembler. Later she became a crocheter at a garment factory in the San Fernando Valley. The work was difficult, and Soon Ja suffered from migraine headaches, but by 1981 the family had saved enough money to buy a market and liquor store in San Fernando, serving a mostly white and Latino clientele. The business succeeded, although the hours were long and Soon Ja Du's headaches continued. After an automobile accident in 1985 she lay comatose for seven days in what doctors described as a "depressed and vegetative" state.

The Dus sold the San Fernando store in 1987 and bought another store in Saugus, a mostly white community north of Los Angeles. By now Joseph Du was working alongside his parents. Mike Du, two years younger than Joseph, became an import supervisor at Korean Airlines. Sandy Du, five years younger than Mike, was attending California State University at Long Beach, with the intention of becoming a nurse. The Dus were making money and wanted to expand. They bought Empire Market from another Korean despite a warning from friends that it was a "bad area." The impetus for the purchase seems to have come from Billy Du. "My father said our family should buy the market," said Sandy Du. "As a parent he always wanted to earn enough to leave something behind for us."[10] But Joseph Du was also willing to give South Central a try. "This was Los Angeles," he said in looking back on the decision. "How bad could it be?"[11]

Empire Liquor was beset by problems from the beginning. The Du family hired a neighborhood teenager but decided he was a gang member who was stealing from them. As the Dus saw it, every black customer was a potential thief. Joseph Du compared the situation to "having to conduct business in a war zone." The family bought guns for protection, and Joseph used one to warn away gang members. He never shot anyone, but everyone in the family knew a gun was handy behind the counter. Soon Ja Du's attitude toward guns would become a matter of dispute in her trial. She showed apparent expertise in wielding the gun that killed Latasha Harlins, but family members said she disapproved on religious grounds of using firearms. Seven out of ten Korean immigrants are regular churchgoers, and Soon Ja Du was a deaconess in the Valley Korean Central Presbyterian Church. She said she had never fired a gun until the day she killed Latasha Harlins.

THE LIFE OF SOON JA DU, AS HARD AS IT WAS, HAD BEEN PRIVILEGED in comparison with the life of Latasha Harlins, who was born to Vester Acoff and Crystal Harlins in 1976, the year the Du family arrived in America. Latasha and her parents lived in East St. Louis, Illinois, one of the nation's most impoverished and violent cities. Her father was an alcoholic and drug addict who physically abused her mother. Latasha witnessed many of these assaults on her mother, who was only sixteen when Latasha was born. When Latasha was four, the house in which she was living burned down, and the family traveled by Greyhound bus to Los Angeles to live with Latasha's grandmother, Ruth. Two other children were born to Vester and Crystal, a boy four years younger than Latasha and a girl six years younger.

On November 27, 1985, when Latasha was nine, her mother was found shot to death at 3:00 A.M. on the floor of the B&B Club on Florence Avenue. The woman who shot Crystal Harlins claimed she had been threatened by her. She received a five-year prison sentence for manslaughter, making her eligible for parole in two years. For all practical purposes, the killing left Latasha an orphan. As a probation officer described it: "In the following year her father deserted the family, providing the victim with no interest, concern or support. The family believes that he may have left because he is a fugitive from justice in California for burglary offenses."[12]

Latasha was angry that her mother's killer had received a short sentence. She told her aunt, Denise, and her grandmother that when she grew up she wanted to become a prosecuting attorney and protect other people. They encouraged this ambition and had high hopes for Latasha, who did well in school and athletics. She was an assistant cheerleader and a member of the drill team at a nearby recreation center, and she won first place in a combined sprint and long jump event at the Jesse Owens Arco Track Meet. Each Sunday she attended services at the Abundance In Christ Church. In June 1990 she graduated from Bret Harte Junior High School, having made the honor roll. The family was so poor that Latasha offered to pick up her diploma to save the money for a graduation dress. But her aunt and grandmother bought her a dress for graduation.

Latasha Harlins entered Westchester High School that September. She was growing rapidly, and some thought her lonely and moody. In a neighborhood full of dangers for young women, Latasha had learned to take care of herself with her fists. Her aunt and her grandmother were worried because her grades had begun to slip. Latasha, who still harbored ambitions of becoming a lawyer, promised to concentrate on her schoolwork. In an assignment for a history class five weeks before her death, she wrote: "The most important thing to me is that my family is always protected by a shield so that they won't be harmed by dangerous, ruthless, uncaring people." After her death the document became known as Latasha's Shield.

The Harlins family was shattered by her death. Her cousin Shenise, also fifteen and close to Latasha, cried for months after the shooting. Her younger brother Montrelle could not talk about what happened but asked his grandmother if he could sleep in her bed. Her sister Christina would say Latasha's name over and over again. What particularly incensed Ruth and Denise Harlins was that members of the Du family circulated a false story that Latasha had intended to rob Empire Liquor. Joseph Du acknowledged when he testified at his mother's trial that he had told a *Los Angeles Times* reporter that Latasha was heading for the cash register. He said this is what his mother had told him and Joseph Du insisted that his mother's perception of Harlins was quite reasonable given what had happened previously at Empire Liquor.

This implicit contempt for Latasha Harlins and a lack of concern for the suffering of her family typified the attitude of the Du family, who persistently depicted Soon Ja as the real victim. Joseph Du even theorized that his mother was being used as a scapegoat by authorities to appease blacks who were angered by the King beating. "Because we are a minority, they think Korean people are weak," he told a reporter.[13]

What the authorities were actually doing, to the extent they were doing anything at all, was trying to prevent a race riot by misrepresenting the racial context of the killing. LAPD commander Michael Bostic, who would later be a prosecution use-of-force witness in the first Rodney King trial, was quoted in the *Los Angeles Times* as saying that there were no racial overtones to the Harlins killing. "This is just a business dispute," he said. The comment infuriated Denise Harlins, as did Bostic's characterization of Latasha as a runaway. "She had some problems at home the night before and went to spend the night with a friend," Harlins said. "We knew where she was."

But Denise Harlins never succeeded in overcoming Billy Du's initial inaccurate depiction of her niece as a "robber lady" who was heading for the cash register when she was shot. This misperception may have been unwittingly reinforced by District Attorney Ira Reiner's withholding of the videotape from the media. Reiner's decision was legally unassailable: He wanted a jury that was untainted by exposure to the videotape and would return a conviction of murder. Whether his decision made a difference in the ultimate public perception of the case is difficult to know. Even when the tape became available to the media at Du's trial, it was considered of inferior quality and shown far less often on television than the dramatic sections of the video of the King beating. Among nonblacks, a widespread impression persisted that Latasha Harlins had entered Empire Liquor with a criminal purpose. Deputy District Attorney Glenn Britton, who had followed the story in the newspapers and was called on to write an appeal brief after Du's trial, was surprised when he read the official trial record. "There was this impression from the news that somehow Latasha had been shoplifting, not that this justified shooting her," he said three years later. "But she hadn't been shoplifting."[14]

WHILE THE POLICE WERE STILL EXAMINING THE BODY OF LATASHA Harlins and conducting interviews, Soon Ja Du was at the hospital being treated for facial injuries and examined for brain damage. She had a black eye, but nothing was seriously wrong. While still at the hospital, Soon Ja Du was arrested and charged with first-degree murder. She was then held for ten days without bail at Sybil Brand Institute for Women.

Soon Ja Du would later say she was assaulted while in jail. Whether or not this is true, her family feared for her safety and concentrated on obtaining her release on bail, which meant persuading a judge that there was no risk of her fleeing to Korea. Her attorney, Charles Lloyd, successfully argued this point, and on March 26, after a hearing in Compton Municipal Court attended by 150 Korean supporters, Judge Morris Jones set bail at $250,000, and Du was freed. Billy Du put his head in his hands and wept in gratitude, but the decision was a disappointment to black activists. "How much are they paying you?" a Harlins supporter said contemptuously to Lloyd.

Disparities in legal skills would be factors in the "Rodney King trilogy," as defense attorney Michael Stone called the three trials arising from the King beating. But no one had reason to quarrel with the quality of legal representation in *The People of the State of California v. Soon Ja Du.* The people were represented by Deputy District Attorney Carvajal, who worked in the Long Beach office. Normally a prosecutor from the Compton office would have been assigned to the case, but Ira Reiner wanted to avoid what Carvajal called a "sticky" situation created by Joseph Du's dual role as a witness for the prosecution against the gang members who had robbed him and as a witness for the defense in his mother's trial. The Compton office was handling the prosecution of the gang members. Carvajal, self-composed and deliberate, had compiled a formidable record as a prosecutor. Reiner thought she was sometimes underestimated, especially by men, because of a deceptively "sweet quality."

On the defense side, Charles Earl Lloyd was one of the city's most successful criminal attorneys. He did not come cheap, but a civil attorney who had represented the Dus advised them that they needed an experienced criminal attorney who was black. Lloyd fit the bill. He was born in 1934 in Indianola, Mississippi, in one of the nation's poorest counties. When he was nine his father sent him to a lawyer's office with a message that he needed two more weeks to pay off a small loan. Lloyd was dazzled by the expensive furnishings and leather chairs in the office and blurted out to the white attorney that he wanted to be a lawyer. The man laughed and told him he might get a good job when he grew up but would never become an attorney.

Lloyd remembered this conversation. He was bright and a natural leader who became class president and quarterback and captain of the Indianola Colored High School football team. He had large ambitions. Nineteen days after his eighteenth birthday he arrived by bus in Los Angeles with a single pair of pants and twelve cents in his pocket. That night there was an earthquake, and he was terrified. "If I had any money at all, I would have left," Lloyd said years later. "But I didn't have any money. I was stuck."[15]

In 1954, when he was twenty, Lloyd graduated from the Los Angeles Police Academy at the top of his class. He saw police work as a stepping stone to becoming a lawyer and attended law school during his six years on the LAPD. Lloyd made the department's racial segregation work to his advantage by going home and studying law whenever no other black officer was available to serve as a partner. In 1961, he graduated from the University of Southern California Law School and passed the bar on his first try.[16] He joined the Los Angeles County District Attorney's Office, where he won his first sixty-nine trials and became chief trial deputy of the Criminal Division. In 1964, he went into private practice. He made no secret of wanting to become rich, and he specialized in criminal defenses of well-heeled clients. But Lloyd also defended poor blacks accused of murder, and he represented Black Panthers, Black Muslims, and the Aryan Brotherhood in politically charged cases. When a middle-class friend said that a black group represented by Lloyd preached a philosophy of hate, Lloyd responded, "I don't give a damn what they preach. I am a defense attorney, and I will represent anybody."[17]

Lloyd prospered and became Tom Bradley's friend and law partner. But Lloyd found the good life more appealing than politics. He was a flashy dresser who drove a black Rolls Royce and promoted himself with the slogan "When you are charged with murder, don't call unto the Lord—call Lloyd." Ira Reiner thought that he was a "hustler." But in 1992, the year after the murder trial of Soon Ja Du, the Los Angeles Bar Association named Lloyd its trial attorney of the year. It was the first time a black lawyer had won such recognition. The award commended "a man whose fortitude, tenacity and dedication to the legal community truly exemplifies the spirit of professionalism of the legendary Atticus Finch," the fictional attorney who defends a black man accused of raping a white girl in To Kill a Mockingbird.

Lloyd had represented a score of Korean Americans in criminal cases involving other Korean Americans. When the Du family came to him, he willingly took the case and brought in a white co-counsel, Richard Leonard.[18] "I took the case because the money was there, it was an interesting case and Charley and I work well together," Leonard said.[19] Leonard specialized in murder cases, and he and Lloyd had tried three capital cases together. They set out to demonstrate that the killing of Latasha Harlins was an act of self-defense by a woman who felt her life was in danger.

The case was more difficult for Lloyd than for Leonard. While Lloyd was secure in his legal skills, he was unprepared for the anger that his representation of Du would arouse among blacks. It had never occurred to Lloyd that both he and his client would become targets of anonymous death threats. Lloyd was bothered even more by criticisms from prominent blacks whose children or friends he had defended in criminal cases. He thought that blacks should realize that minority defendants needed good legal representation in unpopular cases. Yet Lloyd found too many of them "totally willing" to deny a fair trial to Soon Ja Du.[20]

Carvajal called four witnesses and played the videotape in presenting the prosecution's case to the grand jury. There were two eyewitnesses—Lakeshia Rashion Combs and her little brother, Ismail Ali. Lakeshia's testimony was vivid. She told of "the girl" approaching the counter and trying to pay for the orange juice and of "the Oriental lady" grabbing her. She told of the name-calling and the fight and Du pulling the gun from a brown "gun pouch" and shooting Harlins. "I ran," she said.

A grand juror had a question for Lakeshia Combs, submitted through Deputy District Attorney Lawrence Mason, the grand jury adviser. The juror wanted to know if Du understood English and spoke the language well. "Yes," Lakeshia said.

"How do you know that?" Mason asked.

"Because one day she was in the store in another argument with another lady, and she was speaking English very good." Lakeshia said. Lakeshia also said she understood everything that Harlins and Du had said to each other.

Denise Harlins testified. Carvajal played the tape and gently asked her to identify her niece. She did, fighting back tears. The last witness was Gerry Johnson, a detective who had investigated the shooting. He carefully described the weapon used to kill Harlins as a .38 caliber Smith and Wesson five-shot stainless steel revolver with a two-inch barrel. He said the wound was "absolutely" consistent with a wound made by a bullet from such a gun, necessary testimony because the police had been unable to find the bullet despite an extensive search. Johnson had interviewed Mrs. Du after placing her under arrest at the hospital. She admitted firing the gun. He described how Harlins had been shot in the back of the head and the position of the body on the floor. He said the shooting occurred at a distance of three to four feet, while the victim was walking away.

"I ask that you return a murder indictment," Carvajal said.

After two hours and forty minutes of deliberation, the grand jury indicted Soon Ja Du for the murder of Latasha Harlins.

6

CHRISTOPHER'S COURSE

"The Rodney King beating stands as a landmark in the recent history of law enforcement, comparable to the Scottsboro case in 1931 and the Serpico case in 1967. Rightly called 'sickening' by President Bush, and condemned by all segments of society, the King incident provides an opportunity for evaluation and reform of police procedures."

—"Report of the Independent
Commission on the Los Angeles
Police Department, July 9, 1991."[1]

DARYL GATES STRUGGLED TO SAVE HIS JOB AFTER THE RODNEY King incident while Tom Bradley pursued a political strategy that almost cost him the services of the quiet man he chose to investigate the inner workings of the LAPD. "The Los Angeles Police Department is facing a crisis of confidence in light of the intense scrutiny following the brutal beating of Rodney King," the mayor said on April 1, 1991, as he announced formation of the Independent Commission on the Los Angeles Police Department and named Warren Christopher as its chairman. Bradley said his "top priority" was "to restore the public's confidence in the LAPD and to restore the prestige and morale of our officers." He promised that the commission would "produce a report . . . beyond reproach."

But Bradley's behavior during this period did not match the high standard he set for the commission. The mayor had decided that the King incident had handed him an opportunity to oust a police chief he lacked the authority to fire, and the mayor's aides fed a flow of disparaging information about Gates to the media, some of it demonstrably false.[2] Gates dug in his heels. "I'm not going to slink away, defeated, because of some people in the community that are not thinking and who found an opportunity to run me out," he had said on March 13.[3] Two days later, Glenn Bunting of the *Los Angeles Times* reported that Deputy Mayor Mark Fabiani was orchestrating the effort to "turn up the heat" on the chief and pressure him to resign. Bradley had unconvincingly denied responsibility and said in an interview with the *Daily News* on March 24 that any decision on retirement was up to Gates. But then on April 2, the day after he named the Independent Commission, Bradley summoned Gates to his office and bluntly asked for his resignation.

Gates could not believe what he was hearing. Although he and Bradley had little use for each other and rarely talked, the chief had taken the mayor at his word when he said that he wanted an independent inquiry and that he would make no effort to force Gates to quit. Now, out of the blue, Bradley was making a power play. Gates rose from the couch where he had been sitting, told Bradley that he wasn't going to quit, and stalked out of the mayor's office.[4] Bradley, who had planned his next move, went on television to denounce Gates. "The public has lost confidence in Chief Gates since Rodney King was beaten," the mayor said. "I have asked him to show the uncommon courage to retire for the good of the LAPD and the welfare of all of Los Angeles . . . Unfortunately, Chief Gates has not recognized the impact he is having on the LAPD . . . His reactions to the tragic Rodney King beating have made an ugly situation even worse."

Watching Bradley's performance on television in his downtown law offices, Christopher was almost as appalled as Gates had been during his brief meeting with the mayor. Christopher had a low opinion of Gates, and he was a longtime political ally of Bradley. But appearances mattered greatly to Christopher, and he believed Bradley had compromised the commission he had just appointed. How could an inquiry into the LAPD have the appearance of objectivity after such prejudgment? In the process of denouncing Gates, Bradley had expressed his view that the officers accused of abusing Rodney King were guilty. This offended Christopher, who reveres the judicial process and has high expectations of other members of the legal profession, even full-time politicians. Certainly, Bradley should have known better. Christopher later told me that he was so shaken by Bradley's clumsy effort to oust Gates and by his prejudgment of the accused officers that he had been on the verge of backing out of his commitment to head the inquiry.

But history weighed heavily on Christopher. In 1965, as a thirty-nine-year-old attorney, he had been vice-chairman of the McCone Commission during its inquiry into the Watts riot. He had been the principal draftsman of the commission report, which was criticized by liberals for dealing too gently with Chief Parker and derided by an advisory committee to the U.S. Civil Rights Commission as "elemental, superficial, unoriginal and unimaginative." These criticisms stung Christopher. He saw the Independent Commission as an opportunity for redemption and a chance to recommend changes that would make the LAPD more accountable to civilian authority.

Christopher decided that he couldn't walk away from this second chance to make a difference.[5] He swallowed his doubts and stayed on to head the body that would become known as the Christopher Commission.

As Christopher saw it, however, the principal shortcoming of the Mc-Cone report was that there had been no follow-up on its recommendations. The report had identified deficiencies in education, health care, transportation, and housing that acted as barriers to the full equality of blacks and Latinos and had made suggestions to remedy these shortcomings. The McCone Commission report had identified with "the disadvantaged Negro," and posed a passionate question: "Of what shall it avail our nation if we can place a man on the moon but cannot cure the sickness in our cities?" But most of the McCone recommendations had been filed and forgotten. The only exception of consequence was the commission's support of "a new comprehensively-equipped hospital" in South Central, which helped spur the building of the facility now known as the Martin Luther King Jr. Hospital/Drew Medical Center.

Nothing had been done since McCone to improve relations between the LAPD and the black community. The community policing experiments of Chief Davis had been scuttled by Gates and Bradley. The one specific McCone recommendation designed to improve LAPD procedures—creation of an "inspector general" who would take over the functions of the Internal Affairs Division—had not been implemented, and the generalizations about the police and "the Negro community" trying harder to understand one another were largely meaningless. Geoffrey Taylor Gibbs, a black attorney, testified at the first public hearing of the Christopher Commission that "the only thing that has changed in Los Angeles is that the community under siege refers to itself as 'African American,' rather than 'Negro.'"[6]

But Warren Christopher was in a stronger political position in 1991 than he had been in 1965. Then-Governor Edmund G. (Pat) Brown was struggling to show that he could deal firmly with social unrest on university campuses and with riots in inner cities, issues that would contribute to Brown's defeat at the hands of Ronald Reagan when he sought a third term a year later. To mollify conservatives, Brown had named John McCone, a former Central Intelligence Agency director and prominent Los Angeles attorney, as the commission chairman. Christopher, who had worked for Brown in the past, was trapped between the liberal but politically nervous governor and the conservative McCone. "It was an impossible position," wrote Bill Boyarsky. "No wonder the report was a compromise at best, a whitewash at worst."[7]

While Pat Brown in 1965 had worried about alienating white voters, Tom Bradley in 1991 had reason to be concerned that he was not doing enough to please blacks. Bradley had been mayor for nearly eighteen years at the time of the King beating, and he was no longer the visionary leader who had transformed Los Angeles into an engine of diversity. The mayor's mantra of Los Angeles as "world city" resounded with bizarre dissonance in South Central, where blacks felt economic pressure from Latino and Asian immigration compounded by the city's worst economic downturn since the Depression.

Damaged by conflict-of-interest scandals, Bradley had been reelected to a fifth term in 1989 by an unexpectedly small margin.[8] He retained the support of downtown developers who had been the principal economic beneficiaries of his regime, but he no longer stirred the enthusiasm of the liberal coalition that had been his political mainstay. Black activists increasingly viewed the mayor as a distant figure who ignored growing poverty and despair almost literally in his own backyard.

The Rodney King incident gave Bradley an opportunity to reassert leadership with his core constituency. But more than politics was involved in the mayor's response. He had been truly offended by the Holliday videotape, and Chief Gates' dismissal of the King incident as an "aberration" had rekindled Bradley's still smoldering indignation over the humiliations he had suffered on the segregated LAPD. Police officers who had known Bradley when he was an officer (including Jesse Brewer and Ed Davis) knew that he had never forgotten how he had been treated and suspected that he still harbored a grudge. Bradley also remembered the frustrations of his early days on the city council, when the LAPD had brushed aside his efforts to draw attention to police abuses in the black community.

Few white Los Angeles politicians shared the mayor's enthusiasm for taking on the chief, and the reasons for their reluctance were demonstrated by a March 1991 Los Angeles Times poll. A majority of all races and ethnic groups expressed the opinion that police mistreatment of minorities was commonplace but took a wait-and-see attitude on whether Gates should resign. Despite the chief's low approval ratings, fewer than 20 percent of blacks and Latinos and fewer than 10 percent of Anglos (non-Hispanic whites) thought Gates should resign immediately over the King incident. A bare majority of blacks and Latinos wanted Gates to quit if an investigation proved police wrongdoing, while 60 percent of Anglos wanted him to stay no matter what the inquiry found.[9] As always in Los Angeles, city council members mentally adjusted these findings and took into account that Anglos, although only half the city's population, usually made up more than two thirds of the voters.

The upshot was that the city council hesitated to confront Gates. This task was left to the five-member Police Commission appointed by the mayor, theoretically the body to which the chief was accountable. The commission at the time had two black members, Sam Williams and Melanie Lomax, both of whom were quite willing to challenge Gates. But the commission was a part-time body that usually met once a week, depended upon the LAPD for much of its information, and lacked the expertise to analyze the voluminous reports, charts and statistics the department produced to justify even the most questionable police actions. Only in rare moments of heightened public awareness, notably after the 1982 choke-hold death of James Mincey, had the commission been able to impose a significant change.

With Gates damaged by the King incident, however, the commissioners believed that another such moment was at hand. Ignoring California's open-meetings law, they met secretly and decided on a strategy they thought would force Gates out. They summoned the embattled chief on April 4, two days after Bradley had tried to fire him, and told him they were putting him on paid leave pending investigation of "serious allegations of mismanagement" arising from the King affair. Gates stood his ground, stonily telling the commissioners he would fight in court. "I feel that I have been disgraced and defamed," he said after the meeting. "I have done nothing wrong. What they have done is improper, and we're going to prove that." Gates then taped a twelve-minute message of farewell to the members of the LAPD, urging them "to act like professionals" and vowing to fight his forced leave of absence "with every ounce of strength."

By suspending Gates without giving him a chance to defend himself, the Police Commission triggered a backlash of sympathy for the chief. Many city council members believed the suspension had been orchestrated by Bradley because Gates had refused to quit. Council President John Ferraro expressed the prevailing view when he said the Police Commission had "acted illegally and irresponsibly." Ignoring a plea from Bradley, the council voted 10–3 to reinstate Gates. When the Police Commission unwisely insisted on challenging the council's authority, it lost a court decision that further eroded its ability to control the police department.[10]

The city council's action was the first good news Gates had received since he watched the videotape of the King beating. On the day the council reinstated him, Gates met George Holliday for the first time at a $25-a-plate luncheon in the San Fernando Valley sponsored by a police-support group. Gates was in a happy mood. He shook Holliday's hand and told him he had become famous because the high-powered searchlights on the police helicopter had illuminated the scene of the King arrest and improved the conditions for videotaping. "If it wasn't for the helicopter, the lighting would have been horrible," Gates said.[11]

On April 9, City Council President Ferraro, quietly backed by Warren Christopher, brought the police chief and the mayor together and proposed a truce for the duration of the Christopher Commission inquiry. Neither Bradley nor Gates was conciliatory. When Bradley pointedly suggested that

Gates promise to retire after the inquiry, the chief flushed and replied that he would retire immediately if the mayor would do the same or promise not to run for a sixth term. Bradley refused. Gates then accused the mayor of interfering with the police department. Ferraro calmed Gates down, who acknowledged retrospectively that he behaved like "a jerk" in this meeting. But Bradley had provoked the argument. What had set Gates off and would always bother him was the mayor's refusal to recognize that he had been horrified by the Holliday videotape. "If it wasn't for you being so absolutely stupid and your office so crass, you'd have known that this incident broke my heart," Gates told the mayor.[12]

Bradley and Gates emerged from the meeting and held a joint news conference in which they promised to stop their feuding. Bradley said he had not changed his opinions, but he acknowledged that his attempt to force Gates into retirement had been unproductive "and we concluded we would take this step to heal the differences that have developed . . ." Gates concurred. "We do agree that we need to get this city back in shape, get it back in order, get it back to the level of the support from the community we had before the Rodney King incident," Gates said. It would be the last meeting between the mayor and the chief until the riots engulfed Los Angeles a year later. But their wary truce had freed Warren Christopher to pursue his course.

WARREN MINOR CHRISTOPHER WAS THEN SIXTY-FIVE YEARS OLD and arguably the most influential attorney in Southern California. He was chairman of O'Melveny and Myers, a powerful Los Angeles law firm that represented mostly corporate clients. He also had a long record of public service, including a year and a half as deputy U.S. attorney general in the Johnson administration and four years as deputy secretary of state in the Carter administration. In 1981, Christopher had won national acclaim and the Medal of Freedom for negotiating the release of Americans held hostage in Iran.

While Christopher's patrician bearing, impeccable manners, and tailored suits seemed more appropriate to the State Department than to Southern California, he was in fact reflective of Los Angeles, where the establishment is mostly an aristocracy of merit. Indeed, it is an aristocracy only in the libertarian sense used by Owen Wister, who early in the twentieth century had defined the credo of democracy as "Let the best man win." Despite its size and sprawl, Los Angeles remains a frontier city devoted to the gospel of rugged individualism.[13]

Warren Christopher, who had climbed by talent and hard work into the city's millionaire elite, was well suited to the Los Angeles frontier. Born on October 27, 1925, in the farming town of Scranton, North Dakota, to parents of Norwegian origin, he was a product of the egalitarian culture Scandinavians brought from their homelands to the prairies of North America. His father, Ernest, managed a small bank. Warren was only five when the Depression struck Scranton, engulfing the Christopher family. After being forced to foreclose on the properties of friends, Ernest Christopher suffered a massive stroke. His son always blamed the Depression.

Warren Christopher never forgot the misery that pervaded Scranton in those days. The Depression exposed him to social Darwinism, the dark side of the Wister vision, in which those who could not keep pace with change were flung by the wayside to fend for themselves. Christopher became a New Deal liberal in boyhood, and his politics did not change in the conservative climate of Los Angeles, where the family moved in 1937 so that his father could recuperate.

Ernest Christopher, who was only forty-nine when he suffered his first stroke, never recovered. The burden of raising a family fell to his wife, Catherine, who worked as a sales clerk and took care of her invalid husband and their five children in a rented Hollywood apartment. Ernest Christopher died from another stroke four years after the move to Los Angeles. Two of Warren's older brothers found jobs instead of attending college, but Warren won a scholarship to the University of Redlands. He later transferred to the Naval Reserve program at the University of Southern California, from which he graduated magna cum laude in February 1945. Like Daryl Gates, Christopher served on active duty in the Pacific during the closing months of World War II, although he did not see combat. Known to everyone as Chris, he was recognized by his peers for the quiet brilliance that would distinguish him in law and government. Christopher attended Stanford Law School from 1946 to 1949 and became president of the *Law Review*, joining a circle with a strong commitment to liberalism and civil rights. After graduation he landed a coveted clerkship with Supreme Court Justice William O. Douglas. When that ended, he joined O'Melveny and was made a partner at thirty-three. He subsequently became executive secretary to Governor Pat Brown, beginning a long career as an adviser to prominent Democrats.

But the Independent Commission cast Christopher in much more than an advisory role. As he had recognized early on, the trauma of the King beating provided a rare opportunity for fundamental change. "The Rodney King incident has changed the landscape," Christopher said in an opening statement to the commission's first public meeting. "The home video of the incident has become the most widely viewed news video since the tragic *Challenger* explosion. Without prejudging any of the sensitive issues surrounding the incident itself, there can be no doubt that the underlying issue of excessive use of force in the name of the law must be examined on an urgent basis. Few issues have such a polarizing and disruptive potential as this one, and few issues present a more complex challenge to the city of Los Angeles."

Christopher had used his diplomatic skills to head off another investigation that almost certainly would have distracted from his commission's inquiry. The potential competitor was a citizens' panel that Chief Gates had named on March 27. The head of the Gates panel was retired California Supreme Court Justice John Arguelles, another Navy veteran with World War II combat experience in the Pacific. Christopher sought him out, and Arguelles quickly agreed to allow his panel to be absorbed by Christopher's, and he became vice-chairman of the Christopher Commission, which was expanded from seven members to ten.

With or without the new members, the commission seemed too conservative to liberal critics, as Ramona Ripston, executive director of the American Civil Liberties Union Foundation of Southern California made clear when she testified at the panel's first public hearing. She told the commissioners that people have "doubts about your willingness to take controversial stands—stands that may offend the establishment. We wonder whether your ties to the business community are too close—whether your commitment to the status quo is too binding."

On the face of it, Ripston had reason for skepticism. Six of the ten members were lawyers with establishment firms. The other four were Roy Anderson, chairman emeritus of Lockheed Corporation; John Brooks Slaughter, president of Occidental College; Robert Tranquada, former dean of the USC school of medicine, and Leo Estrada, an urban affairs professor at UCLA. Of this group only Estrada, a demographer who had drawn the redistricting map that created the first Latino seat on the Los Angeles Board of Supervisors, had a left-of-center reputation. Ripston might have been even more alarmed if she had known that Estrada had been chosen only after four prominent Latinos, two of them lawyers, had declined appointment. The commissioners, all male except for former U.S. Attorney Andrea Sheridan Ordin, had impressive resumes but as a group did not seem likely to rock any boats.

The commission staff consisted mostly of attorneys, except for Bryce Nelson, a USC journalism professor and former *Los Angeles Times* reporter who served as director of press information, and Lieutenant George Godwin of the LAPD, the technical adviser. Christopher had agreed to complete the inquiry within ninety days, a deadline that seemed rushed to him but helped in the recruiting of top-notch lawyers who might not have been available for longer service. His point man in the recruiting was John Spiegel, who had experience as a prosecutor and as special assistant to Christopher in the State Department.[14] Spiegel had accepted appointment as the commission's general counsel with misgivings. Christopher, whose bland exterior concealed a pungent sense of humor, tried to reassure him. As they were leaving for the press conference at which Bradley announced the commission, Christopher said he was reminded of a story of Marilyn Monroe, "on location in some God-forsaken place and having a miserable time," who had asked a friend: "Who do I have to fuck to get fired from this picture?"[15]

After reaching agreement with Arguelles, Christopher plunged into the inquiry with disciplined curiosity. He held one-on-one lunches with individual commissioners and also met with police officers, community activists and journalists.[16] Christopher was a proficient listener. His aim was to produce a report so factually sound and carefully written that it could not be ignored. The commissioners started out, at Christopher's direction, by reading the McCone Commission report. "As things went on, almost everything McCone did, he did the opposite," Leo Estrada said.[17]

Unlike McCone, Christopher did not depend on official information provided by the LAPD. His staff interviewed 300 current and former LAPD officers, some of whom provided devastating information about Chief Gates, and 150 experts in the fields of policing, law enforcement, psychiatry and medicine. The commissioners and their staff reviewed 1,240 personnel complaints, more than 100,000 pages of transcripts from the Mobile Digital Terminal (MDT) conversations between police officers, and 700 LAPD personnel files. They held five public hearings in different parts of the city, reviewed 8,000 letters sent to the LAPD and conducted 100 telephone interviews with people who called to comment or complain about the police.[18]

The commissioners were profoundly affected by what they learned through this process. John Slaughter, an African American, was "shocked by the testimony of an African-American police officer who confessed that he had apprehensions about driving home from duty, late at night, for fear that he would be harassed by fellow officers who needed no other reason to stop him than that he was a black man driving through their district."[19] Leo Estrada was struck by the harrowing account of a black civilian who had borrowed a car for a date on which he had planned to celebrate a new job. The car had a warrant on it. When the man who had borrowed the car was stopped by police, he pleaded not to be made to lie face down on the ground in his new white suit while the officers checked out his story. The officers nonetheless forced him to the ground in front of his neighbors and put their feet on him before determining that the car was borrowed and releasing him. As the man recalled the indignity, his voice rose. A commissioner asked when the incident had happened. In 1967, the man replied. "He just blew us away," said Estrada. "The way he told the story it could have happened yesterday."[20]

Police witnesses also made an impression. Lieutenant George Aliano, president of the Los Angeles Police Protective League, testified at the commission's first public hearing that the LAPD undervalued "the most important service" of patrol by treating it as a dumping ground for new sergeants and the least experienced officers. Nearly four out of ten officers on patrol had been members of the LAPD for three years or less, and capable officers often transferred to specialized assignments because it was difficult to be promoted from patrol. "Why would you want to stay in patrol?" Aliano asked. "If anything can go wrong, it's going to go wrong on patrol."

Aliano also called for improved psychological tests to weed out unfit officers and for improvement of in-field training. These recommendations would find their way into the Christopher Commission report, although the media rarely noted that they originated with the police union. Significantly, Aliano quoted former LAPD Chiefs Parker and Reddin to make his points. He did not mention Daryl Gates.

WHILE ALIANO'S SILENCE ABOUT GATES SPOKE VOLUMES, IT WAS the direct testimony of Jesse Brewer and Assistant Police Chief David Dotson that inflicted the heaviest damage. Brewer had stayed the course within the LAPD for thirty-eight years. He had survived the humiliations of segregation and the uncertain post-segregation years, when blacks slowly overcame traditional barriers and advanced to positions of leadership within the department. Ed Davis had trusted Brewer and promoted him, and Gates had also learned to depend on him. Brewer had become one of three assistant chiefs to Gates before he retired. It was then the highest rank an African American had ever obtained within the LAPD. Gates had not wanted to lose him and as Brewer recounted it, the chief had tried to keep him by offering him the prestigious job of director of operations, a job then held by Assistant Chief Robert Vernon. The offer was tempting, but Brewer had made up his mind to retire. When he left on February 28, Gates kept the post vacant.[21]

Three days after Brewer retired, the Rodney King incident occurred. The response of the LAPD leadership to the beating ratified Brewer's belief that the department tolerated excessive force by failing to hold senior officers responsible for the conduct of those under their command, an issue on which he clashed many times with Gates and Vernon. Brewer did not think it was sufficient for Gates to describe the incident as an "aberration" and vow to punish the officers involved. As Brewer saw it, Captain McBride, the Foothill Division commander, had ignored previous abuses by Laurence Powell, and McBride should have been immediately reassigned.[22]

Gates, in fact, had shaken up the command structure at the troubled division after the King incident, and Captain Paul Jefferson, an African American, had been transferred to Foothill as patrol commander and

McBride's second in command. But McBride had waged a vigorous fight to avoid reassignment, talking to leaders of a police-support group who enlisted two pro-Gates members of the city council, Ernani Bernardi and Hal Bernson, in his cause. Bernardi had called Gates, who decided to take it easy on McBride. Vernon then praised the embattled Foothill Division commander, saying that "community people" thought he was "doing a wonderful job."[23]

There was nothing Brewer could do about McBride. But he wanted to do something about the LAPD pattern of looking the other way at excessive force, and Bradley gave him a chance by naming him as an adviser to the Christopher Commission. It was a shrewd political decision by the mayor, and as Christopher carefully built a case against Chief Gates, Brewer became his secret weapon.

Gates and Assistant Chiefs Vernon and Dotson testified before the Christopher Commission on June 14, with Brewer strategically held in reserve. Dotson was the key. He had served thirty-three years with the LAPD and as acting chief during the brief suspension of Gates by the Police Commission. While still harboring dreams of becoming chief in his own right, he realized his chances were remote. But Dotson was not ready to retire, which made it harder for him than for Brewer to speak out against Gates. Even though he was not aware that his testimony in closed session would eventually be made public, Dotson suspected that the chief would learn of it and make his life at Parker Center intolerable. He cushioned his criticisms by telling the commission that he held Gates "in very high esteem personally, he is a very good man, and he has been very nice to me . . . but this is a rare opportunity, I believe, to have some influence on the future of the department and the city, and so I'm going to suck up my courage and try to give you my best estimate of whatever it is you wish to hear."

The willingness of Dotson and Brewer to talk candidly gave Christopher an opportunity denied McCone. Using pending lawsuits and coroner's inquests as his rationale, Chief Parker had ordered LAPD officers not to talk after the Watts riot in 1965. The order had been scrupulously obeyed, with productive results for Parker. The police killings of rioters were uniformly ruled "justifiable homicide."[24] Media coverage of Parker was mostly favorable. No LAPD officers broke ranks in testifying before the McCone Commission. While two useful books on the Watts riot—*Burn Baby Burn* and *Rivers of Blood, Years of Darkness*—raised critical questions about police conduct, the LAPD under Parker had maintained its seamless web of silence.

But Parker had an advantage in 1965 that Gates did not enjoy a quarter century later. In the summer of 1964 seven black communities in eastern cities had been stricken by riots that the McCone report called "a symptom of a sickness in the center of our cities." The Watts riot was widely viewed as an extension of this epidemic, which many whites believed could be stamped out only by vigorous police action. It was different in 1991. At the time of the Rodney King beating a new generation of Americans had become less trusting of the police, the media no longer fawned over hard-nosed police chiefs, and Gates did not control subordinates with Parker's iron hand. Christopher knew from Brewer that the facade of LAPD loyalty was fragile. With careful questioning the cracks would be revealed, and Gates might come tumbling down.

The questioning of Gates was conducted entirely by former prosecutor John Spiegel, who led the chief through a series of interrogatories on excessive force, disciplinary procedures, and expressions of racism and sexism on transcripts of patrol car messages. Speaking without notes, Gates gave what even the critical Estrada would call "one of the most incredible, remarkable performances I have ever seen."[25] Exuding charm and self-assurance throughout the first hour and a half of questioning, Gates lectured the commission about police work, discussed the need for psychological profiles of problem officers, and restated the case for the modified carotid choke hold. He promised that officers who had made offensive racial or sexist comments on in-car computers would be disciplined but observed that computer messages were not normally monitored. "Your offices are not bugged, and I guess it's only President Nixon who taped everything," Gates said. The commissioners laughed.

But Gates wasn't laughing. He was disturbed more than the commissioners realized by some of the 260 computer messages that Spiegel called "patently offensive." After comparing the messages to remarks made in locker rooms or military service, Gates said: "All I can tell you is that they are deeply offensive, disappointing to me, very disappointing. . . . Police officers work in the garbage pail all the time, you know. They are constantly working in a very, very difficult arena, and some get very cynical, some get very hard, some of them are frightened, some of them are stressed. When you are frightened or stressed, a lot of these things come out that perhaps might not come out, so I don't know . . . I think we would be remiss if we really didn't dig very deeply and ask ourselves, why is it? Why does this occur?"

Gates testified for nearly three hours in closed session, more than holding his own in the early going and often turning aside barbed questions with one-liners. But the chief became annoyed when Spiegel suggested that he had outlived his usefulness to the LAPD. Spiegel said police experts had told the commission that thirteen years was too long for anyone to remain as chief, although they had somewhat softened the impact of their testimony by expressing high regard for Gates. "They usually do when they think I can identify who they are," Gates shot back. "Bill Parker stayed a long time, probably too long, and probably I've stayed longer than I should, and probably if the people left me alone I would have left some time ago . . ." Gates said.

The chief did not care for this line of questioning. Ever since the King incident, Gates had been suggesting that he might be willing to jump if he wasn't pushed, an idea that became a refrain of the chief's defenders. But the notion that he was clinging to his job simply out of pride contradicted the strong belief within the LAPD—shared by Gates' predecessor Ed Davis—that Gates had a firm goal of breaking Parker's longevity record of nearly sixteen years as chief. This would have meant staying until 1994. Gates was realistic enough to know that the King affair had made this objective unattainable, but he still meant to leave on his own terms.[26]

Late in the questioning, John Spiegel recalled that Gates had once favored a set term for police chiefs. Did he still? Gates hesitated. He suddenly seemed unsure of himself. He recalled once saying that a chief should serve "five years and get out of here . . . that was my intent, to get out of here." Spiegel then backed off and tried to change the subject, but Gates seemed lost in thought. "You gotta be a masochist to stay here much longer than that period of time," Gates said.

As the interview progressed, the chief's charm faded. He "bobbed and weaved," as Estrada saw it, and became annoyed when Spiegel asked about the increasing number of successful lawsuits against the city based on police misconduct. Gates faulted the city attorney's office. "It's badly staffed, badly organized," he said. "I don't think the police department has been represented well." Nor did Gates care for Spiegel's insistent questioning about the LAPD survey conducted by Commander Michael Bostic, which had found that a significant number of officers acknowledged racism within the LAPD. Gates said a poll taken before the King incident had found "that the most believable person in Southern California was the chief of police."

The believability of this chief did not survive the testimony of David Dotson, who gave Gates high ratings for the department's handling of the 1984 Olympics and the Drug Abuse Resistance Education (DARE) program, in which officers teach children the dangers of drug use, but low marks for just about everything else. "Painting with a very broad brush," said Dotson, "we have not had, at the top, very effective leadership" during the Gates years. Dotson faulted Gates for inaccessibility, poor budgeting and incoherent management. "We have a big policy manual full of high-sounding statements of purpose . . . and how we should treat people, and what it is that we're supposed to be doing, what our role is in modern society," Dotson said. "But that stays in the policy manual and is not reflected in our day-to-day operation . . . and there is no clear statement of mission or purpose. In addition to that, we have no priorities set for our operation."

Dotson said that the essence of the LAPD's recurrent excessive-force problem was that the department remained "stuck . . . in a 1950s sort of world view." Officers were rewarded for "hard-nosed, proactive police work," which often meant arresting criminal suspects on suspicion and making a case after they were in custody. But the Supreme Court and the California courts had outlawed such practices, and the suspects knew it. "And so it results in police officers bluffing their way into situations, and when they stop people on the street, frequently the guy knows you don't have anything . . ." Dotson said. Time after time these stops resulted in arrests in which improper force was used, "frequently with manufacturing or at least puffing up of the probable cause." LAPD practice was "inimical" to "what our Constitution says you may do," he said.

Dotson's analysis of LAPD practices ratified the harsh depiction of police lawlessness that had been presented to the commission by Ramona Ripston of the ACLU. And his up-close portrayal of Gates shattered the chief's cultivated public image of decisiveness. With his dapper appearance, determined manner and ready wit, Gates seemed the model of a modern professional police chief. Although the 1992 riots would tarnish his reputation, Gates in 1991 was still widely viewed as a top cop who headed the best police force in the nation. But the chief portrayed by Dotson was an indecisive leader whose most distinguishing trait was an unwillingness to hold anyone accountable. This chief was lax in disciplining those who used excessive force because he did not want to offend officers or their division captains. This chief used his secretary as a gatekeeper to fend off bearers of bad news. He ducked disputes among assistant chiefs by canceling his weekly meetings with them. "Daryl Gates is a very nice man," Dotson said. "He and I get along just great. But he doesn't hold me accountable, either. I screw things up, and the worst he can do is get a pained expression on his face."

Because Dotson was in charge of Internal Affairs, his criticisms about the toleration of excessive force could also have been viewed, as Gates later said, as a self-indictment. Indeed, Dotson sometimes used the first-person plural in finding fault, saying, for instance, that "we have failed miserably" to hold supervisors accountable for excessive force. But Dotson insisted that Gates bore the main responsibility. Like Brewer, Dotson wanted Captain McBride removed from the command of Foothill Division and thought he had persuaded Gates to make the transfer. Gates had agreed, then allowed himself to be talked out of it. As Dotson saw it, such decisions sent a message that supervisors would not be held accountable for the conduct of brutal officers under their command.

Five days later Jesse Brewer added unflattering details about the chief's management style. Brewer, who had been assistant chief for administrative services, said it was "very, very difficult" to see the chief in a one-on-one meeting. And Gates either canceled scheduled meetings with the assistant chiefs or started them too late to complete the agenda. Because Gates spent much of his time "interacting with the citizens," the assistant chiefs were "almost autonomous." While Gates had done "a good job" overall, Brewer said, "I would not give him a good grade in his handling of discipline."

"What grade would you give him?" Spiegel asked.

"I would probably give him a 'D,'" Brewer said. "I think I would be generous in giving him a 'D' in discipline because I felt the way he handled discipline was really not the best for the department, nor for the people of the city."

Then Brewer turned to the King case. He thought Sergeant Koon should have been suspended immediately, the Foothill watch commander removed, and Captain McBride reassigned and replaced by Captain Jefferson. He said that Gates' reluctance to make changes reflected a pattern established by the chief in other cases in which officers had been accused of using excessive force.

Overall, Brewer's overall assessment of Gates was more balanced than Dotson's. "I think he's a good administrator, he has a keen intellect, he's very sharp, he knows how to handle the political establishment well," he said. ". . . He's been innovative, and he's developed some very progressive ideas." But this apparent evenhandedness made Brewer's indictment of Gates' disciplinary policies that much more impressive to the commissioners. At the heart of the problem, said Brewer, was "a culture that exists in the police department that has been growing for a number of years. . ." and was reflected in a belief that "we are better than them," a belief that encouraged officers to take the law into their own hands.

Commissioner Mickey Kantor picked up the issue. Did this cultural attitude extend all the way up the LAPD hiearchy to Chief Gates? "I would think so," Brewer replied. In fact, Brewer said he had brought the issue up with Gates, who had agreed he needed to pay closer attention to such attitudes.

"Did anything happen?" Kantor asked.

"I don't know of anything that happened," Brewer said.

John Arguelles, fair-minded but sympathetic to Gates, realized that Brewer's testimony had done heavy damage to the chief. He pressed Brewer on the issue of discipline, asking him whether there was any occasion when Gates had sided with bureau chiefs or assistant chiefs against the captains and imposed harsher penalties on officers who used excessive force.

"I don't recall him ever siding with me," Brewer replied.

In his quiet way, Brewer had made the strongest case for getting rid of Gates, the issue the commission would grapple with as the original three-month time frame of its inquiry was extended an extra week. If Gates was reluctant to impose heavy penalties for excessive force even when principal subordinates favored it, how could the LAPD be reformed with him in charge? The chief received no help on this point from Vernon, who as director of operations had control of more than 80 percent of the department and supposedly had the best access to Gates. Although Vernon did not join in the systematic criticisms of the chief's management, his testimony reinforced the growing belief of the commission that Gates was lax in dealing with excessive force.

Vernon was also criticized, particularly by Brewer, who said he should be removed as director of operations. Brewer said Vernon was a "devious" person of "very, very conservative" views who promoted police officers who shared his fundamentalist Christian beliefs. "He's the head of the God Squad, as we refer to it," Brewer said. ". . . It's commonly known that the way you get ahead as far as Vernon is concerned is to become aligned either with his church or to profess that you are born again."

This "commonly known" conduct had first been alleged in an anonymous letter to *The Thin Blue Line*, the Police Protective League's newsletter, in November 1987. The letter said that a watch commander at a police roll call had solicited volunteers to attend Vernon's church, the Grace Community Church in Sun Valley. When no one volunteered, four probationary officers had been ordered to attend. The letter also alleged that at least twenty on-duty officers attended a Vernon sermon on police appreciation, leaving others in the field without partners. The churchgoers received Bibles and flashlights "to light the way" and heard Vernon denounce homosexuality, encourage wives to be submissive to their husbands, and advocate corporal punishment. While an LAPD investigation cleared Vernon of misconduct, the *Daily News* reported two days before he testified to the Christopher Commission that Gates had reopened the investigation.[27] Nothing would come of this inquiry either, but the issue was a critical distraction at a time the LAPD leadership could least afford it. Vernon would say later that the "false accusations" had plunged him into depression. "My biggest fear—of bringing discredit to the name of Jesus—had come true," he wrote.[28]

The Christopher Commission had no way of resolving the accusations against Vernon, but the controversy was another sign to commissioners that the LAPD leadership was in disarray. As one commissioner put it privately: "What can you say about a department in which two of the three highest ranking subordinates attack their boss, and the other is busy defending himself?" Gates, in fact, did not know what to say or where to turn. He was not close to Vernon, although he would side with him against the "God Squad" accusations. He felt blindsided and betrayed by Dotson and Brewer. But as adversaries and events closed in on him, the chief was in a state of resolute denial. When the investigations were over, Gates told *Playboy* magazine that the conclusion would be "This is a great department."[29]

Two days before he testified to the Christopher Commission, Gates ordered a daily audit of the computer messages sent over the Mobile Digital Terminals (MDTs) from LAPD patrol cars. This was two days after Superior Court Judge Bernard Kamins decided that he would permit the "gorillas-in-the-mist" message sent by Officer Powell to be introduced into evidence. The Christopher Commission wanted to make an extensive examination of the computer messages, which the LAPD had stored in a data base but not audited. After negotiating with the LAPD, the commission staff settled for six months of random samples drawn from a sixteen-month period between November 1, 1989, and March 4, 1991. All told, said Gates, six million computer messages would be examined.

Although the vast majority of the messages were routine, hundreds contained comments in which officers joked about beating suspects or derogated racial minorities, women, and homosexuals. African Americans were most frequently disparaged, but derogatory comments were also aimed at Mexicans, Salvadorans, Cubans, Asians, and Jews. The compendium of messages included examples of borderline police humor, such as advice on how to obtain a stress-related pension: "just go in twerling your gun on one finger and say who's next." It also included remarks that may genuinely have been stress related: "I shot him once and it had no effect. I shot him a second time and it had no effect. I shot him a third time and it stopped the motherfucker long enough to cuff him." Other messages clearly met Spiegel's description of "patently offensive":

"I would love to drive down Slauson [a street in a black neighborhood] with a flame-thrower . . . We could have a barbecue."

"If you get a chance swing by Westpark and chase the fruits."

". . . I left a 14 year old girl that I met yesterday handcuffed naked to my chin-up bar wearing nothing but a blind-fold and salad oil . . . I'd like to check on her."

"They found something that does the work of 5 women—1 man."

"Death an destruction puts a roof over my head, food in my belly and a new car under my fanny. A day with out violence is like a day without sunshine."

A commission composed of working-class Angelenos might have taken in stride the fact that police officers talked as if they had been plucked from the pages of a Joseph Wambaugh novel, using slang like "macho chick" and "squid" and referring to suspects as "NHI," for "no human involved." But the members of the Christopher Commission and especially its staff were more accustomed to the rarefied atmosphere of the courtroom than the subculture of the LAPD. Except for having taken a few ride arounds in police cars, most of the commissioners lacked firsthand experience of the seamy

side of Los Angeles and had little taste for life on the streets. It took a suggestion from Bryce Nelson, a former journalist, to prod the commission into
visiting the site of the King incident, the first thing a reporter (or a police
officer) might have done. Christopher drove to Foothill and Osborne in his
Mercedes on the day the commission held its first public hearing and expressed amazement that King had been beaten "right out in the open" where
the incident could have been seen by so many people.[30] Nelson was not
amazed.

Christopher found the computer messages "abhorrent," and even commissioners who were not shocked by them recognized that the transcripts
were useful in making a case for reform. Slaughter and Estrada believed the
messages were powerful evidence of racism, and Andrea Ordin said that
they also showed that sexism was embedded within the LAPD. "The computer messages tended to jell the inchoate feelings of commissioners that
something was really wrong within the LAPD," she said. "And they were
concrete evidence that kept the report from being an overly dry statistical
analysis of what went wrong."[31]

Ordin, a former U.S. attorney and deputy state attorney general, played a
decisive role in the way the messages were treated. The other commissioners,
all men, wanted to release MDT messages that reflected racism or excessive
force, but felt that describing the sexually explicit messages was sufficient.
Ordin objected. "As accustomed as I am to say that diversity makes a difference, this was one of the few concrete examples in my life when I could see
the impact," she said later.[32] The male commissioners backed down and included messages with sexual references in the compendium.

Because the computer messages bothered even the most pro-police commissioners, they helped move the panel closer to consensus. John Arguelles
said after the commission's report was released that the messages "affected us
with the impression that racism and a cavalier attitude towards the use of
force was not something that was being particularly concealed by at least
those people that were speaking." When he was asked if the LAPD leadership was aware of the tone of the messages, Arguelles replied, "I'm not so
sure . . . but they should have been."[33]

As Ordin had noted, the computer messages added bite to a report laden
with statistical analysis, and the 693-message compendium certainly engaged the media. But whether racist attitudes and support for excessive force
were as widespread within the LAPD as the commission believed remains
an open question. The commission's analysis of the messages reveals a stunning ignorance of police slang and jargon. The compendium of MDT
messages contains dozens of inoffensive comments that were misinterpreted as having sinister meanings. The most widely quoted of these was,
"It's monkey-slapping time," which the *Los Angeles Times* made the focus

of an advance story on the Christopher Commission report. But the phrase did not indicate that an officer intended to beat up African Americans, as the Christopher Commission and the *Times* assumed. "Monkey-slapping" was originally a euphemistic reference to masturbation that over time became synonymous with "relaxing" or "goofing off." The officer who announced that it was time for monkey-slapping was about to go off duty.

Nor did the commission know that "kick" is police slang for "release." A sergeant who was returning to the field to "kick the suspect" was letting him go. "Queen car" was seen by the commission as a reference to gays; it is actually an LAPD term referring to a unit that observes and controls demonstrations. The compendium of supposedly offensive messages also contained many innocuous comments. Eliminating such expressions of enthusiasm as "I love pursuits" and "Praise the Lord and pass the ammunition" would have resulted in a much shorter list.

Gates later claimed on the basis of an LAPD analysis that only 277 of the released computer messages reflected actual misconduct. He said that of the 44 messages involving racial remarks the majority were jocular exchanges between officers of the same race or ethnic group. Only 12 were messages of a racial nature in which neither party belonged to the racial or ethnic group that was being derogated.[34] But the chief's subtraction was as suspect as the commission's addition because his list did not include some 300 messages that were not subject to discipline because the one-year statute of limitations for punishing this sort of conduct had expired.

Even so, Gates is right in saying that only a tiny percentage of the computer messages sent from the patrol cars were objectionable in any reasonable definition of this term. Even if 600 messages are deemed objectionable, which is probably a stretch, this would amount to one-tenth of 1 percent of all computer transmissions during the period the messages were audited. How many police departments or factory workforces would fare as well from similar monitoring? It is impossible to know, but it is understandable that many LAPD officers believed that the audit of the messages demonstrated the overall professionalism of the department rather than widespread racist or brutal attitudes. In reaching a judgment it is important to realize that some LAPD officers treated the in-car computer system as an electronic-mail bulletin board on which they could send ordinary messages, such as birthday greetings. Officers knew that car-to-car conversations were not monitored by their supervisors, as is demonstrated by various messages that knock LAPD management. Considering the LAPD's fearsome reputation, there were remarkably few officers who boasted about beating suspects or compared black people to "gorillas in the mist."

On the other hand, as Andrea Ordin observed, "There was not a single message in which anyone joked about corruption, stealing the evidence, or using drugs." This suggested to her that the MDT messages truly reflected a police culture "in which certain types of conduct were always impermissible." Ordin believed that if LAPD training and the LAPD culture had proscribed racism and sexism as firmly as it did bribetaking, the computer printouts would have been devoid of crude remarks. "We know there are jokes in bars and locker rooms and gallows humor," Ordin said. "None of us would like to hear what is said when we are on the operating table. But these were work comments typed into a computer while people were on duty. It was the tip of the iceberg."[35]

THE COMMISSION'S MOST DIFFICULT DECISION WAS WHETHER TO call directly for the resignation of Gates or simply to reprimand his management practices. Christopher once told me in customary elliptical fashion that this decision "evolved," which I took to mean that he had not expected at the outset of the inquiry that the commission would seek the chief's resignation. It was not Christopher's style to begin an investigation with a firm conclusion or make decisions before he was required to. He would in any case have withheld judgment until he heard from Gates, as he had wanted Mayor Bradley to do.

"Our focus will be to study the use of excessive force in the name of the law," Christopher said at the commission's initial public meeting. This focus repeatedly exposed the principal deficiency of Gates, an able and innovative police officer who had become an ineffective and unwilling disciplinarian in his later years as chief. Gates was not himself a brutal officer, and his testimony to the commission recounted with emotion how he had cracked down on excessive force as a police commander. Ordin found the testimony credible but also concluded that Gates no longer exercised such control. "He was disconnected in some way as chief," she said. "He didn't believe in excessive force, but the rules he thought were ingrained really weren't. Unfortunately, Gates believed things were the way he wanted them to be."

Especially persuasive was the evidence that a handful of officers— branded "problem officers" in the commission's report—were allowed to continue working on the streets despite repeated complaints of excessive force. Gates barely defended himself against the charge that he had been ineffective in weeding out such officers or the related accusation that he too often reduced penalties in excessive-force cases.

Roy Anderson, the respected Lockheed chairman emeritus, played a significant behind-the-scenes role in deciding the commission's recommendation on Gates. A conservative, no-nonsense businessman who usually did more listening than talking, Anderson said that if he served on a board of directors where senior vice presidents had faulted the management practices of the chief operating officer "we would have no choice in the corporate world than to clean house."[36] Other commissioners concurred, and the issue then became not whether to seek the chief's resignation but how to word the recommendation. This was a task to which Christopher's diplomatic skills were suited. The extent of the discussions on the phrasing is known only to Christopher, who had frequent one-on-one conversations with Richard Mosk and Arguelles, holdovers from the Gates panel who were considered most sympathetic to the chief.[37] From these conversations came a recommendation that put the call for the chief's resignation within the context of a proposed city charter change and offered an olive branch to pro-Gates forces by also seeking changes in the Police Commission:

> Chief Gates has served the LAPD and the City 42 years, the past 13 years as Chief of Police. He has achieved a noteworthy record of public service in a stressful and demanding profession. For the reasons set forth in support of the recommendation that the Chief of Police be limited to two five-year terms, the Commission believes that commencement of a transition in that office is now appropriate. The Commission also believes that the interests of harmony and healing would be served if the Police Commission is now reconstituted with members not identified with the recent controversy involving the Chief.

The message of the 228-page report released by Warren Christopher at a televised news conference on July 9, 1991, was as unmistakable as the wording was roundabout. "Panel Urges Gates to Retire" said the banner headline in the *Los Angeles Times*. Mayor Bradley was predictably ecstatic. "I say to those who would block the road to change: stand aside or we will leave you behind," he said. "We cannot, we will not rest until the Christopher Commission has changed the way we police our city." Ramona Ripston said the ACLU had been "totally vindicated" in its campaign to reform the LAPD. Police Commissioner Stanley Sheinbaum said Gates "knows as well as I do what the tea leaves read."* But Gates read the tea leaves differently. The delicate phrasing that couched the call for "transition" in the context of a change in the city charter limiting the terms of police chiefs had left Gates running room, and he knew it. Hours after Christopher delivered the report, Gates told reporters at Parker Center that he would step down only if Los

---

* Sheinbaum, an influential member of the American Civil Liberties Union, was appointed by Bradley to the Police Commission on March 15, 1991, in a move widely viewed as an effort to turn up the pressure on Gates. But Sheinbaum immediately departed on an overseas trip and played no part in the Police Commission's failed attempt to fire the chief. Two commissioners involved in this effort, Sam Williams and Melanie Lomax, resigned on the day Christopher submitted his report. They were replaced by Jesse Brewer and Ann Reiss Lane, with Sheinbaum taking over from Williams as president.

Angeles voters approved a term limit for police chiefs. LAPD employees crowded into the room as Gates spoke and chanted "Chief, chief" in a calculated display of support. The Los Angeles Times said they had "turned an event some thought would be a farewell speech into a pep rally."

THE REPORT OF THE INDEPENDENT COMMISSION ON THE LOS Angeles Police Department had been completed in one hundred days, exactly the time spent by the McCone Commission on its inquiry into the Watts riot, but the resemblance between the two reports ends there. The McCone Commission report had analyzed the social conditions that formed the context of the riot while saying little about why the police were so unpopular in Watts. The Christopher Commission report focused almost entirely upon the LAPD and made 130 recommendations designed to improve the practices and policies of the department.

True to its mandate and Christopher's disciplined focus, the report concentrated on the use of "excessive force under color of law." A prerequisite of submitting to the rule of law was serious considerations of citizen complaints about illegal police action. "No area of police operations received more adverse comment during the commission's public hearings than the department's handling of citizen complaints," the report said. It noted that Rodney King's brother had tried in vain at Foothill Station to make a formal complaint about the incident. The McCone Commission had recommended appointment of an inspector general who would report to the chief of police. The Christopher Commission went further, calling for establishing this post within the civilian Police Commission outside the chief's control.

The section on the "problem officers," who remained anonymous until their names were published by the Los Angeles Times in 1992, was also significant.[38] "The Commission has found that there is a significant number of LAPD officers who repetitively misuse force and persistently ignore the written policies and guidelines of the Department regarding force," the report said. "The evidence obtained by the commission shows that this group has received inadequate supervisory and management attention." Of 1,800 officers against whom complaints of improper tactics were made from 1986 through 1990, 183 were recipients of four or more allegations and 44 of six or more allegations. It was this group of 44 that Christopher defined as the "problem officers."

The commission also conducted a computerized examination of use-of-force reports involving nearly 6,000 officers from January 1987 to March 1991. Sixty-three officers were involved in twenty or more incidents, and the top 5 percent of them accounted for more than 20 percent of all use-of-force reports. These data also bolstered Christopher's argument that the

LAPD's use-of-force problem was primarily an issue of supervision and discipline. While relatively few LAPD officers used excessive force on a regular basis, those who did were rarely disciplined severely.

It is possible, perhaps probable, that use of force by the LAPD was even more excessive than the Christopher Commission realized. A court order had prohibited the Christopher Commission from examining the records of the officers involved in the King case, on the grounds that this would have interfered with their rights to a fair trial. But even if the examination had been allowed, Officer Powell, the central figure in the beating of Rodney King, would not have made the "problem officer" list. His record, bad as it was, paled in comparison to the records of officers such as Nick Savala, who was identified as "Officer D" in the commission report. In eight years on the LAPD, Savala had been the target of nine sustained and eight unsustained complaints of excessive force. Like Powell, he was nonetheless promoted to serve as a training officer. Savala's conduct had eventually proved intolerable even to Gates, who in 1989 upheld a recommendation that he be fired after a department investigation showed that Savala had punched a handcuffed prisoner for refusing to give his real name. But most of the other 44 problem officers were still working for the LAPD when the Christopher Commission delivered its report.

With complimentary nods to former Chiefs Reddin and Davis, the commission made a strong case for reinstituting community policing but balanced the recommendation with a realistic assessment of the LAPD. "The values underlying community policing, most fundamentally restraint and mutual respect, are most difficult to incorporate into the behavior of officers operating within the LAPD's current professional system," the report said. "LAPD officers are trained to command and to confront, not to communicate. Regardless of their training, officers who are expected to produce high citation and arrest statistics and low response times do not also have time to explain their actions, to apologize when they make a mistake, or even to ask about problems in a neighborhood."

The report cited a declaration issued six weeks after the King incident in which ten metropolitan police chiefs gave their imprimatur to community-based policing. "Our hope is for the Los Angeles tragedy to have a positive outcome by accelerating change toward this new form of policing, in order to better serve our diverse communities," the chiefs said.

Community policing was really an old technique in Los Angeles, as the Christopher Commission recognized. One of the commission's most significant recommendations called for restoration of the community-relations officers eliminated by Gates and Bradley in their notorious concordat after the departure of Chief Davis. "Equally important, the Department must develop and employ tactics that emphasize containment and control, rather than confrontation and physical force," the report said. "Credit for pay advances and promotions should be given not simply for arrest statistics, but for innovation and creativity in developing and implementing crime prevention programs."

Mayor Bradley did not entirely escape criticism, although the commission's rebuke of him was buried deep within the report and received little media attention. The report said that several former police commissioners had complained of a lack of direction from the mayor and added that Bradley's "unwillingness over the years to exert more leadership using the inherent powers of his office has contributed to the Police Commission's ineffectiveness." Furthermore, Bradley had never used his authority under the biennial merit-pay review of the chief to make a critical evaluation of Gates. This discredited Bradley's alibi that he lacked sufficient powers to exert any influence on the police department. But these mild admonishment were from Bradley's standpoint far outweighed by the political benefits of a report calling for Gates' ouster.

The Christopher Commission report was far from perfect. It extrapolated too much about racism and sexism from a small selection of computer messages that were heavily padded with innocuous comments, and it unfairly suggested that Gates was to blame for declining physical standards at the Police Academy, where the traditional 60 percent graduation rate had soared to 90 percent. Gates was right in saying that he was "stuck with lower physical standards as the result of a court-ordered consent decree mandating the hiring of more women and minorities." He also had some basis for saying that he had made the system work despite his own opposition to female police officers.[39]

But in its totality, the Christopher Commission report was an impressive and penetrating indictment of the Los Angeles Police Department and its "siege mentality." The accumulation of data, interviews, and analyses made a case that minorities and, indeed, ordinary citizens of any race or ethnic group had reason to fear the police who were supposed to serve and protect them. The commission had examined the LAPD culture and found it inadequate for a modern, multiethnic society. Most important, the report outlined the path to a more accessible police force, one that would abandon the *Dragnet* legacy, respect the people of Los Angeles, and observe their constitutional rights.

Gates denounced the report as a "travesty." He had given his life to the LAPD, and some of his innovations—especially the DARE program—had become national models. Even the Christopher Commission report had recognized DARE as "one of Chief Gates' major achievements, promoting substantial public goodwill toward the LAPD." Now such innovations seemed to count for nothing. As Gates later complained, "The commission tagged

LAPD as a racist organization, composed of back-slapping cowboys out for a night of brutality on the town. Then they complimented us for our honesty and integrity."[40] Gates could not accept this. He was unwilling to be run out of office by people he believed were ignorant of the hard realities of police work.

The refusal of Gates to set a date for retirement overshadowed his largely professional performance in the ten-and-a-half-month interval between the Christopher Commission report and the Los Angeles riots. Despite his disagreements with the report, Gates set about implementing its recommendations. In-car computer messages were monitored, and officers who had made offensive racial or sexist remarks were disciplined. Citizen complaints were investigated, and captains and commanders no longer looked the other way when an officer was accused of excessive force. Gates also vastly expanded the LAPD's embryonic community-based policing programs.*

While Bradley and Sheinbaum were exasperated by the chief's stubborn refusal to set a retirement date, Gates saw himself as the good soldier who was obeying the Christopher Commission's marching orders. In time he even convinced himself that he was the only person who could make the changes the commission wanted. But despite his professionalism, Gates felt unappreciated, melancholy, and vengeful. He was particularly angry at Dotson and Brewer, whom he viewed as ingrates and traitors. When I asked him about this a year and a half later, his anger flared at the thought of what his once-trusted subordinates had done, particularly Dotson. "To me he was useless," Gates said. "I couldn't trust him any longer. He had totally stabbed me in the back."[41]

Brewer was beyond the chief's reach on the Police Commission, which would not allow Gates to demote Dotson. But Gates retaliated by removing Internal Affairs from Dotson's jurisdiction and isolating him from LAPD decision making. "Get the hell out of here," Gates told Dotson after the Christopher report was released. "I don't want anything to do with you. You're untrustworthy."[42] But the quiet Dotson was no more willing than Gates to retire. He went to his office in Parker Center each day and attended to paperwork. He and Gates never spoke.

---

* Gates and Vernon paid lip service to community policing when testifying to the Christopher Commission. But the programs they extolled did not impress the commission, with the partial exception of DARE. A 1985 pilot community service program in the Wilshire district had been discontinued after police response times to crime calls became the worst in the city. The other "community-policing" plan was "Operation Cul de Sac," under which streets were closed off in high-crime neighborhoods while police patrolled on foot and bicycle. But the Christopher Commission said that many officers believed that Operation Cul de Sac's "impact on crime is illusory: when the police operate in one neighborhood, crime is simply displaced to another."

Vernon by default became the sole functioning assistant chief, running the day-to-day operations of the LAPD. Gates treated him warily. He did not fault Vernon's tepid testimony before the Christopher Commission, and he defended Vernon against Brewer's charge of religious favoritism, but he thought Vernon's judgment tended to be erratic in moments of crisis. "He'd do a lot of things that were really right, and all of a sudden he'd make a decision that was just a screwup," Gates said in a statement that could also have served as a self-assessment.[43] After the Christopher Commission report, Gates clung to a tiny inner circle that included secretary Mary Miller, attorney Jay Grodin and his last ally in the LAPD leadership, Deputy Chief Bill Booth. But the chief's real trust was in himself.

Gates had disappointed the LAPD rank and file in the panicky aftermath of the Rodney King incident by assuming that the officers were guilty and urging their prosecution. "I lost a lot of respect for him when he did that," said Sergeant Gregory Dust, a militant LAPD veteran in Foothill Division and a supporter of Laurence Powell. "He was willing to sacrifice others to save himself."[44] Other officers who did not necessarily approve of Powell's conduct also believed that Gates had been wrong to jettison the defendants because he was under political pressure as a result of the Holliday videotape. But when the Christopher Commission called for Gates' ouster, rank-and-file officers rallied to the chief's defense. Overnight Gates became a symbol of the picked-on police officer who, while valued in the abstract, is castigated when the public is exposed to the realities of life on the streets.

Gates tried to capitalize on these sentiments, saying that the politicians who wanted to oust him did not appreciate the dangers of police work. He noted that in the month before the King affair, ten LAPD officers had been fired on by suspects and five of them hit by gunfire. One of the five was Tina Kerbrat, the wife of a Los Angeles firefighter, mother of two, and a recent graduate of the Police Academy. Kerbrat and her training officer, Earl Valladares, were patrolling a bleak industrial neighborhood when they spotted two men walking down a street drinking beer, a violation of the municipal code. Valladares asked Kerbrat whether she had ever written an "open container" violation. "No," she said. Valladares decided that it would be a good training exercise for his partner to write a ticket for the violation. As Kerbrat stepped out of the car, one of the men drew a revolver and fired four times at her without saying a word. One shot struck Kerbrat in the face, and she fell backward into the patrol car, the first female LAPD officer to be killed in the line of duty.[45]

Kerbrat became a hero to LAPD officers. Laurence Powell knew her slightly, and Stacey Koon would later say that he thought of her after the King affair when reflecting on the danger of approaching an unsearched suspect. But Koon thought it was wrong of Gates to hide behind the shields of fallen officers and make himself the embodiment of the thin blue line. Writing in the *Los Angeles Times* while the Christopher Commission was conducting its inquiry, Koon compared Gates to J. Edgar Hoover, who had made the FBI a "role model for law enforcement," then diminished the agency by treating it as an extension of himself. Gates, like Hoover, had once been an effective and innovative law enforcement officer. But his "inflated self-worth" had led him to a false and selfish belief that he was indispensable. Gates had "metamorphosed himself from an individual into the organization" and therefore interpreted exposure of his own deficiencies as an attack on the LAPD itself.[46]

Koon's low opinion of Gates was shared by his fellow defendants and their attorneys, who had not been idle during the Christopher Commission's inquiry. While public attention was riveted on Gates, they were preparing motions for an attempt to transfer the trial out of Los Angeles County to a place more friendly to the police. This prospect did not trouble the prosecutors. California courts had hardly ever granted such motions, not even in notorious cases such as the Charles Manson murders or the trial of Sirhan Sirhan for killing Robert Kennedy.

The lawyers who led Los Angeles had reason to be pleased with themselves in the summer of 1991, when the city basked in the glow of the Christopher Commission report. Justice was about to be done. The police officers who had beaten Rodney King into submission would surely be convicted, and District Attorney Ira Reiner would win reelection in 1992. King's attorney, Steven Lerman, anticipated winning a record damage award against the LAPD. Mayor Bradley, back in the graces of his core constituents and confident that he would soon be rid of Gates, toyed with the notion of running for a sixth term. It was a time of triumph for Christopher, Spiegel, Bradley, Reiner, and Ripston, lawyers all. They had vanquished Gates and asserted civilian authority over the LAPD.

Warren Christopher and his competent band of lawyers had performed a public service in exposing the excesses of the LAPD and the deficiencies of its chief. But none of them recognized that they faced more formidable barriers within their own profession than any that had been constructed by the police. The most effective adversaries of justice would not be police officers but lawyers who wore judicial robes. As the city celebrated, the judges were about to decide the fate of Los Angeles.

7

KARLIN'S WAY

*"We must feel that our lives have value. We must feel that justice is
equitable, that Latasha's death has meaning."*
—Reverend Cecil (Chip) Murray.[1]

JUDGE JOYCE ANN KARLIN OF THE SUPERIOR COURT WAS AN
unlikely choice to preside over the murder trial of *The People of the State
of California v. Soon Ja Du,* if only because she had never before presided
over a jury trial of any kind. Karlin had been a busy federal prosecutor at the
time of the Latasha Harlins shooting. By the time of the trial six months
later, she was, at forty, the newest and youngest judge in the Compton office of the Court.

It is exceedingly rare for a novice judge to launch her judicial career
with a murder trial. But coincidence and a reluctance of senior jurists to
become involved in controversy combined to hand Karlin the case almost
by default. Before she received the assignment in September 1991, during
her second week on the bench, one experienced judge had been transferred
to a civil case because of an unrelated controversy, another had been removed by a prosecution challenge, and still another removed by a challenge
from the defense. Two other judges had dodged the assignment on the trivial ground that the trial would conflict with their vacations. Karlin also
could have refused to take the case, but she was self-confident and unafraid
of controversy. She believed the trial would be a challenge and accepted it
with alacrity.[2]

Karlin, a talented and fiery lawyer, was a self-described movie brat who
was born in 1951 in Caracas, Venezuela, where her father Myron was a film
distributor. He later became the president of Warner Brothers International.
The family moved every few years—to West Germany, Argentina, and Italy
and then back to the United States. Karlin attended schools in Frankfurt,
Rome, Denver, and Chicago and became fluent in German, Italian, and
Spanish. As a child she read mystery stories voraciously, sometimes rewriting

the endings to suit herself. She was nine when she announced her ambition to become a lawyer. "I decided that I would be a lawyer because I was a girl and as such I didn't need to support a family or make any money, so I could defend poor people who didn't have any money," she said.[3]

Despite her girlhood sympathies, Karlin's professional experience suggested that she might be a more desirable judge for the prosecution than for the defense. While attending Loyola Law School in Chicago, she worked at the U.S. attorney's office for a lawyer she much admired, then joined him as an associate in private practice after she graduated in 1974. But Karlin missed her parents, who now lived in Southern California. She moved to Los Angeles and was hired in 1977 as an assistant U.S. attorney at the federal courthouse on Spring Street. Prosecuting accused criminals became Karlin's life for the next fourteen years.

There is no doubt that Karlin was an effective prosecutor. "I can't think of anybody who is more bulletproof," said James Walsh Jr., her boss in the narcotics division.[4] Known by the nickname Joey, the blonde and vivacious Karlin was a head-turner at the federal courthouse at a time when female assistant U.S. attorneys were a rarity. Karlin looked even younger than she was. "I quickly realized that if I was going to get interesting cases, I was going to have to get them on my own," she said. Get them she did. She prosecuted violent crimes and corruption and narcotics cases. In one celebrated trial she vigorously prosecuted self-styled "porn queen" Catherine Wilson, then the nation's largest distributor of child pornography. Wilson, who had been arrested many times but had never been convicted, received a ten-year sentence.

Karlin had a knack for attracting media attention, but she was respected by her colleagues for the thoroughness with which she prepared her cases. She won a conviction in a high-profile corruption case involving officials at Terminal Island Prison. This led to other prison cases, including the prosecutions of members of the Mexican Mafia and the Aryan Brotherhood for murdering inmates in the Lompoc federal prison. Her associate in some of these cases was an experienced U.S. attorney named William Fahey, who became a friend—and eventually her husband. Fahey had an aggressive courtroom style that Karlin realized did not mesh with her gentler, low-key approach. She believed that jurors paid more attention to a female prosecutor than to a male and worked at establishing rapport with jurors. Because of her diminutive size, she often stood away from the podium so jurors could see her. Only once did she lose a trial, and that was a prison case she tried with Fahey.

Unlike many prosecutors, Karlin cared about the people she convicted, sometimes going so far in her concern as to recommend where youthful offenders should be incarcerated. She exchanged letters with inmates, inquired about their treatment and visited prisons. Inmates knew her as Jailhouse Joey and telephoned her with complaints of poor food or insufficient medical attention.

In January 1991, two months before the Rodney King beating, retiring Governor George Deukmejian offered Karlin a seat on the Superior Court. Her husband was now in private practice, active in Republican politics and planning what would prove to be an unsuccessful run for Congress. Karlin was preoccupied with a high-profile prosecution involving three Drug Enforcement Administration officials accused of moneylaundering and drug-trafficking. It was the biggest corruption scandal in DEA history, and Karlin wanted to see it through. She turned down Deukmejian's offer. The three DEA agents were convicted and the ringleader, Darnell Garcia, was sentenced to eighty years in prison. It was a heady moment, and Karlin decided to quit on a high. When Governor Pete Wilson renewed Deukmejian's offer of a judgeship, she accepted and was appointed to the bench on July 31, 1991.

The trial at which Karlin endured her baptism of fire would have been an ordeal even for an experienced judge. Although the legal issues were not complex, the tension on the streets and in the courtroom made even routine rulings contentious. The trial was set to begin on August 26 in Compton, a blighted city in southern Los Angeles County with a tradition of political activism and a black-majority electorate. Charles Lloyd, the attorney for Soon Ja Du, thought that the pressures of trying the case in Compton would be intolerable and had asked for a more neutral venue.

On June 4, another Korean had shot another black to death in a South Central store. As police recounted the incident, Lee Arthur Mitchell entered Chung's Liquor Market on Western Avenue and attempted to use some jewelry as partial payment for a wine cooler. The shopkeeper, Tae Sam Park, consulted with his wife, who didn't care for the jewelry. Park said he wasn't interested, a response that infuriated Mitchell. He made a motion inside his pocket, faking a movement with a gun, and said he would take the cooler. Park shot him dead. A police investigation supported Park's claim that Mitchell had pretended to be armed, and District Attorney Ira Reiner announced that Park would not be prosecuted.

By now, South Central was seething. A black minister led a boycott of Chung's Liquor Market, and on one hot August weekend, Chung's Liquor Market and two other Korean markets were firebombed. One of the targets was the boarded-up Empire Liquor Market Deli, which had been closed since the Harlins shooting. While damages to all three stores were minor, many Koreans were terrified. Mayor Bradley struggled to keep order, appearing in front of the third firebombed Korean market with a plea for peace that was denounced by black militants.

Meanwhile, every hearing in the Du case became an occasion for a demonstration at the Compton courthouse, where blacks and Koreans jostled each other even within the courtroom. Lloyd asked again to have the trial moved. His request was denied, then abruptly granted by Judge Lois Anderson-Smaltz, who noted that a Korean interpreter had refused to work in the trial if it remained in Compton. "My concern is that jurors and witnesses could be intimidated . . . simply by the trial being held here," the judge said.[5] The trial was moved to the downtown Los Angeles courthouse, where tighter security was available, and delayed until late September. This decision disappointed Latasha Harlins' grandmother, Ruth Harlins, who observed that Koreans had outnumbered blacks at the bail hearing for Soon Ja Du in Compton. "Now that we have more support, they want to move the trial," she said.[6]

DOWNTOWN PROVED NO PICNIC. THE DU FAMILY AND LLOYD WERE showered with insults as they entered and left the courtroom and were also frequent targets of telephoned and mailed threats. "Buddha head, we're going to kill you," said an anonymous letter to Mrs. Du. Jurors complained of being harassed in the corridors. Judge Karlin warned onlookers not to approach the jurors and kept careful order inside the courtroom, where spectators were divided into roughly equal groups of blacks and Asians. But Roxane Carvajal, the deputy district attorney prosecuting the case, thought Karlin singled out blacks, rather than Asians, for criticism of disruptive conduct.

Charles Lloyd wanted to avoid a trial entirely. He explored a deal in which Du would plead guilty to voluntary or involuntary manslaughter with an understanding that she would serve no prison time. He argued that Soon Ja Du had not meant to kill Harlins and that Harlins had threatened to kill the shopkeeper. Neither Carvajal nor Reiner thought Harlins had made any threat, and both believed that Du had falsely portrayed her victim as a thief. The only plea that would have been acceptable to the district attorney was a charge of second-degree murder, which by law would have required a prison sentence. This was out of the question for Lloyd.

Demographics put the defense at a disadvantage during jury selection. California juries are drawn from lists of registered voters and licensed drivers, and Asians are underrepresented on both. Asians have the lowest proportion of voters in relation to population of any ethnic or racial group in California, and inner-city Asians are less likely to be drivers than members of other groups.[7] Lloyd dared not hope for Asian jurors. He used all his peremptory challenges against blacks, prompting Carvajal to complain that he was excluding jurors because of race. Lloyd responded that Carvajal had used a peremptory challenge to remove the sole prospective juror who was Asian. The irony was not lost on Karlin, who knew that prosecutors usually want Asians on a jury because they believe they respect authority and take police testimony at face value. The seated jury confirmed Lloyd's fears. It included five African Americans and no Asians. A black was elected forewoman.

Carvajal called ten witnesses: the two child eyewitnesses, four police of-ficers who had participated in the investigation, three expert witnesses, and Denise Harlins, for the purpose of identifying clothing found in her niece's backpack. Carvajal also made extensive use of the security-camera video and of two slow-motion versions of this tape, as prosecutors would similarly use different versions of the Holliday tape in the trials of the officers accused in the King case. One of the slow-motion versions had been marked to show the money held by Latasha Harlins as she approached the counter and the gun in the hand of Soon Ja Du.

Twelve-year-old Lakeshia Combs was a key witness. Except for minor discrepancies, her story was consistent with what she had told the police after the shooting and with her testimony to the grand jury. Du had called Harlins a "bitch," accused her of shoplifting, and started the fight. Combs stuck to her story under cross-examination, firmly denying Lloyd's sugges-tion that Harlins had ever threatened to kill Du. "She was trying to walk out the door," when she was shot, Combs said.

Officer Ralph Spinello, one of the first officers to arrive at Empire Liquor after the shooting, also scored points for the prosecution. He testified that not all of Du's injuries necessarily were the result of being punched by Harlins. Spinello said that when he entered the store Soon Ja Du was in a chair be-hind the counter. Her husband started slapping her, "at first not so hard, gradually to very hard slaps until I had to stop him . . . because of the force he was using." Billy Du subsequently testified that he had hit his wife so hard because he panicked, thinking she was slipping into unconsciousness.

The trial had been going badly for the defense when David Butler, an LAPD firearms expert called by the prosecution, took the stand to testify about the gun Du had used to shoot Harlins. Charles Lloyd believed that the condition of the weapon was a weak link in the prosecution case, which re-quired a showing of intent to kill. The revolver used by Du had been altered to make it excessively easy to fire, particularly by someone unfamiliar with firearms. Had the "defective" weapon not had a "hair trigger," as Lloyd called it, Du might never have succeeded in firing it.

Butler provided grist for this contention. He testified that Billy Du had purchased the gun in 1981 for self-defense. It was stolen from the Saugus market in 1988 during a robbery, recovered by the LAPD two years later, and returned to Du. But it was no longer in its original condition; some-one had made crude alterations that reduced the pressure needed for firing.

Butler testified that the alteration made it possible to fire the revolver with a trigger pull of only one-and-three-quarters to two pounds of weight, if the hammer was cocked, and with seven to seven and three-quarters pounds of pressure, if not cocked. In addition, the locking mechanism of the hammer and the mainspring tension screw of the gun had been altered so that the hammer could be easily released, and the safety mechanism did not function properly. Defense attorneys Charles Lloyd and Richard Leonard were so pleased with Butler's testimony that they decided not to call the firearms expert they had lined up to testify. "Butler ended up being our witness," Leonard said afterward.[8]

The three Dus were the only defense witnesses. Billy Du was questioned extensively about his 911 call after the shooting, which had been recorded on a police audio tape. He said he had reported a robbery because that is what his wife had said to him. Joseph followed his father to the stand, relating the sad story of Empire Liquor. He told of the December robbery at which gang members wearing bandanas crowded into the store and threatened to kill him. He also said that armed shoplifters entered the store as often as four times a week. The gun that his mother had used was there not to stop shoplifters but for self-defense. Joseph said he had been frightened after the robbery and had pleaded with his parents to sell the store. He had also instructed his mother on the appearance of gang members, who wore light sneakers, caps or headbands, and thick jackets and carried "some kind of satchel." Harlins was wearing a baseball cap and jacket and carrying a backpack. Joseph suggested that her appearance was similar to that of a gang member, although there was no evidence that Harlins had ever been involved with any gang.

Soon Ja Du, in her first public statement since the shooting, testified through an interpreter. Her testimony was vital, but she was a problematic witness for both sides. The defense had no choice except to call her, given the evidence of the videotape, but Lloyd and Leonard realized that Du was at times confused and unconvincing. Carvajal had a problem, too. She needed to impeach Du's credibility without inducing the panicky state of mind that jurors might decide had existed at the shooting and was an excuse for it.

On the witness stand Du seemed frail, vulnerable, and older than her years. Her memory appeared to fail at crucial points. The defense thought this reflected the stress of the shooting and the trial, while the prosecution believed Du was faking. Some of Du's assertions, such as her claim that she did not know the English word "bitch" until it was explained to her by her daughter long after the event, struck Carvajal as outrageously untrue. As a witness, Du was at once unreliable and persuasive: unreliable because she contradicted herself and had memory lapses that seemed excessively convenient; persuasive because her frailty made plausible the vulnerability she said she felt when Harlins approached the counter.

There is no doubt that Du had viewed Harlins as a potential shoplifter, although her belief was based more on past experiences, her attitude toward black people, and perhaps on what her husband and son had told her about the methods used by shoplifters than on anything Harlins did. Du testified that she thought Harlins was stealing the orange juice because shoplifters often hide merchandise they want to steal and then buy inexpensive items. She said her belief was confirmed when she politely asked Harlins to pay for the orange juice and Harlins replied, "What orange juice?" Du said she wanted to take the orange juice out of the backpack but couldn't reach it and grabbed the sweater instead. She said that Harlins hit her so hard that "I thought my eye was going to fall out." And she said that after Harlins struck her with an "iron-like" fist, she fell down and thought, "Oh my God, I'm going to die."

As Du recalled it, she grabbed the chair as she fell behind the counter, hurling it at Harlins. "I threw the chair because I thought she had a weapon in her backpack," Du said, even though the videotape showed that Harlins was no longer holding the backpack when the chair was thrown. When Harlins hit her again and knocked her down a second time, Du said her hand touched the gun under the cash register and she rose and picked it up without thinking. "I had no real purpose in taking the gun out," she said. "It just happened to fall into my hand." Pressed on this point by Carvajal, Du said, "I must have extended my hand. It didn't magically fall into my hand." Du said she blacked out after that. She remembered hearing the shot and seeing Harlins disappear but insisted that she had not pointed the gun.

Carvajal's cross-examination explored Du's knowledge of firearms.

"How do you fire a gun?" Carvajal asked.

"I see it in the movies," Du replied. "You pull the trigger."

Carvajal then painstakingly went over the weapon with her, trying to get Du to demonstrate how she had pulled the trigger. Du wouldn't do it. She said she grabbed the gun and "shook" it. The prosecutor put her finger on the trigger and squeezed it and asked Du if that was what she had done.

"No, I'd never seen that before," Du said.

"Your testimony is that you didn't know until today, until just three minutes ago, that you have to pull the trigger in order for the gun to go off?" Carvajal asked.

"Well, because I haven't seen . . . touch the gun, I do know how, how to discharge a gun. I do not know about the pulling the trigger. Now that the D.A. is showing me, I saw that, how the gun is structured, how the parts are structured," Du said.

Du's testimony seemed inherently unbelievable to Carvajal. The prosecutor was convinced that Du understood very well what she had done and knew far more about firing a gun than she had admitted. Would her husband and son, as protective as they were of Soon Ja, really have told her where the gun was hidden under the counter but never instructed her on how to fire it? But Du stuck to her story that she was ignorant of the workings of guns and could not remember firing the weapon that killed Latasha Harlins. Carvajal played the tape that showed Du bracing herself on the counter and firing at the retreating Harlins, but Du insisted again that she had never pointed the gun.

Trial testimony was completed in three days, ending with Soon Ja Du's cross-examination on October 2, 1991, a Wednesday. Karlin set closing arguments for the following Monday. But on Thursday, outside the presence of the jury, the judge issued a ruling that showed her skepticism of the prosecution's version of the incident. The indictment of Du allowed jurors to consider a range of charges from first-degree murder to involuntary manslaughter. But Karlin felt that no evidence of premeditation had been presented at the trial, and she decided that the jury would not be allowed to consider a first-degree murder charge. Soon Ja Du bowed her head and sobbed at Karlin's ruling, which caused a resentful stir among black spectators.

Carvajal had never expected a first-degree verdict, which would have carried a maximum sentence of twenty-five years to life, but she wanted the jury to be able to consider this possibility. She realized that a compromise verdict was possible, perhaps probable, given the racially charged atmosphere and the sympathy that Du was likely to arouse in some jurors. But Carvajal knew (and knew that Karlin knew) that the range of choices available to a jury often influences the nature of a compromise. As the indictment had been presented by the grand jury, the jurors had five choices: first-degree murder, second-degree murder, voluntary manslaughter, involuntary manslaughter, and not guilty by reason of self-defense. Eliminating first-degree murder as an option made second-degree murder the most serious crime of which Du was accused and therefore an unlikely choice for compromise. Typically, although not always, a trial judge will allow a jury to consider the entire range of possibilities presented in an indictment. While Karlin had the authority under the law to eliminate the first-degree murder charge, the prosecutor thought she had abused judicial discretion. With hindsight, Carvajal came to view the ruling as a disturbing sign that Karlin had accepted the defense's view of the evidence.

In her closing argument on October 7, Carvajal raised an issue that would trouble prosecutors in the trials of the officers accused of beating Rodney King. Videotaped evidence can be powerful in a society where people are accustomed to relying on the visual medium of television. But Carvajal worried that repeated viewings of the videotape of the Harlins shooting might have numbed jurors. She had played the videotape for the jury ten times in three days. "And in a sense by doing that we have desensitized you to what you saw the first time, and I warned you originally that what you were going to see was very graphic," she told the jurors. "And when you first saw it, I'm sure that all of you sat back, opened your eyes a little bit wider and said, 'Now, wait a minute,' and it had an effect on you. And now you have seen the tape over and over and over and over again, and it doesn't have the same effect. Don't lose sight of the fact of why we're here, and what we're asking you to do. Don't lose sight of the fact that you see the defendant Mrs. Du in the courtroom every day and you are able to see her reactions and you are able to see her tears and you are able to hear her answers. . . . But don't lose sight of the fact that you do not see Latasha in the courtroom, and you do not see or hear her point and hear her side of the story."

Then Carvajal played the tape again, at regular and slow speeds, effectively dismantling the contention that Du had acted in self-defense. The Empire Liquor videotape, while of inferior technical quality, had significant advantages over the Holliday tape that would be used so extensively in the King beating trials. For one thing, the Harlins shooting had been taped at much closer range, with the camera focused on the counter where the events occurred. For another, the Empire Liquor videotape encompassed the entire incident, providing a more complete picture than the Holliday tape. Because almost all the action in Empire Liquor involved only two people, the tape was also easier for jurors to follow.

Carvajal realized the importance of using the tape to demonstrate the crucial point that Latasha Harlins was not a threat at the moment she was shot. "The minute Latasha turns around the right of self-defense completely ends," the prosecutor said. "Why? You can't shoot somebody in the back." Reading from Karlin's standard jury instructions, the prosecutor reiterated that Du's actions were incompatible with self-defense. And she reminded the jurors of Du's curious testimony: "I had no real purpose in taking the gun out."

When the jury returned after a luncheon recess, Carvajal methodically dissected Du's claim that she knew nothing about guns and had not fired with intent to kill. "Mrs. Du will only tell you certain things, only certain things that she wants you to know so that you can draw certain inferences and nothing else," Carvajal said. "And you have to continually keep asking yourself, why, why, why?

"When she gets the gun, did she put her finger in the trigger? Well, we don't know from her because she won't tell us. Why did she point it in the direction of Latasha and not shake it like she said [that's] how you shoot a gun? She didn't do that. She pointed it.

"Did she tell us she put the finger in the trigger? She wouldn't tell us that. But she had to. In order for the gun to go off, she had to. Did she tell us why she braced herself on the counter? Look at the tape. She braces herself . . . Did she tell us why she's got two hands on the gun? This is somebody who knows nothing at all about guns, who's hardly ever even seen it on television. She knows now, brace herself and brace the gun with two hands. And if you look at the tape and if you look at the slow motion tape and if you look at the enhanced version, you can see she puts her hand under [the gun], and she braces herself."

Carvajal explored other contradictions in Du's testimony. Du testified that after Harlins was shot, she didn't know where Harlins was: "She was there a minute, and she was gone the next." But the videotape showed Du peering over the counter, and she must have known that the body was there. When Carvajal had asked Du whether she was afraid that "Latasha was going to come up and get you," the defendant had answered, "Yes, I was afraid of that." But the tape showed that Du continued to peer at the body. "She stays right there because she knows Latasha is down," Carvajal said. "She can see her."

Carvajal also reviewed the testimony of Billy Du and Joseph Du, quoting contradictory statements they had made in their efforts to put Soon Ja in the best light. She noted, however, that father and son had been consistent in saying that Soon Ja had told them that Latasha was heading for the cash register. Soon Ja had mentioned this to her husband immediately after the shooting, when she was supposedly dazed and confused. But she had said it again to her son three days later, as Joseph had acknowledged on cross-examination after a pause. Without ever saying so directly, Carvajal suggested that Du was not the frail, confused woman of her self-portrayal but an angry shopkeeper who had made a misjudgment, reached for a gun, and deliberately shot a girl who was walking away from an argument. "You've seen goal-oriented behavior, and you've seen somebody do such a dangerous, intentional act that the natural consequences would be death, and it didn't matter," Carvajal concluded after two-and-a-half hours of argument. "She did it anyway. And that, ladies and gentlemen, is murder, and that's what the defendant is guilty of."

Then it was the defense's turn, with Richard Leonard making the closing argument. While he lacked Charles Lloyd's intensity, he efficiently presented the defense view of the evidence. He called the Harlins shooting "a tragedy . . . a no-win for both sides," and urged jurors to use the videotape to see how hard Du had been struck by Harlins. The lapses in Du's memory resulted not from deception but from the impact of these blows, Leonard argued. "Don't forget this is a woman who was punched repeatedly by this young lady, fell to the floor at least twice, and came back up and got out a gun . . . If you're punched like that . . . you might have a hard time remembering exactly what had happened during that short period of time."

Leonard cited the testimony of a doctor called by the prosecution who had said that Latasha Harlins had scars on her right knuckles that were not the result of recent injuries, suggesting that she knew how to use her fists. "She threw a punch like somebody who had fought before because every time Mrs. Du came back up, she whacked her again. Came back up, whacked her again, punched her down. And those just weren't light punches, ladies and gentlemen, they were forceful punches. And Mrs. Du got hit either three times or four times and went down twice." Later, Leonard returned to this theme, saying of Latasha, "Take a look at her knuckles. She punched awfully hard, possibly tough as any guy at that same age."

The defense attorney urged jurors to walk in Mrs. Du's shoes. "You have to look at Mrs. Du's state of mind that morning, what was happening that morning," Leonard said. "Take a look at the tape and see how fast everything transpired." It was easy to criticize Mrs. Du's actions with "Monday morning quarterbacking," but she was in pain and feared for her life.

Leonard made the obligatory argument that his client was innocent, although he knew there was little realistic chance of a nonguilty verdict. A jury would need to find that Du shot Harlins in self-defense or accidentally in order to acquit her. Leonard's goal was a verdict of involuntary manslaughter, the least serious crime of which Du was charged. "From the defense standpoint [this case is] one of three things," he said. "It's an accidental shooting. [Or] self-defense. And if you don't buy these two, ladies and gentlemen, then at worst you have what we call the imperfect self-defense. In other words, she used too much force, and it's an involuntary manslaughter. Let me tell you what it is not. It is not murder."

Carvajal understood that it was necessary for Leonard to portray Harlins as the aggressor and Du as the victim, but she was angered by the argument nevertheless. Du had shot Harlins to death, falsely depicted her as a thief, and exaggerated her own injuries. In her rebuttal, Carvajal showed the jurors the defense exhibit of Du with a black eye and contrasted it with the picture of Harlins lying dead in a pool of blood. "And they want you to believe that, when you are threatened with this kind of injury, you can do this," she said, pointing to the two pictures. "No, you can't. Absolutely not. The law does not provide for that. That is not the type of society we have."

Carvajal then turned to the "defective" gun, as it had been described by Leonard and Lloyd. "The gun works," she said. "The gun works when it's dry fired or when it's got bullets in it. It is not a defective gun, it is an altered gun. The gun does not work unless you put your finger in the trigger. You have to do that." And that is what Soon Ja Du had done when she shot and killed Latasha Harlins. She had shot her not because of anything that Harlins had done but because Du was fed up with the constant strain of operating the store in a crime-ridden neighborhood. "Her son's been burglarized, threatened, shoplifted," said Carvajal. "She's had it. She doesn't want it, anymore. She doesn't want to deal with it. She's going to deal with it the way she knows how and that was by taking that gun and pointing it at Latasha and shooting and killing Latasha."

Jury deliberations in *People v. Soon Ja Du* began the next day, October 8, a Tuesday. They were interrupted for several hours on Wednesday after two reporters told the judge about an argument between two black male jurors who were talking about the case outside the courtroom in violation of standard instructions that permit discussion only in the jury room when all jurors are present. Andrea Ford, who had covered the trial for the *Los Angeles Times*, quoted one of the jurors as saying: "It's hard to convince a jury that she thought that gun would fire if she shook it. That's insulting to my intelligence."[9] But Karlin found insufficient grounds for declaring a mistrial.

On Friday afternoon, on the fourth day of deliberations, the jury returned a compromise verdict of voluntary manslaughter. Du lowered her head and wept silently. Outside the courtroom, Denise Harlins said Du had "got away with murder. The judicial system let her get away with murder. There is no justice." Carvajal said she was pleased that the verdict was voluntary manslaughter rather than involuntary manslaughter but acknowledged that jurors felt sympathy for Mrs. Du "and may have compromised in her behalf." Lloyd said: "There's no victory for anybody. This was just a really very sad, heart-wrenching, soul-searching case."[10]

It was also the kind of case, a serious crime involving a defendant with no criminal record, in which probation reports traditionally are influential. These reports are based on a review of the facts plus interviews with the defendant, family members, police investigators, attorneys for both sides and other interested parties. While not binding, they often guide a judge's sentence. It seemed especially likely that the probation report would be influential in the Du case because of Karlin's inexperience on the bench. Du faced a maximum term of eleven years in prison on the voluntary manslaughter conviction plus an added five years for using a gun. The district attorney sought the maximum sentence, while the defense asked for probation.

DESPITE THE INITIAL ANGER OF THE HARLINS FAMILY AND BLACK militants, the verdict won grudging acceptance from moderate leaders in both the African-American and Korean communities. "In my view, justice has been done by the verdict," said Joseph Duff, the president of the Los

Angeles chapter of the National Association for the Advancement of Colored People. "A person had been found criminally guilty of killing, and I think that's pretty damn important." Jerry Yu, executive director of the Korean-American Coalition, said there was sympathy for Du among Koreans, "but, on the other hand, just because we are Korean, that doesn't mean we wanted her to get off. There has to be justice."[11]

The probation report in *People v. Soon Ja Du* was thorough and extensive. Patricia Dwyer, the probation officer, went beyond the trial record in trying to form an opinion of Du's intentions and beliefs. She interviewed a police officer and a doctor who had not been called as witnesses, talked to Denise Harlins and Ruth Harlins, and twice interviewed Soon Ja Du, trying to draw out her feelings about Latasha Harlins.

Du did not do well in these interviews. Lloyd had cautioned her to be careful about what she said to the probation officer, particularly in expressing negative opinions of blacks. This canny lawyer from Mississippi had painful experience of racial discrimination. Lloyd had hauled himself up by his brains and his bootstraps to make it in a white man's world, but he had no illusion that race relations in America were improving. Lloyd believed that racism was prevalent among Koreans, who wanted to be accepted in the white world and whose relationships with blacks were often forged on the front lines of the nation's violent urban conflict. He worried that Soon Ja Du might share her negative stereotypes of black people with a white probation officer under the assumption that all whites are racist. And this is exactly what Du did. Responding to Dwyer's question about her impressions of black people, Du said in broken English that they were lazy and spent welfare checks on liquor instead of their children.[12]

When he read Du's comments in the probation report, Lloyd thought they were an honest expression of insensitivity that reflected her naivete. A white defendant in Du's shoes would have known better than to express open prejudice, but Du was unsophisticated. "She thought all white people sided with Koreans," Lloyd said. "And she went to a probation officer who was a white woman, and it was just the opposite. [Dwyer] nailed Mrs. Du to the cross."[13]

Dwyer was certainly bothered by Du's racism, but she was even more concerned with Du's apparent lack of remorse. Soon Ja Du had come to the probation office without an appointment two weeks after the conviction, accompanied by her husband, Joseph Du, Sandy Du and Darryl Dupuy, a family friend. It was a chaotic meeting in which Soon Ja spoke alternately in English and Korean and Sandy translated for her mother. As Dwyer tried to focus on Soon Ja Du's perceptions, family members frequently interrupted in an effort to clarify her answers. Dwyer concluded that Soon Ja "did not accept responsibility for the offense and expressed no remorse for what had occurred." She scheduled another interview to explore Soon Ja's attitudes more fully and saw to it that an official Korean translator was present.

It was at this second interview that Soon Ja, accompanied this time only by her husband and Dupuy, expressed her low opinion of black people. Dwyer was now able to talk to Du through the interpreter, but the probation officer still found her oddly unresponsive. When Dwyer asked Du what she would change if she could live through the situation again, Du said that she was too afraid to work and that blacks had recognized her and shouted threats at her as she entered the building. Dwyer asked Du again about her feelings concerning the event. Du said it was a "painful, painful experience" and that she had not known Harlins was so young. Dwyer once more encouraged Du to express her feelings about Latasha Harlins, but Du's thoughts were on herself and her family. She said she would have done the same thing if the person who hit her was "black, white or yellow" because she had feared she was dying. "I feel pain when I see my family suffering," Du said. "My mother came from Korea. She is 78 years old. . . . I wish the world would change so that everyone trusted each other."

Dupuy must have recognized that the interview was going badly. He interrupted and encouraged Du to relate purported conversations in which she had expressed regret for the death of Harlins. But this produced a response more offensive to the probation officer than anything Du had said previously. "It didn't come to my mind right away. . . . [I] found out she was such a young girl. . . such a painful experience . . . I pray for her, thinking that if she was born in a better family, better situation she could have been leading a much happier life . . . She made me suffer so much, and she suffered tragedy, too."[14]

It is not surprising after this interview that Dwyer took a dim view of Du as a candidate for probation, particularly since there were suggestions that Du had faked the extent of her injuries at the hands of Harlins. Dr. Joann Williams had examined Du at Martin Luther King Jr. Hospital/Drew Medical Center, where she was tested for neurological damage and eye injuries. Du had suffered only a black eye, and the medical staff concluded that she had feigned unconsciousness during her stay at the hospital. "Psychomotor testing indicated that defendant was in fact conscious, and staff observed the defendant sitting up and alert when she believed she was not being watched by hospital personnel," Dwyer wrote after an interview of Dr. Williams.

J.C. Johnson, an LAPD lieutenant who had reviewed the investigating officers' reports and studied the videotape of the shooting, also believed that Du had exaggerated her injuries and feigned symptoms of emotional distress after her arrest. He was persuaded that Du's shooting stance belied her claim that she was unfamiliar with firearms. Johnson concluded that Du had tried "to create a false impression to the jury by claiming complete inexperience with weapons and a lack of knowledge as to how they are held." He advocated the maximum sentence to avoid sending a message that it was acceptable to "shoot a fifteen-year-old kid over a $1.79 bottle of orange juice."

Dwyer was sympathetic to the Harlins family. She quoted Ruth Harlins as saying of Du, "She has taken my granddaughter, my laughing and my joy . . . even my happy memories bring me pain." The probation officer wrote that the entire family believed "that the defendant has no remorse or regret for her actions and that any tears she has shed have been only for herself." Dwyer's report also said that she had no doubt that Du was "the loving wife and mother described by her family, friends and well-wishers and that she has led an exemplary life as a hardworking, law-abiding and Christian woman." She noted that since Du was "unlikely to repeat this or any other crime," the arguments for "leniency or mercy are compelling." But the incident had revealed "serious flaws" in Du's character. "She admits to a regard for black citizens tinged with suspicion, fear and contempt," Dwyer wrote.

> It was this attitude that caused her to set in motion a chain of events which led to the death of a 15-year-old child. The girl who approached the counter with money in her hand, presumably to pay for the orange juice, was confronted by the defendant, accused of theft and physically accosted. While the victim may have responded with excessive force, the defendant's response was horrifying . . . in an uncontrollable rage [she] shot the girl in the back of the head as she attempted to leave.

Du's psychiatrist, family, and friends had expressed regret for the killing and Du had written a letter to Judge Karlin about her feelings, but Dwyer concluded that "any guilt or remorse the defendant holds in regard to this offense is related to the prosecution of the case and the possible consequences. While the defendant's feelings are understandable, they cannot be justified." Dwyer decided that probation was not suitable for Du: "This was an aggravated crime based upon the youth of the victim and the defendant's callousness in shooting her as she was leaving the area," she concluded. "Of considerable concern is the defendant's response immediately after the offense as she took no action to assist the victim, exaggerated her injuries and feigned unconsciousness. This can only be viewed as a deliberate attempt to manipulate public opinion and underscores her unrepentant attitude." Dwyer recommended that Du receive the maximum sentence of sixteen years.

The report pleased Carvajal, who thought that the call for a maximum sentence would make it difficult for Karlin to grant probation. Lloyd was bothered by the report for the same reason. He suspected that Karlin was sympathetic to his client but worried that the negative report would make it impossible for the judge to resist the clamor for a prison sentence. Lloyd had obtained probation for nineteen clients convicted of voluntary manslaughter, some in cases in which the killing was less equivocal than the shooting of Harlins. In none of these cases, however, had there been such pressure on the judge to send his client to prison.

Karlin, who made up in brashness what she lacked in experience, was marching to the beat of other drummers. She had the courage of her convictions. She felt sympathy for Du and her family and empathized with their struggle to succeed under fearful conditions. As the judge watched the videotape, she understood why Du had found Harlins menacing. Karlin also was convinced that Du had been dazed by Harlins' blows and that the altered gun had been too easy to fire.[15] She believed Du's declarations that she had not meant to kill Harlins, a claim the jury had rejected when it reached a verdict of voluntary manslaughter. Most important, Karlin believed Du's claim that she had been attacked in jail and could not withstand time in prison. "If you send me to jail, I will go mad, the ten days spent in jail because of this ordeal has proven that," Du had written in her letter to the judge.

While Karlin was pondering probation, friends suggested that she could defuse the political impact of a lenient sentence by sending Du to prison for a ninety-day medical and psychological evaluation. This procedure is commonly used in California by judges who seek additional medical information before imposing final sentence, particularly if the sentence might be controversial. But Karlin wondered whether such an evaluation had any purpose other than to "take the heat off" her. She had already read a defense-arranged psychiatric evaluation of Du. This confidential report, highly sympathetic to the convicted shopkeeper, reinforced the judge's belief that Du's life was threatened by even a limited prison term.

Still, Karlin paused. She asked whether Du would be separated from the general population if sentenced to an evaluation, and she received conflicting information from authorities. Karlin also inquired whether a Korean-speaking interpreter would be available for Du in prison. Once more, the answers were equivocal. Typically, Karlin decided to find out for herself. She and her husband drove to the California Institution for Women at Frontera near San Bernardino east of Los Angeles, where Du would have been imprisoned during an evaluation.

What Karlin found at Frontera confirmed her worst fears. There was no separate diagnostic center where prisoners who were being evaluated were kept apart from other inmates. There were no Korean prisoners and no interpreter. Karlin happened to arrive at the prison soon after a violent incident in which one inmate had cut the throat of another. The victim was being treated for her wounds while Karlin and Fahey were touring the prison medical center. This incident and the conduct of "mannish women, screaming profanities" reinforced Karlin's belief that prison was no place for Soon Ja Du.

Lloyd's sentencing memorandum skillfully exploited Karlin's fears for Du's safety. He cited the case of a retired police officer who had been convicted of assaulting two homeless people. The officer was granted probation because of a perceived danger to his life if he were sent to prison. "Surely those two homeless persons were more vulnerable to a police officer to whom they had the right to look for care and protection than Latasha Harlins was to Mrs. Du. . . . If the retired officer's safety is an appropriate factor for consideration, so should be Mrs. Du's safety," Lloyd stated. He again reminded Karlin that Du had "reported being attacked in jail and mistreated by the inmates."

The defense attorney's memorandum called the shooting of Harlins an "isolated incident," and once more put the victim on trial—a useful strategy in view of Karlin's sentiments. "The facts clearly demonstrate culpability on the part of the victim in an altercation which led to the fatal shooting," Lloyd wrote. "Although Mrs. Du used a weapon, one cannot characterize her 'armed' in the usual sense of the word. . . . The weapon was seized by Mrs. Du in an act of desperation. Mrs. Du was battered, injured and confused when she reached for the gun."

Lloyd still faced the obstacle, or so he believed, of Du's perceived lack of remorse. In an appeal for probation at the sentencing hearing, Lloyd said that Du was being made a scapegoat for the hard times of the black community. "They're appealing to the ugliest things in our society," Lloyd said. "They are saying Mrs. Du isn't remorseful. As an officer of the court, I can assure this court she is very remorseful, apologizes to the family, and we understand if you don't accept it."

The problem with this argument was that it reflected Lloyd's feelings more than Soon Ja Du's. While the record of Du's statements about the killing is replete with expressions of regret, virtually all of them deal with the impact on Du and her family. This preoccupation was particularly evident in Du's letter to Karlin, dated October 25, written in Korean and translated by Sandy Du. In this letter she described the killing as "a horrifying accident" that happened unexpectedly.

"Even to this day I can't believe something like this could happen to our family," Du wrote.

> I feel like I am suffering in a nightmare. I am sad and overwhelmed by the incident, and I find myself wondering, only if my eyes weren't suffering from the iron like punch, only if I was fully aware what I was doing something like this would have never happened.

Through this accident, I emphasize with Natasia Harlins family and friends. Being a mother myself, I full share in the sorrow Natasia's mother must be feeling.

This statement, more than anything else that Du had said, infuriated the Harlins family and outraged Carvajal. Here it was seven months after the shooting, and Du had not bothered to learn the name of her victim or the most basic facts about her short life.

"Your honor, she doesn't even know that Latasha's mother is dead," Carvajal said, her voice rising. "She doesn't know Latasha's name. She doesn't know anything about Latasha's background. She's made absolutely no effort to get to know who she killed. As I'm sure the court read [in] the psychological report, what bothered me the most is whenever she was discussing how she felt about the killing, it had to do with how it had affected her. It didn't have to do with the fact that she killed a fifteen-year-old girl. It had to do with how it affected her and her family and her husband and her children and the fact that now, back in Korea, she has lost face."

Carvajal scoffed at Lloyd's comparison of Du with the retired policeman who had assaulted two homeless people and received probation. How could assault be compared with the killing of a child? It was wrong of the defense to imply that it was "Latasha's own fault that she was dead." It would be unjust to allow Du to escape punishment because of her fears about being placed in a prison where inmates might despise Koreans or other Asians. "Latasha's life was taken away from her," said Carvajal with great emotion. "She was taken away from her family, from her friends. Defendant has to be punished. She has to suffer. . . . By sentencing the defendant to the maximum term, this court would be protecting society not only by removing the defendant from society but also by demonstrating to the community that our justice system and society do not and will not tolerate the senseless killing of a child by a gun-wielding merchant. Any other sentence, your honor, would create a perception in the mind of the community that young black children do not receive the full protection of the law. The people strongly urge this court not to treat Latasha's life as if it were worthless because it was not."

Neither the prosecution nor the defense knew what to expect from Karlin after this speech. Both sides realized that the judge was sympathetic to Du, but probation seemed a reach in light of the probation report and Du's attitude about the shooting. Lloyd tried again on the latter point, saying that Du's supposed lack of remorse was "a language thing" that reflected her difficulty with English and uncertain translation. Once again Lloyd reminded Karlin of the dangers that Du faced in prison. "Mrs. Du has to have security to come into this courtroom, an American courtroom, in broad open daylight. She was in custody for ten days and complains that she was beaten there. Your honor, it's sad, but I beg you, please, please, don't put her in jail . . ."

Karlin asked what would be gained by putting Du in prison.

"My response to that is the one word, and it's very simple," Carvajal replied. "Justice. And that's what we're supposed to be doing here."

A final plea for punishment was made by Ruth Harlins, Latasha's doting grandmother. She said her family had been devastated by the loss of Latasha. "Soon Ja Du has taken the life of a fifteen-year-old child, my granddaughter, and I believe that she should get the maximum sentence for the crime that she has committed, and I would be very disappointed if Soon Ja Du got away with probation," she said.

The appeals of Carvajal and Ruth Harlins fell on deaf ears. Karlin had decided before she came to court on sentencing day, November 15, 1991, what she wanted to do. She had written out what she wanted to say, although she was not required to comment on her sentence.[16] Unlike the federal system, where judges are bound by rigid guidelines and must explain any departure from the standard sentence, California guidelines allow judges considerable sentencing discretion for many crimes. But Karlin realized that the public expected an explanation of her sentence, and she felt a duty to give one.

Karlin began by saying that nothing anyone could do would lessen the loss suffered by the Harlins family. But something good could come from Latasha's death if it forced the African-American and the Korean communities to confront an "intolerable situation" by "creating solutions" so that similar tragedies would never be repeated. "I agree with Mr. Lloyd that now is a time for healing," Karlin said. "It is not a time for inflicting greater damage in these communities. It is not a time for rhetoric which served no purpose other than to fuel the fire. It's like throwing gasoline on a fire that's already burning and at best is counter-productive. To suggest that any sentence that this court might give results in the conclusion that young black children don't receive full protection of the law—I'm sorry, Miss Carvajal, but that is dangerous rhetoric, and that is unjustified."

Denise Harlins and Ruth Harlins could not believe what they were hearing. Neither could Andrea Ford of the *Los Angeles Times*, who had covered the trial with notable objectivity. Ford was a reporter, but also a black woman with teenage children. She could understand why Karlin might give a lenient sentence but not why the judge was blaming the black community for what had happened. Didn't Karlin know that South Central was on edge? How could freeing Du promote healing? Carvajal, too, was stunned. As Karlin spoke, she realized that the judge had accepted the defense argument that the victim was to blame for her death. The jury's determination that the killing was intentional meant nothing. Soon Ja Du was going to walk.

Karlin continued. "This is not a time for revenge, and it is not my job as a sentencing court to seek revenge for those who demand it," she said. "There are those who have demanded publicly the maximum sentence in the name of justice as Miss Carvajal just did. But it is my opinion that justice is never served when public opinion, prejudice, revenge or unwarranted sympathy are considered by a sentencing court in attempting to resolve a case. In deciding what sentence should be imposed in this case, I am required by law to consider Mrs. Du as an individual in the context of the crime [of] which she's been convicted. No matter what sentence the court imposes and despite arguments to the contrary, Mrs. Du will be punished for the rest of her life. This is a crime that she will have to remember and live with every day of her life. Her failure to verbalize her remorse to the probation department I find to be much more likely a result of cultural and language barriers rather than an indication of a lack of true remorse."

Karlin ticked off the objectives of the California sentencing guidelines: protection of society, punishment, encouragement of the defendant to lead a law-abiding life, deterrence, isolation of the defendant to prevent her from committing other crimes, restitution, and uniformity in sentencing. Although most people convicted of voluntary manslaughter in nonvehicular cases receive prison terms in California, Karlin dismissed the uniformity criterion as inapplicable. "Because of the unique nature of each crime of voluntary manslaughter . . . uniformity in sentencing is virtually impossible to achieve," she said. She then turned to the other sentencing objectives.

"Is the defendant a danger to society? I think not.

"Is state prison needed in order to encourage the defendant to lead a law-abiding life or isolate her so that she cannot commit other crimes? I think not.

"Is state prison needed to punish Mrs. Du? Perhaps. There is, in this case . . . a presumption against probation because a firearm was used. . . . In order to overcome that presumption, the court must find this to be an unusual case. . . . There are three reasons I find this an unusual case: First . . . the statute is aimed at criminals who arm themselves and go out and commit crimes. It is not aimed at shopkeepers who lawfully possess firearms for their own protection. Secondly, the defendant has no recent record, in fact, no record at all, of committing similar crimes or crimes of violence. Third, I find that the defendant participated in the crime under circumstances of great provocation, coercion and duress. . . .

"Should the defendant be placed on probation? One of the questions that a sentencing court is required to ask in answering that question is 'whether the crime was committed because of unusual circumstances, such as great provocation.' I find that it was.

"I must also determine the vulnerability of the victim in deciding whether or not probation is appropriate. Although Latasha Harlins was not armed with a weapon at the time of her death, she had used her fists as weapons just seconds before the shooting. The district attorney argues that Latasha Harlins was justified in her assault on Mrs. Du. Our courts are filled with cases which suggest otherwise. Our courts are filled with the defendants who are charged with assault as a result of attacks on shopkeepers, including shopkeepers who rightfully or wrongfully accuse them of shoplifting. Had Latasha not been shot and had the incident which preceded the shooting been reported, it is my opinion that the district attorney would have relied on the videotape and on Mrs. Du's testimony in making a determination whether to prosecute Latasha Harlins for assault.

"Other questions I am required to address in determining whether probation is appropriate [are] whether the carrying out of a crime suggested criminal sophistication and whether the defendant will be a danger to others if she is not imprisoned. Having observed Mrs. Du on videotape at the time the crime was committed and having observed Mrs. Du in this courtroom during this trial, I cannot conclude that there was any degree of criminal sophistication in her offense. Nor can I conclude that she is a danger to others if she is not incarcerated. Mrs. Du is a fifty-year-old woman with no criminal history and no history of violence. But for the unusual circumstances in this case, including the Du family's history of being victimized and terrorized by gang members, Mrs. Du would not be here. Nor do I believe Mrs. Du would be here today if the gun she grabbed for protection had not been altered. . . . The court has been presented with no evidence, and I do not believe that Mrs. Du knew that the gun had been altered in such a way as to—in effect—make it an automatic weapon with a hairpin trigger. Ordinarily a .38 revolver is one of the safest guns in the world. It cannot go off accidentally. Ordinarily, a woman [of] Mrs. Du's size would have to decide consciously to pull the trigger and to exert considerable strength to do so. But that was not true of the gun used to shoot Latasha Harlins. I have serious questions in my mind whether this crime would have been committed at all but for the altered gun.

"The district attorney would have this court ignore the very real terror that was experienced by the Du family before the shooting, and the fear, whether it was reasonable or unreasonable . . . experienced by Mrs. Du on the day of the shooting. But there are things that I cannot ignore. And I cannot ignore the reason Mrs. Du was in the store that day. The Du's son had begged his parents to close that store because he was afraid. He had been the victim over and over of robberies and terrorism in that same store. And on the day of the shooting Mrs. Du went to work with her husband so that her son would not have to face another day of fear.

"Did Mrs. Du react inappropriately to Latasha Harlins? Absolutely. But was that overreaction understandable? I think it was."

And with that, and the comment that "Mrs. Du had led a crime-free life until the day that Latasha Harlins walked into her store," Karlin imposed and immediately suspended a ten-year prison sentence. Soon Ja Du was placed on probation for five years on the condition that she perform four hundred hours of community service, pay a $500 fine, and "pay full restitution to the victim's immediate family for the out-of-pocket expenses related to Latasha's funeral and any medical expenses if there were any."

The courtroom erupted. "Thank you, God," Du cried in Korean. "Murderer," blacks shrieked at Du, who was surrounded by relatives and hustled away while sheriff's deputies separated jostling blacks and Koreans. "I think justice was done," Lloyd told reporters above the din after Du had fled. But Denise Harlins was bitter. Blacks had been told to work within the system, she said later to Andrea Ford. When they did as they were told, the system simply added insult to injury. Outside the courtroom, as some Harlins supporters vowed to take their case into the streets, Ruth Harlins, weeping, seemed beyond anger. Judge Karlin had ignored her plea to consider the feelings of the Harlins family. "It was an injustice," she said in an unbelieving voice.[17]

JUDGE KARLIN NEVER REALIZED HOW DEEPLY SHE HAD OFFENDED the Harlins family and other black people who looked to the courts for justice. She was focused on Du, whose life Karlin thought she had saved with her sentence. The judge's decision, for which she would pay a high price in career and reputation, was motivated by a compassionate belief that Du could not survive in a prison with a black majority. Other judges with less courage or more experience might have shrunk from such an unpopular decision even if they felt as Karlin did, but Karlin prided herself on doing what she thought was right. "It took a lot of guts," said Richard Leonard. "Given the verdict, most judges who felt the way she did probably would have sentenced her to the minimum time."[18]

Put another way, "most judges" might have bothered to calculate the personal cost of leniency in such a high-profile case. Several judges in the Compton court had already made a calculation of self-interest when they dodged the trial assignment ostensibly because it conflicted with their vacation plans but also because they did not want to face the pickets and the protests. These judges did neither Karlin nor the judicial system any favors. The senior jurists who left *People v. Soon Ja Du* to the literally tender mercies of a novice judge were part of the sad pattern of official negligence that was a recurrent characteristic of the Los Angeles troubles from the day of Rodney King's arrest through the riots in 1992.

What was less defensible than the sentence, given Karlin's belief that she was saving Du's life, was the extraordinary insensitivity of the judge's comments from the bench. Karlin, raised largely overseas and in a wealthy family, had no difficulty seeing herself in Du's shoes. But she failed to put herself in the place of Latasha Harlins. Even some of the judge's defenders were amazed at the coldness of Karlin's claim that Latasha Harlins might have faced assault charges if she had not been shot to death. The statement was an affront to the Harlins family. It was also inaccurate. In her eagerness to spare Du from prison, Karlin ignored the fact that it was Du who started the fight.

Latasha Harlins was not the first victim of a violent crime to be placed on trial by those who had victimized her. Victim blaming is standard strategy in rape and manslaughter trials. To the degree that a manslaughter defense is dependent on an assertion of self-defense, victim blaming could even be said to have roots in common law. The right of shopkeepers to use guns to defend themselves is also well established and has a particular resonance in the American West. Lloyd appealed to this sentiment in the sentencing hearing when he cited the legal maxim that "detached reflection cannot be demanded in the presence of an uplifted knife." If Du really had feared that Harlins was about to kill her or if she were so dazed that she did not know what she was doing when she fired the gun, she was offering "the imperfect self-defense." As Leonard had put it in his closing argument, "in other words, she used too much force, and it's an involuntary manslaughter."

But the victim blaming in the Harlins case went beyond any traditional assertion of self-defense. Du certainly feared Harlins, but what she really feared were the blacks who had terrorized her son, or, perhaps, all black people. Karlin excused Du's conduct because she had been terrorized by others of Harlins' race, which was the basis of Du's accusation of Harlins and the reason she started the fight. While Karlin is a conservative, her sentence upheld a fashionable belief often attributed to liberals that criminal conduct can be excused or mitigated because of social conditions. Such defenses flourish in a society in which it is unfashionable to hold individuals accountable for their actions. Lack of accountability is reinforced by the pop psychology of television talk shows that encourage confession, understanding, and acceptance of the brutal or the bizarre. Inevitably, the belief that all victims contribute to their victimization has invaded the courtroom, where experts trained in identifying the biases and predispositions of potential jurors assist lawyers who are skilled in putting a dead or absent victim on trial.

The victim blaming that was offered as a defense in the Du case was also endemic in the Los Angeles Police Department, where suspects who were choked to death or beaten after traffic stops were invariably held responsible by the police officers who killed or injured them. In the two years after the Du case, defense attorneys in a series of Southern California trials succeeded in blaming Rodney King for being beaten by the police, Reginald Denny for having his skull bashed in by rioters, and the Menendez brothers' parents for being murdered by their sons.

What distinguished these trials from the Du case was that the victim blaming was ratified by a jury rather than a judge. Indeed, in the bitter aftermath to Karlin's decision, it was sometimes forgotten that the jury system functioned admirably in *People v. Soon Ja Du*. Jurors, black and white, rejected the prosecution argument that Du had acted with malice, as would have been required for a conviction of second-degree murder; they rejected defense arguments that the shooting was accidental or unintended. Had the jury believed the defense claim that Du was more vulnerable than Harlins, the verdict would at most have been involuntary manslaughter. A verdict of voluntary manslaughter required a finding that Du had intended to kill. Judge Karlin's contribution to victim blaming was that she based her sentence on a premise that the jury had explicitly rejected.

The sentence barely caused a ripple in white Los Angeles. But to blacks it was a harsh reminder of the double standard that too often prevails in the justice system. "If Latasha had been a blonde, blue-eyed white girl with no record, the person who shot her would be in prison," said Leon Jenkins, the black lawyer who represented the Harlins family in civil proceedings against Soon Ja Du.[19] It is even more likely that Latasha would not have been shot had she been white.

Racial violence would terrify white people five months later when Reginald Denny was dragged from his truck and savagely beaten for no reason except his skin color. But there was no similar white outrage when the killing of Latasha Harlins went unpunished. Nonetheless, the Du sentence was an early warning of the firestorm that would engulf Los Angeles, claiming people of all races as victims and taking a heavy toll of Korean shops and markets.

Within South Central, the warning sounded loud and clear. The sentencing shattered the fragile truce that had ended the boycott of Chung's Liquor Market and another Korean store. Community leaders worked to channel black rage into peaceful protests, but they recognized that the mood was anything but peaceful. At a town meeting at the Bethel African Methodist Episcopal Church, one man showed up wearing a hand-lettered T-shirt that said, "Fuck the judge. Justice B Damned!!!" Inside the church the Harlins family sat in chairs usually reserved for the choir and heard Danny Bakewell, president of the Brotherhood Crusade, vow to disrupt Karlin's life. Denise Harlins said she supported the effort "by whatever means necessary."

The Reverend Cecil (Chip) Murray of the First African Methodist Episcopal Church, a persistent voice for calm, could hear the sounds of the riot to come. Murray was one of many African Americans who feared that allowing Du to go free would trigger the "next Watts" as some called it. "The simmering really started with Latasha Harlins and the judge's decision to give Mrs. Du probation," said Andrea Ford, who sensed the anger of other blacks in South Central. "After that it was only a matter of time."[20] Tim Fowler, an African American who was Rodney King's parole officer, was similarly alarmed. He believed that the Du sentence had done more than the King beating to reinforce black perceptions of injustice.[21]

Many Koreans also saw portents of catastrophe in the Du sentence. David Joo, a gun-store manager in Koreatown, could feel the rage of black people on the streets. So could Angela Oh. "The disposition of the Latasha Harlins case was a major factor in the targeting of Koreans," Oh said in 1994. "Even today if people in South Central were asked to name one Korean, it would be Soon Ja Du."[22] When the riots that some blacks called the Uprising erupted in April 1992, the name of Latasha Harlins would be heard in Koreatown.

District Attorney Ira Reiner had no premonitions of rioting, but he was as offended as Leon Jenkins by Karlin's decision in the Du case. "An outrage doesn't begin to describe it," Reiner said two years later, as full of emotion as if the sentence had been handed down the day before. Normally he had no use for "the liberal speak" that complained of double standards of justice. "And then one judge comes along and does an act that is so unjust there isn't anything you can say because words at that point have no meaning, . . ." Reiner said. "Every single person in the black community understood, or at least they believed they understood, what justice was in our courts when they saw a young black child being shot in the back of the head and the person being let off with a $500 fine and reimbursement to the family for the price of the funeral."[23]

The order for the reimbursement seemed oddly "medieval" to Reiner, something that might have been issued if an animal had been killed. He remembered a case two years earlier in which a postal worker in suburban Pacoima had been sentenced to six months in jail for shooting and killing a dog. Was a dog's life really worth more than the life of a black child? Karlin thought such assertions wildly unfair, but they seemed reasonable to African Americans who knew of cases in which blacks had been sentenced to prison for less than what Du had done. "It wasn't a sentence that was handed down because the judge was racist, but I think that even if it's subconscious sometimes, there tends to be less of a value placed on human life when the individual is black," said Lawrence Middleton, an assistant U.S. attorney and an African American who would play a key role in the civil rights prosecution of the police officers involved in the King beating.[24] Certainly, Denise Harlins was convinced that Judge Karlin placed no value on the life of her dead niece. She refused to take burial compensation from the Du family and paid the $3,400 cost of Latasha's funeral expenses with donations from a victim's rights group and community organizations.

Black activists soon made Karlin's life intolerable. They stormed her Compton courtroom two weeks after the sentence, destroying furniture and injuring a bailiff. They picketed her home and harassed her husband. Reiner, meanwhile, carried on a campaign of retaliation, announcing that he would disqualify Karlin in subsequent criminal cases. This provoked a company-line complaint from various judges that Reiner was assailing the "independence of the judiciary." Karlin was eventually transferred to Juvenile Court where she performed with skill and diligence and came to think of herself as a victim on the altar of political correctness.

Los Angeles would not lack for victims in the months to come, but Latasha Harlins was one of the first and among the most significant. The granting of probation to Soon Ja Du ignited a fire in South Central that was fueled by decades of neglect, indifference, and injustice. The fire smoldered through the warm Los Angeles winter and the spring to come, although few white people even noticed the smoke. It would take the spark of the next trial to set Los Angeles ablaze.

8

JUDICIAL NEGLIGENCE

"Here is Rodney King, racing on the freeway. . . . a black man racing toward Ventura County. Just that juxtaposition alone can influence jurors."

—Deputy District Attorney Roger Gunson[1]

IRA REINER REMEMBERS THE DAY THE TRIAL OF *THE PEOPLE OF the State of California v. Laurence Powell et al.* was transferred to Ventura County as the day when the unflappable Roger Gunson used a four-letter word. Gunson is a devout Mormon who rarely swears or uses crude language. He was then chief deputy of the Special Investigations Division in the Los Angeles County District Attorney's Office, where he had worked for twenty-three years since graduating from law school at UCLA. During this time Gunson had served under five district attorneys, earning their respect for his calm professionalism. But he wasn't calm on November 26, 1991, when Judge Stanley M. Weisberg decided to try the officers accused of using excessive force against Rodney King in the East Ventura County Courthouse in Simi Valley. Gunson desperately wanted Reiner to challenge the decision. Otherwise, he was sure the case would go down the drain and Reiner with it.

The Special Investigations Division prosecutes the bad cops whom Warren Christopher had called "problem officers," and Gunson knew from experience that it was never easy to convict even the worst of them. A few months earlier, despite the testimony of sixteen LAPD officers for the prosecution, a racially diverse downtown Los Angeles jury had acquitted three LAPD officers of misdemeanor charges in the Thirty-ninth Street and Dalton raid, where four apartments inhabited by poor blacks and Latinos had been leveled during a futile search for drugs. These verdicts, a surprise even to Chief Daryl Gates, had deeply disappointed Gunson. During Gunson's years at Special Investigations, civil juries had become sufficiently skeptical of the LAPD to award damages to civilians who suffered at its hands. But the Thirty-ninth and Dalton trial showed that juries still hesitated to send police officers to prison.

This reluctance of juries to convict police officers on criminal charges might have made *People v. Powell* a difficult case anywhere, despite the widespread assumption that the videotape gave prosecutors an insurmountable advantage. Gunson believed that the likelihood of convicting four white police officers of abusing an intoxicated black ex-convict who had driven at dangerously high speeds and resisted arrest was especially remote in Ventura County, where blacks make up only 2.3 percent of the population.

Ventura County, an expanse of rolling hills and pastoral valleys northwest of Los Angeles County where split-level homes and shopping malls have displaced citrus groves and farms, has long been a suburb of choice for white families fleeing the violence of the city. Many whites in Ventura County associated crime with black people, especially young black males such as Rodney King, and didn't want blacks living in their communities or driving their freeways. Gunson considered this such common knowledge that he could not imagine a responsible judge allowing *People v. Powell* to be tried in Ventura County, even with a videotape as evidence. This is what prompted Gunson (as Reiner remembers it) to say "shit" when Weisberg moved the trial to Ventura County.[2] "I have never been so horrified in my life . . . . ," Gunson told me later.[3] He was convinced that the inevitable result of a trial in Ventura County would be across-the-board acquittal of all defendants.

NEITHER REINER NOR GUNSON HAD ANTICIPATED THAT THE TRIAL would be moved or that Weisberg would be the presiding judge. The case had first been assigned to Superior Court Judge Bernard J. Kamins, who wanted a speedy trial in Los Angeles County. Before his five years on the bench, Kamins had served sixteen years as a public defender. This experience had convinced him that police and prosecutors sometimes cut corners to make arrests or gain convictions and made him sensitive to any accusations of official misconduct. Kamins had once dismissed felony drug charges despite evidence so strong that even the defense attorney acknowledged that his client was "guilty as sin."[4] But Kamins ruled that the evidence had been obtained by an illegal search and would not permit its use.

Except for cases involving drunk driving, in which he was known as a tough sentencer, Kamins was preferred by defense attorneys and avoided by prosecutors. But his reservations about the police seemed to make him ideal for the prosecution in *People v. Powell*. During pretrial skirmishing Kamins ruled thirty-five times for the prosecution on procedural issues.

Defense attorneys thought him so one-sided that they began searching for ways to remove him. Their first priority, however, was moving the trial out of Los Angeles County.

History suggested that a change of venue was unlikely. California courts have traditionally frowned on moving trials, and all the more so after local governments became financially pinched by Proposition 13, the 1978 initiative that restricted local taxing authority. No trial had been moved out of Los Angeles since Proposition 13 went into effect, and only two changes of venue had been granted in a quarter of a century—a bribery charge involving a city official in 1969 and a child murder case in 1973. The California courts had been especially resistant to changes of venue in highly publicized cases such as the Charles Manson murders, where it seemed probable that prospective jurors anywhere would know of the crimes. Citing the Manson precedent, Deputy District Attorney Alan Yochelson argued that the *Powell* trial should remain in Los Angeles, the state's largest and most diverse county. The King beating was such a worldwide sensation, he said, that the trial could not be insulated from publicity by moving it somewhere else.

Defense attorneys countered that the political situation in Los Angeles, where Mayor Bradley and others were trying to oust Chief Gates, was too volatile to permit a fair trial. A defense-commissioned survey showed that 81 percent of Los Angeles County's registered voters thought the defendants were "more likely guilty."[5] Darryl Mounger, the former LAPD sergeant who had launched his new career as a defense attorney on behalf of Stacey Koon, said: "A lynch mob atmosphere currently pervades the community at a level not tolerated by the court since the days of the wild, wild West. And until the harmful pretrial publicity subsides, no trial date should be set in this matter."

Judge Kamins agreed with Yochelson. Holding up a set of brass scales, he said that he had spent many hours weighing the arguments and decided that a fair jury could be selected in Los Angeles County. On May 16, Kamins set June 17 as a trial date. This was too hasty for the defense, and all the more so because Koon was ill with pneumonia. "The worst part is that [Kamins] consumed so much time with his long monologues from the bench," said attorney Patrick Thistle, who was then representing Laurence Powell. "We didn't know how we could prepare for trial if he remained as the judge."[6]

The prosecutors were not completely delighted with Kamins, either, despite his apparent favoritism toward them. They thought he demonstrated a distracting proclivity for grandstanding that might lead to reversible legal error. Perhaps because *Powell* was his first high-profile trial, Kamins could not resist commenting on media coverage and the evidence. He held a *Los Angeles Times* reporter in contempt for refusing to identify the source of an LAPD Internal Affairs report on the King incident; he held an assistant city attorney in contempt for commenting on the report. Although Kamins eventually reversed himself on these rulings, his actions and comments fueled controversy in a city already inflamed. Rejecting defense requests for separate trials, Kamins said the officers were blaming each other to evade individual responsibility. "If the effect is a shark biting a shark . . . that cannot be prevented," he said.

The defense appeal of Kamins' decision denying change of venue landed on the desk of Joan Dempsey Klein, presiding justice of the Second District of the California Court of Appeal. Klein, then sixty-six, was a distinguished jurist and political liberal who had gained fame beyond California's borders for her battles for women's rights. She had been appointed to the Municipal Court bench by Governor Edmund G. (Pat) Brown in 1963, elected in her own right to the Superior Court in 1974 and elevated to the appeals court by Pat Brown's son, Governor Edmund G. (Jerry) Brown, Jr., in 1978. Although outspoken and at times abrasive, Klein was considered a fair-minded judge who respected precedents and kept her politics outside the courtroom. Nothing in Klein's record led District Attorney Reiner, who thought well of her, to suspect she would move the trial. Defense attorneys had similar perceptions but believed the appeal for a change of venue was a long shot worth taking. At a minimum the appeal would buy time, allowing some of the passions aroused by the videotape to subside before the trial.

While judges in California are political appointees, the judiciary tends to be apolitical. Trial judges are often selected from the ranks of prosecutors without having participated in partisan politics. Joan Klein was an exception. She had been an active Democrat and forthright feminist in her youth and during eight years as a state deputy attorney general under Pat Brown. As a jurist she maintained a keen interest in politics and public affairs. Klein worried about her city. "Los Angeles was a cauldron, with Gates and the mayor and the Christopher Commission," she told me in 1994. "The tape of the beating was playing on nightly TV, every single night, over and over again. You had all of that. Then you had the effort to move this thing. The defense attorneys submitted a very good brief."[7]

Klein's concerns made her receptive to defense arguments that the situation in Los Angeles was too precarious for the defendants to receive a fair trial. While the impact on the city was uppermost on her mind, Klein's record as a civil libertarian suggests that she was also concerned with the rights of the police officers. "Joan is kind of liberal and political but overall a fair judge," said another judge who has known her for many years. "She probably thought she should get it out of Los Angeles to save the city. She also must have believed that some responsible judge would send it to an appropriate place."[8]

Justice Klein granted the change of venue on July 23, 1991, on behalf of
a unanimous four-member court. Her eighteen-page ruling was devoted more
to discussion of the political situation and the media coverage than to legal
issues, and it is difficult to understand from any plain reading of the opinion how a reasonable person could have concluded that Ventura County was
an "appropriate place" in which to hold the trial. The opinion analyzed the
saturation coverage of the King incident and its aftermath in the Los Angeles
media market, of which Ventura County is an integral part. Ventura County
residents read the *Los Angeles Times* and the *Daily News,* the newspapers that
provided the most extensive coverage of the King affair. They watch Los Angeles television stations, on which the KTLA edited version of the Holliday
tape had been shown hundreds of times. They listen to KNX and KFWB, the
Los Angeles news stations. Klein observed that it was impossible to pick up
a copy of the *Times* without finding a story related to the King case. Television coverage had been "graphic and devastating." Radio news was "available around the clock to persons in their homes and offices and to the
hundreds of thousands of commuters on the freeways. Again, it is impossible to listen to any station without hearing stories relating to the latest developments, including jokes, whether it be coverage of a news conference
with the chief, the mayor, or an interview with the 'person on the street.'"[9]

Klein's ruling took only passing note of the fact that the very poll commissioned by the defense to show that most people thought the defendants
guilty also suggested that at least half a million prospective jurors in Los
Angeles County had not made up their minds. And she found the analogy
with the Manson case irrelevant. Charles Manson had been denied a change
of venue, but the nature of the publicity about Manson was "totally unlike
the publicity surrounding this case. The publicity in *Manson* arose from the
nature of the crimes, the manner in which the murders had been committed, and the persons involved. *Manson* was not entangled in local politics,
did not focus on local politicians, and did not involve issues unique to Los
Angeles County."

Klein issued her decision exactly two weeks after the Christopher Commission report, which she referred to in her ruling, and wrote it when coverage of the LAPD and the furor surrounding Chief Gates was especially
intense. She seems to have had the post-Christopher Commission controversy in mind when she declared that it "becomes increasingly more obvious as each day passes" that a fair trial was impossible in Los Angeles County.
Her summation bundled the political controversy and the media coverage
together, declaring that "the totality of the circumstances" required a change
of venue. "We conclude there is substantial probability Los Angeles County
is so saturated with knowledge of the incident, so influenced by the political controversy surrounding the matter and so permeated with preconceived

opinions that potential jurors cannot try the case solely upon the evidence presented in the courtroom," Klein wrote.[10] Selection of the new venue was left to the trial judge.

With the change of venue secured, defense attorneys focused on removing Judge Kamins from the case. Again they found a friend in Justice Klein, who had been astonished when Kamins attempted to block review of his order denying change of venue on grounds it would delay the trial. Barely concealing her contempt, Klein dismissed this "novel issue" in her order granting the change of venue. But although it was clear that she lacked confidence in Kamins, he would have remained the trial judge except for a stunning misjudgment that handed the defense the evidence it sought of the judge's bias toward the prosecution.

While Kamins' denial of a venue change was still under appeal, he had surprised both sides by saying he might be willing to change his mind if doing so would move the case along. To prosecutors alarmed by this apparently new position, Kamins sent a reassuring message through his law clerk: "Don't panic. You can trust me." On the basis of this message, an ex parte (one-sided) communication with prosecutors, the defense asked that Kamins be removed. After an Orange County Superior Court judge ruled in favor of Kamins, the defense appealed to Klein, who took advantage of her opportunity. In a twenty-six page opinion written for a unanimous court, she reprimanded Kamins for engaging in a "constitutionally unacceptable" practice and removed him as the trial judge. "We conclude as a matter of law that the conduct of Judge Kamins was not only improper but that a reasonable person aware of the facts would reasonably entertain a suspicion concerning the judge's impartiality," Klein wrote.

EXIT JUDGE KAMINS AND ENTER JUDGE STANLEY WEISBERG, WHOSE quizzical expressions, balding forehead and dry humor would soon become familiar to Court TV viewers during a series of nationally televised trials. His appointment did not initially seem cause for rejoicing by the defense. Weisberg was the son of a sheet-metal worker who was raised in a then Jewish and now Latino neighborhood in East Los Angeles. Bookish and bright, he attended UCLA, graduating with a political science degree. He obtained his law degree from UCLA as well and upon graduation was hired by the Los Angeles County District Attorney's Office, where he spent nearly eighteen years as a prosecutor.

Weisberg's most celebrated prosecution involved Marvin Pancoast, who was accused of murdering Vicky Morgan, the mistress of Alfred Bloomingdale, with a baseball bat. Although the LAPD laboratory botched important evidence by allowing fingerprints and blood samples to deteriorate, Weisberg obtained a conviction of first-degree murder. In 1986, Governor George Deukmejian named Weisberg to the Superior Court, where he spent a year in the Juvenile Division. Despite his shyness and reserve, Weisberg demonstrated an empathy with children who lacked many of the advantages he had enjoyed. "He was willing to listen to kids and give them. . . . what they needed," said Jeanette Malouf, who represented children in Weisberg's court.[11]

After this apprenticeship, Weisberg was assigned to the Criminal Division, where he was viewed as a competent judge who tended to give close calls to the prosecution. Weisberg's trademarks on the bench were punctuality and skepticism about expert testimony, which he believed confused juries and unnecessarily prolonged trials. Unlike the accessible and opinionated Kamins, Weisberg avoided the media.[12]

By the time Weisberg took over *People v. Powell*, the defense concern that the four officers would be rushed to trial before an inflamed jury was overshadowed by grumbling from community activists that the case had been too long postponed. Weisberg wanted no further delays. On November 22, the day he was appointed, Weisberg said he could try the case early in February and held a forty-five-minute conference with lawyers from both sides to discuss a new venue. He then disclosed that three counties were under consideration: Ventura; Orange County, south of Los Angeles; and Alameda County in northern California, five hundred miles away.

The district attorney's office wanted to try the case in Alameda County, in which the largest city, Oakland, has a black majority. Weisberg said the prosecution had no legal standing to propose a venue, but he nevertheless allowed Deputy District Attorney Terry White to make a case for Alameda County. Orange County was preferred by Michael Stone, a former Orange County police officer who had replaced Patrick Thistle as Powell's trial counsel, and by John Barnett, an Orange County attorney representing Officer Theodore Briseno. But three days later Weisberg said that Orange County officials had told him they had no courtrooms available, which some attorneys told me really meant that they simply didn't want the trial. After rejecting Alameda County as inconvenient and costly because it was so far away, Weisberg chose Ventura County. He said the site would be close and "convenient" for all parties. Best of all, Ventura County had a new courtroom in Simi Valley that was barely used.

Without fanfare or attention to demographics, Weisberg had made a decision that would prove fateful for Los Angeles. His action shocked both Gunson and Justice Klein, who had never imagined that a judge would keep the trial within the Los Angeles media market. When I asked Klein whether Weisberg's decision had surprised her, she answered tartly, "Surprised? Of course. I know of no one who wasn't surprised."[13] Defense attorneys were delighted at a venue that seemed too good to be true. "We never expected that the trial would be sent to Ventura County," said Thistle, who had initiated the appeal. "We thought it would be sent outside the Los Angeles media market, to Oakland or Sacramento or Fresno."[14]

If Ventura County was favorable for the defense, Simi Valley was ideal. Simi Valley and adjacent Thousand Oaks are home to thousands of law enforcement officers who have flocked with their families to eastern Ventura County in search of safety, good schools, and affordable homes within driving distance of Los Angeles. The two communities boast some of the lowest crime rates in the nation.[15] Simi Valley, a community of 100,000 people sixty miles northwest of downtown Los Angeles, was more ethnically homogeneous than most Southern California cities. In 1991, 80 percent of the population was non-Hispanic white, compared to 66 percent for the county as a whole. Only 1.5 percent of Simi Valley's population was black (compared to 2.3 percent for the county), and the community had a reputation as being inhospitable to African Americans. When Simi Valley was being developed in the 1950s, signs proclaiming "No niggers or dogs allowed" proliferated among the multicolored rock formations that are the community's most beautiful natural feature.

The selection of Simi Valley bothered John R. Hatcher III, president of the Ventura County branch of the NAACP. "It concerns me that we're going to have a criminal jury selected from a community where everybody . . . is either a police officer or is a friend of or related to a police officer," he said.[16] Hatcher lived in Oxnard, an ethnically diverse and relatively tolerant coastal city in western Ventura County that had also felt the sting of prejudice. In 1990 the garage of Hatcher's home had been spray-painted in two-foot-high letters with the message, "We Is Apes."

Trying not to gloat, defense attorneys blandly described Ventura County as "a level playing field." In fact, no other California county would have been as likely to produce a jury favorable to police defendants. Even Orange County, which the defense had proposed as a trial site, had more blacks in jury pools.[17] Jo-Ellan Dimitrius, the defense jury consultant, believes that a racially diverse jury probably would have been impaneled in Orange County, which despite a national reputation for conservatism is more settled and self-contained than Ventura County and less preoccupied with the prospect of invasion from Los Angeles. Rodney King had not been driving toward Orange County. In Ventura County, as Gunson said, King was a potent symbol that stirred white fears.

If Weisberg had been willing to move the trial outside the Los Angeles media market, he had choices besides Alameda County, which might have produced a jury with a disproportionate number of blacks and tilted the "level playing field" toward the prosecution. Racially diverse juries are common in

Sacramento and Fresno counties, for instance. Assuming the necessity of a trial site that was easily accessible by air, Sacramento was the venue outside the media market most similar demographically to Los Angeles.[18]

How could a judge with Weisberg's reputation for fair-mindedness move a trial involving alleged excessive force by white police officers against an unarmed black man to a county where the deck was so stacked against the prosecution? His answer is that he did not consider demographics. "As you are aware, the trial court is required to consider the relative costs of transfer and the hardship of the transfer on the parties and witnesses," Weisberg wrote me. "There was no legal authority which permitted the court to consider the relative demographic characteristics of the counties."[19]

This comment is disingenuous. The appeals court decision had encouraged a trial outside the Los Angeles media market, and I know of no legal authority who believes Weisberg stood a risk of reversal if he had moved the trial to Sacramento or another Northern California jurisdiction. The defendants were entitled to a fair trial, and so were the people of the state of California, and demographics were involved whether or not Weisberg took note of them. "It is naive to think demographics will not be a factor in this case," said Geoffrey Taylor Gibbs of the John Langston Bar Association, a black lawyers group, in reaction to Weisberg's decision to put the trial in Ventura County. "This is one of the most important cases of our time, and it seems to me that no expense is too great to make sure justice is carried out."[20]

Aside from demographics, Weisberg was certainly entitled—some would say obligated—to heed the reasons given in the appellate opinion for the change of venue. Klein's ruling placed almost equal weight upon media coverage and political conditions in Los Angeles County. The venue change was granted because of "the totality of the circumstances," and media coverage was an important part of the totality. Weisberg understood this. During voir dire he made a show of determining the extent of trial coverage by the local Simi Valley newspaper, as if this mattered. Weisberg knew as well as Klein that it was the repeated showing of clips from the Holliday tape on television that was "graphic and devastating," not an article about jury selection in the local newspaper. As another Los Angeles Superior Court judge put it: "Weisberg screwed up. If the court tells you that you have to get out of the media market, how can you put it in Simi Valley? It's the same television, the same news. The only thing different was that the jurors were all white. He complied with the technical letter of the law but not the reason for moving the trial. He just went across the border."[21]

Weisberg must have realized that moving the trial to Ventura County would affect jury composition. He has a college degree in political science, and the demographics of Ventura County and its heavy concentration of law enforcement officers are well-known. The county's representatives in the legislature were then the most conservative in the state, and the pro-police attitude of Ventura County residents had consistently been reflected in the performance of the county's juries. Shortly before the Rodney King incident, a Ventura County jury had exonerated an Oxnard police officer accused of brutality. Weisberg also knew from his experience as a judge how difficult it is to obtain criminal convictions of police officers even when the case is strong. He had just presided over the first-degree murder trial of a former LAPD police officer charged with two contract killings. The case had ended in a mistrial, although the officer subsequently pled guilty to second-degree murder. Under ordinary circumstances it seems unlikely that Weisberg would have chosen Ventura County as the place to try police officers accused of using excessive force. But the Rodney King case was not ordinary. In this trial the prosecution had a supposedly unassailable videotape as evidence of police misconduct.

To a great degree, District Attorney Reiner also depended too much on the power of the videotape, as he has forthrightly acknowledged. "I thought the videotape would overcome even a bad jury situation," said Reiner. "I would have been much more reluctant to try a case [in Ventura County and Simi Valley] if we were relying solely on testimony."[22]

Because of his reliance on the videotape, Reiner did not follow Roger Gunson's advice and appeal Klein's decision ordering a change of venue. His legal grounds for doing so were slim—nonexistent, in Reiner's view—since the law allowed an appeal by the prosecution only if its witnesses were seriously inconvenienced by the new venue.[23] Weisberg said after the trial that prosecutors "could have filed a motion requesting me to reconsider or they could have challenged my ruling in the appellate court before commencement of trial."[24] But there is nothing in the record to suggest that Weisberg was open to further argument.

What Justice Klein would have done if Reiner had appealed Weisberg's selection of Ventura County is not clear, even to her. Long after the riots, Klein said she would have considered a writ if Reiner had filed one, but acknowledges that she doesn't know if there were sufficient legal grounds to overturn Weisberg's decision.[25] Klein also believed that the videotape was persuasive and said there was "a widespread feeling" that the location of the trial would not affect the outcome. In retrospect, she said the appeals court should have suggested "that the case should be moved to a location of comparable diversity with some size."[26] But Klein also believes that Reiner should have appealed her change-of-venue decision to the California Supreme Court if he disagreed with it, which he did.

Four months elapsed between Klein's ruling ordering the change of venue and Weisberg's choice of Ventura County as the trial site. Reiner took Klein's order in stride, believing as she did that the trial would be assigned to a comparable urban county. When Weisberg instead selected Ventura County, Reiner asked appellate experts in his office whether he now had grounds for appeal. No, they told him. Reiner's recourse at this point could have been the bully pulpit of the district attorney's office, which he had used to denounce perceived injustices in other cases and which Gunson wanted him to use again. Gunson had done more than use a four-letter word when Weisberg announced the trial site. He had called a friend in the Ventura County District Attorney's Office, who confirmed his fears by telling him that Ventura County juries inevitably took the testimony of police officers at face value. On the basis of this call, Gunson confronted Reiner and said, "If this case remains in Ventura County, it's a not-guilty verdict."[27] Gunson urged Reiner to sound an alarm, to "tell the community" that sending the case to Simi Valley meant acquittals for the officers who had abused Rodney King.

But Reiner refused to speak out against a decision that he believed would stand no matter what he said. While he knew that Ventura County was an awful venue for the prosecution, he rationalized that the videotape was powerful enough to persuade even the most pro-police of jurors and saw nothing to gain by suggesting that the jury could not be fair. Instead of warning the public, Reiner adopted a strategy of false optimism that led trial attorneys to launch their prosecution with a lie. "No, we are not disappointed," Deputy District Attorney Terry White said after Weisberg announced the venue. "We think we can get a fair trial in Ventura County."[28]

But it is Judge Weisberg, not Klein or Reiner, who bears the blame for putting the trial in a jurisdiction that favored the defense. Why did he do it? Weisberg's comments from the bench are insufficient as an explanation. In support of his decision, Weisberg said, "The focus of the court of appeals was on the political atmosphere that had been generated by the media coverage and the unique events that were occurring . . . the political careers that were at stake." Ventura County was the proper venue, he continued, because it "has its own politics, its own political officials and its own police department." This is a curious interpretation. Justice Klein had given nearly equal weight to the media coverage and the political climate and held that these factors worked together to prevent a fair trial in Los Angeles County. By the mental sleight of hand of subordinating media coverage to its impact on the "political atmosphere," Weisberg was able to ignore any adverse effects of this coverage on prospective jurors and claim that he was satisfying the appellate decision simply by moving the trial to an adjoining county. It was odd reasoning for a judge with a reputation of being reflective and logical.

Prosecution and defense lawyers, as well as neutral attorneys and jurists, told me that Weisberg selected Ventura County because he saw no risk in holding the trial there because of the presumed strength of the videotaped evidence and wanted to spend his evenings at home. Simi Valley is an easy commute from Weisberg's home in western Los Angeles County. The new Simi Valley courthouse theoretically was chosen by Ventura County judicial officials, but they consulted with Weisberg, who knew where the trial would be held when he made his venue decision. The only other venue that would have permitted him a daily commute was Orange County, where he would at best have faced a difficult drive of twice the distance. Weisberg denied to me that he was motivated by personal convenience, but he supplied no reason for choosing Ventura County beyond what can be gleaned from the slim pickings of the trial record.* But defense attorney Darryl Mounger did not find the decision peculiar to Weisberg. When a new venue for a trial is under consideration, Mounger said, "the only question to ask is where the judge lives."[29]

MOVING THE TRIAL TO SIMI VALLEY BOLSTERED THE CONFIDENCE of the defense. In the summer of 1991, defense attorneys had been unprepared for a trial before an unsympathetic judge and a racially diverse jury in a city in which public opinion had been inflamed by the Holliday videotape and the Christopher Commission report. But the delay caused by the appeals had allowed time for preparation, even though all the attorneys except Mounger believed the odds remained against acquittal of their clients. Now, nearly a year after the King incident, the defense attorneys were ready for a trial before a presumably more sympathetic suburban jury. They sought to cement their advantage by seeing that no blacks were on the jury that would determine the fate of the officers who had beaten Rodney King.

Race was the silent issue haunting jury selection. Because the Supreme Court had found it unconstitutional to exclude jurors because of their race, the defense could not proclaim its objective of obtaining an all-white jury. The prosecution's lies about being satisfied with Ventura County as a venue were more than matched by the defense's lies about being willing to accept jurors of any race. As prospective jurors were questioned by Judge Weisberg, attorneys and the court behaved for the benefit of the trial record as if racial attitudes had nothing to do with the case. But everyone in the courtroom knew that this was not true.

* Weisberg said in a letter to me that the accusation he moved the trial to Ventura County for personal convenience is "absolutely false." But he has been more guarded than Klein or Reiner—or Judge Joyce Karlin in the Soon Ja Du case—in discussing the reasons for his decisions. Klein, Reiner, and Karlin answered all my questions in interviews, defending their actions in analyses that were occasionally self-critical. Weisberg answered a few questions in two letters, which to the best of my knowledge are the only comments he has made about the case off the bench. He declined to be interviewed. Two attorneys who know Weisberg have told me that his wife, also a Superior Court judge, was ill at the time he made the decision to move the trial.

It is an axiom in police brutality cases that black jurors tend to disbelieve the police. African Americans are more likely than whites to have had negative experiences with police officers, and they are more aware that police rationalize excessive force by saying that the suspect was resisting arrest. In this case, black suspicion of the police was enhanced by the racial comments in Officer Powell's MDT messages. Powell's attorney, Michael Stone, realized that even if the computer messages were deemed inadmissible they could prove damaging to his client if a juror remembered them. And it was hard to believe that a black juror would not remember the talk about "gorillas in the mist."

Stone is no racist. He is a bright former cop who compensated for lack of legal experience with a high level of energy and theatrical skills. While Stone had never tried a felony case in his life, he had won acquittals against high odds in the misdemeanor trials of the officers accused in the Thirty-ninth and Dalton raid. As general counsel of the Los Angeles Police Protective League, he had been assigned the defense of Powell, who was the most vulnerable of the four defendants. Stone knew black jurors, or any jurors with sympathy for King, would be a problem for Powell if a jury reached a compromise in which some officers were found guilty and others were acquitted. Under such circumstances, it was hard to believe that Powell could escape conviction. And Stone knew that black jurors could create the conditions for compromise verdicts. This view was shared by more experienced trial lawyers, such as Johnnie L. Cochran Jr., the preeminent African-American trial attorney who was himself a former prosecutor. "If they had had blacks on that jury, it would have been a different story," Cochran said. "They would have talked about it differently . . . they would have identified more with King. The white jurors couldn't really identify with King."[30]

Terry White, the black deputy district attorney, wanted blacks on the jury, but there was little he could do about it. The jury pool of 260 people contained only six African Americans, replicating the percentage of blacks in the Ventura County population. With a single possible exception, these potential black jurors wanted no part of a trial of police officers at the East Ventura County Courthouse in Simi Valley, a community they considered hostile.

As jury consultant Jo-Ellan Dimitrius observed, Simi Valley compounded the defense advantage of holding the trial in Ventura County.* Inland Simi Valley is a thirty-five-mile drive from coastal Oxnard, the county's most

* Dimitrius gave the white police defendants an advantage in the jury-selection process at Simi Valley, as she would subsequently give the black defendants accused of assaulting Reginald Denny an advantage in their Los Angeles trial. She tried to identify "strong women" who had the potential to become forewomen and guide juries toward verdicts favorable to the defense—as happened in both trials.

THE SHOTS SEEN ROUND THE WORLD

Above: George Holliday's tape was edited for television. Most viewers never saw this early frame, in which Rodney King, at left, is charging at Officer Laurence Powell, who has cocked his baton. *Right:* Here, Officer Theodore Briseno has raised his hand. Later, he said he was trying to stop the beating.

Left: King struggles to his knees as officers order him to the ground to be handcuffed. *Below:* Briseno's famous "stomp." Briseno cannot see Powell, to the right, reaching for handcuffs in his back pocket. Officer Timothy Wind (in front of police car) has stepped back, his baton at the ready.

(Video by George Holliday)

ELDER STATESMAN

Warren Christopher headed the Independent Commission on the Los Angeles Police Department, appointed by Mayor Bradley after the Rodney King beating. On July 9, 1991, the commission, which had concentrated on excessive use of force by the department, issued a searing indictment of the LAPD and its "siege mentality." (Harold Sweet)

TRIAL AND ERROR

Superior Court Judge Stanley Weisberg (*left*) astonished legal experts by moving the trial of the officers involved in the King beating to Simi Valley, a famously pro-police enclave in Ventura County. (Myung J. Chun/*Los Angeles Daily News*) It was a great boon for defense lawyers like Michael Stone (*right*), who represented Officer Laurence Powell. (Tina Gerson/*Los Angeles Daily News*)

Bryant (Pooh) Allen, a passenger in King's car the night of the beating, told the court about the night of drinking and driving with his friend. (Gus Ruelas/*Los Angeles Daily News*)

Above left: Officer Stacey Koon insisted that he and his fellow officers had acted legally and properly in handling what he saw as a dangerous armed confrontation that might end in violent death. (Tina Gerson/*Los Angeles Daily News*) *Above*: Powell had trouble recognizing himself on the videotape. Less than two hours before the incident, in a demonstration at roll call, he had failed to show proper use of the metal baton he deployed against King. (Tina Gerson/*Los Angeles Daily News*)

Officer Timothy Wind (*above*) was portrayed by
his lawyer as a novice who had just followed orders.
(Kim Kulish/*Los Angeles Daily News*) Officer Theodore
Briseno (*left*), who considered Powell "out of control"
during the beating, was branded a traitor by his peers.
(Kim Kulish/*Los Angeles Daily News*)

After the verdicts, the prosecution team (from left, Los Angeles Deputy District
Attorneys Alan Yochelson and Terry White and District Attorney Ira Reiner)
announced that they would retry the Powell case on the one remaining
count against him. (Larry Bessel/*Los Angeles Times*)

The Rev. Cecil (Chip) Murray, pastor of the city's oldest black church, had worried early on about possible trouble in the wake of the verdicts. "Even in anger, be cool," he warned his congregation. (Steve Dykes/*Los Angeles Times*)

But community anger was already high. A few months before, a Korean woman convicted of killing a fifteen-year-old African American named Latasha Harlins had been set free by a Superior Court judge, reinforcing a perception that there was no justice for blacks. Above, the scene of the Harlins shooting. (Lou Cannon)

A CITY EXPLODES

The initial reaction to the verdicts was nothing less than a cry of black rage. Residents of South Central Los Angeles streamed into the streets, hurling rocks and racial insults at passersby, most of them Asian and Latino. (Dayna Smith/*The Washington Post*) Soon much of the neighborhood was ablaze. Eventually, 862 structures were destroyed by fire. (Fred Sweets/*The Washington Post*)

Above: Many Korean merchants were determined to protect their property by themselves, if necessary. Army veteran Jay Shin, above, guarded his Koreatown liquor store. (Fred Sweets/*The Washington Post*) *Below:* Burned cars at the intersection of Florence and Normandie, where the disturbances began. Despite all the warnings, city officials and police leaders were entirely unprepared for the upheaval. In the first hours, when they had a chance to quash the riot at its roots, police retreated—"abandoning the community," in the words of one officer. (Dayna Smith/*The Washington Post*)

In the absence of the police, the riots continued—and their nature changed.
The first furious reaction to the verdicts gave way to massive looting.
Above: A woman takes toilet paper from a South Central shop. (Dayna Smith/*The Washington Post*) *Below:* Another liberates beer from a burned liquor store.
(Dayna Smith/*The Washington Post*)

TOO LITTLE, TOO LATE

Above: Mayor Tom Bradley (*left*), Police Chief Daryl Gates (*center*), and Captain Donald Manning of the Los Angeles Fire Department meet the press. (Bob Halvorsen/*Los Angeles Daily News*) *Below:* Riot police guard Hollywood Boulevard. During five days of violence, 54 died, 2,328 were injured, and property losses topped $900 million. (Dayna Smith/*The Washington Post*)

With order finally reestablished, the cleanup began, joined by volunteers from all over the city and all walks of life. Above and below, workers clear debris from a burned-out mini-mall in South Central. (Fred Sweets/*The Washington Post*)

Angered by the looting, residents of South Central helped police track down those responsible. Above, people accused of riot-related crimes in Los Angeles Criminal Court. (Dayna Smith/*The Washington Post*)

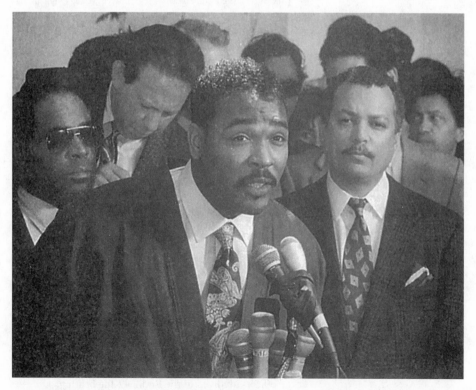

Rodney King had watched on television as people killed, burned, and looted in his name. Horrified, fighting back tears, he stepped before the cameras to utter the most memorable words of the riots: "Can we all get along?" (David Crane/*Los Angeles Daily News*)

UNFINISHED BUSINESS

After the riots, the old order quickly changed. Within less than two months, Willie Williams (*above right*) was sworn in as chief of police to succeed Daryl Gates. (Ray Lustig/*The Washington Post*) By the first anniversary of the riots, Richard Riordan (*left*) was well on his way to replacing Tom Bradley as the city's mayor. (Greg O'Loughlin)

MAKING A FEDERAL CASE OF IT

U.S. v. Koon, the federal trial of the officers involved in the Rodney King beating, had strong political overtones. But U.S. District Judge John Davies was known for a resolute fair-mindedness that was apparent throughout the trial—and in its aftermath. (Youngblood Photography)

The government was represented by Steve Clymer (*above left*), the top trial lawyer in the U.S. attorney's office in Los Angeles, and by Barry Kowalski (*above right*) of the U.S. Justice Department's Civil Rights Division. (Marsha T. Gorman/*Los Angeles Times*) For the defense, Harland Braun (*right*) represented Officer Ted Briseno. (Roger M. Vargo/*Los Angeles Daily News*) Ira Salzman was the attorney for Officer Stacey Koon. (Scott Garrity/*Los Angeles Times*)

Above: Koon (*left*) and his lawyers await sentencing. Judge Davies gave Koon thirty months in jail—a decision that was instantly attacked by African Americans as too lenient, and by police as too punitive. Koon himself thanked the judge for a fair trial. (Myung J. Chun/*Los Angeles Daily News*)

REGINALD DENNY'S TURN

The brutal assault on truck driver Reginald Denny during the riots was inextricably linked in the public mind to the beating of Rodney King: Both had been videotaped, and television stations played the painful footage over and over again, in back-to-back clips. In fact, the two incidents were not comparable— except in symbolizing the city's racial divide. (Robert Durell/*Los Angeles Times*)

In an act of grandstanding that infuriated African Americans—and ultimately backfired—Chief Daryl Gates himself participated in the pre-dawn arrest of defendant Damian (Football) Williams. Above, Williams (*left*) in court with co-defendant Henry (Kiki) Watson. (Myung J. Chun/*Los Angeles Daily News*)

Williams' lawyer Edi Faal argued that his client had been caught up in a "group contagion," and that the attack on Denny had been "a thoughtless and random act of violence" with no intent to kill. The verdict was a major victory for the defense. Williams was convicted only of simple mayhem against Denny and of misdemeanor assault against four other victims. (Ken Lubas/*Los Angeles Times*)

THE NEW ERA

On August 12, 1997, Mayor Richard Riordan (*center*) looked on as a new
police chief was sworn in. Bernard Parks, a highly respected LAPD
veteran known for being a tough-minded manager, was Riordan's
choice to restore order to a badly demoralized police department.
City Councilman Richard Alatorre spoke for many when he called the
appointment "a great day for Los Angeles." His only regret, Alatorre said,
was that it came five years too late. (Ken Lubas/*Los Angeles Times*)

populous and diverse city. Oxnard has more than 40 percent of Ventura County's black population and its largest numbers of Latinos and low-income residents. Oxnard voters frequently serve on juries in the next-door city of Ventura, the county seat, but were underrepresented in the *People v. Powell* jury pool and unrepresented on the jury. The Simi Valley site assured a solidly middle-class jury that gave the defense an advantage of class as well as race. Prospective jurors dependent on public transportation who might have been willing to serve on a jury in the downtown Ventura courthouse were eliminated because Simi Valley is readily accessible only by car. Other prospective jurors potentially unfavorable to the defense were excused on grounds of hardship that in part reflected travel distance. The jury was thus unrepresentative not only of Los Angeles but of Ventura County as a whole.[31]

As Dimitrius had suspected, blacks "self-selected" themselves off the *Powell* jury. She believes that blacks who were called for jury service in Simi Valley "basically were scared" and gave responses on the forty-one-page questionnaire distributed by Weisberg that guaranteed they would be excused. This is not unusual in highly publicized cases, where prospective jurors who do not wish to serve can often be excused by saying they have formed opinions that the evidence cannot overcome. Virtually everyone living in the Los Angeles area had seen the videotape and had an opinion about the Rodney King incident.[32] Four of the six prospective black jurors said on their questionnaires that they had strongly negative opinions of what the police had done to King. Another was disqualified on hardship grounds. Only one black made it into the jury box, and she was removed by a peremptory challenge from Stone. Except for this one black, who had strong opinions and might not have survived a challenge for cause, demographics and Simi Valley's reputation had done the work of the defense. The Supreme Court's prohibition of race-based challenges could not create a racially diverse jury in a jurisdiction where qualified black jurors were in short supply and did not wish to serve.

But the lack of black jurors may not have been the prosecution's biggest problem. As Deputy District Attorney Terry White analyzed responses to the questionnaires, he found a frightening unanimity of opinion. "Everyone seemed to be very conservative, very law enforcement oriented, very pro-police," White said. ". . . They all seemed to come from the same background."[33] Even a prospective juror who had once been stopped because he matched the description of a robbery suspect and was briefly jailed on outstanding traffic warrants harbored no ill feelings toward the police. As he went over the questionnaires, White had a sinking feeling. "I remember thinking as we were rating these jurors [that] we were going to lose this case," he said later.[34] Jo-Ellan Dimitrius, meanwhile, was "absolutely delighted" with the responses to the questionnaires.[35] As she (and White) later observed, the Simi Valley jurors would have been perfect for the prosecution in any case except one in which police officers were on trial.

When a jury was selected, after a month of legal motions and voir dire conducted by Weisberg, the fears of the prosecution and the expectations of the defense were confirmed. Thomas Gorton, fifty, a park ranger and member of the National Rifle Association, said on his questionnaire that "the police have a difficult job to do and for the most part do it well." He was seated as Juror No. 3. Retta Kossow, sixty-five, another NRA member, said: "I would like to know what really happened—not all the 'hype'." She was Juror No. 12. Henry King, forty-nine, was also a member of the NRA. He was a cable splicer for a power company who expressed respect for "the difficult jobs" of police officers. He was Juror No. 8. Charles Sheehan, sixty-five, a retired teacher and Navy veteran who had served in the Shore Patrol, thought that police have a "very tough and demanding job" and believed that the "LAPD is a fine organization." He was Juror No. 6. Gerald Miller, fifty-nine, a retired mental health worker, had been an Air Force military police officer, who said of police that "they try to do a good job in difficult times." He was Juror No. 9.

Best of all from the defense point of view was Dorothy Bailey, a sixty-four-year-old computer specialist and technical writer who had been a civilian employee for the armed services before becoming program manager for a company that prepared technical manuals for the Navy under contract with the federal government. Bailey was circumspect on her questionnaire, saying she had no prejudices for or against the police, but she had the look of a leader, and Dimitrius wanted her on the jury. Believing that she fit the profile of a juror who was likely to hold to a high standard of reasonable doubt, Dimitrius rated Bailey first among the 260 prospective jurors. Bailey became Juror No. 11 and was subsequently elected forewoman of what Dimitrius called "this gem of a jury."[36]

Overall, four of Dimitrius' top ten choices wound up on the jury, and every other juror was in the upper 50 percent of her rankings. Terry White understood what was happening, but his analysis of the questionnaires convinced him that the defense had more peremptory challenges than there were pro-prosecution jurors in the entire pool. White declined to challenge Bailey or other jurors who were low-rated by the prosecution because he was convinced they would have been replaced by jurors who were even more favorable to the defense.

It was a sign of White's desperation that he looked with relative favor on two jurors who had familial ties to the police. Christopher Morgan, forty-three, was a telephone company service technician whose brother was a retired LAPD sergeant. He probably would have been routinely excused in a Los Angeles County trial in which the defendants were police officers, but

White was more concerned with open minds than with family relationships. In his questionnaire, Morgan said that "seeing the partial clips of the video on TV, it had looked to me like excessive force was used. However, I do not know the whole story of what actually happened." While White would be criticized for accepting the brother of a police officer, his assessment of Morgan as fair-minded proved as accurate as Dimitrius' view that Bailey was perfect for the defense. Morgan was seated as Juror No. 1.

Anna Charmaine Whiting, known by her middle name, was a fifty-four-year-old printer and the daughter of a police officer. On the face of it, she seemed a desirable defense juror because of her awareness, expressed in her questionnaire, that police work is highly stressful. "It takes a special kind of person to make a good officer," Whiting said. Her response to the videotaped beating as it had been shown on television was similar to Morgan's. While "sickened" by the sight of the officers hitting King, Whiting believed there was more to the incident than she knew. Again, a juror with Whiting's background and opinions might have drawn a prosecution challenge in Los Angeles County. But she seemed open-minded, which was the best White could hope for in the context of the jury pool. She became Juror No. 5.

White also held hopes for Virginia Loya, forty, a hospital housekeeper who had worked as a security guard and expressed pro-police opinions on her questionnaire. Her twelve-year-old son wanted to become a police officer. But Loya seemed a compassionate person who might respond sympathetically to the ordeal of Rodney King. The only Latino on the jury, Loya was seated as Juror No. 2. White also accepted Kevin Siminski, thirty-eight, a computer programmer and the man who had once been mistaken for a robbery suspect. Despite Siminski's forgiving attitude, White hoped he harbored enough residual resentment toward the police to make him skeptical of contentions that the force used against King was fully justified. Siminski became Juror No. 7.

The jury of seven men and five women was seated on March 2, 1992, one day short of the first anniversary of the Rodney King incident. It became in midtrial a jury of six men and six women after a thirty-four-year-old male garbage collector, the only juror from relatively diverse Oxnard, was excused for personal reasons. His departure may have benefited the defense, for he had written on his questionnaire that police officers who used excessive force "should be treated like everyone else." He was replaced as Juror No. 10 by alternate Alice Debord, forty-three, who said on her questionnaire that police "have a very tough job . . . a hard job. They need to be respected." Statistically, the jury was older, whiter, and less diverse than the population of Ventura County. It included ten non-Hispanic whites, Loya, and one Asian—Amelia Pigeon, a thirty-nine-year-old Filipino-American nurse who was seated as Juror No. 4. The average age was nearly fifty-one, with

Sheehan and Kossow the oldest at sixty-five and Siminski the youngest at thirty-eight. The conservative city of Camarillo was disproportionately represented with three jurors, including Bailey. Morgan and Pigeon were from Simi Valley.

IN RETROSPECT, WHITE AND DIMITRIUS BELIEVE THAT JURY composition was the principal determinant of the trial's outcome. But it was not that clear at the time. Delighted as she was with the jury, Dimitrius did not view the case as a "slam dunk" for the defense. And despite his premonitions of disaster, White clung to the hope that the videotape would persuade even a pro-police jury that the officers, or at least Powell, had used excessive force.

White, who would pay a price in reputation for the mistakes of judges and his superiors, realized that a black prosecutor ran the risk of not connecting with a white, pro-police jury. He briefly considered withdrawing from the case after Weisberg moved the trial to Simi Valley. But that would have left whoever replaced him with little more than two months to prepare for trial. White concluded that the risk of inadequate preparation was greater than the risk that the jury might not warm to an African-American prosecutor. "I said to myself, 'no one knows this case . . . as well as I know it, and no one can be prepared in two months the way I will be prepared,'" White said.[37] But he had no illusions of victory.

Black community leaders who had monitored the case since its inception feared the worst after the trial was moved to Simi Valley, and their fears were heightened by the composition of the jury. "I think this jury means that the four officers have a jury of their peers, but Rodney King and the African-American community don't have a jury of our peers," said John Mack, president of the Los Angeles chapter of the Urban League.[38] Compton city councilwoman Patricia Moore said that black people were "hoping for the best but prepared for the worst. After the Harlins case, how can you blame them?" Moore warned that if justice was not done "this community, and possibly the nation, will see upheavals as never before."[39] Her warning was echoed by Joe Hicks, executive director of the Southern California Leadership Conference, who said conditions throughout South Central Los Angeles resembled those in Watts before the 1965 riot. "In many ways it's even worse," he said. "All the conditions are there, unemployment, crime, people are being driven to survival levels."[40]

But the general public, at least the white general public, did not realize that the prosecution was in peril, and the media sounded no alarms. While the absence of blacks on the jury was noted, most media accounts glossed over the views of the jurors and accepted at face value the lawyers' litany about the "level playing field" of Ventura County. The *Los Angeles Times* set the tone. Its story on the completion of jury selection said in the lead paragraph that the jury contained no blacks but in the third paragraph assured readers of the jury's balance: "Although civil rights groups had expressed concern that moving the trial to predominantly white Ventura County would make it difficult to select a representative jury, prosecutors and defense lawyers said they were satisfied with the selection." The story also said that the twelve jurors had expressed "evenly divided views on the King beating and the Los Angeles Police Department." In fact, eight of the twelve jurors had given strong pro-police opinions on their questionnaires.[41]

The prosecution bears the principal responsibility for such misleading accounts. Instead of warning that prosecutors faced an unsympathetic jury, Reiner continued to maintain his satisfaction with the panel, and the trial attorneys parroted this party line. A week after the riots, when the jury's bias was evident to the world, White would say that the jury was made up of "people who believe there is this 'thin blue line' separating law-abiding citizens from the jungle—the criminal element. They are people who put police officers on a pedestal."[42] But neither White nor Reiner was candid about the attitude of this jury when doing so might have put the public on notice about the realities of Simi Valley.

By accepting the pretrial prosecution propaganda about the jury, the media failed the public. Judge Weisberg preserved the anonymity of the jurors during the trial, but the completed questionnaires, on which the jurors were identified by number, were available to reporters. Had the media focused on the frank pro-police comments of the jurors, rather than on the reassurances of Reiner and White, they might have realized that convictions were not inevitable. But reporters also suffered from the misconception that the Holliday videotape was irrefutable. The videotape seemed so potent, so graphic, and so conclusive that it was hard to believe that anyone could watch it and fail to conclude that the defendants, at least some of them, had engaged in criminal conduct.

As for the much maligned jurors, most of whom had also seen the edited version of the videotape on television, they were also unaware of the burdens that trying the case in Simi Valley had placed on the prosecution. As one juror later told a reporter for *The American Lawyer*, "Most of us believe in law and order, and we haven't been in trouble with the law. If I was the D.A., I would try to get somebody that's sympathetic to minorities or something like that."[43]

But no such sympathizers were available to the prosecution. The world in which the jurors lived was white. During the trial, I became aware that a particular juror flinched whenever a bulky African-American bailiff approached the jury box to escort the jurors to lunch or a recess. It was no doubt an involuntary reaction, but troublesome nonetheless. I wondered how anyone who was frightened in broad daylight by a black man who wore the uniform of the Ventura County Sheriff's Office, could possibly understand the ordeal of Rodney King.[44]

It was not, however, the jury's fault that it was unrepresentative of vast, diverse Los Angeles County, where it certainly would have been possible to seat a representative jury. Justice Klein's ruling forced the trial out of Los Angeles, but it is Judge Weisberg who kept the trial within the media market and changed the venue to a place where it was impossible to obtain a balanced jury. Had Weisberg foreseen that the jurors would be so unresponsive to the videotape, there seems little doubt that he would have chosen a different trial site, for he had no sympathy for the defense. But that hardly excuses Weisberg, who knew as much about juries as his former colleague, the reliable Roger Gunson. Weisberg should have realized, as Gunson did, that the prosecution of police officers is always difficult and that holding the trial in Ventura County stacked the deck in favor of the defense. He probably should have moved the trial to a county that replicated the diversity of Los Angeles, and he should at least have been willing to select a venue that was less convenient to witnesses, attorneys, and himself.

"What crimes are committed in the name of personal convenience," Warren Christopher said to me after the trial. It was a sorrowful comment on the judicial negligence that propelled Los Angeles toward the firestorm.

9

BEYOND THE VIDEOTAPE

"Sometimes police work is brutal. It's just a fact of life."
—Sergeant Stacey Koon[1]

"Witnesses tend to see things in a certain way. The videotape does not lie."
—Johnnie L. Cochran Jr.[2]

PEOPLE V. POWELL EXISTED BECAUSE OF THE COMPELLING evidence of a videotape that the world assumed had caught LAPD officers committing acts of irrefutable brutality. Without the Holliday video, the beating of Rodney King would at most have prompted an Internal Affairs inquiry in which investigators would have faced a tangle of contradictions and uncertainties. King had been too intoxicated at the time of the beating to remember with any clarity what had happened. The police officers had plausible explanations for their conduct. Civilian witnesses had seen only fragments of the incident, and their accounts conflicted.[3]

Without a videotape, investigators would have known that a physically imposing African-American man had led police on a pursuit of nearly eight miles and behaved in a bizarre fashion after he finally stopped. They would have known that the man was shot by an electric stun gun and charged at an officer who hit him with a baton. They might have concluded from medical reports that he had been struck numerous times, but they would not have known that he had been on the ground during many of the blows. Without a videotape, they would have been unable to determine whether the officers had behaved unreasonably. Without a videotape, the victim would have been just another black ex-convict who was injured by the police while supposedly resisting arrest, and no one except friends and family would today know the name of Rodney King.

By catching officers in the act, the tape had solved the central problem of most excessive force cases by making it impossible for the police to deny that they had beaten a suspect. But the video simultaneously undermined the criminal case it created. It became a powerful defense tool for removing from the jury the people who were most appalled by what they had seen.

Only rarely do defense attorneys have an opportunity to question jurors ahead of time about the prosecution's evidence. While prospective jurors in high-profile cases are often asked whether they have formed conclusions based upon news accounts, they cannot be asked to give opinions of evidence they have never seen. But in *People v. Powell*, the Holliday video was the prosecution's best evidence, and it had been seen in edited form by nearly everyone. Defense attorneys could and did ask jury candidates their opinion of this evidence, conducting what attorney John Barnett called "an enormous mock trial" during jury selection.[4] Potential jurors who had decided on the basis of the video that the police officers had used excessive force were promptly excused by Judge Weisberg. The videotape that made a criminal trial possible also eliminated the jurors who were most likely to find the defendants guilty as charged.

Such jurors were plentiful, even in the hot-house, pro-police climate of Simi Valley. Of the first thirty-one prospective jurors questioned by Weisberg, nine were excused because they had formed the opinion that the officers had used unreasonable force. The prosecution objected, but it would have been difficult, and possibly a legally reversible error, for a judge to have seated a juror who was convinced of the defendants' guilt. Nevertheless, the process sharply skewed the jury pool. The remaining jurors either did not share the general revulsion at the videotaped beating or doubted that the video told the full story. "The video gave us a jury panel who had seen the prosecution's best evidence and was not convinced," said Barnett, who represented Officer Theodore Briseno and was the most experienced of the defense attorneys.[5]

Since the videotape was never played during jury selection, the prospective jurors were basing their opinions on the version they had seen on TV, the version from which KTLA had removed the initial three seconds which show King charging toward Officer Laurence Powell and ten subsequent seconds, which are blurred because Holliday had moved the camera. This compounded the prosecution's predicament. The beating was violent enough in any version but seemed mindlessly brutal in the absence of King's charge. If prospective jurors who were shocked by the edited video had seen the full tape, some of them might have been willing to keep an open mind about the officers and probably would have been retained on the panel by Weisberg. If only one or two such jurors had made it to the final twelve-member panel, it might have made a difference in the outcome.

The editing that deleted King's charge also caused a pitfall for the prosecution among the seated jurors, who were in the main conservative and suspicious of the media. Many of them believed that the media had displayed bias against the police in covering the King case. They also suspected that there was more to the story than the media had revealed. Seeing the full, unedited version in court for the first time doubtless reinforced those suspicions. John Barnett believes that jurors "felt cheated" when they realized that a videotaped segment that might at least partially have explained the conduct of the officers had been suppressed.[6] In part because of the television editing, the video that made prosecution possible also offered a way out for the defense. "The video is our best piece of evidence, as bizarre as it sounds," said Sergeant Stacey Koon the weekend before jury selection began.[7]

Deputy District Attorney Terry White did his best to diminish the harmful impact of the editing. Following a basic legal strategy of disclosing damaging information before the other side can do it, White played the entire videotape during his opening statement on March 5, 1992. He acknowledged that King had been intoxicated and uncooperative. He drew attention to King's charge, which he said "could be viewed either as an attack on Officer Powell or running away from Officer Powell."[8] White made no attempt to defend King's behavior. But he said that Powell had responded in an "unreasonable" way, striking King in the face with his baton "much as a baseball batter would swing at a pitch."

Nevertheless, the initial section of the videotape raised questions about the prosecution case before the defense had made its opening statements. Dorothy Bailey, who was to become the jury forewoman, was amazed when she saw the complete video. She so abhorred violence that she closed her eyes or lowered her head during violent scenes at movies, and she had found the televised version of the videotape so brutal that she had left the room whenever it was shown on news broadcasts.[9] But as the tape began to roll during White's opening statement, Bailey's fascination overcame her squeamishness. She had not known about King's charge or realized that Powell had taken out his handcuffs early in the incident. "I was very surprised to see all the things that did happen," Bailey said.[10] The defense would subsequently dissect the tape in slow motion in a process that District Attorney Reiner believes gradually desensitized the jurors.[11] But Bailey never became emotionally comfortable with the video in any version. And for her the unedited tape provided motivation for the actions of the officers. "It was the most powerful evidence that we had, but most of America saw only part of the tape," she said.[12]

Anna Charmaine Whiting was a kindly and open-minded person who deplored the King beating when she first saw it on television. Unlike many of the other jurors, Whiting recognized that police do not always uphold the law. And unlike Bailey she would be skeptical of expert defense witnesses who justified the officers' actions. But Whiting also had not realized until White played the unedited video that King had charged at Powell. While

Whiting would differ with Bailey on many issues, she too found that the unedited tape clearly showed that King had "aggressed" against the police.[13]

The defense took immediate and devastating advantage of the doubts raised by the unedited video. Koon's attorney, Darryl Mounger, used his opening statement to review the attempts to take King peaceably into custody. He then described King's "violent charge" and his repeated attempts to regain his feet after he was knocked down by Powell's first baton blow.

"Ladies and gentlemen, throughout the course of this trial you are going to hear that Rodney King and Rodney King alone was in control of the situation because Sergeant Koon is watching the situation," Mounger said. "He is watching his officers. He can't see everything. He's not going to tell you he saw every blow, but he will tell you that he was watching Rodney King. And when you are reviewing this tape, if you watch what Sergeant Koon watched . . . if you focus on what Rodney King is doing, the evidence will show you that when Rodney King is lying spread eagle in a prone [position], he is not hit."

From opening statements through closing arguments, none of the defense attorneys except Barnett ever deviated from the contention that King was responsible for his ordeal and that the officers who subdued him were doing their duty as they had been trained. While the strategy of shifting blame from the defendants to the victim may have been helped by King's imposing size, and by his race and prison record, it was solidly based on King's combative actions in the opening frames of the unedited video. "How lucky these defendants really are in connection with that videotape," said Officer Wind's attorney, Paul DePasquale, in a closing argument that effectively summarized the defense theme. If George Holliday had turned on the videotape five seconds later, DePasquale said, "Mr. White would be able to say, why that is a damned lie that he [King] got up and charged because, if you will recall, not even all of the police at the scene remember seeing that charge."

THE ADVANTAGES THE DEFENSE OBTAINED FROM THE VIDEO MADE no discernible impression on the media. Most news accounts of the trial conveyed the impression that the video formed the basis of a powerful prosecution case that was moving swiftly to inevitable convictions. With few exceptions, reporters did not recognize that the combination of a pro-police venue and a videotape that had been used to excuse potential jurors who distrusted the police had produced a jury that was exceptionally responsive to the strategy of blaming King. Nor did the media understand that television had given aid and comfort to the defense cause by repeatedly showing the version of the Holliday videotape from which King's charge had been deleted. I know of no story on opening day of the trial, including my own, which emphasized that the jurors had been shown a version of the video they had never seen before.

The media had a reason beyond the video for believing that the prosecution would prevail. It was clear from the first day of the trial that the four defendants did not face the prosecution with a united front. Even if the initial actions of the officers could be explained by King's behavior, the defense still faced the challenge of explaining why the beating had gone on so long. To win its case, the defense had to show that every blow and kick was justified. The defense also had to overcome the testimony of Officer Briseno, whose version of the incident largely supported the prosecution's. Even reporters who understood that the unedited video presented problems for the prosecution could not see how Koon and Powell could escape conviction when the evidence against them included the testimony of a participant in the arrest.

Michael Stone faced the stiffest challenge of the defense attorneys. His client, Laurence Powell had delivered most of the baton blows to King and had sent computer messages that had been described even by Chief Gates as racist. But Stone, despite never having tried a felony case, was a resourceful lawyer who threw himself into the defense with vigor and determination. He was convinced that Powell had been unfairly victimized by the political system, the media, and a spineless LAPD leadership that had bowed to the pressures of political correctness. Influenced by remembered dangers of a cop's life on the streets, both Stone and Mounger almost casually accepted the police premise that officers are justified in using whatever force seems necessary in the heat of battle. DePasquale, who had once served as a district attorney in a rural northern California county, did not fully share this attitude, and Barnett did not share it at all. But Mounger and Stone, viewing the world through grim police lenses, saw suspected criminals as a lower species. King was a "nothing," said Stone, expressing an opinion that was Powell's and his own.[14]

At Simi Valley the zeal of Stone and Mounger served their clients well, and their immense knowledge of arrest procedures impressed jurors inclined to believe the best about the police. When Koon and Powell and their lawyers learned that Briseno would testify that King's arrest was mishandled, they immediately branded him a traitor who was trying to save himself at the expense of his fellow officers. This was an understandable reaction from defendants who faced prison sentences if convicted, but it would not necessarily have been the reaction of lawyers who lacked the police background of Mounger and Stone. More objective attorneys might have acknowledged that it was possible for an officer to have an honest difference of opinion about the arrest without being an enemy. Perhaps Briseno was simply wrong, not a traitor. This possibility did not occur to Mounger and Stone, who had changed professions without changing points of view. As Stone saw it, part of his mission in defending Powell was to destroy Briseno's credibility.

Stone began his attack on Briseno in his opening statement. He said that the video segment in which Briseno raises his hand to stop Powell does not show an officer's attempt to help King. Instead, Stone said, Briseno had raised his hand to prevent Powell from becoming entangled in the wires of the Taser—the stun gun Koon had fired at King—and receiving an electric shock. John Barnett was surprised at this comment, then incensed by it. He was not seeking a confrontation and had planned to explain conflicts among the officers as differences of perception during a volatile and confusing arrest.

Barnett, who had toyed with the idea of not even making an opening statement, revised his strategy after Stone's attack. If Stone insisted on discrediting Briseno, then he would go after Powell. Barnett said the evidence would show that Powell was "out of control." This reinforced the prosecution case against Powell and effectively precluded reconciliation among the defendants during the trial. Outside the courtroom Stone and Barnett continued their verbal battle in an exchange before television cameras that cemented their hostility and set the tone for a trial in which Briseno in effect became a witness for the prosecution.*

It is possible, of course, that Briseno would have been on a collision course with his codefendants even if Stone had not forced the issue. At Barnett's instruction, Briseno sat apart in the courtroom from the opening day of the trial, and he gave no public sign of solidarity with the other defendants when the jury was in the room. To Stone this behavior stamped Briseno as a witness-in-waiting for the prosecution. Stone's suspicions were confirmed by White's comment in his opening statement that Briseno had tried to stop Powell from hitting King. This convinced Stone that Briseno's testimony would buttress the prosecution argument that Powell had behaved brutally, and it persuaded him of the need to launch a "preemptive strike."[15]

Barnett, whose client was less vulnerable than Powell, wanted the defendants to finesse their differences. "I felt that it was unnecessary for the other defendants to directly attack [Briseno] in terms of credibility and in terms of his perception," Barnett said. "My view was that they could present their defense and live with Briseno's perception by showing that his perception as to certain events was inaccurate."[16] Briseno had little to lose in

---

* White told me in an October 5, 1993, interview that he had mixed feelings about prosecuting Briseno. Although he had delivered "a fairly hard stomp," White said, a case could be made that he was telling the truth when he said he had been trying to keep King on the ground. White said Barnett had sounded out prosecutors on the possibility of obtaining immunity for Briseno in return for his testimony. "Our office would have none of that," said White. "I always thought we should have listened to them."

taking this approach, and it is possible that Powell might have gained from it. But Stone's view of Briseno as a betrayer willing to smear other officers to save himself did not allow Stone to take the chance.

The conflict among defense attorneys naturally pleased the prosecution. But the prosecutors had internal problems of their own. As Terry White and Alan Yochelson, second chair on the prosecution team, put on their case in Simi Valley, every move they made was monitored by their superiors at the district attorney's office in downtown Los Angeles, via a satellite dish installed for this purpose.* District Attorney Ira Reiner, Assistant District Attorney Dan Murphy, and Deputy District Attorney Roger Gunson all had opinions, which they did not hesitate to communicate to the trial attorneys. As the trial went on, the prosecution suffered from the debilitating effect of what Yochelson called "decision by committee."[18]

The case had been assigned to White, thirty-five, because he was new to the Special Investigations Division and had a light caseload. This seemed sensible in March 1991, when everyone anticipated that the trial would be conducted in downtown Los Angeles before a multi-racial jury. White was a dedicated attorney with an intense courtroom presence. He had successfully prosecuted drug and pornography cases, including that of ex-Catholic priest John Bauer, the "Priest of Porn," who had been convicted and sentenced to eight years in prison for producing and appearing in child pornography films. Yochelson, thirty-six, had been a deputy district attorney for a decade and assisted in prosecuting serial killer Richard Ramirez, the "Night Stalker," who been convicted and sentenced to death.

Yochelson, who was more methodical and less intense than White, understood as well as his colleague that the prosecution would be difficult. When a young deputy district attorney excitedly proclaimed after the Holliday videotape was shown on television that "we're going to get them now," Yochelson withheld judgment until he had seen the entire tape. And he realized from watching it that King was not "an innocent person who simply got pulled over for no reason and was beaten up." King had "goofed off," refused to obey police commands, and charged at an officer. The case the prosecution would have to prove in court "was a completely different case than the way it had been portrayed" in the news media.[19]

The difficulty of the prosecution case was apparent with the first witnesses. George Holliday described how he had been awakened by helicopters and police sirens just before 1:00 A.M. on March 3, 1991, and had gone to the

---

* Sandi Gibbons, spokeswoman for Reiner, said that one reason for installing the satellite dish was that top officials in the district attorney's office wanted to be aware if television commentators critiqued the courtroom performances of White and Yochelson. Dan Murphy was quoted as saying that the satellite dish saved Gunson a daily trip to Simi Valley.[17]

balcony of his apartment to videotape the incident. So far, so good. But Holliday then testified that he had been amazed by King's apparent lack of response to the baton blows, underscoring the defense contention that King's behavior was abnormal and therefore frightening to the police officers.

Bryant (Pooh) Allen then described the evening of drinking and driving with King. He said that King, an old friend, had picked him up at Allen's mother's home in Altadena just before 6:00 P.M. on March 2. They had gone with Freddie Helms (who died in an unrelated car accident between the time of the incident and the start of the trial) to a liquor store, where each had bought a forty-ounce bottle of Olde English 800. They had gone to a park to drink, then parked in front of Allen's house, where they drank some more as they listened to rap music and sang along with the radio. "It was getting kind of late," Allen said, when King abruptly decided to go for a drive. Allen said under cross-examination that he thought they were "cruising around" with the purpose of "looking for some girls."

Allen denied they had been drinking for two hours before the drive, a statement that proved unpersuasive to the jurors. He also said that King did not seem "drunk," which was even less convincing. Later in the trial, prosecutors would stipulate that King's blood alcohol level was .19 when he was arrested, nearly two-and-a half times the legal limit in California. Allen further damaged his credibility by asserting that King had obeyed all traffic lights and stop signs after exiting the freeway, a claim that would be contradicted by the testimony of the officers who were involved in the pursuit. Indeed, Allen gave the impression that King had been a menace on the highway.

"I said, 'Rodney, why don't you pull over?' a couple of times," Allen testified. "He wasn't saying nothing. He just kept on driving. At one time, I wanted to just jump out of the car . . . He was acting strange."

"You thought he was acting kind of crazy . . . so strange that you were considering jumping out of that car even though it was moving?" Barnett asked.

"Correct," Allen said.

The prosecution could not wait for Allen to leave the stand. "He was an absolutely horrible witness," said Yochelson. Allen's civil attorney had dominated the prosecutors' pre-trial meeting with the witness, and as a result they could not adequately prepare Allen for his testimony. "Every time we would ask him a question, the attorney would answer or suggest an answer," Yochelson said. "It was very, very difficult. We had that problem with a number of witnesses."[20]

Allen was followed by Melanie Singer, the California Highway Patrol officer who, with partner-husband Tim Singer, had pursued King and tried to arrest him before Koon intervened. Singer gave detailed testimony about the chase, then related that Powell had struck King while he was on his hands and knees four times on the left side of his face and once on the right side, "splitting his cheekbone from the top of his ear to the bottom of his jawline . . . Blood spilled out. Blood poured out."

Asked by White whether Powell had any reason to strike King in the head, Singer replied, "In my opinion, no sir, there was no reason for it."

Singer's dramatic testimony gave a momentary lift to the prosecution and exacerbated the conflict between Stone and Barnett, who said outside of court that her "very compelling and important evidence" provided "an understanding into the mind and heart of Mr. Briseno at the time he put his foot on Mr. King's back" to keep him down.[21]

But this "very compelling" evidence did not survive cross-examination.

Under questioning by Stone, Singer said she did not recall King's dashing toward Powell, a movement she acknowledged seeing on the Holliday video. After watching the video, Singer also acknowledged that King had not been on his hands and knees when Powell first hit him with his baton, as she had remembered. When Stone asked Singer to examine photographs of King's injuries, she agreed that they showed a one-inch cut on the right side of King's face and no marks on the left side. She could not account for the disparity between her recollections and the photographic record. Nor could she account for the disparity between her testimony and a memo she had written a day after the incident in which she said that King "became almost violent" and had "kicked and punched" at the police officers. These contradictions persuaded Stone that what Singer remembered was "inherently unbelievable" and "absolutely wrong," a point he would drive home to jurors in his closing argument.[22]

WHILE THE PROSECUTION'S PRIZE WITNESS WAS TURNING INTO A prize headache under cross-examination, Terry White was struggling with another witness problem outside the courtroom. He had known since his early difficult dealings with Rodney King's attorney, Steven Lerman, that King was a problematical witness. King was on the prosecution witness list, but the question of whether to call him had become a matter of "constant discussion" among Reiner, White, Yochelson and other members of the prosecution team.[23]

Putting the victim on the stand so he could tell his story to the jury was accepted practice in excessive-force cases. But in *People v. Powell* the videotape was the best evidence of what had happened, and nothing King could say was likely to improve on it. As White had acknowledged in his opening statement, King had been too drunk the night of his arrest to be a convincing witness to his ordeal. What's more, he had given conflicting

public accounts of the incident, which defense attorneys could use to impeach his credibility. He had originally denied that he was speeding or that
he had refused to obey police commands. He had described every act of
force against him as unprovoked. He had first denied that there had been
any expression of racial animus by the officers, then claimed that they had
been racially derogatory.

King was taking medication, and in their private discussions White
found him surly and uncommunicative. Lerman often answered for him. It
was clear to White that neither King nor his lawyer appreciated the obstacles facing the prosecution. White worried about what King might say on
the witness stand. It was possible that, under cross-examination, he would
tell jurors more about his criminal record than the judge had allowed into
evidence.[24] But White's biggest fear was that King would lose his temper
and antagonize a jury that was not sympathetic to him in the first place.

On the other hand, White knew that allowing jurors to see Rodney King
as a human being could be useful. King had been demonized in defense
opening statements as an imposing, hostile creature of extraordinary
strength who was remarkably resistant to pain and had terrified the officers who confronted him. Prosecution witnesses had subtly contributed to
this dehumanization. Holliday had been amazed at the number of blows
King had taken. Allen said that King had acted strangely. Melanie Singer
said that he had staggered, "almost appearing like a monster," after being hit
by the Taser shots fired by Sergeant Koon. Tim Singer, too, had been reminded of a "scene from a monster movie."

If King took the stand, jurors might see that he was not a monster but a
harmless and vulnerable human being who had been too drunk to follow
police commands. But that presumed King would testify sensibly, and White
saw no sign that King was prepared to deal honestly with his behavior. He
concluded that the risk that King would reinforce the defense's damning
portrayal outweighed the possibility that he might win the jury's sympathy.
Reluctantly, he decided that he dare not call King as a witness.[25]

The issue, which Reiner considered a "close question," was resolved at a
meeting of the prosecution committee. Yochelson made the case for calling
King and White argued against it. Yochelson conceded that King was uncooperative and risky but said "that the jury is going to want to see him regardless."[26] Neither Yochelson nor anyone else on the committee argued that
King would be a good witness. "The people that wanted to call him . . . just
said it may be a worse idea than not calling him," Reiner recalled. "No one
person said it was a good idea."[27]

In the end the committee was evenly divided. Reiner then resolved the
issue in White's favor, deciding that King would not be called. Reiner later
told me that he did not want to burden his lead attorney with an unwanted

witness and that he also basically accepted White's evaluation. "The last thing you want is a witness on the stand who is a victim who is going to get up there and bullshit," Reiner said. "And the second worst thing that you want is somebody [who] under cross-examination is going to lose his temper and get mean and surly and argumentative on the stand."[28] Yochelson, who had argued for calling King partly to ensure that the issue was fully debated, was also persuaded by White's argument. "Terry was absolutely right," he said.[29]

Any lingering doubts were resolved by Rodney King. On Saturday morning, March 7, the day after Melanie Singer testified, White received a call at his office from Lerman, who said King wanted to speak with him. White was greeted with a string of profanities from King. "He was angry, saying, 'Melanie Singer kicked me, Tim Singer kicked me, and they're lying!' It was 'fuck this' and 'motherfucker that,' and right then I knew we had made the right decision," White recalled.[30]

Back in the courtroom, White and Yochelson plowed ahead. While relying largely upon the videotape to make the case of excessive force, the prosecutors sought to show through other evidence that the defendants had behaved callously after the incident. Stone, who realized that Powell's post-incident conduct gave a poor impression of his client, tried to keep the recorded audio transmission in which Powell called for a rescue ambulance out of evidence. But Weisberg allowed jurors to hear the conversation with LAPD dispatcher Leshon Frierson in which Powell said an ambulance was needed for the "victim of ah, ah . . ." and Koon completed the sentence with, "beating." Powell then laughed and said, "Yeah . . . numerous head wounds." Frierson testified that officers rarely used words such as "beating" in radio transmissions. He also testified that he had heard Powell "laugh or giggle."

News accounts had depicted Powell as laughing at what he had done to King, which was certainly a possible interpretation. But in the hushed courtroom, Powell's laughter sounded oddly strained, almost hysterical. Even before the defense argued the point, several jurors concluded that Powell had been scared when he made the call.

That wasn't the only problem for the prosecution posed by the audio-tape. The prosecution sought to show that Koon and Powell had deliberately concealed the severity of the beating. That required showing that Koon and Powell intended to cover up the beating, not just that they had made inaccurate statements. But the audiotape showed that Koon, at least, had refused from the first to sugarcoat the violent incident and it suggested that Powell, at the prompting of his sergeant, had gone along. A beating is what it was, and beating is how Koon described it.

On the other hand, there was no question that Powell had bragged about what he had done to King. Glenda Tosti, an LAPD communications supervisor, testified about the message that Powell sent on his in-car computer to Officer Corina Smith in which he boasted, "I haven't beaten anyone this bad in a long time." This was a revealing comment to Whiting, one of the few jurors who had been distressed by Powell's laughter during the ambulance call. Whiting thought the MDT message demonstrated an arrogance unbecoming in a police officer.[31]

The prosecution contended that this arrogance turned to taunting at Pacifica Hospital in nearby Sun Valley, where King was treated after the beating. Lawrence Davis, the nurse in charge, testified that King started talking about the Los Angeles Dodgers while being examined and said he was an usher at Dodger Stadium. This prompted Powell to say, "Boy, I sure hope we don't ever go to the game and you have to usher us down to the seats." When King made no reply, Powell persisted. "Well, we had a pretty good hardball game tonight, didn't we? . . . Don't you remember? Don't you remember the team we were playing against?" Finally, said Davis, it dawned on King what Powell was talking about. "We won that game, didn't we?" Powell said. "We had quite a few home runs." King nodded in agreement. This testimony was the strongest evidence of Powell's callousness to be presented at the Simi Valley trial. It has endured in the folklore of the incident as confirmation that Powell was a brutal wise guy who mocked his victim after beating him.

What neither the prosecution nor the media realized at the time was that the testimony was suspect. It is by no means certain that much of the conversation described by Davis ever occurred. And even if it did, it is not clear that the officer who taunted King was Laurence Powell.

Davis previously had related the incident to police investigators and the grand jury without identifying the officer who did the taunting. When Powell became aware of the charge, he acknowledged having said to King that he did not want him to be the usher who conducted them to seats in Dodger Stadium, but told his lawyer, Stone, that it was another officer in the hospital room who had taunted King about losing the "ballgame." Powell identified the officer but said he was a friend and did not want to implicate him. In cross-examining Davis, Stone asked why he had not identified Powell as the officer who taunted King when he testified to the grand jury. "They never asked me," Davis said.[32]

Davis' veracity went unchallenged for nearly a year. Then Richard Serrano, who had covered the Simi Valley trial for the Los Angeles Times, reported that the FBI had interviewed Davis and found "discrepancies" in his account. He also reported that Davis had been arrested and charged with felony assault for allegedly putting a pistol into the mouth of former girlfriend, Joan Deneve, and threatening to kill her. Deneve told police that Davis said he made up his testimony because he was interested in a movie deal. "He hoped to get paid for his story," she said.[33] The charges against Davis were eventually dismissed, but prosecutors in the federal trial did not use him as a witness.

Another Pacifica nurse, Carol Denise Edwards, also testified at Simi Valley. She said that she had been placing an intravenous tube in King's body when she heard Powell say, "We played a little hardball tonight. Do you remember who was playing?" In response, "Mr. King said something to the effect, 'I guess so,' and Mr. Powell said, 'We won and you lost' or something to that effect." This testimony seemed to establish that the baseball colloquy had occurred, but it fell short of conclusively establishing Powell's participation. Under cross-examination by Stone, Edwards said that there were eight police officers in the hospital room at the time. She said she had been unable to identify Powell (or Wind, who had been standing silently nearby) when she testified to the state grand jury because she could not "recall" their names at the time. She had learned of their names from reading newspaper accounts, she said.

Nor did King know who had taunted him. When he was questioned in 1992 by Barry Kowalski of the Justice Department before a federal grand jury, King recalled that an officer had said, "Well, we played a little ball tonight, and guess who won?" King said he responded, "You did." King said he remembered only one officer talking to him in this vein, but he was unable to identify the officer.

The prosecution's medical testimony was also confusing. Dr. Antonio Mancia, the Pacifica Hospital emergency-room physician who had applied twenty stitches to King's face and mouth, testified that he did not believe King was under the influence of PCP or alcohol. But Mancia's recollection was contradicted by his own medical report and the testimony of Dr. David Giannetto, a physician at Los Angeles County–USC Medical Center who had examined King at 6:15 A.M., slightly more than five hours after the incident. Giannetto said that Mancia had told him King was being transferred from Pacifica to the medical center "solely because the patient needed to be observed for possible PCP intoxication."

Giannetto, in the third year of a four-year hospital residency, was an earnest witness whose uncertainty on critical points proved helpful to the defense. He testified that King's injuries included a fracture of the zygomatic arch on the right side of his face, a broken right leg and various bruises and lacerations. He was not asked, and did not offer, his opinion of what had caused the injuries. But he did have an opinion that King was "mildly intoxicated" when Giannetto examined him, implying that King was far more intoxicated at the time of his arrest.

The prosecutors knew that the defense would contend that King was under the influence of PCP, and they wanted to discredit this claim with medical evidence. Giannetto was of no help. While tests of King's urine had not detected PCP, Giannetto testified that such tests are not infallible. The cross-examination also revealed that Giannetto lacked PCP expertise. When Barnett asked whether PCP was stored in any particular part of the body, Giannetto replied honestly, "I'm not sure. I would suspect the fat tissue."

"Would the bottom line be that you can't give us any opinion as to his state of intoxication either of alcohol or PCP five hours earlier?" Barnett asked.

"Yes," said Giannetto.

The prosecution rested on March 17, after formally announcing that King would not testify. This belated declaration was a sign of weakness that was misinterpreted by the media and the legal community as a sign of strength. "Keeping King Off Stand Was a Wise Move, Experts Say," said a headline in the *Los Angeles Times*, which quoted criminal defense lawyer Stanley Greenberg as saying that King would have risked diverting attention to his behavior and away from the conduct of the officers "so plainly reflected on the videotape."[34] "King's Absence From Stand Hints Prosecution Is Confident," said a headline in the *Daily News*. The story quoted Peter Arenella, a well-known UCLA professor and nationally recognized expert in criminal law: "The fact they are not calling King is telling you that they are very happy with the way their case has progressed."

But the prosecutors weren't happy. Most of their case had focused on the conduct of Powell; the evidence offered against Koon to this point was scanty and against Wind and Briseno almost nonexistent. And even the case against Powell was equivocal. While prosecutors had shown him to be arrogant and uncaring, they had also planted the seeds of a defense based on inadequate training. Sergeant Richard DiStefano had testified about Powell's demonstration with the baton at Foothill Station two hours before the King incident. "His execution was weak . . . his blows were glancing," DiStefano said, making a point that Stone seized upon to minimize the injuries caused to King. Nor was it lost on jurors that Powell had been sent into the field after demonstrating his incompetence, armed with a metal pipe he did not know how to use.

After the prosecution rested, the defense attorneys except for Stone submitted motions that sought directed verdicts of acquittal on the basis of insufficient evidence. Such motions are normally routine, and the attorneys expected them to be rejected, as they were. But in denying the motions, Weisberg said revealingly that his decision was based "upon a review of the evidence presented and specifically a review of the videotape evidence." It was a recognition by the court that the prosecution case against all the defendants except Powell had become nearly totally dependent on the videotape.

The defense attorneys now faced the challenge of putting on a coherent case of their own. This meant somehow reconciling Briseno's view of what had happened with the perceptions of the other defendants. A more or less unified defense, in which each officer claimed to have acted reasonably based on his own perceptions, might have been sufficient to create reasonable doubt, if jurors believed that all the officers had acted in good faith. Such a defense would have allowed Stone and Mounger to argue that their clients had not set out to hurt King, although they might have made some mistakes. But the total lack of trust between Briseno and his codefendants and between Barnett and Stone made such a defense impossible. Stone and Mounger considered Briseno more dishonest than any prosecution witness, while Barnett was convinced that he needed to distance Briseno from the other defendants to stand any chance of acquittal.

Perhaps most important, Stacey Koon, and to a large degree, Stone and Mounger, were not interested in a defense based on errors of judgment. They wanted to show not only that the officers had been prudent in expecting the worst of King but also that they had been justified in beating him into submission. Had Koon and Powell and their attorneys been willing to admit misjudgments, they might have created a defense that would have been credible beyond the Simi Valley jury box. But Koon especially did not want to be seen as a bungler. He wanted to show the world that he was right.

The defendants faced a total of eleven felony charges. All were accused of assault with a deadly weapon and assault under color of authority. Koon and Powell were also charged with filing false police reports and Koon with being an accessory after the fact. Although Powell was named first in the indictment, giving the case its designation of *People v. Powell*, Stone and Mounger had agreed that Koon, as the officer in charge, would put on his case first. This decision set the tone for the defense.

MOUNGER AND STONE WERE TALENTED LAWYERS WHO HAD DRIFTED into the legal profession in the midst of police careers. As a police officer in the city of Orange, south of Los Angeles, Stone had attended night law classes at Western State University in nearby Fullerton. He passed the bar in 1979 and continued to work as a police officer after becoming an attorney for the city. Then he met George Franscell, an experienced attorney who specialized in police misconduct cases. Stone quit the police force and worked four years with Franscell in police litigation before becoming general counsel of the Los Angeles Police Protective League in 1984.

One of Stone's clients as lawyer for the league was Darryl Mounger, a feisty LAPD sergeant. Mounger, then in the second of his three careers, had built a successful business selling electronic equipment to a law enforcement clientele. But being a police officer had seemed more useful and glamorous, so Mounger sold his business in 1975 and applied for admission to the LAPD. He was resourceful. Told that he was a quarter inch shorter than the LAPD height minimum, he sought out a chiropractor and asked to be stretched. A lenient examiner allowed him into the Police Academy. "Technically, I'm five eight, but not always," Mounger told me.[35]

For a time, Mounger was a rising star in the LAPD. He led his unit in arrests, became a detective and passed the sergeant's test. Then a partner involved in a rooftop shootout mistakenly shot a maintenance man instead of the armed suspect he was pursuing. Internal Affairs investigated, and the partner asked Mounger to serve as his defense representative in administrative proceedings. Mounger reluctantly agreed, and the decision proved a turning point in his life. The shooting was denounced by Daryl Gates, and Commander Matthew Hunt ruled that it was unjustified. Mounger was incensed, and took the unusual step of making a videotape that reenacted the incident. The tape so impressed an LAPD Board of Rights that his partner was cleared.

According to Stone, Mounger was so effective that Internal Affairs launched "a vendetta" against him and obtained access to Mounger's private telephone records "without a search warrant and without authorization of any kind."[36] To protect his privacy, Mounger sued Chief Gates and won, and his case became a milestone in establishing the rights of California police officers. But Stone dropped out during the litigation after a quarrel with Mounger, who thought he knew as much about the law as his attorney. "If you can pass the bar, I can pass the bar," Mounger said to Stone.[37] And he proved it. Mounger resigned from the LAPD, graduated from Southwestern University School of Law in May 1989 and passed the bar in July. He had been in practice for fifteen months when Cliff Ruff called from the Police Protective League to ask him to represent Koon.

Ruff, baffled by Koon's supervisory lapses during the King arrest, realized that Koon needed a lawyer who was also a police peer. Ruff thought Mounger's background as an LAPD sergeant would enable him to understand Koon's behavior and offset his lack of courtroom experience. It was a shrewd judgment, and Mounger was useful to the defense in other ways as well. It was Mounger, with his electronics background and experience in constructing a videotaped defense, who came up with the idea of outlining the figures of King and the officers during the crucial but blurry early frames of the Holliday videotape. Stone believes this device, used as the tape was played in slow motion, helped jurors understand that it was King who started the aggression.[38]

Mounger began the defense presentation with tone-setting witnesses who minimized King's injuries and described his behavior. Los Angeles Fire Department paramedic Kathleen Bosak testified that it looked to her as if King had suffered cuts on the right cheek in "a simple fall to the ground." She said she had not approached King closely enough to determine whether he had alcohol on his breath because he was spitting blood at her. Officer Susan Clemmer, a rookie who was in the fourth LAPD car to arrive at the scene, had observed King, handcuffed and hog-tied at the side of the road. He was laughing and repeatedly saying "fuck you."[39] Clemmer said that Powell, highly agitated, had walked up to her as she was directing traffic at the Foothill-Osborne intersection. "I was scared," Powell said. "The guy threw me off his back. I thought I was going to have to shoot him."

Clemmer, who impressed jurors as straightforward, had been an emergency medical technician before becoming a police officer. She agreed with Bosak that King did not seem seriously injured. Clemmer had been ordered to accompany Wind and the hog-tied King in the ambulance and stayed with them in the hospital emergency room. Reinforcing Bosak's story, she said that King had spit blood at her in the ambulance. There was something about King that intrigued Clemmer and caused her to pay close attention to him. When King muttered words in the emergency room that she could not understand, Clemmer asked him to repeat them. King obliged. Smiling and looking directly at Koon, he said to the sergeant, "I love you."

Mounger's next witness was David Love, the only African American among the LAPD bystanders at the scene. As Mounger realized, Love's very presence was helpful to the defense for it seemed to suggest (at least to a jury with no black members) that the beating of King was not racially motivated. Love was a good witness in other ways as well. He had watched Powell swing his baton as King advanced, and he testified that the first blow had landed on King's upper torso. Love had then been ordered to attend to the passengers in King's car, conveniently removing him as a witness from most of the beating until he participated in the handcuffing of King.

Despite Love's acknowledgment under cross-examination that he had formed an opinion from watching the video that King had been hit an excessive number of times, his testimony underscored an essential theme of the defense. King's combativeness had made Powell's baton use appropriate, Love testified. "The next level of escalation would have to be your gun," he said.

Koon then took command of his defense, as he had meant to take control of the situation at Foothill and Osborne in the early morning of March 3, 1991. Speaking in a calm and measured tone, Koon described his background and his activities at the beginning of the last shift he would ever work as a Los Angeles police officer. He had arrived typically early at

Foothill Station so that the watch commander on the previous shift could leave before 11:00 P.M. when Koon's shift began.[40] As Koon drove away from the station, he heard a radio call from an LAPD dispatcher saying that the California Highway Patrol had requested assistance in a pursuit. Koon soon reached a chaotic scene where officers with drawn guns were confronting an imposing-looking man and yelling at him to lie on the ground with legs and arms spread out. From his first glimpse of King, Koon saw that he was "very buffed out . . . very muscular."

Mounger asked Koon the "significance" of King's muscularity, drawing a quick objection from Yochelson. At the bench, out of hearing of the jury, the prosecutor implored Weisberg to prevent Koon from saying that he believed King was an ex-convict. The judge overruled the objection, the first of several rebuffs for the prosecution during Koon's testimony. Weisberg said Koon's opinion "certainly would be reflective of his state of mind on this issue . . ." Continuing with his testimony, Koon said that "'buffed out' is jargon that I have come to associate with very muscular." Mounger asked Koon what he thought when he saw King. "My initial response was that he was probably an ex-con," Koon said.

During the next two days, Koon gave a compelling account of the incident. He explained that he had taken control of the arrest because he feared the worst as Melanie Singer advanced on King with drawn gun. Koon told of trying vainly to arrest King without hurting him, first with shouted commands, then with the swarm of officers whom King threw off his back and finally with Taser shots, all of this happening before a blow was struck. He described King's charge at Powell and Powell's baton swing that knocked King down. He told of the many blows and kicks that followed from Powell and Wind and the stomp by Briseno. Through all this King showed few signs of pain.

"I'm getting concerned, scared and a little frightened," said Koon. "This gentleman has been subjected to a multitude of blows from metal PR-24 batons, and there was no evidence he was going to comply."

As the beating continued, Koon said he thought of applying the carotid hold to King but didn't "because in Los Angeles the choke hold is associated with the death of blacks." The beating continued until King yelled "Please stop" and raised his hands in what Koon considered "a compliance mode."

Koon said that despite the many times he had watched the video, he had never counted the actual number of blows, but he did not dispute a commonly used estimate of more than fifty. Nor did he shrink from characterizing what had happened under his command. Using a pointer, Koon went frame by frame through the videotape, describing every action of the officers and making no attempt to coat the ugliness of the incident in euphemisms. "It's violent and it's brutal," Koon said.

As prosecutor Terry White acknowledged afterward, Koon was believable because he was sincere. His account of the King affair had remained consistent on fundamental points, if not on every detail, since he first related it to police investigators. He told essentially the same story in Simi Valley that he would subsequently tell in his book and at the 1993 federal trial in Los Angeles. But Koon was more persuasive on the witness stand at Simi Valley than at any other time before or after. He was buoyed by the supportive presence of Mounger, whose knowledge of police work enabled him to frame questions in a way that encouraged Koon to enrich his narrative with police experiences. Koon, like other witnesses, was given wide latitude by the court in explaining his answers, and he was comfortable in dealing with the cross-examination of Yochelson, who was inexperienced in treating a police officer as an adversarial witness. He may also have sensed that the jury was sympathetic.

But the principal reason that Koon did so well at Simi Valley was that he had a need to tell his story to the world. He had talked candidly to Jaxon Van Derbeken of the *Daily News*, describing the King arrest as "a managed and controlled use of force."[41] But this was not enough. Koon was a straight and stubborn man who had overcome a speech impediment, put himself through college, earned two master's degrees, and succeeded in the profession he had chosen as his life work. As a police officer he had sought difficult and demanding assignments. He was proud that he was valued by his peers and of the many commendations he had received from the LAPD. Koon thought of himself not as a hero, although he had performed undisputed acts of valor, but as a professional police officer who did his duty. He was a devoted family man, the father of five, who had been married to the same woman for twenty years.

All this—his police vocation, his family, his Roman Catholic faith—formed a composite portrait that Koon wanted the world to see. He wanted to be known as the good officer he believed himself to be and not as a bad or brutal cop. Koon's pride was simultaneously his strength and his vulnerability. His faith and his strength enabled him to face the potential terrors of prison, but he could not with equanimity accept the loss of reputation. The trial gave Koon an opportunity he knew might never come again to tell his story to the vast audience that was watching the trial on television. It gave him a chance to show that he was in control of events that through no intention of his own had controlled him.

Koon's view of the incident was different from that of George Holliday, from the safety of his balcony, or the views of Powell or Wind or Briseno, on the ground. As Koon saw it, in his first glimpse of the scene and in his mind's eye ever afterward, there had been a dangerous armed confrontation that he thought might end in violent death. What Koon believed he had done was prevent a shooting, perhaps of Melanie Singer—more probably of Rodney King. The world might think of him as a brutal cop, but Stacey Koon was certain that he had acted professionally and well. What animated Koon's testimony and gave it emotional force was his fervent belief that he had saved King's life.

Koon's credibility was enhanced when jurors compared his testimony to the testimony of Melanie Singer, the eyewitness on whom the prosecution most depended. Koon's recollections could be more easily reconciled than Singer's with the video record. For instance, he remembered King's charge at Powell much as it was shown on the videotape, although he was uncertain if Powell and King had collided or precisely where Powell's first blow had landed. Singer did not remember the charge at all, and she said she had turned away from the action after the first blows.

Also, Singer had seemed flustered on the witness stand when her account was challenged by Stone, while Koon calmly repeated under cross-examination the same story he had related during Mounger's direct examination. Some jurors extrapolated from these contrasting courtroom performances to the incident itself. They suspected that Singer might also have been flustered when King was slow to obey her commands, while Koon's steady performance as a witness undergirded his claim to have made a composed and professional assessment on the night of the beating. Even Whiting, the juror most appalled by the force used against King, accepted Koon's contention that it was necessary for him to take control of the arrest. "I think [Koon] may have saved King's life because Melanie Singer or someone would have shot him," Whiting told me.[42]

White had wanted Yochelson to cross-examine Koon because he thought his colleague's less confrontational approach would expose Koon as the "arrogant sonofabitch" that White believed him to be.[43] "I tend to be very aggressive in cross-examination," White said. "I thought that on the stand he would be very arrogant and that we would really clash, that it wouldn't be good for the case."[44] But as White watched the self-possessed Koon answer questions in a "very believable fashion," he had second thoughts. In truth, as White later recognized, it wouldn't have mattered who had cross-examined Koon. "He was going to tell the same story," White said. "He really believed that story. He will go to his deathbed believing that story."[45]

Yochelson tried to shake Koon. His questions emphasized the violence and duration of the beating, trying to cast doubt on Koon's contention that the force used was appropriate. But the prosecutor was attempting to shove his way through an open door, for Koon made no attempt to dodge the fact that King had been brutally subdued.

"Sir, have you ever seen a worse beating applied by members of the Los Angeles Police Department?" Yochelson asked.

"I have seen uses of force of considerable violence, but I have not seen anything that is as violent as this in my fourteen-and-a-half years, no, sir," Koon said.

Mounger then conducted a brief redirect examination. He wanted to show that Koon had made his decisions in a flash without enjoying the luxury of a slow-motion video.

"What were you thinking at the time you saw Melanie Singer approaching with a gun in her hand?" Mounger asked.

"What I thought at the time was a flashback that I had seen at the Academy when we went through a tour of the morgue. They have a picture of—"

Yochelson, who anticipated what Koon was about to say, leaped to his feet. "Excuse me, your honor, that is nonresponsive."

"Overruled," said Weisberg.

"That is also improper redirect," said Yochelson.

"Overruled," said Weisberg again. To Koon he said, "You can answer the question."

Fighting back unbidden tears and struggling to keep his voice from breaking, Koon said, "They show a picture when you are in the Academy [taken] at the morgue, and it is four [highway patrol] officers in full uniform that are on a slab and they are dead, and it is the Newhall shooting."[46]

The courtroom was suddenly quiet. Mounger paused. Jurors and reporters peered at Koon. Yochelson stared straight ahead. No one said anything. There are moments in trials when emotions burst through the procedural boundaries, and stoic witnesses declare what is in their hearts. This was such a moment. Koon, intensely emotional beneath his hard exterior, was so consumed with being in control that he often seemed cold and uncaring to those who did not fathom the depth of his feelings. Mounger had wanted Koon to show more of his feelings on the witness stand, but Koon would have none of it.

But Mounger was a sergeant who understood the sergeant he was questioning and knew how he felt about his work. When Koon thought about Melanie Singer advancing gun in hand on an unsearched suspect, the picture of the slain officers had flashed into his mind and Koon for once could not control himself. It was what Mounger wanted, but Koon seemed embarrassed. He did not want strangers to see him with tears in his eyes.

In allowing the jury and the world an unintended glimpse of his humanity, Koon had provided the trial's most eloquent moment. It was a moment that seemed to last forever in the quiet courtroom, a moment that opened a window into Koon's soul. There was nothing Terry White could do about it. There was nothing anyone could do. That Koon would cry, however briefly, had not occurred to the prosecutors or, indeed, to Koon himself. This human moment had come upon the courtroom unsuspected, revealing the intensity of the emotions that had guided Koon and had been disguised, even to himself, as cool and professional judgment.

Against the revelations of Koon's true feelings, which demolished with equal force the prosecution portrayal of Koon as a brute and his own contrived defense of managed and controlled use of force, even the violent videotape seemed pale and unconvincing.

Against the emotions Koon had sought to conceal from the world, the video could not stand.

10

JUDGMENT AT SIMI

"Duty required Officer Powell to act. Circumstances required him to engage his duty at his own peril. He didn't have the opportunity for calm reflection . . . He didn't have an opportunity to run the scenario backwards and forwards on a video screen in slow motion."

—Michael Stone[1]

"They think they are above the law. And I'm here to tell them and they should know that no man is above the law—not Rodney King, not Stacey Koon, not Ted Briseno, not Timothy Wind and not Laurence Powell."

—Terry White[2]

If Stacey Koon was the compass of the defense, then Sergeant Charles Duke was its anchor. Koon had steered the defense argument beyond the deep waters of reasonable doubt into the safe port of an affirmative defense in which the conduct of the defendants was acclaimed as well as justified. Testifying as an expert witness in Koon's behalf, Duke secured this argument in the hard doctrines of LAPD policy. The officers had been doing what they had been taught in the Police Academy. After repeatedly watching the video, Duke said he was certain that the officers who had so badly beaten and kicked Rodney King had acted on the basis of "reasonable perceptions" in dealing with an unsearched felony suspect whom they had reason to consider a threat.

Duke was a living legend within the LAPD. A hero of the SWAT team, he had received ninety commendations, earned a medal for bravery, and taught self-defense tactics or hostage negotiations to police agencies, the Marine Corps, and the FBI. Even a jury less enamored of police officers than the one assembled in Simi Valley might well have been dazzled by

Duke's background, which was elicited by Mounger in a long preamble to Duke's analysis of the videotape.

For jurors in need of an expert's argument in order to indulge their pro-police sympathies, Duke was the perfect witness. As interpreted by Duke, even Powell's ineptitude with the baton—a failing Sergeant DiStefano had emphasized when he testified for the prosecution about Powell's abysmal performance at roll call—became a point in his favor. As Duke saw it, since Powell was not adept with the baton, he had added reason to fear King. The fact that many of Powell's blows were ineffectively delivered made it seem more likely that King had received only minor injuries, as the officers and the paramedic at the scene had believed.

Duke welcomed the opportunity to testify. Not only did the trial allow him to defend fellow officers whom he believed innocent of criminal wrong-doing, but it gave him a platform to renew his crusade for restoring choke holds as a force option available to LAPD officers. Judge Weisberg did not allow Duke to tell the jury that choke-hold use had been restricted because the technique had been implicated in the deaths of blacks in police custody. But Koon had already testified that he had not used the choke hold on King because he associated it with the death of blacks.

Ever since the metal side-handled PR-24 baton was introduced a decade earlier, Duke had believed that it was a barbaric, bone-breaking weapon that was certain to cause thousands of unnecessary injuries. Duke was a tough guy who was willing to justify every blow to King, but he preferred what he saw as more humane alternatives, including upper-body control holds. In the two years after the choke-hold ban was imposed, Duke had led a counterrevolution against the PR-24 from his vantage point as self-defense and tactics trainer at the Police Academy. Now, in an irony Duke appreciated, he had been asked to defend officers who had provided a devastating example of the perils of the PR-24. Koon had wanted to vindicate himself to the jury and the world; Duke saw the trial as an opportunity to educate the jury and the television audience about the folly of a policy that encouraged officers to beat resistant suspects into submission.

Duke first summarized his views outside the presence of the jury at a hearing at which Mounger sought court permission to explore the history of how batons became the LAPD weapon of choice. White, realizing the danger of allowing experts to argue that policy had compelled the beating, sought to restrict Duke's testimony. But Weisberg heard Duke out. "The proper way to handle this situation would have been with either a net, leg grabbers or upper-body control hold," Duke told the court, adding that the LAPD had failed to equip vehicles with such equipment. "I think with nets and leg grabbers this incident wouldn't have lasted forty-five seconds," Duke said. "With upper-body control holds, it wouldn't have lasted thirty seconds."

"So if I understand you correctly you are saying [the King beating] is within the policy of the Los Angeles Police Department but you don't think it is right?" Mounger asked.

"That's correct," Duke said.

Weisberg permitted Duke to tell the jury that if the officers had been equipped with nets and leg grabbers, he would agree that the actions shown on the video constituted "unnecessary and violent use of force." But since they lacked such options and were confronted with an unsearched and combative suspect, they had no alternative but to beat him with batons until he complied. "It sounds cruel, but it may come to the point that you have to break a bone or so incapacitate a suspect to where he can no longer rise and pose a threat to the officers," Duke said.

Duke plowed frame by frame through the video, offering his opinion that the officers were justified at every point because of a "reasonable perception" that King was resistant. White put Duke through the video again on cross-examination, wringing occasional admissions that it might also have been reasonable to perceive King's movements as an understandable effort to evade the torrent of blows. Near the end of the incident, as King writhed in pain after Briseno's stomp and Powell and Wind resumed the beating, Duke said that the officers had evaluated the situation and used their batons again only after King started "to get into that aggressive mode."

"Can you read their minds, Sergeant Duke?" White asked.

"I can form an opinion based on my training and having trained people, what I can perceive that their perceptions are," Duke said.

"Well, what is Mr. King's perceptions at this time?"

"I've never been a suspect," Duke said. "I don't know."

Duke was also cross-examined by John Barnett, who wanted the sergeant to acknowledge that Briseno's "stomping motion" was as reasonable as the baton blows delivered by Powell and Wind. This Duke refused to do, although he said it "could be a perspective" that Briseno had seen King reaching toward his waistband when he put his foot on his neck. In fact, as Koon himself had conceded after watching the video, King had not been reaching for his waistband at all. He had put a hand on his buttocks, palm up, in utter helplessness. But Duke said Briseno might have had a "reasonable perception . . . that there was a possible threat."

Post-trial interviews with jurors suggest that the back-to-back testimony of Koon and Duke decisively established the defense contention that King had it in his power to prevent what happened to him. He had not been hit until he refused to obey repeated commands and until he threw off his back the officers who were trying to handcuff him. The first and most damaging blow had occurred when King charged at Powell. King had repeatedly attempted to regain his feet until the final stages of the incident. When he finally complied, the blows had stopped.

Although no one realized it at the time, the defense had reached its zenith. Subsequent experts would be less effective than Duke in justifying use of force. Powell would be less persuasive than Koon. Briseno and others would poke holes in the testimony of Koon and Powell that would never be repaired. Gradually, the defense would cloud its own case enough to encourage a second prosecution.

The trouble began during the testimony of retired LAPD Captain Robert Michael, called by Mounger on the heels of Duke as a second use-of-force witness. From viewing the video a hundred times and portions of it as many as three hundred times, Michael concluded that the King incident involved "ten distinct uses of force rather than one continuous use of force." He said all uses were justified because the officers had evaluated and "deescalated" after each force application. He also testified that only about twenty of the fifty-six baton blows delivered by Powell and Wind actually struck King.

But Michael did not fare well under cross-examination. White attacked his credentials, bringing out that he had taken disability leave in 1982, eight years before his retirement, and that he had little street experience or training in the use of force after the 1970s. Michael conceded that two books he had written on law enforcement were self-published and had never been used as training manuals by the LAPD. His least believable moment on the witness stand came when he contended that an intoxicated person feeling pain from numerous baton blows would react more quickly than a sober person who was not in pain. White responded incredulously, and Mounger wisely decided, one witness late, that he would rest his case without calling four others on his list.

The defense now shifted to Stone, who presaged the testimony of his client, Powell, with a parade of police bystander witnesses. The first and most hapless was Officer Louis Turriaga, who could be seen in the video putting his foot on King's face during the handcuffing and was then assisted by Officer Rolando Solano in dragging King to the roadside after he had been handcuffed. Turriaga recalled that King, while on knees and forearms, had lunged at Powell, who hit him with forward and reverse strokes of his baton. But when asked by Barnett to examine the video, Turriaga could not see the blows he had described. Nor could he see himself on the video, which he said he had watched many times. "Can you think of any reason you are not in the picture?" Barnett asked. "No, sir," said Turriaga, who was facing LAPD administrative charges of misconduct for his role in the King arrest and was deep into denial.[3]

Other bystanders told other stories. Officer Christopher Hajduk, a rookie LAPD officer, testified he had been shocked when repeated blows to King's legs had no effect. Hajduk's training officer was the veteran Robert Simpach, who a decade earlier had tried to arrest James Mincey for traffic violations; Mincey's death, at the hands of another officer, had led to the choke-hold ban that Duke so deplored. Simpach had seen Powell deliver only three blows to King. As Simpach remembered it, the blows were delivered to King's thigh as he attempted to rise. Wind then kicked King in the right shoulder area, "which seemed to have the effect of knocking Mr. King to the ground," Simpach said.

The cumulative effect of this testimony was minimal. Even the Simi Valley jury recognized that the bystander officers, none of whom had seen the entire incident, were partial to the defendants. But while volunteering almost nothing that was damaging to the defendants, most of these police witnesses stayed within the boundaries of truthfulness. Simpach and Hajduk, for instance, acknowledged under cross-examination that they had not seen King swing at the officers or regain his feet.

Officer Solano, Stone's next witness, was more than a bystander. As Briseno's partner, he had grabbed King's leg during the unsuccessful attempt to handcuff him. After King hurled Powell and Briseno off his back, Solano had backed away at Koon's direction while the sergeant fired the Taser. Solano was amazed and frightened when the darts from the electric stun gun failed to stop King. As Solano remembered it, King "lunged" toward Koon after the second Taser volley and was confronted by Powell, who flailed away wildly with forward and reverse power strokes of his baton. Solano saw four blows land in the shoulder area and two bounce upward into King's face. He did not like the sound the baton made when it hit King's face and looked away. Solano's obvious distaste for this violence impressed the jurors most appalled by the beating; juror Anna Charmaine Whiting thought Solano was the trial's most reliable witness.[4] He was also the first LAPD witness to support Melanie Singer's assertion that King had been hit in the head. But Solano's account was more credible than Singer's because it seemed compatible with the video and with medical testimony about the location of King's facial injuries.

Solano's testimony offered Stone an escape hatch from a dubious strategy. Prosecutors conceded that Powell was justified in using his baton when King charged, which is when the head blows were said to have occurred. LAPD policy prohibits intentional head strikes with the baton except in self-defense, as Duke had testified. The crucial question was not whether Powell's baton had struck King in the face but whether the blow was intentional. Stone, however, was obsessed with the notion that King's facial injuries were caused entirely by collisions with the pavement. He did not believe that Powell's baton had even struck King in the head.

Stone's approach obscured the vital question of intent. Only in Melanie Singer's account of the incident did Powell seem to be aiming deliberately at King's head, and this portion of her testimony had been discredited by Stone's effective cross-examination. Solano's statement that the baton blows had been deflected into King's face provided Stone with a opportunity to concede the head blows and say that the evidence clearly showed them to be accidental.

As Stone should have known, there was substantial agreement about the head blows among the three officers—Solano, Wind, and Briseno—with the closest view of the incident. Stone can be forgiven for distrusting Briseno, whose path to acquittal was at Powell's expense, but he should have adopted the observations of Solano and Wind. As Wind had told LAPD investigators, for instance, King's head and body came up as Powell swung "and he moved enough that Powell hit him in the face."[5] This was a description of an accident, not a crime.

Stone told me later that he thought it necessary to dispute the head blows because the prosecution had made such a "big deal" of them.[6] Actually, it was Stone who made them into a big deal, to Powell's eventual detriment in the federal trial. In fairness to Stone, who was trying his first felony case, he faced a tougher challenge than his fellow defense attorneys. Powell was the villain of the videotape and obviously the most vulnerable defendant. Koon, the ostensible supervisor, had struck no blows. Wind was a probationary officer. Briseno was charged with a single stomp that was open to interpretation. Considering the heavy odds that Stone believed Powell faced even with a pro-police jury, it is understandable that he was reluctant to concede anything.

Stone also was reluctant to put Powell on the stand, an attitude based on his assessment of his client's stylistic deficiencies, rather than lack of faith in his innocence. Powell habitually avoided direct eye contact, and his high-pitched voice became even higher under pressure. His nervous laugh when he called for a rescue ambulance after the beating was typical of Powell's behavior in stressful situations. Nevertheless, Powell was the focus of the prosecution case, and Stone realized that the jury expected to hear his story. Stone put him on the stand.

In the early stages of direct examination, Powell's nervousness was displayed in rambling, long-winded answers that were punctuated by White's objections, most of them sustained. But eventually Powell settled down. He described the conclusion of the pursuit and the scene after King stopped. Powell had crouched behind the door of his patrol car with gun drawn as the Singers ordered King out of the white Hyundai. He remembered King exiting after a delay and waving at the police helicopter overhead. In an answer struck by the court, he said he had thought that King resembled "a robot" moving "real slow and unnatural." He remembered saying to Wind that King was "dusted," and he recalled his concern as Melanie Singer advanced on King with her gun held out in front of her. He remembered Koon's orders to handcuff King. Assisted by the other officers he had tried to force King's arms behind him and had put his knee in King's back, as he had been taught. He described how King had hurled him off his body.

Powell had been relieved that Koon ordered the officers back and used the Taser. But he was alarmed when King, after being hit by four darts from the electric stun gun, immediately regained his feet. "I saw him get up, turn and come right at me," Powell said. As Powell remembered it, King's charge was more menacing and direct than it seemed on the video, which Powell said "has confused my memory because it is not my perspective." In Powell's memory, King had advanced with arms extended, and they had collided. Powell had swung his baton, aiming at King's chest. "I saw Mr. King fall like a rag doll down on to the ground and his head smashed the pavement. . . . " He had stood over King, hitting him again and again so he wouldn't get up again. He had heard Koon say, "Don't hit him in the head."

Powell became increasingly apprehensive as he recalled the details of the incident. That was fine with Stone, who hoped jurors would sympathize with Powell's mental state even if they did not endorse his version of events. Repeatedly throughout the trial, defense attorneys asked jurors to pay attention to the "state of mind" of the officers rather than to their actions as portrayed on the video. Powell's state of mind seems to have been fearfulness bordering on panic. "I was completely in fear for my life, scared to death that [if] this guy got back up, he was going to take my gun away from me or there was going to be a shooting, and I was doing everything I could to keep him down on the ground," Powell said. He said he had continued to hit King in the arms and legs with Koon shouting at him to keep him down. Finally he heard Koon yell "Do you give?" and saw King put his hands up with his palms facing outward. "I was absolutely exhausted, fatigued, at the end of my energy," Powell said. He gave his handcuffs to Briseno, who grabbed King's arms, "and suddenly a bunch of officers that I hadn't seen up until that point came in and assisted Officer Briseno in handcuffing the suspect."

Powell seemed relieved after telling his story. But Stone knew that Powell's conduct in the aftermath of the incident would also be an issue. The defense attorney wanted to defuse a cross-examination he expected would portray his client as callous, and he led Powell through an explanation of his post-incident behavior, beginning with the call for the rescue ambulance. Powell was now more comfortable on the witness stand, but his answers seemed more evasive. He denied that he had laughed or giggled at the end of the radio call. "I was breathing very heavily, trying to catch my breath," Powell said.

After being instructed by Koon to file a use-of-force report, Powell had driven alone to Pacifica Hospital, following the ambulance in which Wind and Clemmer accompanied King. It was during this drive that Powell called Officer Corina Smith on his in-car computer, the Mobile Digital Terminal or MDT, and bragged that he hadn't "beaten anyone this bad in a long time." This message bothered even jurors sympathetic to the defense, and Powell's attempt to explain it was unconvincing. He blandly dismissed the comment as a way of saying that he had been involved in a "donnybrook" and had "never had to use so much force to control a prisoner."

While trying to minimize the importance of such MDT messages in a series of follow-up questions, Stone made a legal blunder that opened the door to examination of Powell's racial attitudes. His key question was, "Can you describe some other non-essential communications that you made that night over the MDT?" Stone had forgotten that one of these communications was a message to Smith twenty minutes before the King incident in which Powell compared a domestic dispute among African Americans to a scene from the movie *Gorillas in the Mist*.

Outside the presence of the jury, Stone later described this question as "thoughtless" and "unwitting" and said he was mortified. "Obviously, I wasn't soliciting information about *Gorillas in the Mist*; I had completely forgotten about it," Stone told the court. "It has been out of my mind, it has been out of this case . . ." The issue was also out of White's mind. While Stone's blunder is widely remembered, it is rarely recalled that White objected to the question and that Weisberg sustained the objection. Only later, after discussing the issue with colleagues and reflecting on it, did White recognize that Stone had given him a critical opening.

White had agreed at the outset of the trial to give notice to the defense if he intended to raise racial motivation as an issue. Considering that there were no blacks on the jury and that White himself doubted that the beating was racially motivated, this was not much of a concession. The only known racist comment by a defendant was the "gorillas-in-the-mist" MDT message, and it had been sent after an incident in which Powell had behaved professionally. White realized that Weisberg would not let him introduce a statement so obviously prejudicial against Powell unless it could somehow be related to the King incident.

When Stone unexpectedly gave the prosecution an opportunity to brand his client a racist, White made the most of it. "Race could be seen by this jury as the motivating factor by Officer Powell," White told the court after the recess. Weisberg read the transcript of the computer exchange between Powell and Smith, who had replied to the "gorillas" comment by saying, "Let me guess who be the parties." Powell replied, "Good guess." This convinced Weisberg that Powell had displayed racial prejudice. "I don't think it's ambiguous," the judge said, ruling that White could ask about the message in cross-examination.

White went after Powell fiercely, provoking responses that doubtless would have offended black jurors, if there had been any to offend. Even though all participants in the incident that had prompted the "gorillas" message were African American, Powell blandly denied that he had used the word gorillas as a reference to blacks. White then became sarcastic.

"Now this call that involved these African Americans, was it in a jungle?" asked White.

"In a what?" asked Powell.

"A jungle?"

"No," said Powell.

"Was it at the zoo?"

"No."

"Were there any gorillas around?"

"I didn't see any," said Powell.

The cross-examination continued in this vein. Powell denied that "Let me guess who be the parties" was an attempt to parody the speech of African Americans. He could not explain why he had responded, "Good guess." He dismissed his message about not having "beaten anyone this bad in a long time" as "common police jargon," not an admission of inappropriate force. He asserted again that he had not hit King in the head and said he "didn't know for sure" why it had been necessary to call an ambulance for him. The only injuries Powell had seen were "some cuts on his face and some blood."

Powell spent the entire day of March 31, 1992, on the witness stand. By the time Weisberg called a halt at 5:00 P.M. the defense was dispirited. Powell's palpable lies about the racial nature of his first exchange of MDT messages with Smith had seemed unconvincing even to his codefendants. In the press room down the hall, the consensus was that White had inflicted heavy damage. White also believed that he had Powell on the run, and he pressed his advantage when cross-examination resumed the following morning. After Powell again asserted that he believed that King was on PCP the night of the arrest, White explored the defendant's attitudes toward the man he had beaten.*

---

* I thought at the time that Powell's performance on the PCP issue carried a ring of truth that seemed lacking when he tried to explain his MDT communications with Corina Smith. This impression was reinforced after the trial when I read Powell's interview with Internal Affairs investigators. Powell had trouble reconciling anything he saw on the videotape with his recollections of the incident but did remember thinking that King was "dusted," that is, on PCP. He had also anticipated this line of cross-examination and remembered his PCP training and articles he had read on the subject.

"At any time during this evening did it go through your mind that this was not a human being that you were beating?" asked White.

"No," said Powell.

"All right. Mr. King is a human being, isn't he?"

"Yes, sir."

"He should be treated like a human being?"

"Yes, sir."

"Even though he is a suspect and even though he is suspected of committing a crime, this man is still a human being, isn't he?"

"Yes, sir."

"He deserves to be treated like a human being, didn't he?"

"Yes, sir."

"He wasn't an animal, was he?"

"No, sir, just acting like one."

White wasn't finished. Powell's contempt for King angered the emotional prosecutor, as did the readiness of LAPD witnesses to defend the beating on what he considered flimsy grounds. Barnett called these police witnesses participants in a "conspiracy of silence," and White believed that one way to expose the conspiracy was to drive a wedge between Powell and Koon. If Powell really had been "out of control," as White knew Briseno would testify, then Koon's depiction of the incident as a textbook use of force was not believable. White viewed Powell as the moral weak link among the officers. Because Powell was also the defendant most likely to be convicted, White thought he might crack under cross-examination.

Powell was certainly no Koon. Koon was stubbornly proud of his professionalism. As the supervisor who had taken control of the arrest, he considered himself responsible for actions taken by officers at his command. Powell, in contrast, was unwilling to accept blame for anything. By exploiting this trait, White hoped to show that both Koon and Powell—and, to a lesser extent, Wind and Briseno—had acted unreasonably.

White asked Powell a series of questions about his initial reluctance to handcuff King. As the prosecutor had expected, Powell said he didn't think it "safe" to approach King and had done so only because of Koon's orders. White then asked Powell about his police report, which had exaggerated King's resistance and omitted the fact that King was on the ground during most of the beating. Powell was unwilling to take responsibility for these misstatements and omissions. He said he had written at Koon's direction that King had been knocked down and subdued with the "swarm technique."

His voice flashing with anger, White asked Powell whether he would put inaccurate information in his report because of Koon's orders.

"That is why he has the extra stripe," Powell said.

"Because he tells you what to do?"

"Yes, he does."

"He controls you?"

"Yes, he does."

"You are a puppet in his hands?"

"Oh, when he tells me to do things and they're within department policy, and I feel they're reasonable, then by all means you do them or you are in trouble," Powell answered.

White paused a moment and asked, "If there was excessive force out there that night then Sergeant Koon is the one responsible for it?" Powell said he wouldn't carry out unreasonable orders. "That would be like saying, 'Shoot that shoplifter.' I'm not going to do that," he said. But White persisted. "Hypothetically speaking, if there was excessive force used out there that night, would Sergeant Koon be responsible for that excessive force?"

"That is not a question that can be answered," Powell said. "That doesn't make sense."

"It is not a question you want to answer, is it?" White asked.

"No, sir. It doesn't make sense. I can't answer that. You are going to have to rephrase it."

White exploded in fury. Pointing at Koon, he asked Powell, "If there was excessive force used out there that night, you wouldn't say it, you wouldn't testify here in court in front of this jury that this man was responsible, would you?"

"Objection, badgering," Mounger said.

"Overruled," said Weisberg. "The question, you can answer it."

Powell straightened in the witness stand. "If there was excessive force out there that night, I would have reported it to another supervisor," he said in an uncertain voice.

"That is not the question," said White, shouting again. "I'm saying if there was excessive force out there that night, is this man responsible?"

"If there was excessive force out there?"

"Yes," said White.

"He didn't hit anybody," said Powell. "How could he be?"

"Was he controlling it?"

"He was in control, yes."

"He was in control of the force that was used that night? This man was responsible for that force, wasn't he?"

"He was controlling the situation."

"This man was responsible for the force used out there that night, wasn't he?"

"Everybody out there was responsible for their own actions," Powell said.

It was the closest Powell would ever come, in or out of court, to taking responsibility for what he had done. But it was a hollow gesture, for he reiterated throughout the remainder of the cross-examination and ever afterward that all the blows he had delivered were appropriate.

Still, everyone in the courtroom could see that Powell had been shaken by White's probing cross-examination. That would not be wholly damaging to the defense, for several jurors believed that Powell's performance on the witness stand reflected the tendency to panic he must have displayed when confronted with a resistant Rodney King. Juror Whiting, whose sympathy for Powell was slight, had no doubt that he had been terrified by King. Unlike many other jurors, Whiting did not dismiss the computer messages as irrelevant. She understood that they expressed racial prejudice and recognized that Powell's biases had contributed to his fears.

To a jury that admired police officers, Powell was a poor specimen of the profession, but his performance on the witness stand had oddly restored a defense of reasonable doubt. Koon would never in any circumstance have tried to save himself by confessing panic, and he would not have been believable if he had tried. Powell was a different story. Jurors could see that he had been afraid, and it is possible that their own racial fears made it easier for them to put themselves in Powell's shoes. But Stone, knowing nothing of how the jurors felt, realized that Powell had barely held together during cross-examination, and he could not wait to get his client off the witness stand. He soon rested his case.[7]

Because Koon had done so well, Mounger was comfortable with the defense case despite Powell's shaky performance. Stone wasn't. He wanted Wind to take the stand. This puzzled Wind's lawyer, Paul DePasquale, because Stone knew Wind had told police investigators that Powell's first baton blow had struck King in the head. Wind wasn't likely to change his story; DePasquale said his client was showing "the compulsion of an honest man to tell the truth."[8] But whether the truth about the head blow would have been damaging to Powell, as DePasquale believed, is conjectural. It was clear by now to jurors that no two officers had identical perceptions. While Wind would have contradicted Powell on the head blows, he might have reinforced the impression that King had acted in a bizarre fashion that made him seem dangerous.

Unlike Stone and Mounger, DePasquale was not a former officer who felt impelled to defend police conduct. He was interested only in his client's acquittal. He realized that if Wind were the only defendant not to testify, jurors might think he had something to hide. But Wind had seen what White had done to Powell under cross-examination, and he wanted no part of that. He was suffering physically and emotionally from the stress of the trial.[9] Respecting his client's wishes, DePasquale announced that Wind would not testify. He said Wind's defense would be that he was "at the bottom of the chain of authority in this incident."

DePasquale was the Rodney Dangerfield among the many defense lawyers. His bass voice, bombastic manner and Falstaffian appearance made him seem a comic-opera figure. Journalists and lawyers alike underrated him, in part because his courtroom presence could be clumsy and his questions long-winded. But the bumbling appearance was deceptive. DePasquale was a shrewd and observant lawyer. He tried to seat Wind where the jurors could get a good look at him because he realized that Wind was the most handsome of the defendants and that he seemed younger than Powell, even though he was more than two years older.

Portraying Wind as a novice who had followed the instruction of senior officers, DePasquale fought vigorously and with partial success to prevent jurors from learning about Wind's previous police experience in Kansas. He repeatedly pointed out that Wind was a probationary officer and that Powell was his trainer. He used the slow-motion version of the videotape to demonstrate that Wind had stepped back during the beating to evaluate the impact of his blows, as he had been taught. The effect of this minimalist defense was largely lost on the press and the public because of the dramatic testimony of the other defendants. Wind went unmentioned during long stretches of the trial.

One of DePasquale's few witnesses was Officer Jerry Mulford, a twenty-year LAPD veteran and instructor in tactics at the Los Angeles Police Academy who was called as an expert on police training. Under direct examination by DePasquale and cross-examination by Stone, Mulford drew a vivid picture of the perils of arresting a muscular, unsearched suspect who had led police on a long pursuit, stopped his car adjacent to a darkened park and disobeyed officers' commands. Mulford disapproved of advancing on such a suspect with a drawn gun, and he thought it appropriate of a supervisor to take over an arrest from any officer who used such a tactic. He said that on the basis of their training, LAPD officers would have expected Taser shots to stop most suspects. He thought it appropriate for officers to use their batons, even if it took numerous blows to subdue the suspect. In response to a question from Stone, Mulford sounded a basic theme of the defense: "The suspect is the one who sets the rules out there and if he keeps on his attack, then you have to defend yourself."

Stone saw Mulford's testimony as another opportunity to discredit Briseno—an urgent priority after Powell's shaky performance on the witness stand. He asked Mulford if it would be improper to kick a suspect in the neck to keep him on the ground. Mulford replied that LAPD officers were taught to avoid the neck "at all costs" because such a kick "can cause serious injury to the person being handcuffed."

Briseno's lawyer, John Barnett, was livid. He regarded Stone's questions and Mulford's answers as a gratuitous attempt to denigrate Briseno for refusing to justify the King beating. Cross-examining Mulford with a sharpness that matched White's interrogation of Powell, Barnett asked if there was a limit to the number of baton blows an officer could inflict on a suspect on the ground. Mulford said this depended on the situation; it might take only one blow, but it could mean one hundred blows.

"Well, can you beat him to death?" Barnett asked.

"If it is a life-threatening situation, your life or his, yes," Mulford said.

MULFORD, A CAPABLE OFFICER OF THE OLD SCHOOL, REFLECTED THE conflicted attitudes within the LAPD toward the King beating. Most senior officers knew that the incident had been a public relations catastrophe that had encouraged disrespect for police, fueled the drive to oust Chief Gates, and led to the Christopher Commission inquiry. Political consequences aside, many officers were also critical of Powell's inadequacy with the baton and Koon's supervisory lapses. But even officers who thought it was fair to fire Koon or Powell generally believed that it was unjust to prosecute officers for good-faith actions taken against a resistant suspect who had seemed to be on PCP.

By the time *Powell* came to trial, the trauma of the Christopher Commission report had begun to ease, and police sympathies for the defendants, except Briseno, had increased. Many rank-and-file officers were fascinated by the trial, which had become a televised drama of expiation in which they could imagine themselves in the roles of participants. As police officers saw it, Rodney King was the clear villain. Officers saw in him every dangerous or resistant suspect they had ever confronted, as well as a drunken menace who would probably have crashed his car and killed someone if he had not been stopped. Koon, despite his intelligence, was seen as a sergeant with more guts than brains, a principled hero who had put himself at risk by intervening to prevent a shooting. Wind was a promising rookie who had the misfortune to be in the wrong place at the wrong time with the wrong training officer. Powell was Officer Dufus. He had a big mouth and a weak baton swing and was better suited to another line of work, but he had followed orders and was certainly no criminal. Briseno was cast in the unambiguous role of traitor. As Koon later labeled him, he was "Benedict Briseno."

This had not been the rank-and-file reaction to Briseno in the immediate aftermath of the incident, when there was talk of prosecuting even some of the bystander officers. Many officers had thought it unfair to indict Briseno for a single stomp, and his action was defended as readily as Koon's use of the Taser, Powell's baton swings, and Wind's kicks. But this attitude changed when it became known that Briseno would be a witness against the others. Officers who would say nothing critical of Koon or Powell eagerly provided reporters with juicy details of Briseno's previous excessive-force incident and with gossip about domestic problems that included the alleged physical abuse of his former spouse.[10] This get-Briseno attitude spilled over into the trial, where expert police witnesses willing to excuse the most dubious of Powell's actions refused to make any concession to Briseno. Mulford represented this attitude in the extreme. Responding to Stone's hypothetical questions, Mulford said it was not uncommon for officers under stress in training situations to laugh or giggle, as Powell had done after beating King. "I have seen them cry," he said. "I have seen them just turn and walk away. I have seen them quiet up and just stand and stare at the wall. I've watched them urinate and defecate on themselves."

Mulford said that recruits who responded to stress in such extreme ways were not flunked out of the Police Academy "because everybody has a different level of stress response." But he could not imagine that an officer who had watched a suspect repeatedly struck by batons every time he tried to gain his feet might use his foot to keep him down, as Briseno claimed to have done. Suppose, asked Barnett, that an officer used his foot in this manner because he feared being struck by baton blows if he kneeled down and used his hands. "I wouldn't move and put my foot on the suspect until the other officers backed off," Mulford responded.

Taken in its totality, the message of the police experts called as witnesses for Koon, Powell, and Wind was that every blow and kick delivered to King was justified except for Briseno's single stomp. Powell's baton blows had shattered King's face and broken his right leg, and the officer had bragged about the beating afterward. All this could be excused as the actions of an officer under stress, but Briseno's stomp, which had caused no injuries, was indefensible to the police experts who testified for the other officers.

Briseno, never gregarious, had become an extremely lonely man. Like his codefendants, he had not worked since the King incident and had exhausted his savings. Unlike Koon, Powell, and Wind, he had no strong network of emotional support. His brother worked for the LAPD and stuck by him, and a few police friends called occasionally, but they were exceptions. Briseno felt depressed and abandoned. His plight was captured by photographer Joe Kennedy of the Los Angeles Times in a revealing picture that showed Briseno, with eyes downcast, walking alone during a break in the trial.

But Briseno was a good witness. While codefendants scoffed at his claim of having tried to stop the beating, Briseno believed it as much as Koon believed that the incident was a controlled and managed use of force. White had said that Koon was so convinced of his explanation that he could have passed a polygraph test.[11] Briseno actually did pass such a test during the federal trial, although the results were not admissible in court. But his code-fendants were not willing to make the concession to Briseno of sincerity that they expected for themselves. Briseno's reputation was that of a rough-and-ready cop, and his fellow officers assumed he was falsely posing as a hero.

Briseno, however, had formed his opinions about the incident before he knew about the videotape. He complained in profane terms to his partner, Rolando Solano, that Powell was out of control and that Koon had mismanaged the arrest, first in their patrol car after King was subdued and again as they went about their police business, which in the early morning of March 3, 1991, included arresting four robbery suspects.

When Briseno learned that the King incident had been videotaped, he did not share Koon's sanguine misconception that it would make a terrific training film. Briseno believed the beating was excessive. He knew that every officer who had participated in the arrest would be investigated and that he was especially at risk because of his prior suspension for using excessive force. Acting on this knowledge, Briseno ducked Internal Affairs investigators, pleading emotional stress. But his partner, Solano, told the investigators what Briseno had said about Koon and Powell that night. Had Briseno contradicted his opinion at the time, he would have been branded an accomplice in a cover-up and might have been indicted for conspiracy.

Briseno came to court on the morning of April 3, 1992, dressed in a somber black suit. His testimony was focused and dramatic. He described the beginning of the incident, recounting how King had put his hands on the roof of the Hyundai after he had exited and adding the detail that King had slipped his left hand into his left pocket as he began to lie down in response to shouted commands. Briseno then described the attempt to handcuff King, recalling his amazement at King's strength. Briseno, who had weighed only 140 pounds, had been unable to move King's arm into a handcuffing position behind his back. He told how King had risen to a kneeling position, hitting him in the chest with his arms and "causing me to fall like in a backward crab position." He described how he and the other officers had scrambled away as Koon shot King twice with the Taser. He remembered that King had regained his feet after the second Taser shot and charged toward Powell. Briseno decided then and there that King was probably under the influence of PCP.

Until King's charge, Briseno's testimony reinforced the recollections of the other defendants. But his account then diverged. Wielding a PR-24 baton, a prosecution exhibit, Briseno demonstrated for the jury how Powell had reacted to King's "quick charge," swinging his baton in a downward, reflexive motion as King nearly collided with him. Briseno had not seen Powell's baton before he swung, but he saw the blow land on the right side of King's face and knock him down. Briseno thought the location of the blow was "accidental," for King had moved too swiftly for Powell to take aim. (Although Briseno didn't know it, his account of this first blow closely matched Wind's account to Internal Affairs.) But after this first swing, Briseno became alarmed when he saw Powell standing over the fallen King and delivering a series of forward and reverse power strokes with his baton. It seemed to Briseno that these blows were directed at the head and that Powell was now "out of control." Using a pointer as Barnett advanced the video, Briseno described these blows. Barnett stopped the video at the point at which Briseno put up his hand in what he said was an attempt to stop Powell from hitting King again. "Get the hell off," Briseno remembered telling Powell. Six seconds later Barnett stopped the video again.

"What were you thinking at this point?" Barnett asked.

"I didn't understand it . . . I just didn't understand what was going on out there," Briseno said. "I just didn't understand it. It didn't make any sense to me. I couldn't see why they were doing what they were doing."

"What do you mean doing what they were doing?"

"It was like he moved, they hit him," replied Briseno, as if still perplexed. "I couldn't see it. I can't understand it. I couldn't understand. . . . I understood a lot of things that night, but I'm thinking evidently they saw something I didn't see."

What Briseno suspected the other officers might have seen was a weapon. He had shouted that the suspect's hands were free, trying to tell Koon and the officers who were beating King that he wasn't armed. But the beating continued. Briseno recalled making eye contact with Powell at one point and Powell staring back at him as if he were not there.

"Officer Powell had a look I'd never seen before," Briseno said during Stone's cross-examination. "It was a look of just pure exhaustion. His eyes looked like they [had] exploded, like they were coming out." Powell was "continually gasping" for breath. It was Briseno's fear that Powell would not stop hitting King, he said, that eventually led him to place his left foot on King's left shoulder to keep him down. Briseno said he had not dropped down and put his knee on King as policy dictated because he was afraid of being hit by Powell's wild baton swings.[12]

Briseno's account supported Powell's recollection that he had been scared and exhausted but contradicted Koon's depiction of the arrest as managed and controlled. Briseno had not heard Koon's shouted commands, and it had not seemed to him that Koon was directing the arrest at all. Briseno testified that he was so concerned about Koon's lack of supervision that he had approached the sergeant and yelled, "What the fuck is going on out here?" Koon gave no response. He told me outside court that he did not recall Briseno saying anything to him. But Briseno certainly gave Solano an earful when the two of them returned to their patrol car. Briseno testified that he had taken out "my anger and my frustrations" on Solano "because I was upset with my sergeant."

"Tell the jury what you said to him," Barnett said.

"I told him . . . Goddamn, sergeant should have handled this a lot different. He should have handled it a lot better . . . The officers should have their asses reamed."

Briseno made a better case for the prosecution than any prosecution witness, and the videotape of his trial testimony would in time prove as damaging to Koon and Powell as the Holliday videotape. White, who had wanted Briseno as an out-and-out prosecution witness rather than a defendant, appreciated the value of his eyewitness account and in skillful cross-examination used him to bring out points the prosecution had hoped to make during its own presentation. Over and over again White returned to the excessiveness of the beating.

"You thought that if they didn't stop they were going to beat this man to death, didn't you?" White asked.

"The thought crossed my mind," Briseno said.

"That they were either going to beat this man to death or shoot him, is that right?"

"Yes," Briseno said.

Briseno spent an entire day on the witness stand, holding up well to White's questioning and Stone's more skeptical cross-examination. He remembered events with greater clarity than Melanie Singer or Powell and was a match for Koon in reconciling his recollections with the videotape. Although he initially balked at describing the force used against King as "excessive," he conceded to White that "too much force was used" and eventually that Powell, Wind, and Koon had engaged in "misconduct." Briseno also acknowledged to White that he was aware that a "code of silence" discouraged reporting of officer misconduct.

Stone tried to diminish the impact of Briseno's testimony by suggesting that he had done little to help the other officers arrest King. Stone brought out that Briseno had left his baton in his patrol car. He questioned Briseno's account of the stomp. He insinuated that Briseno's concern for King's safety was exaggerated and belated.

"You'd rather see this unjustified use of force rather than do anything to stop it other than put your foot on Mr. King?" Stone asked.

"That's your interpretation, not mine," Briseno replied curtly.

Briseno's interpretation, which he clung to during cross-examination, was that he had been King's protector. He had helped try to handcuff King before a blow was struck. He had tried to stop Powell from hitting him. He had handcuffed King at the conclusion of the incident. When Stone asked Briseno what he had done, Briseno replied firmly, "I attempted to stop it."

But Briseno, like Powell, had difficulty explaining his post-incident conduct. Briseno testified that he had returned briefly to Foothill Station and had seen Koon's MDT message about "big-time use of force" on the computer screen in the watch commander's office. He believed that such a message surely meant the incident would be investigated, which became Briseno's excuse for not filing his own report.

It was a weak excuse, even if true. LAPD officers are required to report misconduct, as other officers had reported Briseno's misconduct when he had used excessive force in 1987. Attorneys for the other defendants were quick to suggest that Briseno's failure to report the King beating cast doubt on his entire testimony, which proved an effective tactic with pro-police jurors who were prepared to see Briseno as a turncoat.

Stone, trying to destroy Briseno's credibility as a witness against Powell and Koon, sought to show that Briseno had lied when he said he had returned to Foothill Station after the incident. Stone called police dispatcher Leslie Wiley, who said she had not seen Briseno return to the station. She also testified that Koon's MDT message about the beating had been removed from the computer screen before Briseno could have seen it. Wiley had responded to Koon's report of a beating with the message, "Oh, well. I'm sure the lizard didn't deserve it. Ha, ha. I'll let them know. OK." Wiley said she could not have sent this message without first clearing Koon's message off her screen.

After a weekend recess, Stone continued his anti-Briseno campaign, calling Officer Dennis Watkins and former Officer Gerald Williams as witnesses. They said they had volunteered to testify because they were offended by Briseno's "lying" on the witness stand. Watkins, a twenty-seven-year veteran of the LAPD, recounted an alleged conversation with Briseno in the watch commander's office at Foothill at 10:45 P.M., on March 4, 1991, a half hour after the edited Holliday videotape had first aired on KTLA. Watkins said he had told Briseno about the videotape. "Oh yeah, that arrest," Watkins quoted Briseno as saying. "We had to kick a little ass that night."

Williams, who wore a cowboy outfit and a ponytail and answered to the nickname "Psycho," had retired from the LAPD the previous July with twenty years of service. He called himself "a loyal police officer," as he had once been a "loyal Marine," and claimed to have overheard the exchange between Watkins and Briseno. Williams said he had then had a brief conversation of his own with Briseno in which he told him that the stomp of King "looked bad" on the videotape. But Briseno had said he wasn't worried about an investigation. "We didn't do anything wrong," Williams quoted Briseno as saying. "That asshole deserved it anyway."

Barnett had anticipated such an attack since Stone's opening statement. He understood that Stone felt a need to impeach the testimony of the most powerful witness against Powell, and he also realized that the old-guard, self-protective LAPD was embarked on a mission that went beyond Powell's defense. To officers reared in the Parker tradition of the LAPD as a law unto itself, Briseno threatened the culture that Barnett sometimes called "the brotherhood." Officers who broke ranks were dangerous, especially when the LAPD was particularly vulnerable to its critics in the ACLU, the black community, and the media. Had the LAPD old guard taken the trouble to draw up an enemies list, Briseno would have been right near the top with Mayor Bradley and Warren Christopher. The brotherhood's punishment for Briseno was to brand him a disloyal cop and a perjurer.

The next witness was Officer Glen King, a twenty-year veteran and longtime friend of Briseno whom Barnett had intended to call to the stand. But in an effort to defuse testimony that he suspected would undermine Watkins and Williams, Stone called him first. King testified that he had responded to the pursuit call on March 3, 1991, but had arrived at Foothill and Osborne after Rodney King had been subdued. He spotted Briseno and yelled at him, in reference to the hog-tied King, "Didn't he want to go along with the program?" Briseno told his friend that the suspect had been "dusted," that Koon had shot him with a Taser and that "Powell came out of nowhere and took him down with his baton."

Glen King next saw Briseno on March 4, in the locker room at Foothill Station at 10:45 P.M., the time at which Watkins and Williams had placed him in the watch commander's office. Briseno had dressed for his shift, which began at 11:00, when Glen King told him about the videotape, which he had just seen on television. "What tape?" Briseno asked. King said it showed Briseno kicking a suspect while he was on the ground. Briseno immediately responded that he had used his foot to keep the suspect down. "He said he was afraid that if he got up they would have beat him to death," King said.

Glen King's account poked a large hole in the testimony of Watkins and Williams. Briseno could hardly have been bragging about the beating in the watch commander's office while he was talking with King in the locker room. In any case, Watkins' story was premised on the claim that he had first told Briseno about the videotape. In addition to discrediting Watkins and Williams, Officer King's testimony showed that Briseno's dramatic declaration that he feared Rodney King might be beaten to death had not been invented for the trial.

If Glen King had stopped there, his testimony would have been of unmitigated benefit to Briseno. But Stone called King back the next day and pressed him for details about his locker-room conversation with Briseno. His persistence bore fruit. On the third try, Stone elicited an acknowledgment from King that he recalled another portion of the conversation. King said he had warned Briseno that "with your . . . prior complaint this isn't going to look good." This answer provoked a furious reaction from Barnett, who at the bench moved for a mistrial and accused Stone of "clear misconduct" for eliciting a reference to Briseno's 1987 suspension for excessive force, which Weisberg had earlier ruled inadmissible. Weisberg questioned Stone pointedly, asking if he had anticipated Glen King's response. "Absolutely not, your honor," Stone replied. "I had no idea of what he was going to say."

Weisberg took the issue seriously. Throughout the trial the judge displayed sensitivity to prosecution concerns that the jury might be prejudiced by Rodney King's robbery conviction and to defense concerns that information about prior use-of-force incidents involving their clients would be similarly prejudicial. The judge had allowed the jury to know that King was on parole, realizing that this was a possible explanation for his refusal to pull over and his subsequent resistance to arrest, but it had not been told about his robbery conviction. Nor, until Briseno's friend Glen King let the cat out of the bag, did the jury know that Briseno had a prior record involving the use of excessive force.[13]

After sending the jury out of the room, Weisberg questioned King, asking him when he had first recalled reminding Briseno about his prior record. King said he had remembered it while driving to work that morning. Weisberg asked King what Briseno had told him after he made this comment. "Oh God, they're going to hang me," Briseno had replied. Weisberg then sent King out of the courtroom while the lawyers debated whether this response should be heard by the jury. Before calling King back into court for further questioning, Weisberg said dryly, "Maybe now [that] he is out in the hallway, he has remembered something else."

Eventually, after much wrangling among the lawyers, Weisberg decided that Stone had not known that King was going to mention Briseno's prior record. The judge denied the motion for a mistrial. He also denied Stone's request to allow Briseno's response into evidence. Stone's determined attempt to discredit Briseno had ended in an uneasy stalemate from which none of the participants had emerged unscathed. But Barnett successfully rebutted the testimony of the police dispatcher Wiley. He recalled her supervisor, Glenda Tosti, who testified that Koon's computer message would not have been automatically removed from the screen when Wiley sent her reply. If Briseno had in fact gone back to the station, he could very well have seen the message on the screen.

As the locker-room conversation demonstrated, even Briseno's friends did not think of him as a hero. During his questioning by Weisberg, Glen King said that as the conversation continued, Briseno had declared he hadn't done anything wrong. "Goddamn it, Ted, you kicked him," King had replied. Briseno, highly agitated, had reiterated that he had feared Rodney King would be beaten to death or shot and had yelled at Koon to do something to stop it. "Well, Ted, there is no audio on that tape that I heard and they will just construe that to be self-serving statements," Glen King said.

None of this was heard by the jury, but it made a strong impression on Weisberg, who told the attorneys that a "compelling argument" could be made that Briseno's "activity in grabbing Mr. Powell's arm and running around and going in different directions as depicted on the videotape and putting his foot on Mr. King all could very well have been related to the fact that he had been the subject of some prior disciplinary proceedings and was aware of the consequences of having so many witnesses around . . ." The implication of Weisberg's statement was that Briseno had indeed tried to intervene, not because he was a hero but because he knew from experience what could happen to an officer who used excessive force when witnesses were present, even when there was no videotape.

Briseno was an ordinary officer who liked his work and did it reasonably well. While he was hardly a hero cop in the Duke mold, neither was he one of the "problem officers" described by the Christopher Commission. As his reaction to Glen King in the locker room demonstrated, Briseno knew that he faced dismissal from the LAPD if he was again charged with using excessive force. He had been much chastened by his suspension and had not been the subject of any excessive-force complaint in the years between the 1987 incident and the Rodney King affair. But Briseno had a temper, as he had showed in sounding off to Koon and Solano. Cliff Ruff told me that he thought Briseno suffered from "a little-guy complex," in which he compensated for his small size with aggressive behavior.[14] Briseno had been startled and upset when he could not force King's hands behind him to handcuff him and when King had raised himself up and thrown the officer off his back. When Powell started wildly swinging his baton and Koon seemed oblivious to what was happening, Briseno had not known what to do. He had indeed, as Weisberg said, run around in different directions. But he was also the only officer who had tried in any way to stop the beating of King. This was something on a night when heroes were in short supply.

WHILE THE DEFENSE ATTORNEYS WERE BATTLING OVER BRISENO'S credibility, the prosecutors were struggling to find a credible expert who would testify that the King beating had violated LAPD policy. The defense had put on three experts with LAPD connections to justify every baton blow. These witnesses, particularly Duke, gave a pro-police jury a solid basis for indulging its pro-police sympathies. If experts found this force justified, then how could it be disputed? White realized that countering the defense experts was crucial for the prosecution.

The principal obstacle was the LAPD. Deputy District Attorney Roger Gunson talked to nationally recognized experts outside Los Angeles County, authorities in police work who were in private business as consultants, and three expressed interest in testifying. All eventually backed out, one after candidly acknowledging to Gunson that he feared never being hired again by the LAPD if he testified for the prosecution. "None of them wanted to testify in an LAPD case where it would be against an LAPD officer," Gunson said.[15] Gunson persevered, and White announced in court on April 7 that the well-regarded Bruce Siddel, a consultant based in St. Louis, would testify. DePasquale objected, saying he had previously consulted with Siddel about testifying in behalf of Wind. A day later White announced in court that Siddel had withdrawn because of this perceived conflict of interest.

Even without an outside expert, prosecutors might have fared well enough if they had been allowed to call an LAPD witness of their choice. They talked to Sergeant Mark Conta, who would become a hero to federal prosecutors for defying peer pressure to testify at the subsequent civil rights trial, where he proved an effective witness. But Conta was no hero to Gunson. After the LAPD suggested him as a witness, prosecutors sat down with him to discuss the case. Conta said his career would be damaged if he testified. He also denied he would be a good witness. "I can be a witness, but I am not going to be any good under cross-examination," he told Gunson. "I am going to fall apart under cross-examination."[16]

The prosecution then turned to Sergeant Fred Nichols, who had been in charge of the LAPD's physical training and self-defense section at the Police Academy at the time of the King incident. After viewing the videotape Nichols had no doubt that the officers had used excessive force. He expressed this opinion to Internal Affairs investigators and to the grand jury that indicted the four officers. He later expressed the same view to the Christopher Commission. Gunson believed that Nichols "would have made a great witness because he spoke in such layperson's terms, and he spoke of it from experience as well as training."[17] Yochelson thought Nichols had been "wonderful" before the grand jury.[18]

But after Nichols testified before the Christopher Commission he had been reassigned from his prestigious post to a desk job and replaced by Conta. Badly shaken, he took stress leave for several months, returning only after he was told that he would be placed on unpaid leave if he did not come back to work. Nichols wanted nothing more to do with the King case. The prosecutors decided they needed him as a witness and subpoenaed him. He fought the subpoena. His attorney Richard Wilson said Nichols suffered from a "stress disability" and submitted medical reports to the court saying that his condition would be aggravated if he was forced to testify. Weisberg ordered a hearing.

At the hearing, White expressed his frustration scoffing at Nichols' claim of stress. "He is just trying to get out from under a subpoena," White said. "There is no stress-related disability and there is no medical disability, there is no psychiatric disability. Sergeant Nichols just does not want to come in and take an oath and tell the world that he believes these officers used excessive force . . ." Weisberg refused to quash the subpoena.

Still, Nichols resisted. He told Weisberg that he shouldn't be allowed to testify because his opinions had been influenced by his reviewing of the statements Koon, Powell, and Wind had made to Internal Affairs investigators. Yochelson, managing the prosecution's rebuttal case, insisted that Nichols was lying. He pointed out that Nichols had never said anything about reading the statements before testifying to the grand jury, and he said Nichols was using stress as an excuse because he had been told not to testify against fellow officers. Nichols complained in a quavering voice that the "prosecution has been relentless in harassing me" but conceded under Yochelson's questioning that he had "heard that I shouldn't testify."

"I didn't answer or give any notion that I even heard it because I've got a task at hand," Nichols said.

"What is that task?" Yochelson asked.

"Trying to preserve my sanity," Nichols said.

Weisberg finally had enough. The judge had reservations about the worth of expert witnesses, and he especially questioned the value of such a reluctant expert. During the stress hearing Weisberg had agreed with Stone that it might be difficult for Nichols to give an objective opinion in light of his feelings. Then the judge had ruled that this was a matter for the district attorney to decide. Now, after a lengthy second hearing in which Nichols claimed that it was "humanly impossible" for him to distinguish between opinions he had formed from watching the videotape and those he has formed from reading the compelled statements, Weisberg made the decision himself.

The judge decided that forcing Nichols to testify would be a mistake. If Nichols was lying, then prosecutors were asking the jury to rely on the testimony of a perjurer. If he was telling the truth, then forcing him to testify could become grounds for reversing a conviction. Either way, the conclusion was the same. Weisberg ruled that the prosecution had failed to establish that Nichols was lying, and excused him. Asked outside court about the appearance that he had invented a story to avoid testifying, Nichols said, "To be honest with you, I'm not concerned about appearance. I'm concerned with my well-being."

The prosecution's problem of finding an acceptable use-of-force expert could have been solved by Daryl Gates, whose popularity with whites had not yet been ruined by the riots. The LAPD chief at this time was probably more popular in Ventura County than in Los Angeles and was especially well regarded by the Simi Valley jurors, as White had noticed in reviewing their questionnaires. White had no doubt that Gates could help the prosecution if he was willing to testify. "I thought it was critical that Daryl Gates get on the stand and tell everybody . . . that these officers used unreasonable force," White said.[19]

Other members of the prosecution team did not share White's enthusiasm for using Gates. Yochelson wasn't keen on calling any use-of-force witness, believing that a battle among experts might divert jurors from the videotaped evidence of excessive force. When Duke's effective testimony made it obvious that the prosecution needed a rival expert, Yochelson decided that even a reluctant Nichols was preferable to the chief. "I felt that Gates was a loose cannon," Yochelson said.[20] Gunson agreed with White that Gates would be influential with the jurors and with Yochelson about the chief's unpredictability. On balance he opposed using Gates because he feared the chief was still preoccupied with the choke hold and would testify that the choke-hold ban had left police officers with a choice of beating suspects or shooting them. Gunson dismissed this as "baloney" but thought it might seem credible to a Ventura County jury.[21]

The decision was left to Reiner, who had first suggested using Gates as a witness. Since the district attorney and the chief were barely on speaking terms, Gunson and White explored the idea through Commander Michael Bostic, a Gates loyalist. Gates was hesitant. Detective Addison Arce had called him after Duke's testimony and told him that the SWAT sergeant had been "brilliant" on the witness stand.[22] The LAPD rank and file had rallied to the cause of the defendants as the trial progressed, and Gates was reluctant to forfeit the backing of officers by testifying for the prosecution even though he was on the way out as chief. "In the back of my mind I dreaded the worst possible designation by police officers everywhere: the chief's a wimp," Gates later wrote.[23]

While the chief pondered his decision, a federal jury returned an unexpected verdict in a civil lawsuit resulting from a 1990 shooting by members of the LAPD's controversial Special Investigations Section (SIS). Nineteen SIS members had followed four suspects in a string of restaurant robberies to a McDonald's in Sunland. The officers waited outside as the suspects robbed a lone employee, then poured handgun and shotgun fire into them as they entered their getaway car. Three robbers were killed and the fourth seriously wounded. The survivor and family members of the slain robbers charged that the SIS had conducted a "death squad" execution and sued for damages, naming Gates as one of ten defendants. The judge allowed into evidence portions of the Christopher Commission report that faulted the chief's management. The jury agreed that excessive force had been used and found Gates liable for $20,505 in damages.[24] Gates was stunned. He knew that if a jury could find him liable in the SIS case, he might also be held liable for damages in the King beating. From White's point of view, the timing could not have been worse.

Gates promptly sent word through Bostic that he would not testify. While he could have been subpoenaed, even White doubted that the prosecution needed "an angry Daryl Gates" on the witness stand.[25] Reiner viewed Gates as an "X factor." He might "take an absolutely perfectly great case and destroy it," the district attorney later said, but he could also rescue a lost case.[26] The comment is revealing. Had Reiner realized how poorly the prosecution was faring with the Simi Valley jurors, he might have thrown the dice and subpoenaed Gates. But Reiner, along with most people, believed that Powell at least would be convicted. Only White, the pessimistic realist of the prosecution team, was willing to risk calling Gates. He was overruled by his boss.

The burden of serving as a prosecution expert fell on Bostic, a handsome and well-connected officer who claimed to be the author of the LAPD's use-of-force guidelines. Although Bostic had never testified in any trial, he chaired the board that reviewed police shootings and had been designated by Gates as the LAPD's use-of-force expert. In this capacity, Bostic had a bureaucratic responsibility to represent the LAPD, and he took it seriously. Gates was stepping down. If Bostic also refused to testify, it would have been apparent that the surviving leadership of the LAPD embraced the "code of silence" of which White so often complained. While Bostic was not confident about his ability to counteract Duke, he was willing to try. "You can do it, Michael," White said, trying to encourage an inexperienced witness whom Reiner would later disparage as "less than third tier."[27]

Bostic worked to become an overnight expert. He watched the video six times, at regular speed and in slow motion, and read the reports of the Singers, Koon's sergeant's log, and Powell's police report. Bostic testified that all the force used against King after the first nineteen seconds of the video—shortly before Briseno held up his hand to restrain Powell—was unwarranted. He said the officers should have swarmed King, as they had tried unsuccessfully to do before the video began. Bostic discussed the concept of "reasonable and necessary" force, defining it as "the minimum amount of force necessary to take control of the suspect without causing injury to the officer or the suspect." Baton use was appropriate if an officer perceived "some aggressive resistance by a suspect . . . in a self-defense situation." The perception must be objectively reasonable. "An officer's use of force must be in direct response to some action by the suspect," Bostic said.

Bostic was comfortable when reciting policy, but cross-examination exposed him as a desk officer who possessed little contemporary knowledge of how officers actually behaved on the mean streets of Los Angeles. Barnett drew an admission from Bostic that the Police Commission had prepared the use-of-force guidelines Bostic was supposed to have written. Bostic said he had "interpreted" the guidelines. Then, he acknowledged having spent fewer than four of his nineteen years in the LAPD in the field and not having made an arrest since 1978. Bostic had used his baton ten to twelve times during his career and had never witnessed "actual excessive force." Only once had he felt endangered by a suspect. On that occasion, also in 1978, Bostic had struck the suspect once on the arm with his baton, and two other officers had joined in wrestling the offender to the ground. Barnett asked if it was "just a little unfair for you to sit in your living room" and say that "I, Commander Bostic, would have done things correctly." "No," said Bostic. "It is not my purpose to determine what I would have done at the scene."

Under Stone's cross-examination Bostic acknowledged that it was important to consider an officer's perceptions in determining if use of force was justified. But the commander proved remarkably unfamiliar with the perceptions of Officer Powell, the focus of the trial in which Bostic was testifying as an expert. Bostic said he had not watched Powell testify or read his testimony. Stone's tone of voice reflected his incredulity when Bostic explained that he could nonetheless understand Powell's perceptions from watching the video because "I'm watching some of the same things I'm sure he was watching."

"Now is it your opinion that Officer Powell had tunnel vision?" Stone asked.

"I have no way of knowing that," Bostic said.

"Would that factor be important in your determination?"

"It could be."

Bostic's pathetic performance as a witness probably extinguished the embers of the prosecution's flickering hopes. Even the minority of jurors who were critical of Powell realized that Bostic's analysis paled in comparison with Duke's. But Bostic had done as well as he could, considering his inexperience as either expert or witness, and he did not deserve the calumny heaped on him by police and prosecutors alike (White excepted) after the trial. The prosecution made numerous blunders at Simi Valley, and Bostic was just one more key witness who was miscast in the role he was asked to play.

For Daryl Gates the Simi Valley trial was a missed opportunity. It is understandable that he did not want to forfeit the goodwill of the men and women of the department that he had led, usually ably, for fourteen years. He was not a rich man, and the verdict in the SIS case had given him reason for concern about personal liability. Even so, the trial was a last chance for Gates to send to officers who still admired him an unmistakable message that excessive force would not be tolerated. It was a chance to show that he meant it when he described the King beating as a "very, *very* extreme use of force" and an "impossible" use of force for a department "considered by many to be perhaps the finest, most professional police department in the world."[28] The trial was an opportunity for Gates to express this view in an arena where his opinion might have made the crucial difference. He chose not to do so, at great cost to the people of the State of California and to his own reputation. More than anyone else, Gates was to blame for the prosecution's failure to present a credible use-of-force expert. The code of silence did the rest.

White and Yochelson did not give up. As the trial careened toward closing arguments, they struggled to plug holes in their leaky case. Dr. Norman Shore, a Beverly Hills ophthalmologist and reconstructive surgeon who had repaired bone fractures around King's right eye, testified that King's injuries were "more likely" the result of a blow from a blunt object such as a baton than from a fall to the ground. Shore said the way the cheekbone was pressed downward into the face suggested that the force had come from above. He testified that in a fall to a flat surface the forehead would have acted as a "bumper" to protect King's eye and cheekbone from injury.

The prosecution also won a pair of skirmishes with DePasquale, who wanted the jury to learn that a test of King's urine taken five hours after the beating had revealed traces of marijuana. DePasquale argued that marijuana possession was a parole violation that could have motivated King to resist arrest. But after Yochelson argued that chemicals derived from marijuana could have been in King's body for several months, Weisberg refused to allow the test into evidence.

While prosecutors fought to keep damaging information about King out of evidence, they wanted to inform jurors that Wind had spent seven years on the Shawnee, Kansas, police force before joining the LAPD. Yochelson told the court that this was necessary to counter the impression given by DePasquale that Wind was "an innocent babe in the woods." DePasquale responded that he had only tried to show that Wind was the least experienced defendant, not "Toto coming from Kansas with no experience—no background." Wind's experience on the fifty-six-member Shawnee force was irrelevant to police work in Los Angeles, DePasquale said. In Kansas "perhaps more time is spent getting cattle out of the street than in dealing with unruly subjects." Weisberg, after commenting that DePasquale made Shawnee sound "like a scene out of *Gunsmoke*," ruled in favor of the defense attorney but reversed himself after a review of the trial transcript showed that Powell had acknowledged Wind's previous experience during cross-examination. The judge said prosecutors could refer to this testimony in closing arguments but could not go beyond it. But DePasquale succeeded in his larger purpose of making jurors realize that his client was a novice LAPD officer who had followed instructions he believed to be lawful.

WHITE BEGAN HIS ARGUMENT ON THE AFTERNOON OF MONDAY, April 20, by urging jurors to base their verdicts on the videotape. "This videotape is the central piece of evidence in this case," White said. "We don't need to rely on Stacey Koon's words. We don't need to rely on Laurence Powell's words. . . . We don't need to rely on what Mr. King says happened that night. We have the videotape and the videotape shows conclusively what occurred that night, and it is something that can't be rebutted. It is there for everyone to see."

White's argument was heavily focused on what Powell had done. "On that videotape, you see . . . unnecessary, excessive, unreasonable brutality by Officer Powell," he said. Powell had struck the majority of the baton blows, including the blows that shattered King's cheekbone and broke his right leg. The videotape showed King writhing helplessly on the ground in a vain attempt to escape the ceaseless beating. "When you look at this video, what you see is a man feeling the pain of these batons. This was a man in pain. You can clearly see it on the video. They continued to hit him and hit him and hit him. And you've got to at some point say: Enough is enough. Stop it!"

When Powell had written a police report that omitted any mention of his "deliberate, intentional baton strike" to King's head, he had not known that his words would be refuted by the videotape. Powell, White said, had lied at least twenty-six times in his police report or his testimony, and many of the lies had been exposed by the video. Other lies were revealed by computer or audiotape records. Powell's racism had been shown by the exchange of computer messages with Officer Corina Smith. Powell's insensitivity had been shown by his laughter in calling for the ambulance. "He just punished this man, and he thought it was funny," White said. Powell had bragged about the beating in another computer message to Smith. When Powell said he hadn't beaten anyone so badly in a long time he was admitting that he had used unreasonable force against King.

Such were White's arguments over three-and-a-half hours in which he used sixteen charts to illustrate his points but returned repeatedly to the videotape. The tape contained the most significant evidence against Powell and most of the evidence against Wind and Briseno. White played the seven-second segment in which Briseno moves in and stomps King. Holding up Briseno's black boots, White said that Briseno "just got caught up in the frenzy." As for Koon, a comparison of the videotape with his sergeant's log contradicted the claim that King's arrest had been a managed and controlled use of force. "I would say this is a managed and controlled cover-up," White said.

The prosecutor concluded his argument as he had begun his case, playing the video for a jury that had become weary of seeing it. Facing the jurors, White asked softly, "Now, who are you going to believe, the defendants or your own eyes?"

Stone, nattily attired and wearing a familiar bow tie, answered the next day in a closing argument of nearly seven hours. He began in a conversational tone, eliciting smiles from jurors with a reference to his short and somewhat ragged haircut. But he was soon launched on a bold and serious argument that would impress the federal prosecutors who later watched the videotape of the trial as a masterful appeal to the prejudices of the white, suburban Simi Valley jury.

Stone was not as confident as he seemed. He knew the videotape was potentially devastating to Powell, and he did not want jurors sitting around debating the video as they decided his client's fate. He really did not want them to watch the video at all, not even in the frame-by-frame reconstruction favored by the defense. Stone wanted jurors to think about how it had felt to be a tired police officer at Foothill and Osborne in the middle of the night facing a presumably drug-crazed suspect who outweighed him by sixty to eighty pounds. He wanted jurors to remember that King had picked himself up after being hit by high-voltage electric darts that supposedly could stop an ox. Stone knew that the men and women who would determine Powell's guilt or innocence looked upon the police as their protectors and expected them to be around when they needed them. They did not want these protectors to take unnecessary risks. Powell was a protector, not a brute. He was the barrier between the comfortable, ordered world of Ventura County and the lawlessness of Los Angeles as epitomized by Rodney King.

This was not the only conceivable approach. As Barnett and, later, Harland Braun suggested, it could be argued that Koon and Powell had made an honest miscalculation after the Taser failed to halt King. While the subsequent arrest was unavoidably violent, the officers had done nothing that was criminally wrong. Koon had seen the danger of Melanie Singer's armed advance on an uncooperative, unsearched suspect, and King's bizarre behavior had given the officers reason for concern. But Koon had miscalculated and Powell had panicked when King charged toward him.

But Stone and Mounger had not based their defense upon blunders. They had explained the incident as proper police work that had turned violent only because of King's behavior. Even so, a last chance for changing strategies had emerged before closing arguments when the defendants and their lawyers discussed whether the jury should be allowed to consider verdicts on lesser offenses, such as simple assault. This option had a potential advantage if the jury leaned toward convictions, for it would permit guilty verdicts on relatively minor crimes that might spare the officers prison sentences. The downside was that it might also increase the risk of conviction.

After their lawyers explained the options, the defendants chose the all-or-nothing course. Koon, certain that he had done right, never even toyed with the idea of allowing the jury the face-saving compromise of lesser verdicts. The other defendants, while less self-assured, knew that conviction on any charge would make it impossible for them to work again as police officers. Stone strongly favored the all-or-nothing approach, even though Powell was the defendant who stood to benefit most from the option of conviction on a lesser charge. Powell was either "a courageous, faithful responsible police officer" or a "brutal thug in uniform who abused and beat another human being with no justification," Stone told the jury. "There's no compromise. It has to be one or the other."

Stone had been a police officer longer than he had been a lawyer, and he was able to see the world through Powell's eyes. He knew that if he could also make the jurors share Powell's perceptions and fears, they would be well on the way to a verdict of not guilty. With this in mind, Stone recalled a sign that hung in the police gymnasium when he had worked as an officer. "There are no second-place ribbons in a street fight," it said.

"These officers, these defendants," Stone continued, "do not get paid to lose street fights. They don't get paid to roll around in the dirt with the likes of Rodney Glen King. That is not their job. That is not their duty. And if we as members of the community demand that they do that, the thin blue line that separates the law abiding from the not-law abiding will disintegrate. These are not Robocops, ladies and gentlemen. They hurt, they feel pain, they bleed and they die, just like everyone else. And we leave it to them to take care of the mean streets so that we can safely enjoy our lives, so that we can raise our families in neighborhoods . . ."

In doing his duty as a police officer, Powell had not acted on his own. To see the incident through Powell's eyes meant remembering that Powell had done what Koon had ordered him to do. But Stone did not distance Powell from the sergeant who had commanded him. To the contrary, Stone's defense urged jurors to decide that Koon had given the proper orders and that Powell had carried them out. In trying to persuade jurors to see Powell as society's defender, Stone wrapped him in the protective mantle of Stacey Koon.

It was the right argument for jurors who Stone accurately suspected had been more impressed by Koon than by Powell. Koon had come into court and taken responsibility for every blow and every kick. "Even though we expect that kind of unwillingness to pass the buck, I'm still in awe of Sergeant Koon," Stone said. "I'm still impressed with his courage and his guts. He didn't come into this courtroom sniffling, back-peddling, turning on his own men one bit. You didn't see or hear one bit of that in an effort by Sergeant Koon to save his own skin."

Despite this backhanded swipe at Briseno, Stone said that every officer on the scene, Briseno included, had acted "in good faith for the right reason." Only Rodney King had behaved wrongly. King had chosen to drink, he had chosen to speed on the freeway, he had chosen to violate traffic laws on city streets, he had chosen to resist arrest. From beginning to end, it was King alone who had controlled his destiny. "Rodney Glen King made the choice every time he had the opportunity to make a choice . . . and every choice was the wrong one." Stone said. "Now whose fault is that?"

Then Stone took up the conflicting testimony about whether Powell's first baton blow had hit King in the head. He reminded jurors that Melanie Singer's vivid recollections had been contradicted by her own subsequent testimony. He observed that King had not testified. "It would seem to me if we can't decide whether or not Mr. King was hit in the head with the baton maybe we would want to ask the person who owns the head," Stone said. He conceded inaccuracies and "sloppiness" in Powell's police report but reminded jurors that the Singers, who were prosecution witnesses and not charged with anything, had also filed an "incorrect report." Powell had checked the box for "use of force" on his report and had written "use of force" on every page, as LAPD policy required. While his report was incomplete, it was no cover-up.

The jury seemed weary and Stone himself was tired when he finished late in the afternoon. He wondered afterward whether he had talked too long, but Stone's calm discussion of jury instructions in the latter stages of his address would be better remembered in the jury room than his dramatic remarks about the duty of police officers to win "street fights." Jurors would particularly focus on two instructions by Judge Weisberg to which Stone drew attention. One called upon jurors to put themselves in the place of a "reasonable officer at the scene confronted with the same or similar circumstances" in deciding if the defendants had reacted appropriately. The other instruction concerned circumstantial evidence. "If circumstantial evidence is susceptible of two reasonable interpretations, the jury must—must—(Stone emphasized) adopt that which points to the defendant's innocence and reject that which points to his guilt."

Stone was followed by DePasquale, who began his argument late Tuesday afternoon and finished it the following morning. While also blaming

Rodney King for the incident, DePasquale took pains to disassociate himself from any inference that King deserved to be beaten. He also distanced
Wind, a rookie officer in a "chain of police command," from Powell and
Briseno. "All Tim Wind did that night was his job," DePasquale said. "He
didn't make jokes and he didn't have fun and he didn't take cheap shots."

Then came Barnett, who soon demonstrated why Stone and Mounger
had not wanted him to be the last defense lawyer to address the jury. Barnett
asked jurors to see the King beating through the eyes of Briseno, an LAPD
veteran who truly believed Powell would beat King to death and had "intervened in a holocaust of batons and boots and blood and tried to stop it."
With clarity and command of the evidence, Barnett described the seamy un-
derside of the police culture that Stone had celebrated as the "thin blue line."
This was a culture of "us against them" where the world was divided into
"good citizens" on the one hand and "subhumans," "gorillas" and "lizards" on
the other. In Stone's opening statement the police brotherhood who ruled
this world had sent Briseno a warning not to testify against the other officers. It had sent another warning in the testimony of Officer Jerry Mulford,
who had justified every blow and every kick except Briseno's single stomp.
Mulford was willing to justify this too, if only Briseno would say that he had
seen King reaching for a gun. "What Mr. Mulford is telling [Briseno] is either
accept the joint defense, he was going for a gun, or suffer the consequences,"
Barnett said. "Either join the team or become the enemy."

But Ted Briseno had refused to join the team, and the police culture had
retaliated by inventing a "phantom conversation" in which Briseno boasted
of "kicking ass." The lie had been exposed by Officer Glen King, whose
testimony had revealed the "situational morality" operating within the police culture. Within the culture it was permissible "to misrepresent the truth
for the greater good," as Briseno's accusers had done. "They truly believe,"
said Barnett, "that there is a jungle and that there is this thin blue line and
that . . . if coming in here to tarnish a good man is necessary, it is okay . . ."

Barnett, no less than White, believed that police officers were willing to
lie to protect themselves from the truth, but he thought White was telling
only part of the truth. The truth was that the beating was unjustifiable. The
lie was that Briseno had done nothing to stop it.

"You heard Officer Briseno testify," Barnett said. "You saw his face and
his eyes as he described his fear and his frustration at what he saw. You felt
the emotion as he transported us back in time as clearly and as accurately as
Mr. Holliday's video. You felt the shock and horror as he described the blow
after blow, the terrible scene. He was thrust into a crucible of cross-examination. He was vilified. He was defamed, he was labeled a liar for telling the
truth, belittled and accused of . . . not taking a more active role. His detractors reached into the depths of the sewer of perjury to blunt this truthful

testimony and to no avail. Ted Briseno stood and stands alone against the power of the state and against the cruel weapons of slander, deceit and perjury and the extortion of his former comrades."

Barnett's passionate defense of Briseno was an indictment of the police culture as telling as the Christopher Commission report. He had, with good reason, devoted more of his argument (and more of his case) to answering the LAPD campaign against his client than in rebutting the tenuous prosecution contention that Briseno's single "stomp" constituted excessive force. As Barnett observed, even the prosecutor's presentation against Briseno had raised an issue of reasonable doubt. The case that would matter more with the pro-police jury was the one made against Briseno by his fellow officers, to whom he was indeed Benedict Briseno.

Mounger, the last defense attorney to address the jury, was handicapped by a persistent virus and a hacking cough. But alone among the defense attorneys he had no need to refurbish the reputation of his client. Sergeant Koon had been his own best witness in the trial, and Mounger knew there was nothing he could do to improve on his testimony. Koon had unblinkingly acknowledged the violence of the beating and had taken responsibility even for blows he had not seen. He had done everything except take responsibility for the incident itself, which Koon—and Mounger—firmly believed was attributable solely to the absent Rodney King. Barnett had used his closing argument to put the LAPD on trial. Mounger responded by trying King.

All the defense attorneys asked the jurors to see the incident through the eyes of their clients. But Mounger, even more than Stone, saw the events that way himself. He was so completely the police sergeant that he had made jurors feel what it was like to confront a felony suspect at the end of a heart-pounding pursuit in the middle of the night. "You don't know what you have in that car," Mounger said. "You don't know what that person has done, you don't know whether they are a rapist or a robber, you don't know whether somebody was just the victim in the wake of their driving and there is a little mayhem or maybe death that has lurked a few blocks back." All an officer could know was that the driver of the car had been running from something, and "that is a clue in law enforcement, ladies and gentlemen, that is a clue that there is something wrong."

Mounger scornfully recalled that White had described King's conduct as "silly." It was the wrong word. "Silly . . . is what a high school girl does at her senior prom," Mounger said. "It is not something you do at one o'clock in the morning when a bunch of police officers are pointing guns at you. That is not silly." King's actions had convinced Koon, as they would have persuaded any prudent sergeant, that he was potentially dangerous. Koon had not tried to hurt him for that. He had tried to take King into custody with commands, with a swarm, and with the Taser. These were the tools Koon had been given, and he had used them to the best of his ability before a blow was struck. He did not have the nets or leg grabbers that the LAPD considered too expensive. He was not supposed to use a choke hold. He had used the officers who were on hand to make the arrest. "I'm sure he would have rather have had four Charlie Dukes standing there to help him take this big guy into custody, but he didn't have that," Mounger said. "He didn't have a platoon of Green Berets that were well trained . . . He is playing the cards that he is dealt."

King had been on parole for only sixty-five days, with recent memories of prison, which Mounger said "is a real good motive for you to run the risk of letting a policeman use force." Mounger reminded the jurors of King's size and strength. He recalled that officers had trained their guns on King as Melanie Singer advanced upon him in the dark with her own weapon outstretched. Koon had seen a catastrophe in the making. "Either she is going to shoot [King], he's going to shoot her . . . or some of these little young officers are going to open up fire and shoot them both."

It was to prevent such a disaster that Koon had intervened. "Whether you like it or not, on this particular evening Sergeant Stacey Koon did more to save Rodney King's life than Rodney King ever did to save his own," Mounger said. Had Koon not been on hand, "there would inevitably have been a shooting." Had Koon not exercised control, King would not be home watching the trial of the sergeant who had saved him. King was a menace, not a "loving little drunk." Koon was a responsible officer who did not deserve to be prosecuted. None of the officers deserved to be prosecuted. What had caused the incident was "not the conduct of the officers" but "the conduct of Mr. King."

Terry White was exhausted and frustrated as he rose to deliver the prosecution's rebuttal. He was also bothered by a virus and a cough, and the cards he had been dealt at the trial had been no better than those given to Koon at the King arrest. White could not understand why the media did not realize that the opening frames of the videotape posed a problem for the prosecution that had been compounded when Judge Weisberg moved the trial to Ventura County. The trial itself had turned into a paradigm of the event that caused it, when a more-or-less ordinary arrest became a nightmare. Melanie Singer had self-destructed. King had refused to cooperate. Gates had not come through. Duke had testified powerfully, and the LAPD had prevented the prosecution from finding an effective expert to counter him. As in an actual nightmare, White wanted to cry out but couldn't speak. He couldn't say that the jurors adored police officers and probably detested Rodney King. He couldn't say that the LAPD and King himself had undermined the prosecution. He couldn't make reporters understand what was really happening at the trial they were confidently recounting to the world. He couldn't tell anyone that the prosecution case was hanging by a thread. All he could do was make a final, emotional argument in which his accumulated frustrations poured out on the one defendant he abhorred.

White began calmly enough by challenging the notion that police officers are somehow above the law. For Koon and Powell and Wind to "hide behind the very badges that they wear by talking about this thin blue line, by talking about these hordes of criminals out there that they are protecting us from is embarrassing," White said. "Men and women across this country do their job every day as law enforcement officers without resorting to the violence and brutality . . . that you have seen on this screen over the last six weeks. What these officers say in here implicitly, if not explicitly, is that they are immune from prosecution."

White then reviewed Powell's police report. As he discussed its inaccuracies and omissions, he grew more agitated. Why was it that every time any evidence pointed to Powell, he blamed someone else? Why was nothing ever Powell's fault? All at once, White's pent-up frustration erupted in a rage. He dashed across the courtroom and confronted Powell. Jabbing his right index finger within inches of the startled officer's face, White screamed at him. "This is the man—and look at him," White said. "This man laughed." Stone came to his feet, objecting. "This man taunted," White continued. Weisberg looked at the prosecutor. "Mr. White get back to the podium," he said softly. "Please confine your argument to the podium."

White walked back to the podium. "I'm sorry," he said to the judge. But he continued in the same vein. "This man laughed," White said again. "This man taunted. And he's denying it."

Later White apologized to the jurors, who had seemed as startled as Powell when the prosecutor dashed across the courtroom. "That was uncalled for," White said. But he was not sorry he had confronted Powell. It had been a long trial, and White had reasons for his rage. He was still boiling inside as he returned to the podium, where he completely forgot that he had been discussing Powell's police report. All he could remember was what Powell had done to Rodney King.

"They treated him like an animal, and yet Michael Stone does not . . . want me to call his client a thug," White yelled. "Okay," he said with a glance at Powell. "You are not a thug but you are acting like one, just like Mr. King wasn't an animal but he was acting like one . . . So you are not a thug, you are just acting like a thug." And to the jurors, White said, "That is what he was doing. There is no reason for that."

Judge Weisberg instructed the jury the following morning, taking ninety minutes to read the seventy-eight pages of instructions. He urged the jurors to rely on their own impressions of the videotape rather than on what experts had said about it and told them to "reach a just verdict, regardless of the consequences." It was a few minutes after noon on Thursday, April 23, and *People v. Powell* had been submitted to the jury after seven weeks of trial and testimony from fifty-five witnesses. The jury was sequestered at a nearby TraveLodge.

A TERRIBLE CALM NOW DESCENDED OVER SOUTH CENTRAL LOS Angeles, where an unrelated court decision had reopened a wound that had never fully healed. The conclusion of the *Powell* trial coincided with a state appeals court decision upholding Judge Joyce Karlin's sentence of probation for Soon Ja Du, the liquor store owner who had killed Latasha Harlins with a shot to the back of the head. Karlin's lawyer, Donald Etra, called the court's ruling a "marvelous victory," but it was a decision, as the *Los Angeles Times* observed, that "renewed ethnic discord" in the city.[29] Compton Councilwoman Patricia Moore, an African-American activist who would later be tried and convicted on federal charges of extortion, attempted to use the ruling to revive a lagging recall campaign against Karlin. It was a busy time for Moore. While the *Powell* jury was deliberating, she led a pilgrimage of blacks to Simi Valley and held a news conference outside the courthouse to express concern about possible acquittals.

Most whites did not share Moore's apprehension. Every public opinion poll showed that huge majorities of all races and ethnic groups thought the accused officers had used excessive force. This was true in Ventura County as well as Los Angeles County.[30] The view that the videotape guaranteed convictions was widespread. Most local television stations used these clips on the day *Powell* went to the jury, again omitting the frames in which King charges toward Powell.

The certainty that the videotape guaranteed convictions was so pervasive that it influenced even the lawyers who were familiar with the case's ambiguities. "The media said the officers didn't have a chance," recalled Barnett. "Reporters who I knew from other cases said I was fooling myself to think that any of them had a chance, even Briseno. Even the president had pronounced them guilty. I didn't view Rodney King as a hero, but I thought the evidence was very strong."[31] Stone thought much the same. He knew he had put on a strong case but expected Powell to be found guilty and prudently inquired of the prosecutors what the bail would be while the presumed conviction was appealed.

The assumption that Powell would be convicted was shared within the LAPD. It was shared by Chief Gates, by his deputy chiefs and by officers in the field. It was shared by officers at the dilapidated 77th Street Station in the heart of South Central, where more than half the young black males were unemployed. Gates believed that Powell would be convicted for using excessive force and that Koon would be convicted (unfairly, the chief thought) for filing a false police report.[32] Captain Paul Jefferson, an African American in charge of 77th Street Station, believed that Powell and maybe Wind would be found guilty and Koon acquitted "because I didn't see any place in the penal code where there's a criminal penalty for being a poor supervisor."[33] Jefferson knew that the troubled, gang-ridden 77th Street area was a powder keg. While the jury was deliberating, he asked people he knew in the community what would happen if the police officers were acquitted. "What are you talking about?" they responded. "It's on tape."[34]

The LAPD, which was supposed to be prepared anyway, did little more than go through the motions of preparing for reaction to the verdict. Gates allocated $1 million for police overtime and videotaped a five-minute message that was shown at police roll calls throughout the city. The message urged officers to disregard community leaders and "irresponsible people" who had suggested that verdicts with which they did not agree would be met with "very serious uprisings." The duty of LAPD officers, Gates said, was "to approach the verdict in the Rodney King case with maturity and calmness and professionalism." Gates had no doubt that LAPD officers would perform well in a crisis, but he did not expect a crisis. He was sure there would be convictions in Simi Valley and equally certain that there would be no "very serious uprisings" in South Central.

His certitude was shared by Mayor Bradley. The mayor talked to community leaders, who planned a solidarity rally at the First African Methodist Episcopal Church in South Central after the verdicts were returned. The rally was to be the centerpiece of an appeal for calm called "Operation Cool Response." But Bradley saw no need to pick up the telephone and talk to Gates, to whom he rarely spoke. It was business as usual at the mayor's office and business as usual within the LAPD, where eighteen patrol captains made plans to attend a three-day training seminar, beginning April 29, at the Harborside Inn in Ventura, an eighty-minute drive from South Central.

When the jury had deliberated for three days without reaching a verdict, the Reverend Cecil Murray, a former Air Force navigator, had visions of the upheaval to come. Murray was pastor of First AME, the city's oldest and most politically active black church. When he had arrived in Los Angeles from Seattle in 1977, First AME was on a downward slide with a congregation of 300 "mostly status-conscious elderly women who didn't take kindly to change."[35] Murray brought in music that appealed to young blacks and hired an artist to darken the skin and kink the hair of the images of Mary, Jesus, and Joseph that hung over the altar. Fourteen years later First AME had 8,500 members, including 3,500 males, and was the most influential black church in the city.

Murray tried to use that influence to save South Central. In his Sunday sermon on April 26 he tried to divert the latent anger he knew was ready to explode in surrounding neighborhoods. "Be cool," Murray implored his congregation in a throaty baritone. "Even in anger, be cool. And if you're gonna burn something down, don't burn down the house of the victims, brother! Burn down the Legislature! Burn down the courtroom! Burn it down by voting, brother! Burn it down by standing with us at Parker Center, brother! Burn it down by saying to Daryl Gates, 'This far, and no farther!'" But Murray had few illusions that his impassioned plea for peace would carry the day. "Much is at stake for our city, and the longer the jury stays out, the more we tremble," Murray told me the day after this sermon. "The possibility of the verdict being a flash point is very high."[36]

Black leaders were more aware than their white counterparts of the potential for violence. But with the exception of Murray, they tended to be captives of a particularized historical view in which violence was caused by police as well as criminals. Harking back to the Watts riot of 1965, these leaders worried about the potential overreaction of the police, not about whether the police would respond in time.

The black politician concerned most about police overreaction was Councilman Mark Ridley-Thomas, whose vast district included some of the most blighted stretches of South Central. Ridley-Thomas did most of the talking at a news conference of African-American leaders at First AME Church on Tuesday, April 28. He was incensed that Gates had allocated money for police overtime, although this was one of the few sensible precautions taken by the chief or anyone else before the riots. Ridley-Thomas also denounced the videotaped message sent by Gates to LAPD officers, saying it had "caused people to be concerned as to whether the department was arming itself" in preparation for a riot. "We should not repeat the errors of the past," he said. "A massive show of force would be a mistake. These are very tense times."[37]

IT HAD ALSO BECOME TENSE WITHIN THE PLAIN, SECOND-FLOOR room in the Simi Valley courthouse where the jurors were deliberating the fate of the defendants—and unknowingly, the fate of Los Angeles. While Ridley-Thomas was warning about the LAPD, jurors were nearing deadlock on the only charge on which there was a chance of conviction.

The *Powell* jury had demonstrated from its first deliberations that it was in thrall of neither the videotape nor the conventional view that the beating of King was a self-evident case of police brutality. Gunson had been right when he said that only in Parker Center could the defendants have found a more sympathetic jury. Juror Retta Kossow, a retired real estate broker, later expressed the attitude of the jury majority to D. M. Osborne of *The American Lawyer:* "[King] is the only criminal, and he's free. And these four men have lost their careers."[38]

Kossow was sixty-five years old, the same age as Dorothy Bailey, the program manager for military contracts whom Jo-Ellan Dimitrius had rated number one for the defense among all the prospective jurors. The first day of deliberations happened to be Bailey's sixty-fifth birthday, and Kossow suggested to Henry King, a cable splicer for Southern California Edison, that he nominate Bailey as forewoman. King did, and Bailey was elected by a secret ballot on a 9–3 vote over Kevin Siminski, a thirty-eight-year-old computer programmer who had been nominated by Anna Charmaine Whiting.

The election was more than a birthday present. Kossow and King, two of the most pro-police jurors, sensed that Bailey was a kindred spirit. She was also experienced at chairing meetings and forging consensus. As soon as Bailey was elected, she said she needed a right-hand man and designated Siminski as deputy foreman. Her second action was to establish a ground rule requiring that jurors who believed a defendant to be guilty to accept the burden of convincing others "because that's the way our system is set up."

Siminski was probably the most conflicted of the jurors. Although he was conservative and pro-law enforcement, Siminski had been mistakenly arrested as a teenager because he matched the description of a robbery suspect. White hoped that this youthful experience had taught Siminski that police can make mistakes and that it would enable him to see the arrest from the viewpoint of Rodney King as well as the defendants. The prosecutor had been as accurate in this perception as Dimitrius had been in seeing that Bailey was a boon for the defense. For a long time after his arrest, Siminski told Osborne, "I was always afraid that I was going to get pulled over for no reason."[39]

After their organizational meeting, the jurors had dinner in the banquet room of an International House of Pancakes and celebrated Bailey's birthday. She was in high spirits. "It's not every sixty-five-year-old broad who gets elected a jury forewoman and sequestered all in the same day," Bailey told juror Charles Sheehan.[40] But she was all business the next morning, when jurors took up the two assault charges against Briseno. Their discussion quickly revealed the majority's sympathies. Sheehan had been surprised by Barnett's announcement that Briseno would testify Powell was "out of control." He had not believed Briseno, who he thought had been "lying through his teeth."[41] Sheehan's view echoed throughout the jury room.

Briseno's bold testimony against his fellow officers proved unpopular even with jurors who disapproved of Powell's conduct. "Nobody bought the choir-boy defense," Siminski said.[42]

But jurors were willing to give every defendant, Briseno included, the benefit of the doubt. Briseno's police boots were among the 150 exhibits stacked on a card table in the jury room. The jurors passed the boots around. Sheehan, who had expected them to be steel-toed, said he was surprised at how light they were. When the jurors played the video, focusing on the Briseno segment, they saw that his action had been a two-step motion in which he appeared to lose his balance before bringing his left foot firmly down on King. The jurors still disapproved of Briseno's testimony against his fellow officers, but they believed the crucial point of his defense and voted to acquit him on both counts.

The jury then turned to the assault charges against Wind, who at both trials benefited most from juror examination of the videotape. The tape clearly showed that Wind had stepped back several times to evaluate the impact of his and Powell's baton strikes. Sergeant Duke had testified that such evaluation was a key element of LAPD instruction. Jurors agreed unanimously that Wind had tried to assess the results of his sixteen baton blows and several kicks. They voted to acquit Wind on both assault charges and went back to the International House of Pancakes for Friday dinner, having disposed in a single day of the allegations against two officers.

While the decisions on Briseno and Wind had been reached with relative ease, the discussion that had taken place among the jurors was revealing. Most respected Wind for refusing to break ranks as much as they disliked Briseno for testifying against his fellow officers. These jurors were not offended by the "code of silence." But they were offended by White's sarcastic cross-examination of Powell and especially by his emotional confrontation of Powell during the closing argument. The discussion about Wind also revealed that the jurors accepted Duke as a reliable expert on police procedures and rejected Bostic as inexperienced. Sheehan thought Duke was "streetwise" and "agreed with every thing he said."[43] Bailey was similarly impressed. She later said that the principal issue facing the jurors was deciding "whether the officers were out of policy" when they repeatedly hit King.[44] Based on Duke's testimony, Bailey concluded that all blows were "in policy" and therefore justifiable. "In my opinion it's not right or morally acceptable to beat any human being, but if LAPD policy has determined it's right in certain circumstances, we had to go with that and we did," Bailey said.[45]

In fact, Judge Weisberg had charged the jury with determining whether the defendants had acted reasonably under the law, not whether they had complied with LAPD policy. Weisberg had told the jurors to make independent assessments of the videotape, but this instruction does not seem to have registered. Most of the jurors were mesmerized by Duke and relied on his testimony. Once they equated Duke's interpretations of LAPD policy with determinations of reasonable force, they were well down the road toward acquitting all the defendants.

The only defendant whose case caused real debate was Laurence Powell. On Saturday, Bailey polled the jurors and found them leaning 9–2 for acquittal, with Siminski undecided. The votes for conviction were cast by Whiting and Virginia Loya, the hospital housekeeper whose young son wanted to be a police officer.

Whiting, a printer, was the jury's most working-class member. She was straightforward and emotional and tended to see many sides of an issue but make her own judgments. Loya was the only Latino on the jury in a county where Latinos constitute 26 percent of the population. She had a strong feeling that Powell had behaved brutally but found it difficult to express herself in a group of strangers. Siminski was articulate and technical. He drew a grid on a blackboard in the jury room and wrote down the major points of the two counts against Powell. The principal questions, as Siminski saw them, were "Was it an unlawful beating?" and "Was there deadly force used?"[46]

In considering the charges against Powell, the jury basically divided into three groups. At one end of the spectrum were Whiting and Loya. At the other end were four hard-liners who totally accepted the argument that King was to blame for everything. A dominant group, led by Bailey, disapproved of the violence used to subdue King but thought there was reasonable doubt as to whether Powell's conduct had been unlawful. Siminski wavered between this middle group and the Whiting minority.

Bailey's rules of procedure wore down Whiting, since they gave her, as the juror most convinced of Powell's guilt, the burden of convincing her fellow jurors. It was an unfair burden. Whiting, forceful and fair-minded, became frustrated at her inability to make the others see the excessive force she thought was plainly revealed on the videotape. "She felt pressured," said Bailey.[47] Siminski was seen as an honest broker by both Bailey and Whiting, but his painstaking analysis of the prosecution case left him with reasonable doubt. In his view, Melanie Singer had been persuasive on direct testimony, but the cross-examination had revealed that she was wrong. No one, Whiting included, had liked White's confrontation of Powell. The medical evidence was inconclusive. So, ultimately, was the video, for all the jurors agreed that it showed that King had been the initial aggressor.

Whiting was particularly disturbed that the other jurors, Loya and Siminski excepted, were unconcerned about Powell's racial attitudes and bragging. "I felt very strongly that he had an attitude," Whiting said. She based her view on the totality of Powell's conduct, including the message he sent before the beating to Corina Smith where he compared African Americans to gorillas, and the message he sent afterward in which he boasted about not having beaten anyone so badly in a long time. She also thought that the audiotape showed that Powell had laughed while calling the ambulance. "You can't make excuses for every action that a person does," Whiting said. "You can say this is an exception or that is an exception, but you can't make exceptions for everything that they presented to us."[48]

But the majority did make exceptions for everything. Many jurors agreed with Powell that his "laughter" on the audiotape was just "heavy breathing." Sheehan, who had naval combat experience, knew laughter when he heard it, but thought that Powell's laughter had been a nervous reaction based on fear. Whiting realized he had a point. "There [were] extenuating circumstances," she said. "Here's a guy who had a racist attitude, who was inadequately trained in the use of his baton, and he . . . was scared to death."[49]

Most jurors were less willing to listen to Whiting than she was willing to listen to them. Stone himself could hardly have done more to excuse Powell than Kossow, who said Powell's message about gorillas was "merely chatter" and a way of releasing tension after a "dangerous" domestic call.[50] Not even Powell had described the call as dangerous or thought to make this defense of a remark that seemed "racist" to Chief Gates and almost everyone else except the Simi Valley jurors.

The jurors adjourned on Saturday without reaching a decision. When they resumed deliberations on Sunday, April 26, a heated argument erupted between Whiting and Alice Debord, and Loya started to cry. Bailey calmed the jurors, urging them to focus on the evidence and not make personal attacks. She read from the instructions on reasonable doubt and once more asked Whiting and Loya to show the others that an unlawful assault had occurred. Whiting backed down. She was convinced that Powell had acted unreasonably, but she could not find a single specific blow that other jurors would agree was excessive force. Siminski had a similar problem. He tearfully told Osborne that he had wanted to find Powell guilty, but could not identify any one blow that established guilt beyond a reasonable doubt. Just before lunch on Sunday, while Reverend Murray was completing his impassioned plea to the First AME congregation to "be cool," the three pro-conviction jurors abandoned their fight and voted with the majority to acquit Powell of the principal assault count.

After lunch, the jurors quickly disposed of the false report counts against Koon and Powell. Contrary to the expectations of Chief Gates, no juror felt that Koon had attempted to cover up the ferocity of the beating. Koon had impressed all the jurors with his forthright testimony taking full responsibility. After voting to acquit Koon and Powell of the false report charges, the jurors acquitted Koon of the other, more serious charges against him and quit for the day with the second assault count against Powell undecided.

Whiting felt so bad about acquiescing in the acquittal of Powell on the first assault charge that she could not sleep. She talked with Loya about making a stand. On Monday morning, the two women announced to their fellow jurors that they planned to ask Judge Weisberg to excuse them from the jury on the ground that they had been pressured to acquit Powell. This alarmed Bailey. She knew that if Weisberg granted their requests, he would also declare a mistrial or name alternate jurors to the panel and order deliberations to begin again. To keep the jury intact, Bailey scrapped her rule requiring that jurors who favored conviction accept the burden of convincing others. Instead, the discussion would be conducted in turn around the jury table. This concession spared Whiting from the bombardment of questions she had faced when she advocated that Powell be convicted on the first assault count. A poll on the second count against Powell—assault under color of authority—showed the jury split 9–3 in favor of acquittal with Whiting, Loya, and Siminski voting for conviction.

But the three advocates of a guilty verdict could not overcome Duke's interpretation of the videotape. Duke had testified that LAPD officers had a right to use their batons to keep an unsearched felony suspect on the ground, which seemed reasonable to a majority of the jurors. Siminski, who had taken over the burden of arguing for conviction, played a section of the video in an effort to show that Powell had continued to whale away at King long after he stopped resisting. "I felt that Powell did not give King a chance to just lie there," Siminski said.[51] This was the essence of the prosecution case, essentially a restatement of White's plea to the jurors to trust their eyes. Instead, the jurors relied on what Duke and Koon had told them. By Tuesday evening, at the end of two days of debate, a vote by show of hands found the jury still deadlocked 9–3 for acquittal.

When jurors reassembled on Wednesday morning, Bailey and Siminski suggested that they look again at the videotape and vote another time on each charge. It was a responsible effort, but the jurors were in no mood to change their minds. Whiting no longer saw any reason for holding out; she knew she could never change the opinions of the most pro-police jurors.[52] The only change in the final voting was by Christopher Morgan, the telephone technician whose brother was a retired LAPD sergeant. He joined Whiting, Loya, and Siminski in voting to convict Powell of assault under color of authority. The jurors deadlocked 8–4 for acquittal. They voted unanimously to acquit the four defendants of the ten other charges. After seven days that included thirty-two hours of deliberation, the jury had completed its work.

IT IS UNLIKELY THAT ANY PROSECUTORS, NO MATTER HOW SKILLED, could have overcome the obstacles that faced White and his colleagues. They started with the disastrous change of venue, which virtually guaranteed a jury that would have deep sympathy for the defendants and little for Rodney King. The very videotape that had made the prosecution possible simultaneously undermined its case: Prospective jurors who had been outraged by it—and might have voted for convictions—were automatically excused, and perhaps more important, the unedited tape that was played in court, which included King's charge toward Powell, was a powerful advantage for the defense. These basic problems were compounded by contradictory and ill-prepared prosecution witnesses and by a creative defense presentation that, while far from error free, was persistent and effective. Sergeant Duke, in particular, was believable and professional, and set the standard by which most jurors determined reasonable use of force.

In post-trial interviews, forewoman Bailey consistently pointed to two of Judge Weisberg's instructions as the basis for the acquittals. One called upon jurors to put themselves in the place of a "reasonable officer . . . confronted with the same or similar circumstances." The other was an instruction on circumstantial evidence. As Bailey paraphrased it: "If there are two interpretations of an event and both are reasonable, we must [adopt] the interpretation that favored the defendant. That gave the benefit of the doubt to Powell."[53] Later, Bailey told ABC's Ted Koppel that she had a "vague, nagging feeling" that Powell and Koon were guilty but could not convict them on such a basis.

Some of the jurors were so pro-police that they might have favored acquittal under almost any circumstances. But others, such as Siminski, struggled to find a basis for conviction before reluctantly deciding that reasonable doubt existed on every count except the second assault charge against Powell. While the Simi Valley jurors were condemned and hounded for their decisions—some received death threats—most of them did their best in light of their backgrounds and the evidence.

Ultimately it was Rodney King's behavior that persuaded the jury to exonerate the officers. This is a hard truth that critics of the Simi Valley jury rarely acknowledge, any more than most defenders of the jury admit the possibility of subconscious racial bias. Even Bryant Allen, King's boyhood friend, could not explain King's bizarre actions, and the jurors were convinced that the officers believed King had been under the influence of PCP. And truth to tell, *People v. Powell* was always a close case, once the videotape was seen in its entirety. Even before the trial was transferred to Ventura County, Terry White wanted to tell the world: "The first ten seconds on the video are not exactly very good for us. . . ."[54] He could not have been more right.

WHILE CECIL MURRAY BECAME STEADILY MORE PESSIMISTIC AS SIX days passed without a verdict, the spirits of the defendants rose. Outside the courthouse on April 28, Powell said he remained "very apprehensive" but was becoming more optimistic every day. He had no regrets. Powell said that it was "maddening" to think that King would become wealthy while the officers who had arrested him would lose their careers and possibly their freedom. "He's no victim at all," Powell said of King. "He's just a civil attorney's client and a political puppet." Powell was even harsher on Gates, accusing him of betraying the officers. "I thought he'd support us and support our policies, but he didn't," Powell said.[55]

On April 29, at 1:00 P.M., Bailey sent word to Judge Weisberg that the jury had reached ten verdicts and was hopelessly deadlocked on the remaining charge. Weisberg had agreed to withhold announcement of any verdicts for two hours—a procedure intended to give the lawyers time to reach the courtroom but that also provided a warning to the LAPD. Reporters rushed to Simi Valley to hear the verdicts read in open court at 3:00. So many reporters were admitted that only eight members of the public could squeeze into the courtroom, much to the disgust of scores who were turned away. "The jurors, that's who I want to see," said John Aguirre, one of the lucky few who got in. "And justice, I want to see a just verdict."

The jurors showed no emotion as they filed into the courtroom, but Weisberg's face registered surprise when he saw the verdicts. DePasquale turned to Wind and said, "Judging by how unhappy Judge Weisberg looks, that verdict is very good for you."[56] King's attorney, Steven Lerman, was perplexed by Weisberg's reaction. "What's he staring at that paper for?" wondered Lerman, who had assumed that the defendants would be convicted.[57] The defense attorneys also did not expect acquittals. When Barnett learned that the jury was deadlocked on one charge, he hoped this meant a mistrial for Briseno because he was convinced that the other defendants would be found guilty. He could not believe it when the clerk began to read "not guilty" over and over again. Aguirre, the fortunate citizen who been allowed into the courtroom, gasped, and silently began to weep.

Most people in the courtroom were as shocked as Weisberg and Aguirre. "This is heavy shit," thought Lerman, who would remember Alan Yochelson coming up to him with tears in his eyes.[58] The officers listened stoically until all the verdicts were read, then joyously hugged their attorneys. Powell also hugged Wind. Family members wept in happiness and relief. Powell's sister, Leanne, a paralegal who lived with her brother, said, "I am so ecstatic, so relieved . . . He did nothing wrong and today I saw his first real smile since March 3, 1991." Darryl Mounger was happy, too, but he told reporters that the officers had lost their livelihoods. "Nobody wins," he said prophetically.

A crowd outside the courthouse shouted "guilty, guilty" as Koon and Powell were hustled out behind a wall of Ventura County sheriff's deputies. A few rocks were thrown harmlessly in Powell's direction. Many in the crowd wandered aimlessly about the parking lot. Patricia Moore, her voice full of anger, tried to mobilize a demonstration. "Our justice system does not respect blacks," she told the crowd. Another African American who had attended the trial asked what she should tell her teenage son. "Tell him that this is our system, the jury has spoken," a man shouted from the back of the crowd.

Inside the crowded press room, reporters could not believe what they had heard. "I was dumbfounded and shocked by the verdicts," said Barbara Murphy, who had capably covered the trial for the *Daily News*. "The black leaders from Los Angeles had warned us, and we hadn't paid any attention to them." As reporters filed their first dispatches or talked to their editors, veteran Associated Press trial reporter Linda Deutsch told them that disturbances had begun in South Central.

The verdicts confirmed the fears of Cecil Murray, who had gathered with friends and members of his ministry before a television set in a basement office of the First AME Church. He could see the city burn in his mind's eye. "If something in you can die, that something died," he said.[59] Pearl Bell, who had joined a crowd at the church, said, "There is no justice for black people in Los Angeles—first Latasha Harlins and now Rodney King."[60]

King watched the verdicts on television at his apartment in Studio City in the company of his friend and bodyguard Tom Owens. Both had camcorders, and they had decided to videotape each other watching the verdicts being read. "King's reaction was one of pure disbelief," said Owens. "It took him a while to fully comprehend what had occurred. He sat absolutely motionless throughout the entire reading, all fifteen minutes of reading the verdicts."[61] Then King picked up a roller device he used on his right cheek, where he had suffered nerve damage from the beating. He began to move it, slowly at first, then faster, "literally gouging his face with this roller in very short, very forceful strokes."[62]

But it was a jubilant scene at Parker Center. Officer Corina Smith, who had exchanged the controversial computer messages with Powell, raised her fist in jubilation. "I'm elated, absolutely elated," she said. "I'm proud to be a Foothill officer, and I'm proud to be an LAPD officer. It's like this sick feeling is finally going to go away."[63]

For others the sick feeling was just beginning. Ed Davis, the tough cop who had been LAPD chief before Gates and left to go into politics, was almost incoherent with disbelief. "If this is okay, what's not okay?" he said. "This beating was terrible. It was not okay. There is a defect in the law." At 77th Street Station, deep in South Central, Lieutenant Michael Moulin worried that the community would react. "I was scared to death that they were going to burn our city down," Moulin said.[64]

Anna Charmaine Whiting was scared, too—at first of the reporters who pursued the jurors when they were dropped off in the sheriff's parking lot where their cars were parked. The state was done with the jurors, and they were left to fend for themselves. Whiting lived far away, on the western edge of the county, and reporters who were following her abandoned the pursuit in favor of closer targets.[65] But Whiting could not flee the decisions in which she had participated.

Almost thirty years earlier, Whiting had switched on a television set in time to see Jack Ruby shoot Lee Harvey Oswald to death in a Dallas police station. The moment flashed in her mind when she finally reached the safety of her home and turned on the television just as it showed black men dragging Reginald Denny from his cement truck at Florence and Normandie and beating him nearly to death. Whiting began to cry. She cried for two hours.[66]

Many others would weep that night as Los Angeles burned and people died. And even before the riots, when she heard the verdicts that she feared, Joan Dempsey Klein had buried her head in her hands and cried inconsolably.

There was not "enough gray area in the verdicts," Cecil Murray would say later, to persuade blacks to respond rationally. In fact, there was no gray area at all. As South Central viewed the judgment at Simi Valley, white jurors had justified the beating of a black man by white police officers.

Blacks would wreak a terrible vengeance.

11

ANATOMY OF
A BREAKDOWN

"It was the Pearl Harbor of the LAPD."

—Zev Yaroslavsky[1]

"It was the LAPD's Vietnam."

—LAPD Sergeant Charles Duke[2]

DARYL GATES BELIEVED THAT THE WATTS RIOT HAD TAUGHT enduring lessons to the LAPD and to African Americans in South Central Los Angeles. Reflecting on the riot twenty years later, he said that blacks realized "it would be total insanity to do that again." But if another disorder on the scale of Watts ever did occur, he vowed, the LAPD would be ready: ". . . The Los Angeles Police Department would not allow it to go the way it did before. We would stop it the first night."[3]

Gates was a thirty-eight-year-old field commander at Watts and in the thick of the action. On August 11, 1965, the first night of the riot, he had established a command post at a strategic location and tried to close off the area. "Once the area was sealed off, it was our opinion that the activity would subside," Gates said in a memo afterward. "A sweep of the area on foot was thought to be inadvisable at this time, primarily because of a lack of sufficient personnel and a belief that the disorder would subside by itself."[4] But instead of subsiding, the disorder spread. Defiant youths stoned patrol cars. Under orders not to fire unless their lives were in danger, police officers fell back. Although his post-riot memo did not mention it, Gates said in a book written a quarter of a century later that Deputy Chief Roger Murdock had ordered him to leave the area.

Whether ordered out or not, Gates had no choice except to withdraw. "We did not know how to handle guerrilla warfare," he acknowledged.[5] Nor

did he have enough police officers at his disposal. By the time order was restored six days later by the National Guard and a task force of various police forces under LAPD command, thirty-four people had been killed and
1,032 injured. The central district of Watts had been burned to the ground,
and the riot had triggered kindred disturbances in Long Beach, Pasadena,
Pacoima, and San Diego.

While the McCone Commission absolved the LAPD, the department's
ineffective performance during the early stages of the riot was embarrassing
to Gates and other line officers. After the riot, said one officer, "we spent
years dissecting what went wrong and decided we had to move in quickly
should a similar situation develop."[6] Police leaders decided on a doctrine
that was a variation of what Gates had hoped to do on the first night of
Watts. No longer would the LAPD allow a riot to burn itself out. Instead,
the LAPD would "overwhelm and arrest everybody and prosecute them and
cordon off the area and take the territory in a military-type operation and
hold the territory and restore order as quickly and as rapidly as possible."[7]
Since a military response required military equipment, the LAPD purchased
two V-100 armored personnel carriers equipped with battering rams as an
alternative to sending police officers into battle in vulnerable patrol cars.

Gates and other senior officers in crucial decision-making positions during the Simi Valley trial believed that any potential disturbances would
likely follow the pattern of Watts, where rioting had flared by night and
subsided during the day. When Lieutenant Michael Hillmann asked permission a week before the 1992 riots to deploy the department's elite Metro
unit during daytime hours, he was told by Deputy Chief Ronald Frankle,
"Riots don't happen during the daytime."[8]

The assumption by LAPD leaders that they could wait until dark undermined the strategy of striking quickly to crush a civil disorder before it
developed momentum. Even more damaging was the widespread assumption that there would be no disorder to crush. "If we were not prepared for
any one thing, we were not prepared for four not-guilty verdicts," said Commander Bayan Lewis. "We did not plan for a worst-case scenario."[9] This attitude filtered down through the ranks. "Preparedness also involves mental
readiness," observed an LAPD internal review written more than two
months after the riots.[10] Because police officials did not anticipate acquittals, they were not ready for the riots.

The 1965 Watts riot had flared by spontaneous combustion late on a
hot day after a drunk-driving arrest initiated by the California Highway
Patrol. In contrast, the LAPD in 1992 had a full week, as the Simi Valley
jurors deliberated, to mobilize for any scenario, including the "worst case."
By April 29, the day of the verdicts, the jury had been out so long that
black leaders and even the defendants were openly speculating about a

mistrial or acquittals. And on the day of the verdicts the LAPD was given two hours notice that they would be read in court soon after 3:00 P.M., when shifts changed in many LAPD police stations. Shifts were held over at 77th Street and seven other stations, but officers at ten stations were allowed to go off-duty. Only 838 LAPD officers were on duty in the entire city when the verdicts were read at 3:15.

South Central had been on edge since March 1991 when the Holliday videotape was first televised. Parker Center had been a target of periodic demonstrations. In June, three police defendants accused of demolishing apartments inhabited by African Americans and Latinos were acquitted by a Los Angeles jury. In August three Korean markets were firebombed, among them the store where Soon Ja Du had fatally shot Latasha Harlins. In November contentious demonstrations erupted after Du was granted probation.

Despite all these warnings, the blue-ribbon commission that investigated the Los Angeles riots of 1992 found no "meaningful preparation" for the trouble that followed the trial. "There was no city-wide planning effort, no specific coordination with county, state, and federal authorities and, indeed, no event-specific planning within the LAPD itself," concluded the commission, which was headed by former FBI and CIA director William Webster and former Newark police chief Hubert Williams. "The city's standing emergency 'plan' was so general and unspecific, untested, unfamiliar to those who were later called upon to carry it out, and in large part nonresponsive to the nature of the civil disturbance that occurred, that it proved to be essentially useless."[11]

As the Webster report makes clear, Mayor Bradley and Chief Gates had the authority to prepare and to mobilize for a riot, and they share the responsibility for failing to do so. Bradley had possessed broad emergency powers since he became mayor in 1973, and those powers were strengthened by a 1980 city ordinance. He headed the Emergency Operations Organization; under that was an Emergency Operations Board directed by the chief. Both were served by a staff called the Emergency Management Committee. The chief was empowered to arrange with local governments and state and federal agencies for "cooperation, mutual aid, and protection during a local emergency." Gates did not use this authority. He believed that the LAPD was the finest force in the nation, fully capable of handling any disorder on its own, and had been mortified that it had been necessary to call in the National Guard to suppress the Watts riot. As a result, he did not ask for help until forced to do so.

Mayor Bradley did not reach out either, nor did he exercise his own emergency authority. He was also deficient in dealing with the police chief he was trying to force into retirement. Bradley had not talked to Gates for thirteen months. After the riots, the mayor said he had believed the chief's assessment that the LAPD was prepared to cope with civil disorder. This is disingenuous, in light of Bradley's ongoing skepticism about anything Gates said. In fact, Bradley was aware, thanks to conversations with black leaders and with Deputy Chief Matthew Hunt and Jesse Brewer, that South Central was ripe for rebellion. The mayor was simply too stiff-necked to make his peace with Gates.

That Bradley was well aware of the possibility of unrest is shown by his backing of the Reverend Cecil Murray's plan for "Operation Cool Response." This was a well-intentioned effort that depended on friendly persuasion to quell post-verdict protests, instead of the extensive legal authority the city's emergency ordinance gave the mayor. The 1980 measure authorized the mayor to activate the Emergency Operations Organization whenever he determined that there had been "an occurrence which by reason of its magnitude *is or is likely to become* beyond the control of the normal [capacities] of the city government."[12] Once it was activated, the mayor had what the Webster Commission called "extraordinarily broad discretionary power during the period of the emergency to promulgate, issue and enforce rules, regulations and orders for the purpose of protecting life and property."

Bradley saw no need to exercise powers that would have brought Los Angeles to the brink of martial law. While he was clearly more aware than Gates of the potential for violence in South Central, the mayor shared the chief's view that the videotape of the Rodney King beating would produce convictions. And Bradley's judgment was further clouded by an attitude that he shared with many black leaders: He feared the LAPD more than he feared the prospect of mob violence.

Gates and Bradley were operating, in fact, on the basis of contrary assumptions. The chief believed that South Central was supportive of the police unless ignited by "irresponsible people." The mayor worried that police provocation might ignite a riot, just as a seemingly insignificant arrest had set off the disturbances in Watts. Neither view prepared the city for what actually happened in 1992. The number of "irresponsible people" who needed no goading to cause trouble was multiplied by verdicts that were widely considered a miscarriage of justice. And Bradley's fear that police provocations might set off a riot ignored the impact of the Rodney King beating and the Christopher Commission inquiry on the once-aggressive LAPD. As plummeting arrest statistics reflected long before the riots, LAPD officers had been cowed by the prosecutions and administrative discipline stemming from the King case. Officers worried about being second-guessed for any use of force and hesitated to arrest resistant suspects for minor crimes. Overall police morale was low. Even before the riots the LAPD was in retreat.

Gates, also in a retreating mood, exhibited little of the fiery defiance he had shown in the aftermath of the Christopher Commission report. Worn out by political struggles, he had abandoned his dream of breaking Bill Parker's longevity record as LAPD chief. But he had set no firm date for his retirement, and he still enjoyed civil service protection that allowed removal only for cause. Mindful that the Police Commission's bungled attempt to dismiss Gates had been overturned in court in 1991, his critics on the reconstituted commission and city council a year later tacitly accepted the contention of the chief's defenders that he would leave quietly if he wasn't pushed. This created an uncomfortable truce in the period before the riots. No one wanted to offend Gates, and no one pressed the chief on his plans for dealing with potential civil disturbances.

Within the LAPD, the Gates transition had a paralyzing impact. High-ranking officers who hoped to be considered as the chief's successor deferred to their departing leader. They were reluctant to rock the boat with bold suggestions for riot preparation or anything else that might offend police commissioners or community leaders. "The general attitude was not to act decisively," said Hubert Williams. "The prevailing attitude was that if you don't make any decisions, you can't get hurt."[13]

The department was "heavily reliant" on the chief, and Gates wasn't telling anyone what he wanted.[14] Much as Richard Nixon asserted without specifics during the 1968 presidential campaign that he had a "plan" for ending the Vietnam War, so did Gates declare that he had a "plan" for dealing with any disorders that might arise from the trial of the officers accused of using excessive force against Rodney King. Even the chief's staunchest critics thought it inconceivable that Gates would *not* have a plan. But what Gates thought of as a plan was a twenty-nine-page section of the LAPD tactical manual that he had helped write after the Watts riot. Each of the city's eighteen geographic police divisions also had "standing plans" for responding to civil disorders.

All of these were little more than guidelines. None addressed the specific conditions existing in South Central at the time of the verdicts. Indeed, the manual that Gates would later cite in his defense called for preparing specific plans to deal with anticipated crises, just as the LAPD had done before the 1984 Olympics.

ROBERT VERNON MADE NO SECRET THAT HE WANTED TO BECOME chief. Passed over when Daryl Gates was chosen in 1978, he had waited patiently for another opportunity. As assistant chief in charge of operations, Vernon controlled 85 percent of the LAPD and ran the department on a daily basis. He was a competent officer who under normal circumstances would have been a logical successor to Gates. But ever since the Christopher Commission hearings, he had waged a defensive struggle against charges that he headed a "God Squad" within the LAPD and used religious affiliation as a criterion for promotions. After the Police Commission told Vernon in February 1992 that he had not made the list of finalists to replace Gates, he decided he would retire early in June.

Although he was now a short-timer, Vernon recognized the potential for trouble in South Central and knew that more than generalities were needed to prepare for civil unrest. He had been thinking about the possibility of riots since the summer of 1991, when Parker Center was picketed and the Korean stores firebombed.[15] In August, he had dispatched Deputy Chief Matthew Hunt, the commander of South Bureau, to New York City to analyze police response to a disturbance in Crown Heights triggered when a car driven by a Hasidic Jew jumped a curb and killed a black child. A mob formed. Three hours later, Yankel Rosenbaum, a visiting Hasidic scholar from Australia, was stabbed to death by marauding black youths. Reporting on the New York disorder at a September 15 staff meeting, Hunt said the police response had been tardy and that the field commander "had failed to allocate sufficient personnel resources quickly enough to control the problem."[16] Vernon agreed with Hunt's analysis.

In January 1992, before the Simi Valley trial began, Vernon ordered the city's four police bureaus to train their staffs in operating field command posts. Each bureau designated a cadre of officers to operate command posts during a civil disorder, and they were tested on March 19 in the Dodger Stadium parking lot. On April 1, Vernon met informally with platoon leaders from the elite Metropolitan Division at the Police Academy bar, a location Lieutenant Pete Durham thought "kind of unusual" for the devout Vernon, a teetotaler. Over drinks (a glass of water for Vernon), they discussed Metro's needs. Durham, an ex-Marine who had once been Vernon's aide, realized that the assistant chief "wasn't happy" with the department's state of readiness. Metro leaders gave Vernon an earful for two hours. "Some of the things were rather elementary," Durham said. "We didn't have enough ammunition to train with, we didn't have the kind of protective equipment that's routine in other police departments."[17] The platoon leaders also warned Vernon that there was no up-to-date riot plan and confessed to feelings of neglect, saying that past warnings had been disregarded.

Metro had the theoretical capability to crush a riot at its inception. It was at once the Marine Corps, Green Berets and praetorian guard of the Los Angeles Police Department, proud of its record and can-do attitude. One of its standard techniques was to flood an area with more patrol cars than an entire police station could field. Durham, a platoon commander in the Vietnam War, had become infatuated with Metro when the SWAT team gave a demonstration at Camp Pendleton in 1972. He retired from the Marines, joined the LAPD and spent eighteen years trying to become a member of

Metro, which finally accepted him in 1990. Many other Metro officers had military backgrounds, and John O'Connell, one of the Metro platoon commanders, had won the Silver Star in Vietnam. Gates traditionally lavished attention and resources on the division, which he said was entitled to "special things for special people."[18]

Metropolitan Division had been created during the 1930s, when the LAPD was the enforcement branch of a corrupt and reactionary municipal government that took a dim view of radicals and militant trade unionists. Long after reformers cleaned up the corruption, Metro continued as an elite and mobile force within a force. It was expanded after the Watts riot from 70 to 200 officers. SWAT, originally a separate unit, merged with Metro in 1971. Its success in handling hostage negotiations and other high-risk assignments was copied nationwide.

At the time of the 1992 riots, Metro had 233 officers, less than 3 percent of the LAPD's sworn personnel. It was divided into four platoons, one of them administrative. The SWAT unit was D Platoon. B Platoon was assigned to the San Fernando Valley and the western part of the city and C Platoon to downtown and South Los Angeles. In practice, geographical distinctions often blurred, and all Metro units were called upon for crime suppression in gang-ridden South Central. Metro had its own armory, stocked with submachine guns and explosives. It controlled the two V-100 personnel carriers with battering rams and its officers did not have to respond to non-emergency calls. They roamed over a wide area, seeking suspects and making "observation-based" arrests.

Metro cops often viewed themselves as the shock troops of the *New Centurions* described in Joseph Wambaugh's novel. Lieutenant Thomas Lorenzen, in charge of SWAT at the time of the riots, said other units often feared Metro because it was staffed "by very aggressive, very skilled leaders."[19] But some officers took a dim view of Metro's detachment and elitism. John Sheriff, an LAPD street cop who reached out to black youths in South Central, thought Metro was a menace. "The people in Metro have no ties to the community," he said. He described Metro cops as "freelancers" who had a mission to "crush crime . . . kick ass and take names."[20]

But Vernon knew that an effective performance by Metro was the key to quashing a riot. As much as other units might resent this elite unit, they depended upon it in crises. On April 8, 1992, Vernon directed Metro to update antiriot plans "and develop necessary tactics and training to cope with an impending major unusual occurrence." He brought captains of the LAPD's divisions to Parker Center on April 10 to review plans for "unusual occurrences." Vernon also proposed that the LAPD declare a citywide tactical alert at the time of the verdicts. Gates later said this proposal met resistance from other high-ranking officers who thought it would be a waste of resources in the event of guilty verdicts. According to Gates, Vernon then backed down and said that a tactical alert should be declared after the verdicts if there were any sign of trouble on the streets.[21]

Vernon would subsequently point to the April 10 meeting as an example of his efforts to prepare the department. But despite his sense of urgency, it had no galvanizing impact on the LAPD. The objections to Vernon's proposals for a citywide alert showed that the LAPD leadership was distanced from the realities of the Simi Valley trial. And the euphemism that the LAPD was preparing for unspecified "unusual occurrences" cluttered the meeting with talk of earthquakes and Operation Rescue demonstrations. For reasons that have never been explained, three of the eighteen LAPD divisions did not even send representatives to the meeting. Among them was the 77th Street Division, which would be at the epicenter of the riots.

Secrecy also proved an enemy of preparation. Gates was worried that the media would learn of LAPD planning and ordered that no instructions be given in writing at the April 10 meeting. He told Vernon: "Make sure they understand I don't want to put the LAPD in the position of predicting a riot. I don't want us to be accused of issuing a self-fulfilling prophecy."[22] Vernon obediently instructed the captains to say nothing to the media. "The message to me from both of them was we don't want this to come out in the press . . . but we want you to be prepared because there may be a riot," said Captain Tim McBride, who then commanded Foothill Division.[23]

This obsession with secrecy had a devastating side effect: It kept critical information from police officers in strategic positions. Lieutenant Michael Moulin, who would be thrown into command during the crucial first engagement at Florence and Normandie, was unaware of any planning for civil disorders. His ignorance was shared by many others in the 77th Street Division. A post-riot LAPD internal review found that many 77th Street officers believed there "were no specific plans devoted to the potential aftermath of the King verdict." This review suggested that "the political climate of the day dictated a mindset that may have stifled open discussion regarding planning and preparation."*

Mayor Bradley and various African-American leaders, especially Councilman Mark Ridley-Thomas, encouraged this mind set. Their repeated warnings about the dangers of police provocation discouraged LAPD commanders from sending a public signal that the police were mobilized and

---

* After the riots, Gates ordered the LAPD's Inspection and Control Section to review preparation for the events that occurred during the riot's first six hours. Lieutenant Gary Williams and his staff conducted dozens of interviews and reviewed videotapes, radio transmissions, computer messages and logs. On July 8, 1992, they produced a document called "Analysis of the Los Angeles Police Department's Planning, Preparedness and Response to the 1992 Riot (The First Six Hours)." This document, used as a source in this book, has never been made public.

ready. Bradley, Ridley-Thomas, and many other leaders who later lamented the LAPD's slow response in South Central never acknowledged that their own attempts to restrain the police had contributed to inadequate deployment and preparation.

Still, blaming lack of LAPD preparedness on the bad judgment of politicians is a poor alibi for a chief who had often shown the courage to disregard political pressure. Gates had the prestige and authority to deploy the LAPD in a visible manner. That he shrank from the decision to do so seems to have reflected his weariness of political combat and an unwillingness to be blamed for any police-caused incident. Gates might have behaved differently if he had not believed that Powell and Koon would be convicted. But that is no excuse. He had a professional responsibility to see that the LAPD was prepared for a "worst-case scenario."

The chief and his principal subordinates defaulted on this responsibility. "Without proper planning, it is difficult to give proper training," declared the Webster Commission report. "Without proper training, the best planning may be wasted." Even the LAPD internal review acknowledged that the department had been inadequately prepared. "Planning and preparedness are two separate issues," the review said. "Planning can be done surreptitiously, but preparedness requires realistic and ongoing training as well as rather obvious deployment of personnel and equipment."

Perhaps more than any other LAPD officer, Metro's Lieutenant Mike Hillmann recognized the need for such training. Hillmann had grown up near downtown Los Angeles and, after brief Army service, had joined the LAPD in 1966 when he was twenty-one. He had spent all but four of the intervening years in South Central. Trim, hard-working and dedicated, Hillmann had a national reputation as a tactician and "policeman's policeman." Gates and Vernon valued his leadership abilities. Early in April, 1992, when Gates transferred Captain Patrick McKinley, Metro's longtime commander, he named Hillmann as interim commander.

Hillmann foresaw a post-trial confrontation that would be "much more violent" than Watts.[24] His opinion was based on observance of pre-riot incidents, including a rise in gang activity, and an understanding of economic conditions and attitudes in the community. He urged a highly visible LAPD deployment that followed the advice of the tactical manual—"present a dominant appearance"—and a strategy in which Metro would serve as a quick-response force to deal with "a very violent type of a confrontation where police officers with conventional resources were overwhelmed."[25]

Hillmann did not dismiss the concern that the LAPD could create a "self-fulfilling prophecy" with a provocation, and he thought it important that zealous officers not give activists an excuse to riot. What he advocated was a police version of Theodore Roosevelt's dictum: "Speak softly and carry a big stick." Officers should be disciplined so that they did not invite trouble but ready if trouble came along. "That has always been my philosophy," he said. "I always want to be prepared, and I want to be in the shadows. I want to be sensitive to the community's needs. We are going to be professional police officers, but if the situation happens where the civil rights of people are infringed upon, I want to be able to deal with it."[26]

In the weeks before the riots, Hillmann found LAPD management "very apathetic." He became, as he later described it, a "madman" as the trial neared conclusion "because people were not paying attention" to his warnings.[27] Frustrated at his inability to persuade superiors that big trouble was in the offing, Hillmann did his best to get Metro ready. He took a night helicopter flight to San Luis Obispo, some 200 miles up the California coast, to borrow bullet-proof vests and helmets for a hundred Metro officers who lacked such equipment. He studied a deployment model that had been used to quell demonstrations in Dade County, Florida. On April 13, he adopted a similar plan, dividing Metro into eight "tactical support elements" armed with shotguns and assault rifles.

Hillmann and the Metro commanders also developed potential scenarios. "Riot crowd control scenario #1" began with a crowd throwing rocks and bottles at Los Angeles Housing Authority Police. By the time Metro squads arrived, the crowd would have grown and refused to disperse. Other scenarios included a confrontation with an "unruly mob" in which officers came under fire from snipers, a protest at Foothill Station and a mission to escort firefighters to an industrial blaze amid rioting. Each of these mock incidents would be replicated on the first night of rioting.

Hillmann, at least, grasped the distinction between planning and preparedness. Metro units trained secretly at Todd Shipyards in San Pedro south of Los Angeles between April 20 and April 24 in crowd-control tactics, tear-gas use, hostage rescue, and antisniper tactics. But Metro's Pete Durham found it "embarrassing" that no one in the LAPD above the rank of lieutenant bothered to attend the training sessions. Durham would say later of his department's ranking officials that they "didn't have a clue" about what was happening.[28]

While the Simi Valley jury deliberated, Hillmann twice briefed Commander Lewis and Deputy Chief Frankle on Metro's preparations. Hillmann urged that Metro be deployed between 10:00 A.M. and 6:00 P.M., the time frame he thought most likely for verdicts in Simi Valley. He requested that the department's two armored personnel carriers be put on duty in South Central. And he asked that Metro officers be outfitted in body armor and ballistic helmets in advance of the verdicts, patrolling with AR-15 assault rifles at the ready.

Lewis deferred to Frankle, the balding, bespectacled head of the Operations Headquarters Division, who had served in the LAPD since 1961. Frankle, then nearly fifty-six, suffered from hypertension and was faulted by some rank-and-file officers for being out of touch with the realities of police work. But he was an accomplished bureaucrat who worried about overtime costs and was mindful of the pressure on the LAPD to keep a low profile. Hillmann had not gone far in his presentation before Frankle started grilling him about the AR-15s. Frankle wanted them kept out of sight, preferably locked in the vault at Metro's downtown headquarters. Hillmann said there would be no time to send officers back to the armory in an emergency. Frankle conceded, but insisted that the AR-15s be locked in the trunks of patrol cars so they would not be visible.

Hillmann then pressed his views on deployment, drawing the comment from Frankle that riots don't happen during the day. The Metro commander suggested as a compromise that Metro could be deployed from the midafternoon into the evening.

"No, I don't think we ought to do that," Frankle said.

"Chief, we need to do that," Hillmann replied. "It's not a question of whether I think we should do it, we need to do it . . ."[29]

Frankle would not yield. As the conversation grew heated, Hillmann argued that Metro needed a "first-strike capability." This was the last thing Frankle wanted to hear. He vetoed any daytime deployment of Metro, prompting Hillmann to tell his boss that he was making "a giant-assed mistake."

"Well, that's how I want it done," Frankle said.

"All right, we'll do it that way," Hillmann said.[30]

Lewis reprimanded Hillmann for his aggressive confrontation of Frankle. Hillmann recognized that he had been on the borderline of insubordination, accepted the reprimand, and reluctantly abided by the decision.[31] As the department after-action report delicately described what happened, Metro was deployed at night in a "soft patrol" mode. "Soft patrol" meant that Metro officers were in regular platoons, instead of self-supporting tactical squads, and their forces divided, instead of concentrated. They wore regular uniforms instead of riot gear and presented a "very friendly, high profile demeanor with no proactive police enforcement to be initiated unless necessary." It was a deployment better suited to a public relations offensive than to averting a riot.

Of all the decisions that prevented the LAPD from quickly responding to the riots, the refusal to allow Metro to deploy in battle array is most significant. The "giant-assed mistake" was compounded by the deployment of the V-100 personnel carriers, which Frankle kept out of South Central and unavailable for duty in the early hours of the riots. These decisions all but eliminated Metro's utility as a quick-response force and with it the possibility of suppressing a massive riot in its early stages. While Metro was small in numbers, it was the only LAPD unit with the will and training to carry out this mission. "Metropolitan Division pre-riot recommendations for deployment, tactics and training were ignored," said Lieutenant Durham's after-action report. "A request to obtain, train with and deploy non-lethal weapons well in advance of the riots was ignored. Advice concerning the most effective way to pre-position the division was similarly ignored."

By "non-lethal" weapons, Durham meant rubber bullets, 37-millimeter cartridge rounds that are fired from a gas gun similar to those used to deliver tear-gas canisters. Each round delivered five foam-rubber projectiles about the density of racquet balls at a maximum distance of fifty feet. A study by Metro's tactics review committee, headed by Hillmann, found that rubber bullets had been effective in crowd control and in quelling jail disorders. Metro had obtained thirty rounds and tested them on its officers, who wore protective gear and were not injured. Citing Hillmann's study, Metro commander McKinley sent a March 17 memo to Frankle requesting allocation of the cartridges for training and riot use.

The request wound up on the desk of Lieutenant Dan Koenig, whom Vernon had assigned to obtain the equipment Metro platoon leaders had requested during the meeting at the Police Academy bar. Koenig, a Parker Center insider known for his administrative prowess, was skeptical of Metro claims about the safety of "non-lethal munitions." He vividly remembered a 1970 incident in which Ruben Salazar, news director for a Spanish-language television station and Los Angeles Times columnist, was killed by a tear gas canister fired into a bar by Los Angeles County sheriff's deputies during an antiwar protest. Koenig thought rubber bullets had been insufficiently tested. If they had been used against a crowd and killed someone, he said later, the LAPD officials responsible would have been "absolutely crucified."[32] Because Koenig shared the conventional view that the Simi Valley trial would produce convictions, he did not share Metro's sense of urgency. He rejected Metro's request, and his decision was upheld by Vernon.

Metro has since been equipped with rubber bullets, and they have proven nonlethal and effective. But in the early stages of the 1992 riots, outnumbered LAPD officers had only the unpalatable alternative of retreating or using deadly force against civilians armed with rocks and bottles. This was the precise situation LAPD officers had faced in Watts.

Rubber bullets were not the only option: LAPD officers might have been able to disperse the crowd at Florence and Normandie with tear gas. A post-riot study by University of New Mexico sociologist Bert Useem and the LAPD's David Gascon contended that non-burning "cold" tear gas could have cleared stores of looters "without causing enduring harm to the looters or to the facility."[33] But the study noted that LAPD policy was "prohibitive," requiring that "chemical agents could be used only when expressly authorized by a command level officer of commander or above." Officers at Florence and Normandie were commanded by a lieutenant who had no authority to use tear gas, even if the option had been available.

INSTEAD OF FOCUSING ON RIOT PREPARATION, LAPD LEADERS WERE consumed by Gates' impending retirement and the struggle for succession. As the Webster Commission politely put it, a "morale problem arose in the LAPD's top command" in August 1991 after Gates said he would step down within a year. Seven top LAPD officers—Vernon, Frankle, Hunt, and Assistant Chief David Dotson among them—sought to succeed Gates. Others positioned themselves for promotion, producing what Webster called "finger-pointing and hard feelings among the competitors" and what Vernon saw as "disloyalty and insubordination" by high-ranking officers.[34] "For almost one year before the 1992 civil disturbance, the top LAPD commanders appear to have functioned with a seriously impaired working relationship characterized by poor or non-existent communication and little coordination of their respective commands," the Webster report found. "This prolonged period of infighting and isolation severely impacted the LAPD's command and control."

Gates became increasingly disengaged as his retirement, now expected in June, neared. He held no staff meetings during April and remained aloof from riot preparations except for his warnings to Vernon and the captains to keep information about riot planning from the media. The highest echelon of the LAPD was virtually dysfunctional. The chief had viewed Dotson as a traitor ever since his criticisms of Gates to the Christopher Commission and kept him isolated from LAPD decision making. Despite sharing with Vernon the lofty title of "assistant chief," Dotson was devoid of operational authority. He went home on the first night of the riots as if it had been the end of an ordinary workday.

Vernon was also among the missing, and his absence was far more critical. Vernon did not share Gates' delusion that the LAPD was ready to stop a riot, and had, as we have seen, made genuine efforts to increase LAPD readiness. But Vernon left the department in the lurch by scheduling a vacation in Florida in advance of his retirement and before the trial was resolved. It was an astonishing decision, considering Vernon's view that a riot was likely no matter what the verdicts. Vernon returned to Los Angeles from a business trip on the first day of the riots and departed for his vacation the following day, leaving behind a city in flames. He telephoned Gates on both days, offering to return to work. Gates turned down the offer, not wanting to interfere with Vernon's vacation. It was a well-meaning gesture that Gates later acknowledged was also "a big mistake."[35]

Deputy Chief Hunt, in command of South Bureau, was on the job but largely out of the loop. Hunt, who spoke in a brogue that revealed his Irish origins, had a mixed reputation within the LAPD. Some militant officers believed that he cultivated approval from the black community at the expense of hard-nosed police work. Gates later contended that Hunt "froze" during the riots because he was "so sensitive to overreaction that he didn't want to move out too quickly."[36] But there is no doubt Hunt tried to warn Gates that the riots were coming. Hunt's adjutant, then-lieutenant Paul Pesqueira, recalled that Hunt often expressed frustration during the concluding weeks of the trial, saying he could not persuade anyone that there would be disorders if the principal defendants were acquitted: "He kept bringing up that issue time and time again, telling people we need to prepare for these things, and we need to do more than what we're doing."[37]

Ironically, Hunt's ability to mobilize LAPD forces when the crisis came was hindered by the reintroduction of community-based policing, a concept he strongly favored in principle. Fourteen years earlier, after becoming chief, Gates had joined forces with Mayor Bradley to eliminate a successful community-policing program that had been instigated by his predecessor, Ed Davis. But after the Rodney King affair, Gates came under heavy pressure from the Police Commission and African-American leaders to reintroduce community policing as a means of improving relations between the LAPD and blacks. Following a recommendation of the Christopher Commission, Gates in January 1992 introduced a pilot community-policing program in six of the LAPD's eighteen divisions. When Councilman Mark Ridley-Thomas objected that the 77th Street Division was not included in the pilot program, Gates added it to the list. The captains of these seven divisions were told to report directly to Gates, bypassing deputy chiefs and creating an administrative vacuum. Not even a fully engaged chief could have adequately supervised seven far-flung divisions. The "Magnificent Seven" divisions, as they sarcastically became known within the LAPD, were largely left to their own devices. As Ira Reiner put it, "When you say that people at that level are reporting to the chief, as a practical matter, you are saying they are on their own and reporting to no one."[38]

While the reintroduction of community policing served the long-term interests of the LAPD and South Central, the timing of the decision proved disastrous. Hunt was deprived of control over the 77th Street Division, where the riots started, and of Harbor and Southeast Divisions, through which they soon spread. The Webster Commission found that removal of these three divisions from Hunt's command had "a deleterious effect on decision-making during the civil disorder." In fairness to Gates, it must be said that the chief would never have initiated such a dubious decision to disrupt the vital chain of police command. His action was an attempt to show that he was responsive to the Christopher Commission's call for reform and to the clamor of black leaders for restoration of community-based policing. Where Gates can be faulted is for waiting too long to restore an appropriate chain of command after the riots began. Not until 5:00 P.M., forty-five minutes after the first reports of disorders, did Gates return the three divisions to Hunt's control.

Vernon's absence and the dilution of Hunt's authority were compounded by the transfer of Metro commander Patrick McKinley to Valley Bureau a month before the riots. The transfer seems to have been an attempt to reward a highly competent cop with a deserved promotion.[39] Still, it is inconceivable Gates would have made this transfer if he had anticipated a riot. McKinley's absence threw the entire load of preparing Metro for the disorders on the shoulders of Hillmann. These were capable shoulders, but Hillmann essentially was forced to do McKinley's job as well as his own in the three weeks before the verdicts. McKinley's replacement, Captain David Gascon, took command of Metro only two days before the verdicts.

Inexperience and absences also afflicted the 77th Street Division. Captain Paul Jefferson, an African American, had been in command of the 77th for only four months and was mindful of the many admonitions not to cause a provocation. Talking to officers before the verdicts, Jefferson repeatedly urged restraint "in case some motormouth started talking about Rodney King after a traffic stop."[40] The station's other captain, patrol commander Robert Hansohn, was attending a training seminar in Ventura, more than seventy miles away, on the day of the verdicts. His absence put Lieutenant Moulin in charge of the fateful patrol that responded to the first disturbance call in the vicinity of Florence and Normandie. Sergeant Andy Simone, who was responsible for the station's response to "unusual occurrences," had the day off. Simone, formerly with SWAT, was the only officer in the station with recent riot training.

Overall, the LAPD was shockingly unprepared for even a mild disorder, let alone a full-scale riot. This was recognized in Metro, where a mood of fatalism prevailed. On Sunday, April 26, the day Cecil Murray admonished his parishioners at First AME Church to "be cool" and the jurors who wanted to convict Officer Laurence Powell gave up their fight in Simi Valley, then-Sergeant Greg Meyer went golfing with friends in Long Beach. Meyer, who shared the concerns about unpreparedness of the Metro platoon leaders who had met with Vernon at the Police Academy bar, realized there was nothing he could do about the LAPD's lack of preparation. In the parking lot of the golf course one of his golfing partners asked what would happen when the verdicts were returned.

"Oh, that's easy," Meyer said. "There's going to be across-the-board acquittals and a full-scale riot. The city will burn down."[41]

APRIL 29, A WEDNESDAY, DAWNED WARM AND CLOUDLESS EXCEPT for the usual morning fog along the Pacific coast. Temperatures would reach the eighties by the afternoon, above normal for Los Angeles in late April, and purple jacaranda bloomed in the planting strips between the streets and the sidewalks at Florence and Normandie Avenues. But it was not the weather or the spring foliage that dominated conversation at the dilapidated 77th Street Station, where officers were unusually jittery.

"We came to work that day, fully realizing the possibility that something was going to happen," Sergeant Charlie Strong would remember. "We didn't know exactly what."[42] Soon thereafter, about 8:30 A.M. the station received the first of a series of anonymous telephone calls threatening violence. One call seemed particularly worrisome to Strong, the assistant watch commander. "I'm a member of the Eight Tray Gangster Crips, and come this weekend you'll know who we are," the caller said.[43]

Strong conferred with Sergeant Roger Vian, the watch commander, and they agreed to prepare for trouble. After talking by telephone with Andy Simone, Strong decided to post two officers on the station roof and send two others into the surrounding neighborhoods to see what was happening. When Lieutenant Bruce Hagerty, head of detectives in the 77th Street Division arrived, Strong briefed him on what was happening. Hagerty asked Strong if he had informed LAPD higher-ups about the phone calls. Strong said he had not yet done so but planned to notify Metro and Detective Headquarters Division. While they talked, Sergeant Jerry Stokes, the adjutant for Jefferson, joined in the conversation. Stokes told Strong to proceed with the rest of his plan but not to notify anyone until he had talked to the captain.

The officers at the station that morning knew they were likely to be at the center of any violence that erupted in Los Angeles. Their cramped and crumbling station at 77th and Broadway was at the center of nearly everything, including some of the nation's most demanding police work. If the LAPD had truly been an army of occupation, as its critics contended, then the 77th Division would have been a garrison in enemy territory. From it, officers patrolled nearly twelve square miles awash in poverty, drugs, and violence—the highest murder rate in the city. The station, built in 1925, was a mess. Piles of confiscated rifles and assault weapons accumulated in the dank basement, where investigators worked without heat or ventilation, waiting for an open telephone line. The second story had been torn down for safety reasons, leaving a door that led nowhere and forcing vice and community-relations details to work out of trailers in the parking lot. One of the running gags played on police rookies at the 77th was to tell them to take something to the second floor.

But "working 77th" was a badge of honor and sometimes a path to advancement within the LAPD, where it was said that an officer who succeeded in 77th could succeed anywhere. Officers took a perverse pride in the primitive accommodations of their roach-infested station. Many, including Sergeant Strong, had a highly developed ethic of community service and a sense of solidarity with Stacey Koon, a respected veteran of the division. When the station was torn down nearly three years after the riots, a reporter noted that 77th was "police work boiled down to its essence: everyone pulling together because so much was stacked against them."[44]

Sergeant Strong was well suited to the rigors of life in this most primitive of LAPD assignments. He had been a telescope lens-maker in 1978 when he answered what he believed to be a divine call and sought to become a police officer. Accepted by the LAPD on his second try, Strong had worked on downtown foot patrol on Skid Row, where in a confrontation with a suspect he had suffered a serious back injury that almost forced him off the force. He returned to active duty six months later and eventually made sergeant at the 77th. Strong was forty years old and usually happy with his work, but he was much frustrated this Wednesday morning when Stokes told him not to notify Metro and Detectives Headquarters Division about the threatening phone calls. Stokes said Captain Jefferson had made some calls of his own and "doesn't feel that the threats are serious."

Long after the riots, Strong still wondered what would have happened if he had notified Metro that morning. "Maybe nothing," he added, and that is probably right. The urgency Strong felt was absent at Parker Center. Gates did nothing when he was notified that the verdicts would be announced in two hours and nothing when they were read. The chief could have declared a tactical alert, as Vernon had proposed at the April 10 meeting. As Gates belatedly acknowledged, "a citywide tactical alert, put into effect as the verdicts were read, could have speeded our response somewhat."[45]

But Gates practiced a leadership of denial while Frankle, Hunt, and other officers in the depleted high command waited for him to act. At the 77th, Captain Jefferson was also reluctant to move aggressively. He watched television in his office with disbelief as the verdicts were read. "It took a while to sink in," he said. "I knew there would be some reactions and the possibility of disturbances."[46] But Jefferson said he thought the reaction would come in the form of a march or demonstration.[47]

When the verdicts were announced, the incoming shift was at roll call in a trailer at the back of the station. Lieutenant Moulin, the watch commander and a twenty-one-year veteran of the LAPD, watched the announcement on a television in the squad room.[48] He was an emotional man of progressive views who was convinced that the officers on trial in Simi Valley had used excessive force. Moulin knew from experience that LAPD officers sometimes did "horrible" things to uncooperative suspects, and he thought the King incident was an "aberration" only in that it had been videotaped. When the verdicts were read, several officers in 77th cheered or clapped, particularly at the acquittal of Koon. Moulin was disgusted. "White officers were prancing around like someone just had a baby," recalled Moulin, who is white. "Frankly, I was disappointed. I thought the criminal justice system had failed the people of Los Angeles."[49]

Moulin's was a minority view among LAPD officers, but not unique. Theresa (Terry) Tatreau, the assistant watch commander, would recall a "range and gamut of emotions" as she glanced around the roll-call room. Some officers seemed bewildered. A few looked at the table and said nothing. The emotions of the officers were further stirred by Moulin, who as watch commander addressed them at the beginning of their shift. "I don't know why you mother-fuckers are happy because now the shit's going to hit the fan," Officer John Edwards recalled Moulin saying. "And his exact words were, 'I hope you are all proud of yourselves and happy. I wish those guys had been found guilty because now there's going to be a whole lot of trouble'." Edwards, an African American, resented Moulin's comments. "I couldn't believe he was saying that he wished police officers had been found guilty," Edwards said.[50]

Moulin would remember reaction in the roll-call room as dividing mostly along lines of race and gender. "Many of the white officers were elated, but the black officers and women were sad, and many of them were crying," he said. Moulin believed that blacks in Los Angeles had reacted patiently to the videotape of the King beating, giving the justice system a chance to work. Now he was "scared that they were going to burn our city down." He felt a need to express these feelings to the officers he knew would bear the brunt of the judicial system's failure. "I talked to them as best I could," Moulin recalled. "I said it was going to be a horrible day in the history of Los Angeles, a day on which many of them could well lose their lives. I told them they had to depend on themselves and the equipment they had. I said, 'we have no weapons beyond what you have in your lockers, no tear-gas masks, no reserve ammunition.' I told them to take whatever they could in their police cars and make sure their cars were full of gas."[51]

Many officers who disagreed with Moulin's assessment of the verdicts shared his fears about the reaction on the streets. For all their pride and professionalism, most officers at the 77th were not trained to deal with civil disturbances. Officer Renee Minnick, in her fifth year on the LAPD, later said there had been "nothing, no preparation at all" and that officers had not even been told there might be protests.[52] But the protests were swift in coming. Soon after the verdicts, people began honking horns and shouting outside the station. Angry crowds gathered at 55th and Normandie at 3:20 P.M., five minutes after the verdicts, and far to the north, at the Lake View Terrace site where King had been beaten. "There was no plan at that point, no direction was given to us," Strong said. "[We] were on our own."[53]

Strong, who had been held over from the day shift, scooped up maps of designated police command posts and left the station by the back gate in a car with Sergeant Don Schwartzer, as people on the street screamed obscenities at them. Their destination was a nearby doughnut shop, where they intended to get a bite to eat and improvise a plan of action. But the two sergeants were met at the shop by a jeering crowd. A man handed Strong a flyer from the "Revolutionary Communist Party" denouncing the verdicts and urging revolt. The sergeants returned to the station.

Shortly after 4:00, five young black males made a beer run to the Pay-less Liquor and Deli at Florence and Dalton Avenues, a Korean-owned store three short blocks west of Normandie that was known in the neighborhood as "Mr. Lee's." Their beverage of choice was Olde English 800, the malt liquor consumed by Rodney King in quantity before his fateful drive nearly fourteen months earlier. At the store each youth scooped up four or five bottles of the malt liquor and walked toward the entrance, where their path was blocked by David Lee, son of the owner. One of the youths struck Lee in the head with a bottle, and two others hurled bottles at the glass door of the store, shattering it. "This is for Rodney King," one yelled. From behind a bullet-proof counter Lee's father, Samuel, pushed a silent alarm button that alerted the 77th Street Station of the robbery. It was 4:17 P.M., and one of the deadliest urban riots in the nation's history had begun.*

THE NEIGHBORHOOD IN WHICH THE RIOT ERUPTED IS PART OF THE relatively well off western side of vast South Central Los Angeles. It is stable by South Central standards, blending into even more affluent Hyde Park on the west. Just west of Hyde Park is Inglewood, home of Hollywood Park and the Great Western Forum, where basketball's Los Angeles Lakers and hockey's Los Angeles Kings play their home games. The 1991 crime rate in the Florence-Normandie census tract of 10,000 people was only slightly

---

* The first known emergency call came at 3:43 P.M. at West Sixty-seventh Street and Eleventh Avenue when a young man hurled a brick at a passing pickup truck but missed. The Webster Commission report cites looting of the Lee liquor store (using a time of 4:15 P.M.) as the riot's initial incident. This seems the most appropriate incident, as it is the first one in which a confrontation is known to have occurred that resulted in both damage and injury. The time used here is the time when the alarm was sounded.

above the city's average and far below the crime rate for South Central as a whole. While nearly 25 percent of the 672,000 residents of South Central were then on public assistance, the welfare rate in the Florence-Normandie and Hyde Park (5,700 population) census tracts was less than 9 percent. More than 60 percent of the residents in Florence-Normandie and Hyde Park owned their own homes, which were typically surrounded by neatly trimmed lawns and gardens. Viewed strictly in demographic terms, Florence-Normandie may have been the most secure and affluent inner-city neighborhood ever to become the flash point of a riot.

But the disorders that erupted on April 29, 1992, had more to do with racial attitudes than with the economy of the neighborhood in which they began. Viewed in their totality, the riots had many causes. Poverty and social instability would contribute to violence and looting as the disorders spread through South Central and beyond its boundaries. The extent and ferocity of the riots, which eventually involved slightly more Latino than black participants, prompted some sociologists to describe them as an "uprising" or a "rebellion" against harsh economic conditions and social oppression. Social activist Larry Aubry called the disturbances an "upheaval," encompassing concepts of both riot and rebellion. Police analysts emphasized the role of organized gangs, noting that even the five youths involved in the original attack on Mr. Lee's were gang associates. Other analysts blamed the LAPD for making it clear, in its inadequate early response, that the police had abandoned the defense of South Central.

But in their origins, the riots were neither a gang conspiracy nor a revolt against harsh conditions but a cry of black rage. The riots were indeed "for Rodney King," as the youth said when he hurled the bottle of malt liquor at the glass door of Mr. Lee's. And they were for Latasha Harlins, whose name was invoked by sign-waving demonstrators on Florence Avenue and in the systematic destruction of Korean-owned stores throughout the riots. The rebellious blacks who took to the streets in the aftermath of the verdicts shared with Lieutenant Moulin the belief that the judicial system had failed the people of Los Angeles.

Officers James Lumpkin and Ricky Banks were having a snack at a bakery down the block and across the street from Pay-less Liquor when it was robbed. They felt at home in the neighborhood, for Banks had been raised a few blocks away and Lumpkin in nearby Compton. Both officers were African Americans who stood out in a crowd, with Banks towering six feet six inches and Lumpkin six-five. When they heard that Mr. Lee's was being robbed, they ran to the liquor store to find the robbers had fled. They interviewed the Lees, inspected the damage and wrote a police report describing the robbery and the assault on David Lee. As they were finishing their report, they received a radio call of a disturbance only a hundred yards away at Florence and Halldale.

Officer John Ayala and partner Ty Hansen were in their patrol car near the corner of Florence and Halldale a block west of Normandie when they heard the same radio call. Reaching the scene at 5:23 P.M., they found a slender young black man with a goatee and shaved head swinging a silver-and-black aluminum baseball bat at the windshield of a Cadillac with two white men inside. Black youths cheered on the bat wielder, who did not immediately stop at the sight of the police car. "Goddamn, look at this guy," said Ayala, who was amazed that the youth seemed undeterred by the presence of police.[54] But when Ayala got out of the car the youths fled, pursued on foot by the two officers, who put in a call for assistance that brought Banks and Lumpkin sprinting to the scene.

The chase ended in an alley behind an apartment complex known as a favorite hangout of the Eight Tray Gangster Crips. Ayala arrested the young man with the baseball bat at 5:27. Four sergeants, including Schwartzer and Strong, were now at the scene, and a crowd had assembled, drawing the attention of a TV news crew. Sergeant Tom Tavares would remember the crowd as fairly quiet until the camera crew arrived. People then began shouting, "Rodney King, Rodney King, Rodney King." Schwartzer detected a "palpable" mood change. "It got ugly," he said. "It was the first call after the verdicts . . . We were the friendly neighborhood cops one minute, the next minute we were lunch meat. It didn't take a genius to figure out we needed to do something. . . . We got out of there."[55]

Among those departing were Ayala and Hansen, who took in their patrol car the youth they had arrested. On the way to the 77th Street Station the youth said repeatedly that he had just been expressing anger at the verdicts. Without defending the verdicts, Ayala and Hansen patiently explained that he had no right to commit a crime because of his frustration. The youth paid no attention. "This is right, this is right, this is right," he said until Ayala finally told him to shut up. By the time they reached the station, the radio was crackling with calls for assistance, and Ayala and Hansen did not want to lose time booking a suspect for a minor crime. They turned the youth over to a night-duty officer, who released him. Ayala and Hansen never learned his name or saw him again.

It was now past 5:30 P.M. and even the most sanguine officers in the 77th Division sensed that the neighborhood was ripe for a riot that would put the LAPD to the test. Their concerns were not shared at Parker Center. Chief Gates had activated the Emergency Operations Center in the sub-basement of City Hall East across the street from Parker Center at 3:55 P.M., but this "activation" was a just formality. "In fact, all that appears to have happened was the doors were opened, the lights turned on and the coffee pot plugged in," according to the Webster Commission report. Members of the EOC staff went off shift at their usual time of 4 P.M. and were not called back until several hours later. "In the meantime, the EOC was an almost empty room," the Webster report said.

Mayor Bradley had watched the verdicts in his office, shaking with anger. His fury had not subsided two hours later, when he appeared on television and proclaimed that the "senseless" verdicts had rendered him "speechless." It might have better if this had been literally true, for Bradley's language was unusually incendiary. "Today, the jury told the world that what we all saw with our own eyes was not a crime," he said. "Today that jury said we should tolerate such conduct by those who are sworn to protect and serve. My friends, I am here to tell the jury . . . our eyes did not deceive us. We saw what we saw, and what we saw was a crime. No, we will not tolerate the savage beating of our citizens by a few renegade cops."

Bradley then issued what he afterward described as a plea for calm. While saying it was necessary to express "our great frustration" and "our profound outrage, our anger . . . we must do so in ways that bring honor to ourselves and our community. We must not bury the gains we have made in the rubble caused by destructive behavior. We must not endanger the reforms we have achieved by resorting to mindless acts. We must not push back progress by striking back blindly."

Police officers and many others who heard these comments felt the mayor was inviting a riot, even though he followed his expressions of outrage with an appeal for calm. Noting an upsurge of incidents in the hour after the Bradley statement, Vernon maintained that the mayor's words were taken "as a signal" by "irresponsible activists" to take to the streets. But the rioters who would within two hours savagely attack bystanders were already on the streets when the mayor spoke.

Bradley's comments sounded worse at the time than they do when read today because he condemned the verdicts with an emotional intensity unusual for the mayor. Later, he explained that had he not spoken forcefully, he would not have had the credibility to call for a peaceful reaction. "I would have been laughed out of town if I said, just be cool, don't react . . . this verdict was something which was quite appropriate," Bradley said.[56] But in fact, his comments seem to have reflected his personal feelings rather than a calculated effort to stop any disorders. His words did not cause the disorders, but a more thoughtful mayor would not have heaped extra fuel on a fire already beginning to burn out of control.

If Bradley was hasty in his condemnation of the verdicts, Chief Gates was far too slow in responding to the situation they had created. Post-Watts LAPD doctrine called for police to strike quickly and with massive force when civil disturbance threatened. But perhaps deluded by the Watts-based belief that nothing serious would happen until after dark, Gates did not do much else. He watched the mayor's statement in his office, and afterward criticized Bradley for taking issue with the verdicts. At 5:38, about the time Officers Ayala and Hansen were depositing the bat-wielding youth they had arrested for vandalism at 77th Street Station, Gates made a statement in Parker Center Auditorium. "If we have disturbances, we are prepared," he said.

As Gates spoke, the LAPD's lack of preparation was already evident. Near Florence and Normandie, outnumbered officers in vulnerable patrol cars faced roving bands of rock-throwing youths. The first police targets were four officers in two cars who had responded late to Officer Ayala's call for help and arrived at the scene where the youth with the baseball bat had been arrested. They proceeded through the Florence-Normandie intersection, where people on the sidewalks yelled obscenities at them. Officer Phyllis D'Elia, driving the lead car, tried desperately to make the light but was blocked by a truck. Suddenly, the cars were showered with rocks and bottles. Officer Timothy McGrath, in the second car, put out a radio call at 5:34. "Officer needs help. We're taking rocks and bottles from Florence and Normandie," he said.

McGrath, an African American and former gang officer who grew up in South Central, was considered an expert on the Eight Tray Gangster Crips. He spotted a youth approaching the passenger side of his car with brick-sized stones in both hands. McGrath jumped out and drew his gun. He recognized the youth as Seandel Daniels, a sixteen-year-old gang associate. Daniels cocked an arm and McGrath commanded: "Don't do it. Drop the rocks."[57] Daniels looked at McGrath's gun, dropped the rocks, and fled. Within five minutes, eighteen patrol cars and more than thirty officers had reached the scene in response to McGrath's call for assistance.

One of the first to arrive was Sergeant Sam Arase, a beefy Asian LAPD veteran. He found people milling around McGrath's police car. When Daniels reappeared, carrying more stones, McGrath identified him as one of the youths who had been throwing rocks at the police cars. "We're not going to tolerate that," Arase said. "He's mine." He then set out in pursuit of Daniels, who fled up an alley between Seventy-first Street and Normandie, northwest of the intersection. McGrath put in another call that brought Air 3, a police helicopter, to the scene of the chase. The pursuing officers grabbed Daniels as he climbed a chain-link fence, and they handcuffed him in a yard. "I can't breathe," Daniels yelled as his face was pressed to the ground. "Don't do him like that, you don't have to do him like that," responded people in the crowd. "Don't make this another Rodney King beating," a black officer said.[58] As Arase turned toward the crowd with the handcuffed Daniels, it seemed to him that there were "millions of people, not only on the sidewalk but in the middle of the street."[59]

Daniels was hog-tied and placed in a patrol car as the crowd screamed in fury at white officers to "get the fuck out of here" and taunted black officers as "kiss-ass niggers." Officer Brian Liddy drove to the scene with two partners in an unmarked car, headlights flashing. He later testified that he saw a rock hurled at Arase as he arrived. Liddy, who had a reputation for aggressiveness, and his partner Terry Keenan arrested former gang associates Cerman Cunningham, twenty-eight, for the rock throwing and Mark Jackson, twenty-nine, for grabbing at police batons and trying to kick the officers. Bart Bartholomew, a free-lance photographer for *The New York Times*, saw officers push the struggling Cunningham against a squad-car door as he resisted.[60] "Kill me . . . why don't you just kill me?" Cunningham screamed in rage.[61] Keenan believed there was "a strong possibility of violent confrontation" and wanted to remove Cunningham quickly before he could "motivate the crowd into violence."[62]

The scene was now what Sergeant Strong would describe as a "confusing mess." Officer Perry Alvarez would remember it as "chaos, constant chaos," with bottles flying everywhere and people yelling "fuck the police."[63] Four helicopters from local television stations and the police helicopter circled overhead, adding to the din. The police formed a loose skirmish line around their cars so the arrested men could be taken away, but their passive behavior reflected the legacy of the Rodney King case more than the "proactive" reputation of the LAPD.

As the skirmish line formed, the officers could see they were being videotaped by two black men at the edge of the crowd. The scenes portrayed on these amateur videos would show the police in a defensive posture. Instead of locking arms and aggressively jabbing people back with their batons in a standard crowd-control technique, many officers stood passively with hands at their sides, and some female officers tried to calm individuals in the crowd by talking to them. Several officers, both male and female, did not even have batons.

The skirmish line faced west against the bulk of the eastbound crowd, but there were patrol cars parked on both sides of the line and people were pouring in from the west, near the Florence-Normandie intersection. The thirty to thirty-five officers were now outnumbered by a crowd of perhaps two hundred people.[64] Sergeant Tom Tavares, who was helping supervise deployment of the skirmish line, kept looking behind him. "I was very cognizant of the fact that the crowd in back of us was also growing, but they hadn't breached the intersection yet," he said.[65]

The crowd to the west grew bolder as its size increased, and the situation became riskier for the embattled officers. "White bitch," a woman in braids screamed at Officer D'Elia, spitting on her. D'Elia kept a tight rein on her emotions, realizing she could be jumped if she broke ranks to arrest her tormentor. Bartholomew, coolly photographing the action, heard someone behind him say chillingly, "Cops going to die tonight" and another voice cry, "It's Uzi time."[66]

Lieutenant Moulin, the ranking officer, had driven to the scene from 77th Street Station. "I found utter chaos, an intersection that was uncontrollable," he said afterward. "The officers were being subjected to bricks, to huge pieces of concrete, to boards, to flying objects."[67] Moulin knew how ill-equipped the officers were. "Most of the policemen had no helmets. They had no bulletproof vests, no tear gas, no face shields . . . I think we're going to have to use deadly force, we could have a massacre here. So I ordered a pullout."[68] Moulin sounded the order to retreat at 5:43 P.M. over a squad-car public-address system and repeated it two minutes later. "I want everybody out of the area of Florence and Normandie," Moulin said. "Everybody get out of the area."

The officers obeyed, although not all agreed with the order to retreat. One skeptic was Sergeant Strong, who had been trying to firm up the skirmish line by pushing everyone to the east, in effect creating one crowd and allowing the officers to get control of their vehicles. Then an officer told Strong that a man had taken something from a police car. Strong's first thought was that the missing item was a weapon and that the person who had taken it was behind the skirmish line where he could menace the officers. He sent officers through the line to apprehend the man, who had taken only a flashlight and was not arrested. After Moulin ordered the retreat, a sergeant's voice could be heard over the police public address system, "Forget the flashlight. It's not worth it. Let's go, the flashlight's not worth it."[69]

Strong could not believe that Moulin would retreat. "I felt that we had to make a stand," he said later. But Strong assumed his superior officer must know more than he did. "When he ordered us to leave, I thought . . . he's aware of something I'm not—I'm too locked into the situation, therefore, he sees something I don't see. There's got to be some reasoning to this."[70]

Officer Danny Calderon, who had accompanied Moulin to the scene, also questioned the retreat. There was bad blood between the two, stemming from Moulin's objections to what he considered Calderon's harsh treatment of a rookie. Moulin designated Calderon at roll call as his driver in a move that Calderon suspected was really the boss' attempt to keep his eye on him. Whatever the reason, Moulin did all the driving that day, while Calderon became increasingly embittered. "When you turn your back on an angry crowd, they're going to start throwing stuff, and this one did," Calderon said.[71]

The police departed so quickly that D'Elia, first on the scene when she had been unable to make the traffic light, was almost left behind. Transfixed by the crowd, she stood momentarily alone as other officers left and her partner beckoned to her to join the exodus. D'Elia finally fled, and Bartholomew shot a picture of her as she ran. "The crowd was very empowered by this," Bartholomew said. "It was clearly a victory for them."[72]

PHOTOGRAPHER BART BARTHOLOMEW HAD DRIVEN TO THE 77TH Street Station after the verdicts and introduced himself so that police would recognize him later. He had then donned a bullet-proof vest he carried in his Volvo but had never worn and asked an officer where the trouble would start. "Go to the liquor stores," the officer said. Bartholomew had followed this advice and been in the vicinity of Pay-less Liquors when he saw police cars race by, responding to McGrath's call for help at Florence and Normandie.[73]

Bartholomew followed the police cars and the subsequent chase of Daniels up the alley. But when the police abruptly pulled out from Seventy-first and Normandie in response to Moulin's order ten minutes later, Bartholomew was suddenly the only white person in the crowd. As he walked to his car, which he had parked on Seventy-first Street, someone smashed the photographer under the chin with a two by four and a man in dreadlocks said, "Give me the fuckin' film, give me the fuckin' film." Bartholomew had taken thirty-six frames with one camera and shoved the roll into his pocket. He had taken two frames in another camera, and he gave this film to the man who was demanding it. As he did so, he continued walking toward his car as deliberately as he could, convinced the crowd would rush him if he ran.[74] By the time Bartholomew reached his Volvo several black men were dancing on the hood and one had broken the windshield, reached in and flung open the doors of the car, which was then looted of expensive cameras.

But not everyone joined in savaging the photographer. Bartholomew believes his life may have been saved by an anonymous black man who "felt like a middle linebacker on my right flank" as he helped the photographer to his car and told him to "get out of here." As Bartholomew pulled away, a piece of concrete came through the window and hit him in the face. He made a left turn through the Florence-Normandie intersection, spotted a single remaining police car, and tapped its rear bumper with his front one. The officer turned around. "You and me," Bartholomew said, motioning to himself and the officer. "You and me." He then followed the police car away from the intersection that he later realized had been "ground zero," the flash point of the riots.[75]

DAMIAN MONROE (FOOTBALL) WILLIAMS, THEN NINETEEN, WAS IN the crowd as Bartholomew fled. Williams belonged to the 71 Hustlers, a feeder gang for the Eight Tray Gangster Crips, and had been arrested eight times for auto theft, burglary, and other crimes, but had never been convicted. Williams had been at Florence and Halldale when the youth with the baseball bat was arrested, and he watched as Daniels, Cunningham and Jackson were taken into custody. Jackson was his half-brother, and Williams later claimed to have been caught up in the post-verdict anger of the neighborhood. This may have been true. But the immediate source of his rage seems to have been a girl's taunt. After Williams stood by and did nothing to interfere with the arrest of Jackson, a girl he knew called him a "pussy." Williams took down his trousers and undershorts and mooned the girl and the police.[76]

Just as Florence-Normandie was more affluent than most other South Central neighborhoods, so was Williams better off than most of his peers. He lived on Seventy-first Street, the toniest street in the neighborhood. "Our parents gave us everything," said Mark Jackson. "We had bikes, motorcycles, and minibikes, and we had more than other kids. . . . We made custom go-carts, we had show ten-speeds, all kinds of stuff."[77] Jackson was the oldest and Damian Williams the youngest son of Georgiana Williams, a church-going woman who had labored in Mississippi cotton fields before attending nursing school and moving to Los Angeles where she worked as a nurse, married and gave birth to two sons and a daughter. She was divorced and recovering from a serious illness when she became pregnant a fourth time. Williams thought of having an abortion, but decided the pregnancy was God's purpose and gave birth to Damian, whom she called her "miracle baby."

Although Damian Williams would symbolize violent black racism to many who witnessed his conduct on television during the early evening of April 29, he was not considered prejudiced toward whites. Notably more light skinned than his siblings, Williams had white friends and had wondered as a child if his father were white. Neighbors spoke of Damian's generosity with younger children, and his mother of the loving way he cared for her brother after he was badly beaten in a robbery and moved into the Williams home. But as a teenager, Damian chafed at discipline. During the tenth grade, he dropped out of the strict Christian academy where his mother had enrolled him, and he fathered a child when he was sixteen. His mother could now do little with her one-time miracle baby, who wore gang tattoos and became known in the neighborhood as an "O.G.," or original gangster.

Mark Jackson was working as a stereo repairman at the time of the riots. He had tried to be a father to his little brother, enrolling Damian in community sports programs. Damian did so well in football and baseball that his mother put a trophy case in the front hall to hold his numerous awards.

When Damian was eighteen, he tried out as a running back with the LA Mustangs, a semi-pro football team. He showed ability but again balked at discipline and stopped attending practices. After he left the team, Damian still bragged that he would play pro football and "have me a big mansion." But all he had to show for the season were color photographs of himself in a football uniform and his "Football" nickname.

When the police fled the Florence-Normandie neighborhood at 5:45, the two crowds converged. They became a purposeful mob that attacked, beat and robbed helpless civilians. Damian Williams was in the forefront of a dozen youths who hurled rocks and racial insults at whites, Latinos, and Asians as they drove by. Their conduct was captured on amateur videotapes and by the cameras of the news-station helicopters overhead. Voices can be heard on one videotape yelling, "Get the Buddha heads and the white boys." Williams directed traffic through the intersection, allowing blacks to proceed unharmed while all others became targets for a shower of stones and debris. Since few whites were in the neighborhood, most of the early victims of the mob were poor Latinos and Asians.

Marisa Bejar, her husband Francisco Aragon and their seven-month-old baby, Josh, were the first to be attacked. As Bejar drove through the intersection, their car was showered with bricks, rocks, and a metal-covered phone book that opened a deep cut on her forehead. A man leaned through the window and told the terrified Aragon, "I'm going to kill you." The baby suffered cuts from a metal sign board that a youth hurled through the rear window. The car crashed, and Bejar could not get it started again. But passers-by picked up the family, and an LAPD car that had responded to a call for help from the police helicopter led them to safety. As Officers Kris Owen and Steve Zaby neared the intersection, a rock came through an open window of their patrol car and hit their in-car computer. The officers deemed the situation too dangerous to leave their car but used their public-address system to direct the driver who had rescued Bejar, Aragon, and their baby to follow them. They drove three miles to Daniel Freeman Memorial Hospital, which became a principal receiving center for riot victims.

Another poor Latino family was less fortunate. As Manuel Vaca drove his worn 1973 Buick through the intersection, gang members showered him with rocks. Vaca swerved in terror and his car fishtailed, smashing into a pickup truck. Antoine Miller leaped jubilantly, and ran with Damian Williams to the wrecked car to lead an assault on Vaca, his wife, and his brother. Badly beaten, the Vacas struggled away on foot. When Sylvia Castillo, a community activist who had been outraged by the verdicts, drove through the intersection, her car also was struck by rocks. As blood streamed down her nose, a black man leaned in through the window and said, "Bitch, you're going to die." Unlike the Vacas, she managed to drive away. As Castillo fled, she thought, "Why are they doing this to me?"[78]

Although television viewers were struck by the absence of the LAPD, not every officer obeyed when Moulin sounded the retreat from Seventy-first and Normandie. Two who decided to remain in the vicinity were Lumpkin and Banks, the imposing African Americans who had grown up nearby and felt a personal responsibility for protecting the neighborhood. After taking the robbery report at Pay-less Liquor and sprinting to Florence and Halldale where the young man had taken a baseball bat to the Cadillac, Lumpkin and Banks had responded to McGrath's call for help at Florence and Normandie. When other officers pursued Daniels and became involved in the confrontation with the crowd a block away, Lumpkin and Banks had stayed in the intersection, attempting to divert traffic. Lumpkin thought the order to retreat was "bullshit."[79] When they heard it over the public address system, he and Banks wordlessly agreed to ignore it. "You had innocent people that were being hurt and needed our assistance," Lumpkin said later.[80]

A block away, once more at Florence and Halldale, they spotted a Latino couple running down the street. The Latinos were bleeding from head wounds and said they had been badly beaten. The officers radioed for an ambulance, and Lumpkin stood guard with a shotgun as paramedics who responded to their call attended the couple. While this was happening, a terrified white couple in a white car with a smashed windshield drove up. The man, bleeding from the side of his head, told Banks he was from Utah and had been driving to Los Angeles International Airport when he left the freeway and became lost. Blacks had stopped the couple's car on Florence Avenue and attacked them.

The officers could see that the mob was coming in their direction. A police car with Tavares and another sergeant pulled up, and the four officers organized an impromptu convoy. One car led the way, followed by the ambulance, the white car, and the second police car. They escorted the ambulance to the Inglewood city limits, then took the white car to a street that led directly to the airport. Lumpkin and Banks were later criticized, although not disciplined, for refusing to obey the order to retreat. But they believed their action may have saved lives. "I'm still happy I made that decision," Lumpkin said two-and-a-half years after the riots.[81]

Unlike Lumpkin and Banks, most officers awaited orders, believing they would be sent back to the Florence-Normandie intersection. "We thought we were beating a tactical retreat and would return in force," an officer involved in the pullout told me ten days later. "We didn't know we were abandoning the community."[82] This was also Sergeant Strong's view. "We pulled out thinking we were going to regroup," he said.[83] But Moulin did not believe he had enough officers available to retake the intersection. His first move was to confer with sergeants six blocks away at Florence Avenue and Hoover Street. Bartholomew, following the police car, drove up during this conference with a contusion on the side of his face "as big as a grapefruit" and gave Moulin the film he had saved, asking him to get it to *The New York Times*. Moulin promised he would, put the photographer in the backseat of his car, told officers to drive Bartholomew's car to the station and radioed for paramedics to meet them.[84]

Meanwhile, at Florence and Normandie, the situation had gone from bad to worse. At 5:59 P.M. a police dispatcher in the basement of City Hall relayed a report of a "major 415" (disturbance) at the intersection with "approximately five hundred male blacks throwing bottles at passing cars." The dispatcher directed units to the area but was interrupted by a radio message from Sergeant Tavares, who instructed LAPD units to disregard calls to help civilians "unless specified otherwise by Lieutenant Moulin." Tavares said he felt that lives of officers would have been at risk if they responded.[85]

At 6:00 P.M. Moulin and Captain Jefferson met tensely at the 77th Street Station. While Jefferson changed from civilian clothes into his uniform, Moulin told him the LAPD had "lost control of the streets" and urged the captain to declare a tactical alert. Jefferson said he would reserve a decision on whether to call a tactical alert and directed Moulin to return to the intersection and "assess" the situation before proceeding to a pre-designated emergency police command post at Fifty-fourth Street and Arlington Avenue.[86]

This, at any rate, was Moulin's recollection of a discussion that produced one of the critical police misunderstandings of the riots. Jefferson's account diverges on the crucial point of the specific orders he gave Moulin. Jefferson maintains that he instructed Moulin to return to Florence and Normandie and restore order. "I said to get back there and deal with the situation," Jefferson said. "I thought he would take the troops and do what needed to be done."[87]

Neither the Webster report, the post-riot LAPD internal review nor my interviews with Jefferson and Moulin resolved the contradiction of the two accounts, and the behavior of the officers in the post-verdict hours is consistent with either version. It is clear that Moulin never believed he had sufficient forces available to retake the intersection. Calderon recalls him emerging from the meeting with Jefferson and announcing that they were going to set up the command post. While Jefferson may indeed have expected Moulin to return to the intersection in force, the captain himself behaved cautiously throughout the afternoon and early evening. Gates subsequently suggested that Jefferson, as an African American, may have been "influenced by some of our black leaders who pleaded caution."[88] This may have been true, but white officers, including Gates, Frankle, and Hunt,

were similarly influenced. As for Moulin, who is also white, he had anticipated a riot when he heard the verdicts and glimpsed for himself the ferocity of the reaction on the streets. What Moulin seems to have done after
meeting with Jefferson was narrowly interpret an ambiguous order in the
only way he thought it could be carried out. Moulin told me "we would have
needed a thousand men" to retake the Florence-Normandie intersection.[89]
Instead of attempting to retake it, he drove back through Florence and Normandie to observe the violent scene, then sped on to the designated command post at Fifty-fourth and Arlington.

While Calderon was disgusted with Moulin for not stopping to assist
civilians on his return trip through the intersection, it seems unlikely that
the two officers by themselves could have done much more than endanger
themselves. It is also doubtful if Moulin, even if he had interpreted Jefferson's instructions as a direct order to retake the intersection, could have
achieved this goal without outside reinforcements. In any case, by the time
Moulin passed through the intersection again, he felt an understandable
imperative to establish the command post at Fifty-fourth and Arlington.

The pertinent issue concerning Moulin's conduct is whether he should
have immediately regrouped his forces after retreating. On this issue the
Webster Commission and Gates are in rare agreement. "The lieutenant
rightfully pulled the people out, but he should have formed up in squads
and gone back in," Gates told me.[90] The Webster report concluded that
Moulin made a "critical error" in not returning immediately to Florence
and Normandie. Hubert Williams said Moulin should have gone back "unless there was an absolute order to the contrary. . . . We may never know
what the truth was, but Moulin had a lot of power and authority to act on
his own," Williams said.[91]

During the forty-five minutes after this retreat the LAPD lost its chance
to stop the riot in its tracks. As disorders spread beyond the Florence-
Normandie flash point, isolated teams of officers skirmished with rioters
and two of them conducted an especially brave rescue, but the 77th Street
Division overall operated without effective direction and had scant communication with units outside the area. Citizens watching television at
home had a better grasp of what was happening than did most officers.
Seven news helicopters were hovering near Florence and Normandie,
recording the rock throwing and attacks on vehicles, and their pilots asked
the police helicopter why the LAPD was ignoring so many calls for help.
"We explained that there were too many people and not enough officers at
the present time to maintain control," said Stan Brittsan, the observer in
the police helicopter.[92]

The bewilderment of the pilots in the air was shared on the ground by
gang members, who were emboldened when the police did not return to

contest their control of Florence and Normandie. After the riots, several gang members told Lieutenant Hagerty that there would have been a fight if police had come back, but that the gangs would have backed down.[93] A similar conclusion was reached by the Webster Commission, which said that the "failure to respond aggressively and in force appears to have been a significant tactical mistake."

The absence of Metro during this period was crucial. In theory, this elite force should have been seeking out trouble spots and providing reinforcements for the embattled officers of the 77th Street Station. In practice, the battle for control of the streets was mostly lost by the time Metro swung into action. This was not the fault of Moulin, who at the first sign of trouble had instructed Sergeant Tatreau, the assistant watch commander, to call Metro. Nor was it the fault of Lieutenant Hillmann, who took Tatreau's call and a follow-up message from her at about 6:00 P.M., saying that "all hell had broken loose at Florence and Normandie."[94] Hillmann had wanted Metro officers in riot gear and on the streets at the time of the verdicts. Had they been so deployed, they might have assisted in the original response to McGrath's call and made a retreat unnecessary. Or they might have moved back to Florence and Normandie after the original retreat and dispersed the gang members when the mob was relatively small. But Metro had lost this capability when Hillmann's request for daytime deployment was denied.

When the riots broke out during the daylight hours of April 29, most Metro officers were off-duty or out of position. B Platoon was twenty miles away in the San Fernando Valley. C Platoon was scheduled to report at 6:00 P.M. D Platoon, the SWAT team, reported at 4:00 to Metro's downtown headquarters, where officers did weight training while awaiting instructions. But even SWAT was not at full strength: Two of its squads were undergoing sniper training at Angeles Rifle Range, more than fifteen miles away. David Gascon, Metro's newly appointed commander, had the day off and was tracked down by Hillmann at a restaurant in his hometown, San Pedro. Hillmann spent the day at Metro headquarters and set up a 5:00 P.M. meeting at Southeast Station at 108th and Broadway to brief commanders on Metro capabilities. But except for Gascon and some Metro sergeants Hillmann brought along, almost no one showed up. Only then did Hillmann learn that two-thirds of the LAPD's captains were out of the city attending a training seminar in Ventura. "I went absolutely nuts," Hillmann said, "thinking, what in the hell has happened here?"[95]

What was happening was an uncontrolled civil disorder that in the absence of the police and with the help of stolen liquor was well on its way to becoming a monumental riot. South Central had the city's highest proportion of liquor stores, and one of them, Tom's Liquor 2, was on the corner of

Florence and Seventy-first Street. Wes Wade, the night manager of Tom's Liquor, had closed the store and padlocked its metal front gate at the first sign of trouble. But at 6:03 P.M. black youths smashed the padlock and opened the gate. A youth wearing a Malcolm X T-shirt hurled a steel light pole through the window, and looters poured in to the store. "Everything's free," said a young woman on a videotape of the looting, which was seen as it happened on television.

Two veteran LAPD sergeants from 77th Street Station drove up while the looting was in progress. The driver, J. J. May, aimed the police cruiser at the looters, who threw rocks and a whisky bottle that came so close that the other sergeant, Nick Titiriga, was able to read the label. Most of the looters then scattered, encouraging May. "They took off running so I knew we could control the intersection," May said. "And that's what I was going to do."[96] Titiriga, however, heard Moulin instructing officers over the radio to assemble at the command post, and he insisted they had to obey. Within an hour after the departure of the police car every bottle in Tom's Liquor had been stolen or smashed. While much of the loot was carted away, several bottles of malt liquor were consumed by Damian Williams and other gang members. Their drinking fueled the fury on the streets.

The situation in the Florence-Normandie neighborhood had become perilous for officers and life threatening for the helpless civilians, mostly Asian or Latino, who had the bad fortune to be on the streets. At 6:07 P.M., Officers Lisa Phillips and Daniel Nee heard a dispatcher broadcast "an ADW [assault with a deadly weapon] in progress." The call reported "fifty male blacks throwing rocks at a gray vehicle with a female locked inside. Any 77th unit?" Moulin came on the air, ordering 77th Street units to assemble at the command post, concluding, "I don't want anybody chasing rocks." But Moulin was not as oblivious to the plight of trapped civilians as his detractors later claimed. At 6:10 P.M. he was back on the air, saying: "The call that was just broadcast regarding the lone female that was being rocked and bottled by fifty or so individuals . . . Make that a Code 3 [emergency] call."

The Code 3 was at Normandie and Seventy-first Street, just north of the intersection from which the officers had retreated. Nee and Phillips were young, idealistic officers who had been among the last to leave and had then helped an elderly man who had wandered away from home. They were two miles away from Normandie and Seventy-first when they heard the radio call about the trapped woman. Twice they called for a police helicopter to fly over and assess the situation but were told there was "no airship available, sorry, you're out of luck." Nee and Phillips drove back through the gang-controlled intersection of Florence and Normandie, where youths rushed up, bombarding their car with rocks and bottles and breaking the windows. Phillips watched a car crash in front of her and another roll down the street on fire before it struck a telephone pole. "I remember just mayhem," Phillips said afterward. "Hordes of people, yelling, screaming and throwing huge 40-ounce liquor bottles and beer bottles . . . Just crazy. It looked like Beirut, it looked like pictures on the news of Beirut."[97]

As Nee and Phillips drove west on Seventy-first Street, the crowd followed, continuing to throw rocks and bottles. They spotted a smaller crowd gathered around a car, which they knew must be where the woman was trapped. Nee floored the accelerator, aiming the police car at the people around the vehicle. Most of them ran, although one man remained for several moments on the hood of the car, smashing the windshield with a two-by-four while another reached in through the driver's side, punching the person inside. The rest of the group melted back into the larger crowd that had followed Nee and Phillips up the street and surrounded their police car. "We were scared to death, very, very scared," Phillips said.[98] At 6:14 P.M. she radioed, "Be advised we've got a large 415 group here at this Code 3 call, this ADW call. We're Code 3, taking rocks and bottles." Nee then added his plea, "We're at Normandie and Seventy-first . . . we need help, we need help."

The two officers quickly devised a plan. Nee would get the woman out of the car while Phillips covered him. Phillips jumped out the passenger side of the police car with her gun drawn, "yelling and screaming, and they probably thought I was just a crazy, crazy cop."[99] She then ran around the back to Nee's side. Nee emerged, and the two officers circled the perimeter of the two cars with their backs to each other. Nee made it to the woman, who was covered with blood and unconscious. He holstered his weapon, leaned in and unbuckled her seat belt, and scooped her into his arms. As Nee turned toward the police car, he was struck in the back of his head and legs with rocks and bottles. He fell, still holding the woman.

"The street had probably a quarter inch of glass on it from all the broken bottles and everything," Phillips said. "I can remember when Dan hit the ground, the crowd started laughing. And I'll never forget that . . . I thought, 'animals.' . . . I just couldn't believe humankind had sunk to such depths. This woman was just destroyed, she was a total bloody mess, limp, we thought she was dead already." Then Phillips took a chance. To help her partner she holstered her gun in front of the crowd, briefly leaving the two officers and the woman they had come to rescue defenseless. Now Phillips had another thought about the crowd. "They could have killed us anytime they wanted to, they just didn't," she said. "They somehow had some amazing group conscience that they weren't going to kill two cops that day. I don't know why."[100]

Nee regained his feet with the help of his partner. He put the unconscious woman in the backseat of the police car, which was covered with glass from the broken windows. Phillips, her weapon drawn again, covered him. As they pulled away, a brick smashed through the back windshield, spraying more glass inside. The situation seemed unreal to Phillips, who imagined that they were in a scene from a movie in which everything was occurring in slow motion. Although to Phillips the rescue seemed to take forever, the entire incident had lasted only forty seconds.

The officers had rescued Soon Oh, forty-six, a Korean American who lived in the Wilshire district. Nee and Phillips took her to Daniel Freeman Hospital and stayed with her as she was revived. Phillips then called Oh's daughter and told her that her mother had been in a car accident and was safe but not to come to the hospital.[101] Oh's head wounds were not as serious as the officers had thought, but there seems little doubt she would have been killed or bled to death had she been left in the car. Nee and Phillips reported the rescue by radio at 6:15 P.M. en route to the hospital, and the incident was also reported by the police helicopter, which arrived for the tail end of the rescue. A minute later a dispatcher repeated Moulin's order to assemble at the command post. The message was greeted by the voices of excited officers, who said over the radio, "We don't know what the fuck is going on. What the fuck is going on here?"

At 6:18 a sergeant suggested by radio to Moulin that he or Jefferson call a tactical alert to eliminate non-emergency radio calls. Moulin, who had just reached the command post at Fifty-fourth and Arlington, replied that Jefferson was on the way, and said, "we're going to make that decision momentarily." The narrow escape of Nee and Phillips had persuaded Moulin that it was too dangerous to allow officers to attempt further rescues. When a dispatcher at 6:19 reported another possible assault at Seventy-first and Normandie, Moulin said, "We'll just take that information . . . for the present time we are not going to go into that area and search any further for anybody. I want all my units at Fifty-fourth and Arlington."

The site where Moulin tried to regroup his troops was a nine-and-a-half-acre municipal bus yard that had been designated in the division's standing plan as a command post in the event of an "unusual occurrence." But as Useem and Gascon put it, the demands on this particular post quickly "outstripped its capabilities."[102] Rank-and-file officers preferred to work out of the 77th Street Station and several of them had grumbled when Moulin announced the command post location, which was 2.3 miles northwest of Florence and Normandie. When ordered to the command post, officers deployed south of the intersection had the choice of detouring or driving through the heart of the developing riot. At the command post, confusion prevailed. "We just showed up and said we're taking over the bus yard," Moulin recalled. "There were hundreds of buses there. We had to get them out one at a time. It took us hours to establish the command post."[103]

But when Moulin started setting up the command post, the LAPD had minutes, not hours, to keep the disorder from spreading uncontrollably. No one seems to have realized that at the time. Arriving officers were given pink-and-blue "unusual occurrence" cards to fill out, a device the LAPD uses to keep track of officers during emergencies. This procedure exasperated Sergeant May, who wanted officers to "rock and roll and go out there and do what we're paid to do."[104]

Chief Gates would later say that officers should have been formed into squads—four to a car—and immediately sent back into the field, as May wanted. But neither Moulin nor Jefferson, who arrived at the command post about a half hour after Moulin, believed they had sufficient forces to reestablish order without Metro's assistance. The first Metro officer to reach the bus yard was Sergeant Andy Lamprey, who had heard radio reports of the disturbance at Florence and Normandie. "Thank God, here comes Metro," someone said when he arrived at 6:25. But Metro was not there in force. "They felt like we were coming in with an army," Lamprey said. "Well, in fact . . . we were coming in with a couple of squads."[105]

Neither the command post nor Metro received any guidance from the Emergency Operations Center (EOC) or from Parker Center, where a demonstration against the verdicts was beginning to form and where the police high command was dependent on commercial radio and television for most of its information. George Morrison, Gates' longtime chief of staff, learned of the breakdown at Florence and Normandie through an open line to KFWB, an all-news station that had close relations with the department. Using information from KFWB, Morrison was able to inform the Emergency Operations Center at 5:45 P.M. that police vehicles were being "rocked and bottled" at the intersection. Soon afterward, he stuck his head into the chief's office and said that it was "getting bad" on the streets.[106]

That should have sent an alarm signal to Gates, who except for his brief statement in Parker Center auditorium at 5:40 spent the three hours after the verdicts closeted in his office. But the chief seemed oddly oblivious. At a time when civilians were being attacked in South Central and Moulin was struggling to get the command post in gear, Gates put Deputy Chief Frankle in command and departed for faraway Brentwood to address a political fund-raiser. When he left Parker Center at 6:30, the chief told a reporter that LAPD officers were dealing with the crisis "calmly, maturely, professionally."[107]

According to Gates, he summoned Frankle to his office "right after the verdicts were read" and told him he would be department commander. Gates said Frankle informed him that "Metro was fully deployed in the South Central area."[108] This seems an unlikely statement for Frankle in midafternoon, when one of Metro's three platoons had not reported for duty and another was far away in the San Fernando Valley. Frankle, after all, had given the order that scattered Metro—"to the four winds," as Hillmann put it—and he certainly knew that one of its platoons had not started its shift.

Frankle does not recall Gates putting him in command—or even that they talked the first day of the riots. Although Frankle acknowledges that he and Gates may have talked, he finds aspects of Gates' account preposterous. In the paperback edition of his memoirs, Gates writes that he told Frankle to deploy officers in riot gear formed into four-officer squads in the event of *any kind* (Gates' emphasis) of violence.[109] Frankle insists that this was simply basic doctrine, and that Gates would no more have instructed him that officers should wear riot gear and deploy in squads than he would have told him to make sure that the officers "bring their cars and their guns and their shoes."[110]*

Morrison gives yet another version of the transfer of power. He recalls going to Frankle when he learned that Gates was about to leave Parker Center to ask whether Frankle would be department commander in the chief's absence. Frankle said he didn't know, and Morrison urged him to talk to Gates. "Well, I guess I'm it," Frankle said a few moments later.[111] Morrison assumed that Gates had formally put Frankle in command. If so, the transfer of power occurred because Frankle went to Gates and not the other way around. And if the only conversation between the two men about transfer of command occurred just after 6:00 instead of right after the verdicts, Frankle might indeed have been reassuring about Metro, whose units had by then reported to duty.

In any case, Gates should have known from the EOC logs alone that he had a riot on his hands. In addition to the Morrison message at 5:45, a message at 6:00 from an intelligence officer said the situation at Florence and Normandie was "out of control" and that Metro had been called in to help. Other reports on the logs before Gates left the building told of a crowd gathering at the Foothill Station and of telephone threats to the Hollywood Station: "We are going to start to kill fucking cops."

---

* Frankle told me on October 10, 1995, that he was unaware of Gates' account of what happened on the first night of the riots until I quoted it in a letter requesting an interview. Frankle read Gates' memoirs in the hardcover edition, written before the riots. The account to which Frankle objects is from an afterword to the paperback edition of the memoirs and is consistent with what Gates said in an interview for this book.

Among all the dubious actions by public officials during the disturbances none is as troubling as Gates' astounding decision to leave his post. This action probably would have led to a court-martial if the LAPD were a true military organization. The chief's political foes had a field day at his expense. Even the loyal Morrison was baffled, and in its report six months later, the Webster Commission called Gates' action "mystifying." As the commission saw it, Gates' absence "compounded all of the department's command and control problems." The report added: "Chief Gates himself cannot justify his decision to take a leisurely car ride to a Brentwood political event at this critical time."

In fact, Gates made no attempt to justify the decision. He told me that attending the fundraiser was "a dumb thing to do" and acknowledged as much in the afterword to the paperback edition of his memoirs.[112] So why did he do it? Doubtless the major reason was that he wanted to help the hard-pressed opponents of Charter Amendment F, a pending city charter amendment to limit the tenure of police chiefs and make the LAPD more subject to civilian control. Charter Amendment F was the fruit of the Christopher Commission inquiry that had been prompted by the King affair. While its provisions did not apply to Gates himself, the chief knew its passage would mean that Bradley and the LAPD's liberal critics had accomplished their long-term objective of bringing the department to heel.

Ironically, the LAPD was unprepared for the riots largely because Gates had not demonstrated the independence he feared would be stripped from future chiefs. Instead of standing up to Mayor Bradley and the black leaders who feared that aggressive police deployment might cause a provocation, Gates had attempted to appease politicians by ordering the department to keep a low profile during jury deliberations. This cautious approach in turn led the LAPD to ignore the doctrines of quick and massive response that Gates had helped develop after Watts. Because he declined to exercise the independence he valued in the abstract, Gates had set a passive tone for the LAPD in the crucial pre-riot period. This passivity had been reflected in Frankle's decision denying Hillmann permission to deploy Metro during daytime—the single most damaging mistake of riot preparation.

Gates acknowledged "apprehension" when he departed for the fundraiser, but said "from past experience with riotous behavior I doubted anything substantial would happen until much later, or possibly the next day. Like the police, it takes rioters time to gear up, too."[113] It seems never to have occurred to Gates that people reacting in blind rage to verdicts they viewed as wildly unjust needed little time to "gear up." Nor did it occur to the chief that the leadership of his department had become dysfunctional. He seems to have believed that the LAPD could function on automatic pilot and was shocked when it did not. "I should never have gone to that thing [the fund-raiser], but

I thought I had given clear instructions," Gates told me. "I thought every-thing was in order. I thought we were okay, that we would be able to handle anything."[114]

The chief's abandonment of his post cost him the support he had main-tained throughout the Rodney King affair among the city's white, middle-class homeowners in West Los Angeles and the San Fernando Valley. Even conservatives who consistently took Gates' side when he came under fire from liberal critics were disappointed by the chief's lapse in judgment. But it is not clear that Gates' absence had any more impact on the LAPD re-sponse to the disorders than the mayor's intemperate reaction to the verdicts had on the behavior of the rioters. The sad truth is that Gates did not take charge even when he was on duty, perhaps because he really believed that "everything was in order" despite the abundant evidence that it was not. Whatever the reasons for the chief's behavior, the Webster Commission noted that the "leadership void" continued when Gates resumed command nearly two hours later. "During the entire crisis the chief of police appears never actively to have taken command of the department and its response, preferring to leave that critical responsibility in the hands of less experi-enced subordinates," the commission found.

While the absence of Gates from Parker Center may have had a negligi-ble impact on the LAPD's actual performance, it had immense symbolic consequences. More even than Moulin's retreat, the chief's departure sig-naled to street gangs and the law-abiding majority alike that the LAPD had abandoned a needy community. The people of South Central deserved pro-tection from their police, as Gates had realized at Watts. But instead of mov-ing swiftly, the LAPD magnified the mistakes of Watts, abandoning a vital intersection to a mob and producing a chain reaction that allowed a reign of terror to prevail in many of the city's poorest neighborhoods. In leaving his post at a crucial hour Gates sent an unfortunate message to South Cen-tral that his political agenda meant more to him than the welfare of the community.

This message, unintended by Gates, certainly did not represent the pre-vailing view of the officers on the front lines. Hillmann later said that some officers at the command post were afraid, and Tavares acknowledged that a few officers were so disgusted by media and community criticism of the LAPD that they cynically thought, "It's their neighborhood, if they want to burn their houses, let them."[115] But most of those in the 77th Street Divi-sion were dedicated cops who cared about the community in which they worked. Many had not wanted to retreat from Florence and Normandie in the first place. Others accepted the retreat as a tactical necessity, but be-lieved that they would soon return in force. The conduct of Lumpkin, Banks, Nee, and Phillips, among others, suggests that rank-and-file LAPD officers wanted to do what was right. That they were limited to saving isolated victims reflects not on their skills or courage but on the inadequate LAPD leadership.

Gates was not uncaring, either. He was a deeply committed police officer who had devoted his life to the LAPD, but lost touch with the realities of the city he was pledged to serve and protect—and with some of the realities of his department as well. When Gates left Parker Center to attend a political event during the nation's worst modern riot, he abandoned not only South Central Los Angeles but the police department he had served and loved.

12

NIGHTMARE CITY

"There are going to be situations where people are going to be without assistance. That's just the facts of life."

—Chief Daryl Gates[1]

"There's no doubt in my mind that we could have saved the city."

—Metro Officer Greg Baltad[2]

No ONE NOTICED DARYL GATES AS HE WAS DRIVEN NORTH TO Brentwood on the San Diego Freeway, following the route that O. J. Simpson would take two years later in the famous slow-speed chase that ended in his arrest. On April 29, 1992, the eyes of the world were focused on the bloody intersection of Florence and Normandie, where in the wake of the LAPD's withdrawal a gang-led mob took control and attacked anyone who was not African American. Because the police had failed to seal off this well-traveled route through South Central, targets were plentiful. Whites, Asians, and Latinos were hauled from vehicles and beaten or attacked on the streets. Most of the victims were poor, small, or frail. None had any connection with the LAPD or Rodney King.

These racially charged assaults were recorded by television cameras on news helicopters hovering over the intersection as horrified pilots added commentary. "And there's no police presence down here!" an observer in one helicopter said at the height of the violence. "They will not enter the area. This is attempted murder! Tell LAPD to shut Florence Boulevard down, and Normandie."[3]

While the savagery at Florence and Normandie was witnessed by the nation live on television, it was not seen by the mayor, the police chief, or many high-ranking LAPD officers. Chief Gates learned of "a major incident" at Florence and Normandie by radio as he was heading for the fund-raiser, but he could not see what was happening. Neither could Mayor Bradley, who after denouncing the verdicts had left City Hall for the First African

Methodist Episcopal Church and the rally that was intended to launch "Operation Cool Response." Deputy Chief Matthew Hunt, in charge of South Bureau, was also at the rally. Twelve LAPD captains, two-thirds of the department's division leaders, were still on the freeways returning from the distant training seminar in Ventura. And most 77th Street Station officers were awaiting redeployment at the command post at Fifty-fourth and Arlington, which lacked a television set.

What the police could not see was hell for those traveling through Florence and Normandie during the nearly three hours the intersection was under gang control. At 6:43 P.M., an hour after Lieutenant Moulin ordered the police retreat, a white man driving for a black-owned company entered the intersection in a white delivery truck filled with medical equipment destined for Chile. Larry Tarvin, then fifty-two, was unaware of the verdicts because his truck had no radio. He did not realize anything was wrong until he saw a man jumping on two cars at the southwest corner of Florence and Normandie.

Too late, Tarvin tried to turn back. Before he could do so, Henry Keith (Kiki) Watson pulled Tarvin from his truck and hurled him to the ground as if he were a rag doll. Tarvin, who stood five feet seven inches and weighed 130 pounds, would under any circumstance have had little chance against Watson, who was six feet one and weighed 215 pounds. And Watson was aided by other youths who joined in beating the hapless driver. One of the first blows knocked off Tarvin's eyeglasses, and he was hit again each time he reached for them. "I just wanted to get out of there, but every time I tried to get up, they knocked me back down," Tarvin said later.[4] He lay unconscious in the street for more than a minute, bleeding profusely. Nearby, an onlooker said, "No pity for the white man. Let his white ass down. Now you know how Rodney King felt, white boy."[5]

Reginald Oliver Denny had loaded his fire-red eighteen-wheel truck with twenty-seven tons of sand at an Azusa quarry at 5:39 P.M., just as Gates was assuring reporters at Parker Center that the LAPD was prepared to cope with any disturbance. Denny was thirty-six years old, slight of build and mild mannered. He deplored violence and fighting and rarely listened to the news. He was listening to country music when he left the Santa Monica Freeway and took a familiar shortcut across Florence Avenue to his plant in Inglewood.

Denny entered the Normandie intersection at 6:46 P.M., a minute after a bystander had helped the battered Tarvin drive away in his looted truck. Although Denny had not seen what happened to Tarvin, he had noticed from his cab's high vantage point that people were taking items from a truck in front of him. Briefly, he considered making a U-turn, but his truck lacked power steering. Since he knew his cargo was of no value to looters, Denny reasoned he could "tiptoe across this intersection and get on down the road."[6] But then he heard people shouting at him to stop. Rocks flew through his window. Denny would not remember the events that followed this volley of rocks, but they formed a tableau of brutality that much of America would be unable to forget.

As Denny's truck slowly entered the intersection, Antoine Miller yanked open the door of the cab, allowing others to pull Denny into the street. Henry Watson held Denny's head down with his foot. Another man kicked him in the belly. And the man in the Malcolm X T-shirt who had led the liquor store break-in hurled a five-pound piece of medical equipment from Tarvin's truck at Denny's head and hit him three times with a claw hammer. The most damaging blow was administered by Damian Williams, who at point-blank range hurled a slab of concrete (often called a "brick" in news accounts) at Denny's head. It struck Denny on the right temple and knocked him unconscious. Williams did a victory dance over the hapless man, imitating a football receiver who had caught a touchdown pass. He then flashed the sign of the Eight Tray Gangster Crips and gleefully pointed out Denny's crumpled figure to the helicopter pilots. Gang member Anthony Brown spit on Denny and walked away with Williams, leaving the trucker bleeding and unconscious in the street.

Various men then approached the fallen Denny, hurling liquor bottles at him. Gary Williams, a drug user who often hung out at the Unocal gas station at the corner, strolled over from the station and rifled Denny's pockets, holding a liquor bottle in his free hand. As Denny lay unconscious, Lance Parker passed by on his motorcycle and stopped. Parker, a process server for a law firm, took a shotgun from his gym bag and fired a shot at the gas tank of the truck. He missed, which probably spared Denny from being incinerated.

The Denny beating was the most horrific television image of the Los Angeles riots. It would be shown repeatedly during and after the disorders, frequently in tandem with clips of the Rodney King beating. Although commentators and activists found easy symmetry in the brutality of white police and black gang members, the behavior of the officers charged in the King incident cannot be equated with the conduct of Denny's assailants. King had refused to respond to police commands after a high-speed chase and had charged at one of the officers who had tried to arrest him. While the police arguably misjudged the threat King posed, Sergeant Stacey Koon had tried hard to take him into custody before the first baton blow was struck. Even Officer Laurence Powell, whose baton use was excessive, acted largely out of panic. Damian Williams and his fellow gang members had the unresistant Denny totally in their power and inflicted far graver injuries than the officers did to King. Denny was entirely a victim who had done nothing to provoke the attack against him. His only crimes were to be on the wrong street at the wrong time and to be white.

The paramedics who attended Denny said he came within a few minutes of dying. His skull was fractured in ninety-one places and pieces of it pushed into his brain. His left eye was so badly dislocated that it would have collapsed into his sinus cavity had surgeons not been able to replace a crushed bone with a piece of plastic. A permanent crater remains in Denny's face despite three reconstructive operations. Tarvin's injuries were less serious but hardly trivial. He suffered a cracked pelvis, fractured ribs, a broken nose, and permanent facial scars.

Except for Denny and Tarvin, most of the victims badly hurt by the small band of gang members who controlled the intersection were Latinos or Asians. Raul Aguilar, a slender immigrant from Belize, was beaten into a coma and his legs run over by a car. Takao Hirata, a print-shop owner returning home from work, was pulled from his car and beaten unconscious. He did not know until he saw pictures of Damian Williams, after Williams was arrested, that the same man had assaulted him and Denny. Williams and his cohorts also assaulted Fidel Lopez, who was beaten senseless. Then Williams pulled down the pants of the helpless, bleeding Lopez and sprayed black paint on his genitals and body.[7] A voice on an amateur videotape of the assault can be heard saying, "He's black now." Through all this violence and degradation, not a single police officer was in sight.

In the aftermath of the riots, Gates would complain that television coverage distorted what happened in South Central after the verdicts. He disputed the notion that Florence and Normandie was the "flash point" of the riots, saying that the media focus on the intersection obscured "outbreaks of violence" that occurred over thirty square miles of South Central. Defending himself against the charge that abandonment of the site had set the riots in motion, Gates offered the excuse that LAPD officers had been preoccupied with too many calls to focus on a single intersection.

That self-serving argument was inconsistent with the chief's criticism of Moulin, who Gates said had sent the wrong message when he did not try to retake Florence and Normandie. The reason the message was important was that Florence and Normandie at the time was the focus of violence in South Central, not simply one incident among many. This is clear from the well-documented analysis of the riot's first six hours prepared at Gates' behest by the LAPD's Inspection and Control Section. This report dutifully repeats the chief's assertion that "the media declared" Florence and Normandie the flash point of the riots. But it goes on to show that the declaration was accurate. Of thirty-seven "riot-related" incidents reported in South Central during the ninety minutes between 5:15 P.M. and 6:45 P.M., almost all were of isolated looting except for the criminal assaults at Florence and Normandie.

The LAPD report went on to describe the "unique" details of the violence at the intersection. "The crimes committed at Florence and Normandie were perpetrated by a core group of individuals who remained in the area, literally taking it over as their own, for a protracted period of time. This contrasted to other areas of the city where criminals fled after the commission of a crime, or upon the presence of authority." While "crimes against property were predominant in other locations," the report observed, the crimes at Florence and Normandie were violent assaults against civilians. It is another way of saying that Florence and Normandie was indeed the flash point, where the riots might have been stopped if the LAPD had responded promptly and with force.

Far from inventing some phony flash point, as Gates suggested they had, the media actually helped fill the vacuum left by the police. According to department doctrine, the LAPD should have sealed off the intersection early on. While there were not enough 77th Division officers to provide traffic control, a single call from Parker Center could have flooded the approaches to Florence and Normandie from nearby freeways with police cars and kept most unsuspecting motorists away. Instead, the task of warning motorists away from the area was left to radio and television, and especially to the alert news-helicopter pilots who witnessed the Denny beating. Motorists in Southern California tend to listen to news stations for traffic reports, and these warnings led many to avoid the danger zone. But the stations could not help drivers like Tarvin who lacked radios or those like Denny who were not listening to the news. It was the poor and the unsophisticated who suffered most from the failure of the police.

While the news judgment of the broadcast media in focusing on Florence and Normandie cannot be faulted, the televised scenes of violence advertised to criminals that the LAPD would not stand in their way and almost certainly fanned the spread of the riots. As Ted Koppel put it in describing the Denny beating: "It is television at its most riveting and horrifying. But live TV also becomes the carrier of a virus. At one and the same time, television conveys the fever of street violence and the impotence of the police. The beatings, the looting, the arson spread."[8]

Television coverage also may have contributed to a demonic view of African Americans. All the assailants and none of the victims at Florence and Normandie were blacks. As the helicopters moved from one incident of violence to another, they necessarily neglected much that happened in the wake of the attacks. The edited videotape of the King beating had failed to explain why the officers had acted as they did; the vivid televised accounts from Florence and Normandie inevitably missed or minimized brave and humane actions of African Americans who were appalled by the assaults. While the racial identity of Denny's assailants and the mob in the intersection was apparent to viewers, few knew about the heroic actions of blacks who stood up to the mob and rescued whites, Latinos, and Asians from death.

One of these heroes was Donald Jones, a burly off-duty firefighter and former LAPD reserve officer who had watched the verdicts on TV. He was appalled when the officers were not convicted, and was driving north on Normandie to a friend's house to discuss the verdicts when he spotted the crowd at the Florence intersection. Jones was curious—"nosy," he said later—and headed toward the crowd. Soon, he was enveloped in a chaos of flying bottles and debris. He parked his pickup at Seventy-fourth and Normandie and walked two blocks to the intersection. Standing at the Unocal station on the southwest corner, he saw a fire burning at the looted liquor store and black youths throwing stones at cars. When the cars slowed down, the youths ran in and beat the drivers. Jones saw helicopters circling overhead. He realized the youths must know they were being filmed but were too "out of control" to care.

Then Jones saw an Asian man in a black Ford Fiesta whose car windows had been shattered. The driver stopped as a brick went through his windshield, later testifying he was afraid he would "bump into people" if he kept going. The crowd closed in, pulled the driver from his car and kicked and beat him repeatedly as he clung to his ignition keys and covered his face with his hands. Jones could see that the Asian man was not going to get away. "I was not going to sit here and watch this guy being beaten to death," Jones said later. "I'm thinking to myself, how am I going to get him out of here?"[9]

Jones, with help from another man, picked up the driver and put him in the passenger side. He then told the crowd to get back. A heavy-set man with a ponytail and a cellular phone gave Jones a menacing look and warned, "You have only a few more seconds at this intersection." Jones took it to mean that he wasn't going to be spared because he was black. The car door would not shut all the way, but Jones held it with one hand and with the other steered the car to a fire station at Seventy-ninth and Vermont, where he called for an ambulance. He had rescued Sai-Choi Choi, a Chinese immigrant who had been returning home from his bookkeeping job. Choi suffered severe head and back injuries and neurological damage and would not work again as a bookkeeper.

Reginald Denny was rescued by four black strangers, one of them a woman, who had watched on television as he was dragged from his truck and beaten. As Titus Murphy, an unemployed aerospace engineer, remembered it, the four friends said to one another, "Somebody's got to get that guy out of there," and they decided to do it themselves.[10] They piled into a car and in less than fifteen minutes reached the intersection, where they were surprised to find that police were nowhere in sight. One of the group was Bobby Green, a trucker with the special license required to drive

Denny's eighteen-wheel truck, which was in gear with the engine running. With his friends driving ahead of him, Green steered the truck three miles to Daniel Freeman Memorial Hospital, ten minutes away. Denny then had a seizure, and Green thought he was going to die on the spot. But paramedics and five doctors, two of them African American, brought him back. The doctors had no doubt that the prompt action of Green and his friends saved Denny's life. Larry Tarvin, who had driven into the intersection ahead of Denny, was also rescued by a black stranger who picked him off the street, put him in the passenger's side, and drove him to the 77th Street Police Station. Tarvin knew his rescuer only as "Rodney."

The most heroic rescue may have been performed by Bennie Newton, an ex-convict and former pimp who ran an inner-city ministry. Newton came to the aid of Fidel Lopez, pleading with black youths to stop hitting him. When Damian Williams spray-painted Lopez and the crowd closed in on the unconscious man, Newton could stand it no longer. He threw himself over Lopez's body, Bible in hand, saying, "Kill him and you have to kill me, too."[11] The mob backed off. Newton drove Lopez to the hospital and later started a fund-raising drive in his church for the badly injured man.

Other blacks also intervened, with life-saving results. Television actor and writer Gregory Alan-Williams stopped the beating of Takao Hirata. John Henry left his porch near the intersection of Florence and Normandie to save Raul Aguilar, who was in a coma after he had been beaten and his legs run over by a car. John Mitchell, a *Los Angeles Times* reporter, rescued Tam Tran after the thirty-four-year-old Vietnamese woman had been robbed and hit in the head with a brick.

POLICE OFFICERS IN THE VICINITY SAW NEITHER ATTACKS NOR rescues. The command post was without a television, and there were no uniformed patrol officers remaining at the 77th Street Station to send into the field. Lieutenant Bruce Hagerty, head of 77th Street detectives, learned of the Denny beating when his wife called in tears. South Bureau called soon afterward with the same information, and Sergeant Theresa Tatreau, the assistant watch commander, sent a desk officer scurrying to find a television. Only then could she see the "carnage" occurring little more than a mile away. Tatreau put out a radio call to the command center for Moulin, who responded on his cellular phone.

"Mike, they're killing people at Florence and Normandie, they're really killing people," Tatreau said. "We need police officers at Florence and Normandie—what are you guys doing?"

"We're meeting and planning," Moulin said.

"What's Metro doing, where's Metro?"

"They're dressing," Moulin said.[12]

Hagerty came into the watch office as they were talking. He was livid. "Terry, are you getting through [to Moulin] with the information we're sending you?" he asked.

"I told him six times about Florence and Normandie," she replied.

Hagerty took the phone. "Mike, what the fuck are you doing?" he asked.

"We're making a plan," Moulin said.

"Forget your plan, get somebody to Florence and Normandie . . . I'm giving you a direct order to get officers to Florence and Normandie."

Moulin told Hagerty he should talk to Captain Paul Jefferson, the field commander, and handed the phone to Jefferson. Hagerty thought Jefferson seemed surprised at the report from Florence and Normandie, but the captain said the command post would respond. Hagerty found the conversation "very frustrating."[13]

It was frustrating for Jefferson too. Everyone was suddenly calling him on cellular phones about the Denny incident, including Deputy Chief Hunt from the church, but "I didn't know what the hell was going on."[14] Part of the problem was the LAPD's antiquated communications system. During Chief Parker's heyday, the LAPD had boasted the nation's most up-to-date police radio communications, but the system had become a relic by the time of the riots. There were not nearly enough hand-held radios, for instance, for use outside of vehicles. Moulin had requested one hundred such radios soon after setting up the command post but was told that only seven were available.

The radio breakdown was not the fault of Gates, who had persistently asked Mayor Bradley and the city council to upgrade the department's outmoded system. When the politicians pleaded poverty, the LAPD turned to the people for help. But voters in 1990 and again in 1991 rejected LAPD-sponsored bond issues that would have authorized $230 million for a new communications system. "This is a cheap city," Gates said, and its citizens paid a price for their cheapness.[15] One of the reasons Jefferson did not know what was going on was that Metro had its own frequencies which the LAPD's outdated system did not allow him to monitor.

On the other hand, it seemed to Sergeant J. J. May and many others at the command post that the command staff didn't use the resources it had. These officers also lacked up-to-date information about events at Florence and Normandie, but they sensed that a riot was spreading and were eager to return to the field. It seemed to May that Jefferson and Moulin, soon joined by Commander Ron Banks, conferred endlessly without reaching decisions. This was also the view of the Webster Commission, which determined that 480 officers had reached the command post by 7:00 P.M., when Tatreau was pleading with Moulin to rescue the civilians at Florence and Normandie. The Webster inquiry concluded that "the leaders of the 77th froze."

But the failure was more widespread. Deputy Chief Hunt had made a point of demanding return to his command of the three divisions Gates had controlled in South Bureau. After the chief released the divisions to him late in the afternoon, however, Hunt virtually ignored the fruits of his victory, put Commander Banks in charge of South Bureau, and departed for the rally at the First AME Church, where he was as much out of the loop as Gates was at the Brentwood fund-raiser. Hunt meant well, but rank-and-file officers and Gates alike thought he was overly reluctant to use sufficient force. Soon after receiving word of the assault on Reginald Denny, he called Jefferson and then departed for the command post.

In the interim, Banks was indecisive. He showed up at the command post but neither took command nor declared a tactical alert, which would have cleared cluttered radio frequencies of all but emergency messages. In this he was no less remiss than Gates, who later acknowledged that he should have called a tactical alert early in the afternoon. Not until 6:45, as Denny's truck approached the Florence-Normandie intersection, was a tactical alert declared by Lieutenant George Godwin of Communications Division at Parker Center. This action made radio communication easier, but decision making remained in slow motion at the command post, where no one wanted to take charge. During the buck passing of post-riot analysis, Gates suggested that Banks and Jefferson, as African Americans, were inhibited by the concerns of black leaders that vigorous police action would provoke disorders. Hubert Williams found some merit to this point but thought it was transcended by Gates' failure to take charge. Banks said he believed that Jefferson was capable of dealing with the situation at Florence and Normandie as area commander of 77th. Jefferson said he was "surprised" that Banks did not assume command. "It was obvious to me that it was larger than 77th," Jefferson said.

Helicopter mishaps, tactical blunders, and congestion at the command post magnified the problems. As emergency equipment poured into the bus yard, bolt cutters were used to open additional gates and hundreds of officers milled around, waiting for orders. "Witnesses stated that the 77th Street officers were not organized in a state of readiness," said the LAPD internal review in laconic understatement. Jefferson described it more vividly. "It was chaos," he said. "There were these stories afterward about all these officers who were there, but I honestly [didn't] know how many were there because my line of sight was blocked off by the buses. It's a mess. Where were the tactical vehicles? Where were the maps? . . . Things kept going wrong."[16]

One of the things that went wrong and stayed wrong was communication between the command post and other LAPD units. Telephones at the command post were linked to a transit-district communications system and could not be used for outgoing calls. Moulin took two cellular phones with him when he set up the command post, but these were usually busy in the early, critical hours of the riots. When the Emergency Operations Center tried to reach the command post after the Denny beating, operators called South Bureau, which called the 77th Street Station, resulting in Tatreau's radio call to the command post and Moulin's response on his cellular phone. Moulin aggravated the problem by directing that 911 emergency calls to 77th be re-routed to the command post.

"Without a computer terminal and with virtually no telephones, this decision reduced management of the response to a primitive paper and pencil exercise," said the Webster report. As officers poured into the bus yard, a site intended as the command post for the 77th Division became the riot-response center for all South Central. The Useem-Gascon study concluded this was the "crux of the problem" because "the demands of the command post outstripped its capabilities." Jefferson, as usual, put it more bluntly. He said the command post suffered a "breakdown."[17]

While others hesitated, a squad of Metro officers tried to reach Florence and Normandie. At 6:53, Lieutenant Thomas Lorenzen dispatched a "rescue probe" of ten officers under command of Sergeant Andy Lamprey in response to a report that a victim trapped in a black Thunderbird was under assault. Traveling in unmarked cars and wearing bulletproof vests over their uniforms, the officers encountered a raging crowd within five blocks of the intersection. Black youths raced wildly by, "hanging out of their cars, throwing gang signs, and careening from the curb into the opposing lanes of traffic . . . at speeds of forty to sixty miles an hour."[18]

As the officers came within a block of Florence and Normandie, they were greeted with a barrage of rocks, bricks and bottles. Lamprey had never seen anything like this "absolute war zone" in twenty-five years as a police officer. He could hear automatic rifle fire and see a building burning. As his squad advanced within 150 feet north of the intersection, Lamprey estimated the size of the crowd at three hundred. He realized his small force would be unable to penetrate the intersection without using deadly force. Instead of trying to retake the intersection, Lamprey ordered his squad to skirt it and try to find the trapped person in the Thunderbird. But they could not locate any such car. Lamprey radioed the command post with this information, and Lorenzen told him that the officers should return to the command post. "Do not engage," Lorenzen said. Lamprey obeyed.[19] Once more, the LAPD retreated from Florence and Normandie.

The LAPD fared no better in the air. The helicopter Air 3, piloted by Officer Teresa McIntosh, landed at the command post at 6:44 P.M., just missing the Denny assault. Desperate for first-hand information, Lorenzen wanted to send the chopper back aloft with Commander Banks and Sergeant Mike Albanese on board.[20] But the helicopter had room for only one person in addition to McIntosh and Stan Brittsan, the other crew member. Banks deferred to Albanese, who had more tactical experience, but later said this decision was a mistake. As the highest-ranking officer present at the command post, Banks said he would have been able "to scream bloody murder to South Bureau or whoever else would listen that this was far beyond anything we'd anticipated . . ."[21]

By 7:06 P.M., Air 3 was back over Florence and Normandie. Brittsan could see Denny's eighteen-wheeler and a man lying at its side. Although the officers in Air 3 had no way of knowing it, their return coincided with the arrival of Denny's rescuers. By the time Air 3 made a second pass over the intersection, the truck was moving away. After missing the attack on Denny, the LAPD helicopter had also missed his rescue.

It was 7:10 now, and Albanese inspected the scene below. The moon-faced LAPD veteran, who two years later would engineer the surrender of O. J. Simpson, was an expert in hostage negotiations. He was terrified of flying, which he had been careful not to mention when Lorenzen and Banks were discussing who should make the flight. As Air 3 circled the intersection, Albanese saw a fire at the liquor store and "a Latin couple in a brown pickup truck, stopped, pulled out, and beaten, and then running for their life." Albanese was thinking about how the LAPD might regain control of Florence and Normandie when the helicopter made a third pass over the intersection. "Did you feel that?" McIntosh said abruptly, a note of urgency in her voice. Albanese hadn't felt anything, but fear of flying came to the fore. He threw his radio down, thinking, "I'm going to fucking die in the first two minutes of this riot because this helicopter is going to crash and burn."[22]

By then, McIntosh was having difficulty controlling the chopper. "We need to set it down now," she said and landed in the parking lot of a "swap meet," or indoor flea market, at Slauson and Western, where they were met by armed security guards. McIntosh thought the helicopter was suffering from a mechanical failure or had been hit by a bullet, but it was later determined that Air 3 had been caught in the "prop wash"—air turbulence from other helicopters at the scene. Albanese waited for another chopper while the riot raged and the command post remained oblivious.

CHIEF GATES KNEW NOTHING OF THE TRAVAILS AT THE COMMAND post. After a forty-five-minute drive at rush hour, he had reached the fund-raiser on Westridge Road in the Mandeville Canyon area of Brentwood, a community of expensive wooded estates thirteen miles northwest and a world away from Florence and Normandie. The affair had been promoted as a "mixer" in which the chief would discuss Charter Amendment F, described in a leaflet promoting the event as a "power grab" by politicians. The chief was applauded as he entered. One woman wanted to know if the riots would affect the outcome of this city ballot measure and Gates told her it could "impact us favorably" or "very unfavorably," depending on what happened.[23]

Gates answered questions for twenty-five minutes from a wealthy, white audience of thirty-five people who normally would have been outraged at the thought that Mayor Bradley and the polyglot city council would seek to bring the LAPD under their control. But those present had watched television coverage of the riots as they waited for the chief, and some seem to have had a better grasp than Gates of what was happening in South Central. One woman said she had watched three people pulled from their cars "and just literally beaten to death." Where were the police? Gates tried to reassure her, saying they had learned from Watts that police deployment had to be different during riots. "You have to deploy in a special fashion," he said. "What we're doing is pulling our people back and putting them in squads, redeploying them . . . That takes a little bit of time, but we're ready for it—they should be out in squads by now. There are going to be situations where people are going to be without assistance. That's just the facts of life. There are not enough of us to be everywhere."[24]

When the chief had finished, the hostess thanked him and said, "I know he should be elsewhere." That much was clear. The riots had spread as Gates spoke, and the peaceful crowd in front of Parker Center in the downtown Civic Center area had turned ugly. As at the 77th Street Station, key Parker Center personnel were away on routine assignments. And as happened at many stations, the decision makers who were on hand misgauged the potential of the disorders. When the verdicts were read, the lieutenant who was serving as acting commander of the Central Patrol Division in charge of protecting Parker Center asked Deputy Chief Bernard Parks and Commander Maurice Moore if he should hold over personnel from the day watch. They told him such action was unnecessary.[25]

But at 6:40, ten minutes after Gates departed for Brentwood, a crowd of 150 persons rushed toward the front door of Parker Center, throwing rocks and bottles and uprooting plants near the glass doors at the front of the building. A call for help was broadcast at 6:58, telling officers to go to the front of the building. Instead, they "responded to several different locations around the building," according to the LAPD post-riot report. A skirmish line was eventually established in front of Parker Center, however, and the crowd retreated, content for a time to hurl occasional objects and obscenities at the officers.

Then at 7:30, a portion of the crowd ran to an unoccupied guard shack at the entrance to Parker Center's north parking lot. They pushed it over and set it on fire. Fifteen minutes later the bulk of the crowd moved south and broke windows in the New Otani Hotel. Police pushed the remaining demonstrators away from the front of Parker Center and occupied the intersection at First and Los Angeles Streets to protect the hotel. The crowd then broke apart. Demonstrators spread through the Civic Center area and vandalized businesses, including City Hall East, the *Los Angeles Times* building and the Criminal Courts Building. They overturned three vehicles and set fire to a police car and palm trees. But with the crowd scattered, the police organized into mobile units and cleared the Civic Center area. By 8:30, the LAPD once more controlled its headquarters and downtown.

The Webster Commission found "tactical errors" at Parker Center similar to those made in the 77th Street Division, and the LAPD post-riot report also criticized the performance of Parker Center commanders. Parks and Moore did not face the humiliating post-riot criticism inflicted on Gates, Frankle, Moulin, and Jefferson (and to a lesser degree Hunt and Banks), but they demonstrated comparable obliviousness when they decided not to hold over the day watch. As in the 77th Street Division, lower-ranking officers had warned that the verdicts might provoke disturbances. Watch commanders and sergeants at Parker Center who raised this issue "did not perceive that their superiors had serious concern about potential riots," said the LAPD post-riot report.

Unlike the mostly spontaneous eruption of black rage at Florence and Normandie, the racially mixed and well-organized Parker Center demonstration began as a conventional political protest similar to others that had taken place there since the Rodney King affair. But since the Parker Center confrontation came on the heels of the Denny assault and was also widely televised, it reinforced a public impression that Los Angeles was an undefended city under siege. "Both [incidents] communicated the same explosive message—the police were not going to act," the Webster report found.

> Regardless of public statements by elected officials and community leaders, many angry people in Los Angeles learned shortly after the verdicts that they would be allowed to take their anger to the streets. We are confident this was an unintended message, but the failure of the police to act quickly and forcefully to uphold the law was shown graphically on television for all to see. Television thus acted as a catalyst for the events to follow.

The Parker Center demonstration also had the unfortunate effect of diverting police resources from the riot epicenter in South Central. Metro's Lieutenant Mike Hillmann was driving toward the command post at 7:00 when he received a radio message that demonstrators were about to breach the front doors at Parker Center. Metro's C Platoon was mobilizing at its headquarters nearby, and Hillmann sent it to Parker Center. But with other units also fast arriving, the cautious commanders did not use C Platoon to engage the demonstrators. For Metro, as the post-riot LAPD report put it, the Parker Center episode proved a "significant distraction," diverting a platoon urgently needed in South Central.[26]

While driving across South Central to the command post in an unmarked brown Ford, Hillmann became aware of how desperate the situation had become. He saw people running through the streets and others being pulled from their cars, and he heard gunfire. At one intersection, a man jumped on the hood of Hillmann's car and swung a fire ax at his windshield while another beat on the car windows. Hillmann managed to shake off his attackers and reach the command post. So did Captain David Gascon, the newly appointed Metro commander who was following in another car but had become separated from Hillmann during the wild drive across South Central.

All in all, it was a difficult and at times embarrassing evening for the vaunted Metro Division, supposedly capable of crushing a riot at its inception. Despite some intrepid individual efforts, Metro never surmounted the disadvantages of being widely dispersed and partially mobilized when the riots began. One of the two armored personnel carriers designed for riot control was out of position at Piper Technical Center behind Parker Center, and the other was slow to swing into action.

Even if Metro had been fully mobilized, this small, elite unit would have had its hands full. And as it turned out, 76 of Metro's 233 officers and supervisors were off duty at 6:00 P.M. when the mob became ascendant at Florence and Normandie. Of the other 157 Metro officers, 46 were far from the central action with B Platoon in the San Fernando Valley and another 29 were with C Platoon when it was dispatched to Parker Center. That left Metro with only 82 officers in South Central. Although Metro's officers were valiant and capable, they were too few and too scattered to contain a full-scale riot.[27]

And despite Hillmann's pre-riot planning, even Metro was not immune to the odd lassitude that overcame the LAPD during the early hours of the riots. Sergeant John Christensen, who arrived at the command post at 6:40 with the first Metro contingent and wrote a post-riot evaluation, believes Metro failed to realize how rapidly the disorder had spread after the initial retreat from Florence and Normandie. Christensen had agreed with Moulin's order to retreat because he knew from experience that the presence of police cars can provoke demonstrations. But Metro, along with the rest of the LAPD, was in the dark about events after the pullout. Christensen concluded that the "downfall" of the officers at the command post came from relying on police radio instead of on commercial news broadcasts. Had officers listened to these broadcasts, he said, "perhaps things would have changed or been changed drastically." The failed helicopter reconnaissance also contributed to Metro's ignorance and provoked an outburst from Hillmann after he reached the command post. "I said, 'Goddamn it, we've got seventeen helicopters in the city of Los Angeles, and sixteen ought to be flyable,' " Hillmann recalled. "Now get me a couple of them down here."[28]

Another helicopter was sent while Christensen tried to prod Moulin into rapid deployment of the officers streaming into the command post. But not until Lamprey's squad returned from its unproductive Florence-Normandie mission did Metro commanders realize the extent of the calamity. The Metro sergeant bluntly told Banks and Jefferson that the LAPD faced "an absolute hostile, hostile situation" requiring use of deadly force. Banks looked at Lamprey with what the Metro sergeant thought was an uncomprehending stare. According to another Metro sergeant, Banks told Lamprey the riots would burn themselves out.[29] Lamprey was furious. "I've been an angry man about this for two and a half years," he said when interviewed in 1994. "There was a total and complete lack of any air of decisiveness. . . . It has haunted me ever since because had I to do it all over again, I would have taken a stand at that intersection."[30]

Metro now set up its own command post within the command post at Fifth-fourth and Arlington. This was a decision that the LAPD post-riot report would find contributed to the confusion, but at the time Hillmann thought he had no other choice. With the situation in the field rapidly disintegrating, Hillmann decided that he had to put police officers into the field as quickly as possible, and he did not want to lose time explaining what he was doing to other commanders. First, he told Sergeant Henry (Grady) Dublin to bring C Platoon back from Parker Center because "we're up to our ass in alligators." Dublin was eager to comply, but his platoon made slow progress amid the growing congestion in the streets. Hillmann also radioed Lieutenant John O'Connell, commander of B Platoon, which Gascon had earlier told to make its way to South Central. "I want you to get your people and go out and engage the rioters," Hillmann said. "I'm trying to get these people off their duff, light a fire under them to make some decisions on what they're going to do."[31]

But these decisions came too late to save South Central from devastation. At 7:30, ten minutes after Lamprey's squad returned to the command post, an LAPD helicopter reported a conflagration north of Florence and Normandie. Soon the skies were filled with billowing smoke and an acrid burning smell as the first arson-caused fires swept through South Central.

LOS ANGELES HAD REASON TO BE PROUD OF ITS LARGE AND highly professional fire department, which in some respects was better prepared than the LAPD for a civil disorder. Unlike the LAPD, firefighters had long been viewed positively in South Central and had traditionally enjoyed the status of neutrals, even during racial conflicts. This had changed in the 1990s, as crime rates soared. Firefighters and paramedics who reached scenes of violence before the police were often threatened and sometimes attacked. Responding to this trend six months before the riots, Fire Chief Donald O. Manning issued a training bulletin detailing precautions for firefighters in hostile situations. The department also issued body armor and strengthened the walls of fire stations.

Manning watched the verdicts on television at his office in the Civic Center and went home at 5:15. But it soon became obvious that South Central was seething, and he headed back to headquarters. As he left the freeway on his way downtown, Manning encountered a "large, hostile crowd," took a detour, and was back in his office by 7:00. He recalled his staff and set up a command center on the tenth floor of City Hall East. He then issued instructions that gave priority to protecting public buildings and homes and the safety of firefighters, who were ordered not to work on roofs or use ladders, on which they could become easy targets.

The fire chief had personal as well as professional concerns. The Los Angeles Fire Department is divided into sixteen geographical districts called battalions, and two of those in South Central were headed by Manning's sons, Terrance and Timothy. Terry Manning was nearly halfway through a twenty-four-hour shift when he went to Southeast Station late in the afternoon to meet with Captain David Gascon, with whom he had worked in the past. But Manning learned at the station that Gascon had been transferred to Metro. He met instead with the new captain, Willie Pannell, who seemed harassed. When Manning requested police escorts for firefighters, Pannell told him: "I'll do what I can [but] I don't have anybody now."[32]

Firefighters knew from the first that police escorts would be needed. As department officials watched the Denny assault on television at headquarters, dispatchers were already receiving calls that firefighters were being hassled. Engine 57, sent to Florence and Normandie at the time of the Denny incident, was redirected to the command post for an escort. At Fire Station 33, a mile and a half east of Florence and Normandie, Captain Robert Munoa reported at 6:52 to the Operations Control Division at headquarters. Munoa said "we have a little situation down here" and warned that paramedics should not go on rescues without escorts. "We just had a run to Florence and Normandie and it was ugly," Munoa said.[33]

But LAPD dispatchers, flooded with calls, did not respond to the frantic efforts of Fire Department dispatchers to reach them on a private line. At 6:54, a crew from Fire Station 64 told of being pelted with rocks en route to a fire at Ninety-third and Hoover and requested police officers to meet them at the scene. "We're ringing LAPD and getting no answer," the dispatcher told the fire crew.

Among the fire officials recalled to duty by Donald Manning was Timothy Manning, who headed Battalion 3. He was sent to the command post at Fifty-fourth and Arlington, where he arrived at 7:15 as police were donning riot gear and Lamprey was briefing Banks. Timothy Manning recognized that heavy casualties were likely and asked the Fire Department to send medical personnel to the command post. But the riot arrived first. As Manning waited for the medical units, he saw a Molotov cocktail soar over the wall of the command post, igniting an empty bus.

The disorders were now spreading west toward the University of Southern California and the adjoining Coliseum. A mob that quickly swelled from fifty people to three hundred hurled concrete bus benches into the intersection of Martin Luther King Boulevard and Coliseum Street. Following the pattern of Florence and Normandie, passing motorists were pelted with rocks and bottles and one was dragged from his car and beaten. Members of the mob displayed gang colors and weapons. At 7:15, firefighters at nearby Station 94 reported that they were trapped inside and needed police assistance.

But the LAPD was receiving more calls for assistance from firefighters than it had escorts. When police cars from the command post accompanied one fire crew and rescue ambulance to a reported shooting, they were turned back by a rock-throwing crowd before they could reach their destination. Fire officials radioed that it was too dangerous for firefighters to travel to the command post for escorts and requested that police be sent to the fire stations. Captain Pannell at Southeast Station responded by sending police officers to two vulnerable fire stations, but most other stations went without escorts for many hours. At 7:30, officers who were passing Fire Station 14 in a patrol car saw four black men smash the station door with a piece of concrete. When the officers tried to arrest them, the men opened fire on the police. The officers fired back, wounding one of them, who fled but was arrested two days later.

Terry Manning, meanwhile, was responding to a fire call a mile north of Florence and Normandie. With Fred Mathis at the wheel of his red-and-white patrol car, Manning reached the chaotic intersection at 7:38 and saw a milling mob. He told Mathis to slow down, turn off the siren, and move through as quickly as possible. As they entered the intersection, a man wielding a thirty-six-inch red pick ax charged at them and struck a resounding blow on the car's roof. It made a four-inch gash but did not penetrate the lining above Manning's head. Later, at the trial of Damian Williams, Manning could not identify the ax-wielder, but he had no difficulty in "identifying every inch of that ax."[34]

As they continued through the intersection, someone hurled an unopened bottle of champagne, which shattered the windshield and stuck in the shards of glass. The car was then pelted with bottles and rocks. "Where do rocks come from in South Central Los Angeles?" Manning wondered. He later realized that rioters made them by smashing concrete bus benches and using the pieces as projectiles.

Terry Manning and Mathis reached the fire scene at Sixtieth and Normandie, where two police sergeants from the 77th Division—Charlie Strong and Don Schwartzer—had formed a skirmish line to protect firefighters battling a large blaze from an "extremely belligerent" crowd. It had been a long day for these two sergeants. Nearly twelve hours earlier, Strong had warned of prospective disorders after the 77th Street Station received threatening telephone calls. Strong and Schwartzer had been present at the first arrest of the young man with the baseball bat and at the retreat from Florence and Normandie. Now they headed a squad of 77th Division officers who had been hastily assembled at the command post and sent out to protect the fire trucks. But there were not enough police officers to hold back the crowd, and the sergeants told Manning they would have to pull out. They departed in a convoy of LAPD cars and Fire Department vehicles, including Terry Manning's patrol car.[35] Manning radioed the dispatch center not to send any more fire engines into the riot area without police escorts.

When the convoy reached Slauson and Western where three fires blazed, the first fire truck stopped, bringing the procession to a halt. Manning was trapped behind a fire truck, and his car was again peppered with rocks and bottles. He was attacked again, this time by a man with a crowbar who smashed the side window on the passenger's side and hit Manning on the shoulder and neck. Manning tried reaching for the in-car microphone to call the police escorts but couldn't move his right arm. "Fred, he broke my fucking arm," Manning said. In fact, the arm was only bruised but Manning felt helpless and immobilized in his seat belt, not knowing if his attacker would strike again. Then the convoy began to move, and the attacker vanished. On the radio, Manning could hear firefighters pleading for escorts. "Let's go to Fifty-fourth and Arlington," he told his driver, and they drove to the command post where his younger brother, Timothy, was waiting.

Timothy Manning was not the only anxious brother at the command post that night. Greg Baltad was an assistant squad leader in Metro's B Platoon. His younger brother, Brian, was a firefighter, and Baltad worried that he would become a target for the rioters. B Platoon had reached the command center at 7:10, and Greg Baltad had been sent into action as part of yet another Metro probe into the riot area. Under Sergeant Doug Reid, B Platoon moved east of Normandie and observed looting on Slauson. The platoon reported its findings to the command post but was told not to engage. This disgusted Baltad.

"We could have stopped the looting," Baltad said. "People ran when they saw the police cars." At Vermont and Slauson, a looter emerged from a store with a shopping cart so heavily laden with batteries that he lost control of it as he crossed the street in front of the police. The cart slammed into a police car. Baltad opened the door of his car to confront the looter but was immediately ordered back into his vehicle. He did as he was told, unhappily. "To this day, I wished I'd disobeyed that order," he said two years later.[36]

B Platoon made a rescue and returned to the command post just ahead of the police-and-fire convoy that included Terry Manning's patrol car. Manning and Reid were neighbors in suburban Valencia, and they commiserated about the difficulty the LAPD was having in providing escorts. "God, we could really use you," Manning said. Reid told him that Metro hadn't been authorized to provide escorts. As they talked, unescorted firefighters streamed into the command post. "Firemen love coming to the aid of other firemen, and police officers love coming to the aid of firefighters," Terry Manning said. "We felt like we were really hamstrung."[37]

Brian Baltad was a member of an unescorted fire crew that reached the command post, where he sought out his brother. "Couldn't you have at least protected us?" he said. Greg Baltad knew his brother had reason to be angry. Greg was angry, too, and not just about the escort breakdown. To Baltad, who had once been an officer in the 77th, it seemed that the LAPD command staff was practicing "an ostrich technique of riot control" while officers piled up at the command post and the community outside was looted and destroyed. Baltad couldn't fathom it. He had been taught that the LAPD was the best and that Metro was the best of the best, and he was shocked and embarrassed by what was happening. He took refuge in the belief that there were really "two LAPDs." One was composed of rank-and-file officers and sergeants who were eager to engage rioters and looters. The other consisted of cautious members of the command staff who "were trying to protect their own careers, not stop the riots."[38]

Greg Baltad may be right in his opinion that police "could have saved the city" if their commanders had behaved more aggressively. Certainly, they could have saved more of it than they did. As Baltad noted, an extensive business district along Vermont Avenue was virtually unscathed when B Platoon was ordered back to the command post the first night of the riots. But by the time the platoon returned the following day, it had been burned to the ground. The burning was mostly the work of arsonists using Molotov cocktails.

These arsonists usually worked unopposed. Sergeant Julio Nunez, a plainclothes vice officer from the 77th Street Division, posed as a journalist the first night of the riots and interviewed a group of arsonists who told him and his partner to "get your asses out of this area or we're going to blow you up." The undercover officers left but soon observed another group of youths loading brown beer bottles with protruding wicks into their car. Nunez took the license plate number of the car and called the command center on his cellular phone but no one responded.[39] Even if someone had come, it is unlikely any arrests would have been made. The great frustration of rank-and-file officers from the 77th Street Division and Metro on the first night of the riots is that they were consistently instructed not to engage or arrest rioters. Few arrests were made in the 77th during the first nine hours of the riots—indeed, only fifty arrests were made throughout the entire city during this period. As the Webster Commission concluded: "During the first evening of the disorder, the LAPD seems to have lost all control over the mobs of demonstrators in South Bureau, who looted and burned at will."

The work of the arsonists was assisted by the dangerous conditions facing the firefighters. Mobs and gunfire made it too risky for firefighters to linger at fires or work inside buildings. Instead, they relied on "hit-and-run" tactics, quickly pouring water on a fire and moving on to the next blaze before a crowd could form. As a result, many fires were only partially extinguished and flared up again or were easily relit. Even so, firefighters might have saved much that was lost that first night had the LAPD been quicker to provide escorts. Terry Manning, like Greg Baltad, blamed the command staff. Manning understood that police officers and sergeants wanted to provide escorts "but it was somebody up above who wouldn't press the magic button to unloose the guys."[40]

At 8:31, SWAT teams were sent to rescue firefighters from three stations. Meanwhile, firefighters who had reached the command post were organized into strike teams of five engine companies and a battalion chief. But they still lacked escorts, despite the presence of at least 200 unassigned officers at the command post. Although Deputy Fire Chief Davis Parsons arrived at the command post at 8:58 and complained to Captain Jefferson about "unacceptable delays," the first escorted strike team did not leave the bus yard until 9:43. As other teams waited impatiently, Parsons continued to lobby the police command staff. Finally, at 10:00, Deputy Chief Hunt promised to "expedite" the process of providing escorts.[41]

By then, however, the fires were spreading unchecked. Only fifteen were burning throughout Los Angeles at 8:00 P.M., and nine of these were within a thirty-six-block area bounded by Fifty-first Street on the north and Manchester Avenue on the south. Within an hour the number of fires had doubled and had burned across a wide expanse of the hundred and five square miles of South Central. By 10:00 P.M., at least forty-seven fires blazed simultaneously and mostly unattended, lighting the night skies of a dream city that had become a nightmare.

THE FIRST RIOT DEATH OCCURRED AT 8:15 P.M. WHEN SHOOTING erupted at one of the many Korean-owned swap meets that are a conspicuous feature of neighborhood business districts in the city's working-class neighborhoods. This swap meet was at Vernon and Vermont, north of Florence and less than two miles northeast of the police command post. The victim was Louis Watson, an eighteen-year-old county employee, who was guiding two elderly women across a parking lot to a bus stop. "He bent over and told them to get on the first bus that came, no matter where it was going," a witness said. "And he told them to keep their heads down." But Watson did not heed his own advice. He was killed instantly by a bullet to the forehead.

Michael Bell, standing on the opposite side of Vermont Street, saw Watson fall. Bell was waiting for a friend, Dwight Taylor, who had darted inside a supermarket on an urgent errand. Taylor had recently been released from jail after serving three months for violating a judge's restraining order to stay away from his estranged wife. After his release, his wife relented and said he could visit, providing he brought milk for their two children. At the fish market where he and Bell worked, Taylor had talked happily throughout the day about seeing his family again. He wore new clothes and sported a fresh haircut for the occasion and was carrying the milk in his hands when he walked out of the market and into a hail of gunfire. Bell watched as his friend fell, blood staining his brand-new shirt. "Tell my kids I love them, and tell my wife I said goodbye," Taylor said to Bell before he died.[42]

The deaths of Watson and Taylor set the pattern for riot fatalities, most of which occurred from gunfire at the hands of unknown assailants. It is not even known whether those who did the shooting were aiming at the victims. Random gunfire broke out after the police pullout, and it continued sporadically even after officers began patrolling again, for it was evident to rioters that the police had no desire to engage unless they were themselves under fire. This contrasted with the 1965 Watts riot, when the LAPD was less inhibited. Twenty-six of the thirty-two Watts deaths investigated by the coroner (out of a total of thirty-four) resulted from police shootings. All were ruled justifiable, including the killing of a looter who was shot in the back. Of fifty-four deaths during the 1992 riots, thirty-six were the result of shootings, but only ten were by peace officers and only six by the LAPD. All the LAPD shootings involved incidents in which officers were fired upon or seemed to be in imminent danger.

The law-abiding population of South Central paid a high price for LAPD restraint. Louis Watson, Dwight Taylor, and many others might still be alive if the LAPD had crushed the riots at their inception or used deadly force during one of the early Metro forays into the riot area. It is also possible that the civilian toll would have been higher if LAPD officers had used their weapons freely; Lieutenant Moulin, for one, believes the police retreat he ordered at Florence and Normandie averted a "bloodbath." But interviews with gang members after the riots suggest that rioters felt free to break the law because they realized that the police were not opposing them. Daryl Gates eventually came to the view that a more militant police response would have saved lives and property.

GATES WAS LESS MILITANT WHILE IN COMMAND. HE RETURNED AT 8:15 to the Emergency Operations Center and almost immediately commandeered a helicopter for an aerial tour of the riot area. Gates recalled that Chief Parker had remained in his office during the Watts riot and "kept barking out orders that did not fit the situation in the field."[43] He said he wanted to "get a bird's eye view of what in the hell was happening."[44]

William Webster was caustic in his appraisal of the chief's helicopter flight, which he found as baffling as his attendance at the fund-raiser. "He could have gone to a saloon and watched [television] if he wanted to see what was happening," said Webster.[45] Or he could have switched on the television set in his office. Television had tracked the spread of the riots from the air since their inception. Terry Manning said that after firefighters obtained police escorts, they responded to several outdated calls and arrived at buildings that had been burned to the ground. They then turned to local television for guidance.[46] Gates could have done the same. "The mystery to me is the helicopter ride," said Webster. "He took something like an hour-and-a-half ride and never issued any instructions as far as I could determine . . . So he is just up there watching Rome burn."[47]

Still, during his aerial inspection, Gates formed the accurate if belated opinion that police and firefighters had a chance to control this "damn thing" if they would move into the streets.[48] His assessment may have been optimistic at the time he made it, but it was the message his hesitant command staff at the bus yard needed to hear. Hubert Williams, experienced in police command, believes the staff had to hear this message from Gates himself, since the LAPD is "very militaristic" and "heavily reliant on the chief and his policies."[49] Gates seemed to have recognized this, for his impulse was to land at the command post and tell the staff what to do. But he was undone by faulty LAPD communications. When Gates tried to obtain permission to land, he found the helicopter radios weren't working. He wanted to land anyway, but the pilot told him that regulations required that he alert the command post first. The frustrated chief returned to the Emergency Operations Center.

By now Gates realized that his earlier confidence in the LAPD's riot readiness had been misplaced. "Where the hell is Metro?" he said to Frankle. "I didn't see them deploying."[50] Frankle sought to reassure him, and Gates was soon drawn from riot-response tactics into larger strategic issues. With the riots spreading and the LAPD seemingly powerless to stop them, Mayor Bradley had decided to seek assistance from outside the city.

The impetus for calling out the National Guard came from neither the chief nor the mayor but from Governor Pete Wilson in Sacramento. Along with the rest of the world, Wilson, a onetime mayor of San Diego, had been watching the events in Los Angeles on television. He was an adept and decisive politician who remembered that Lieutenant Governor Glenn Anderson had been criticized for temporizing before calling out the Guard when Governor Edmund (Pat) Brown was out of the country during the Watts riot. Wilson was not about to make a similar mistake. He called Bradley at 7:00 and asked him if he wanted the Guard. Bradley, who was out of position at the First AME Church and in touch with his staff in City Hall by cellular phone, said he didn't think the Guard was needed but would call back after he was briefed.

Bradley's initial reluctance to call out the Guard reflected less his own indecisiveness than the disadvantage caused by Gates' absence. Hubert Williams believes that the most harmful aspect of the chief's helicopter flight was that it "caused the mayor to equivocate . . . he has to rely on the chief."[51] But Gates was still aloft when Bradley returned to City Hall. The mayor and his chief of staff, Mark Fabiani, talked about obtaining outside help in the car ride back to City Hall, but Bradley also wanted to discuss the situation with Frankle and with Police Commissioners Stanley Sheinbaum and Jesse Brewer. They agreed that Bradley should accept Wilson's offer. At 8:45, the mayor told the governor that he had decided to declare a city emergency and asked for the National Guard. Wilson said he would act immediately. At 9:00, the governor's cabinet secretary, Larry Goldzband, called Adjutant General Robert Thrasher, the director of the Guard, and informed him of the decision.

Fifteen minutes after Goldzband's call, Thrasher issued a mobilization order for 2,000 National Guard troops. At 10:13, Wilson, Bradley, Gates, Thrasher, and Los Angeles County Sheriff Sherman Block held a conference call in which officials from the California Highway Patrol, the State Office of Emergency Planning, and the California Attorney General's Office also participated. Wilson thought Block was forceful but that both Bradley and Gates seemed shaken. Gates said he believed the riots could be put down without the Guard but that he had no objection to the call-up. This wasn't good enough for Wilson, who near the end of the conversation again asked the chief and Block if they agreed with the decision to send in the Guard. Both men said they did.[52]

As soon as the call was over, Gates ordered his driver to take him to the command post at Fifty-fourth and Arlington. His anxiety increased along the way because he saw no police cars. More shocks were in store. When Gates reached the command post, he found it clogged with officers and cars. He then inspected the sector board to find out where units were deployed and found many areas without a police presence. Gates was appalled. "My God, this thing has been going on for hours," Gates said to the lieutenant who was briefing him.[53]

Soon after, Gates flew into a rage. "Goddamn it, Jefferson, how could you let a thing like this happen?" he said to the captain of 77th Street Division.[54] He was so angry he knocked over his coffee cup, spilling the contents on the ground. "He didn't spill it on himself or me," Jefferson said. "I don't think he threw it. But he was angry and upset at the way things were going."[55]

The chief then stalked to a trailer that Hunt was using as his headquarters and vented his anger on the cautious commander of South Bureau. "Matt, where in the hell are your people?" he asked. Hunt told him that fifty officers had arrived at the command post on a bus and that he intended to send them into the field in the same bus.

"No, fill the sectors with squads," said Gates. He wanted Hunt to use a standard tactic of putting four officers instead of the usual two into a car, which would free patrol cars for additional squads.

"We don't have enough cars," Hunt replied.

But the bus yard was filled with cars, as Gates could see, and Hunt's response made no sense to the chief. He began yelling again. It was uncharacteristic of the chief to berate a senior officer in front of subordinates, but he could not control himself. "I had to get out of there because I totally, completely lost my temper," Gates said.[56] Later, he learned that many of the patrol cars he saw at the command post were locked. "You're supposed to have a guy that stands there . . . takes the keys to the cars, puts them on a board, deploys people in those cars, and provides the keys to them," Gates explained.[57] But no one had been there to take the keys when the officers arrived, so they had locked their cars and taken their keys with them when they were redeployed in other vehicles.

Even the Webster Commission report, otherwise so critical of Gates, found the chief had "reason to be upset" with Hunt and Jefferson. They had failed, the report said in a section written by the knowledgeable Hubert Williams, to utilize basic and widely taught riot-control strategies. The strategy known as "containment" called upon police to deploy as a "blocking force" along a roadway or geographic barrier perpendicular to access roads into the riot area. They were then supposed to cordon off the area. This would have been followed by "sectoring" or dividing the enclosed area into small units that could be recaptured one by one as reinforcements arrived. Hunt and Jefferson had discussed containment but in the confusion did not attempt to implement it until after 9:00, "and by then it was too late."[58]

Whether a bolder or more adept performance by Hunt would have made a difference is unclear. Williams believes the LAPD had only until 7:00 P.M. to stop the riots by containment, and Hunt had not by then reached the command post. Scores of officers at the bus yard have attested to the disorganization and seeming indecisiveness of their superiors, both before and after Hunt arrived. "There was no movement," said veteran Sergeant Scott Landsman, who led two squads of officers into the bus yard midway through the evening. "Officers were just standing there, doing nothing." By midnight, according to the Webster report, 1,790 officers had reached the command post and many were stuck there awaiting assignments. As police commanders struggled to break the logjam, officers were rushed into the field without assignment or supervision, "just sent out," as Landsman put it.[59]

Gates subsequently said he made a mistake in assuming that his senior officers were prepared to deal with a civil disorder. "Since I'd been through it, I kind of thought that fellow members of the top command knew what to do," Gates told me eight months after the riots. "They didn't."[60] But the bigger problem, as Williams has suggested, may have been that the "fellow members of the top command" were waiting for Gates to make decisions. And the LAPD might have been better off if Gates had made them, for the chief was a more talented and experienced tactician than most of his subordinates. Had Gates remained at Parker Center or, alternatively, arrived earlier at the field command post, he might have prodded his command staff into a more responsive performance.

After leaving the command post, Gates roamed the streets throughout the night with a driver and another aide and did not return to the Emergency Operation Center until 6:00 A.M. Sergeant Landsman would remember a strange encounter with the chief at 2:00 A.M. after Landsman had encountered four officers who had been sent out from the command post without clear assignment. They were huddled against a building, not knowing what they were supposed to do. Landsman was interviewing the officers when Gates pulled up and got out of his car. The chief walked over and asked Landsman what the officers were doing. "I have no idea," Landsman replied. Normally deferential to authority, Landsman had been seething since he left the command post and the unexpected appearance of Gates gave him a target for his anger. "Your command post is out of control," he told the chief. "There is no command."[61] Gates did not dispute him. He made a wry face, climbed back into his car, and drove away.

Later that morning Gates had another strange encounter, this time with two police heroes of the early hours of the riots. Officers Daniel Nee and Lisa Phillips, who had defied the mob to rescue the unconscious Soon Oh from her car at Seventy-first and Normandie, had been sent to a deserted intersection that was the dividing line between two police jurisdictions. They pulled their patrol car into the intersection so it could be used for cover and stood guard at a church at the corner of Arlington and Vernon. Gates drove up, chatted with them, and asked if they needed anything. Phillips was thirsty and asked the chief if he would mind bringing them diet Cokes from a nearby store. "No problem," said Gates. He drove off but did not return with the sodas. Instead, he sent his driver back to tell the officers that it would be safer if they put out flares so their car would be more visible. Nee was amused. "There's a riot going on, and the chief is micromanaging how our car is parked," he said afterwards. "Thanks, chief."[62]

But Phillips thought back to the rescue of the night before. What had the chief been doing then? She wanted the diet Cokes he had promised, not safety instructions. "He didn't just put his butt on the line at Florence and Normandie," said Phillips. "I was pissed."[63]

The long night had been an ordeal for Los Angeles. The early failure of the police to establish a perimeter had permitted mobs to roam at will through South Central, and the disorders had spread north toward downtown and west along Wilshire through Koreatown, lapping into Hollywood, the fringes of West Los Angeles and the San Fernando Valley. Southern California was gripped by terror, and some residents guarded their homes with rifles and shotguns. Others panicked and fled. Hotels in Ventura and Santa Barbara along the Pacific coast to the west and north were filled for the next five days, as if it were midsummer. Most of the panic was born of rumor and the dread that "they" were on the way to the privileged west side, Molotov cocktails in hand. In fact, with the conspicuous exception of South Central, Koreatown, and the surrounding mid-Wilshire area, police held control of the streets. The true nightmare city was South Central, where residents stayed inside as the riots raged, and the sick and the needy were unable to obtain emergency medical or fire help.

One of those in need of help in South Central that night was Donzell Gooden, seventy-four, who awoke in a stifling heat caused by the burning of a bank building on the nearby corner of Eighty-ninth and Western. Her husband was moaning in pain. "Everything was on fire, and he was sick," she recalled later. Fred Gooden, seventy-nine, was a retired city maintenance worker who was suffering from pancreatic cancer. After vainly dialing 911, Gooden realized that it was up to her to obtain medical attention for her husband. Fearful and praying, she put her husband in the car with a neighbor's help and drove through South Central, trying to avoid crowds and burning buildings. Heading west where there were fewer fires lighting up the skies, she made it to Centinela Hospital in Inglewood.

The LAPD receives 6,500 calls on the 911 number during an average twenty-four hours and the Fire Department 900 calls during the same period. But during the twenty-four hours beginning on the first night of the riots, the police received 29,623 calls and the Fire Department, 3,881 calls. The "sheer number of calls inundated the system," according to the Fire Department's post-riot report, and produced a breakdown that greatly added to the burden of the firefighters.

By the time the Fire Department's insistent lobbying persuaded the LAPD command staff to press Metro into escort duty late on the first night of the riots, firefighters were backlogged. Racing from fire to fire around South Central, they became targets of deliberate and random gunfire. In terms of casualties it was the Fire Department, not the LAPD, that bore the brunt of the riots. Fifty-nine firefighters were injured, four by gunfire, and several trucks and ambulances were hit. Almost all the shooting occurred the first night.

The worst single incident for firefighters happened at 9:48 P.M., when a dark car with its headlights out drove up alongside a fifty-two-foot hook and ladder that was heading north on Western Avenue with sirens blaring. Driver Scott Miller could see looters ahead at Thirty-first and Western. As he slowed the huge rig from thirty-five to fifteen miles an hour, the dark car passed on the driver's side. A gun reached out, and crew member Tom Carroll saw a flash. Miller slumped over the wheel, blood gushing from his cheek. Captain Francis Howard, a fifty-nine-year-old veteran of the Watts riot, pulled the air brake on the steering column, managing to stop the truck just before it plowed into cars parked at the curb. "We have a fireman shot!" shouted firefighter Paul Jordan, "We have a fireman shot! Need help immediately!" Carroll was trained as a paramedic. He ran to Miller, who fell unconscious and bleeding into his arms.

A rescue ambulance was dispatched from the command post, but Captain Howard decided the best hope for saving Miller's life was to drive to Cedars-Sinai Medical Center, a full trauma hospital. With Paul Jordan at the wheel, the hook and ladder maneuvered north on Western through looters and onto the Santa Monica Freeway. As with Reginald Denny, the truck reached the hospital just in time. Miller, a thirty-two-year-old father of two and brother of an LAPD sergeant who helped investigate the Rodney King beating, spent five and a half hours in surgery as doctors removed a bullet that had penetrated his right cheek, entered his interior carotid artery, and lodged in his neck.

Seven minutes after the Miller shooting, more than a mile away at Vermont and Vernon, a crowd watched as a six-man firefighting crew tried to stop a department store blaze from spreading. Alonzo Williams, the only African-American member of the crew, thought there was a "strange quiet" to the crowd. He was attaching a hose to a hydrant when he felt bullets whiz by his head. As he turned toward the fire truck, wrenches in hand, a black man with an AK-47 ran toward him, shouting. Williams put his hands up. "You're not going to put out anything, I'm going to kill you," the gunman said. "I'm going to kill all these motherfuckers with you." Williams tried to calm the gunman in a loud voice, hoping to alert other members of the crew. Engineer Kelly Kilmartin was nearby at the instrument panel of the truck but could not hear Williams above the noise of the water pumper. When he turned, he saw the gunman pressing the AK-47 against Williams' head. Then the gunman pointed the weapon at Kilmartin.

While the gunman confronted Kilmartin, Williams managed to warn Rick Reyes, another crew member, who sent an emergency call over a hand-held radio. The gunman told him to stop, and Reyes did. The gunman then focused his attention on Captain Carl Butler, the crew leader, a twenty-four-year department veteran with a reputation for aggressiveness. Butler thought about charging the gunman and trying to disarm him, but realized that he had been joined by three other armed men. Still, it seemed to Butler that the original gunman was the principal menace. He talked in-coherently, muttering obscenities and pointing the AK-47. The firefighters would later learn that the gunman was Trynon Lee Jefferson, known in the Eight Tray Gangster Crips as "Psycho." His message, repeated over and over again, was, "Motherfuckers, let the fire burn, or I'll shoot you."[64]

Butler tried to reason with the angry man. "Please don't shoot us, we're just here to put out the fire, we're not here to hurt anybody, or do anything else," he said.[65] Unmoved, the gunman demanded Butler's radio, and the crew chief handed over the $3,000 piece of equipment. Then the gunman told Butler to turn around and pointed the weapon at the back of his head. Butler feared he would be shot, but the gunman instead told him and his crew to abandon their trucks and leave. They fled through a corner parking lot with the crowd yelling, "Kill 'em, shoot 'em!"

In the panic of their flight, the firefighters did not realize that Williams had become separated from them and that Kilmartin had never heard the gunman's order. Left alone, Kilmartin crouched inside the fire truck as the men sprayed it with gunfire. The other firefighters, meanwhile, took refuge in the home of Bertila Pozo, a Salvadoran pillow-maker. Butler had entered the first home he could find where the residents were not African Ameri-can. At the time, said Butler, "black was death, Latino was life."[66]

But after drinking ice water provided by Pozo and her two daughters, the firefighters decided to rescue Kilmartin and Williams. They left the house and walked fearfully back toward their truck, shouting and waving to attract Kilmartin's attention. Kilmartin, who had cautiously left the truck, sprinted to join them. They then found Williams nearby and returned to the house. Later that night they were rescued by a SWAT team headed by Sergeant Albanese, the observer in the luckless helicopter flight. The SWAT team arrived in an armored personnel carrier, a vehicle that might have made a difference had it been available at Florence and Normandie.

The incident emphasized racial feelings that were common among firefighters on that first night of the riots. Butler lived in a remote Santa Barbara County community that is home to many Latinos but few African Americans. After his perilous encounter, it is not surprising that he equated blacks with death and Latinos with life. As word of the Miller shooting and the incident with Butler's crew spread, even racially diverse crews tended to regard African Americans as potentially dangerous and Latinos as likely to be helpful. These feelings were reinforced by another incident involving a crew from Butler's Fire Station 50. The crew was trying to prevent a strip-mall fire at Fifty-fourth and Main from spreading to an apartment complex. Suddenly, the firefighters were surrounded by Latinos wielding machetes who said they lived in the apartment building and had come to prevent anyone from interfering with the fire fighting effort. Reassured by their guards, the crew saved the apartments where the Latinos lived.[67]

Only a handful of blacks in South Central attacked or threatened firefighters. "It was just a few bad people that really stood out," Terry Manning said. Much public attention was paid to these "bad people," however, and little to the numerous black bystanders who joined in picking up fire hoses, blocking off streets, and otherwise helping the fire-fighting effort. Firefighters were highly vulnerable, even with police protection, but they were rarely shot at after the first hours of the riots. "If they were targeting firemen, we would have lost them by the dozen," Manning said.[68]

This analysis, however, became possible only with the comfort of hindsight. At the time every firefighter had reason to fear he might become the next Scott Miller. Nevertheless, they stuck to their dangerous and grueling work, saving hundreds of homes and apartment buildings from being consumed by arson-caused fires.

The arsonists rarely set fire to dwellings; they were not, in fact, trying to "burn their houses," as an LAPD officer had put it cynically. But strip malls and stores are interspersed with residences in South Central and the mid-Wilshire area. During the rioting, 862 structures suffered fire damage, including scores of apartment buildings and homes that were ignited by flames that spread from commercial fires. Firefighters tried to get water on every residential blaze. By 11:00 the first night, 122 fire companies and 25 rescue ambulances were working in South Central. Every available piece of fire equipment in the San Fernando Valley was pressed into service in the riot area. By the second day, firefighters were arriving from hundreds of miles away.

Although the assignment of Metro officers as escorts for firefighters was criticized by the Webster Commission and the LAPD post-riot report, the decision assisted the fire-fighting effort on the critical first night. Ideally, Metro would have been deployed directly in riot-suppression rather than riding shotgun for the Fire Department, but the use of Metro officers as escorts brought them into engagements with violent rioters. The most extensive police shootout of the riots, at Nickerson Gardens late on the first night, was a byproduct of Metro's escort role.[69]

Nickerson Gardens, the largest government housing project west of the Mississippi, hugs the borderline of Watts near the Century Freeway and the Martin Luther King Jr. Hospital/Drew Medical Center. It was home to 3,707 people, of whom 60 percent were black and most others Latino. In contrast to relatively self-sufficient Hyde Park and Florence-Normandie, drug-ridden Nickerson Gardens was at the bottom of the economic and social scrap heap and heavily dependent on public assistance. Its residents were dirt poor, with an average income of $722 a month including welfare payments. Gangs of young African Americans ruled the curving streets within the sixty-eight-acre project, terrorizing other residents and removing street signs in order to confuse rookie police officers. These gangs hated the LAPD.

The first police shooting of the riots occurred at 114th and Central, just outside Nickerson Gardens. Four officers from the Southeast Station, responding in a single patrol car to the report of an arson and burglary at a liquor store, encountered a crowd of looters, one of whom opened fire with an assault rifle. The bullets kicked up fragments of pavement and flattened the left rear tire of the patrol car. Officer John Alviani, driving with his nine-millimeter gun on his lap, fired sixteen rounds in response and another officer in the backseat fired thirteen rounds. One of Alviani's bullets mortally wounded Deandre Harrison, seventeen, the youth who police said had fired at them. His mother, Anita Lewis, said her son had left home two hours before the shooting. She never heard from him again.

Less than fifteen minutes after the Harrison shooting, three fire engines and two squads of Metro officers arrived at the liquor store, where the spreading fire threatened a small medical building. They knew nothing of the shootout, nor did Southeast officers know Metro was in the area. Police units were operating independently, observed Metro Sergeant Grady Dublin, because the dysfunctional command staff had "completely broken down."[70]

Chris Schnitker, a lanky six-foot-eight firefighter, was attaching a hose to a hydrant in front of the medical building when a gunman in Nickerson Gardens opened fire. Metro officers returned fire, and Schnitker dropped to the pavement to avoid being caught in the crossfire. It was the beginning of a two-hour gun battle in which Metro officers claimed to have fired more rounds than in any LAPD engagement since the 1974 assault on the headquarters of the Symbionese Liberation Army.

The battle pitted desperate black men who knew the terrain against twenty-five members of one of the nation's best-trained police units. While the Nickerson Gardens shooters were resourceful, the Metro officers had better weapons, bulletproof vests, and much more patience. The outcome of such an engagement was a foregone conclusion, but the shooters surprised the police with their tenacity and managed to pin down both Metro squads. "The aggressive actions of these suspects toward the police was just amazing," said Sergeant Roger Blackwell, who headed one of the Metro squads. "I just could not believe that none of us got hurt. It's like standing in front of a firing squad and everybody missed."[71]

In the end, the battle was won, as battles often are, by courage and superior firepower. Officer John Puis was equipped with a state-of-the-art AR-15 with a laser-assisted aiming device, and had the help of a trained spotter, Officer Jim Moody. At 1:40 A.M., Puis saw two armed men moving along the side of a building in an attempt to outflank the Metro squad commanded by Sergeant Richard Beardslee. One of the men fired a dozen rounds from an assault rifle at Beardslee's pinned-down squad. Puis stepped out without cover and fired twenty rounds—the entire magazine of his weapon—at the gunman, who fell wounded. Another gunman then fired at Beardslee's squad. Puis reloaded and fired twelve shots at the man, who sprayed the area with a sweeping arc of gunfire before fleeing.

This ended the battle. After the shooting subsided, an elderly man emerged from the projects to tell officers that two bodies were lying in front of one of the project units. The SWAT team arrived and went into the projects in an armored personnel carrier to remove the bodies of Anthony Taylor, thirty-one, and Dennis Jackson, thirty-eight. SWAT also extricated the firefighters, who had moved their trucks into a V-formation during the battle and used them as shields. The Metro officers urged the firefighters to cut their hoses and leave before more shooting started. A grizzled fire captain resisted the suggestion. Firefighters in budget-strained Los Angeles are trained to recover their equipment, and the captain insisted that the brass hose fittings were expensive. Get Mayor Bradley to buy you new fire hoses, said Sergeant Dublin. The captain was unimpressed. The dispute was finally resolved by an exasperated Albanese, who told the fire captain, "Cut them, or you're here on your own."[72] The hoses were cut, and the firefighters moved out with Metro once more riding shotgun.

Metro commanders were pleased with the professional performance of their officers in Nickerson Gardens. They had done what they were trained to do and emerged unscathed, protecting firefighters in the process. But the shootout was an aberration in the context of overall LAPD performance during the riots. Most of the public was barely aware of the incident, which happened under cover of darkness and out of sight of television cameras.

ELSEWHERE MOBS RANSACKED AND BURNED AT WILL. THEY WERE especially destructive in attacking Korean-owned stores, which were demolished with a systematic ferocity reminiscent of attacks on Jewish-owned shops in Nazi Germany. Black ownership, when the rioters were aware of it, did not necessarily protect a store from looting but often saved it from arson. Korean-owned stores were burned to the ground. One of the few exceptions was the boarded-up Empire Liquor Market Deli on Figueroa Street where Soon Ja Du had fatally shot Latasha Harlins. Neighborhood blacks protected the store from being torched, partly to shield an adjoining black-owned business and partly to preserve it as a memorial to Harlins.[73]

The targeting of Korean shops was in some respects a legacy of the Harlins affair. African Americans viewed Judge Joyce Karlin's light sentence as an extreme injustice, and memories of the case had been revived just before the riots by an appellate ruling upholding her decision. But it is likely that Korean stores in South Central, many of them isolated from other business or concentrated in distinctive pastel-colored strip malls, would have been singled out even without the provocation of the Harlins affair, given the combustible mix of racial and cultural misunderstanding between African Americans and Korean Americans. In the early stages of the riots, most Korean shopkeepers in South Central were quick to realize what might happen. Taking with them what they could, they abandoned their stores and fled.

It was different in Koreatown, on the fringes of the mid-Wilshire district, where Korean shopkeepers were less isolated, more numerous, and well-armed. Some had received military training in Korea, and a few members of the older generation had served in the Korean War. These Koreans were ready and willing to defend themselves by force of arms.

Richard Rhee, a leader of the Korean resistance in the riots, was barely twenty when he came to Los Angeles in 1957 with boyhood memories of hardships during the Korean War and dreams of affluence. Rhee spoke no English, but he found work in Chinatown as a dishwasher by day and a janitor by night. In time he learned English well enough to be accepted as a business major at UCLA, but he was then working seven days a week and sleeping only four hours a night. Eventually, he dropped out of college. By then Rhee had saved enough money to purchase a small garment factory. He made money, sold the factory at a profit, and bought a neglected Mayfair grocery store near the corner of Fifth Street and Western Avenue. Rhee transformed the store into the California Market, a modern grocery that featured Asian delicacies and also catered to the diverse tastes of multicultural Los Angeles.

By the time of the riots, Rhee was a wealthy family man with a comfortable house in Hancock Park and fourteen commercial and residential properties in Southern California. But he devoted most of his time and energies to his beloved market, where prices were reasonable and security stringent. Store managers posted a rogue's gallery of persons arrested for shoplifting, most of them black. State officials would later accuse Rhee of violating numerous labor laws, but he was respected among Koreans for determination and courage. These were qualities that would prove useful in the riots.

Rhee was in the office of his market watching customers through a one-way mirror when he heard about the first protests against the verdicts. Soon rumors spread through Koreatown that black rioters were on their way. Rhee turned on CNN and watched the Denny beating, then summoned his security chief and told him to round up reinforcements. By nightfall, Rhee had posted guards with loaded guns on the roof, where they would soon see the smoke rising from South Central.

The mob did not reach Koreatown until Thursday, April 30, the second day of the riots. By then Rhee had assembled twenty armed men in the parking lot of the California Market, where they were barricaded behind an odd assortment of trucks and luxury cars. One man had brought an old machine gun, but most had shotguns and rifles. Rhee ate and slept in the parking lot for three days, leaving only to use the bathroom inside the store. "Burn this down after thirty-three years?" Rhee said. "They don't know how hard I've worked. This is my market, and I'm going to protect it."[74]

Looters roamed the area around the California Market during the daylight hours of Thursday, but avoided the armed Koreans in the parking lot. Late that afternoon, however, a fire erupted at a mini-mall a block away, and Rhee sent some of his guards to help extinguish it. The looters became bolder. As night fell, they advanced in force, yelling obscenities and threats. The Koreans greeted them by firing several volleys into the air and a few near the feet of the first rank of looters. The looters hesitated, then retreated. Rhee later remembered pointing his rifle directly at one armed looter, who saw him and turned away. He believes that the machine gun made a strong impression. No one was hurt, although there is little doubt the Koreans would have shot the looters if they had continued their advance. The result of this show of force was as telling as the deadly firefight in Nickerson Gardens about what might have happened had rioters faced early armed resistance from the police. Although Rhee's men heard rumors that the looters were coming back, they made no more attempts to overrun the market.[75]

At about the time the Koreans were making their stand at California Market, Jay Rhee (no relation to Richard) and two employees were using similar tactics and considerably less firepower to repel a large crowd of looters at a mini-mall at Santa Monica and Vermont. The looters retreated whenever police officers drove by, then advanced when they were gone. Jay Rhee and his helpers fired a total of five hundred rounds in the air and succeeded in saving the mini-mall, but Rhee was disillusioned by the experience. "We have lost our faith in the police," he told the Los Angeles Times. "Where were you when we needed you?"[76]

This was a common lament among Koreans, who were soon as angry about the absence of the LAPD as they were about the behavior of the rioters. David Joo, who managed a gun store on Western Avenue, helped defend a nearby jewelry store where the Korean owner tried to transfer his wares to a safe while police cars were on the street. Someone in a crowd of rioters across the street began shooting at the store, and the Koreans returned the fire. Instead of intervening, the police drove away. The Koreans held off the rioters for a time but left when they ran out of ammunition. After they were gone, the store was looted.[77]

The LAPD never addressed its failure to protect Koreans and their property. After the riots, an officer told me that Koreans had seemed capable of defending themselves, which begs the question of police responsibility. According to Richard Rhee, a police car pulled up to the California Market on the first night of the riots, and an officer commanded the security guards to raise their hands. They complied but the officer left after seeing that the armed men were Korean. Soon afterward, an African-American police officer who was well-known in the neighborhood pulled up in another patrol car. Rhee spoke to him by name and asked him to stay and protect the store. "I wish I could," the officer said and drove away. He was the last officer Rhee saw during the riots.

Where Koreans were armed and organized, as at the California Market or the mini-mall defended by Jay Rhee, they succeeded admirably in protecting themselves and their property. But such incidents were exceptions. Korean shopkeepers who were isolated and outnumbered in the vast reaches of South Central had no chance of making a similar defense.

As a result, Koreans suffered more from the riots than any other ethnic group. A post-riot study found that rioters destroyed more than two thousand Korean-American businesses with a value of $400 million, which represented nearly half the entire personal property loss. Forty Koreans were injured. Edward Song Lee, an eighteen-year-old freshman at Santa Monica City College, was shot to death on the second night of the riots at Third and Hobart when caught in a crossfire. Lee, hearing radio reports that Koreatown was besieged by rioters, had loaded a car with friends and gone to help the shopkeepers. He may have been killed by other Koreans who mistook him for a rioter; the coroner never conclusively determined the origin of the fatal bullet. Koreans blamed rioters and the police. David Joo vowed that Koreans would be better armed and trained for any future disorder and would never again rely on the LAPD. Soon Cho, an editor at the *Korean Times*, said that Koreans paid their taxes and were entitled to police protection they had not received. What happened during the riots, Cho added, was a "betrayal by the police."[78]

ABANDONMENT BY THE POLICE WAS NOT THE ONLY SURPRISE FOR Korean shopkeepers, who had expected to be overrun by blacks streaming north and west from South Central. But Richard Rhee was astonished to find that a majority of the looters repulsed by his guards—70 percent by his estimate—were Latino.

Latinos had been involved in the first stage of the riots mostly as victims. The African-American gang members who took control of Florence and Normandie attacked Latinos, whites, and Asians without distinction. Much of this gang rage spent itself in the first night of arson and destruction, and the disorders might have ended then if police had been deployed in force. Because a police presence was lacking, however, the riots that began as an expression of black rage became a massive looting spree. So many Latinos were involved that one analyst concluded "this wasn't a black riot so much as a minority riot."[79]

Such assessments view the riots as one continuous disorder and tend to equate property crimes, in which Latinos were most prominent, with crimes of violence. In fact, the disorders were a series of events with varying causes and differing degrees of criminality. On the first day, they were mostly a race riot pitting blacks against everyone else. They became a "minority riot" on the second and third days, as the police breakdown created tempting targets of looting opportunity, especially in South Central. Since Latinos are the majority in the area, they provided the most looters.

But it is important to note that most of the 3 million Latinos who live in Los Angeles County did not participate in the riots in any way. Latinos live in every zip code in Los Angeles, but their population is centered in East Los Angeles, which sprawls across the city limits into the county. Together with adjoining cities in the San Gabriel Valley, this area contains more people of Mexican descent than any place in the world except Mexico City. East Los Angeles has serious social and economic problems, including gangs and grinding poverty. But the area stayed calm throughout the riots, with only four minor criminal incidents reported.

Most of the Latinos who participated in the riots lived in unstable, transitional neighborhoods and had been born abroad. An analysis of court records by the *Los Angeles Times* showed that 80 percent of Latinos convicted of riot-related crimes were foreign born and that 25 percent of them had arrived in the United States within the past two years. These Latinos lived in South Central, where they made up 49 percent of the population, or in the midcity communities of Westlake, Pico-Union or Koreatown, where they constituted 66 percent of the legal population. Most of the Latinos in Westlake and Pico-Union were desperately poor young immigrants who had fled poverty or political repression in Central America and Mexico, lived in conditions of hideous overcrowding, and worked for subminimum wages under constant fear of deportation. Mothers did not hesitate to take food, clothing, and diapers from half-looted and unguarded stores. The eminent demographer Leo Estrada concluded from post-riot interviews that looters from Central America behaved much as they would have in their homelands after a raid by a government or rebel army. Since stores often did not reopen for weeks after such depredations, civilians took what they could. That is what happened in the riots. "People would not have wandered into a grocery store that was being guarded to take Pampers," Estrada said. "The looting was preventable."

Necessity and opportunity also spurred preventable looting by African Americans. Vanessa Coleman was watching a television report of the looting when she thought, "Well, I better get out there and get stuff for my kids, too . . . We didn't know if there were going to be any stores standing. We didn't know if we were going to have food."[80] Coleman and three women friends, who had eighteen children among them, went to a grocery store where she filled a laundry bag with diapers, canned goods, and potatoes. Her companions stole food and beauty supplies. One of these women told Lynne Duke of *The Washington Post* that her grandmother had similarly looted stores during the Watts riot.

Television spread the contagion of the looting. Like Vanessa Coleman, thousands of needy people could see that looters were unopposed by the police, and they rushed to join in the pillaging. It did not occur to most of those caught up in the frenzy that videotape records of their looting would later be used to convict them. But most looters responded rationally to police activity. Looting never started in areas where police maintained a presence. Once mass arrests began in riot-ravaged areas, the looting ceased.

The looting had nothing to do with Rodney King. A useful *Los Angeles Times* study of 694 court files found that King's name was invoked only once during any of these incidents—ironically during the robbery of an African-American grocer by a white and a Latino. These two robbers entered a San Fernando Valley store, knocking over display cases and grabbing several six-packs of beer. "Fuck Rodney King," one of the men said. As they left, the Latino robber pointed at Donald Johnson, the storekeeper, and told his partner, "Shoot the black motherfucker." The white man raised his rifle, but Johnson brought up a .357 magnum from behind the counter and fired first.

He wounded the white robber, who fell to the floor while the Latino fled. The incident reminded Johnson of his first firefight in Vietnam, where he had been an Army machine gunner. "This was far more senseless and stupid than anything I saw in the war," he said.

Tom Bradley and Daryl Gates also thought the riots were senseless. For all their faults and lapses, they were proud and honorable public men who believed in Los Angeles and found it incomprehensible that people would destroy their own neighborhoods. Gates and Bradley had been surprised when disorders erupted so quickly after the verdicts, and they were surprised again when looting and arson continued on the second day. Deputy Mayor Mark Fabiani, Bradley's chief of staff, said they and many others were blinded by the conventional wisdom of the Watts riot, which held that rioting would ebb during daylight hours and give police a chance to regroup. Instead, it continued to spread.

With Los Angeles burning, Gates and Bradley finally put aside their feud. On the morning of the second day, Gates went to City Hall to brief the mayor and discuss the restoration of order. The only lapse in the chief's professionalism was a mild expression of approval that rioters had managed to include the building of his nemesis, the *Los Angeles Times,* among their targets. Bradley treated Gates with respect. The crisis had created a bond between the old mayor and the old chief that would last for the duration of the riots. When Gates learned later that his adult son Scott was in critical condition in a hospital after a drug overdose, he confided in Bradley and left for the hospital. The mayor told no one that the chief was again away from his post, this time for good reason. Scott Gates recovered after two days on the critical list. Daryl Gates was thankful for Bradley's understanding.[81]

At 12:15 A.M. Thursday, Bradley had declared a sunset-to-sunrise curfew order applying to most of South Central. Gates wanted to extend it to the entire city, saying that it would help clear the streets and free police to make arrests. Bradley knew businesses outside the riot areas would resent a sweeping curfew order, but he agreed when Gates pressed the issue. During the day the mayor three times amended his original curfew order, finally applying it citywide. He made exceptions for "activities that are necessary and essential for health, safety, or emergency-related purposes."

The curfew had force of law under the mayor's emergency powers and should have made life easier for the police. It freed police officers from the burden of determining whether people who were out after sunset had engaged in criminal activity; anyone could be arrested simply for being on the streets. But the mayor defused the effectiveness of the curfew by giving the impression that the curfew was voluntary. Bradley told a news conference that he was "calling upon business people of this city to cooperate, asking that if you don't have to be on the streets of Los Angeles tonight after dark, please don't go." He tried to distinguish between "legitimate" and unlawful reasons that people could be out after dark and assured a reporter that the police are "not trying to arrest everybody in town, not trying to prevent them from carrying on their normal lives." Television reports added to the confusion by saying that the curfew was voluntary. Press accounts the next day had it right, but the curfew was inconsistently enforced on the second night. The Webster Commission concluded that "ambiguities in the presentation of the curfew substantially undercut its effectiveness as a tool to keep people off the streets."

Common sense suggested that the best way to stop the rioting was by arresting the rioters, but police were reluctant to do so, partly because they did not know what to do with the people they arrested. The LAPD was slow to set up its field jails, which in any case had been designed for misdemeanor bookings arising from mass demonstrations, not for felony arrests requiring extensive paperwork. Bookings were continuously backlogged, and the Webster Commission found that it took forty-five minutes to process a single felony arrest.[82] Officers who knew they were needed on the streets were discouraged from making arrests by the cumbersome booking procedures and by a shortage of buses for transporting prisoners. The alternative was taking prisoners to often distant jails in patrol cars, a practice the Webster report understatedly called "an inefficient use of those vehicles."

Inefficiency was a hallmark of police performance during the riots. When the LAPD failed to stop the riots quickly, its thin blue line was rapidly stretched to the breaking point. Once the disorders spread beyond South Central, the LAPD lacked the resources to quell them even if it had lived up to its reputation for aggressiveness. Nearby law enforcement agencies had hundreds of officers available, but the LAPD tradition of self-reliance and what the Webster Commission called an "attitude of superiority" inhibited department commanders from seeking assistance. It was a long-standing problem. On the first night of the 1965 Watts riot, Los Angeles County Sheriff Peter Pitchess had offered to send three hundred officers to help the LAPD. Chief Parker had rejected the offer.

By 1992, Los Angeles County Sheriff Sherman Block was midway through his third four-year term. He was a resourceful cop and a masterful politician who rarely faced more than token opposition at the polls. Block cultivated the media and showed a Reaganesque flair for remaining disentangled from periodic scandals that convulsed his department. While deputies had been accused of using excessive force as often as LAPD officers, Block defused the issue after the Rodney King beating by commissioning an independent study which was pending at the time of the riots. He had responded to the Simi Valley verdicts by immediately calling a tactical alert and mobilizing his department, as Gates should have done. When

East Los Angeles stayed calm, Block knew that he could spare five hundred deputies to assist the LAPD—as he informed Wilson, Bradley, and Gates in their conference call. But Block, while friendly with Gates, did not want to risk a repeat of the rebuff inflicted on his predecessor during the Watts riot. If the LAPD wanted help from Sheriff Block, it would have to ask.

The Los Angeles County Sheriff's Department is larger than many metropolitan police forces and is deployed over an area twice the size of Delaware. In addition to serving the county's unincorporated areas, it provides contract police service to forty-one cities. Sheriff's deputies had dealt with civil disturbances and undergone riot training, and Block was regional coordinator of the California Law Enforcement Mutual Aid Plan. In this capacity, he received several offers of assistance to the LAPD from law enforcement agencies on the first night of the riots but rejected them because the LAPD had made no request for help.

As it turned out, the LAPD found it difficult to accept help even when it requested it. On the first night of the riots, the LAPD Emergency Operations Center asked the sheriff's office for two platoons of deputies, but the field command post countermanded the order before they could be sent. Only after Block talked to Gates at 10:00 A.M. the next day and told him that the deputies were still available were the platoons deployed.[83] These 112 deputies made an immediate difference. They were ordered to arrest anyone engaged in criminal activity, and they promptly began rounding up looters.

The LAPD's insularity also initially prevented it from using the considerable resources of the California Highway Patrol, which the Webster report said could have provided perimeter control. By 9:00 on the first night, two companies of California Highway Patrol officers had been mobilized in Los Angeles, awaiting instructions. In the conference call initiated by Wilson, California Highway Patrol Commissioner Maurice Hannigan offered to send in 1,500 officers. Gates accepted the offer, but his commanders made no use of the CHP officers who were already in Los Angeles. The two companies, with a complement of 120 men and women, spent the night watching television at headquarters. On the morning of the second day, the LAPD asked that the two platoons be sent to the Coliseum to help conduct a sweep of the area. When they arrived, no one from the LAPD was there to meet them. The highway patrol did not see action until the afternoon of the second day, when it replaced Metro in escorting fire engines and ambulances, freeing Metro officers for duties for which they were better suited.

The Webster report concluded that Bradley should have utilized the sheriff's deputies and CHP officers before requesting the National Guard, but the mayor apparently did not realize that hundreds of trained law enforcement officers were already in Los Angeles County if the LAPD had been willing to use them. As for the Guard, the deployment went well at first. Many of the Guard's citizen-soldiers had been watching the riots on television and had expected to be sent to Los Angeles. Most units had up-to-date recall plans because of the Persian Gulf war. Guard soldiers were directed to be in their armories by 6:00 A.M. Thursday, but most troops had assembled by four.

The Guard soldiers remained in their armories for most of Thursday, as their commanders struggled to supply them with riot gear and ammunition and state, county, and city officials wrangled about their mission. The comedian Robin Williams later satirized the effort: A National Guard soldier deployed in Los Angeles without ammunition tries to stop rioters by singing, "We Are The World." But it wasn't funny at the time for Guard commanders, who learned in the middle of the night that live ammunition for the rifles of the troops they were deploying was stored at Camp Roberts, 230 miles north of Los Angeles.

What followed was a series of delays reminiscent of the foul-ups at the LAPD field command post. Guard commanders decided to ferry the ammunition by helicopter to a principal armory at Los Alamitos south of Los Angeles. The truck drivers who transported the ammunition to the helicopter were slow to arrive and lacked the right equipment for loading it onto the aircraft. The ammunition and other equipment did not reach Los Alamitos until 1:50 P.M., and it was several hours more before troops were armed and equipped. A distraught Bradley called Wilson at 12:30 P.M. and asked when the Guard would be deployed. The State Office of Emergency Services was trying to cover up the problem by saying that the troops could not be deployed until the LAPD had used the sheriff's department and the highway patrol. Wilson wisely avoided becoming entangled in this ruse. He made three telephone calls to prod deployment of the Guard and flew to Los Angeles to oversee it. "This ammunition problem should not have occurred," Wilson acknowledged on Friday. "It will not again."[84]

While Wilson was flying to Los Angeles, the city's most influential private citizen was driving home from his downtown office under soot-filled skies. No troops were on the street, and radio reports said that arson and looting were increasing. Warren Christopher thought of Watts, when delays in deploying the National Guard had needlessly prolonged the riot. When he reached home at 4:30 P.M., he called the mayor's office and urged Bradley to request federal troops. "I felt things were out of control . . ." Christopher said later. "The National Guard was very slow to move in and that's fairly typical, too. The National Guard is not very effective in these situations."

The phone call to Bradley was decisive, according to Mark Fabiani. Christopher recalled that when he had been a deputy attorney general in the Justice Department during the 1960s it had been necessary to send federal

troops to quell riots in Detroit and Chicago. Bradley respected Christopher's judgment. He authorized a request for federal troops.

Gates and Block were opposed to federal troops, which the chief, in particular, thought were unneeded. It appears in retrospect that he may have
been right. The tide began to turn with the deployment of the Guard, which
started appearing on the streets Thursday night. The Guard soldiers proved
effective and disciplined and worked well with the LAPD. But Bradley had
made his decision to seek federal troops four hours before the Guard was
on the street. He had no way of knowing at the time of Christopher's call
when they would actually be deployed. The weekend was approaching, and
the mayor feared that violence might escalate. Wilson, distressed by the
slow deployment of the Guard, shared this fear. Declaring that "public safety
is the paramount concern," the governor backed the call for federal troops.

At 1:00 A.M. on Friday, May 1, Wilson formally made the request for
federal troops to President Bush, and at 3:30 the first detachments of 3,500
soldiers and Marines were sent from Fort Ord in northern California to Los
Angeles. Bush also federalized the National Guard. While everything looked
fine on paper, the federal troop deployment proved as star-crossed as almost
every other aspect of the riot response. When Army Major General Marvin
Covault met with Gates and Block at 10:00 A.M. Friday to discuss use of
the federal troops, it soon became apparent that the three of them had different ideas. Gates wanted soldiers posted in highly visible positions on the
streets in various neighborhoods. Block wanted the troops for specific mis-
sions in what the Webster Commission described as "rent-a-soldier" deployment. Covault had just enough legal knowledge to be dangerous. He
knew that the federal Posse Comitatus Act ordinarily prevented the use of
soldiers as peace officers, but did not realize that the president's authority
to use troops to quell domestic violence is exempt from restrictions of this
law. Covault might have learned this by reading the proclamation, which
specifically provided for soldiers to be used in a law enforcement capacity.

The general's misunderstanding was shared by National Guard officers
and, in the opinion of the Webster Commission, had a "serious dilatory impact on the responsiveness" of the Guard. Before the federalization order,
Guard troops fulfilled every request made of them by the police. After federalization, military commanders evaluated every police request in terms of
whether troops were being asked to perform a "military" or "law enforcement" function. As a result, the Guard fulfilled only 20 percent of police requests. This foolish restriction on the use of troops undoubtedly prolonged the
riots. After they started making mass arrests, the LAPD and sheriff's office
were tied up in transporting prisoners, a task that Guard soldiers easily could
have performed had they been allowed to do so by their commanders.

The unnecessary delays in bringing the riots under control greatly increased the death toll. More than a score of people died in Los Angeles County on Thursday, the worst of the five days of rioting. Another ten deaths occurred on Friday, nine on the two weekend days, and six more on Monday, May 4, the final day of the disorders.

Ira McCurry, forty-five, was shot to death in the middle of the night because he tried single-handedly to stop a looting that was unopposed by police. McCurry, a white county employee, was described as "a solitary man in a squalid little house" who was trying to prevent the looting of "the sorry liquor store next door."[85]

Howard Epstein, also forty-five and white, flew from northern California to Los Angeles, rented a car, and drove to a machine shop he owned in the riot area. As his car approached the shop he was shot in the head. Looters ransacked his car as he died.

Meeker Gibson, thirty-five, an African American, left the auto shop where he worked to get cigarettes. He was calling his estranged wife from a pay telephone when she heard the sound of gunfire. The phone booth was riddled with bullets; Meeker was hit in the upper torso by two shotgun blasts. A love letter to his wife was found on his body.

Thanh Lam, twenty-five, born in Vietnam of Chinese parents, was delivering a package when he was shot to death. Kevin Evanshen, twenty-four and white, fell through the roof of a burning building as he tried to extinguish the fire with a five-gallon container of bottled water. Juana Espanoza, sixty-five, waited until it seemed calm in her mostly Latino neighborhood before going out to buy two bottles of cola. On the way home she dropped the bottles and cried out for her husband and four daughters. A daughter arrived and found smoke rising from a pencil-sized hole in her mother's blouse. Police later said she had been shot by a sniper, although no one in the neighborhood had heard gunfire. Espanoza died on the way to the hospital.

Cesar Aguilar, eighteen, was an illegal immigrant from Honduras who delivered newspapers. Rounded up with forty others during the looting of a liquor store, he pulled what appeared to be a gun from his waistband and pointed it at LAPD Officers James McDonald and Joan Leuck who shot him in the chest. Aguilar died at the scene, and his weapon turned out to be a plastic toy. No weapon at all was found on the body of Mark Garcia, fifteen, who was shot to death by Los Angeles County sheriff's deputies pursuing six youths who had looted a jewelry store. The deputies were returning the fire of another youth, who was unharmed in the incident.

Charles Orebo, twenty-two, an African American, was driving a car that cut off a vehicle driven by a white man near a Harbor Freeway off-ramp late Friday afternoon. Two friends were with him in the car. "They were yelling, we're going to kill you, white ass, we're going to kill you, white boy," the driver of the other car recalled later. He was Brian Liddy, the aggressive LAPD officer who made the arrests that enraged the crowd at Seventy-first and Normandie after the Simi Valley verdicts. But Liddy was in civilian clothes and returning to 77th Street Station alone after three hours sleep in a Firebird which was nearly out of gas. Liddy knew he was in trouble when he missed a traffic light at the bottom of the ramp and the other car tried to force him off the road. Then one of the passengers pulled out a handgun and fired. Liddy fired back. "They missed, and I didn't," he said in describing the incident. But he hit Orebo, not the passenger who had fired the shots. Then Liddy's car stalled. He scrambled out on the street while the passenger continued shooting and Orebo's car swerved wildly, plowed into a wall, and caught fire. Orebo was dead with a bullet in the head. The passengers ran away.

Liddy then saw another armed black man across the street, wearing a white T-shirt and carrying something shiny in his hand. "Where did he come from?" wondered Liddy, who briefly thought that one of the passengers had managed to get in back of him. But when the man approached, Liddy saw that the shiny something was a star. "Don't shoot, I'm a deputy sheriff," said the man, an off-duty deputy named Tony Taylor who had heard the shooting and rushed to Liddy's aid. "Don't shoot, I'm LAPD," Liddy responded.[86]

Orebo was the last to die at LAPD hands during the riots, but another African American was slain on Saturday by Pasadena police. He was Howard Martin, twenty-two, killed in a shootout that developed when police tried to disperse a group of partygoers who fired on them. Martin had grown up three blocks away from Rodney King. He was known to his friends as "Nine Lives" because as a passenger he had twice survived car crashes in which the driver died.

National Guard troops patrolled streets without bloodshed until the waning hours of the riots. Their presence, the Webster Commission would later say on the basis of a telephone survey, was "important psychologically to the restoration of order." Some 7,000 Guard soldiers were called up. By Sunday, May 3, they were part of a combined force of 13,000 that included the 3,500 federal troops and law enforcement officers from various federal, state and local agencies. On Sunday night Marvin Rivas, thirty-one, a former Salvadoran policeman, tried to drive a decrepit blue Datsun through barricades that had been set up by the Guard at Pico Boulevard and Vermont Avenue. A Guardsman pointed a rifle but withheld fire, and Rivas sped off unharmed. He returned a few minutes later, however, and aimed his car at the barricade and the Guard troops alongside it. They ordered him to stop. Rivas kept going, and soldiers fired sixteen rounds from their M-16 rifles. Three of the bullets hit Rivas, blowing away the back of his head. A sister said Rivas was out of work and drinking heavily on the last day of his life. She said the American dream had not worked out for him.[87]

Nor had it worked for Los Angeles during five spring days in which the protests of the Simi Valley verdicts were allowed to escalate. No one was more distressed at the nightmare than Rodney King, who watched on television in disbelief as people killed, burned, and looted in his name. He wanted to do something to stop it, as did his attorney, Steve Lerman, who wrote something for King to say to reporters. King told Lerman he knew what to say. Outside Lerman's Beverly Hills office in bright sunlight, King fought to keep from crying on Friday as he uttered the riot's most memorable words: "People, I just want to say . . . can we all get along? Can we all get along? Can we stop making it horrible for the older people and the kids?"

Officer Ricky Banks, who had responded to the first robbery call of the riots, had always wanted people to get along. Near the end of the first day of the riots he returned to the Florence and Normandie neighborhood where he had grown up and gazed in disbelief at the devastation he saw all around him. Banks, the son of a construction worker, had been a young child during the Watts riot. His parents were dead, and Banks thought about them and their fervent hope that the riot would never be repeated. Banks felt bad as a black man that people of his race had killed innocent people to make a point. "It wasn't a consensus or something that was voted on," he said later. But Banks also knew there was reason for frustration and anger in the black community. He thought about Latasha Harlins and the sentence he believed had pushed the neighborhood near the boiling point. The acquittals in the King case had been the last straw, and the neighborhood had boiled over. Banks understood what had happened, but he could not accept it. "I almost cried," he said.[88]

Richard Rhee also could not accept the riots. He knew he had been fortunate that his market had survived a disturbance that had reduced so many Korean-owned stores to rubble, but he realized that it would never be the same for him again, nor for the city where he had made his fortune. Rhee was sad. "A light has gone out of Los Angeles," he said.[89]

13

AFTER THE FALL

"Los Angeles, you broke my heart. And I'm not sure I'll love you again."

—George Ramos[1]

"We in Los Angeles cannot begin the healing and the stabilization process until and when we make peace with ourselves and each other. As Martin Luther King once said, 'True peace is not merely the absence of tension. It is the presence of justice.'"

—LAPD Chief Willie L. Williams[2]

MAYOR TOM BRADLEY LIFTED THE DUSK-TO-DAWN CURFEW AT 5:15 P.M. on Monday, May 4, officially ending the riots. Fifty-four people had lost their lives during five days of violence, the highest toll in an American civil disturbance since the Draft Riot of 1863 in New York City.[3] Twenty-six of the dead were African American, fourteen were Latino, nine were non-Hispanic whites, and two were Asian. Three persons who died in fires had been too badly burned to determine their race or ethnicity. Another 2,328 people had been treated for injuries in emergency rooms by doctors who practiced what one hospital official called "battlefield medicine."[4] Property losses exceeded $900 million, the most ever in any U.S. riot. Eight hundred and sixty-two structures had been destroyed by fire, more than four times as many as in the 1965 Watts riot. Thousands of businesses were damaged or looted, and many "mom-and-pop" stores were gone forever.

In South Central, Pico-Union, Westlake, and Koreatown, the lifting of the curfew and the withdrawal of troops marked the end of one ordeal and the beginning of another. The riots had wrecked the infrastructure of the city's poorest neighborhoods. In a sprawling city where public transportation is at best inadequate, hard lives became especially hard for those without an automobile. Many neighborhoods no longer had any grocery stores, and most of the mini-malls where the poor had done their shopping had disappeared.

Gone with the groceries were drugstores, clothing stores, and discount variety stores. Gone, too, were jobs, at least 30,000 of them, in neighborhoods where they had been scarce to begin with.[5]

The 1992 riots were particularly painful for Watts. One of the prouder legacies of the 1965 riot aftermath had been the Watts Labor Community Action Committee, a social-action organization that had brought jobs and social services into the area. But the committee and its thriving commercial center did not survive the 1992 riots. On the second day a mob smashed the gates of the complex in broad daylight and poured inside. "We've been here for you; we're black," pleaded Teryl Watkins, the center's administrative assistant and daughter of its founder. "We're helping the community." The mob paid no heed. It threatened and chased away the Watkins family and staff and burned sixteen vehicles used to take Watts residents shopping and to medical appointments. The commercial center was looted, then burned to the ground. It included a coin laundry, toy store, youth enterprise project, furniture and appliance shop, and food stamp office, whose earnings helped pay for a homeless center, job training center, and a senior citizens housing project.[6]

Such disgraceful marauding turned some residents of South Central against the rioters. After the Watts riot, many blacks who had played no role in the disorder expressed pride that Negroes had risen up against the police. But after the 1992 riots a number of poor people of all races and ethnic groups expressed anger at the police—to the Webster Commission and various interviewers—for failing to cut the riot short at Florence and Normandie. One of these angry people was Dorean Miles, a twenty-seven-year-old black social worker who lived in the heart of South Central. As she washed her clothes at a surviving laundromat, Miles reflected on what happened: "Here were my friends and neighbors, burning down their own neighborhood. A week from now, when the people who looted are hungry, and there are no stores to buy anything in, what are they going to do with that stereo they grabbed, or with the six shirts, all the same color, all the same size?"[7]

While it became fashionable in liberal circles to depict the disorders as an uprising against harsh social and economic conditions, residents of South Central tended to be less charitable. They demonstrated their feelings in several instances by cooperating even with the unpopular LAPD, which after the riots made a belated attempt to arrest large-scale looters. The police were aided by abundant videotapes of the looting but even more by South Central residents who, often anonymously, turned in neighbors who had stored stolen goods in homes and garages. Often, South Central residents drew a distinction between those who had stolen for profit and those who had taken food or diapers out of need. It was the needier looters whom Maria Posadas, a Guatemalan immigrant devastated by the riots, had in mind when she said, "Poor people don't have the means to pay for their sins."[8]

The Watts riot, self-contained within a small area of South Central, had never directly threatened white Southern Californians. But whites felt personally menaced by the 1992 disturbances, which spread over a hundred square miles of the city and then jumped its boundaries like a runaway forest fire hurdling fire lines. An offshoot of the deadly conflagration erupted in Long Beach, scene of one of the riots' most brutal killings. The victim was Matthew Haines, a thirty-two-year-old white motorcyclist with a reputation as a good samaritan, who had responded to a plea for help from a friend, an African-American woman. Black gang members pulled him from his bike and beat him, then shot him to death.

The riots also leaped police lines in Hollywood and the Hollywood hills north and west of the principal disturbance. Fear transcended all boundaries, invading even affluent, well-protected communities that were never in danger. On posh Rodeo Drive, panicked diners fled a hotel coffee shop after seeing smoke they interpreted as the arrival of rioters in Beverly Hills. The smoke came from an accidental trash can fire that was quickly extinguished.

The unrest was not confined to Los Angeles County. News of the verdicts touched off two nights of mass protests in San Francisco, where police arrested 1,500 demonstrators. Nevada Governor Bob Miller activated the National Guard in Las Vegas, and police kept black marchers away from downtown casinos. Two people died in the Las Vegas outbreak, including a twelve-year-old boy who was burned to death in a shopping center firefighters refused to enter, afraid they would be attacked by gangs. In New York, 200 protesters rushed the doors of Madison Square Garden, chanting "Prosecute the cops . . . Justice now." Protests and isolated acts of violence occurred in Denver, Buffalo, Peoria, Toledo, Bridgeport, Providence, Atlanta, and other cities.

The breadth of the contagion suggests that the riots, in their origins, were indeed a reaction to the Simi Valley verdicts rather than a generalized response to economic and social conditions. But the disorders were also rooted in a tradition of black protest that included unrest in seven eastern cities during the summer of 1964, the Watts riot of 1965, the Detroit and Newark riots of 1967, and explosive outbreaks in Washington, D.C. and Chicago after the 1968 assassination of Martin Luther King Jr. The Kerner Commission appointed by President Lyndon Johnson to analyze the Detroit riots blamed them on inequalities in a nation "with two societies—one white, one black." This theme re-emerged after the 1992 Los Angeles riots, which Lynne Duke described in The Washington Post as "a manifestation of America's racial pain" and Janet Clayton in the Los Angeles Times as a reflection of the "everydayness of racism."

The riots also provided easy grist for ideological mills. On the left they were frequently called an "uprising" or an "insurrection" that reflected simmering black anger at discrimination and lack of economic opportunity. On the right they were described as a product of liberal permissiveness and family breakdown. Assistant LAPD Chief Robert Vernon, whose presence during the riots had been sorely missed, identified the "root causes" as abandonment of children, hedonism, neglect of principles, and "arrogant elitism."[9]

Peter Morrison, of the Population Research Center at RAND in Santa Monica, more broadly saw the riots as a product of "ethnic tensions over territory, which in South Central produced an accumulation of grievances against ethnically different neighbors who were accessible for reprisal." Similarly, demographer Leo Estrada observed that Latino riot participants were apt to be new immigrants who were in conflict with African Americans and Asians over jobs and living space.

Morrison's analysis encompassed both the right-wing concern that young black males lacked adult supervision and the left-wing concern that they lacked jobs. Using census and employment data, Morrison found that only 50 percent of South Central's teenage males lived with their fathers and that 42 percent of males between sixteen and thirty-four were unemployed. These jobless, fatherless young men had no workplace to report to on Thursday morning, April 30, after the initial night of rioting and no one to keep them off the streets. They could—and did—continue in daytime the lawless activity that the LAPD high command had anticipated only after dark. Morrison calculated that 50,000 males in the sixteen-to-thirty-four age group were "available" to participate in the riots. "Demographically, South Central Los Angeles was ripe for civil disturbance," he wrote. "It contained a critical mass of young males who had no regular occupation, little reason to feel bound by social rules, and the physical energy needed to stone, loot, burn, and run from the police. The jury's exoneration of the police who beat Rodney King triggered the action, but the resulting explosion of human energy lacked political focus."[10]

And that explosion of energy met little early resistance from the LAPD. Sheriff Sherman Block, who had refrained during the riots from publicly criticizing the police, afterward told the Los Angeles County Board of Supervisors that the LAPD's initial hesitation at Florence and Normandie "made no sense at all to me." Block said, "A show of force at that location at that time might not have stopped everything, but certainly would have had a significant impact." He said he had watched the events on television, expecting the LAPD to appear at any moment, and would have sent sheriff's deputies to the scene had he known that police would not respond. Block also said that LAPD officers had given an "aura of legitimacy" to looters by standing by as they ransacked stores.[11]

Block's criticism signaled that LAPD Chief Daryl Gates at last had lost his political base among middle-class white homeowners in West Los Angeles and the San Fernando Valley. Many whites, even those shocked by the King beating, were willing to tolerate some police excessiveness as the price of being safe in their homes and cars. But they had been frightened by the riots. While they might have found it difficult to put themselves in Rodney King's shoes, they had little trouble identifying with Reginald Denny. In the days after the riots, as the media reported more details about police hesitation and unpreparedness, white anger and resentment at Gates and the LAPD increased.

Black leaders sensed that Gates was on the ropes. Before the riots they had warned against aggressive preparation and expressed fears that police provocation would ignite civil disorder. After the riots they faulted Gates for the LAPD's timidity. Their cause was aided by Deputy Chief Matthew Hunt, who told the Los Angeles Times that Gates had ignored his repeated warnings about the possibility of unrest after the verdicts. Gates was furious at Hunt, whom he believed was trying to divert attention from his own hesitant leadership, but focused his criticism on the politicians and the media he claimed had inhibited the LAPD with recurrent complaints about excessive force. "I know police officers on the street [who] are scared to death to use any kind of force because they think they're going to be second-guessed," Gates told radio talk-show host Michael Jackson.

It was a bold performance. But Gates was as heartsick as anyone at the ineptitude of LAPD leadership during the early phases of the riots. He could not defend the retreat from Florence and Normandie or the lapses at the field command post. He was weary of political strife and shaken by the near death of his son from a drug overdose. What kept Gates going after the riots was his determination to defeat Charter Amendment F, the ballot measure proposed by the Christopher Commission to limit the tenure and authority of future police chiefs. Enactment would mean the end of the LAPD's precious independence from political control. Gates had left his post and risked his reputation as the riots were unfolding to speak out against Charter Amendment F. After the riots the issue for him became a dual crusade to rescue his reputation and rally public support for the LAPD. The measure was to be decided at the June 2 election, less than a month after the end of the riots.

The June 2 election was also the California presidential primary, in which President Bush faced Patrick Buchanan and the frontrunning Democrat, Bill Clinton, was opposed by former California Governor Jerry Brown. The crowded ballot included contests for two U.S. Senate seats, one a full six-year term and the other the two-year balance of the Senate term Pete Wilson had vacated in 1990 when he won the governorship. After the riots the media lost interest in these races, and candidates were able to draw attention only by commenting on the disorders. The temptation proved irresistible. Most of the candidates knew little about what had actually happened in South Central, but they could not resist exploiting the hot topic of the day.

The Bush administration at first blamed the riots on the late Lyndon Johnson, using White House press secretary Marlin Fitzwater to explain that Great Society anti-poverty programs had failed to give poor people an adequate stake in their communities. When this approach was criticized as a partisan attempt to take advantage of a tragedy, Bush changed course and took the high road. He told reporters that Fitzwater's comments had been "grossly misinterpreted" and said it was time to heal wounds rather than assign blame. The president then flew to Los Angeles for a two-day inspection of the riot area. At a disaster center he met with Javier Iniquez, a furniture painter who had been dragged from his car and beaten on the second day of the riots. Iniquez had suffered a badly broken hand and was worried about keeping his job, but Bush re-assured him. "He said I would have no problem getting what I needed and I believed him," Iniquez said.[12]

Clinton also campaigned in Los Angeles, touring South Central and Koreatown. "I am convinced if we can heal the wounds of racial division in this community, we can do it anywhere," he told Latino activists. But Clinton wanted support from white voters as well as from minorities, and he hedged his bets. Determined to be seen as a "new Democrat" who was skeptical of traditional liberal solutions, Clinton distanced himself from the Great Society programs that had been scapegoated by the White House. He said he favored a "third way," in which recovery would be achieved by "empowering" poor people through economic development.

Some Senate candidates were even less edifying than the presidential contenders. Bruce Herschensohn, a television commentator seeking the Republican nomination for the six-year Senate seat, defended the Simi Valley verdicts and decried attempts to identify an "underlying cause" of the riots. "The underlying cause for burning, looting, stealing, and murder is that some people are rotten," he said. Barbara Boxer, a liberal Democrat, followed Bush's example in blaming presidential policies—in this case, those of Bush and his predecessor, Ronald Reagan. "We finally saw the 1,000 points of light that George Bush has been talking about, but unfortunately they were the fires lit up by a decade of neglect," Boxer said. Not all Democrats agreed. Mel Levine, a wealthy Senate candidate with liberal credentials, sounded more like Herschensohn than Boxer as he tried to revive his lagging campaign with what he called a "law and order" TV spot. "It's a failure of political leadership," Levine said of the riots in the widely used commercial. "A democratic society can't tolerate mob rule."

Joyce Karlin, the judge who had spared the killer of black teenager Latasha Harlins from a prison term, was also on the June 2 ballot. Karlin's life had been an ordeal since November 1991, when she granted Soon Ja Du probation after a jury convicted the Korean grocer of voluntary manslaughter in the shooting death of Harlins. The decision had contributed to the hostile climate in South Central. And it had enraged District Attorney Ira Reiner, who denounced the "stunning miscarriage of justice" and filed an affidavit to prevent Karlin from presiding over any future criminal case.[13] Karlin was transferred to Juvenile Court, beyond reach of Reiner.

Reiner appealed the sentence Karlin had granted, arguing that she had disregarded the jury's verdict. Black activists mounted a recall campaign and picketed her home. Three candidates opposed her in the June 2 election. These combined challenges were emotionally draining and expensive, but Karlin was equal to them. She had seemed dogmatic, even arrogant, while lecturing blacks during the sentencing of Soon Ja Du but showed a plucky resolution when under political attack. While Karlin could not prevent Reiner from disqualifying her in criminal cases, she was stubbornly determined not to be driven from the bench. Demonstrators put Karlin to the test. She was cursed and harassed when she showed up at political events.

Within the legal community, Karlin's sentence was widely deplored, but many were even more alarmed by what they saw as the district attorney's political vendetta against a sitting judge. Writing in the *Los Angeles Times*, Loyola Law School professor Laurie Levenson, a former federal prosecutor and erstwhile colleague of Karlin's, said that Reiner's "blanket threat" to disqualify the judge was an effort "to intimidate and control the judiciary."[14] Members of the judges' union took the cue. Although few judges defended her sentence, many rallied around the banner of judicial independence. On April 21, 1992, eight days before the Simi Valley verdicts, Karlin's sentence was unanimously upheld by a three-judge panel of the Second District Court of Appeal written by Justice Herbert Ashby. He found that Reiner had taken Karlin's remarks "out of context" when he said she had disregarded the jury verdict.

Reading Ashby's twenty-six-page opinion, it is hard to escape the feeling that the court was eager to discredit Reiner and uphold Karlin's authority regardless of anything the judge had said in court. The jury had convicted Du of voluntary manslaughter, which under California law is an intentional killing. Karlin believed the killing was accidental (which would have made it involuntary manslaughter) and that Du had pulled the trigger only because the weapon had been altered to make it easier to fire. "I have serious questions in my mind whether this crime would have been committed at all but for the altered gun," Karlin had said. The appeals court nonetheless decided that Karlin's comment about the gun did not mean she had disregarded the jury's verdict. The court found Karlin's statement was "an isolated or ambiguous remark" that did not overcome the presumption that the trial court had acted properly. "The record does not support the district attorney's interpretation of the court's remarks," the decision said.

Any plain reading of Karlin's sentencing comments shows she believed Du did not intend to kill Harlins. Karlin's comments reiterated, sometimes dramatically, defense arguments that had been rejected by the jury and ignored much of the evidence presented by the prosecution. Had the jury seen the case through Karlin's eyes, it could not have returned a verdict of voluntary manslaughter. Certainly, Karlin herself would not have rendered such a verdict, as attorneys on both sides realized. Karlin found it difficult even to say directly that Du had committed a crime, declaring instead that Du had "participated in the crime under circumstances of great provocation, coercion, and duress."

Was Harlins also a participant? It would be reasonable to conclude that Karlin believed so, based on her unsupported assertion that Harlins would have been investigated on assault charges if Du had not killed her. The worst Karlin could bring herself to say about Du's crime—the intentional killing of a minor with a shot to the back of the head—was that it was "inappropriate." Du had been in "real terror" when she fired. She had been dazed from blows to the face. Karlin saw no evidence that Du "consciously" decided to fire the gun. She ignored Du's lie to police that Harlins had been trying to rob the cash register and information in the probation report about Du's bias against blacks. Reiner certainly had not quoted the judge out of context. Karlin's remarks were "isolated or ambiguous" only to an appeals court bent on upholding judicial sentencing discretion at nearly any cost.

And a case can be made that there *is* a cost to unlimited judicial discretion. The growing movement in the late 1980s and early 1990s for mandatory minimum sentences was fueled by public perception that judges were often too lenient. This perception contributed in 1994 to passage by California voters of a far-reaching "three-strikes" amendment to the state constitution, requiring sentences of twenty-five years to life for a third felony conviction even when the crime was not violent. This initiative was decried by many judges and its scope subsequently limited by the California Supreme Court.[15] Even so, the three-strikes initiative sent a message that the public wanted judges to show more concern for victims and their families and less for criminals. In *People v. Soon Ja Du,* first Judge Karlin and then Justice Ashby and his colleagues had almost entirely ignored Harlins and her family—along with the jury that had convicted her killer. The decision offended African Americans, who knew that black people who are convicted of intentional killings do prison time, and ratified the cynicism of those who believe that justice is rarely color-blind. Justice Ashby's ruling was a milepost on the journey to three strikes.

To Karlin, however, Ashby's decision was a vindication.[16] Buoyed by the victory, she plunged into her election campaign. The riots had heightened public awareness of the Latasha Harlins case, and Karlin might have been vulnerable against a well-qualified and well-funded opponent. Instead, she faced three poorly financed and inexperienced candidates who split the anti-Karlin vote. Karlin squeaked through with 50.7 percent of the vote in the June 2 election, avoiding a runoff. She was helped by low turnout in black neighborhoods still reeling from the riots. A month later Karlin won another victory when Compton Councilwoman Patricia Moore announced she was 50,000 signatures short of the 304,000 names needed to qualify a recall for the November ballot.* Karlin still faced intermittent picketing, but the collapse of the recall campaign ended attempts to remove her from the bench.

Bush and Clinton also won their primaries, although in Bush's case the results were deceptive. California's economy was mired in recession, and the president's once commanding lead over Clinton was shrinking. Bush's approval rating dropped with particular rapidity after the riots, which polls suggested had reinforced the dissatisfaction of Californians with political leaders. The voters did not respond to the attempt to blame the riots on the permissive policies of past presidents or to Levine's effort to revive his expensive Senate campaign by recasting himself as the "law and order" candidate. Barbara Boxer won the primary, while Levine finished a distant third. Herschensohn narrowly won the Republican nomination.

The election transformed the political landscape of Los Angeles. District Attorney Reiner struggled into a runoff behind former deputy Gil Garcetti after a campaign in which opponents blamed him for the failed prosecution of the LAPD police officers in Simi Valley. Reiner, an astute politician, realized he had no chance of winning in November and took the unusual step of withdrawing from the runoff. Garcetti was elected without a contest.

Mayor Bradley, whose term would expire in 1993, had also lost the confidence of Los Angeles. While the riots were still raging, the *Daily News* published a front-page article quoting politicians and community leaders who faulted Bradley's leadership and indirectly blamed him for the riots. "I think you're going to see this is the downfall of Mayor Bradley," predicted Richard Close, president of the Sherman Oaks Homeowners Association. Bradley reached a similar conclusion. He kept his decision to himself until

* On October 4, 1996, during the federal extortion trial of Moore, a secretly taped conversation of Moore with an FBI operative quoted her as saying about the recall: "I hope we recall [Karlin]. But that's not my goal. My goal is to keep the issue alive until the election." Latasha Harlins' aunt, Denise, described the revelation as "sickening." Moore was convicted on October 9 on thirteen counts of extorting money from firms doing business with the city of Compton.

September 24, then announced he would not seek a sixth term. "The time for change has come," Bradley said.

Daryl Gates was not on the June 1992 ballot either, but he lost the referendum on his leadership provided by Charter Amendment F, the measure that limited future police chiefs to two five-year terms and made it easier to discipline officers for misconduct. The initiative was the brainchild of Warren Christopher, who was uncertain of its prospects despite the impetus for reform provided by the Rodney King case and the Christopher Commission inquiry. Reformers had been trying since Chief Parker's heyday to put a leash on the LAPD but had never been able to surmount the opposition of the chiefs. After the riots, however, Charter Amendment F became less an abstract political science question about civilian control of the LAPD and more a concrete issue of public confidence in Gates. Charter Amendment F won by 2–1, with a majority in every section of the city and among all races and ethnic groups. An exultant John Mack, president of the Los Angeles chapter of the Urban League, said: "It sends out the message to officers on the street that says, 'Hey, this is a new day, you can't brutalize people, anymore.'"[17]

The vote also sent a blunt message of farewell to Gates. Two weeks before the riots, the Police Commission had selected Philadelphia Police Commissioner Willie L. Williams as the chief's successor. Commission President Stanley Sheinbaum announced the choice, anticipating that Gates would retire and Williams would take over near the end of June. Gates, however, declined to set a specific retirement date, and passage of Charter Amendment F gave him an opportunity for mischief making. Since the measure changed the legal procedures for selecting a police chief, it would have nullified the selection of Williams unless he became chief before the election results were certified. The prospect that the Police Commission might have to start from scratch alarmed Christopher, who accused Gates of game-playing and "arrogance."

While Gates enjoyed discomforting Christopher and Sheinbaum, he had no real intention of blocking Williams on a technicality. On June 25, Gates delivered a videotaped message to LAPD officers at roll call, cheerfully acknowledging that Williams would be a public-relations improvement for the department. "I suppose that the politicians probably get a little tired when I tell them, 'Screw them all'," Gates said. "Those are comments that I'm sure you will not hear from Chief Williams, and that's good." Gates cleaned out his office and retired on June 26. Williams was sworn in the same day at a private ceremony before the election results were certified.

THE SELECTION OF THE NEW POLICE CHIEF HAD BEEN GUIDED BY Sheinbaum, a political activist and civil libertarian whom Bradley named to

the Police Commission soon after the Rodney King incident in 1991.
His appointment was lauded by the American Civil Liberties Union, of
which Sheinbaum was a prominent member, and by liberals in general.
Mark Ridley-Thomas, then running for the city council from South Central, called Sheinbaum "one more nail in Daryl Gates' career coffin."

But Sheinbaum was no knee-jerk liberal. He was seventy at the time of
his appointment, and his age, wealth, and capacity for bold thinking freed
him from dependence on Bradley or anyone else. Sheinbaum had become estranged from the Jewish community during the Carter years by daring to
take the "premature" action of meeting Palestinian leader Yasir Arafat to explore the beginning steps of a Middle East peace process.[18] Although Gates
never realized it, Sheinbaum also did his own thinking about the LAPD.
He had studied police cultures, empathized with officers on the street, and
was strongly committed to substantial expansion of the undermanned police department.

Sheinbaum deplored the feuding between Gates and Bradley. He wanted
a police chief who would cooperate with the city's elected officials rather
than use them as a foil. This goal of finding a cooperative chief, while never
loudly enunciated, was built into the search for Gates' successor. The first
step in the process was a review of the thirty-two applications for the chief's
job by a citizens committee whose members were well aware of the damage
done by the Gates-Bradley conflict. The committee winnowed the list to
twelve applicants, then interviewed and graded them. Williams, with a mark
of ninety-eight, had the highest score. He finished just ahead of LAPD
Deputy Chief Bernard Parks, also an African American, who had a ninety-
seven. The Police Commission then chose from a list of six: the top five
LAPD candidates and Williams.

The LAPD had been managed by an insider since Bill Parker took over
in 1950, and police commissioners believed the department needed a breath
of outside air. This gave Williams an advantage among the finalists. Sheinbaum sent Commissioners Jesse Brewer and Anne Reiss Lane to Philadelphia to find out more about him, and they brought back glowing reports
about Williams' success in fostering inter-racial harmony in a city as divided as Los Angeles. Williams became the unanimous choice of the police
commissioners. His appointment was hailed by Mayor Bradley and black
community leaders, perhaps mostly because Williams seemed to be the polar
opposite of Gates.

Willie Luther Williams, a hulking son of a meat cutter, was forty-eight
years old and had spent twenty-nine years in the Philadelphia Police
Department at the time he became LAPD chief. He had begun as a park
guard, worked a foot beat, and risen through the ranks to the top job of commissioner in a department that was investigated for brutality by the Justice

Department in the 1970s and rocked by narcotics scandals in the 1980s. To many the department was epitomized by Frank Rizzo, the bombastic former police commissioner and mayor who had died of a heart attack during a last-hurrah campaign in 1991. Older Philadelphia cops remembered Rizzo's reign with fondness and resented the gentler, kinder approach to police work that Williams favored when he became commissioner in 1988. Their suspicions were ratified when Williams expanded community policing, fired nineteen officers for brutality, and transferred one hundred others who were accused of misconduct. Mayor Edward Rendell said that Los Angeles and the LAPD were "very lucky" to get Williams, but the police union was glad to see him go. Whether he had made fundamental changes in the department, however, was in dispute. Stefan Presser, director of the area chapter of the American Civil Liberties Union, said Williams' heart is "clearly in the right place" but contended that changes had been mostly cosmetic. "I am pessimistic that he will be able to enforce his will on the L.A. department because he never really got a handle on it here in Philadelphia, despite his good intentions," Presser said.[19]

Williams also faced skepticism from old-guard officers on the LAPD and greater fiscal obstacles than any chief in Philadelphia. Los Angeles was financially pressed and frugal (or "cheap," as Gates had put it), and the percentage of the city budget devoted to the police department had been declining for many years. In 1978, the year Gates became chief and California voters approved the tax-limiting Proposition 13, Los Angeles spent 20 percent of the city budget on the LAPD. By the time Williams became chief, Los Angeles was spending 14 percent of its budget on police. It had fewer than 8,000 police officers—only 1,400 more than Philadelphia to serve a city three times the geographic size and with twice the population.

Since the city's earliest days, politicians had prided themselves on having a police department that did more with less than its eastern counterparts. Traditionally the LAPD made up for a shortage of personnel with modern equipment and advanced technology, especially communications systems. But the technological edge that was a significant element of the *Dragnet* legacy was long gone by 1992. Many LAPD patrol cars were in sorry condition and had been driven far too long; officers sometimes drove them until the axles literally fell off. The outmoded communications system, which became overloaded to the point of breakdown during the riots, was in even worse shape. And even when cars and radios worked properly, the LAPD had so few officers that it sent patrol cars only to the most serious emergencies. This triage was a shock to Williams, who came from a city where police responded to every emergency call.

When the new chief was inaugurated in a televised public ceremony at the Police Academy, Mayor Bradley hurled the fiscal condition of Los

Angeles in his face. Williams spoke passionately, promising that he would heal the city's wounds and refuse to tolerate racism, sexism, or excessive force by police officers. He said he would add officers and expand community policing, enabling citizens to "reclaim their streets and [their] neighborhoods." But Bradley followed the new chief to the podium and bluntly warned that there was no money in the treasury for expanding anything. "Don't come soon to ask for money," Bradley said. "It simply isn't there."

This was too much for Sheinbaum, who was presiding. When Bradley had finished speaking, Sheinbaum boldly contradicted him. "I will tell you that the money is there," he said. "It just takes the intelligence and the wisdom of the people in government to get it for us."

One solution was to ask the people for help. Sheinbaum joined with Warren Christopher in campaigning for two measures on the November ballot that would have slightly raised property taxes to finance a new police emergency-communications system and add 1,000 officers. Williams, basking in the honeymoon glow of media approval, threw himself into the campaign. His most telling argument was that community policing required substantial expansion of the LAPD.

The outcome in November demonstrated both the willingness of voters to help the LAPD and the effectiveness of Proposition 13's constraints on majority rule. Proposition M, the measure providing for the communications system, passed with 75 percent of the vote. But Proposition N to add 1,000 police officers received 63 percent of the vote—just short of the two-thirds margin required by Proposition 13 for a tax increase. African Americans were the only constituency to give Proposition N a two-thirds majority. Wealthy white property owners with private security gave Proposition N the least support, but even they gave it a majority.

IN THE MONTHS AFTER THE RIOTS, WILLIE WILLIAMS SHARED THE spotlight with Peter Ueberroth. Williams faced the challenge of trying to restore public confidence in the LAPD; Ueberroth had the even more daunting task of persuading private companies to reinvest in shattered South Central. On May 2, as troops and police began to regain control of the riot area, Mayor Bradley named Ueberroth to head a non-profit task force called Rebuild L.A. and later RLA, as in "our L.A." At a City Hall news conference where he was flanked by Bradley and Governor Wilson, Ueberroth said he would make South Central a better place than it was before the riots.

Peter Victor Ueberroth was the first and only choice of his old ally, Bradley, to head the rebuilding effort. Ueberroth had been the millionaire owner of the nation's second largest travel firm but publicly unknown in 1979 when Bradley tapped him to direct the Los Angeles Olympic Organizing

Committee. He sold his firm and performed spectacularly in the drive to obtain the 1984 Olympic Games and persuade corporate sponsors to invest in them. The games, which were boycotted by the Soviet Union, returned a $222 million profit and fueled an outpouring of patriotism. *Time* named Ueberroth man of the year in 1984 and major league owners prevailed on him to become the commissioner of baseball.

Ueberroth's high-visibility success made him an attractive political prospect in celebrity-conscious Southern California, where it was widely believed he would someday seek the governorship, probably as a Republican. But Ueberroth never ran. He did not fit neatly into a partisan or ideological pigeonhole, and he had an entrepreneur's impatience with the compromises and insincerity of politics. According to biographer Kenneth Reich, "Ueberroth always insisted on being in control, and politics struck him as essentially uncontrollable."[20] The reconstruction effort was not controllable either, but Ueberroth seemed dazzlingly self-confident. Few doubted his capability or commitment to Los Angeles, even though he lived and worked in Orange County. "Mr. Goodwrench is back on the scene," declared Robert Scheer in the *Los Angeles Times,* summarizing the prevailing reaction to Ueberroth's agreement to head the rebuilding effort.[21] Ueberroth had a reputation as a miracle worker, and miracles were needed in Los Angeles.

Behind the facade of self-confidence, Mr. Goodwrench was a moody and persistent striver. Born in Evanston, Illinois, in 1937, he was the second of three children. His mother died when he was five, and his father, an alcoholic and an itinerant building-products salesman, moved so often that his middle child attended six elementary schools and three high schools. Ueberroth worked his way through San Jose State College as a business major, holding various jobs, including recreation director at a center for children from broken homes. He loved contact sports, which he played with such abandon that his nose was broken several times. Good enough in water polo to win a partial athletic scholarship, he tried out in 1956 for the U.S. Olympic team. Ueberroth didn't make the team but the experience stayed with him. Years later he approvingly quoted the exhortation of a team manager, who asked each athlete: "Are you going to spectate or participate?"[22]

Ueberroth himself was a vigorous participant. He detested "do-nothing critics" who stood on the sidelines, a category in which he put most of the media.[23] Reich, a senior reporter at the *Los Angeles Times* who became close to Ueberroth, believes he exhibited traits, especially the desire to be in control, often associated with children of alcoholics.[24] "He is engaging and impossible," Reich said. "He can be very moody, and he has a tremendous desire for secrecy in financial dealings. He is manipulative and tries as almost an intentional tactic to keep people off balance. He makes things up. He is like a de Gaulle or a MacArthur in that things have to be done his way or not at all. But Ueberroth also has a deep sense of obligation. He abhors racial prejudice. He is an idealist who believes in helping others. The mayor asked him to take charge of the rebuilding, and he felt it was his duty to do it."[25]

Ueberroth's idealism was demonstrated by his premise that corporate America had an obligation to rebuild the shattered inner city of Los Angeles. Although his principal trust was in the marketplace, he welcomed and valued the participation of government. Indeed, RLA adopted as its logo a futuristic "city blossom" drawn by the artist Sammy Loh with three rings representing "the community, the government, and the private sector." In the heady days after the riots much was expected from each of these elements. On May 5, Ueberroth held a news conference near the riot area and said that the answering machine on his home telephone had recorded 120 offers of assistance before it stopped working. He called upon corporations to make long-term investments in inner-city neighborhoods, creating "sustainable jobs on a profitable basis."

To accomplish this far-reaching goal, Ueberroth enlisted powerful movers and shakers. The board of RLA was decorated with the names of Hollywood moguls, prominent politicians and executives from such important corporations as Atlantic Richfield, Southern California Edison, IBM, Bank of America, Hughes Aircraft, and Kaiser Permanente. When community groups protested that they were under-represented, Ueberroth expanded the RLA board, then expanded it again so that it more closely reflected the racial and ethnic diversity of Los Angeles. The sixty-seven-member panel included twenty-seven Anglos, sixteen African Americans, sixteen Latinos, and eight Asian Americans. Bernard Kinsey, an African American and former high-ranking Xerox executive, was named operations officer. "I see this opportunity as a vehicle to satisfy my dreams," Kinsey said with an optimism equal to Ueberroth's. "I have a passion for doing things for people based on the American dream."

No week went by in the months after the riots that some corporation did not announce a financial commitment to RLA: $35 million from Southern California Edison "to help rebuild and re-energize the greater Los Angeles area," $5 million from Nissan for economic development in South Central, $100 million from the Vons Companies to build new supermarkets in the inner city, $18 million from General Motors and Hughes Aircraft for a joint redevelopment venture, $10 million from Shell Oil. Ueberroth met with the RLA board on July 28, twelve weeks after the riots, and announced that corporations had pledged $500 million in investment to create 10,000 jobs over a two-year period. This was supposed to be only the beginning. Robert Taylor, a management consultant employed by RLA, told the board that $6 billion was needed to revitalize the poorer neighborhoods of Los Angeles and create at least 75,000 jobs.

Tom Bradley, disconsolate in the aftermath of the riots, was heartened by the promised investment. "There's enough power in this room to lift this building off the foundation," Bradley said at the RLA board meeting. "And that's what we need to do." During two decades as mayor he had encouraged corporate development of downtown Los Angeles and presided over its transformation from a backward, low-rise commercial district into a gleaming complex of modern skyscrapers. The hope that corporate investment could also transform South Central inspired the tired mayor into a final burst of enthusiasm for his dream city. He gave Ueberroth and RLA free rein to manage a rebuilding effort that in most cities would have been run by government.

In fact, Bradley had missed his main chance to rebuild South Central long before the riots. Community activists such as Karen Bass argued that corporate investors might have been enticed into South Central as a condition of participating in the downtown revitalization, which had been highly profitable. By 1992, the opportunity for such economic linkage was long gone, and Bradley was left to contend that corporations had a social duty to rebuild South Central.

This argument was made with force by Ueberroth. Speaking to the national convention of the Urban League in San Diego on the same day as the RLA board meeting, he honestly confronted one of the fundamental reasons that South Central had been so ripe for rebellion. "For forty years, corporate America, and I'm part of that, has moved every decent job out of the inner city," Ueberroth said. "I had three hundred offices and not one was in the inner city." Ueberroth had taken enough hard knocks to know that life was different in these inner cities than it was outside them. "I live in Laguna Beach, a mostly white area, but I know that the people of South Central must have a chance to have jobs, hope, to pay fair prices for food, everything the suburbs have but that the inner city does not have," he said.

But economic reality undermined Ueberroth's idealism and dashed the dream he shared with Bradley. The end of the Cold War had sent the aerospace industry into a tailspin, plunging the economy into a crash and shattering the myth that California was recession proof. Los Angeles County bore the brunt of the state's worst downturn since the Depression, losing more than 200,000 jobs in 1991 and another 100,000 in 1992. By mid-1993, the official unemployment rate in Los Angeles County had reached nearly 10 percent. It was 15 percent in South Central, where corporations had closed factories even in boom times, and more like 40 percent for black teenagers and young adults. The notion that private industry could create 75,000 jobs in the city's poorest neighborhoods with the economy in free fall was fantasy.

Ueberroth, of all people, should have recognized the problem. He had just headed a commission on competitiveness for Governor Wilson that had finished its work shortly before the riots. "The state of California has developed the most highly tuned, finely honed job-killing machine that the country has ever seen," Ueberroth said in submitting the report. The RLA attempt to spur investment in South Central coincided with a business flight from Southern California—and a flight of well-paid, middle-class professionals—that was spurred by declining profits, high taxes, and extensive regulations. The exodus from South Central was particularly acute. Middle-class blacks had been leaving Los Angeles for a decade, seeking the amenities of home ownership and better schools in the distant suburbs of San Bernardino and Riverside Counties known as the Inland Empire. The riots had accelerated their departure.

As chairman of RLA, Ueberroth ignored facts he had embraced in directing the competitiveness inquiry. In his new role he claimed that "negative thinking" was the principal barrier to corporate investment. When General Motors and Hughes Aircraft executives appeared with Ueberroth in July to announce their joint venture to "revitalize" Los Angeles, a skeptical reporter wondered how the corporations could invest $18 million in the inner city while GM was closing factories and Hughes laying off thousands of workers in California. Ueberroth was outraged. He would have ended the news conference on the spot except for the intervention of Hughes Chairman C. Michael Armstrong, who acknowledged the legitimacy of the question and tried to answer it. "I was wrong; the reporter was right," Ueberroth later acknowledged.[26] But he was bothered that the media kept noticing the gaps between RLA's promises and achievements. "I think Los Angeles should take offense at how we are being portrayed around the world," he told the RLA board.[27]

While RLA focused on the big picture, activists in the African-American, Latino, and Korean communities struggled for small breakthroughs. Danny Bakewell, a black real estate developer and head of a community group known as the Brotherhood Crusade, passed a construction site soon after the riots and noticed that hardly any of the workers were African American. Bakewell launched a picketing campaign aimed at obtaining a larger share of construction jobs for blacks. The Brotherhood Crusade also donated $500,000 to finance the opening of "Mom and Pop's Community Convenience Store" in the heart of South Central. "What we're trying to do is give people an example of how things could and should be in our community," said Bakewell, who was also a member of the RLA board. "This is an experiment based on the premise that all of the outside assistance in the world won't really make much of a difference unless we [black people] help ourselves."[28]

Bakewell's activities were resented by Latino and Korean activists, who also believed they were being short-changed on jobs and opportunities. Tensions between blacks and newly arrived immigrants in transitional neighborhoods in South Central and Pico-Union were exacerbated after the riots because jobs were scarcer. Latinos, vastly under-represented on local and state government bodies because so few of them voted, were particularly powerless. The Union of Latino and Affiliated Merchants complained they had received no help in rebuilding stores that had been burned or looted. "I lost eight years of work in one day," said Juan Zamora, an El Salvadoran shoe salesman, whose store was sacked in the riots.[29] A more militant group known as the Southern California Organizing Committee marched on the offices of Councilman Mark Ridley-Thomas, accusing him of favoring blacks over Latinos.

Ridley-Thomas represented the Eighth Council District, the city's poorest, and had been a member of the council for less than a year at the time of the riots. He had served capably for a decade as executive director of the Southern Christian Leadership Conference of Greater Los Angeles, and saw himself as a grass-roots politician committed to "self-empowerment." One of his first actions as a council member had been to open a constituent services center to provide "instant access" to city departments for residents of his far-flung district. But the center burned to the ground during the riots.

Ridley-Thomas was a member of the RLA board and was even more doubtful than Bakewell about its prospects for success. Dismissing Ueberroth's endeavors as a "dog and pony show," Ridley-Thomas argued that corporations could be encouraged to invest in South Central not out of do-goodism but because there was money to be made in selling goods and services to poor people, especially if government provided services with tax incentives and low-cost loans. Ridley-Thomas aggressively promoted business opportunities in South Central with little support on the council except from Rita Walters, also an African American whose constituents were poor.

On the whole, however, black officeholders were far from united. Instead of pooling their resources after the riots, black politicians blamed one another for lack of leadership and competed to take credit for even the most marginal rebuilding. Leading the competition was Congresswoman Maxine Waters, who favored a "Marshall Plan" to rebuild South Central as Europe had been rebuilt after World War II. Waters started her own community development organization to compete with Ridley-Thomas. She was condescending to Bradley, telling Robert Scheer that blacks had supported him only because of their pride in having "this first black mayor. And the white liberal community kind of romanticized this tall, black, modest, non-threatening black man because they felt comfortable and safe. Until they had a rebellion, and then they thought he didn't do what he was supposed to do. He didn't keep them quiet."[30] Bradley, Ridley-Thomas and Walters responded in a letter to the Los Angeles Times accusing Waters of "self-serving cynicism" and of doing little to help blacks during fourteen years in the state legislature and two in the House.

The lack of black unity made it easier for white city council members and members of Congress to sidetrack aid proposals meant for South Central. Meanwhile, an effort in Sacramento to provide a "fast track" that would lift regulatory barriers to development in the riot area foundered on conflicts between black and Latino legislators. "Even after this incredible unrest, people were unable to come together," said Deputy Mayor Mark Fabiani. "The old thinking still existed and wasn't cast aside."

The "old thinking" emerged in a fierce struggle over the rebuilding of riot-destroyed liquor stores, a conflict that widened resentments between blacks and Korean Americans. Liquor stores were a fixture on nearly every block of South Central, which had seventeen liquor licenses per square mile. The ratio in the rest of Los Angeles was one liquor license in every 1.6 square miles. Medical researchers at the University of Southern California correlated the presence of liquor stores with violent crime, and community activists had been trying for a decade and a half before the riots to reduce the heavy concentration. They had no success in the state legislature, where the liquor lobby was strong, but in 1984 persuaded the city council to impose conditions on new licenses.

While the ordinance did not reduce the total number of liquor licenses in South Central, it made ownership less desirable and triggered a flood of sales by African Americans, many of whom felt pressure from the community. They found willing buyers in Korean realtors, who enticed Korean merchants into business. Most of the new store owners had limited capital and less knowledge of South Central. These Korean-owned stores became flash points of conflict and cultural misunderstanding, most tragically in the killing of Latasha Harlins. But the liquor stores would have been political targets no matter who owned them because they were symbols of destruction in the African-American community.

A 1990 conference on crack cocaine at the University of Southern California spurred formation of a new organization, the Community Coalition for Substance Abuse Prevention and Treatment, with a predominantly older middle-class black membership. The Coalition's director and moving force was Karen Bass, a lifelong resident of South Central and a physician assistant at the USC Medical School. Bass, an African American who was thirty-nine years old at the time of the riots, was a self-styled "'60s kid" with a long record of community involvement. Convinced that crack posed a particular danger to African Americans because it had rooted itself in the economy of the community, Bass dropped other activities and devoted her energies exclusively to the Coalition. This work soon led her to the liquor stores. Recovering addicts told Bass that the worst of the stores surreptitiously sold crack pipes and other drug paraphernalia.

Even the liquor stores that did not were often a dangerous nuisance. Many were congregating places for alcoholics who drank the cheap wine widely sold throughout South Central. Because there were so many stores, competition was cutthroat and owners were often lax in enforcing laws that prohibit selling liquor to minors or persons who are obviously intoxicated. "The merchants knew the kids could just go down the street and buy booze if they didn't sell it to them," Bass said. The Coalition decided it would try to shut down what Bass called the "bad stores."

But when half the "bad stores" were destroyed in the riots, the Coalition changed its focus—to a campaign against rebuilding them. Coalition organizers quickly obtained 34,000 signatures on petitions that were turned over to Mayor Bradley. The city council adopted an amendment offered by Rita Walters that exempted liquor stores from the streamlined rebuilding procedures allowed other businesses. Liquor-store owners were required to improve security and sanitation and forced through an expensive process that included review by the Planning Commission and other boards. The store owners were opposed at hearings by Coalition witnesses and often by Ridley-Thomas and Walters. The Coalition also formed what Bass called "a tactical alliance" with station captains and Vice Squad officers in South Central. "The LAPD was institutionally hopeless, but officers who had to deal with the problems were concerned about the impact of the liquor stores on crime," Bass said. "They didn't want the stores reopened."

Korean merchants were outraged. They described the liquor stores, which often offered a few high-priced grocery items and junk food, as "convenience markets" and thought that the campaign to prevent them from reopening added insult to injury. Koreans had suffered nearly as much economic damage in the riots as everyone else combined, an estimated $400 million of a total $800 million to $900 million in property losses, including $40 million in stores with liquor licenses. Most of the losses were under-insured or not insured at all. By one assessment, 1,867 of 3,100 businesses destroyed or looted in the riots were Korean owned; another calculation used a figure of 2,000.[31] Of slightly more than 200 liquor stores that the Coalition sought to prevent from reopening, 175 were operated by Koreans.

After the riots, Koreans pleaded in vain for reparations. They picketed City Hall and beat drums to draw attention to their cause. On July 7, on the seventeenth day of picketing, Koreans were pelted with ink bottles, thumbtacks, and other office supplies hurled from City Hall windows. The incident violated Bradley's sense of decency. From the steps of City Hall the

mayor apologized for the violence, saying that, "We are proud of our tradi-
tions that permit people to express their point of view." But Bradley would
not meet with the Koreans. He told reporters that the city couldn't single
out any group for help—as if Korean property had not been singled out for
attack in the riots.[32]

With the assistance of the liquor lobby, the Koreans for a time did better in Sacramento. They stopped legislation by Assemblywoman Marguerite
Archie-Hudson, an African American from South Central, that would have
invalidated liquor licenses for riot-destroyed stores in high-crime neighborhoods. But it was a rare and partial victory. When an Orange County assemblyman submitted a bill backed by the liquor lobby to prevent local
governments from regulating liquor licenses, Los Angeles legislators blocked
it. Eventually the legislature passed and Governor Wilson signed a bill by
Assemblyman Louis Caldera, a rising Latino politician, that restricted liquor
licenses in high-crime areas.

The Koreans fared even worse in the courts, where they fought the city's
restrictions on the rebuilding of liquor stores. The Los Angeles ordinance
was upheld by lower courts and eventually by the California Supreme Court
in a decision that was a bitter blow to merchants such as Sung Ho Joo,
whose liquor store had been burned to the ground on the first night of the
riots. "Where is justice?" Joo said after the ruling. "This is like a second
riot—this time in the hands of the highest judges in the state."[33] The frustration of Korean Americans cannot be overstated. They felt abandoned, by
the police during the riots and by the politicians and judges afterward.
Along with blacks who mourned Latasha Harlins, Koreans believed there
was no justice for them in Los Angeles.

But what happened to owners of liquor stores in South Central after
the riots concerned politics and economics as much as justice. Community
organizations had opposed the liquor stores when they were black owned
in the 1980s; the Coalition's aversion to rebuilding them was based on
the impact of the stores, not on the ethnicity of the owners. Bass and others saw the riots as an opportunity to prevent stores from being rebuilt
that never should have been allowed into South Central in the first place.
They were assisted by the stark economic realities of the post-riot period.
Many uninsured owners would have lacked financing to rebuild even if
there had been no campaign against them. Others were prevented from rebuilding by landowners, frequently white, who decided they no longer
wanted liquor stores on their property. The potent combination of riots,
economics, city regulations, and political activism achieved the Coalition
goal of severely reducing the number of liquor stores in South Central.
More than three years after the riots, permits for rebuilding had been
granted to owners of 55 of the 200 liquor stores, and only 40 had been

rebuilt. Bass was especially pleased that 31 of the former liquor stores had reopened as other businesses.[34]

Meanwhile, relations between blacks and Koreans, never very good, were in shambles. Six years before the riots, well-intentioned African Americans and Koreans had formed a Black-Korean Alliance to ease racial and cultural conflicts. Although the Alliance lacked broad support, it had played a calming role after the Harlins incident in March 1991 and again that summer, after another black was shot by a Korean grocer and Korean stores were boycotted. But the Alliance was too fragile to withstand the strain of the riots and the battle over the liquor stores. As a prominent black member put it, the Black-Korean Alliance became "a group talking about dialogue in an era where the two sides are polarized."[35] The Alliance disbanded in November 1992, leaving Los Angeles without a forum to mediate its most troubling racial and cultural conflict.

What was also lost in South Central were many of the small stores that had been a mainstay of the economy. Bradley and Ueberroth wanted dramatic successes on the model of the downtown revitalization. They lost sight of the bootstrap realities of South Central and its mundane need for storefront replacement. Ueberroth's admirable goal of "long-term" solutions that would make South Central a showcase conflicted with the less dramatic but more achievable objective of enticing small stores to return. South Central had long been lacking in large-scale manufacturing; most of the jobs lost in the riots were in small retail enterprises that urgently needed capital, security, low-cost loans, and encouragement to rebuild.

Ueberroth, for all his dedication and acumen, seemed not to understand this. He moved for a time from his home in Laguna Hills to a hotel room in the downtown Westin Bonaventure and worked long hours jawboning executives of major corporations he hoped to entice to South Central. But in this hotel he was as effectively sealed off from the people he was trying to help as he would have been if he had stayed in Orange County. As summer turned into fall, Ueberroth talked more and more of his personal "sacrifices" and became testy when reporters asked for evidence of corporate interest in South Central.

In October, Ueberroth went before the RLA board, by then up to eighty members, and distributed a report that said sixty-eight corporations "were in the process of determining their first commitments" to the rebuilding effort. *Los Angeles Times* reporters Nancy Rivera Brooks and Henry Weinstein called executives from the listed companies to determine the extent of their commitments. The result of their inquiry was published in the *Times* on November 18, inflicting damage from which Ueberroth never recovered. The reporters found that nineteen of the firms had no plans whatsoever to invest in Los Angeles and that many of the other companies were engaged in preliminary discussions and had made no commitments. Only seven of the sixty-eight companies on Ueberroth's list had Los Angeles projects in the works.

When informed that nineteen corporations on his list had no plans for investment in Los Angeles, Ueberroth insisted that the reporters had talked to the wrong people or that the companies were concealing their plans for business reasons. The reporters reinterviewed company executives, who repeated their earlier assertions. Ueberroth continued to deny reality. It may have been, as Ken Reich believed, that he often wasn't truthful with the media, but it is more likely that Ueberroth so truly wanted to be Mr. Goodwrench that he romanticized the corporate interest in the rebuilding on the basis of casual expressions of support. On balance, Ueberroth deceived the public less than he deceived himself.

If Ueberroth had spent less time in the Westin, talking to corporate executives, and more time in Watts, he might have realized the extent of the obstacles faced by RLA in trying to encourage massive corporate investment in crime-ridden neighborhoods that lack skilled laborers. Long after Ueberroth was gone, Felicia Bragg would observe that much of Watts had not been rebuilt "after the 1965 insurrection, let alone the last one." Bragg had grown up in Watts, where her mother still lived. "Recovery has been largely forgotten," she said two years after the 1992 riots. "It is a charade."[36]

Bragg believed, however, that there was long-term economic potential in South Central, which had railroad transportation and abandoned manufacturing sites. She shared the Ridley-Thomas view that corporate investors could be enticed to the area not out of high-mindedness but because there was money to be made. In this belief, African-American community activists were more realistic than Ueberroth. And their belief had particular resonance during the midst of a recession when falling profits squeezed corporate discretionary spending. It is no accident that the outside businesses that returned most readily to South Central were those that stood to make a profit, notably supermarkets and gas stations.

What is remarkable in retrospect is not that Ueberroth failed to accomplish his objectives but that he was surprised by the outcome. "There are virtually no examples of success in restoring strong economic activity and job creation to an inner-city area the size of South Central Los Angeles," observed the Urban Institute.[37] On balance, and largely because of Ueberroth, corporations did more to reinvest in South Central than they had done in eastern cities after the riots of the 1960s. As Johnnie Cochran Jr., an RLA board member who would later achieve national fame as O. J. Simpson's lead defense attorney, observed in 1993: "It took them twenty-five years to get a grocery store into Newark after the riots."[38] RLA promoted perhaps $500 million of development in the riot area, but far short of the $6 billion that Ue-berroth had estimated was needed, but more than most people realized.

Government did worse, as Ueberroth often pointed out. Ridley-Thomas chaired a city council committee that conducted twenty-five hearings on the rebuilding of South Central, but the city had no money to help burned-out businesses and its procedures did little to encourage investment. Despite passage of an emergency ordinance that was supposed to speed the granting of building permits, small merchants complained of persistent, bureaucratic obstacles.

At least the city was sympathetic. Nothing except gridlock came from a spate of election-year promises in Washington and Sacramento, where the executive branches were controlled by Republicans and the legislative branches by Democrats. Few Republicans and not many Democrats outside the Congressional Black Caucus were interested in spending money in the cities in the manner of the Great Society, let alone in grandiose knockoffs of the Marshall Plan promoted by liberals like Maxine Waters and Jesse Jackson. Conservative solutions were also of little benefit. "Enterprise zones" giving tax breaks to businesses for locating in the inner city had existed in Los Angeles for four years before the riots. But only 837 jobs had been cre-ated in these zones by 1993, the majority by companies that had already been operating in the inner city.

The euphoria of the late spring and early summer of 1992 faded quickly, and with it the expectation that a better city would arise from the ashes of burned-out South Central. Defeat of Proposition N dashed hopes for a bet-ter, bigger LAPD in which community policing would be the order of the day. The Crips and the Bloods, the two principal African-American gangs, declared a truce after the riots that for a time reduced gang warfare, but ran-dom violence continued on the streets. Within the LAPD's South Bureau, which covers much of South Central, police were pleased that drive-by shoot-ings declined by nearly 50 percent after the truce. Even so, there were eighty-five such shootings in South Bureau in the six weeks after the truce. Lamoun Thames, fifteen, who lived in South Central, was stabbed to death while wait-ing for a bus in Woodland Hills when youths mistook him for a rival gang member. Random violence against civilians increased. Kimberly Horton, twenty-one, a UCLA student, was shot to death because someone wanted her Honda. Anita Robertson, thirty, was shot to death in front of her children after a robber stuck his head in her van and demanded her purse. These vic-tims, as well as their suspected assailants, were all African Americans.

The anguish of Los Angeles was reflected in the hit movie *Falling Down*, in which Michael Douglas plays an aerospace worker who loses his job and embarks on a hate-filled odyssey across the city. The Douglas character is a California Everyman who becomes a violent urban vigilante plagued by smog,

graffiti, a hostile Korean merchant, Latino gang bangers, neo-Nazi survival-
ists, gratuitous liberals, and the indifferent rich. The film was promoted by
its maker, Warner Bros., as "a tale of urban reality." As critics observed, *Falling
Down* presented a vision of Los Angeles as "melting-pot nightmare" and "hell
on earth."[39]

By the time of the riot's first anniversary in April 1993 such visions had
become the self-image of Los Angeles. Ueberroth's phone no longer rang
off the hook. Richard Riordan, the leading candidate to succeed Bradley,
often referred to Los Angeles as "a dysfunctional city." His opponent, City
Councilman Michael Woo, warned that "the enormous anger of the have-
nots" could trigger new violence. In the midst of their gloomy campaign,
Dan Garcia, a board member, released an internal RLA report that said reconstruction had been frustrated by an unresponsive city bureaucracy, inadequate insurance settlements, and a lack of financing for merchants who
were seeking to rebuild.

On the first anniversary of the riots, the *Los Angeles Times* examined the
riot-changed image of the City of the Angels. "World Sees Lotus Land as
Badlands," said the front-page headline over the thirty-five-hundred-word
article. Before the riots, wrote David Ferrell, Los Angeles had "seemed the
wayward child—spoiled, precocious, a strapping youth running wild on the
world stage." After the riots, a "horrified world realized that the pampered
child had grown into a troubled creature harboring deep fears and hatreds."
A *Times* editorial praising the post-riot work of community groups began
with the words of playwright Eugene O'Neill: "The past is the present, isn't
it? It's the future, too. We all tried to lie out of that but life won't let us."

The past was everywhere present on the first anniversary, when the rescuers of Reginald Denny were honored at one ceremony and the firefighters
of Station 66 at another. Governor Pete Wilson said the firefighters had performed "many selfless acts of heroism . . . without protection" and paid tribute to Donald Jones, the black firefighter who had rescued Sai-Choi Choi
near Florence and Normandie. A rally was held at the intersection by supporters of Damian Williams, who faced trial for assaulting Denny and others
luckless enough to drive through Florence and Normandie at the wrong time.
Two hundred persons, including Williams' mother, Georgiana, and rap artist
Ice-T attended the "Gangs United for Peace Town Hall Summit" at an airport hotel. At the Congregational Church of Christian Fellowship, near the
border of South Central and Koreatown, the Reverend Williams Epps of the
Second Baptist Church called for harmony among diverse races and cultures.
Eighteen Korean-American ministers sang "We Shall Overcome" in Korean.
At another rally, the Latino Coalition announced a citywide "campaign for
peace." Author Kevin Starr said that "future historians may say that the riots
were the beginning of a great awakening in Los Angeles."

But the failures of the reconstruction contradicted the songs and prophecies of reconciliation. The plight of the victims was epitomized by Javier Iniquez, the furniture painter whose right hand had been shattered when he was dragged from his car and beaten on the second night of the riots. During a photo opportunity at a disaster center, President Bush had comforted Iniquez and assured him he would receive any help he needed. Most of Iniquez's medical bills had been paid, but a year later, his hand remained swollen and misshapen and he had lost his job because he couldn't hold a spray gun. Iniquez didn't know where to turn. His request for rental aid had been denied, and he and his wife owed $2,500 in back rent and faced eviction from their modest home. Their plight was not unusual. In the year after the riots, a record 10,600 families were evicted in Los Angeles County. Most of these evictions occurred in riot-damaged neighborhoods or involved riot victims.

Demonstrators representing Justice for Janitors and other low-paid workers held an observance on the first anniversary of the riots. They marched through downtown and occupied the lobby of RLA, bearing a red-and-white banner that proclaimed: "L.A.'s Two Faces. Glamour and Wealth. Poverty and Despair." The demonstrators demanded the resignation of Ueberroth and the departure from the RLA board of Governor Wilson and mayoral candidate Riordan. One of the janitors was Rosa Ayala, forty-nine, who said she worked ten or eleven hours a night cleaning a Westwood high-rise for $5 an hour and no benefits. "No one did anything for us during last year's disturbance, and RLA is not doing anything for us now," Ayala said.[40]

But Ueberroth had done what he could, and he felt tired and unappreciated. He resented the criticism from community activists and the media, and he was particularly frustrated by the absence of a coordinated government response to the problems of South Central. While he never said so directly, Ueberroth hinted that he was also disappointed with corporate executives who had promised more than they had delivered. In any case, he had had enough. On May 21, 1993, he abruptly quit as cochairman of RLA while saying he would remain a member of the board. Ueberroth said he was giving up "the best non-paid job in America" because he had become too much the focus of the coverage. "It's been exciting," he said. "It's been fun. But it's time for a change."[41]

14

PRESUMED GUILTY

"Prosecutors are the good guys."

—Steven Clymer[1]

"This is a political case, not a legal case."

—Harland Braun[2]

T HE RESTORATION OF RIOT-TORN LOS ANGELES WAS A VAST AND difficult undertaking that proved beyond the capacity of federal and local governments. But it was easy and convenient for the powerful law-enforcement arms of these governments to retaliate against the relatively resourceless men whose videotaped conduct symbolized the injustices that produced the riots—or the injustices of the riots themselves. As the disorders spread, President George Bush and Attorney General William Barr swiftly set in motion the process that led to the federal indictment of the four white LAPD officers who had been acquitted of using excessive force against Rodney King. Soon afterward, Los Angeles Police Chief Daryl Gates personally took charge of a high-visibility foray that arrested the alleged ringleader of the four young black men accused of the assault on Reginald Denny and others at Florence and Normandie. After the arrests, District Attorney Ira Reiner produced a long list of charges that had the potential to put the defendants behind bars for the rest of their lives.

Bush's reaction was essentially a political response to a social upheaval that baffled and bothered him. The president had assumed with most other Americans that the videotape of the King beating (Bush said it had "sickened" him) would result in convictions. After the riots that followed the verdicts, Bush was at a loss. He wanted to calm passions.

On the morning of April 30, Bush met in the Oval Office with White House spokesman Marlin Fitzwater, who had drafted a proposed statement. "Yesterday's verdict in the Los Angeles police case has left us all with a deep sense of personal frustration and anguish," it began. When Fitzwater read the statement at a senior staff meeting after his meeting with the president, William Kristol, chief of staff to Vice President Dan Quayle, objected that the "frustration and anguish" phrase was too conciliatory to the rioters.[3] While Bush allowed the statement to be issued as Fitzwater had written it, he took a harder line as the violence escalated. Speaking to a group of broadcasters later in the day, the president denounced "mob brutality" and "wanton destruction" and said, "We simply cannot condone violence as a way of changing the system."

On Friday May 1, the third day of the riots, Bush gave a prime-time television speech in which he virtually promised federal prosecution of the acquitted police officers. He met beforehand with the Congressional Black Caucus, Benjamin Hooks of the NAACP, and other civil rights leaders. According to Earl Ofari Hutchinson, an influential African-American writer in Los Angeles, Bush "scribbled furiously on a note pad" while Hooks and others "laid into him about the racism in the justice system [and] demanded that Bush instruct the Justice Department to bring federal charges against the four officers."[4] White House conservatives were focused on Bush's rhetoric, not his actions, and they did not oppose indictment of the officers. As Kristol remembers it, conservatives wanted Bush to speak out firmly against mob violence and lawlessness—as Quayle would do on a subsequent trip to California. Kristol had talked to Barr and realized that the president and the attorney general felt the prosecutions were politically imperative. "Legally it was a questionable thing, but they felt they had to do it for obvious reasons," Kristol said.[5]

The "obvious reasons" were apparent in Bush's televised speech, in which he said civil rights leaders felt "betrayed" by the verdicts and left no doubt that he agreed with them. "Viewed from outside the trial, it was hard to understand how the verdict could possibly square with the video," Bush said. "Those civil rights leaders with whom I met were stunned, and so was I, and so was Barbara and so were my kids. But the verdict Wednesday was not the end of the process." Bush said that within an hour of the verdicts he had "directed the Justice Department to move into high gear on its own independent criminal investigation into the case," and observed that Justice had prosecuted one hundred officials for use of excessive force during his administration. "I'm confident that in this case the Department of Justice will act as it should," he said.

These were marching orders, issued to a department already on the move. Within an hour of the verdicts, Attorney General Barr had devised a strategy to defuse their impact, and he discussed it with the president. Barr remembers telling Bush of the availability of a "federal alternative" of trying the police officers for violating King's civil rights.[6] This idea appealed to Bush, and the first step in the process was promptly announced by John

Dunne, head of Justice's Civil Rights Division, who said that the division, "in conjunction with the U.S. attorney's office for the Central District of California will now undertake a review of this incident to determine what, if any, action may be taken under federal civil rights laws."

Barr hoped that the announcement would take the edge off the wave of protests that was rippling across the nation. But the statement went almost unnoticed as people focused on the gripping television coverage of the Los Angeles riots. Barr tried again the next day. He issued a more detailed statement: "The verdicts yesterday on state charges are not the end of the process . . . We have now moved forward with our own federal investigation of this incident to determine whether there was a violation of the civil rights laws." At a news conference with Dunne and FBI Director William Sessions, Barr announced that a Justice Department team had been sent to Los Angeles under the direction of Associate Attorney General Wayne Budd, the department's number-three man and an African American.

What Barr didn't say was that Budd's team had struggled to reach Los Angeles. The riots had closed Los Angeles International Airport, and the plane with the Justice Department lawyers was diverted to Las Vegas, where it was met by U.S. marshals. They drove the Justice Department lawyers five hours across the desert to Los Angeles, where they arrived at the Century Plaza Hotel at 2:00 A.M. Barr awakened Budd with a telephone call four hours later and instructed him to confer immediately with Lourdes Baird, the U.S. attorney for California's Central District. By the time Bush addressed the nation on television the following night, Baird had already begun selecting the Los Angeles members of what became the prosecution trial team.

After the president's speech, no one at the White House doubted that the officers would be prosecuted. Bush and Barr had made a basically political decision, but one well within the boundaries of federal law enforcement practices. The Justice Department conducted 123 civil rights prosecutions during the Bush presidency, and in all likelihood would have prosecuted the Los Angeles officers had they not been tried in a state court. Bush based his opinions of the case almost entirely on what he had seen on television and thought the remedy of a second federal trial perfectly appropriate. He might very well have felt that way even if he had not faced election-year pressure from black leaders. Although Barr's predecessor, Richard Thornburgh, had said a year earlier that the Justice Department probably wouldn't prosecute the officers if they were acquitted, the riots had changed the calculus. The administration wanted to control events and head off far-reaching investigations into police conduct then being urged by congressional militants.[7] The prosecution of the officers accomplished the administration goal of defusing the concerns of civil rights activists.

This strategy had a broader dimension. White House polls found that most Americans deplored the actions of the rioters, particularly the beating of Reginald Denny, but also disagreed with the Simi Valley verdicts which had triggered the disturbances. Bush's formula of denouncing mob rule while simultaneously endorsing a federal prosecution of the officers mirrored the public mood. There is no evidence that the president based his decision to endorse a second prosecution on survey data, but he may have been pushed along by his own rhetoric. Conservatives in his party had criticized him for retreating from his 1988 "read my lips" pledge that he would not accept a tax increase, and Bill Clinton had taken up the theme. Bush wanted no more accusations, fair or not, of broken promises, and he knew that his televised statement that the Simi Valley verdicts were "not the end of the process" had been interpreted as a pledge to prosecute the officers in federal court.

Barr played by the book procedurally. Officially he merely reactivated an investigation that the FBI began after the King beating and closed down when the state prosecutions began. It was an investigation that soon took on a life of its own, as Bush and Barr had anticipated. The official line that the attorney general had ordered an investigation, not prosecutions, proved a distinction without a difference.

Barr knew that the grand jury would do whatever the prosecutors recommended, and he counted on the prosecutors to recommend prosecution. Steven Clymer, the assistant U.S. attorney who became the government's lead trial lawyer, told me long afterward that he believes Barr would have declined to prosecute had the prosecutors recommended against it.[8] Maybe so, but Barr's acknowledgment that his decision was based in part on his analysis of the videotape suggests that he reserved the right to make the final decision no matter what the prosecutors said. "It was a difficult decision," Barr said. "While there was no technical double jeopardy, I was worried about whether it was fair to prosecute a second time and also about whether [the police officers] could receive a fair trial. What was presented to me by the prosecutors and also what I could see on the videotape convinced me that the officers had definitely crossed the line and could properly be indicted for using excessive and unreasonable force. On balance, I decided that the state had not adequately presented the case and that the indictment was justifiable." When asked if the decision to retry the officers was political, Barr said, "There was certainly a highly charged political atmosphere which made decision making difficult. But you can't just walk away from the decision for this reason . . . I believe, then and now, that justice was served by the indictment."[9]

On May 7, six days after Bush's speech, federal prosecutors began presenting evidence in Los Angeles to a grand jury of twenty-three Southern

Californians. By August 5, the prosecutors had unveiled a two-count indictment. Lourdes Baird said that Laurence Powell, Timothy Wind, and Theodore Briseno had "willfully and intentionally used unreasonable force" during their arrest of Rodney King, depriving him of a right provided by the United States Constitution. The indictment's second count charged Stacey Koon with "depriving King of a constitutionally protected right by willfully permitting and failing to take action to stop the unlawful assault by the other defendants, who were under Koon's supervision."

The indictments were saluted by civil rights leaders and much of the media.[10] They were criticized by the LAPD rank and file, whose morale had not recovered from the King beating, the Christopher Commission inquiry, and the public criticism of ineffective police response in the early hours of the riots. The department's high command cooperated with the government, but most officers of lower rank were appalled. Even Internal Affairs investigators who had assembled evidence for the original case sympathized with the defendants who had been bankrupted and had seen their careers ruined despite the acquittals. Among the four defendants only Koon, who completed his book the month he was indicted, approached a second trial with a semblance of equanimity. The indictments were a heavy blow to Wind, whose physical and emotional health was shaky, and to Briseno, who was such a marginal participant that he had persuaded himself he might escape a second trial. "I'm upset, and I'm angry," Briseno said. "I don't understand why they're putting me through this again."

Normally, defendants facing a second trial for conduct on which they already had been acquitted could have counted on help from the American Civil Liberties Union. The Double Jeopardy Clause of the Fifth Amendment to the Constitution provides that no person shall "be subjected for the same offense to be twice put in jeopardy of life or limb." The ACLU took this language literally and had opposed Supreme Court decisions that reduced the protections of the clause. The court had by narrow votes over several decades accepted a doctrine known as "dual sovereignty" that permits successive state and federal prosecutions for essentially the same crime. This doctrine was anathema to the ACLU and was also opposed by conservative scholars such as Robert Bork, who believe it violates the original intent of the Constitution. The position of civil libertarians was most famously enunciated by Supreme Court Justice Hugo Black in a dissent to the 1959 *Bartkus* decision, which upheld the doctrine on a 5–4 vote:

> The court apparently takes the position that a second trial for the same act is somehow less offensive if one of the trials is conducted by the Federal Government and the other by a State. Looked at from the standpoint of the individual who is being prosecuted, this notion is too subtle for me to

grasp. If double punishment is what is feared, it hurts no less for two "Sovereigns" to inflict it than for one.

The indictment of the four officers forced the ACLU to choose between two nemeses: double jeopardy and police misconduct. No organization in Los Angeles has done more than the ACLU Foundation of Southern California to oppose police excesses. It had challenged LAPD misconduct since the days of Chief Parker, and it had led the call for Gates' ouster after the King beating. In this clash of priorities, the Southern California chapter of the ACLU decided that it detested the LAPD more than it loved the Double Jeopardy Clause. But the chapter failed to persuade the national board of the ACLU, which after long debate narrowly reaffirmed its opposition to double jeopardy without exceptions.

That was of little consequence in Los Angeles, however, where polls showed the heaviest support for the proposition that the Simi Valley verdicts were a miscarriage of justice. Whether the officers involved in the Rodney King incident could have received a fair trial in Los Angeles is problematical, and all the more so because of widespread public fears of new disturbances if they were acquitted again. The cause of these defendants should have been tailor-made for the ACLU, with its proud record of defending political outcasts in fearful times. By endorsing the prosecutions, the Southern California chapter deprived the defendants of significant support outside the police community.

The principal ACLU advocate of the federal prosecutions was Paul Hoffman, the respected legal affairs director of the ACLU Foundation of Southern California. He argued that there are "compelling reasons" for a civil rights exception to the Double Jeopardy Clause. Summarizing his views in the UCLA *Law Review* after the federal trial, Hoffman observed that federal prosecutions had played a key role in extending constitutional protections to blacks during the critical days of the civil rights movement. As an example he cited the federal prosecution of two Ku Klux Klan members whom a Georgia jury packed with Klan sympathizers had acquitted of the 1964 murder of African-American serviceman Lemuel Penn. The Klansmen were then convicted in federal court for violating Penn's civil rights. Hoffman also took note of the 1965 murder of civil rights worker Viola Liuzzo in Alabama. Again the federal government obtained convictions after Liuzzo's killers were acquitted—twice—in state court.

Hoffman agreed that the gravity of the actions of the four LAPD officers did not compare with these offenses, but wrote that "the constitutional equality values embodied in the federal criminal civil rights statutes are not limited to the most extreme forms of racist violence." In Hoffman's view, police brutality was of "sufficient national importance to justify the most vigorous use of federal criminal civil rights prosecutions to end the impunity with which many police officers act toward members of the community. The federal reprosecution of the four LAPD officers in the *Koon* case was an emphatic statement that the federal government would no longer tolerate this situation."[11]

Hoffman tried to bolster his argument with a recent incident closer to home than the Penn and Liuzzo murders. He used the example of Dana Patrick Hansen, an LAPD officer who in 1986 had dragged seventeen-year-old Jesus Martinez Vidales from his car and had beaten him so severely that Vidales suffered a fractured skull and was hospitalized for several weeks. The LAPD treated this brutality leniently. Hansen was suspended for only fifteen days and a civil lawsuit settled for $42,000. The federal government then prosecuted Hansen for civil rights violations, and he was convicted and sent to prison in March 1992 after a trial that attracted little attention. In contrast to *Koon*, this case was a textbook example of how a federal prosecution can serve the interests of justice when the state fails to act.

But Hoffman inaccurately equated the conduct of the officers who arrested King with Hansen's treatment of Vidales. "The Rodney King beating exemplified the 'street justice' experienced by large numbers of young African-American and Latino men in Los Angeles," Hoffman wrote. Quoting from the closing address of Powell's attorney Michael Stone at the federal trial, Hoffman maintained there was "no middle ground" in the King case and that what happened either was "'street justice' in violation of basic constitutional protections or it was acceptable police behavior." The change of venue to Ventura County had "led to the selection of a jury that was widely perceived as biased in favor of the defendants." The second prosecution resolved "any lingering doubts about jury nullification" and dispelled a "gnawing fear that the officers were acquitted against the evidence" out of sympathy for the police. But the second trial would also raise the gnawing fear that the jurors returned convictions against the evidence because they feared that acquittals might start another riot.

In fact, a constructive "middle ground" was available and in the process of being occupied when the Bush administration made its political decision to prosecute. What is often forgotten is that the much maligned Simi Valley jury had deadlocked on the charge that Officer Powell had assaulted King under the color of authority. Even if there had been no riots, Powell faced a second state trial on this felony charge and an almost certain prison sentence if convicted.

Although Powell was not without a defense for his actions, he had struck the vast majority of the baton blows. Briseno and Wind played minor roles. Even Hoffman, who contended that "the weight of the evidence" was grounds for reprosecution, said in a little-noticed footnote to his *UCLA*

Law Review article that "the Justice Department might be criticized for re-prosecuting officers Briseno and Wind given the relatively weaker evidence against them." If Hoffman's standard is applied, then the federal prosecution was needed only to try Sergeant Koon, who struck no blows and, according to *uncontested testimony*, attempted to take King into custody without hurting him. Is there a relevant analogy for a second prosecution of an officer who behaved as Koon did? Neither Hoffman nor any of the other advocates of this particular prosecution have ever cited a comparable case.

The state proceedings under which Powell would have been tried a second time for assault under color of authority were well under way by the time the federal grand jury returned its indictments. Shaken by the verdicts and the resulting riots, Judge Weisberg had decided to retry Powell in Los Angeles. Denying Powell's request for another change of venue, Weisberg said: "No one in the state of California . . . is unaware of the verdict in the first trial. In my view at this time, the potential jurors in this case would have the same state of mind whether they are selected from Los Angeles County or another county." Had Weisberg's reasoning been used by the appeals court that granted the original change of venue, there never would have been a Simi Valley trial.

Weisberg's ruling locked the barn door after the barn had been demolished and the horse was out of sight. But it would have produced a second state trial with a jury panel potentially more favorable to the prosecution than the panel in the federal trial. Federal jurors were chosen from a vast seven-county area of Southern California in which blacks were a small minority. The state trial would have drawn on a jury pool within a twenty-mile radius of downtown Los Angeles, where the black population was considerably higher and where the impact of the riots had been directly felt.

While it is perilous to predict the outcome of any trial in Los Angeles, it seems likely that Powell would have been convicted in a state trial. From a legal standpoint, the federal government would have lost nothing by waiting, for it would have retained its ability to file civil rights charges under its interpretation of the Double Jeopardy Clause. But waiting could have been politically disastrous for President Bush, who would have been perceived as reneging on his perceived promise of prosecution. And after the federal government initiated its civil rights prosecution, Weisberg dismissed the remaining state charge against Powell.

POLITICAL CONSIDERATIONS WERE JUST AS EVIDENT IN ACTIONS taken against the black defendants accused of assaulting Reginald Denny. LAPD officers and FBI agents swooped down in predawn raids on May 12 and arrested Damian (Football) Williams, Henry (Kiki) Watson, and

Antoine (Twan) Miller for the Denny assault. The arrest of Williams was led by Daryl Gates, who held a news conference afterward and quipped that, "I did it all by myself with the aid of about two hundred police officers."* Reporters and photographers laughed, but the chief's participation in the arrest angered African Americans. It would be remembered in the jury room to the detriment of the prosecution.

Gates never stopped to think that his grandstanding might backfire. He had long displayed a cowboy streak that led him to impulsively chase "bad guys," and collaring Damian Williams was a kind of last hurrah before retirement. Gates even managed to persuade himself that his actions compensated for the dismal LAPD performance at Florence and Normandie. "As you know, the Los Angeles Police Department was very, very concerned about our inability to reach Mr. Denny at the time he was being assaulted and after and assist him," Gates told reporters after the arrest. "We are hopeful that at least this will atone for some of that [by] bringing these very, very vicious criminals to be prosecuted."

District Attorney Ira Reiner, who ought to have known better, contributed to the legal martyrdom of Damian Williams with some grandstanding of his own. Reiner was then clinging to his job. He was being second-guessed for the Simi Valley trial, and he was less than a month away from the primary election that would force him into retirement. Reiner's conduct can be compared to that of Bush and Barr, who were genuinely appalled by the Simi Valley verdicts and the riots but sought to gain from them a measure of political advantage. Reiner was, if anything, even more outraged by what had happened to Reginald Denny and the other victims at Florence and Normandie, but he also hoped that his high-visibility prosecution of those responsible would impress the voters.

On May 13, a day after the arrest of Williams, Reiner held a news conference with U.S. Attorney Baird to announce the filing of state and federal charges against Williams, Watson, and Miller. The state charges against Williams included attempted murder, aggravated mayhem, and robbery, all of which may have been justified. But Reiner added the charge of torture, using the statute for a different purpose than it had been designed. Baird charged the defendants with violating the federal Street Terrorism Enforcement Act. The federal charges were never pursued, but Reiner continued to pile on new counts in the preprimary period. On May 28, the week before the election, he announced that Williams faced thirteen additional counts involving six victims. Miller was charged with seventeen additional counts and Watson

---

* Williams was awakened from a sound sleep by the officers who arrested him and recognized Gates. "Chief, you are going," he said, in reference to his upcoming retirement. "Yeah, Football, but you are going first," Gates replied.

with six. If the defendants had been convicted on all counts, they could have spent most of their lives in prison.

The cumulative effect of Reiner's actions was to create a broad climate of sympathy for the defendants in South Central, where an activist, fund-raising group called the "Free the L.A. 4 Defense Committee" was formed. The fourth defendant was Gary Williams (no relation to Damian), who was charged with robbing Denny after he had been beaten into unconsciousness. Gary Williams surrendered to police after the others were arrested and tried separately, but the committee continued to use the name of the "L.A. 4."[12]

The belief that Damian Williams, Miller, and Watson were being singled out for harsh treatment because of their race was enhanced by Reiner's action in removing the black judge assigned to preside over their trial. Each side in a California criminal trial is allowed one peremptory challenge in which a judge can be removed without a statement of cause. At a hearing conducted by a then obscure judge named Lance Ito, Reiner used his challenge to disqualify Judge Roosevelt F. Dorn, the only African-American judge who regularly presided over criminal trials in the downtown courts building.

Dorn had been assigned to the case by Cecil Mills, the criminal courts supervising judge. While Mills did not give a reason, it was widely believed in the legal community that he wanted Dorn as the trial judge to avert accusations of racism. But Reiner considered Dorn "a very bad judge."[13] His objections had nothing to do with race but with Dorn's reputation for being abrasive and confrontational during his tenure on the Juvenile Court. After an investigation Dorn had been reassigned to criminal trials in Superior Court.

Reiner felt he had to challenge Dorn even though he knew it would cause an "explosion." But he deliberately misstated the reasons for his actions in an attempt to spare Dorn's feelings. Instead of saying he considered Dorn unfit or saying nothing, Reiner explained through a spokeswoman that he had removed Dorn because of problems involving the judge's court calendar. This was too much for Dorn, who held a news conference to accuse Reiner of lying and charge that he had been removed because of his race. Reiner then acknowledged he had removed Dorn because of his temperament. Outraged supporters of the defendants held a demonstration on the courthouse steps and chanted, "No justice, no peace." Yolanda Madison, a twenty-one-year-old UCLA student, told a reporter, "People need to see the double standard here. If they do get convicted, I suggest that people burn the city down."[14]

THE FEAR THAT BLACKS WOULD RESORT TO SUCH VIOLENCE pervaded Los Angeles in the summer of 1992 as the federal case against the police officers and the state proceedings against the Denny defendants moved forward. The two incidents were not equivalent. Rodney King had been driving drunk and speeding and had resisted arrest before he was harmed. Reginald Denny had done nothing except drive into an intersection where he was attacked without provocation. While King's injuries were far from trivial, they did not begin to compare with those inflicted on Denny, who nearly died. The two incidents were also less representative than was widely believed. Despite its seriousness, the King beating was borderline in comparison to incidents in which LAPD officers had shot, choked, or beaten suspects without provocation. And even the brutal Denny assault paled in comparison to several deliberate killings during the riots. What made the two incidents exceptional—and linked them symbolically in the public's mind—was that they had been videotaped. Local television stations enhanced the illusion that the two events were equivalent by showing back-to-back clips whenever a development occurred in either case.

This mindless juxtaposition was exploited by the Free the L.A. 4 Defense Committee. The committee complained that the defendants were being unfairly held in jail because they could not meet the high bail: $585,000 for Damian Williams and $500,000 for the others. Meanwhile, the officers remained free on $5,000 bonds. "That rankles many of the protesters, but the surface similarities obscure significant differences between the two cases," the reliable Jim Newton reported in the *Los Angeles Times*. "The officers all had steady jobs, clean arrest records and a history of making their court dates when bail was set for them. That is not the case of the other defendants."[15] Newton's assessment was accurate, but it was not persuasive in South Central.

One significant difference between the two cases in their formative stages was that state proceedings were held in open court where every misstep was visible, while federal proceedings were cloaked in the secrecy of the grand jury. Not everything went smoothly in the federal case, and defense attorneys would later complain that police witnesses were intimidated. But this issue was not raised publicly until the trial and never gained wide currency. Shut out of federal proceedings in the late summer and autumn of 1992, the media focused on the maneuverings and blunders that plagued the state trial.

After Reiner disqualified Dorn, Judge Mills selected Judge George Trammell, who is white. The defense promptly used its peremptory challenge to disqualify Trammell. Mills then appointed another white judge, John Reid. Reiner, seeking to regain some of the ground he had lost with blacks when he disqualified Dorn, asked defense attorneys to join in petitioning Mills to replace Reid with Donald Pitts, a black judge who often heard cases in Compton. The defense agreed, but Mills was upset with both sides for emphasizing racial tensions instead of legal issues and decided to keep Reid on the case. One of the defense attorneys appealed on a technicality, and Reid eventually was removed. On October 2, Mills appointed Judge John Ouderkirk, a former police officer and deputy district attorney with a proprosecution reputation.

Before this happened, public attention had been fixed on a bizarre sideshow involving the lawyer hired by Georgiana Williams to defend her son Damian. Dennis Palmieri was newly affiliated with the Center for Constitutional Law and Justice, a public-service group, and, according to writer Peter Boyer, was "desperate to prove himself on a big case."[16] He made a flamboyant presentation at the preliminary hearing but was fired soon afterward by the center for "highly questionable behavior and poor judgment." Fred Sebastian, the center's deputy director, said Palmieri's resume claimed such achievements as the advocacy of a lunar mining colony and a Martian expedition plus the "edifying re-examination of the Christian Principal in its substance and essence." Palmieri said his ideas had been responsible for "dismantling the Berlin Wall, raising the Iron Curtain, unifying Germany, bringing democracy to Eastern Europe and the individual republics of the Soviet Union."[17] Georgiana Williams replaced him with Edi M.O. Faal, a tall, soft-spoken, and dignified black immigrant from the West African nation of Gambia who practiced law in Orange County. It was a fortuitous selection for the defense.

No controversy surrounded the selection of a federal judge to preside over the trial of the police officers. U.S. District Judge John G. Davies, randomly assigned to the case, was also a naturalized citizen. Born in Sydney, he had represented Australia in the 200-meter breast stroke in the 1948 Olympic Games in London, where he qualified for the finals but finished fourth. After the Olympics he returned home by way of the United States and decided to enroll at the University of Michigan. He took time off from his studies in 1952 to again represent Australia in the Olympics. This time he won the gold medal. After earning a law degree from UCLA in 1959, he practiced business law for twenty-seven years in Los Angeles before being named to the federal bench by President Reagan.

Davies, tall and austere, spoke with only a hint of an Australian accent. He was a registered Republican who was relatively unfamiliar with the civil rights statutes and had more experience in civil litigation than in criminal cases. But he had substantial trial experience as an attorney and a judge, a droll sense of humor, a grasp of evidentiary detail, and a penchant for controlling the courtroom. Federal prosecutors thought him too conservative, while defense lawyer Harland Braun believed that Davies was overly deferential to federal authority. These perceived deficiencies were transcended by the judge's resolute fair-mindedness, which was evident throughout the trial.

Although he formed opinions of the case, as judges often do, he did not allow his feelings to govern his actions on the bench.

U.S. Attorney Terree Bowers, who replaced Baird after she was named to the federal bench, later called the lawyers who prosecuted the King civil rights case "one of the most formidable trial teams ever assembled." This was no exaggeration. The lead prosecutors on the four-man trial team were Steven David Clymer, the top trial lawyer in the U.S. Attorney's Office in Los Angeles, and Barry Kowalski of the Justice Department's Civil Rights Division. Their backups were Lawrence Middleton from the U.S. Attorney's Office and Alan Tieger, a colleague of Kowalski in the Civil Rights Division.

Kowalski, diminutive and feisty, was sometimes called the "pit bull" of the Justice Department and was the most famous of the four. The son of a former Democratic House member from Connecticut, he had served with distinction as a Marine rifle-platoon leader in Vietnam. During eleven years at Justice, in which he became the nation's best-known civil rights prosecutor, Kowalski won convictions against an assortment of Ku Klux Klan members, skinheads, and brutal police officers. His cases included the 1981 trial of the Klansmen who killed Michael Donald in the nation's last racial lynching. Their conviction led to a civil rights lawsuit and a $7-million judgment that forced what was then the Klan's largest branch into bankruptcy. In 1983, Kowalski successfully prosecuted neo-Nazis in the Denver killing of Alan Berg, a Jewish talk-show host. Kowalski lost the 1982 prosecution of an avowed white supremacist who was accused of shooting civil rights leader Vernon Jordan. But he had won many more cases than he had lost and believed strongly in the necessity of prosecuting police officers who committed crimes under the color of authority. "I'm very concerned about the abuse of power by people in public authority, by police abuse of power," he said.[18]

Kowalski was forty-eight years old when the King civil rights trial began, much the oldest of the prosecutors, and unhappy with the prospect of spending as much as a year away from Washington. He glumly compared the trial to going with his platoon to Vietnam. Although it was not widely known, Kowalski was worn out by the strain of incessant prosecutions, and the pressure of what he called the "twenty-six-hour days" of the King trial would take a personal toll. Still, he had a worldly view, enjoyed good food and country music, and was more comfortable than Steven Clymer with the limelight and the media. When Seth Mydans of The New York Times interviewed the prosecutors early in the trial, Kowalski impishly suggested, "Why don't you call me the brooding, intense one and Clymer the light, conversational one?"[19]

"Intense" was an appropriate description of Clymer, a brainy lawyer with a capacity for hard work and an ability to charm jurors with his earnestness. Clymer saw himself as a risk taker who never shrank from hard decisions. He admitted to a certain impatience with lawyers (including Kowalski) who liked to talk out strategy. Clymer was a man in a hurry. He had graduated magna cum laude from Cornell Law School and had become an assistant district attorney in Philadelphia, where he obtained the indictments of several police officers involved in a bribery and gambling ring. In 1987, he joined the U.S. Attorney's Office in Los Angeles and soon became a rising star. Displaying a commanding courtroom presence, Clymer became the office's principal prosecutor of drug and money-laundering cases.

Clymer, thirty-four years old when the King civil rights trial began, was secure in his judgments and chock full of energy and moral righteousness. He was committed to color-blind justice and was convinced, as he told Jim Newton, that "from the day of the Simi Valley verdicts, this case raised the question of whether the criminal justice system worked the same for black people as it does for white people." The case was more complicated than that, but Clymer was uncomfortable with ambiguity and easily persuaded himself that the Bush administration's motives were pure.

Clymer no doubt could have passed a polygraph test when he insisted that the federal prosecution was not political, just as Stacey Koon could have passed such a test when he claimed that the King arrest was a managed use of force. Ironically, Clymer and Koon were much alike: strong, dedicated, and professionally impervious to anything that might dent their self-images as "the good guys." Had Koon been a lawyer, it would not be hard to imagine him as an unforgiving prosecutor of the cops who had beaten Rodney King. Nor is it difficult to imagine Clymer, as a police officer, taking control of the King arrest because he feared someone would be shot if he did not interfere. Both Koon and Clymer are decent and honorable men—and both are also true believers who find it almost impossible to acknowledge misjudgments. Koon, the more stubborn of the two, gave himself the impossible task of proving that the King arrest was exemplary police work. Clymer claimed reservations about double jeopardy, but refused to acknowledge that President Bush (with Barr's connivance) had reopened the investigation to appease election-year critics.

What both men lacked was humility. Koon's image of himself as the professional sergeant kept him from examining the possibility that he might have inadequately supervised officers under his command or that one of those officers had panicked and used his baton excessively. Clymer's belief that he served the cause of justice without fear or favor precluded him from questioning the motives of his superiors or the impartiality of his own beliefs.

Whether the actions of the officers in the King arrest, considered in their totality, constituted criminal conduct is a close question. The rationale for a second prosecution, particularly one influenced by a perception of political advantage, is even narrower. But neither Koon nor Clymer was comfortable with close questions, and both tended to resolve doubts, as police officers and prosecutors often do, by demonizing their adversaries. What the officers had done was justified in Koon's eyes because Rodney King was a threat. What the prosecutors did was right from Clymer's point of view because the defendants were bad cops.

Clymer and Kowalski would have been formidable as a team if left to their own devices. But they were mightily bolstered by Tieger and Middleton. Tieger was the son of two survivors of a Nazi concentration camp who had immigrated to San Jose, California, after World War II. He was a gentle, devout Jew with a passion for justice and a preoccupation with genocide that after the trial led him to become involved in the prosecution of Bosnian war crimes. As a prosecutor with the Justice Department's Civil Rights Division, Tieger had obtained convictions of skinheads and brutal prison guards. He was quiet in manner and tended to see both sides of any argument. When the lead prosecutors were at loggerheads, Tieger tried to play a mediating role.

Middleton, the only African-American member of the team, had been an Air Force lawyer before joining the U.S. Attorney's Office in 1990. Two years later he received an award from the Department of Health and Human Services for successfully prosecuting the largest ever individual case of Social Security fraud. Usually, Middleton was even more reserved than Tieger, but he was so forceful when he did speak out that Kowalski compared him to the broker in the E. F. Hutton commercials for whom everybody stops and listens. "Lawrence was the tiebreaker," said Clymer, who thought Middleton sometimes saw aspects of the case that others missed.

With one exception, the defense lawyers were no match for the prosecution in savvy or experience. Michael Stone and Paul DePasquale returned for a second trial as attorneys for Officers Laurence Powell and Timothy Wind, respectively. Stone had made mistakes but also displayed flashes of brilliance at Simi Valley. Overall, he had given a remarkable performance considering that it was his first felony trial, but he was still a novice criminal attorney who had never tried a case in federal court. Darryl Mounger had bowed out as Koon's attorney. He was upset with the Los Angeles Police Protective League for reducing legal fees for the federal trial, and he also had a trial conflict and a feeling he should move along in his legal career after spending so much of his life as a cop.[20] There may have been more to it. Cliff Ruff, a veteran LAPD officer and league director who interviewed prospective attorneys for the officers before both trials, thought that Mounger and Koon had experienced a falling out.

Mounger was replaced by Ira Salzman, a gentlemanly civil litigator in a one-man office who made a good impression on Koon. "There was a bond between them," said Ruff, who also thought Koon wanted an attorney who would not be controlled by Stone.[21] Salzman saw himself as a legal defender of the underdog, but he lacked Mounger's commanding personality or his background in police work, and he also had never tried a criminal case in federal court. These potential deficiencies didn't matter to Koon, who was absolutely certain that he would never be convicted by a jury that learned the full story of what had happened the night of the King arrest. He wanted a dignified attorney to represent him, and Salzman fit the bill.

The standout among the defense attorneys was Briseno's lawyer, Harland Braun, an ebullient legal warrior with broad interests in history, theology, and politics. Braun made the law review at UCLA Law School, an honor reserved for the top 10 percent of the class. After graduating in 1967, he joined what he later called a losing war on poverty and spent a year in Washington working for the Office of Economic Opportunity. He returned to Los Angeles to seek a job with the public defender's office. Because there were no immediate openings, he went to work instead for the Los Angeles County District Attorney's Office, then rapidly expanding. Within six months Braun was trying felony cases.

During five years as a deputy district attorney, Braun tried some minor members of the Charles Manson family and was befriended by the mercurial Vincent Bugliosi, principal prosecutor of Manson himself. Braun had left the district attorney's office in 1973 to go into private practice. Bugliosi was charged with perjury and hired Braun to defend him. As Braun later said, "It was a big break for a young lawyer," and it became an even bigger break when the charges were dropped.[22] The case made Braun's reputation and launched him on a successful career. By the time of the King civil rights trial, Braun was fifty years old and the most experienced trial lawyer on either side. As prosecutor and as defense attorney, he had participated in more than three hundred criminal trials.

Braun bore his experience lightly. He was relentlessly cheerful, a happy family man. His optimism sometimes grated on those for whom life is burdensome, while his studied irreverence for authority tended to annoy judges, including Davies. But Braun's insouciance masked impressive legal skills. He was at once intuitive and analytical in courtroom arguments and a creative legal strategist with the ability to focus on essentials and see a case through the eyes of a jury. Braun had a realistic view of human nature and understood that government was not inevitably on the side of the angels. He also had a capacity for self-criticism and the ability to change his mind. Of the eight principal attorneys involved in the King civil rights trial, Braun was the only one to change his opinion of what had happened on the night of March 3, 1991.

Braun's original opinion was that the arresting officers had beaten King brutally and without provocation—a view shared by millions of people who watched the truncated Holliday video on television. Braun saw the tape for the first time while visiting in rural Florida. Although he thought of the area as backward, he noticed that even people he considered racially bigoted thought the officers were out of line and had probably beaten King because he was black. While in Florida, Braun received a telephone call from another attorney asking him if he would represent Briseno in the state trial. Braun turned down the request out of hand. "I'm a liberal Democrat and even Daryl Gates had condemned the beatings," said Braun. "How much more did you need to know?"[23]

But Braun watched the Simi Valley trial on television and gradually changed his mind about Officer Briseno, if not about the other defendants. He knew that police officers usually abided by the "code of silence," and he was impressed by Briseno's account of the incident and by John Barnett's defense. After the verdicts, Braun received a telephone call from Greg Petersen, the attorney who had called him in Florida after the King beating. They knew each other from a trial in which Braun had successfully defended the producer of Twilight Zone: The Movie against manslaughter charges.[24] Peterson, who was representing Briseno in civil matters, said that Barnett would not be able to stay with the case and asked Braun to take over. Braun said he was interested but wanted to talk to a client before making any commitment. The client was Eazy-E, a black rap singer whose real name was Eric Wright. He was a founder of NWA (the initials for "Niggers With Attitude"), whose members Braun had represented in various criminal proceedings. Braun asked Eazy-E if it would bother him if he represented a police officer in the federal civil rights trial. "No," the singer said, without bothering to ask the name of the officer. Braun called Peterson back and took the case.

Braun still felt "tremendous dislike" for Koon and Powell and thought they posed a greater danger to his client than the government did. In discussing the case, he was candid and likable, but presented a one-dimensional analysis that cast Briseno as the hero and the other officers as villains.[25] But Braun did not stand pat with the opinion that all the officers were wrong except Briseno. He soon developed a sophisticated understanding of the incident that would lead him to question his cherished premises about the police.

Braun's revisionist analysis was spurred by a strategic impulse. He recognized that Officer Powell's attorney, Michael Stone, was capable of damaging Briseno. As recounted previously, Briseno in the first trial described Powell as being "out of control" when he repeatedly hit King with his baton. Stone had anticipated this testimony in his opening statement, portraying Briseno as a dishonest officer who was trying to save himself by vilifying the other defendants, and John Barnett, representing Briseno, had responded by attacking Powell. Braun wanted to avoid a repetition of this confrontation, believing it could be harmful to Briseno. His solution was to propose a "unified defense" to Stone and Salzman in which the defendants would seek to minimize their differences. While the purpose of this strategy was to help Briseno, Braun learned so much in the course of constructing it that he fundamentally changed his opinion of the case.

In going over the incident with his client, Braun realized that the officers had indeed been fearful of King and were certain he was under the influence of PCP. Whether they were right is another question, but it was evident to Braun that the PCP story had not been made up after the fact, as prosecutors maintained at both trials. When Braun watched the full video, he also learned of King's charge at Powell, which he had never seen before. He talked to Sergeant Charles Duke and learned about the history of the choke hold and the LAPD policy of not tying up with suspects. He was impressed by Koon's straightforward manner and direct answers. Braun had read widely about the Nazis and concluded that Koon "in some weird way" was making the opposite of the notorious Nuremburg defense that he had only followed orders. Koon blamed neither orders nor others. He took responsibility for everything the officers had done, although Braun had begun to wonder whether Koon actually had been responsible. His behavior surprised Braun, who was used to defendants who denied everything.

It is conceivable that the federal trial might have taken a different turn had Braun represented Koon. Braun believed in what he called "the value of truth" and thought that truth required a better explanation than describing the King incident as an exemplary arrest in which everything had gone according to plan. The Simi Valley jurors had accepted the argument that King was to blame for everything that had happened to him, but Braun thought it unlikely that such an approach could prevail again. He also believed that jurors might be persuaded by a different defense that was solidly grounded in reality: that Koon did his best to arrest King without hurting him and had been frustrated by King's resistance and then by Powell's panicked ineptitude. This was the truth, as Braun came to see it, and it was not particularly flattering to anyone. Braun believes he could have persuaded Koon at least to acknowledge that he did not know everything that was going on during the arrest. But Salzman accepted Koon's no-errors explanation at face value, and Stone believed he needed to replicate the defense that had worked so well at Simi Valley.

By any measure the federal prosecutors possessed enormous advantages in the second trial. The federal government used a score of attorneys on one or another aspect of the case and spared no expense on investigation. Justice Department officials have consistently refused to put a price tag on their efforts, probably because doing so would reveal the disproportionate expenditures of the prosecution and the defense, but one department source privately estimated the cost of the civil rights trial at $5 million, exclusive of security costs. Against this the Los Angeles Police Protective League spent only $320,000 on the federal trial. Money talks in the justice system, as in other aspects of American life. The reduction in each defense attorney's fee from $100,000 in the state trial to $80,000 in the federal trial was one of the reasons the capable Darryl Mounger left the case.[26] There were other consequences, as well. One prosecutor found it hard to believe when Braun confided to him after the trial that the investigative budget for all four defendants was only $5,000.

The disparity in resources encouraged the defense not to seek a change in venue—a mistake that may have been critical. Judge Davies subsequently told me that he had anticipated a request for a venue change and would have granted it. But the defense attorneys didn't know this. They thought from a stray remark of Braun that the venue decision might be made by another judge. They also worried that the trial could wind up in a less favorable place than Los Angeles—although it is hard to imagine what could have been worse than trying the case in a city where deadly riots had occurred and fears of another were widespread.

But it is doubtful that the defense would have sought to move the trial even if assured a favorable venue. Braun was convinced Briseno would be acquitted no matter where the trial was held. Salzman thought Koon, with his large, young family, would be more relaxed at home. Stone had wanted the trial moved when Powell faced retrial on the state charge before a Los Angeles jury, but he believed the venue was unimportant in the federal case because the jurors would be drawn from a seven-county area. Braun and Stone told me the issue was resolved in a brief conversation among the attorneys, most of whom could not have afforded to live for weeks in a remote city and to pay the costs of flying in witnesses. "We all agreed on that," said Braun. "A change of venue was really out of the question with our resources."[27]

The government had no such limitations. It was able and willing to spend whatever it took, as Stacey Koon learned in retrospect when he and Salzman sought access, under the Privacy Act, to the government's information on Koon's case. A letter from Deval Patrick, assistant attorney general in the Civil Rights Division, informed them that Justice had amassed 262,000 pages on the case. The charge for copies at ten cents a page was $26,200, with one-fourth of this payable in advance. Koon and Salzman decided they could not afford the documents.

Another example of the government's resources, as well as of its thoroughness, was demonstrated by the FBI investigation of Powell's statement that he had never been taught to subdue a suspect with the "swarm technique." The statement was true, as the government could have learned by discussing the issue with the LAPD officials who were cooperating with the prosecution. FBI agents nonetheless interviewed every one of the other eighty-eight members of Powell's class, ostensibly to see if they had been taught the swarm. Diane Marchant, the Police Protective League lawyer who attended the interviews, thought they were "a stunning example of overkill. You would have thought that after the first dozen people told them they had not been taught the swarm technique they would have got the idea," she said.[28]

Clymer and Kowalski observed with pride after the federal trial that police officers had been less inclined to testify for the defense than they had been at Simi Valley. The same point was made in a critical way by Marchant, who said the conduct of the prosecutors and the FBI was designed to intimidate officers and had the intended "chilling effect." Whether such "chilling" was necessary to offset the "code of silence" is a matter of opinion, but Marchant is surely right in saying that the FBI "had money to burn."

And Clymer is right in saying that the prosecution made effective use of the grand jury. The federal grand jury is a powerful prosecutorial tool that operates according to strict rules of secrecy and such loose rules of evidence that even hearsay is admissible. Federal prosecutors privately criticized state prosecutors for not making similar use of their own grand jury. But California grand jury proceedings follow trial rules of evidence, and some of the questions put to witnesses during the federal grand jury proceedings would have been inadmissible under state law. The secrecy of federal grand jury testimony also gave federal prosecutors an edge. Since testimony before California grand juries becomes a public record once an indictment is returned, defense attorneys at Simi Valley knew everything that every witness had said. Under federal rules, the government does not have to reveal grand jury testimony to the defense unless the person who testified is called as a government witness. And as it turned out, the defense was damaged by witnesses who testified one way before the grand jury and another way when called as defense witnesses.[29]

But the prosecution's greatest advantage was simply the fact that this was a second trial. Double jeopardy imposes almost insurmountable burdens for defendants in a high-profile case, particularly one with a videotape. As two advocates of a strict interpretation of the Double Jeopardy Clause observed, an erroneous conviction becomes possible whenever the government employs "its vast resources against an individual in successive prosecutions" and is even more likely "in successive prosecutions . . . fueled by a politically motivated government substituting its judgment for that of the previous jury."[30] Even if the two sides had been equally matched in resources and legal skills, prosecutors would have been able to correct the many mistakes of the state trial, an advantage that would have been difficult for any defendants to overcome.

But with all these advantages, not everything went the government's way. One disappointment for the prosecution was Edward Nowicki, executive director of the American Society of Law Enforcement Trainers at the time of the King beating. Nowicki was an experienced police officer who had worked for ten years on the Chicago force, where he was involved in six shootings. He subsequently served as police chief in Silver Lake, Wisconsin, before taking an advanced degree and becoming a police trainer in Milwaukee.

Nowicki had been outraged when he saw clips of the King beating on television. "I thought it was brutal and horrific, racism at its pinnacle," he said. He denounced the officers, in class and publicly. Kowalski learned about Nowicki's views from an FBI agent who was one of his students. Eventually he called Nowicki to ask if he would testify in the federal trial. The government had money to pay for experts, Kowalski said. What would Nowicki charge to testify for the government? Nowicki said he didn't want anything except expenses. The Justice Department flew Nowicki to Los Angeles on October 1, 1992, where he and Kowalski chatted about their Polish ancestries and Kowalski showed him the menu of a Polish restaurant where he suggested they could have dinner.

Then Nowicki met with the prosecution team and heard a detailed account of the Rodney King pursuit. Nowicki had not watched the state trial on television and hadn't realized that the California Highway Patrol had been involved. The story of the high-speed pursuit gave him pause. The prosecutors led Nowicki through the incident, recounting the attempts to arrest King by swarming him and with the Taser. "That was news to me, too," Nowicki recalled later. "I thought they had stopped some black guy for speeding and just beat the living hell out of him."[31] The prosecutors then played the video at varying speeds. Nowicki was still appalled by the violence shown on the tape, which he thought of as "a movie that you hate." But like the jurors at Simi Valley, Nowicki realized from the full videotape that King had charged at Powell. "I had never seen that before either," Nowicki said. By now he was beginning to wonder if the officers had used excessive force. "I had to tell them I'm not sure," he said. The demeanor of the prosecutors changed. They remained polite, but wanted nothing more to do with him. Instead of dining with the prosecutors, Nowicki took the overnight plane back to Milwaukee. He took with him as a memento the menu of the Polish restaurant.[32]

AS THE FEDERAL PROSECUTORS READIED THEIR CASE AGAINST THE officers and the state prosecutors prepared to try the accused assailants of Reginald Denny, LAPD Chief Willie Williams worried about the prospect of a second riot. Williams, new to the city, had relatively little understanding of its politics, but he could read the danger signals in the black community, where activists increasingly insisted on the equivalency of the two trials. The chief assumed that the Denny defendants would be convicted. If the trials coincided and the officers were acquitted, Williams anticipated another revolt.

Williams was not alone. A *Los Angeles Times* poll on the eve of the federal trial found that two thirds of those surveyed feared another riot but also thought the LAPD would respond more effectively. Williams tried to defuse expectations. "As much as we all hope that nothing occurs, the realities are that this is a big city and these are very tense times," he said on January 27, 1993. "The police department, in and of itself, cannot prevent another riot, big or small. Our job is to ensure that we are prepared to suppress these events when they occur by shows of force, increased visibility [and] coordination with other law enforcement agencies." The most Williams would claim was that the LAPD was better prepared for a disturbance than it had been in April 1992.

This much was true, and Williams was a principal reason. Like a general who has learned the most important lesson of the most recent war, Williams was determined that the LAPD would be prepared for any civil disturbance. After the Webster Commission report was issued with its many criticisms of LAPD preparedness, Williams ordered that every officer receive sixteen hours of riot training. The training focused on maneuvering officers in ten-person squads, using tear gas for crowd control, and hostage rescue. With Metro playing a prominent role, the LAPD conducted tactical training at the Police Academy and nearby Dodger Stadium. No longer was this preparation kept secret from other LAPD units or the media. No longer did black leaders argue that such high-visibility preparation was unnecessarily provocative. "Never again" might have been the LAPD's new motto as Los Angeles braced for violent reactions to potentially unpopular verdicts. But the new police resolve was challenged before the trials at the intersection that had been the epicenter of the April riots.

Appropriately, LAPD preparedness was tested by the Free the L.A. 4 Defense Committee, which gathered at Florence and Normandie in the midafternoon hours of December 14, a Monday. At first it was a peaceful demonstration, with members handing out leaflets that urged bail reduction for Damian Williams and his codefendants. But it was not long before the leafleteers were joined by boisterous young African-American men who seemed to have been drinking and were later described as gang members by Deputy Chief Matthew Hunt. The youths began taunting passersby and hurled bottles and rocks at police cars and other vehicles. The police dispersed the crowd and left. But in an uncomfortable echo of April 29, a crowd gathered again as soon as the police withdrew and began looting a gas station at the corner of the intersection.

This time police cars returned to the intersection and scattered the crowd for good. During the next two hours, in the early December darkness, LAPD officers, some in riot gear, conducted a street-by-street sweep. They arrested fifty-five people. Department management and the media celebrated the incident as a textbook case of preventive force.*

But rank-and-file officers were unconvinced. They claimed that Hunt was as reluctant as ever to be seen as provocative and had ordered the first withdrawal to appease demonstrators in a repeat of Lieutenant Moulin's actions on April 29. In this cop-in-the-street version of events, Officer Greg Baltad and Sergeant Nick Titiriga had refused to leave the intersection either because they wouldn't (according to one account) or because they were pinned down at the gas station.[33] Police commanders then sent in units to rescue the officers and quelled the disturbance. In this unofficial version, LAPD management was still slow on the switch, and only the stubbornness of two veteran officers had saved the day. But the media reported the official version of the incident. Local television was especially restrained, perhaps reacting to criticism of inflammatory coverage during the riots. Instead of interrupting regular programs, most stations confined reports of the December 14 "mini-riot," as it came to be called, to regular newscasts.[34]

Chief Williams went to Florence and Normandie at 8:00 P.M. and held a televised news conference in which he declared victory and praised the "quick and measured" response of the LAPD. His statements were reported uncritically and praised by the media, which gave the LAPD unusually positive coverage in the months after Gates' departure. In a page-one story on December 16 headed "LAPD Widely Saluted for Swiftly Quelling Incident," the Los Angeles Times said Williams was "far more engaged" than Gates "in coordinating the overall response, including maintaining contact with field commanders and advising political leaders." The story also lauded the chief for alerting other law enforcement agencies and the governor's office. Williams basked in the glow of his media honeymoon, but he knew that Los Angeles remained a city on the brink.

In fact, the violent texture of South Central was grimly evident a mile away from Florence and Normandie at the very time police officers were arresting the rock-throwers on December 14. The incident occurred at a

---

* This time the elite Metro Division was ready for a disturbance. Some of its officers were equipped with the new .37 millimeter gas guns with foam-rubber bullets that Metro had sought in vain before the riots. They worked as advertised, providing a stinging impact that dispersed the rock throwers without injuring them.

Manchester Boulevard electronics store owned by Raul Calvin Delcomber, a thirty-three-year-old African American described by a woman friend as "a low-key, slacks-and-polo-shirt kind of guy, hair always groomed, a wholesome All-American type."

Delcomber was a pillar of the community. After his mother died when he was only thirteen, Delcomber tried to escape his grief by losing himself in his hobby of CB radio. He also became an Explorer Scout and a good samaritan. At nineteen he saved the life of a woman in a burning house, winning the first of several commendations from the Fire Department and the sheriff's office for rescues he made after monitoring police radios. After graduating from Inglewood High School, he worked as an ambulance driver and sold electronic beepers on the side. In 1985 he opened the electronics store on Manchester Boulevard and was soon the largest supplier of beepers in South Central. His business grew, and he opened another store in Inglewood and then a third in Lomita. From habit he monitored emergency radio frequencies, as he was doing at his Inglewood store on December 14.

When he heard calls for help from officers at Florence and Normandie, Delcomber realized that the neighborhood was ripe for another riot. His Manchester Boulevard store had been looted in April, and Delcomber told his Inglewood employees that he needed to remove valuable equipment before it was stolen. The employees tried to dissuade him, telling him that it was dangerous in the Florence-Normandie neighborhood after dark. Delcomber went anyway. At 6:40 P.M., he was shot to death in the parking lot of his Manchester Boulevard store by robbers who had come to loot it, as Delcomber feared. No one was ever charged.[35]

In South Central, it was widely believed that police had provoked the December 14 incident by arresting peaceful protesters. This explanation was promoted by Georgiana Williams in her efforts to rally community support for her son, Damian, and by Lawrence Montgomery, a thirty-year-old barber who was among the first arrested. Montgomery said he had taken his two small children to attend the rally, where music was blaring loudly on various radios. Police officers told the demonstrators to turn down the volume. The demonstrators refused. Montgomery said he was urging people to stay calm in the face of police provocation when he was chased and arrested by an officer who called him a "smart-ass." The barber said the LAPD had "converted a peaceful demonstration into a potential riot."[36]

POLICE MILITANCY ON THE STREETS OF SOUTH CENTRAL WAS matched by legal militancy toward those the LAPD blamed for igniting the April riots. Their principal targets were two African Americans, Mark Jackson and Cerman Cunningham, whose scuffles with officers at Seventy-first and Normandie had precipitated Lieutenant Moulin's controversial retreat. The officers of the 77th Street Division were embarrassed by the retreat, and some focused their resentments on Cunningham and Jackson, who had long arrest records. Jackson was also the half-brother of Damian Williams (Georgiana was their mother), whom the videotape had cast as the principal villain of the riots. Blacks in the Florence and Normandie neighborhood believed that Jackson was being singled out because of his relationship to Damian, and their suspicions were ratified when nine misdemeanor charges were filed against Jackson for resisting arrest and grabbing at police batons.

Cerman Cunningham, who had supposedly thrown two fist-size rocks at LAPD Sergeant Sam Arase, was charged with five misdemeanors, including inciting a riot. He was the man who had showered police with obscenities and yelled, "Kill me, kill me, why don't you just kill me?" when he was arrested in the formative moments of the April 29 riots. He was arrested again on December 14, this time for allegedly hurling a ten-inch metal pipe at a police officer. While Cunningham had not harmed anyone in either encounter, the LAPD considered him a troublesome agitator and wanted him off the streets.

Given the jittery atmosphere in the Florence-Normandie neighborhood and a prevailing opinion among officers of 77th Street Division that Jackson and Cunningham had provoked the first clash of the riots, it is understandable that the police wanted to throw the book at them. Certainly, neither defendant was a candidate for sainthood. Cunningham had served a prison term for manslaughter. Jackson was an active gang member (according to police) or a former gang associate (according to Jackson). But the heavy aggregation of charges arising from the brief incident suggests that police and prosecutors may have gone overboard, as the district attorney had gone overboard in charging Damian Williams with torture and as the federal government went overboard in retrying the four LAPD officers, especially Wind and Briseno. Going overboard was the prosecutorial norm in Los Angeles after the riots, where presumptions of guilt abounded on all sides.

Jackson and Cunningham were tried together late in November 1992 for their role in the events of April 29. The list of charges had been pared down by the trial judge, who dismissed two charges against Jackson and one against Cunningham. Jackson was tried on seven misdemeanor counts and Cunningham on four, but Cunningham was more at risk because he was on parole for his manslaughter conviction. This meant that he probably would have been returned to prison if convicted, while Jackson faced a likely county-jail term. The prosecution appeared to have the upper hand against Cunningham—and for the same reason the prosecution had been favored in Simi Valley: Like the officers who had arrested Rodney King, Cunningham had been videotaped by an amateur cameraman. But as at Simi Valley, the video proved ambiguous enough for the defense to turn it to its own purpose.

The racially mixed Los Angeles jury that considered the charges against Cunningham and Jackson did not assume that police were always right. As these jurors afterward told attorneys in the case, they were skeptical about several of the nine police witnesses, especially Brian Liddy, the pugnacious officer who had arrested Cunningham, and his partner, Terry Keenan. Liddy and Keenan were the ones who testified that they saw Cunningham throw the rocks at Sergeant Arase.

Liddy and Keenan are white. So is Cunningham's principal attorney, Michael Evans, who had been a criminal defense attorney for six years. Jackson's attorney was the experienced Leon Jenkins, an African American we met earlier as civil attorney for the Latasha Harlins family. Deputy City Attorney Vivienne Swanigan, the well-regarded prosecutor, is also an African American. In Los Angeles, misdemeanors are prosecuted by the city attorney and felonies by the district attorney, a county official. Swanigan had been prosecuting misdemeanors for nine years. Despite the video she realized that she could probably not obtain a conviction of Cunningham unless the jury believed Officer Liddy. Swanigan worried about Liddy's "self-important" attitude, which some jurors found arrogant. "He had been on the street a long time and forgotten that it is important to deal with people in a human way," she said.[37]

Cunningham testified in his own defense, claiming that his unruly conduct was not in protest to the Simi Valley verdicts but to the rough treatment of teenager Seandel Daniels, whom police had captured in a nearby yard after he threw rocks at patrol cars at Florence and Normandie. Prosecutor Swanigan thought Cunningham an effective and soft-spoken witness. Swanigan used the video to show that Cunningham was already in police custody when Daniels was arrested. But as in Simi Valley, the video did not tell the full story. Cunningham had not yet been arrested when Daniels was chased and, as Evans put it in his closing argument, passed over a fence "like a piece of meat." And the video did not conclusively establish that Cunningham had thrown rocks at Arase. The prosecution case was not helped by the honest testimony of Arase, who had been too busy with the mob to notice what was being thrown at him.

The trial was frustrating for Swanigan, who had survived a harrowing experience in the riots. She had taken her three-year-old boy to Disneyland for his birthday and driven back to her mother's home in Los Angeles to pick up her other son, then eighteen months old. Although she had learned about the verdicts and the Denny beating over the car radio, Swanigan lived on the peaceful west side of Los Angeles and thought she could make it home. She might have done so without incident had the LAPD not barricaded Venice

Boulevard to keep rioters away from Wilshire Station. This diverted motorists into an area where rioters roamed. Swanigan's white Volvo station wagon was set upon by a mob of young blacks, one of whom shattered a window of the vehicle and caused glass to fly over her sleeping children. Swanigan turned the Volvo around, floored the accelerator, and headed into the mob, which parted "as if it were the Red Sea."[38] She then crashed through the police barricade at Wilshire and would have run the red light at La Brea except that she could see that the mob was not pursuing. When Swanigan reached home, she called Wilshire Station to tell police that the barricade was diverting cars into the riot. An officer brushed off her complaint, telling her that the situation outside the station was "not life threatening." Swanigan knew better. She demanded the officer's name. "Officer Smith," said the voice on the phone. She never learned his real name.

Still, Swanigan believed Officer Liddy was telling the truth about what Cunningham had done, and she did her best to prepare him for trial. She would remember yelling at the officer one day, asking if he could be "more human" and respectful in his testimony. Liddy tried, but his attitude did not impress the jurors. Neither did the video. Swanigan decided afterward that she would have been as well off without it. "Better off just have one person's word against another," she said.[39] On December 9, after five days of deliberations and a weekend off, the jury returned its verdicts. Jackson was acquitted on all counts. Cunningham was acquitted of inciting to riot, resisting arrest, and one of the two assault counts. The jury deadlocked 11–1 for acquittal on the other assault count. This was good enough for Swanigan, who made no attempt to try Cunningham again on the remaining count. "I had done my best and accepted the verdict of the jury," she said.

There the prosecution of Cunningham should have ended, but Swanigan's sensible standard of justice was not accepted by the police or the district attorney. Liddy was the arresting officer again when Cunningham was taken into custody at the December 14 rally. This time the district attorney charged Cunningham with felony assault. When Swanigan learned that Cunningham had been arrested again by Liddy, she called the district attorney's office to warn that prosecution would be a waste of time. "I knew a jury wouldn't believe Liddy," she said. "I thought trying him again was a waste of taxpayer's money, that it was strictly a no-win case." She was right. Cunningham was tried for the felony assault in August 1993. Jurors acquitted him after only half an hour's deliberation and then told Evans, again his attorney, that they had not believed the police.

Most people in Los Angeles were unaware of the Cunningham trials. The media virtually ignored the first trial, which was overshadowed by the upcoming federal trial of the officers accused of violating Rodney King's civil rights. The second Cunningham trial was upstaged by the pending state trial

of the defendants accused of assaulting Reginald Denny. But the verdicts in
the Cunningham trials were instructive. They suggested that it could be
counterproductive for prosecutors to pile on unnecessary charges, either for
political reasons or to satisfy police grudges. Such perceived "overcharging"
would become an issue in the Damian Williams trial. The Cunningham verdicts also suggested that jurors who disbelieve or dislike police witnesses may
give defendants the benefit of any doubt, not just reasonable doubt. This
would later become one of the explanations for O. J. Simpson's acquittal on
two murder charges.

Juries reach independent decisions for various reasons. They are capable
of ignoring evidence that prosecutors regard as significant and court instructions that may be inconvenient to their views. They are apt to give
weight to personal experiences and to their own perceptions of the police.
They are sensitive to the attitudes of prosecution witnesses who seem eager
to convict. When weighing evidence against defendants with whom they
sympathize, jurors often cling to a presumption of innocence. In Los
Angeles, as in Simi Valley, this presumption proved too powerful for even a
videotape to overcome.

15

PLAYING THE RACE CARD

*"I'm not absolutely sure which word it was, if it was killer or nigger.
I'm not sure."*

—Rodney King[1]

THE UNNOTICED VERDICTS IN THE FIRST TRIAL OF CERMAN
Cunningham, the unsolved murder of Raul Delcomber, and the rout of
the rally turned "mini-riot" at Florence and Normandie occurred in December 1992, as one of the most tumultuous years in the history of Los Angeles drew to a close. The stage was now set for two trials that many feared
could spark new disorders. Although procedural issues had delayed the trial
of *The People of the State of California v. Damian Monroe Williams and Henry
Keith Watson*, a top-notch trial team was prepared to try *United States of
America v. Stacey C. Koon et al.*, in which Koon, Laurence Powell, Timothy Wind, and Theodore Briseno were accused of violating the civil rights
of Rodney King. The federal prosecutors enjoyed a favorable venue and superior resources and were confident of the merits of their case. But they
were nervous, and security was tight at the federal courthouse in downtown
Los Angeles. Both the security and the nervousness were prompted by fears
that the government had a "mole" in its midst.

The prosecutors had reason for concern. While going through his mail
at his downtown law office on a warm August morning four months earlier,
Officer Powell's lawyer, Michael Stone, had come across what appeared to
be a memorandum to the U.S. Attorney from the federal trial team. Instead
of sharing his discovery with his fellow defense attorneys, Stone telephoned
Steven Clymer at the U.S. Attorney's Office a few blocks away and asked if
he had sent him anything. Not recently, Clymer replied. Stone told him
about the memorandum, and Clymer asked if he had read it. Stone said he
had begun to read it but stopped after a couple of pages when he realized the
memo was not meant for him. Clymer told Stone not to read any more of
the document or copy it and sent FBI agents to his office to confiscate it.

After the trial, Clymer effusively praised Stone for his "tremendous integrity" in returning a document that might have helped his client.[2] But at the time, when it mattered, the government did not trust Stone. FBI agents searched his office, inspected his copying machine, and fingerprinted the attorney and his secretary. They found nothing. The memo had been mailed in a plain brown envelope with no return address.

The memorandum, a strategic analysis of the government's case by the prosecution trial team, candidly assessed the strengths and weaknesses of prospective witnesses. While the document has never been made public, those familiar with its contents said it discussed the problematic potential testimony of Rodney King and California Highway Patrol Officer Melanie Singer, a key prosecution eyewitness at Simi Valley who had contradicted herself under Stone's cross-examination and damaged the state's case.

Federal sources later told me the memo did not contain much that the defense could not have figured out for itself. But the fact that the government has kept it secret to this day leads Koon and others to suspect that it revealed the political nature of the prosecution. My suspicion is that the government would be embarrassed by publication of its unflattering opinions of Melanie Singer and—even more—of Rodney King.

At the time, however, prosecutors were most concerned that someone on the government team, or someone with access to its documents, was disloyal. The trial was months away, and legal strategy could be changed. But someone who betrayed the government once might do it again. In Washington, Justice Department officials directed their Public Integrity Section to undertake a criminal investigation. In Los Angeles, locks were changed and special doors installed at prosecution offices. Government prosecutors went into court in secret session and asked Judge Davies to issue an order compelling other defense attorneys to return the memo. During the hearing, Davies praised Stone for returning the document, which was how other defense lawyers learned what he had done. Ira Salzman, representing Koon, told Davies he had not received the memo. Wind's attorney, Paul DePasquale, said the same.*

But Harland Braun, who represented Briseno, refused to say whether he had a copy of the memorandum. Braun contended that Davies couldn't order

---

* The public did not become aware of the leaked memo until November 20, when a story about it was published by the *Los Angeles Times*. It caused an uproar in Congress, where Senate Judiciary Chairman Joseph R. Biden Jr., Democrat from Delaware, called it "an inexcusable leak of security in a highly sensitive case of national importance." Representative John Conyers Jr., Democrat from Michigan and a senior member of the House Judiciary Committee, said the leaked memo "effectively sabotaged" the prosecution. These assessments were overblown. The leak occurred too early to have any profound effect on the prosecution, as former federal prosecutor Laurie Levenson observed at the time. But as she also noted, the incident had shaken up the prosecution team. "It cost us time," Clymer said later.

him to return the document unless he knew he had it and said he would take the Fifth Amendment if the judge asked. This tactic annoyed Davies, but he was not eager for a confrontation. Davies issued the prosecution's requested order but told Braun he could move to set it aside and allow the question to be decided on appeal. Braun would not be required to do anything until the appellate court ruled. Since Davies gave Braun no deadline for making the motion, Braun never made it. This legalistic sleight of hand, tacitly condoned by the disapproving judge, allowed Braun to maintain throughout the trial that the government could not force him to return the memorandum.

As Davies suspected, however, Braun was engaging in legal gamesmanship and had never seen the document. Braun viewed the government as the enemy and sought every permissible edge for the defense. He told me after the trial that he would have consulted an attorney to make certain of his legal grounds and used the memorandum in any way the law allowed. Courts usually have held that lawyers can use material that comes to them innocently, as this document had come to Stone. Even one of the trial prosecutors acknowledged to me that a defense attorney clearly had a right to read a government memorandum that came to him unsolicited.

Whether Stone was ethically bound to inform the government and return the memorandum once he read it are closer questions. When his action in returning the memo became public shortly before the trial, Braun told *The New York Times* that it was "unbelievable a lawyer would jeopardize his own client's case."[3] Braun believed "whatever is legal in defense of a client is by definition ethical."[4] As he saw it, lawyers have a transcendent duty to their clients that is limited only by the requirement to obey the law.

But Braun had tried hundreds of criminal cases. Stone had never tried a case in federal court, and the Simi Valley trial had been his first felony trial. He had been a police officer much of his life and as a lawyer, had represented police officers. Stone was deferential to authority by nature and training, tacitly sharing Clymer's assumption that prosecutors were usually the "good guys." He had no idea who had sent him the memo and told me later it crossed his mind that he was being set up. This seems far-fetched. It is more likely that Stone simply did what he thought was right, much like Henry Stimson, Secretary of War during a crucial period in the nation's history, who mistakenly closed the War Department's code-breaking section with the explanation that "gentlemen do not read each other's mail."[5] Stone was a gentleman too.

In terms of Officer Powell's interests, Stone's action was also a mistake, as he might have realized with more experience. At the time he returned the memo, Stone was only four months removed from the Simi Valley trial and the stunning acquittal of Powell on every charge but one. He was confident

Powell would be acquitted again. But this time, he faced a more high-powered prosecution, and he needed all the help he could get. Trying the officers in a city that had been wracked by riots for which the police were partly blamed was advantageous for the government. So was the opportunity to review the televised and written record of the state trial and correct prosecution mistakes. The unknown sympathizer who mailed Stone the memorandum had handed the defense a document that might have been a potential equalizer. But Stone failed to realize that the deck was stacked against his client.

Instead of equalizing the odds, the memorandum damaged the defense it was intended to help. The other defense attorneys did not follow Braun's lead in criticizing Stone publicly, but they were similarly scandalized. Privately, DePasquale complained that Stone had undermined a unified defense by sharing information with the government. Stone's action enhanced his reputation as a lone wolf and left wounds that never fully healed.

IN TRUTH, POWELL AND KOON WOULD HAVE FACED ENORMOUS obstacles even if Clymer had mailed the defense attorneys the transcripts of every prosecution strategy conference. The unfavorable venue of the trial was difficult for the defense to overcome, and the federal prosecutors were talented trial attorneys. They spent long days and weekends preparing, concentrating on correcting the defects of the first prosecution. The federal prosecutors were convinced that the state had botched its case, although as Clymer said much later, "We had the advantage of seeing everything that had gone wrong at the first trial."[6]

Some of the biggest gaps in the state's case had been caused by the absence of key witnesses, notably Rodney King. Stone had made a point of this in his closing argument and said out of court, "How many cases have you seen . . . where they don't call the victim?"[7] While it is doubtful that King's presence would have saved the day for the prosecution at Simi Valley, his absence made it easier, Assistant U.S. Attorney Lawrence Middleton observed, for the defense to depict King as a "wild, PCP-crazed monster."[8] Calling King as a witness in the federal trial was a given. The responsibility of preparing him to testify was assigned to Kowalski and Middleton, the only African American among the prosecutors.

Another gaping hole in the state case had been the lack of a credible use-of-force expert. The LAPD had discouraged qualified experts from testifying, sticking prosecutor Terry White with an LAPD commander who lacked street experience. But under new leadership and after the sobering impact of the riots, the LAPD had climbed aboard the prosecution train. The LAPD witness in the federal trial was Sergeant Mark Conta, who taught physical training and self-defense tactics at the Police Academy.

There were other holes that needed filling. Prosecutors at both trials contended that King's facial injuries were caused by Powell's baton blows, while Stone argued that they resulted from hard falls to the pavement. The weight of medical evidence in the state trial favored the prosecution but left ambiguities. Federal prosecutors set out to resolve them by calling an expert in the field of biomechanics, which includes the study of how injuries are caused. They turned to Dr. James Benedict of San Antonio, Texas, a recognized expert in this field.

Federal prosecutors steered around other smaller holes in the state case. They were determined to refrain from calling witnesses likely to raise more questions than they could answer. This eliminated Melanie Singer, the CHP officer who had begun the pursuit of King and reacted in horror to his beating. While her testimony had emotional impact, she had unraveled under Stone's cross-examination and acknowledged that her dramatic recollections did not jibe with the videotape.

JURY SELECTION IN *UNITED STATES V. KOON* BEGAN ON FEBRUARY 3, 1993. The day before, Judge Davies had denied a motion by Salzman to delay the trial until the passions of the riots had cooled. Salzman cited a CBS poll showing that 75 percent of Los Angeles residents believed new riots were likely if the defendants were acquitted. Nearly two-thirds of those surveyed— and four-fifths of African Americans—thought the defendants should be found guilty. Salzman said he had been "jolted out of his chair" by the poll. But the findings were no surprise. The likelihood that fear of new riots would jeopardize a fair trial is what had caused Judge Davies to anticipate a change-of-venue request by the defense. But defense attorneys had not pursued this option, and Davies saw no legal ground for postponing the trial.

The media had underestimated the significance of venue at Simi Valley and would do so again two years later when the district attorney decided to try O. J. Simpson for murder in downtown Los Angeles instead of Santa Monica. But the media understood that a pervasive fear of new riots was, as the McClatchy News Service put it, the "emotional wild card" in the civil rights trial.

This context of fear was cogently addressed by the *Los Angeles Times* on the first day of jury selection. Under a headline, "2nd Trial Revives L.A.'s Fears and Hopes," the *Times* said in a page-one article that "with many of the thorniest problems wrought by last spring's civil upheaval still unresolved, there is apprehension throughout Los Angeles and beyond that more destruction and bloodshed could result if federal prosecutors fail to win convictions."[9] The story quoted worried statements by members of principal ethnic groups. It said federal marshals were beefing up security around the

building where the trial would be held while the LAPD and the National
Guard were holding tactical exercises. Lieutenant Michael Hillmann, who
before the Simi Valley verdicts had been a voice crying in the LAPD wilder-
ness for riot preparation, was quoted as saying, "We're not going to let the
people of Los Angeles go through what they went through last time."[10]

It was in this milieu that Judge Davies directed the mailing of what he
called "invitations" to 6,000 residents of seven Southern California counties, informing them that they had been selected as jury candidates for an
"important trial" beginning February 3, 1993. As Davies later acknowledged,
there was not much mystery about which important trial was pending. The
media glare had remained intense for two years. In September 1992, a li-
brarian in the U.S. Attorney's Office had conducted a computer search and
turned up 14,000 newspaper articles referring to the Rodney King case. A
Los Angeles Times search covering the four months before the trial found
1,745 additional newspaper and magazine references, twice the number of
references to Dianne Feinstein at the time she was winning election to the
Senate.[11] As prosecutors said in a pretrial motion, "It is unlikely that any potential jurors are unexposed to the publicity surrounding the beating of Rodney King and related events."

Most of the 6,000 persons who received the mailed invitations did not
respond. Of those who did, only 380 (6.3 percent) said they would be
available to serve on the jury, and 47 in this group did not show up on the
designated date. Davies tried to reassure the 333 jury candidates who came
to the federal courthouse in downtown Los Angeles, some of whom were
visibly nervous at the sight of cameras and reporters. He told them they
would have "an extraordinarily interesting experience" if chosen to serve.
"I think you will look back on this case as a true highlight in your life,"
Davies said.

After the indictments were read, Davies introduced the defendants and
the lawyers, who stood with him in a sprawling jury assembly area. Prospective jurors had been handed 53-page questionnaires exploring their attitudes on issues ranging from police misconduct to inter-racial marriage.
Davies urged them to answer each of the 148 questions candidly. "You have
our assurance that [the questionnaire] will be confidential and treated as
such forever, I hope." But as jury candidates were being sworn, a middle-
aged white man among them loudly addressed the judge: "You are asking
us to solemnly swear, but you are not solemnly swearing that our questionnaires will be kept confidential. Why don't you take an oath?" Marshals
tried to shush the man, but Davies said the question was fair. He said he had
issued an order directing that the questionnaires be kept confidential but
would excuse anyone who feared it would be violated. No one came forward, but Salzman said that the outburst demonstrated he had been right

in "arguing until I was blue in the face" for a postponement. "This community still has not cooled off," he said.[12]

Nor was cooling off promoted by jury selection, which shifted to the
nearby Edward R. Roybal Federal Building, where Davies had been assigned
a new courtroom. To those familiar with Los Angeles history, Roybal was a
resonant and appropriate name for a trial centering on allegations of police
misconduct. Roybal, who had retired in 1992 after a thirty-year career in
the House of Representatives, was the first Mexican American to win a seat
on the city council and in the early 1950s had led a campaign to hold Chief
William Parker accountable for LAPD excesses against minorities.

Demonstrators, mostly black, ringed the Roybal Building as jury selection began. They demanded "justice" for King and the Denny defendants
and a racially diverse jury in the civil rights trial. The demonstrators stirred
the city's fears. Even Angelenos who did not ascribe the Simi Valley verdicts
to lack of diversity among the jurors shuddered at the thought of what might
happen in their city if four white police officers were acquitted a second
time by a jury without black members. But the federal jury pool, although
more diverse than the one in Ventura County, did not guarantee a mixed-
race jury. African Americans made up slightly more than 8 percent of the
population in the seven counties from which the federal jury was drawn and
about 10 percent of the jury candidates.[13]

The selection process was shrouded in a pretense of color blindness. "My
only goal, and I mean this very sincerely, was fair and open-minded people,"
said Salzman.[14] "I wanted jurors who would be fair, irrespective of race," said
Clymer.[15] Each side accused the other of racially charged jury selection, but
Braun argued that such emphasis was inevitable and appropriate. "Fair had
nothing to do with it," he said. "This was a trial. The defense wanted jurors
who would acquit, and the prosecution wanted jurors who would convict.
The defense wanted white jurors, and the prosecution wanted black jurors."[16]

Braun's assessment was accurate and his bluntness appealing, but he carried candor too far when he told an African-American reporter that it
might be impossible for black jurors to be impartial. Braun's point, better
left unsaid, was that blacks would find it difficult to face family and friends
if they voted to acquit. For good measure, he rebuked the government for encouraging a "mob mentality" toward the defendants.

These comments irritated Davies, who issued a sharply worded three-
page gag order prohibiting Braun from discussing the motives of jurors or (at
Clymer's request) from criticizing the government. "Such comments are
purely speculative and highly improper and have evoked understandable
anger from elected officials and the public," Davies said. Braun was willing
to hold his tongue about jurors but unwilling to go easy on the government.
Represented by the ACLU, he appealed this section of the ruling to the

Ninth Circuit Court of Appeals, which overturned Davies and upheld Braun's freedom of speech.* But Braun's frankness had sent a message to even the densest trial watchers that the defense intended to keep blacks off the jury. His comments distressed Salzman, who said it was "totally offensive to imply that a person who is black cannot be fair."

Offensive or not, the question of whether black jurors could be fair to the white police officers who had beaten Rodney King had occurred to Davies. The judge demonstrated his commitment to an impartial jury by refusing to take responses on the questionnaires at face value and by asking probing questions of potential jurors without waiting for defense attorneys to do it. Davies dismissed one African American who acknowledged that he remained "angry" about the Simi Valley verdicts. Several others were excused because Davies did not find their responses credible even though they said they could be fair.

But African Americans who wanted to correct the perceived injustice of Simi Valley were not the only biased jury candidates, as Davies knew. Many whites expressed sympathy for the police in answers on their questionnaires. One white candidate said that Rodney King was responsible for everything that had happened to him. Another branded the trial as "unfair and a waste of taxpayers' money." Davies excused these candidates for cause, but prosecutors wondered how many more like them lurked behind innocuous answers on the questionnaires.

Indeed, because of the high-profile nature of the case and the likelihood that most candidates had realized the nature of the "invitations" sent them by Davies, attorneys on both sides suspected that the panel might be infiltrated by "agenda jurors" willing to endure the hardships of a long trial and sequestration because they had a mission to convict or acquit the defendants. Because of the requirement of unanimous verdicts, Clymer worried that a single, determined pro-police juror would cause a mistrial. DePasquale observed that all the jury candidates were volunteers auditioning for a role in an historical drama. But defense attorneys failed to realize how many of these role players feared another round of rioting in Los Angeles. Had the defense known the extent of these fears, it might have sought the change of venue it had not pursued for reasons of resources and convenience.

Salzman had belatedly raised this vital issue with his rejected motion to postpone the trial, but defense lawyers then turned their attention to other

---

* While Braun was under the gag order, he circumvented it by sarcastically telling the *Los Angeles Times:* "I think these prosecutors are wonderful guys. If they're single, I hope my daughter marries one of them. And you know what, it was really nice of them to indict my client. In fact, my client wants to know their address so he can send them a thank-you letter."

matters. Juror concern about new riots should have been explored at greater length by the defense, even in the limited questioning allowed in voir dire. While the federal jury was being selected, the Ventura County *Star Free Press* interviewed the Simi Valley jurors and found them living in fear and anger ten months after the verdicts. This story was picked up by the Los Angeles media and was known to some of the federal jurors, who had not yet been sequestered. But no one in court took notice.

Clymer, meanwhile, worried about the high proportion of jury candidates who had a personal or familial connection with law enforcement. "I thought it would be very difficult to find a jury that would find the defendants guilty," he said.[17] But Clymer had the Supreme Court on his side. Prosecutors could remove jurors they considered too close to the police. The defense had the misfortune to try its case a year after a ruling by the Supreme Court that prohibited defense use of peremptory challenges to remove jurors because of race. Without this restriction, the defense probably would have used all of its fourteen peremptory challenges against blacks and might have succeeded in its goal of obtaining a jury that had no African Americans. Defense attorneys tried to reach that goal through a different route by subjecting black jurors to withering questioning in the hope of drawing an admission that would prompt Davies to remove them for cause. The tactic left Clymer seething. "These defense attorneys are treating black jurors differently than white jurors—they're doing it wholesale," he complained.

Clymer's comment was provoked by Salzman's attempt to oust a black jury candidate who was a former Marine and longtime resident of Watts. The man told Stone during voir dire that he was "a little angry" at the Simi Valley verdicts but "didn't know the exact details" and would have an open mind toward the defendants. Salzman was skeptical, as were Stone and De-Pasquale. Braun was willing to accept the Watts man because his client Briseno (who knew many blacks) thought he would be fair but was outvoted by his colleagues. As part of a unified defense, of which Braun was the leading advocate, the defense lawyers had decided to make decisions on jurors by majority vote.

The defense majority viewed the Watts man as a prototype of an agenda juror and grilled him assertively. The government wanted him on the jury. When Clymer accused the defense of trying to oust the Watts man because of his race, Salzman insisted his questions were "race neutral" and aimed at exposing "inconsistencies" in the Watts man's answers. "If that gentleman was white and lived in Beverly Hills, I would question him the same way," Salzman said. Davies was unimpressed. The judge refused to dismiss the Watts man for cause or allow the defense to exercise a peremptory challenge. The seating of the Watts man on February 22 completed selection of a jury that had two black members.

Both government and defense lawyers presumed much and knew little about the jury candidates whose merits they debated. The Watts man proved a competent juror who listened to the evidence, leaned initially toward acquittals, and eventually went along with the majority. Other jurors thought him unbiased. Based on his performance, Braun was wrong in asserting that no black juror could be impartial, Salzman wrong in believing him to be an agenda juror, and Clymer wrong in believing that he was a boon to the government. Black jurors, as Davies had said in evaluating his own performance as a judge, do not come out of a cookie-cutter.

If Clymer was wrong about this particular juror, he was probably right in believing that the defense focus on race backfired. The defense attorneys became so preoccupied with the unattainable objective of keeping blacks off the jury that they failed to challenge whites whose attitudes and responses were unfavorable to the defendants. "They were afraid to use peremptories against these jurors because they thought they might be replaced by blacks," Clymer observed.[18] As a result, the defense wound up with the worst of all worlds—a jury with black members and a majority of whites who were receptive to the prosecution case and fearful that acquittals would lead to another riot.

In preferring any white juror, even an unsympathetic one, to any African American, the defense turned its back on its own best perception of the King incident. From beginning to end, in and out of court, the defendants and their attorneys resisted the assumption of the media and most African Americans that Rodney King was beaten because he was black. They were right to do so, for the preponderance of the evidence suggests that King was beaten because he was resistant (in the defense view) or disrespectful (as the prosecution saw it), not because of his race. But when push came to shove during jury selection, the defense implicitly accepted the conventional definition of the incident as a racial case, preferring to take its chances with unsympathetic white jurors rather than with blacks who might be fair.

Ironically, this preoccupation with race did not protect the defense from a black juror who would ratify their fears. She was Maria Escobel, a widowed Orange County postal worker and mother of a four-year-old son. On her questionnaire and in voir dire, Escobel acknowledged that she disagreed with the Simi Valley verdicts but said she would be guided by the evidence. She was seated as Juror No. 7 without a murmur of protest from the defense lawyers who soon afterward put up such a brisk fight against the Watts man. "I want her on my jury!" Braun told the *Los Angeles Times*. "I like her. She's a good juror!"[19] Salzman went further, describing the woman who would play a key role in sending his client to prison as the "perfect juror."[20]

Not everyone on the defense team was taken with Escobel. Jo-Ellan Dimitrius, in a return engagement as jury consultant, noticed that

Escobel wore black gloves in court in an "obvious sort of disregard for what was common."[21] To Dimitrius, this was a sure sign of a strong juror, and the last person she wanted on this particular jury was a strong, black woman. Dimitrius is a mother, and Escobel's willingness to leave her young son in the care of a nanny while she served on a sequestered jury was another danger signal that she might be an agenda juror.

But nothing in Escobel's written or verbal responses provided a basis to challenge her for cause. The overenthusiastic praise of Escobel by Salzman and Braun was in part a recognition of the reality that she was going to be a juror no matter what they said. Accepting Escobel with open arms had the public relations value of allowing the defense lawyers to defuse the charge that they were opposed to any and all black jurors.

Once the Watts man was seated and the jury accepted, however, Salzman received a shock. At 7:00 A.M. on February 23, he received a telephone call from an excused juror, a reserve police officer who worked for the telephone company. He told Salzman that during a break Juror No. 7 had "disdainfully" blamed defense attorneys for seating a racially unbalanced jury in Simi Valley. Furthermore, she had complained that defense attorneys in the federal case were also trying to keep blacks off the jury. On the basis of this information, Salzman refused to accept the jury and moved for a mistrial. Clymer went into orbit. "This is an attempt to provoke a mistrial after the jury is sworn because the defense is unhappy with the composition of the jury," he said.

Salzman was angered by Clymer's charge. He pointed out that he was acting on the basis of new information, not out of bias. Davies calmed the excited attorneys and directed marshals to bring the excused juror to court. The judge talked to him in chambers, then separately questioned Escobel— most courteously, she later said. Escobel said Davies told her that the excused juror had accused her of making a whispered comment that the defense was trying to exclude any juror who was black. Without denying that she held this opinion, Escobel said she did not recall making the comment and reiterated her willingness to be fair.[22] Davies realized that the statement attributed to Escobel by the excused juror accurately described the defense strategy. In a decision as important as any he would make during the trial, Davies ruled that the defense had made "no appropriate showing of bias" and denied the motion for a mistrial.

THE PROSECUTION CASE OPENED DRAMATICALLY ON FEBRUARY 25, signaling that the federal trial would be different from the one in Simi Valley. Clymer announced in his opening statement that Rodney King would testify. He said that Sergeant Mark Conta, who taught physical training at the Police Academy and had "worked on the streets of Los Angeles as both a patrol officer and a sergeant for about seventeen years of his life," would testify that Powell, Wind, and Briseno violated LAPD policy and training when they beat and kicked King, who "was not combatant or aggressive." Koon, Clymer said, had violated policy and training when he failed to stop the beating.

The highlight of this meticulously organized opening statement, which Clymer delivered with passionate intensity, was the disclosure that Powell and Wind had not taken King directly from Pacifica Hospital, where he was first treated for his injuries, to Los Angeles County–USC Medical Center. Instead, disobeying Koon's orders, they had driven to Foothill Station, where Powell had officers "go out and look at Rodney King in the car." The officers had then covered up their side trip by putting down the wrong times on their logs, omitting the fact they had gone to the station before taking King to the USC Medical Center. This apparent treatment of King as a trophy was a bombshell that gave reporters a lead for their first-day story. State prosecutors had not known of the side trip. Clymer had learned of it in an Internal Affairs document and confirmed it by grilling LAPD officers before the grand jury. The defense would present the stop at the station in a different light, but was never able to explain it away. While the trial would have ups and downs, as trials do, Clymer captured the high ground in his opening statement and never yielded it.[23]

Clymer's opening statement also demonstrated that federal prosecutors had learned important lessons about the value and limitations of the Holliday videotape. In the wake of the state trial, a galaxy of experts had seconded District Attorney Ira Reiner's theory that familiarity with the videotape desensitized jurors. The defense in the state trial supposedly had taken advantage of this phenomenon by playing the video repeatedly in slow motion and breaking it down frame by frame until its overall emotional impact was lost.

Clymer was skeptical about this conventional wisdom. He was appalled every time he watched the video at any speed by what he saw as the inexcusable brutality of the officers, particularly Powell. Clymer's concern was that the video was confusing. "There was a lot happening out there that night, involving a lot of people," he said.[24] Clymer believed the government had to explain the entire video, "not just throw it up on the screen and expect it to convict the defendants all by itself."[25]

The way Clymer went about accomplishing this objective demonstrated his devotion to detail and the technological prowess of the FBI, which had enhanced the video since the state trial. Long before the federal trial, Clymer visited the FBI laboratory to familiarize himself with a "jog-shuttle switch" that moved the video forward and backward a frame at a time. This useful feature was an improvement over the living room remote control used by the state prosecutors. Clymer used the jog-shuttle switch thirteen times in the opening statement alone as he led jurors step by step through the videotape. This careful approach paid off in the jury room. Even jurors who did not agree with all of Clymer's interpretations gained an understanding of fine points of the videotape that had been lacking at Simi Valley.

Also, as former federal prosecutor Laurie Levenson observed, the government avoided overuse of the videotape. It was the prosecution's best evidence, and there would have been no prosecution without it. But as the state trial had demonstrated, the complete videotape offered evidence for the defense as well, especially in the opening frames, where King charges toward Powell. Clymer used his best evidence creatively. He made the video the centerpiece of a narrative that was enriched by the testimony of civilian and police witnesses and by the supposedly damning trail left by defendants after the beating. It was a masterful presentation.

The first day of the federal trial was different on the defense side as well. The opening day of the state trial had been marked by a fiery exchange between defense lawyers Michael Stone and John Barnett. Stone had described Theodore Briseno as a liar who was trying to save himself by attributing misconduct to the other officers. Barnett had portrayed Briseno as a good cop who realized that Powell was "out of control" when he repeatedly hit Rodney King with his baton and had tried to stop the beating. In the Barnett depiction, Briseno had been attacked by Stone because he dared to break the police "code of silence" and tell the truth.

Harland Braun, representing Briseno in the federal trial, sought to avoid a repetition of this conflict. Braun believed his client would be acquitted under any theory of the case because of his minimal involvement. Powell had delivered scores of blows to King, and Wind had added many blows and kicks. Koon was the supervisor. The entire case against the right-footed Briseno was that he had delivered one stomp to King's back or neck area with his left foot—a stomp that Briseno had claimed at Simi Valley was intended to keep King down and prevent his being hit again by Powell. Since the videotaped evidence against Briseno was ambiguous, Braun was confident he had a winning case. His main concern was that defense attorneys for Powell and Koon would try to discredit his client.

It was to protect Briseno from the other defendants that Braun devised the unified defense. Its essence was that every officer had acted legally based on his perceptions. Braun relied on the FBI-enhanced videotape, which he said shed new light on the conduct of the defendants. The video shows that Powell was reaching for the handcuffs in his police belt when Briseno put his foot on King. Briseno could not see this because King blocked his view. Powell, in turn, did not see that Briseno had stomped King and caused him to move.

When King began to rise, Powell hit him again with his baton. As Braun explained the incident in a brief opening statement, every officer had acted reasonably and Briseno's earlier attempt to stop the beating was merely a "remarkable momentary disagreement" among police professionals. This was the "unified defense" that Braun preached and practiced.

Stone, a reluctant convert to coexistence between the Powell and Briseno defenses, went along. His two-hour opening statement mostly ignored Briseno and dwelt on the defense dogmas that had prevailed at Simi Valley. Rodney King was an unsearched felony suspect who led police on a high-speed pursuit. The officers feared King, whom they believed was under the influence of PCP, and followed the dictates of LAPD use-of-force policy. King had disobeyed commands, resisted arrest, and charged at Powell. The force used to arrest King had been managed and controlled by Sergeant Koon and ceased when King stopped resisting. "The conduct that was engaged in was not illegal, but was directly in response to the conduct of Mr. King," Stone said.

After opening statements, the government called civilian witnesses who had appeared before the federal grand jury but not testified at Simi Valley. Dorothy Gibson, a middle-aged African-American woman and registered nurse for twenty years, lived directly under George Holliday's apartment. Awakened by the police helicopter, she went onto the patio of her apartment to see what was happening across the street. Gibson saw a black man "laying on the ground face down on his stomach with hands stretched out like in a cross." When he jumped up, an officer hit him with a "black stick or something." Other officers also hit him with their sticks and kicked him. The man screamed, "Please stop," but the officers did not stop. "Any way they could get a lick in they was kicking," Gibson said, her emotions rising as Barry Kowalski led her through a reconstruction of the incident. She said the officers had handcuffed the man's arms and legs and "drug him to the side of the road." When Kowalski asked what they did next, Gibson was near tears. "They were talking and laughing as they were getting in their cars . . ." Gibson said, her voice cracking. "I didn't want to see anymore."

The next witness was Robert Hill, a county probation officer who supervised juveniles in a detention home and lived in the same apartment complex as Gibson and Holliday. He had been driving home from work when he observed police cars at Foothill and Osborne. Hill, an African American, had parked his car at his apartment, then walked back to the iron fence surrounding the complex to watch through a grating. From a distance of thirty yards, he had seen officers knock a man to the ground and continue to hit him on the upper body and legs while he was down. The man had screamed. Hill had also seen an officer "put his foot close to the head of the man" but didn't know if the foot struck the head.

These witnesses had been interviewed soon after the incident by an investigator from the district attorney's office but not called as witnesses at Simi Valley, for reasons that became apparent—at least in Dorothy Gibson's case—during cross-examination by Michael Stone and Paul DePasquale. The defense attorneys assumed Gibson was telling the truth as she remembered it. But their gentle cross-examination revealed that portions of Gibson's testimony conflicted with what she had told the investigator. Gibson acknowledged to Stone that she didn't "know exactly" who had cried "Please stop." She acknowledged to DePasquale that she had told the investigator four days after the incident that she had seen five officers hitting the man. DePasquale showed her a portion of the transcript of this interview where Gibson had referred to the Holliday video as a basis for her comments. Gibson then denied she had seen the video before being interviewed.

Hill fared somewhat better on cross-examination, perhaps because his direct testimony was more limited. He acknowledged he had seen the televised version of the videotape before he was interviewed by the district attorney's investigator and that he subsequently watched the video many times with Clymer. Whether Hill's recollections had been altered by his viewings of the video could not be determined, but his testimony was little changed from his account to the investigator. A small discrepancy emerged during cross-examination by DePasquale: Hill had told the investigator that King had been hit in the leg area, not on the torso and legs.

The defense conceded that Gibson and Hill were honest witnesses. The problem with their testimony was that their eyewitness accounts were contradicted by the Holliday video and their recollections clouded by exposure to it. Over time, memory and observation had fused into a more or less coherent narrative that may have been additionally enriched by what they later learned. In this respect, Gibson and Hill resembled the participants. Laurence Powell and Rodney King, at the center of the violent and fast-moving incident, had even more difficulty squaring their recollections with what they later saw on the video. Try as they might, they could not reconcile images from the mind's eye with the videotaped record. The fearful Powell remembered his panic and the intoxicated King his pain. The sober video, unencumbered by emotions or memory, impeached the recollections of every witness.

Because state prosecutors had presumed the videotape to be unassailable evidence, they had not wanted to distract jurors by exposing them to witnesses whose recollections conflicted with what could be seen on the tape. State prosecutors also hesitated to call African-American witnesses whom jurors might assume were favorable to King. But federal prosecutors realized that human voices were needed in the King narrative, even if they contradicted the videotape. "The civilian witnesses enriched the picture," said Laurie Levenson.[26] This was evident in the courtroom as jurors listened raptly to Gibson and Hill. The cross-examination finished late Friday afternoon, leaving jurors to reflect on this emotional testimony during their first weekend of sequestration.

The civilian narrative continued the following week with testimony through an interpreter of two musicians from Banda El Rincon, a Spanish-language band that had performed in the San Fernando Valley and was returning by bus to its home base of San Jose. Some band members had seen fragments of the incident through the windows after the bus was stopped in the road by police cars responding to the King pursuit. Benjamin Avila testified that he saw four police officers hit King "all over his body" with billy clubs or baseball bats. Felipe Lopez saw officers knock King down seven or eight times.

The value of this testimony was marginal. Avila had turned his head away at a crucial point, and Lopez's view had been partially blocked from his position on the bus. Taken together or separately, the accounts given by the musicians conflicted even more substantially with the videotaped record than had the accounts of Gibson and Hill. Stone complained outside the courtroom that the statements by civilian witnesses provided "a dramatic example of the untrustworthiness of eyewitness testimony."[27] He had a point, but the civilian witnesses helped set a tone for the trial. Gibson, Hill, Avila, and Lopez were part of a diverse chorus in an historical docudrama produced by the government to show that what happened to Rodney King was unacceptably brutal. The civilian witnesses enhanced the value of the videotape, which remained the star of the show.

After the chorus, the government brought on the supporting cast. It was led by Mark Conta, the LAPD sergeant who had refused to testify at Simi Valley. Conta's excuses were that he was a shaky witness who would do poorly on cross-examination and damage his career by testifying. But circumstances had changed. At the time of Simi Valley, Conta was number two in the unit that taught physical training and self-defense tactics at the Police Academy. He had since replaced Sergeant Fred Nichols as the officer in charge.

Federal prosecutors were determined to make use of Conta's expertise. He was no longer in a position to refuse, for LAPD management was allied with the government in the federal trial, and Conta was the department's resident use-of-force expert. Some LAPD officers have suggested that Conta was reluctant to testify, but he seemed a willing witness when he took the stand on March 3, 1993, the second anniversary of the incident, to provide a crucial evaluation of the defendants' conduct.[28]

The defense made a determined effort to keep the jury from hearing Conta's analysis. Ira Salzman and Michael Stone argued in a hearing outside the jury's presence that Conta had been exposed through conversations with Nichols to statements about the King incident that Koon and Powell had given to Internal Affairs investigators. LAPD officers are required as a condition of employment to answer questions of department investigators. The results of these interviews are known legally as "compelled statements" and cannot be used in a criminal trial because they would violate the defendants' protection against self-incrimination guaranteed by the Fifth Amendment to the Constitution. When Nichols was waging his battle to be disqualified as an expert witness in the state trial, he claimed to have read the compelled statements of Koon, Powell, and Wind.

Conta acknowledged talking with Nichols about the King case but said that he had not read the compelled statements. Conta said his only known exposure to information from any of the statements occurred when he watched a January 29, 1993, TV broadcast that cited a passage of Wind's statement—Wind's potentially significant observation that Powell had struck the charging King in the head. But this information had circulated widely within the department and was also well known to reporters. Conta said his evaluation of the King incident was not based on this thirty-second television segment or anything Nichols had said to him. Judge Davies allowed Conta to testify.

As a witness, Conta was all the government had hoped for and more. In contrast to Commander Michael Bostic, who was discounted by Simi Valley jurors after confessing to minimal street experience, Conta had spent seventeen of twenty-two years in the LAPD as a patrol officer. He was also, in Jim Newton's phrase, a "Charles Bronson look-alike." Trim and immaculate in his neatly pressed blue uniform, Conta seemed an embodiment of police professionalism as he explained LAPD use-of-force policy and analyzed the videotape. Jurors peered over the jury box to watch as Conta left the stand and demonstrated the proper use of the side-handle metal baton that Powell had wielded against King. When he returned to the stand, Barry Kowalski asked him if baton instruction at the Police Academy "ever included teaching someone how to strike somebody who is down on the ground."

"Absolutely not," Conta replied.

Conta's thesis was that the incident began as a lawful arrest and remained lawful during the first thirty-two to thirty-five seconds recorded on the videotape before degenerating into an inappropriate use of force. He excused Powell's apparent head blow near the start of the video, presuming it was not intentional, because it had been delivered defensively in response to King's charge. Subsequent blows, when King was in a crouched, "semi-standing position," were also deemed "within policy" by Conta. During this period, King presented "an objective threat because he's in a position where he could attack the officers," Conta said. Kowalski then advanced the FBI-enhanced video in slow motion, stopping it after 35:28 seconds.

"What is your opinion now?" Kowalski asked.

"My opinion is that he [Powell] has violated policy," Conta said.

"And why is that?"

"Rodney King is on the ground now," Conta said. "He's not displaying any behavior of being combative or aggressive, and in my opinion, that would not constitute an objective threat."

Conta continued through the tape, pointing out what he considered other policy violations as Powell hit King while he was on the ground. He became particularly animated when Kowalski stopped the tape at 55:15 seconds, with King on his back and his knees up as Powell delivered a baton stroke to his chest.

"And to me this is one of the most flagrant violations that I have seen in this entire video," Conta said. "It's clearly out of policy. And I don't see any objective threat, any real threat, anything remotely close to any type of combative or aggressive behavior."

After analyzing Powell's conduct, Conta turned his attention to the other officers. Wind had been out of policy because he delivered baton blows and "brutal kicks" while King was on the ground. Briseno had behaved in a "highly commendable" way seventeen seconds into the video when he attempted to prevent Powell from striking King. But later Briseno stomped King while he was "flat on the ground in a prone position" in what was "clearly a violation of Los Angeles police policy." As for Sergeant Koon, he had failed fifteen seconds into the video to take advantage of what Conta alternately called a "golden opportunity" and a "great opportunity" to take King into custody without further use of force.

"Right now, Sergeant Koon has an opportunity to take control of this situation," Conta testified. "He should tell those officers to put their batons away, and grab arms and legs, and the different appendages, and apply body weight, and handcuff and cord cuff Rodney King and control the situation immediately."

Conta's after-the-fact advice could have served as an accurate description of the tactics Koon had used a few seconds earlier, before the video began, when he ordered Powell, Wind, Briseno, and Officer Rolando Solano to swarm King and handcuff him. The tactic had failed. King had thrown the officers off his back, climbed to his feet even after being hit with two volleys of the electric stun gun that Koon had fired into him, and charged at Powell. Under the circumstances, it is hardly surprising that Koon failed to seize the "golden opportunity" that was so apparent to Conta in retrospect. Salzman thought Conta's criticism unfair, but he had difficulty formulating an acceptable legal objection. Indeed, as Davies observed, defense attorneys offered few objections to any portion of Conta's testimony. When Salzman belatedly asked Davies to strike the criticism of Koon's tactics, the judge allowed it to remain in the record.

In Conta's view, Koon's missed "golden opportunity" fifteen seconds into the video was not necessarily a violation of LAPD policy. He told Kowalski that it was "a gross tactical error that resulted in excessive force" shown later on the videotape. But Conta was not finished with Koon. As Kowalski advanced the video to 37:28 seconds and baton blows continued, Conta intensified his criticism. "He's failed to intervene, and at this point he needs to take some action," Conta said. "He's seen what's going on. He needs to intervene, either by verbal commands or physical force, I mean physically grabbing an officer and removing him, if necessary. And that is his role as a field supervisor, to take control and take charge of that situation."

By the time the tape reached 42:15 seconds, Conta was convinced that "Sergeant Koon is clearly violating the Los Angeles police policy" by failing to intervene. Koon had watched Powell and Wind hitting King with their batons while he was on the ground but "failed to take appropriate actions" to stop them. Responding to a follow-up question from Kowalski, Conta said, "Rodney King did not demonstrate any combative or aggressive behavior while he was on the ground. [He] just does not constitute any objective threat."

Conta's testimony incensed Koon, who otherwise remained fatalistic about a trial that he considered an unjust political response to the riots. Koon realized that the prosecutors had a job to do and respected their legal skills, even while questioning their knowledge of police work. He also bore no animus to King. (Powell, in contrast, became livid at the mention of King and the thought that this "nothing" stood to receive millions of dollars in damages while the officers who arrested him faced prison terms.) Koon could understand why people who had seen the videotape on television thought the treatment of King was unnecessarily brutal; he could even understand why other LAPD officers might disagree with his tactics. But Koon's image of himself as the good sergeant made him unable to accept any suggestion that he had failed to supervise. He found it especially hard to take such criticism from Conta, who Koon believed had deliberately misrepresented LAPD policy in analyzing the video. After he was released from prison, Koon told me that the only time he "lost it" during the trial was when Conta "lied" on the witness stand. While Koon remained impassive in court, he said in the courtyard outside the Roybal Building that Conta was a "whore" who was trying to ingratiate himself with LAPD management.

Koon thought Conta was particularly duplicitous in his contention that the swarm technique was routinely taught to recruits at the Police Academy. Bostic had made a similar if less sweeping claim in the state trial. Both Conta and Bostic relied on a 1984 lesson plan that had been circulated among instructors at the Police Academy but never incorporated into a training bulletin. Under Salzman's cross-examination, Conta acknowledged that the swarm technique was not part of the core curriculum but was taught as "enrichment." Conta claimed that only about 10 percent of Academy graduates "slipped through the cracks" and failed to receive training in the swarm technique. This claim was contradicted by statements made to the FBI by members of Powell's graduating class, none of whom remembered being taught the swarm. But Conta was not pinned down on this discrepancy by Salzman.

Stone took over cross-examination the next day and asked Conta if he was holding officers responsible for using techniques they had not been taught. The question riled Conta, who said, "I would not allow someone to leave the Academy if he didn't know these [swarm] techniques." But all the defendants except Wind had graduated from the Academy before Conta became training chief, and Conta acknowledged that he didn't know if any of them had been taught the swarm.

Braun also scored some points on behalf of his client. Pulling a tape recorder from his suit pocket, he asked Conta if he had ever expressed an opinion of Briseno's stomp that conflicted with his trial testimony. Clymer objected, complaining at a sidebar conference outside the jury's earshot, that Braun was behaving like a "clown." Davies instructed the jury to disregard the tape recorder, but Braun's theatrical maneuver accomplished its intended purpose of stimulating Conta's memory. When testimony resumed, Conta remembered telling Briseno's police defense representative that it was possible Briseno had put his foot on King to keep him on the ground. Conta also remembered that the conversation had been tape-recorded with his permission. Even so, Conta maintained that the stomp was "out of policy" and dangerous to King regardless of Briseno's motive.

Many jurors found Conta persuasive, and a specific point in his analysis of the video would become crucial during jury deliberations. As Jim Newton later described the significance of Conta's testimony: "Here was a police officer with strong credentials who looked good on the stand and testified knowledgeably that LAPD officers had violated policy. It wasn't an outsider saying that what the LAPD had done was wrong but the LAPD itself."[29] Conta's credibility was enhanced by his concession that the officers had reason to use force during the early portion of the beating, when King suffered his facial injuries. In acknowledging that everything that occurred during the first thirty-two seconds of the tape was "within policy," Conta went further than Bostic had gone at Simi Valley in allowing latitude in dealing with a combative suspect. Some of the jurors most sympathetic to the officers were impressed by this apparent reasonableness. In trying to prove less, Conta accomplished more.

It is a tribute to Conta's effectiveness that the defense viewed him with more hostility than any other prosecution witness. But Koon and the defense attorneys also resented Conta because they saw him as the spokesman for a determined LAPD cover-up of the nature of police training. As the defense saw it, the purpose of the cover-up was to take the LAPD off the hook for encouraging officers to subdue combative suspects with bone-breaking metal batons.

Chief Daryl Gates had accurately predicted that reliance on the metal baton, after the use of choke holds was outlawed in 1982, would cause an increase in broken bones and other injuries. But in the furor after the King incident, Gates had described excessive baton use as an "aberration" rather than a logical culmination of a deficient policy. Some of the LAPD's critics, as well as some officers, believed that the beating of King was aberrant only because it had been captured on videotape and was otherwise too typical of what happened when officers tried to arrest a combative suspect without choking or shooting him.

As the defense saw it, Conta was rewriting history when he asserted that LAPD policy required officers to jump on King and handcuff him rather than keep him down with their batons. What particularly incensed Koon was Conta's attempt to invest the swarm with an importance it never possessed in actual training. The LAPD did not issue a training bulletin on the swarm until March 1993, shortly after Conta testified, and it was not actually published for several months after that. Koon and Salzman suspected nefarious reasons for this longer than usual delay, especially since the bulletin warned against using the swarm on a suspect who was in a "push-up position" and trying to reach his feet as King was trying to do when he received several of the blows deemed out of policy by Conta.

But the defense failed to persuade the jurors that lapses in police training excused the beating of King. The jurors found the defense presentation on the swarm issue confusing and beside the point. Even those who were able to follow the Byzantine argument wondered what the fuss was about. Koon surely must have known about the swarm, they reasoned, since he had ordered the officers to jump on King and handcuff him before the violence recorded on the videotape began. This seemed to the jurors—and to Clymer—a matter of common sense regardless of whether the swarm had been taught in the Police Academy.

Swarming King had also seemed common sense to Koon on the night of March 3, 1991. While he had not been taught the swarm or "team takedown," in the Academy, he had participated in station-house conversations with other officers about tactics for subduing resistant suspects as LAPD policy evolved after the restrictions were placed on the choke hold. On the night of the King arrest, Koon had to make many decisions in a hurry. As defense expert-witness Sergeant Charles Duke pointed out later in the trial,

Koon violated accepted tactical guidelines when he ordered Powell, Wind, Briseno, and Solano to grab King's arms and legs and handcuff him because King was an unsearched felony suspect. But Koon was trying to take King into custody without hurting him, and it seemed a logical tactic at the time.

The tactic backfired, on the scene and in the federal trial. When King hurled the officers off his back, they became aware of his tremendous strength. Their fears perpetuated the violence that was initiated by King's charge at Powell. Not wanting to "tie up" with King again, Powell and Wind kept their distance and beat him with their batons.

Logically the fact Koon had ordered a swarm in violation of his tactical training could have been seen as evidence that he had no intention of hurting King. But it didn't have that impact at the trial, probably because the swarm was attempted before the videotape began, and the recounting of it lacked the emotional impact of the violent beating that jurors saw over and over again on their television monitors. Koon was a double loser: He received no credit for trying to avoid use of force, but was faulted because he didn't try the swarm again after the torrent of baton blows began.

CONTA'S ROLE WAS TO ESTABLISH THAT THE DEFENDANTS HAD violated LAPD policy. Rodney King's role was to show that they had failed to understand that he was not some dangerous, drug-crazed monster who needed to be beaten into submission. The prosecutors set the stage for King's performance with medical witnesses who described his numerous head and facial injuries. Dr. Charles Aronberg, an ophthalmologist who had treated King, said these injuries included a broken right cheekbone and eye socket and extensive sinus damage. In the sinus areas, Aronberg testified, "there were innumerable small fractures [and] in some areas the bones were reduced to a very fine powder, like sand."

The impact of Aronberg's testimony was enhanced by a surprising and damaging lapse by the usually adept Braun. Aronberg had not dealt with any alleged injury caused by Briseno's stomp, and Braun had no reason to cross-examine him. He did anyway, asking the physician if he had been asked to form an opinion on whether any of King's injuries had been caused by illegal use of force. Over prosecutor Alan Tieger's objection, Davies allowed Aronberg to say he had opinions on this subject but hadn't been asked by the government to disclose them.

Aronberg had been called solely to testify about King's injuries, not as an expert on use of force. Under the legal rules applying to his testimony, he normally would have been precluded from expressing an opinion on whether King had been injured as the result of illegal acts. But Braun had opened up the subject, and Tieger realized that the question to which he had objected had given him an opportunity. He seized it. As soon as Braun finished, Tieger asked Aronberg for his opinion of the cause of King's facial injuries. "I think the injuries were caused by blows to the face and head from batons," Aronberg said.

Aronberg's pointed answer undermined a principal defense argument that King's facial injuries were the result of falls to the pavement. It was an opportunity that Aronberg, who was disappointed he had not been asked to testify in Simi Valley, had been waiting for. Braun had no way of knowing that, but he should not have asked an aimless question that could not have helped Briseno and had the potential to harm the other defendants. Braun's cross-examination of Aronberg, as he honestly acknowledged, reflected his desire to play a larger part in a trial in which he had a peripheral role. "The next time I need something to do at a trial, I'll take a book," Braun told me long afterward.[30] Salzman was livid, but Stone took the lapse calmly. "What you're going to have to do to make up for this is cross-examine Rodney King," he told Braun.[31]

Aronberg was followed to the stand by Dr. Stanley Cohen, a neurologist who had examined King eight days after the beating and found evidence of memory loss. This helped the government, for memory loss might explain some of the contradictory statements King had made after the incident. Cohen said King had suffered a concussion from the beating and had difficulty recalling specifics. "He described having his eyes open, but his mind blank," Cohen said. "Those were his exact words."

The stage was set for King, who took the stand on March 9 in the trial's main media event. King had not been seen in public since his emotional plea at the height of the riots ("People, I just want to say . . . can we all get along?"), and the televised clip of that speech had added to his celebrity status in a city that dotes on celebrities. A line formed outside the Roybal Building at 6:00 A.M., more than seven hours before King testified, for the dozen public courtroom seats. The throng outside the building included a score of television crews from eight countries. Police and federal marshals ringed the area as a precaution, but the large crowd was curious, not troublesome. Jurors were curious, too. Their eyes were riveted on King as he strode commandingly into the courtroom at 1:30 P.M., flanked by FBI agents.

King had been carefully prepared for his moment in the spotlight. He was neatly dressed in a tailored dark-gray suit, light-colored shirt, and multicolored tie and had lost so much weight that one account described him as "gaunt-looking."* His trim appearance was an outward manifestation of

---

* King testified that he had lost eleven pounds and weighed 214, which meant he would have weighed 225 at the time of the incident. Officers at the scene had put King's weight at 240 or more. Koon had estimated at the time that King weighed 250.

deeper changes in his attitude. Deputy District Attorney Terry White had made an anguished decision not to call King at the state trial because he feared that King would lose his temper on the witness stand and alienate the conservative jury.

But the Simi Valley verdicts had hit King and his civil attorney, Steven Lerman, in pride and pocketbook. The verdicts had emboldened the Los Angeles city council to resist the massive damage award sought by Lerman. And the verdicts had shocked King into realizing that the officers who had beaten him might never be held accountable unless he cooperated. In case there was any doubt, Barry Kowalski patiently explained the situation to King when the federal prosecution team met privately with him, avoiding what Terry White considered the obstacle of Lerman. But Lerman was no obstacle to the federal prosecution. Humbled by the verdicts, he realized King needed to be prepared to perform on the witness stand. Lerman willingly stood out of the way.

Although overshadowed by Clymer during much of the trial, Kowalski made a significant contribution to the prosecution in his patient preparation of King. Experienced in dealing with unsophisticated victims of police abuse, Kowalski did not rush King or talk down to him. They discussed fishing and baseball and found they liked each other. Within a short time, King came to trust Kowalski, and he paid close attention to his instruction to keep his temper at all costs. Lawrence Middleton also played a key role. Posing as a defense attorney, he subjected King to a stiff mock cross-examination that Kowalski said was much tougher than the real thing.[32]

Other factors helped spare federal prosecutors a repetition of White's tribulations. Melanie Singer was not a government witness. The federal jury was racially mixed, younger, and presumably more open-minded than the state jury had been. King had improved his public image with his plea for peace during the riots. He was no hero to the jurors, white or black, but he seemed at least a well-meaning man who regretted that his televised arrest had led indirectly to death and destruction in Los Angeles.

Kowalski kept a taut hold on King as he led him through the opening stages of testimony, pausing to allow his prize witness a glass of water. The Justice Department civil rights attorney realized that King's value as a witness was the emotional dimension he brought to the trial, not the precision of his recollections, and he knew better than to present him as a saintly, law-abiding citizen. Rather than let the defense do it, Kowalski brought out King's prison record early in the testimony as well as his heavy drinking on the night of the incident. He then guided King to the jail ward of County-USC Medical Center, where he had awakened "horrible and confused and in an enormous amount of pain" on the morning of March 3, 1991. "I couldn't move my arms and it hurt when I would try to move any part of my body," King testified. "My head felt real hot. I was having an enormous amount of headaches."

Kowalski then led King back to the incident that had produced his injuries. King said he had not stopped when he saw flashing lights and heard sirens from police cars because he had been drinking heavily and feared he would be sent back to prison for violating his parole. King then described how officers barked confusing commands and how a "police lady" approached him as he lay face down on the ground. She had pointed her gun at him and said over and over again, "I mean it, I mean it, I mean it." King said he turned his head away and made a clicking sound because "I didn't want to watch her shoot me." When he did, he said, he received either a kick or a blow with a hard object on the right side of his face.

King then hesitantly and with some confusion described the police attempt to handcuff him, including the shots he received from the Taser. When he was first hit by a dart from the stun gun, he felt "like my blood was boiling inside of me." After he was hit, an officer had asked, "How do you feel now?" King said he "just kind of laughed it off." He was now "coughing and laughing blood out of my mouth. . . . I didn't want them to get the satisfaction of them knowing what they were doing was getting to me." It was at this point that an officer said to him, "We're going to kill you, nigger. Run." King said he looked for a space between the car he had been driving and the police car pulled up beside it. As he ran toward this space, he recalled being "struck across the side of the face again." Pointing to the top right side of his face, he said, "To this day there is a bump right here."

"And then what happened, Mr. King?" Kowalski asked.

"And it was at that point, I'm not exactly sure, but . . . as they were hitting me, they were chanting either "What's up, killer? How do you feel, killer? [or] What's up, nigger?"

King chanted the words in a high-pitched, almost falsetto voice in the hushed courtroom.

"Mr. King, do you remember whether the word that was being used was killer or nigger?" Kowalski asked.

"I'm not sure," King said. "I'm not absolutely sure which word it was, if it was killer or nigger. I'm not sure."

Sure or not, King's testimony made the trial a racial case—although he himself had initially denied that the officers had called him racial names. He subsequently changed his story, saying he had withheld this information because of a plea his mother had made to him while he was still in custody. But King said nothing about racial epithets when he testified to a federal grand jury more than sixteen months after the incident when he was a free man who knew he would not be prosecuted or returned to prison for violating parole.

In going over prospective trial testimony with Kowalski and Middleton, King had become aware that portions of it, such as his tale of being hit while he lay face down on the ground after complying with Melanie Singer's commands, conflicted with every other eyewitness account. Government lawyers knew the account was not factual, whether or not King remembered it this way, and they had not relied upon King's version of events in preparing the government's case. The unsubstantiated accusation that the officers called King "nigger" and told him to run was supported neither by eyewitnesses, nor by government analysis of the audiotape, nor by King's grand jury testimony. But lack of evidence did not deter the government from putting this most prejudicial of accusations before the jury.

Defense attorneys were furious at what seemed to them a highly cynical strategy and were particularly incensed by Kowalski's little trick of asking King if he was "sure" the officers had said "killer" or "nigger." This seemed to Braun a "deceitful" attempt to have it both ways.[33] The jurors did not know that the government had attempted to prove King's charge of racial derogation and found no evidence to support it. By asking King if he was "sure," prosecutors could pretend they were seeking truth while actually prejudicing the jury. Defense attorneys tried to comfort themselves with the thought that King's inventions about being racially derogated would make it easier to discredit him on other counts. Trying to make the best of the situation, Braun said of King outside court, "I think it's good that he said it was on a racial basis. His case is going to rise and fall on whether they used racial epithets."[34]

This proved to be wishful thinking. Although King's accusation of racial charges raised the temperature in the courtroom, the trial did not turn on these allegations. Even jurors who had little or no sympathy for the defendants could see that King was shaky in his recollections. Maria Escobel, the African-American juror who would play a key role in deliberations, was skeptical of most of King's testimony, which she viewed as a protracted exercise in denial.

But King's seeming inability to remember what happened had the ironic impact of defusing what otherwise would have been bombshell testimony. Had jurors viewed King as sophisticated or intelligent, or even sober at the time of his arrest, it is conceivable they would have faulted him for concocting an improbable story or penalized the government for stirring the pot of racial prejudice. But the jury saw King as a simple man who had been too drunk and perhaps too badly beaten to remember with any clarity what had happened to him. His evident unreliability diminished the shock value of defense suggestions that King or his lawyers had invented the racial episode to improve his chances of winning a significant damage award. Kowalski's trick of asking King if he was "sure" of his accusations may have been a shoddy tactic for a civil rights lawyer of such distinction, but it distanced the government enough from the charge to get it off the hook.

The jury's common-sense approach negated the impact of a cross-examination that sought to expose King as a liar who would say anything to advance his purposes. Since jurors were skeptical of King's account to begin with, the defense expose of its limitations seemed overwrought. The jury's response ratified the prosecution strategy in calling King as a witness. Jurors were not dependent on King's testimony to know he had been brutally beaten—they had the videotape for that. What mattered was not King's testimony but his humanity. "This man was a human being and no human being deserved to be beat like a wild animal, and that's the only thing that King did for me," Escobel said later. As for everything King said about the incident, Escobel said, "I was squirming in my seat."[35]

What made Escobel squirm most was King's reaction to copies of statements shown him by Stone and DePasquale as part of a standard courtroom practice of "refreshing recollection" about prior statements that conflicted with what King said on the witness stand. King pretended to read these documents but asked the lawyers to repeat their questions. It soon dawned on everyone in the courtroom that King could not read. King finally blurted out the truth after DePasquale handed him a document. "I can't read it," he said. To the intelligent Escobel, this admission was "the most embarrassing thing" that occurred during the trial. Davies, who had not realized that King could not read, gently intervened and stopped the attorneys from showing him additional documents.

The episode vividly illustrated the defense predicament during King's two days on the stand. The defense attorneys needed to avoid what was sometimes called "a second beating" of King by ridiculing or bullying him while at the same time exposing the many contradictions in his statements. Stone picked his way through the minefield with care. Over Kowalski's objections he extracted a series of admissions. King said he hoped to win "a lot of money" in damages. (A lot of money was "more than I have now," King said in response to a follow-up question.) King admitted to lying when he said that he had not been drinking and that he had not known police were pursuing him. He had lied when he said that he had obeyed police commands after he stopped. But King explained all of these lies by repeating the story he had told under Kowalski's guidance in direct testimony: He feared he would be sent back to prison for violating the conditions of his parole if he told the truth. Stone was determined to show, as he put it in a motion outside the presence of the jury, that King had engaged in a "pattern of fabrication" and would lie whenever it suited his purpose. But whenever Stone pressed King into a corner, the witness took refuge in his clouded memory.

"You did not ever say in that grand jury testimony the word nigger, did you?" Stone asked.

"Sometimes I forget a lot of things," King replied. "Sometimes I remember. Sometimes I don't."

Braun followed up with a thoughtful cross-examination that in Stone's eyes considerably atoned for his lapse in questioning Aronberg. Under Braun's polite prodding, King contritely admitted he had lied repeatedly. "I lied, sir, and I do not feel happy or proud of it," King said. "I have nothing to brag about." He then acknowledged he was not certain the police officers had called him the racial epithets he had accused them of using only the day before.

Read in retrospect, King's testimony seems a triumph for the defense. In addition to retreating from his provocative racial accusations and admitting lies, King continued to deny behavior in which he had undoubtedly engaged. Under questioning from Salzman, for instance, King claimed he never wiggled his buttocks at Melanie Singer. This behavior was not in dispute. The best that can charitably be said of the factual content of King's testimony is that he was too drunk to remember much of what happened.

But the transcript does not convey the emotional impact that King made on the jury as he struggled earnestly through recollected pain to provide a coherent account of his ordeal. Stone had no doubt that King had connected with the jury. "He looked very good," Stone said after King's first day on the witness stand. "He appears very polite and mild-mannered and thoughtful. That all spells credibility to me."[36]

The well-conducted cross-examination dented this credibility but did not destroy it. Defense attorneys poked holes in King's version of events without discrediting the human dimension of his testimony. They could not have gone after King any harder than they did, given the risks of subjecting him to a verbal beating, but King on balance proved a definite plus for the prosecution. The government had sought merely to show that King was a human victim, not a "wild animal" or a drug-crazed monster who could be subdued only by metal clubs. Ever since childhood, King had impressed others as decent, friendly, vulnerable, and intellectually limited. He was a different person when in an alcohol-triggered rage, but this side was not on display in the courtroom.

King accomplished more than the minimal task the government had set for his testimony. Despite his difficulty keeping the facts straight, his emotional memories of his ordeal seemed genuine, as did his unwavering insistence that he kept moving to avoid a brutal beating. "I was just try-ing to stay alive, sir, just trying to stay alive," King said to Kowalski. "They never gave me a chance to stay still."

While King changed his story many times, he was consistent on this point, and his words had a ring of truth. Through a haze of alcohol or drugs, King had truly feared that the officers who were beating him would kill him—or so it seemed to a sympathetic jury. His declaration that he was try-ing to stay alive seemed a cry from the heart.

16

THE OTHER VIDEOTAPE

"Look, folks, policing is done this way. You may like to live in Santa Monica and have your little wine party in the backyard and drive your Jaguar and do your little barbecue. . . . Know that the reason you are allowed to do that in the safety of your community is because police officers go out and they clean up the streets and deal with all the scum that you don't want to know about·. . ."

—Stacey Koon[1]

"We've survived the prosecution case just fine. The question is whether we can survive the defense."

—Harland Braun[2]

HAVING ESTABLISHED KING'S HUMANITY, PROSECUTORS RETURNED to the theme that the defendants had treated him inhumanely. Their next witness was Dr. Harry Smith, who was called to show that King's facial injuries were caused by baton blows. Smith was substituting for biomechanics expert Dr. James Benedict, who on the second day of the trial dismayed the prosecutors by calling from his office in San Antonio and telling them that a medical condition prevented him from flying. He offered his associate Smith, and Steven Clymer and Alan Tieger flew to San Antonio to interview him. They came back all smiles. In addition to expertise in biomechanics, Smith had a background as an emergency-room physician and radiologist and the confident manner of an expert who had testified at many trials.

Smith spent three hours on the witness stand on March 11, smoothly translating medical terms into layman's language and using a pair of gleaming plastic skulls to trace the patterns of King's facial and head injuries. He took dead aim at the defense theory that these injuries were caused by falls to the pavement. King had suffered fifteen facial fractures, including a broken cheekbone and eye socket and a dislocated jaw, but his nose had not been broken, as Smith said would have happened if the injuries had been the result of face-first falls. "The patterns I have discussed here today are not caused or causable by a fall," Smith said under Michael Stone's cross-examination. "These are baton injuries."

Overall, the prosecution case on the issue of head blows was compelling. The FBI enhancement had improved the blurry section in the initial thirteen seconds of the videotape, and the result suggested that at least one of Powell's first blows had clipped King on the head. If the tape was not fully conclusive (and it wasn't for every juror), the prosecution had the eyewitness observation of Officer Rolando Solano, who testified that one of Powell's deflected baton blows struck King in the face.

As Clymer realized, however, the enhanced videotape was potentially a double-edged sword. On the one hand, it provided visual evidence of a head blow; on the other, it showed that Powell had swung his baton in response to King's charge. Armed with the enhanced videotape, Stone had a valid reason for abandoning the strategy he had used at Simi Valley: maintaining that King's facial injuries were caused by falls to the pavement. Solano's account also contradicted the pavement theory, as did the statement given to Internal Affairs by Timothy Wind, who had said that Powell hit King twice on the arms as he charged at him. King, from Wind's perspective, then raised his head and body and "moved enough that Powell hit him in the face." The Wind statement was not in evidence, but Stone had read it. The combination of the enhanced video and the Solano and Wind observations gave Stone a basis for contending that Powell had acted in self-defense or had hit King accidentally or both. Or he could have conceded that Powell was so panicked when King charged that he had swung wildly without knowing where his blows had landed or what injuries they had caused. This defense would have had the added value of accuracy.

Since only intentional head blows violated LAPD policy, a concession by Stone that Powell had struck King in the face accidentally or in self-defense would have rendered most of Dr. Smith's impressive testimony unnecessary and perhaps irrelevant. The prosecution was concerned about the possibility that Stone would shift gears and offer this more common-sense defense.* As late as his closing argument, Clymer was trying to inoculate jurors against a suggestion of accidental head blows by using the enhanced videotape to show that Powell cocked his legs and arms before swinging at the charging King. But Stone never budged from his contention that King's facial injuries were caused by a collision with the pavement, not with his client's baton.

---

* Stone believes that even if he had conceded head blows the government would have found a way to put Dr. Smith through his paces before the jury. He may be right, for Smith was too good a witness not to be used.

Stone's unwillingness to make any concessions on this issue gave prosecutors an opportunity to dwell on the nature of King's injuries, and they made the most of it. But it should be remembered, on this point and others, that Stone was trying his first federal criminal case and his second felony trial of any kind. Would any attorney with similar experience have abandoned a defense that had achieved such success the first time around? This seems unlikely, particularly if the attorney assumed that the composition of the two juries was similar, as Stone did.

The prosecution was riding high after Smith's testimony: All its key witnesses had met or exceeded expectations. But that changed with the testimony of LAPD Officer Daniel Gonzalez, who was supposed to deliver on the sensational suggestion in Clymer's opening statement that Powell had shown off the battered King to fellow officers at Foothill Station.

Gonzalez was earnest, intense, and, as he said repeatedly on the witness stand, "very nervous" about testifying. He had been a Police Academy classmate and friend of Tina Kerbrat, the first woman LAPD officer slain in the line of duty, and wore a black armband on his uniform and a wrist bracelet with Kerbrat's name on it. On the night of March 3, 1991, Gonzalez had been a probationary officer in a car driven by Officer Martin Garcia that arrived at the scene of King's arrest soon after the incident ended. Two hours later, at 3:30 A.M., Gonzalez was preparing a robbery report in the squad room of Foothill Station when he noticed Powell leaning over a desk and "telling a war story" about the King encounter to seven or eight other officers. King at the time was being guarded by Wind in Powell's patrol car in the station parking lot.

Gonzalez had been interviewed by Internal Affairs investigators on April 8, 1991, thirty-seven days after the King incident. At the time he said that Powell was "happy" and "calm" as he related his war story in the squad room. When he did not recall the "happy" comment during his testimony at the trial, Clymer used a transcript of the Internal Affairs interview to remind him. So far, so good. But in further testimony, Gonzalez denied that Powell had sent him out to the parking lot. Gonzalez said he had asked to see King and that Powell had given him and Garcia permission to take a peek. Gonzalez opened the door of the patrol car and shined his flashlight at King, who complained of pain in his right eye. Wind, who was using his own flashlight to write his daily activity report, told Gonzalez that he was making King "upset" and to go away. Gonzalez and Garcia retreated. The so-called showing off of King had lasted no more than three minutes, involved two officers, and was initiated at their request. It was a far cry from what Clymer had suggested in his opening statement.

Still, it was obvious to jurors that Gonzalez wanted to help Powell. And his stated reason for wanting to see King in the patrol car seemed far-fetched. Gonzalez said under cross-examination that he had previously worked as a security guard and spent nine days in the hospital after being run over by a shoplifter who went free because Gonzalez could not identify him. After that incident, Gonzalez said, he had vowed to get a good look at anyone "who tries to hurt another officer" and he had wanted to see King for this reason. Clymer thought it was an incredible explanation. When Gonzalez then mentioned the slaying of Officer Kerbrat, Clymer objected and complained that the defense was engaged in "inflammatory" conduct designed to prejudice jurors by reminding them of the risks police officers face. After protracted argument outside the presence of the jury, Davies sustained the objection.

But the government was on the defensive for the first time in the trial. Wind's attorney, Paul DePasquale, alleged "bad faith by the prosecution" and asked Davies to dismiss the charges against his client. DePasquale said prosecutors had falsely claimed that Powell had tried "to exhibit Mr. King in the nature of a trophy" even though Gonzalez had told them he had initiated the request. Joining in the motion, Braun compared the government's "trophy" claim with its "bad faith" on the racial issue. Davies didn't accept this argument. He said he saw "not a shred of bad faith on the part of the government," merely a failure of a witness to live up to expectations. "It's a common experience," Davies said.

This particular "common experience" had an ironic result. Gonzalez was a witness against Powell, whom the government portrayed as indifferent to the welfare of anyone but himself. As Clymer saw it, Powell's act of leaving King in the police car while he told "war stories" in the station was part of a pattern of callous conduct. The pattern included Powell's high-pitched "laugh" when he reported the incident over the radio, his in-car computer message that he hadn't beaten anyone so badly in a long time, and his alleged taunting of King at Pacifica Hospital.

These actions may indeed have formed a pattern, but the "trophy" episode contributed little to it. Most jurors whom I interviewed later had a negative impression of Powell, but only one cited the station episode as an explanation for disliking him. (In contrast, the computer message in which Powell said he hadn't beaten anyone so badly in a long time registered with every juror.) At least two jurors considered the station episode an example of overreaching by the prosecution. But if the testimony of Gonzalez had no apparent impact on Powell, it was clearly beneficial to Wind. Maria Escobel, who on most issues accepted the prosecution view, thought Wind's shooing away of the officers who shined a flashlight at King was an act of "compassion." And jury foreman Robert (Bob) Almond, who at first leaned to acquitting all defendants, was moved by the episode to reflect on how "very poorly" rookies were treated by fellow officers.

The government completed its case on March 15 with police witnesses who said that Powell's reports of the incident had failed to mention King was on the ground at any time when he was struck with batons and that Koon's report had downplayed King's injuries. The prosecution had produced thirty-five witnesses and directed most of its case against Powell and Koon. So little evidence had been offered against Briseno that Braun hoped Davies might seriously entertain the motion he made for dismissal after the government rested. Outside the courtroom, Braun's rap client, Eazy-E, joined in calling for Briseno's acquittal. "They should have let Briseno go," he said. "He's the cop who tried to stop this."[3] Such motions are routinely denied, however, and Davies denied this one.

CLYMER LATER TOLD ME THAT HE "LIKED COPS," BUT THIS WAS NOT apparent to the scores of LAPD officers who were grilled first by FBI agents and then by prosecutors before the grand jury during the investigation phase of the federal case. The prosecutors assumed that bystander officers present at the King arrest had knowingly witnessed misconduct and conspired to cover it up. As Koon put it, they looked at any information that hinted of a conspiracy and "threw aside" any information that contradicted it.[4]

Prosecutors were so committed to a conspiracy theory that they wasted time and resources in investigating the unlikely possibility that bystander officers actually had convened to discuss a cover story. No such meeting ever took place, but prosecutors remained suspicious. An officer's failure to remember a detail prosecutors thought he should remember made him a presumptive participant in a cover-up or at least a disciple of the "code of silence." Kowalski was familiar with police cover-ups from other civil rights cases and took a tough line with officers suspected of withholding information. When Officer Garcia did not remember talking to Powell at the King arrest, Kowalski hauled him before the grand jury and pressed him to recall the conversation.

"I don't recall," Garcia said. "I'm being honest."

"Don't tell me you are trying to recall," Kowalski said. "I want you to recall."

But Garcia stood his ground and did not identify Powell.

Clymer was as suspicious of police testimony as Kowalski but eventually decided that the bystander officers were less interested in protecting the defendants than in protecting themselves. The LAPD requires officers to report observed misconduct, and none had done so after the King beating. When the bystanders subsequently learned that the incident had been videotaped, it became what Clymer called "cover your ass" time.[5] Clymer, convinced that any reasonable person would share his view that misconduct in the King incident was obvious, rejected the notion that some officers did not report misconduct either because they did not see it or because they thought the use of force appropriate.

A particular target of Clymer's wrath was Officer Rolando Solano, the probationary officer paired with Briseno who had participated in the attempt to swarm and handcuff King before the beating. Solano had been one of the prosecution's few effective witnesses in the state trial, where he testified that he "didn't like the sound" of Powell's baton hitting King's head and turned away after the blow. He also vividly remembered King's "hostile" or "crazed" look, which he thought was probably a sign that King had been using PCP. This had not reconciled Solano to the head blow. He told Internal Affairs investigators and later two grand juries that he was shocked when Powell hit King in the head.

Solano was considered a promising officer. He was also arguably the only officer at the scene who demonstrated compassion toward King. After King was handcuffed, Officer Louis Turriaga started to drag the battered man face down to the side of the road. Solano rushed over to lift King's body so it cleared the ground, an action for which he was commended by the LAPD.

But Clymer was so committed to the notion of a cover-up that he believed Solano must have been lying when he described the incident to Internal Affairs investigators as a "fight" and said King was on one knee when handcuffed. Clymer wanted Solano to admit he had seen King beaten into submission on the ground. Solano refused. He testified under cross-examination at the federal trial that Clymer threatened to prosecute him for perjury unless he changed his story, but Solano would not budge. After the trial, Clymer compared Solano to a husband cheating on his wife. When his wife asked where he had spent the night, the husband said he had slept on a hammock in the yard. She then told him she had taken the hammock down two months earlier. "That's my story, and I'm sticking to it," the husband replied.[6]

The analogy was defective, however. In Solano's case it was as if the husband knew before he told his story that the hammock had been removed. When Internal Affairs investigators interviewed Solano, he was aware that the King arrest had been videotaped and knew that anything he said would be compared with what could be seen on the tape. His great concern was not that he would be disciplined for failing to report misconduct (the eventual basis of his suspension) but that he would be fired for giving an account that was contradicted by the videotape. Solano had a motive to tell the truth because he was aware that probationary officers were routinely fired for lying to Internal Affairs.

Even so, Solano had trouble reconstructing a coherent version of events. He was less hardened to violence than other officers involved in the incident and during five months on the LAPD had witnessed only one previous use-of-force incident. On the night of the King arrest, events moved in a swift blur, with only a minute and twenty-one seconds elapsing between King's charge at Powell and the handcuffing. Solano had turned away at Powell's first blow and did not watch the subsequent beating closely. What he remembered was filtered through his fear of King, his horror at what Powell had done, and perhaps through Briseno's profane anger at what he considered Koon's mismanagement of the arrest.

Solano could not even remember whether he and Briseno had returned to Foothill Station, a detail important to the government case against Briseno and one that Clymer thought Solano ought to recall. But he did not. The issue of where Briseno and Solano drove after the beating was not significant until later, and the rest of the shift had also been an exciting time for the probationary officer. Four hours later, Solano had helped Briseno chase and arrest four robbery suspects.

Internal Affairs detectives realized that Solano's memory was shaky. They were accustomed to dealing with police officers who were willing to lie to save themselves, and not even Clymer and Kowalski thought Internal Affairs was part of any cover-up. If anything, the Internal Affairs detectives had been under too much political pressure to get to the bottom of the King affair, and they were extremely skeptical of alibis offered by the officers at the scene of the King arrest.

The result of the pressure and the consequent desire to make an example of the officers was mass discipline of the bystanders—mass discipline carried to a ludicrous extreme. The observer in the police helicopter, for instance, was suspended for failing to intervene in an incident that ended before the helicopter could have landed. Solano would have been fired without hesitation if Internal Affairs thought he was lying. He received a relatively minor punishment because his superiors thought he had done his best to tell the truth about a violent incident for which he was emotionally unprepared.

But if Clymer was wrong to brand Solano a perjurer, he was surely right in believing that some bystanders saw or knew more than they had acknowledged during the state trial. Passage of time had not improved the memories or the dispositions of these officers. They resented the punishments imposed by the LAPD as a political reaction by the high command and were hostile to the federal prosecutions, which they regarded as even more political. The bystanders' attitude mirrored the sentiments of the LAPD rank and file. Kowalski and Clymer had no hope of sweet-talking the bystanders or other prospective police witnesses into cooperation. They had good reason for believing that threats of perjury prosecutions were necessary.

Kowalski knew from experience that officers who were treated roughly before a grand jury would think twice before exposing themselves to the bruising cross-examination of a trial. He had no illusion that Garcia or Solano would change his story or that many LAPD officers would volunteer as government witnesses, but he hoped to keep them from testifying for the defense. He succeeded. The flood of police witnesses who had bolstered the defense at Simi Valley slowed to a trickle in the civil rights trial. And the police witnesses who did testify often left the stand feeling as if it were they who were being prosecuted.

The perils of being a police witness were demonstrated in the opening rounds of the defense case, as attorney Ira Salzman began calling witnesses for Stacey Koon. Even Officer Susan Clemmer, the first and best of these witnesses, did not have an easy time. Clemmer, repeating her testimony from the state trial, said she had been directing traffic at the scene of the King arrest when Powell, sweating on a cold night, approached and told her he had been "scared" when King threw him off his back. "I thought I was going to have to shoot him," Powell had said to her. Clymer at first tried to block Clemmer's testimony. When Davies allowed it, he tried to impugn her credibility. Clemmer was composed and held her own. But Clymer's rough cross-examination of Clemmer was a signal to weaker defense police witnesses that they faced an ordeal if they testified.

Paul Beauregard, a police officer for the Los Angeles Unified School District and a friend of Powell, had participated in the pursuit of King. He testified that King had refused to comply with police commands and had thrown off officers who tried to handcuff him. His testimony was intended to set the stage for the standard defense version of the incident: King was uncooperative and resistant. LAPD officers had feared he was on PCP. King had not been stopped by two bursts of the electric stun gun. When King charged at Powell, he brought the beating on himself.

But under skillful cross-examination by Alan Tieger, the school district officer retreated. Prodded by transcripts of his 1991 testimony to the state grand jury, Beauregard acknowledged that his account conflicted with the videotaped record. In his grand jury testimony, Beauregard had minimized the beating. He said that Powell hit King nine times with one-handed baton blows and that King remained standing most of the time and was largely unaffected by the blows. Beauregard also told the grand jury that he had joked with King after he was beaten and hog-tied. When Beauregard informed King that he was a school officer, King replied, "Oh, I guess I'll have to do detention now," and began laughing. Powell and Beauregard had joined in the laughter. According to Beauregard's grand jury testimony, Powell had laughed again as he called an ambulance for King.

Tieger took on this testimony head on:

"And then Officer Powell laughed and then completed the call [for the ambulance] by saying, 'numerous head wounds.' You remember that, right?"

"I'm not sure if he was laughing or what it was," Beauregard replied. "It sounded like a laugh."

"It sounded like laughter to you, didn't it?"

"I'm not sure what it was at that time."

"Well, you were sure in the past, sir, and didn't you describe it as a laugh in the past?"

"I'm not sure if I did or didn't."

"Well, did you ever describe it as anything other than a laugh?"

"No, sir," Beauregard said.

MICHAEL STONE SAID TIEGER HAD USED BEAUREGARD'S GRAND jury testimony to "fillet" him, and Harland Braun called Beauregard's hapless performance the trial's low point for the defense. But there were many other low points. LAPD Officer Joseph Napolitano, who followed Beauregard to the stand, had driven to the scene with a young probationary officer and stood ten feet from Koon during the subduing of King. He testified that Powell and Wind had hit King "six or seven times" because he was trying to regain his feet. In testimony before the federal grand jury, however, Napolitano said he had "assumed" King was trying to get up because otherwise officers would not have been hitting him. The difference was significant, and Napolitano acknowledged as much under cross-examination by Clymer. He also acknowledged that King had not been combative.

The Beauregard and Napolitano episodes demonstrated to courtroom observers (and some jurors) that Koon's attorney, Salzman, was overmatched by the experienced government team. Salzman was conscientious, but he was trying his first federal criminal case and was uncomfortable with some of the procedures. In California, for instance, transcripts of grand jury proceedings are public records after an indictment has been returned. Under federal grand jury rules, prosecutors are required to furnish the defense only with the transcripts of prosecution witnesses. Federal prosecutors took advantage of this rule by interrogating before the grand jury any police officer who might have knowledge of the case. If the officer then appeared in the trial as a defense witness, he could be cross-examined on the basis of grand jury testimony the defense attorneys had never seen. But this was no excuse for Salzman's mistake in calling Beauregard, whose testimony before the state grand jury was a matter of public record.

But it was not just police officers who faced a rough going over from the prosecutors. Los Angeles City Councilman Hal Bernson was the first witness called by Salzman, as part of his effort to put LAPD policy on trial. Davies allowed Salzman to ask Bernson a few narrow questions about the origin of LAPD policy limiting the use of choke holds. Bernson testified that the council had imposed a moratorium in 1982 despite evidence that reliance on the metal baton would increase injuries. Seeing an opportunity to raise a racial issue again, Kowalski jumped on Bernson's testimony.

"Was the reason for putting a moratorium on the upper-body chokehold because so many black people were getting killed?" he asked.

"I think that was one reason," Bernson said.

The prosecution cross-examination was particularly effective on the crucial PCP issue. Salzman started off well by calling Edgar Oglesby, a thirty-one-year LAPD veteran and author of *Angel Dust: What Everyone Should Know About PCP*. Oglesby testified that the "classic symptoms" officers observed in King—a blank stare, incoherent speech, failure to respond to commands, and unusual rigidity—were consistent with consumption of PCP, which often renders its users impervious to pain. Oglesby said PCP sometimes fails to show up in blood or urine samples unless the tests are given repetitively over a number of hours. This had not been done with King. Oglesby seemed to have laid the foundation for a successful PCP defense.

But police defense witnesses did not fulfill the promise of this testimony. Clemmer, who had accompanied Wind in the ambulance that took King to Pacifica Hospital, acknowledged that she had heard no mention of PCP in the ambulance or in the hospital ward. Napolitano said he had assumed that King was on PCP when Koon's Taser failed to stop him, even though there had been testimony that Tasers do not work about 20 percent of the time. Officer Paul Gebhardt testified that when he walked up to Powell at the scene to inform him that backup had arrived, Powell said of King, "Look out, this guy's dusted." Powell then delivered a series of blows that Gebhardt said did not "faze" King. But in a biting cross-examination, Kowalski raised doubts with jurors about Gebhardt's credibility. He established that Gebhardt, a friend of Wind, had refused to talk to LAPD investigators after the incident. Instead of buttressing Powell's argument for using force, Gebhardt's testimony lent credence to the prosecution contention that the PCP story had been concocted to justify an unjustifiable beating.

Overall the government may have scored more points when defense witnesses were on the stand than when government witnesses testified. Prosecutors succeeded in persuading many jurors that police witnesses were friends or colleagues of the defendants and were seeking to help them. This was one of the most significant differences between the attitudes of jurors in the state and federal trials.

On the second day of the defense presentation, Sergeant Robert Ontiveros was called to make the case that Powell and Wind had speeded up the booking of King by detouring to Foothill Station after leaving Pacifica Hospital. The defense case was strong on this technical point, for the station was equipped with a modern computer that enabled Powell, who was skilled in computer use, to tap into state records in Sacramento, learn that King was a paroled felon, and place what is known as a "felony hold" on him. But under Clymer's cross-examination, Ontiveros conceded that taking King to the station instead of to USC Medical Center might have delayed medical treatment.

There was less to this point than Clymer made of it. Under procedures in use at the USC Medical Center jail ward, King would not have received any treatment until he was booked—a procedure that almost certainly would have taken longer on the single manual typewriter then available than at the station. Furthermore, the physician who treated King at Pacifica Hospital had not found his injuries to be serious. That judgment may have been questionable, but police officers are not supposed to substitute their own medical assessments. Had the physician who treated King determined that he needed immediate treatment, he would have been transported to USC Medical Center by ambulance, not in Powell's police car.

Unfortunately for the defense, however, the officers had not mentioned the ninety-minute Foothill Station detour in their reports of the King arrest or in the log they kept that night. The prosecution suggested the omission showed a cover-up; the defense claimed it was sloppiness. Wind had kept the log, and Ontiveros said probationary officers often make such errors. Some jurors thought Ontiveros was reaching to help the defendants, especially after he said that he had not known that Powell had told "war stories" while inside the station.

Then Ontiveros made the mistake of saying it could take as much as twenty minutes to drive from Pacifica Hospital to Foothill Station, less than two miles away. Clymer pounced. "Is your testimony that it takes sixteen to twenty minutes to drive to Foothill Station as truthful as the other testimony that you have given here today?" he asked. Ontiveros often drove from the station to the hospital as part of his police assignment, usually slowly, in order to look for criminal activity. But he failed to make this point until prompted by Wind's attorney, Paul DePasquale. On balance, Ontiveros—a respected police officer—was an inept witness. Outside the jury's hearing, Clymer characterized him as "dishonest," an undeserved slur against an officer who might better have been described as unconvincing.

The police retreat ended on the third day of the defense presentation when the highly decorated LAPD Sergeant Charles Duke took the stand as Salzman's use-of-force expert. Duke was a star of the department's famous SWAT team, the defense hero of Simi Valley, and the antidote to Sergeant Mark Conta. But unlike Conta, he was not permitted by his superiors to wear his uniform—a telltale sign of the LAPD leadership's partiality to the prosecution. Alone among the LAPD witnesses who testified for the defense, Duke had the respect of Clymer, who knew he was a top cop and told me after the trial that Duke would have put Rodney King in handcuffs within seconds without hitting him. But Clymer also believed that Duke was vulnerable as a witness because of his consistent tendency to see any incident through a police officer's eyes.

Duke made a mighty effort to rescue a defense case that was in shambles when he took the stand. As he had done in Simi Valley, he reviewed the videotape frame by frame and over frequent objections from Clymer defended each and every blow and kick by Powell and Wind as warranted by LAPD policy. Duke had no doubt that the officers had perceived King as a credible threat. He suggested that their actions were commendable because they may have saved King's life. As Duke saw it, the incident could have escalated into a "deadly force situation" in which someone, probably King, would have been shot. "The safest place for him, and it may be very hard to understand, is on the ground," Duke said.

Where Conta had seen numerous "golden opportunities" to jump on King and handcuff him, Duke did not see any at all. Duke thought Koon had committed a "tactical error" when he ordered Powell, Wind, Briseno, and Solano to grab King's legs and arms and attempt to handcuff him before he used the Taser or commanded baton blows to keep him on the ground. Duke said that the swarm was designed for use against thinly clothed misdemeanor suspects who had been searched, and that it was "extremely dangerous" with suspects such as Rodney King. "The swarm was not intended to be used on an unsearched felony suspect," Duke said. "The likelihood of disaster is very real." Duke also thought it unfair to hold officers accountable for failing to use a technique they had not been taught: "You can't hold officers responsible for something they don't train in because you're going to get them killed."

Duke supported Koon's argument that the ban on upper-body control holds had made LAPD officers overly reliant on a primitive metal baton that causes bone-breaking injuries. This was much more than a theoretical issue to Duke, who, it will be recalled, had been a training officer at the Police Academy in 1982 when the choke-hold restrictions forced drastic changes. LAPD officers who traditionally had been taught to apply upper-body control holds to restrain resistant suspects were now told to keep away and use batons. Duke was sure the new doctrine would result in more injuries to officers and suspects alike, and he didn't want to teach it. When arrest statistics confirmed his belief, Duke protested. It took a direct order from Commander Matthew Hunt to force him to teach the new policy to LAPD recruits.

Prosecutors in both King trials recognized that LAPD policy implicitly endorsed bone-breaking baton use against resistant suspects, if not beating them into submission. They knew the defendants were likely to be acquitted if they persuaded jurors that they had complied with LAPD policy, even a brutal policy. The defense had carried the day at Simi Valley by persuading jurors that the officers had done what they were trained to do. Federal prosecutors sought to show that the defendants had violated both policy and training, especially by beating King when he was no longer perceived as a threat.

Conta and Duke agreed on the significant point that the blows which supposedly caused King's facial injuries were permissible under LAPD policy. They also agreed that every blow and kick during the first thirty-two seconds of the videotape complied with LAPD policy because King was trying to regain his feet. In a case that was supposedly a premier example of police brutality, the two experienced LAPD sergeants who were adversarial use-of-force experts were in accord that King's facial injuries were not caused by police misconduct. Had the beating stopped at the thirty-two-second point of the videotape, it would have been lawful by Conta's analysis no less than by Duke's. King would nevertheless have been a badly beaten man.

Duke thought it unfair for Conta or anyone else to decide retroactively that the defendants should have made a split-second determination at the thirty-two second mark that King was no longer capable of resistance. Such determinations are considerably more difficult on the dark streets than in a marbled courtroom where a videotape can be played at leisure in slow motion. In Duke's eyes, King was an unsearched felony suspect, and the arresting officers were required to play it safe. This meant using batons to keep King on the ground. The King arrest was the nightmare Duke had envisioned when the LAPD discarded the choke hold, which Koon could have used to subdue King without bloodshed. But the city's political leaders had insisted on changing the policy, and the LAPD had complied. As Duke saw it, the officers were doing their best with the inadequate tools at their disposal.

Duke's testimony in the federal trial remains the most authoritative exposition of the defense position in the King case. He testified on Friday, March 19, providing a rare weekend for jurors to reflect on material favorable to the defense. On Monday, he expanded on his analysis under questioning from Stone and cross-examination by Clymer. The prosecutor zeroed in on Duke's assertion that officers could use an unlimited number of baton blows to overcome a suspect's resistance.

"You, in your mind as an expert, equate overcoming resistance with beating into submission?" Clymer asked in a tone of incredulity.

"If that's what it takes," Duke responded firmly. "If it takes one blow . . . if it takes eight thousand blows to overcome resistance, then that's what it takes."[7]

Clymer and Duke were well matched and equally tenacious. When Clymer said that Duke's analysis interpreted evidence in the light most favorable to Powell, the SWAT sergeant bluntly responded, "That's absolutely right." Clymer replayed segments of the video to show that King had been beaten when no longer resistant; Duke used the same segments to show that King was moving and could reasonably be perceived as a threat. Even jurors unsympathetic to the defendants respected Duke and recognized that he was a good witness. But Duke was not testifying in the vacuum of Simi Valley, where prosecutors lacked an effective use-of-force expert. Jurors told me after the trial that they found both Duke and Conta knowledgeable and did not know which of these experienced sergeants to believe. As foreman Bob Almond explained it, this encouraged jurors to rely on their own analysis of the videotape.

Ironically, Duke's testimony in the federal trial was most beneficial to Briseno, the one defendant he believed had violated LAPD use-of-force policy. Duke took a harsh view of Briseno's stomp on King's neck or back. LAPD officers are allowed to use their feet against resistant suspects but are taught to avoid the neck area because of its susceptibility to injury. Testifying at the state trial, Duke had defended every blow and kick by Powell and Wind but said that Briseno's stomp was an inappropriate use of force.

Appropriate or not, the stomp had clearly prolonged the beating. Duke could see on the videotape that King writhed in pain when Briseno put his foot on him, and he began to move again. Powell, who was taking his handcuffs out of his back pocket, could see the movement but not the stomp that caused it. He resumed hitting King with his baton. But the vital question about Briseno's stomp was not its result but its motivation. Briseno was blocked by King and could not see what Powell was doing, nor could Powell see him. Had Briseno, as he claimed, tried to keep King down so he would not be hit again? Or had he jumped in to make a cowardly contribution to the abuse of a submissive suspect?

Duke's opinion on this question would have been harmful to Briseno if he had given it, but he was never asked. This was largely the doing of Briseno's lawyer, Harland Braun, who feared Duke would be a damaging witness against Briseno with jurors who identified with the police. In conversations before and during the trial, Braun strove to persuade Duke that Briseno had acted in good faith. Duke was unconvinced. Braun knew better than to suggest to Duke that he lie to benefit Briseno, but he did say that the overall defense would be harmed if Duke volunteered his opinion of Briseno's stomp. The liberal defense attorney and the conservative police sergeant reached an uneasy concordat. Because Duke deplored the prosecution and realized that Briseno could damage other defendants, he was willing to withhold his opinion of Briseno's stomp as long as no one asked him about it. Counting his blessings, Braun declined to cross-examine Duke.

For reasons of their own, the other attorneys went along with Braun. Stone wanted to avoid a repetition of Briseno's vivid testimony at Simi Valley in which he said that Powell had been out of control during the beating of King. To demonstrate his commitment to a unified defense, Braun had told the other defense attorneys that he would not call Briseno as a witness unless they wanted him to do so. Stone reciprocated by not asking Duke about Briseno's stomp. Despite nagging doubts about the value of a unified defense to Koon, Salzman also did not ask about it. Neither did Wind's attorney, Paul DePasquale, who respected Braun.

Nor did the government solicit Duke's analysis of what Briseno had done. The prosecutors did not know that Braun had promised the other defense attorneys that he would let them decide whether Briseno should testify. They reasoned that if Briseno repeated what he had said at the state trial, the other defense attorneys would go after him. If he did not testify, the government hoped to introduce a videotape of his state trial testimony. Either way, the government had nothing to gain by discrediting such a potentially powerful witness against Powell and Koon. Briseno was therefore the beneficiary of the unified defense and the contingent calculations of co-defendants and prosecutors who had no use for him.

The defense next called Edward Nowicki, the Wisconsin police trainer whom the government had planned to use as an expert. Nowicki, executive director of the American Society of Law Enforcement Trainers at the time of the King incident, had denounced the beating after seeing clips of it on television but changed his mind after prosecutors flew him to Los Angeles and showed him the unedited videotape. Nowicki told an acquaintance that he had declined to be a government witness because the unedited tape made him see the beating in a different light. The acquaintance passed on this story to Stone, who asked Nowicki to testify for the defense.[8]

Embarrassed prosecutors sought to prevent jurors from learning that the defense was using an expert witness that the government had failed to recruit. Davies was unsympathetic. Over heated objections from Clymer, the judge ruled that the story of Nowicki's government-sponsored trip to Los Angeles was relevant. "So the government thought they had a live one, and they didn't," Davies said. "That happens all the time in this business of expert shopping."

After relating his conversation with the prosecutors to the jury, Nowicki analyzed Powell's baton techniques during the subduing of King. He said Powell's blows were "absolutely appropriate" but mostly ineffectual.

The police trainer blamed Powell's deficiency with the baton on "substandard" training. The LAPD had taught the baton's use with stationary targets which failed to prepare officers for street encounters. Powell had used his baton in a "weak and ineffective" manner. "He had no power," Nowicki said. "He did not know how to use his body to lower his center [of gravity] and use baton strikes effectively." This evaluation echoed the opinion Powell's superiors had expressed less than two hours before the King incident.

Juror reaction to Nowicki's testimony demonstrated the magnitude of the defense predicament. While jurors found him credible, they did not agree that Powell's incompetence with the baton was sufficient justification for the beating. Professional analysis could not prevail against the power of the videotape, the sympathetic impression made by Rodney King, and the fears of jurors in a riot-wracked city. With so much going for the government, Braun believed that the actual burden of proof had shifted to the defense despite the standard jury instruction that the prosecution must prove its case beyond a reasonable doubt.

After repeatedly watching the grim videotape on the courtroom television monitor and hearing King's sad story and the reports of the physicians who had examined him, most jurors did not identify with the defendants. The arresting officers urgently needed to convey to the jurors the fear and confusion they felt in the middle of the night when confronted by an imposing suspect who seemed impervious to pain and two charges of fifty thousand volts of electricity that could literally fell an ox. The formidable task of humanizing the defense fell to Stacey Koon.

The sergeant at the center of the storm had waited through a month of testimony to tell his story. Despite his respect for Duke, Koon did not care much for experts. How could Conta say he had passed up a golden chance to order a second swarm of King, and how could Duke contend that he never should have tried a swarm in the first place? It all seemed so political. Koon believed he had averted a shooting and probably saved King's life. But here he was undergoing a second criminal trial because blacks who could not accept the Simi Valley verdicts had reacted violently and the LAPD had responded slowly to a riot for which it was unprepared.

Koon tried as best he could to make sense of what had happened the night of the King arrest. He believed he had relied on training and policy to arrest a fleeing felony suspect who had thrown "eight hundred pounds of officers off his back" and then struggled to his feet after two volleys from the Taser. It had been obvious to Koon that King was on PCP, as the sergeant matter-of-factly told police investigators after the incident, and he thought it should have been obvious to everyone else. The suggestions that he had ordered the beating because King was black or because he was running away were offensive to Koon. The accusation that he had violated King's civil rights was absurd. As Koon saw it, liberal politicians had decreed that the "Rodney King officers" must be sacrificed, and the LAPD leadership had gone along.

But since Koon believed that everything in life is part of God's plan, it followed that his ordeal must have a larger purpose. On a temporal level, Koon was convinced that any hope the defendants had for acquittal or public acceptance depended on a recognition of how the LAPD had become dependent on metal batons. Salzman's examination of this history seemed irrelevant to most jurors, but it was a defense that respected the wishes of his determined client.

Koon made a good witness for history but did poorly in humanizing the defense. His imperturbability made him seem distant and aloof on the stand, almost as if he were relating a memorized version of events. Koon was less concerned that he might be sent to prison than that he would be forever branded a bad cop. To succeed as a witness, he needed to re-create the anxious emotional and mental state he had felt at critical moments of the King arrest. But Koon believed his mission as a witness was to explain how his decisions were rooted in LAPD policy. He was a natural teacher who at lunch enjoyed evaluating testimony for reporters in the Roybal Building cafeteria.* While his codefendants were uncomfortable around reporters, Koon viewed them as conduits to the larger audience he was seeking to persuade of his professionalism.

Perhaps Koon had explained the King incident so often by the time he testified that he was incapable of the burst of passion that had surprised prosecutors at Simi Valley. Perhaps he needed to be examined by a peer who could arouse the sense of danger Koon had felt when King shook off the effects of the Taser and charged at Powell. This had happened in Simi Valley where attorney Darryl Mounger, a former LAPD sergeant, had brought Koon to the brink of tears by recalling a morgue picture of four California Highway Patrol officers who carelessly approached two suspects and were shot to death. Federal prosecutors realized the effectiveness of this testimony and stood ready to block it with objections had Salzman tried to elicit it. He did not try.

Whatever the reason, much of Koon's testimony at the federal trial was so remote and technical that it annoyed rather than instructed the jurors. Maria Escobel thought that his crisp answers to Salzman's questions were "practiced" and "pat," and Bob Almond considered Koon "cocky" and at

---

* For a time, Koon and all of the defense attorneys—and occasionally Powell—also made their case before television cameras in a plaza outside the Roybal Building during lunch recesses. The practice was frowned on but not forbidden by Davies. As the trial progressed, however, these noontime gatherings began to attract demonstrators and were virtually discontinued by the defense.

times "obnoxious." Koon's answers on direct testimony were squeezed of emotional content. "I had a duty and a responsibility, according to the policy, to manage and control the situation," Koon said, as if describing a boardroom decision.

Koon was not as detached or composed as jurors believed. He was anxious about his testimony but believed it necessary to show confidence on the witness stand as he explained how LAPD policy had governed his decisions. He did not realize that it was also important for him to let jurors glimpse the fear he felt that night. This shortcoming was reinforced by Salzman, who failed to understand that his client could not be saved by policy analysis alone. Koon had wanted a dignified and honest lawyer who would avoid courtroom theatrics. While Salzman fully fit this bill, he failed to appreciate the emotional dimension of a trial in which the government held the high cards.

Unlike Mounger in the first trial, Salzman had only a theoretical understanding of the hard realities of police work. Many jurors had even less such understanding, and Koon needed to persuade them that the videotape that so horrified them reflected prudent police conduct rather than callous and deviant behavior. But he could not bring himself to beg for understanding that he was doing his duty or bare his soul on the witness stand, as much as he wanted to rescue his lost career and preserve his freedom. There was a stubbornness to Koon that was at once admirable and exasperating. Police are like butchers, Koon told me years later. People do not want to know what police do to keep them safe anymore than they want to see what a butcher does to provide them with meat.[9] This was not a comparison that would have helped Koon in the federal trial, even had he been able to make it.

What Koon was able to do as a witness, and did admirably, was take responsibility for all the force used against Rodney King. Even Maria Escobel, who otherwise lacked empathy with Koon, was impressed by this. "He stood by everything that he did," she said.[10] Koon also stood by everything that Powell and Wind did, even while acknowledging that he had not seen every blow and kick. And he also stood by what Briseno had done, although he had privately concluded that Sergeant Duke had been right at Simi Valley when he testified that Briseno's stomp was inappropriate.

As the ranking officer who had taken control of the arrest, Koon was certainly accountable for what occurred. But police investigators concluded that Koon was not responsible for the early baton blows, especially Powell's panicked first swing that hit King in the face and caused his most severe injuries. Even Conta, who was unforgiving of Koon, believed that Powell's first swing was a reaction to King's charge and not to Koon's shouted commands. Powell independently told Internal Affairs investigators that he was acting on his own when he delivered that first blow. Detective Taky Tzimeas of Internal

Affairs concluded that there was no evidence that Powell had heard any of Koon's commands or that Koon was really directing the arrest at all.

But this was not what Koon told the jury. He believed he had directed the entire arrest from the moment he took control of it and that Powell had followed his orders throughout. Koon was persuasive on this point, to his own detriment. If Koon had exercised such sweeping authority, as he and many jurors believed, then it made sense to hold him responsible for King's injuries. Koon said the only order that Powell disobeyed was his instruction to take King directly to USC Medical Center from Pacifica Hospital. Even on this point, however, Koon excused Powell by agreeing that the detour to Foothill Station had speeded booking procedures and followed LAPD policy.

Answering Salzman's questions for four-and-a-half hours on consecutive days, Koon described his failed attempts to arrest King with shouted commands, the swarm, and the shots from the Taser. As Koon explained it, King could have stopped the beating at any time, as he eventually did by complying with police commands. "Rodney King has control of the situation," Koon said. "I have control of the officers." Koon left no doubt that he had intentionally used this control to hurt King. "My intent was to cripple Rodney King," Koon said. "That is a better option than having to use deadly force, having to choke, or having to shoot Rodney King."

The option of applying a carotid choke hold to King had occurred to Koon. This might have been defensible even under the limited circumstances under which LAPD policy permits such holds. Since officers had drawn their guns, Koon might have choked King into unconsciousness and argued that he used the hold because he was involved in a deadly force situation. But this seemed a dangerous course to Koon, who testified that he remembered that choke-hold use had been restricted because of the "perception that the choke hold was killing blacks."

"That inhibited me from using the choke hold," he said.

On the third day of his testimony, Koon was questioned by Clymer, who viewed him as a "bright, articulate and very polished witness" whom he was unlikely to rattle. Clymer approached the cross-examination, he said afterward, as an exercise in "Ohio State football, three yards and a cloud of dust." The prosecutor knew that Koon would make no dramatic concessions. As his football analogy suggests, Clymer hoped only for a series of small gains. He wanted to show that Koon exaggerated and "always slanted things in his favor."[11]

Clymer also had an unannounced objective of inflaming the jury or at least its two African-American members. He sought to ask Koon about his description of the confrontation between King and Highway Patrol Officer Melanie Singer as a "Mandingo sexual encounter," a phrase used by Koon in the manuscript of his book about the case, *Presumed Guilty*, which the

FBI had confiscated from his house. (The phrase was deleted from the published book after Koon's use of it was reported in the *Los Angeles Times*.) Davies would not allow this line of questioning, but Clymer managed to get the "Mandingo" phrase before the jury before the judge upheld Salzman's objection. Clymer tried a similar tactic when he asked Koon about a five-day suspension he had received for a 1986 use-of-force incident. Although Davies had previously ruled this incident inadmissible, Clymer contended he should be allowed to raise it in cross-examination to challenge Koon's credibility. Again Davies would not allow it, saying "there is substantial potential for undue prejudice."

Salzman considered "Mandingo" and the second raising of the 1986 incident as low blows that took advantage of Davies' practice of allowing attorneys to complete their questions before he entertained objections. The questions may have been unfair, but I found no showing in post-trial interviews that these references influenced jurors. The trial did not turn on the tricks or marginal tactics of the competing lawyers.

Whether the outcome turned on Koon's testimony is more difficult to determine, even with the benefit of juror interviews. Clymer believed that Koon's testimony was crucial and that all the defendants would have been acquitted if the jurors had believed him. Maybe, although we shall see that there were other explanations for the jury's decisions. But Clymer is right in saying that Koon failed to persuade the jurors that the officers were simply following LAPD policy when they beat and kicked King. In addition to his difficulty in connecting emotionally with the jurors, Koon was hampered by Clymer's careful cross-examination. Clymer was especially effective on the PCP issue, where he wrung a concession from Koon that he had failed to follow LAPD guidelines for dealing with a PCP suspect. The guidelines say that officers facing a PCP suspect should "wait the situation out" if possible. Waiting out Rodney King had not seemed an option to Koon on March 3, 1991.

Clymer and Koon fought to a draw on another issue in which Koon needed better than a tie. This was the matter of whether Koon, in the period before the videotape began, had waited long enough for King to comply with verbal commands before ordering Powell, Wind, Briseno, and Solano to swarm and handcuff him. Koon remembered waiting five minutes. Clymer attempted to show from records of radio calls that only a minute and forty-five seconds had elapsed before Koon ordered the swarm.

"Mr. Koon, you are exaggerating, are you not, the amount of time that elapsed before you ordered officers to swarm Rodney King?" Clymer asked.

"No, Mr. Clymer, I am telling you my recollection," Koon said.

Even if Clymer was right, a minute and forty-five seconds can seem a long time to police officers in the middle of the night when facing a muscular, noncompliant suspect they believe to be on PCP. The videotaped portion of the incident from the moment of King's charge at Powell to his hand-cuffing takes eighty-one seconds. If Clymer's calculation is right, this is twenty-four seconds less than the time King was allowed to remain un-bothered on the ground before the charge after disobeying police com-mands. And the time King was on the ground, whether a minute and forty-five seconds or five minutes, was followed by the swarm, King's throw-ing the officers off his back, and the unproductive Taser bursts. These com-bined events took several minutes and seemed an eternity to Koon and the other defendants. Unfortunately for the defendants, none of this action was videotaped.

The Rodney King incident was an exercise in *Rashomon* in which every participant saw dramatic events from differing perspectives but a *Rashomon* in which only one version was preserved. The videotape's one-dimensional record omitted almost every action exculpatory to the defendants except the King charge while including every action that was damning. Clymer was therefore able to use the videotape to drive home his opinion that King was a helpless drunk who had been beaten because he did not obey commands quickly enough to suit the officers. Koon's perceptions were similarly honest and consistent, but his record of the incident existed only in his mind. Even had he been a more compelling witness, Koon's narrative would have been unable to compete with the visual realism of the Holliday videotape.

Clymer understood the visual power of the videotape and pressed his ad-vantage. Turning repeatedly to the video, he mocked Koon's perceptions.

"It was your perception that evening that what you saw by Mr. King was a martial arts tactic designed to take an officer's baton and use it against him?" Clymer asked as he pointed to a frame in which King was on one knee raising his arm to block a blow.

"This is my training," Koon said.

"I take it that what you saw that night you did not interpret as a drunken man trying to protect himself?" Clymer asked.

"No, sir, I did not," Koon said.

The polarities of the Clymer and Koon versions of events obscured an al-ternative explanation that neither side wanted jurors to consider—and that was never really put before them. This third version was suggested by the In-ternal Affairs investigation of the incident, which was conducted when memories were fresh and before attitudes had been hardened by multiple prosecutions and riots. According to this view, the King incident was nei-ther textbook use of force nor street justice but a bungled arrest in which officers made a series of well-intentioned mistakes that were compounded by King's intractability.

This third version was propounded most coherently in interviews outside the courtroom by Taky Tzimeas, the level-headed Internal Affairs investigator who thought Koon went "brain dead" after the swarm and Taser shots failed to subdue King. Tzimeas compared the stories told by the participants with what he could see on the video and hear on the audiotape. He concluded that Powell, in his panic, had never heard the shouted commands of Koon and that the sergeant in turn had deluded himself into thinking that he was directing the arrest.[12]

Tzimeas had an acquired skepticism toward claims by police officers that they had used force against a suspect because he was crazed by PCP. But as he analyzed the incident, it became evident to Tzimeas that King had not responded to the beating like a typical drunk. Tzimeas persuaded his superiors to send a specimen of King's urine to an outside laboratory, which found it contained traces of an analogue of marijuana. The laboratory tests did not solve the mystery of what substances King had been using, for no blood or urine samples were taken until hours after the incident. In any case, tests based on these samples do not always detect PCP.

As the police officer who had taken the compelled statements from the defendants, Tzimeas could not be called as a witness, and no attorney on either side—with the partial exception of Braun—was much interested in alternative explanations of events. Clymer was convinced that all the defendants except Wind were bad cops. In any case, he could not have stood before a jury and said, "Ladies and gentlemen, here is a case where fearful police officers and their dysfunctional sergeant used excessive force against a noncompliant suspect who may have been using PCP. I ask that you convict them for violating Rodney King's civil rights." Koon was even less interested than Clymer in alternative explanations. The choice between gaining his freedom on the grounds of incompetence and doing time as a political martyr was easy for him. It never would have occurred to him to blame the King beating on an inept, frightened officer under his command.

For historians who seek to make determinations that reach beyond the verdicts, one anecdote stands out. After King was handcuffed and hog-tied, Koon asked any officers who had participated in the use of force to raise their hands. Powell and Wind promptly did, and each learned for the first time that the other had been involved. This was a tell-tale sign to Tzimeas that both officers were terrified and had "tunneled in" on King. But this story was never related to the jury.

As a result, the federal jurors were left to choose between the video-based prosecution depiction of the officers as brutes or Koon's account that he had conducted a by-the-book arrest. Koon's version became the defense case, all the more so because he was the only defendant to testify. Despite the wishes of his attorney, Wind once again declined to take the stand, knowing that he was too frail emotionally to withstand cross-examination. He also knew that his testimony would have undermined a key defense contention, for Wind had no doubt that Powell had hit King in the face with his baton.

Testifying was a closer question for Powell and attorney Mike Stone, who had put his client on the stand at Simi Valley and wanted to call him again. But Stone was now participating in a unified defense, and the attorneys for the other defendants did not want Powell to testify. The case for putting Powell on the stand was that he had delivered most of the baton blows and was the focus of the government case. Stone knew that the jury would expect to hear Powell's side of the story. The case against calling him was that Powell was a poor witness who had a nervous laugh and a habit of evading eye contact. Even in Simi Valley, Powell had not made a favorable impression. The clinching argument was that Koon had made the case for all the officers. "The theme of the case is that [the defendants] functioned as a team led by the sergeant," Stone said after deciding not to call Powell. He stuck by this analysis, saying after the trial: "If the jury believes Stacey, [Powell] doesn't need to testify. If the jury doesn't believe Stacey, it doesn't matter what he says."[13]

Powell knew he had the right to decide whether or not to take the stand, and Stone was scrupulous in telling his client that it was his decision. But Powell agreed with his attorney that he was unlikely to do better on his own behalf than Koon had done for him. So he agreed not to testify, although with some misgivings. "It would have been nice to tell my story without the government gumming it up," Powell told me moments after he made his decision. He acknowledged he had been "nervous" at the prospect of being cross-examined by Clymer. "They had a big folder and boxes with my name on it," he said. "It was going to be one helluva cross-examination."

Nevertheless, courtroom spectators gasped when Stone rested his case without calling Powell. Dan Caplis, a lawyer and television analyst who was monitoring the trial, thought the decision showed Stone had abandoned any hope of acquittal and was seeking a deadlocked jury.[14] In fact, Stone would have been happy at any time with a mistrial. Even in the pro-police milieu of Simi Valley before the riots, four jurors had held out for convicting Powell for using force under color of authority.

Without Powell, Stone focused on responding to medical experts who had testified that King's facial injuries were caused by baton blows. Dr. Dallas Long, an emergency room physician who had studied King's medical records, testified that the injuries were "most consistent" with "a fall on a broad surface, such as pavement." Long said his opinion was reinforced by a deeply embedded grain of sand removed from King's lip by plastic surgery five months after the beating.

Stone also called Carley Ward, a biomedical engineer specializing in injury analysis whom Judge Stanley Weisberg had refused to allow to testify in the state trial. Ward said King would have received more facial damage and might even have been killed if he had received a series of full-faced baton blows. "All of the facial fractures were caused by the fall," she testified.

Neither of Stone's witnesses was as persuasive with jurors as the prosecution medical experts, and Ward fared poorly on cross-examination. Alan Tieger challenged Ward's qualifications and produced evidence that a California appeals court had reversed a conviction in which she testified for the prosecution because of "flagrant loopholes in the acceptability of [Ward's] procedures and calculations." Stone objected, but Davies said he had invited Tieger's questions by eliciting information from Ward that she had testified as an expert witness in numerous trials. "It's the price you pay for gilding the lily," Davies said. "You've spread too much butter on the slice of bread."

Another significant setback for the defense was provided by Melanie Singer, the California Highway Patrol officer who had initiated the pursuit of Rodney King. The state trial had been a humiliating experience for Singer, who as a prosecution witness had given a riveting account of how Powell, without provocation, savagely struck King in the face with his baton, "splitting his cheekbone from the top of his ear to the bottom of his jawline." On cross-examination, however, Stone had skillfully used the videotape to force Singer to admit inaccuracies in her recollections. Singer did not recall that King had charged at Powell before the baton blows. She could not explain why most of King's injuries were on the right side of his face, for she had seen baton blows to both sides of his head. Singer seemed so confused after Stone had finished that the jurors understandably discounted her testimony.

Kowalski and Clymer had decided before the trial that Singer, while sincere, was so unreliable in her observations that she would hurt which ever side called her to testify. They excluded her from their witness list and were pleasantly surprised when Stone decided to put her on the stand for the defense. Other defense attorneys have suggested that Stone was blinded by his success in cross-examining Singer at Simi Valley, which may be true. But Stone had a practical reason for calling Singer. He wanted to establish that King was a dangerous driver who had hurtled down the freeway at speeds of up to 115 miles an hour and had then driven up to 85 miles an hour on residential streets. Stone thought it necessary to establish this because an earlier defense witness, school district officer Paul Beauregard, had minimized King's speeding.

Singer began with a composed recitation of King's wild drive over 7.8 miles of freeway and city streets. But her voice rose as she described the arrest scene, where Koon ordered her back as she was advancing on King with her gun drawn. In her mind's eye, Singer again saw Powell running up to King and hitting him repeatedly in the face with his baton as the blood ran freely from his shattered cheekbone and jaw. The memory was too much for her, and she abruptly buried her face in her hands and began to weep. Stone did not know what to do. The defendants and their lawyers also felt like crying. Officer Briseno put his hand over his eyes and shook his head. His attorney Harland Braun, his customary good nature deserting him, was angry. "What the hell was she doing up there?" Braun told reporters later. "Even I can't put a spin control on this."[15]

This disaster was compounded the next day when Singer became emotional again under cross-examination by Alan Tieger. Singer said King's face was bleeding so profusely from Powell's blows that she considered giving him medical assistance but refrained because other officers were "joking around" and she did not want them to heckle her. "There is no doubt in my mind that he struck him [King] in the face," Singer said, her voice choking and her eyes again full of tears. "I will never forget it until the day I die."

Stone tried to repair the damage. He showed Singer the opening section of the videotape, and she acknowledged that she did not recall the charge by King that she could see on the video monitor. She also acknowledged that other actions shown on the videotape, as well as the medical evidence, contradicted what she remembered. But the emotional power of Singer's memories and tears were more compelling than her corrections. Stone had given the government an unencumbered gift.

"What do you think of the Dr. Kevorkian defense?" Dan Caplis asked Clymer in the elevator after Singer's second day on the stand. Breaking a self-imposed rule against responding to reporters during trial, the usually sober-sided prosecutor laughed. "I hope the jury sees it the same way you do," he told Caplis.

Not all the jurors did. Singer was on balance a detriment to the defense, but some jurors wondered if she had cried for King or the careers of herself and her husband, neither of which were advanced by their participation in the King incident. "I couldn't figure out why she was crying," said Bob Almond, who had seen his share of injuries in Vietnam. "She's a highway patrolman. She's seen blood and guts on the freeway every day. She's seen little kids run over or burned up." But Maria Escobel sympathized with Singer. While she thought that Singer may have overreacted on the witness stand, Escobel also believed that the California Highway Patrol officer had seen something that bothered her.

The Singer debacle prodded Stone to wrap up his beleaguered presentation. Salzman and Braun believed that Singer was a diversion (as were Ward and other witnesses) which undercut Koon's argument that the defendants had followed LAPD policy. At a thirty-minute meeting the day after Singer's testimony, the other attorneys persuaded Stone. "We agreed that the best thing we could do was to wind it up as fast as we could," Stone said after the meeting. He did not call several witnesses on his list.

Neither Paul DePasquale, representing Wind, nor Braun saw any need to put on an elaborate case. Although Sergeant Conta had said that Wind's kicks and Briseno's stomp violated LAPD policy, the government had all but ignored Wind and Briseno. "Have you kept track of how many times my name was mentioned in court?" Briseno said to a reporter moments before the defense rested. "Sometimes I thought I was in the wrong trial." He could have added that some of the few references to him by prosecution witnesses were positive, especially Conta's acknowledgement that Briseno had tried to stop the beating. Wind had been cast in a positive light as well by the account of the detour to Foothill Station in which he shooed away the officer who shined a light in King's face.

DePasquale had a clumsy courtroom manner, but he had shrewdly analyzed the case against his client. Wind was a rookie LAPD officer and not an instigator of the beating. The videotape showed that Wind had evaluated the results of his blows and kicks, as policy dictated. DePasquale suspected that these factors would persuade the jurors to give Wind the benefit of the doubt, unless they believed he had acted with racial animus. With this in mind, DePasquale called Bryant Allen, King's drinking buddy and passenger the night of the arrest. Allen did not remember hearing racial epithets. To underscore this point, DePasquale melodramatically read into the record two accounts of the incident that King had given while in custody in which he denied that officers had called him racial names.

Braun's presentation was even more minimal than DePasquale's. He called no witnesses and submitted as his only exhibit one of Briseno's size eight black police boots, which Braun fancifully compared to a ballet slipper. The purpose of the exhibit was to suggest that Briseno, who weighed only 135 pounds, had not harmed the burly King with his single, off-balance stomp. It was an astute move by Braun. When the boot was examined by jurors during deliberations, jury foreman Almond was surprised at how much lighter it was than the military boots he had worn in Vietnam.

Braun was the most accomplished of the defense attorneys, with the easiest client to defend. The videotaped evidence against Briseno consisted entirely of the single stomp. Not only was this "foot motion" (as Braun blandly called it) ambiguous, but it seemed inconsequential to jurors when compared to the torrent of blows and kicks delivered by Powell and Wind. Less ambiguously, the videotape showed Briseno lifting his hand to stop Powell from hitting King. The prosecution had made a point of this video segment, which in itself might have been enough to acquit Briseno.

But Braun had changed his opinion of the case. When he agreed to represent Briseno, he had done so in the belief that he would be representing the one officer who had tried to stop an unjustified beating. But in the process of devising a unified defense, which had begun as an effort to spare Briseno from the attacks of his codefendants, Braun had learned that the case was not the uncomplicated incident of police brutality he had assumed from watching the edited videotape on television. Most important, he had discovered that Koon was an honorable police professional who had done his best to peaceably arrest a defiant suspect. So for Braun, a defense that started as a strategic ploy became a cause. Discarding his earlier views as uninformed and naive, Braun realized that Koon was telling the truth and concluded that all the defendants were innocent.

This epiphany gave moral weight to Braun's position, but it carried a risk for Briseno. As long as Briseno was a dissident cop who had tried to stop the beating, his chances of conviction were scant. If he refused to disassociate himself from Powell and Koon, there was always a chance a jury might decide that the beating was egregious enough to find every defendant guilty.

Briseno, however, was comfortable with Braun's strategy. He realized, after watching the enhanced video and listening to his attorney, that the other defendants had reasons for perceptions that differed from his own. He had lived in exile since testifying against Powell and Koon in Simi Valley, and he was weary of being seen as Benedict Briseno, the turncoat who had sacrificed other officers to save himself.

The other defense attorneys rejected Braun's analysis, however. Stacey Koon called the tune for the defense, and for him to concede that the King arrest was bungled by tactical misjudgments and Powell's panicky incompetence would have been to abandon his claim that he had supervised a managed and controlled use of force. Koon clung to this dogma as if it were an article of faith and admitted no possibility of a middle ground. Braun's revised theory may have had the value of truth, but it was a shadowy, unsatisfactory truth in which the defendants emerged neither as criminals nor as exemplary officers. It was a truth that could not prevail in a criminal trial held in a city where so many people had died.

Still, Braun's fellow defense attorneys embraced the unified defense. Briseno had been a prosecution witness in all but name at Simi Valley, where he had testified that Powell had been out of control as he repeatedly hit King. It was obviously in the interest of Koon and Powell to keep Briseno from testifying in the federal trial, and they were willing in return to go easy on him. Stone avoided any repetition of the preemptive strike he had launched against Briseno at Simi Valley. Sergeant Duke did not repeat his firm opinion that Briseno's stomp on King violated use-of-force policy. And Koon avoided criticizing Briseno in his protracted testimony.

Clymer and Kowalski considered the unified defense a fraud. To them it meant that Briseno had joined a continuing police conspiracy to misrepresent the King beating. To break this code of silence, they asked the court to allow them to show jurors a videotape of Briseno's Simi Valley testimony during the government rebuttal case. This was an unusual procedure and, as Clymer later acknowledged, a high-risk legal maneuver. Rebuttal testimony is supposed to answer points that have been made by the other side, and Briseno's videotaped testimony went far beyond that.

But Clymer creatively argued that Briseno's testimony rebutted Koon's contention that the King arrest had been a managed use of force that followed LAPD policy. Braun, with equal vigor, contended that the tape was improper rebuttal. Both attorneys believed they had the law on their side, but Clymer was particularly worried about how Davies would rule. Neither he nor Kowalski considered the judge a friend of the government. While the prosecutors believed they had precedents for their motion, they had been similarly convinced early in the trial that there were valid grounds for introducing past use-of-force incidents involving Koon and Briseno. Davies had ruled against them.

Mike Stone also argued with passion against admitting the videotape of Briseno's testimony. He pointed out that he could not cross-examine the videotape. What remedy existed for Powell if this maneuver were allowed? Davies wavered, appearing to agree first with one side and then with the other. Finally, he decided that the taped testimony could be admitted. The defense attorneys filed an emergency appeal with the Ninth Circuit Court of Appeals, asking that the decision be overturned. Courts rarely interfere on such matters in the middle of a trial, and Davies was upheld.

Ironically, the ruling was a huge boon for Briseno. "I couldn't have planned anything that would have helped Briseno more and hurt the other defendants as much as this ruling by the court," Braun said afterward.[16] Because the tape was supposedly rebuttal, prosecutors were required to delete testimony that did not relate to issues raised in the federal trial. What remained after extensive and skillful editing under standards determined by the court was a compelling two-hour-and-twenty-five-minute videotape with the gripping quality of a television courtroom drama. Briseno was cast as an understated cop in the *Dragnet* mold who gave "just the facts, ma'am." The editing made him look less opinionated and less emotional than he had been and gave added bite to his crisp criticisms of the "misconduct" of Powell and Koon. Briseno looked so terrific in the edited version that he impressed even skeptical juror Maria Escobel as a highly professional officer.

The "other videotape," as this edited testimony came to be called, may have been decisive. For one thing, it dealt a devastating blow to Koon's key contention that King was arrested by "managed and controlled use of force" that followed policy guidelines. Before he or any other officer knew of the existence of the Holliday videotape, Briseno had seen the King arrest as an ugly and largely unsupervised mess and had profanely confided his views of Koon's mismanagement to his partner Rolando Solano. "I was very angry, very upset, very frustrated," Briseno had said. "I was upset with the sergeant."

As the perceptive *Los Angeles Times* reporter Jim Newton observed, the admission of the Briseno videotape put jurors "in the unusual position of watching a defendant on one videotape describe yet another videotape."[17] Braun thought jurors would be "perplexed" by this surreal version of reality, but they were products of a television age, in which on-screen images often seem more authentic than actual events.

Viewing Briseno's testimony on videotape unquestionably enhanced its impact. Briseno, a small man, was larger than life on the oversize television screen in the courtroom and certainly larger than he had loomed at Simi Valley, where his credibility had been impugned by police witnesses. In the federal trial, Briseno's videotaped testimony impressed even jurors who were sympathetic to Koon and Powell—a bad sign for these defendants. Jurors who already leaned to the government side were even more impressed. Here was a veteran LAPD officer and a witness to the arrest who thought the beating of King brutal and unjustified. What more was needed for conviction?

Davies, an evenhanded jurist with a good reputation, was not trying to stack the deck in favor of the government when he allowed the Briseno videotape to be shown. But he was under enormous pressure. From the beginning of the trial, the Los Angeles media had reported on police precautions to guard against disturbances and had speculated on the possibility of civil unrest. Davies and the lawyers in the case had discussed contingency plans, also reported in the media, to evacuate them and the defendants by helicopter from the roof of the Roybal Building, which is near the borderline of South Central. In this milieu it would have been difficult for any judge to deny the introduction of evidence that the government insisted was essential to its case. Braun believes that the pressure became too much for Davies and that he buckled under it.

One does not have to accept Braun's harsh assessment to realize that the judge's decision to admit the videotape of Briseno's state trial testimony compounded the immense advantages enjoyed by the government. It added to the double-jeopardy burden imposed on the defendants by a second trial and made mincemeat of any theoretical right of Koon and Powell to confront their accusers. As Stone had put it so plaintively: How could he cross-examine a videotape? The attorneys in the case knew that Briseno claimed to have changed his opinion of the incident based on the FBI-enhanced videotape, which did not exist at the time of the Simi Valley trial. The enhanced tape had given him a better understanding of matters that had been a blur at the time: He could see, for instance, that at the time he stomped King, Powell had been reaching for his handcuffs. While Briseno still asserted that he had put his foot on King to keep him down, he now conceded that this action was unnecessary. But the judge's ruling froze Briseno's perception as it had existed at the time of the state trial—to the considerable detriment of Powell and Koon.

The government knew when it introduced the videotaped testimony—and Davies knew when he admitted it—that Briseno was not going to testify, thus putting himself at risk to save the other defendants. That was fine with the prosecutors, for it was Koon and Powell that they most wanted to convict. Later, when Briseno no longer faced criminal prosecution, he gave his revised account of the incident to a civil jury and an LAPD Board of Rights hearing. But the federal criminal jury never heard how the enhanced tape had changed his mind.

Skeptics, including the prosecutors and the other defendants, believed that after being acquitted in Simi Valley, Briseno was motivated to change his story so he would no longer be viewed as a pariah by other officers. Perhaps. But sincere or not, Briseno would have been in a no-win situation if he had testified in the federal criminal trial. Prosecutors would have described him as a perjurer if he had recanted his Simi Valley testimony. Had he not recanted, he would have been savaged by Stone and Salzman. No experienced criminal attorney, and certainly not Braun, would have wanted to put Briseno on the stand under these circumstances.*

It will be remembered that Deputy District Attorney Terry White, the lead prosecutor in the state trial, had mixed feelings about indicting Briseno. White thought Briseno's stomp was clearly wrong but that it may have been outweighed by his attempt to restrain Powell. An alternative, which White's superiors rejected, would have been to grant Briseno immunity from prosecution and call him as a witness. This would have required him to testify under penalty of perjury. If he had, Briseno presumably would have been a prosecution witness in the federal trial as well, and Stone and

---

* The prosecutors were ready to go after Briseno if he testified. They had in their possession a videotape taken by a security guard in the same apartment complex from which Holliday had videotaped the King arrest. The guard's videotape showed little of the incident itself but continued after the Holliday video and recorded when various police cars left the scene. Calculating from the times on this video, Clymer decided that Briseno could not have returned to the Foothill Station as he had testified in Simi Valley. Whether this evidence was as conclusive as Clymer believed is a matter of dispute. What is undisputed is that the prosecution was prepared to use it if Briseno recanted his state trial testimony.

Salzman could have questioned him to their hearts' content. This procedure would have been fairer to Powell and Koon.

But when District Attorney Ira Reiner made the decision to seek an indictment of Briseno, he had no inkling that the trial would be held in Simi Valley. In the furor produced by the King beating, Reiner assumed that every officer who used any amount of force against King had to be prosecuted. Under the political conditions that then prevailed, the decision to indict Briseno was not a close question.

Later, prosecutors saw the Briseno indictment in strategic terms: They could undergird their principal evidence, the Holliday videotape, with the testimony of a police witness who was critical of Koon and Powell. The Briseno indictment became an invitation to him to break ranks with his codefendants and become a prosecution wedge in the middle of the defense. Briseno accepted the invitation. Because the state trial was videotaped, the strategy survived to be used by the federal government in the form of Briseno's potent testimony. The government used this wedge to break apart the unified defense and push a fearful and divided jury over the edge.

CLYMER AND KOWALSKI SUSPECTED THAT THE BRISENO VIDEOTAPE had impressed the jurors and decided to quit while they were ahead. Had they appeared in the Roybal Building plaza to announce that they had dropped all charges against Briseno, their intentions could not have been clearer. Briseno was now a backdoor prosecution witness, this time against his wishes. A disconsolate Salzman realized this too. "It appears that the government was not truly intent on prosecuting Mr. Briseno," Salzman observed. "It's clear that the government's strategy was that Briseno was to be employed to get at my client and at Mr. Powell."[18]

Braun was mortified. He had refused to believe that Davies would allow the videotape to be introduced during rebuttal. While Braun's only legal duty was to Briseno, he had long passed the point of wanting his client acquitted at the expense of the other officers. Braun liked and respected Koon, so much so that he told me he would have been willing to represent him despite the anguish this would have caused his liberal friends.

His personal feelings aside, Braun realized he could face a practical problem. With the government no longer interested in his client, Braun had to worry that Koon might abandon the unified defense, which no longer served him, and take on the burden of discrediting Briseno. Braun would not have blamed Koon if he had done that, but he had to be prepared to deal with it.

But neither Koon nor any of the other defense attorneys went after Briseno. They did not blame him for the court's ruling allowing the videotaped testimony into evidence. The other attorneys also credited Braun for having led the legal charge against admitting the videotape. Salzman and Stone were suspicious of Braun, but they had formed a working relationship with him during the trial that was not easily discarded. They also had a practical problem: Braun would give the defense's last closing argument, and they wanted him to make the case for Koon and Powell as well as for Briseno.

Koon was well aware of the various strategic considerations and was in any case disinclined to lash out at Briseno. Koon's great virtue is loyalty, carried sometimes to such extremes that some might say it is also a vice. Koon stuck by Powell after he disobeyed his order to take King directly to USC Medical Center. He defended Salzman against critics who questioned his legal abilities. And he clung to the unified defense after it no longer benefited him.

In a goading cross-examination of Koon after his rebuttal testimony, Clymer asked the stubborn sergeant about Briseno's state-trial testimony that Powell was "out of control." Koon calmly replied that Briseno "had a different perspective than I had." Watching Koon testify, Braun was relieved and pleased. He afterward described Koon's conduct as honorable, which was true enough but of no discernible help to the sergeant.

17

THE THIRTEENTH JUROR

"There is fear for my family. I'm in there, and I don't even know if there is a riot going on outside. I don't know what my family is doing. I'm locked in this closet."

—Jury Foreman Bob Almond[1]

THE PROSECUTION WAS IN CONTROL AFTER THE SHOWING OF THE Briseno videotape. What little remained for the government to do was accomplished by Steven Clymer in a closing argument that was a masterpiece of the lawyer's art. While he knew the government had presented a strong case, Clymer is pessimistic by nature. A single determined juror could cause a mistrial, and trying the officers a third time would be difficult if not impossible. Clymer felt a need to connect with the jurors and make every possible point. He clung rigidly to the lectern and looked at his notes as he began. Then he paced, stopping to look directly into the eyes of the jurors as he spoke.

After a brief outline of his argument, Clymer began by discussing King's behavior. "On March 3, 1991, Rodney King was drunk," Clymer said. "He was disrespectful. In the words of Melanie Singer, he was a wiseacre. He was slow to listen and to comply with the commands the police gave him. When they tried to handcuff him, he tried to resist. . . . He got up and tried to run away [and] escape. In response to that, these defendants taught Rodney King a lesson. They went far beyond what was reasonable and what was necessary to arrest Rodney King."

Clymer described the beating of King and the inaccurate descriptions of it given in the various reports filed by the defendants. He recalled Briseno's testimony that King had not been combative. "Why did [Briseno] tell you he tried to stop Powell, and he tried to stop Koon, and they didn't respond to his request to stop?" Clymer asked. "The answer to all of that is simple, ladies and gentlemen. Something went very, very wrong at the intersection of Foothill and Osborne that night."

Now passionately launched into his argument, Clymer accused the defense of a persistent effort to deny and then to cover up what went wrong. "They have sought to convince you by exaggeration that Rodney King is the most dangerous person on the planet Earth," he said. "Rodney King is the biggest danger any police officer anywhere has ever faced. They've sought to convince you that the defendants had no choice that night but to continue to beat and beat and beat and kick and stomp Rodney King as he lay on the ground. . . . They would turn the world upside down for you. They would say to you that the man laying on the ground being beaten is the aggressor and the people with the batons are the victims."

Clymer reminded the jurors that King was not on trial and hadn't killed or robbed anyone the night of his arrest. Even so, he said, King had broken the law by driving while intoxicated. " . . . Rodney King should have been arrested that night, and Rodney King should have gone to jail, and Rodney King should have gone to court," Clymer said. "And if these defendants had done their job the way they were trained to, instead of beating Rodney King into submission, that's exactly what would have happened."

Instead of allowing the law to take its course, "the defendants tried Rodney King at Foothill and Osborne," Clymer said. "They tried him for being disrespectful, for being contemptuous to police officers. And with Stacey Koon as the judge and Powell, Wind, and Briseno as the executioners, they found him guilty and punished him."

Clymer's best ally in his three-hour-and-fifteen-minute argument was the Holliday videotape, which he played repeatedly at regular and slow speeds. "You will never get a better indication of reality than that video tape two years after the fact," he said. "Unlike witnesses, it doesn't change. Its story doesn't change. It doesn't lose its memory. It doesn't have biases or prejudices or loyalty one way or the other. It is what it is." Pointing to the videotape frame in which Briseno holds up his hand to stop the beating, Clymer said: "What Briseno does within the first eighteen seconds of this video shows that every person had a chance to think about what was happening and had a chance to stop what was wrong."

Then Clymer focused on the PCP defense, which he realized had the potential for providing pro-police jurors with a rationale for acquittal. He conceded it was "possible" King had used PCP but said the defendants had lied in saying they were "certain" of it. PCP was the "magic word." Since PCP could endow users with "superhuman strength" and make them impervious to pain, the officers had invented the PCP defense to justify an unjustifiable beating.

If closing arguments were judged on fairness rather than effectiveness, the PCP section of Clymer's presentation would receive a low grade. In arguing that the defendants had invented their PCP defense after the fact,

Clymer cited Wind's use-of-force report. Wind had marked a box saying that King had used alcohol, skipped a box labeled "PCP", and checked another box that said "other, possibly under the influence of another drug." Although the jury did not know it, Wind had never before filled out such a report. He had asked Powell which boxes to check, and he had done as Powell told him. After the incident, Wind told Internal Affairs investigators that King was on PCP. Powell also believed this—he told an officer during the incident that King was "dusted"—but with typical sloppiness he had instructed Wind to mark a box on the report he considered more inclusive.[2]

Briseno, who had more experience with PCP users than Powell or Wind, also believed that King was dusted. When he touched King during the initial swarm, he had noticed that King was perspiring profusely on what was a cold night. King had seemed unbelievably powerful to Briseno, who realized that King had ingested something stronger than alcohol and so testified in the state trial. Although Clymer relied on Briseno's testimony to ridicule Koon's contention that the force used against King was justified, he took no note of Briseno's unqualified belief that King had been using PCP.

As we have seen, the Internal Affairs investigation concluded that the officers at the scene believed King was on PCP. Detective Taky Tzimeas, who headed this inquiry, did not excuse the defendants' conduct because of this, but he had no doubt they believed it. On this issue, Clymer had things backward. The officers' *belief* that King was on PCP was not in question. The question is whether they were right.

Nonetheless, Clymer was persuasive with the jury. This was partly because of the absence of chemical evidence but mostly because no mention of PCP had been made in the booking of King. This lapse was not unusual: Arresting officers often book suspects on the most serious charge possible—in King's case, the crime of "felony evading"—and omit other charges. Koon told me he always followed this practice.

Dr. Antonio Mancia's treatment of King at Pacifica Hospital, cited by Clymer in his closing argument, helped the government on the PCP issue. Despite having been told by officers that King was on PCP, Mancia cavalierly put his hand into King's mouth and stitched up his cuts. (This baffled the officers at the time, and Koon told me nearly three years after the trial that he never would have put his own hand into King's mouth.) But Mancia also failed to notice that King had suffered fifteen facial fractures, which is why the doctor sent him to USC Medical Center in a police car and not in an ambulance.

Clymer argued that Koon would not have ordered officers to swarm and handcuff King if he believed he was on PCP. This was not necessarily true. Koon was often bold and sometimes reckless in command, and even his expert witness Duke had disapproved of swarming an unsearched felony suspect who might be on PCP. If Koon had conceded this point and said he had ordered the swarm to spare King injury, he might have won over the jurors. But since Koon conceded nothing, Clymer was able to use the swarm to undermine the sergeant's contention that he believed King was on PCP as well as his claim that the arrest had followed LAPD procedures.

Clymer rolled on, systematically picking apart Koon's defense. He dismissed King's apparent imperviousness to the Taser shots by saying that the darts Koon fired had not connected properly on King's clothing. (The Internal Affairs investigation had concluded otherwise.) As Clymer saw it, Koon's claim that King was not affected by two jolts of 50,000 volts of electricity was an exaggeration to make King seem dangerous, "another slanted perception in [Koon's] interest and the interest of the defense."

Even the contention that Powell had swung his baton in panic was "slanted," Clymer said. He stopped the enhanced videotape at the two-second mark, when King is on his knees after being hit by one of the Taser shots and pointed to Powell. "What does Powell do?" he asked. "Watch the foot. Powell starts to lift that foot off the ground like a batter waiting for the pitch. The pitch is coming in. Rodney King still hasn't begun to move in defendant Powell's direction. He's still getting up off the ground. Powell is already starting his swing."

This particular point was not persuasive to every juror and might have been even less so if Powell had testified. Powell had no memory of starting his swing or cocking his baton, and his behavior may have been reflexive. Even Sergeant Conta, the prosecution expert, found no fault with Powell's first swing. But Clymer's analysis undergirded the argument that the defendants sought to punish King. Braun sat riveted, admiring Clymer's skills even while rejecting his analysis. "Given the constraints of his case, I don't think anyone could do better than Clymer did," Braun said afterward.[3]

As good as he was, even Clymer was not flawless. His voice became oddly melodramatic when he described Melanie Singer's performance on the witness stand. He seemed to have no inkling that jurors might wonder if her tears had flowed too often and easily. When Clymer demonstrated Briseno's stomp on King, he used his right foot instead of his left, a technical error that gave Braun an opening. That an attorney of Clymer's skills would miss such a detail shows how much more interested he was in Briseno as a witness than as a defendant. Clymer missed nothing in Briseno's testimony that was harmful to Koon and Powell, and he also said that Briseno had made a "very commendable" effort to stop the beating. The prosecutor explained Briseno's stomp by saying that he had "decided to become one of the boys" as the use of force continued.

Clymer devoted only four short paragraphs of his argument to Timothy Wind, saying he had delivered six or seven "unreasonable" kicks and falsified a use-of-force report. This benign neglect may have reflected Clymer's sympathies as much as his legal analysis. The prosecutor thought Wind had been properly charged but also believed he had been unlucky in having Powell as his training officer and Koon as his supervisor. Wind had been in the wrong place at the wrong time, Clymer told me after the trial. He kept the focus of his argument on Koon and Powell.

Clymer ended his argument by invoking the Constitution, which had protected "rights that kept us from being a police state, rights that we have fought for in wars." Facing the jurors, he said, "You have to decide what you think police officers ought to do in a free country. You have to decide if what you see on this videotape is reasonable. You have to decide if police officers should use enough force to overcome resistance, or if police officers should be able to beat disrespectful subjects into submission."

Salzman, who led off the series of defense closing arguments, lacked Clymer's rhetorical flair and analytical ability. He delivered a long, rambling presentation that touched on the Iran-contra scandal and the movie *Chinatown* and included a baffling anecdote about a former Pittsburgh mayor. Jurors had listened raptly to Clymer; they began to fidget early in Salzman's argument.

Buried beneath Salzman's distracting oratory was a legitimate perception that the defendants were scapegoats who were being tried a second time because of political pressure generated by the riots. Instead of developing this point, however, Salzman blamed the riots on King's resistance to arrest. "Because of that, people died," Salzman said. "People lost their homes because someone wanted to get to Hansen Dam without interruption." It was an argument that failed to take into account the impression that King had made on the jury.

Salzman did better in tracing the historical decisions that left LAPD officers dependent on metal batons. He argued that the defendants were paying the price of official negligence by the city council and LAPD management. The city's 1982 decision to limit choke-hold use had left officers with a choice of hitting resistant suspects with batons or shooting them. Duke and others had warned that the policy change would lead to an increase of injuries during arrests, but the warnings were ignored until the Holliday videotape created a "public relations nightmare." The authorities had responded by making "sacrificial lambs" of the defendants.

Salzman then turned to the videotape, which he said the prosecutors and their experts had played backward and forward three hundred times to determine that unreasonable force had been used. The arresting officers had no such luxury. "Stacey didn't have a videotape," he said. "He didn't have a stop button. He didn't know how this was going to end up."

As Salzman saw it, the videotape really was the "best evidence" for the defense. "Everything that happened on the tape happened for a reason, not unreasonable reasons, not evil reasons, but the right reason," he said. The tape showed King's charge. It showed officers using force and evaluating the results and stopping the force when King finally complied with their commands. If the defendants had intended to teach King a lesson, "you would see [an] unrelenting, continuous rain of blows," Salzman said. "If it was not a managed, controlled use of force, the blows would be nonstop. . . . But that didn't happen." Attorney Darryl Mounger had made a similar argument for Koon at Simi Valley. But Mounger was a former LAPD sergeant with a dramatic flair who had no trouble persuading the jurors to put themselves in Koon's shoes. Whether Mounger could have accomplished the same result with jurors who were younger, more skeptical of the police, and frightened by the riots is unknowable. But Salzman's argument did not get through to them.

Mike Stone, who had spent fifteen years as a police officer, did get through. Walking back and forth and wielding a baton as he talked, sometimes in a cajoling tone and sometimes in a shout, Stone commanded the jury's attention during a passionate four-hour argument that repeated much of what he had said at Simi Valley. The officers were a thin blue line that stood between the public and the likes of Rodney King. "We leave it to them to face the mean streets," Stone said. "We leave it to them to protect us from the criminal predators that prey upon victims in our community every day. We depend upon them to remove from our freeways and streets those, who with reckless and callous indifference to human safety and human life, run from the police, drive speeds of eighty miles an hour on city streets, one hundred miles on the freeway, with a bellyful of Olde English 800."

Stone gave the jurors a stark choice of seeing the officers as heroes or as thugs. "There is no middle ground," he said. "There is no compromise. It's not a little bit one way and a little bit the other. It's one or the other. Either Officer Powell and his companions—Sergeant Koon, Theodore Briseno and Timmy Wind—acted as reasonable police officers . . . or they acted like uniformed hoodlums, and that is all there is to it."

Stone mocked the hindsight analysis made possible by the videotape. When Powell faced King he had "no opportunity for calm reflection" or tactical discussions. "He had no opportunity to run the scenario backwards and forwards in his mind like a videotape with still frames," he said. Powell had done what he was trained to do. Duty had required him to act, and Powell had acted instead of preserving his own safety. "He chose to stand his ground," Stone said. "He chose to do his duty."

Stone's sincerity impressed even those jurors who had made up their minds against Powell. But in trying to persuade jurors that Powell was scared, Stone had a steeper hill to climb than at Simi Valley, where Powell's testimony had conveyed the panic the officer felt during King's charge. King had not testified at the first trial. For the Simi Valley jurors, King was a demonized presence seen dimly in black and white on a one-dimensional screen and described in testimony even by prosecution witnesses as a "monster" or an "incredible hulk."

The situation was reversed in the federal trial, where King testified and Powell did not. Powell was now the shadowy figure on the screen who was easily demonized by prosecutors as a brutal cop meting out street justice. This was as much a caricature as the "monster" portrayal of King had been, but it worked because there was nothing to counter it. State jurors exaggerated the menace of the absent King and identified with Powell, the flesh-and-blood officer on the witness stand. Federal jurors expected Powell to testify, and his failure to do so encouraged them to sympathize with King, whose testimony had demonstrated his vulnerability.

Paul DePasquale knew from experience as prosecutor and defense attorney that jurors expect accused police officers to take the stand. But Tim Wind was suffering too much emotionally and physically to do so. In the absence of his testimony, the burden of distancing Wind from Powell and Koon was left to DePasquale, who began by complimenting Clymer for an "excellent and impassioned argument" that was flawed only by a unitary description of the defense. Clymer had referred to "the defense theory, the defense experts, the defense interpretation, the defense attitude—they, they, they." This was wrong. The charges against each defendant must be considered separately. "This is not a team sport," DePasquale said.

In differentiating Wind's conduct from that of the other defendants, DePasaquale did not abandon the unified defense. Indeed, he advanced it by suggesting that Koon's presence "saved lives," perhaps Melanie Singer's and perhaps King's. But DePasquale also drew distinctions. He pointed out that Wind, despite police experience in Kansas, was a rookie LAPD officer who had acted under direction of Koon, his sergeant and supervisor, and Powell, his training officer. DePasquale mocked Sergeant Conta's suggestion that Wind somehow should have disobeyed Koon's commands in the middle of the incident. Over an objection by Clymer that was overruled, DePasquale described Conta as "the mouthpiece of command authority for the Los Angeles Police Department." The LAPD had decided to scapegoat the defendants because of political pressure, and the "hypocrite" Conta had testified accordingly to advance his "careerist position."

Playing off Clymer's contention that Powell had cocked his arms before swinging at King and using the same baseball metaphor, DePasquale observed that Wind had pulled back on a swing that could have hit King in the head. DePasquale then pointed to segments of the videotape which showed Wind had stepped back between swings to evaluate the results, as LAPD policy requires. He disputed Clymer's assertion that King was on the ground when Wind kicked him at one point in the incident, stopping the tape to show that King was on his haunches. At a later point, DePasquale said the tape showed a tired Wind pushing King to the ground with his foot, which "probably hurt a heck of a lot less than a baton strike."

As this statement suggests, DePasquale recognized that not all the defendants were in the same boat. If jurors were determined to convict Powell, DePasquale wanted them to make allowances for Wind. With this in mind, he steered clear of Mike Stone's all-or-nothing argument that urged jurors to decide that the defendants as a group were heroes or hoodlums. The jury had no duty to "elect a hero," DePasquale said. He paused and added, "There are no heroes in this story, ladies and gentlemen."

DePasquale did not dazzle the jury, nor did his monotonous delivery impress the court. But his closing argument was a triumph of substance over style that recognized ambiguities denied by the other attorneys. DePasquale managed to criticize King without demonizing him, and he was far more measured than Stone and Salzman in his praise of the defendants. DePasquale saw the defendants as ordinary officers who had done a dangerous job to the best of their ability and who lacked the malicious intent to harm King that was required for a finding of guilty. If not heroes, they surely were not villains, and they did not deserve to go to jail.

This common-sense argument resonated with jurors during their deliberations. As they debated Wind's fate, they could see on the videotape that he had stepped back to evaluate the results of the force used against King. The observant Maria Escobel, among others, decided that Wind had tried to restrain his use of force while Powell had not. The jurors also recalled that Wind had shooed away the officer who had shone his flashlight in King's eyes at Foothill Station, another point emphasized by DePasquale in his closing argument. As Harland Braun observed in another context, "There is a tactical value to the truth."[4]

Braun delivered the final defense closing argument the following morning, the Saturday before Easter. He was as confident as an attorney can be after such a bruising trial—and with good reason. Every possible break had gone Briseno's way. The court had kept out evidence of Briseno's prior use of force, which also involved kicking. The court had admitted Briseno's taped testimony from Simi Valley, in which he cast himself as the hero of the incident. Briseno's attempt to stop the beating and his condemnation of Koon and Powell had commended him to jurors who wanted to convict these defendants. The government's reluctance to introduce evidence that would have challenged Briseno's credibility and possibly weakened the impact of his taped testimony had left him in good stead with the more pro-police members of the jury.

Even so, Braun was frustrated with a trial he had decided was a political exercise engineered to quiet the clamor arising from the riots and thereby help reelect President Bush. He was disgusted with the government for playing a racial card that had the capacity to inflame South Central and cause another riot if the defendants were acquitted. Braun believed that African Americans everywhere would remember the racial accusations if they recalled nothing else about the trial.

Braun was equally frustrated with the defense. While he believed that the officers had acted lawfully, he strongly disagreed with the strategy of insisting that the arrest was a textbook example of use of force. It seemed unlikely that a jury would agree that LAPD policy required using fifty baton blows to subdue an unarmed man. Furthermore, by refusing to concede that King's facial injuries were caused by baton blows, Stone had created a straw man that the government had easily demolished. Braun's frustration was compounded by the realization that he had made Stone's dubious position worse by giving Dr. Aronberg an opening to say that King's injuries were caused by baton blows, not falls to the pavement.

Most of all, Braun was frustrated with Davies for the excessive deference he thought the judge had shown the government. The gag order silencing Braun during jury selection for criticizing the government, although quickly overturned, had been a telltale sign. Had Braun heeded this omen, he might have anticipated that Davies would permit the videotape of Briseno's Simi Valley testimony to be introduced during rebuttal. Instead, Braun had been surprised by a ruling that helped Briseno at the expense of Koon and Powell and left him with the burden of arguing the case for these defendants as well as for his own client.

Braun responded creatively to the challenge. He felt keenly that the entire trial was unfair, and as he prepared his closing argument during Passover, his thoughts turned to another trial that had taken place nearly two thousand years ago. It seemed to Braun that Pontius Pilate had capitulated to the mob for political reasons, as jurors were being asked to do in the trial of the four officers. It was an apt analogy if not pushed too far; Braun realized that jurors were unlikely to confuse any of the defendants with Jesus Christ.*

"Preachers have their texts and lawyers their precedents, but it seems to me that on the Saturday between Good Friday and Easter we should remember a

---

* Braun, a Catholic whose father was Jewish, has an interest in religious issues and an awareness that biblical accounts of the trial of Jesus are a potent historical source of anti-Semitism.[5] Before preparing his closing argument, he checked with jury consultant Jo-Ellan Dimitrius, who told him that there were no Jews on the jury.

trial two thousand years ago," Braun said in his closing argument. "When the prisoner was brought by the authorities before the judge, Pontius Pilate asked the simple question, 'What evil has this man done?' . . . And the authorities really had no answer. But when you read Matthew you find in it an eerie echo of this case, that the man was condemned, the prisoner was condemned, because there were riots in the city."

Speaking so softly that Judge Davies asked him to raise his voice, Braun compared Pilate's decision to the task facing the jurors. "No man should be condemned in this country because there is a threat of a riot," Braun said. Juries have a duty to bear witness to the truth. "So in a sense, my client is on trial, but you are also on trial, it's your courage that's on trial."

Braun scorned the prosecutors for portraying Briseno as a liar while simultaneously urging that jurors accept him as a reliable witness against Koon and Powell. Clymer had called Briseno's stomp on King "an act of cowardice." Instead, Braun said of the prosecutors: "It seems to me that they're the cowards, that they're the liars. . . . It seems to me it's an act of cowardice to indict a man simply so that you can use him as some instrument against another citizen. They should have called him as a witness. He took an oath in Simi, and he took that oath seriously, and he told the truth. It hurt. No officer likes to testify that he disagreed with another officer, that's just human nature, but he did that. He would have taken an oath for either the defendants or for the prosecution and told the truth again, but, no, they had to indict him. As Pontius Pilate said, 'What evil has this man done?'"

In order to argue that Powell also had done no evil, Braun had to acknowledge that Briseno was wrong in trying to stop the beating. He conceded this without hesitation, saying Briseno held up his hand to stop Powell from hitting King because he could not see that King was trying to regain his feet and was near Briseno's holstered gun. Later in the incident, when he put his foot on King, Briseno could not see that Powell was ready to handcuff him. These were "instant calculations," made during a dangerous situation where everyone had different perceptions. "If officers can't see things the same way, how can we hold them responsible as criminals if they misperceive something?" Braun asked. "The only thing unique about this situation was that a big portion of [the videotape] was broadcast worldwide, and there was an instantaneous rush to judgment, an electronic lynch mob, if you will."

Braun spoke for two hours in an argument as old-fashioned in form as it was bold in concept. The other attorneys had used copious exhibits, diagrams, and the enhanced videotape to make their points; Braun avoided props and talked conversationally from a one-page outline. He examined the origins of the jury system, analyzed the charges against each defendant, praised Koon for taking control of the arrest and preventing a shooting, and described

Powell as a "scared kid." He again scorned prosecutors for describing Briseno as a coward. ("If he was a coward, then I wish we had more cowards like Ted Briseno, who at least tried.") In a prescient passage, he said the government had tried Briseno so that the jurors "can condemn Larry Powell or Stacey Koon but feel good that they released someone." Raising his voice slightly, Braun said, "Don't use my client for that purpose. That's wrong. It's despicable."

Also despicable to Braun was the prosecution's attempt to make the trial a racial case when the prosecutors knew that King had not been beaten because he was black. Braun threw the racial card back in the government's face. Even Rodney King, who was drunk and "did stupid things" but was not "an evil man," had sensed the "monstrousness" of the racial charge and tried to withdraw it by saying he wasn't sure what the officers had said. But the prosecutors knew for certain that the defendants had not used racial epithets and raised the issue nonetheless. "You have to ask yourself why does the United States government . . . put on Mr. King to use that racial epithet, which is the vilest of all racial epithets that is used by a white person, when Mr. King himself says I'm not sure [that 'nigger'] was used?"

In the final passages of his argument, Braun returned to his analogy with the trial of Jesus. He said that prosecutors would suspect the apostles of lying because their accounts of the trial conflicted. "I'm sort of glad Clymer wasn't around in those days because he would have indicted the apostles," Braun said, drawing a burst of laughter in the courtroom and even a smile at the government table from Barry Kowalski; Clymer stared stonily ahead. Matthew and John were men of integrity who "weren't covering up anything" even though their versions of the trial conflicted. Matthew believed Pontius Pilate had been worried about a riot in the city. John, who said nothing about a riot, wrote that when Jesus announced that he had come to bear witness to the truth, Pilate had asked, "What is truth?" Braun imagined that Pilate had chuckled cynically when he said this, attesting to the absurdity of such a claim. But the jury must answer the question. Braun told the jurors that they must bear witness to the truth that the defendants were innocent.

PROSECUTORS HAVE THE LAST WORD IN CRIMINAL TRIALS, AND Kowalski delivered a scrappy rebuttal argument for the government, filled with folksiness and catchy phrases. He labeled the defendants "bullies with badges" and urged jurors to remember childhood lessons about fighting fair. "Watch the videotape, use your common sense," Kowalski said. "It's wrong to beat a man who's lying on the ground. You know that in the schoolyard when you're a kid. You don't kick a man when he's down. . . . The law demands that you follow that schoolyard rule."

In his impact on the jury, Kowalski can be compared with DePasquale. While jurors were not overly impressed with either lawyer, they remembered their arguments. Foreman Bob Almond said that many jurors could see that Kowalski "grated" on Judge Davies, whom they liked and respected. Almond believes that this attitude rubbed off on the jurors.[6] Many jurors also found Kowalski's two-hour-and-thirty-minute argument long and repetitious, an opinion perhaps reinforced by Davies, who interrupted near the end to ask Kowalski when he would finish. But Kowalski's central point stuck with jurors, who remembered during deliberations that Powell had repeatedly hit King while he was on the ground.

Had Kowalski stayed within the confines of his bullies-in-the-school-yard analogy, his argument would have been an unqualified success. But he intensely disliked the defendants, and his zeal led him beyond the schoolyard. Kowalski's argument included an appeal to jurors to act as the "conscience of the community," and he seems to have had a global village in mind. "When the video was played, people may have noticed different details about what was occurring in the video, but there was one thing that everyone from Paris to Tokyo noticed, one thing that everyone saw," Kowalski said. "There was one thing that caused horror and outrage throughout this world. There was one thing that neither you nor anyone else missed when they saw that videotape, even if they saw it for five or ten seconds. And the thing that everybody saw, that everybody was so outraged about was that the defendants were beating a man who was on the ground. That's why there was such outrage. That's why there was such uproar."[7]

Clymer would later acknowledge to an appeals court, in a remarkable admission from one prosecutor about the conduct of another, that Kowalski's argument was improper because it was inflammatory. But defense attorneys made no objection at the time to Kowalski's statement, which was surely accurate and far less inflammatory than the government's raising of the race issue when King was on the witness stand. In his closing argument, Kowalski was trying forcefully to make the point that it was wrong to hit someone on the ground. He slid from this contention into an offhand appeal to world opinion.

Kowalski's "Paris to Tokyo" remark perfectly captured the mind-set that then prevailed in much of Southern California. People were beset by fear of new riots, and they were also conscious that the eyes of the world were upon them. "Los Angeles: Is the City of Angels Going to Hell?" asked *Time* magazine's cover story two days after the trial ended. Clymer and Kowalski had put on a powerful case, but their greatest success in the jury room lay in reminding jurors about the deadly riots that had engulfed Los Angeles less than a year earlier—and arousing fears of more to come.

No one doubted the city was on edge as Judge Davies completed his instructions and submitted the case to the jury at 3:07 P.M. on Saturday, April 10. Television, radio, and newspaper stories that day and the next took extensive notice of the widespread jitters. "Civil War," said a headline on a report by KCOP-TV. "Will It Happen Again?" asked KCAL-TV. At midnight, the LAPD went on a heightened state of readiness, adding the first 600 of an eventual 1,000 extra officers to patrol duties. Volunteers from Mayor Tom Bradley's "Neighbor to Neighbor" program went door to door in South Central to advocate a non-violent response to the verdicts. "The prospect of new rioting has haunted the federal trial from its opening moments," Jim Newton wrote in the Los Angeles Times.[8]

Judge Davies was well aware of this prospect and concerned that it might influence the jury. Without being asked by either side to do so, he decided to bring up the issue. "You should not be influenced by the anticipation of any external consequences of your verdict," Davies told the jurors before sending them to deliberate.

This was more than a pro-forma instruction. Davies was a high-minded and impartial judge who wanted verdicts based on the evidence. Nevertheless, his well-intentioned words accomplished nothing except to underscore the jurors' anxieties. The truth about whether Pilate's judgment of Jesus was influenced by fear of a riot is lost in the mists of history. But there is no doubt that jurors in U.S. v. Koon were aware of the possibility of new riots in Los Angeles.

PERHAPS THE MOST AWARE WAS ROBERT ALMOND, AN OBSERVANT civil engineer and Army combat veteran of Vietnam who was Juror No. 5. The jury of which he became the foreman was sequestered on the tenth floor of the downtown Los Angeles Hilton Hotel, where Almond's room had a commanding view of South Central. Each night, Almond would peer out at this vast area that began a few blocks from the hotel and stretched to the horizon. The next day he would tell his fellow jurors that he had seen no fires burning in the city.[9]

Almond regarded the report from his window command post as gallows humor. He had learned while serving on an automatic-weapons crew in Vietnam that humor helps to ease tensions. Long before deliberations began, Almond saw signs of stress among the jurors that reminded him of the behavior of scared and battle-weary soldiers. He considered himself more stress resistant than others but recognized he was not immune to pressure. He worried about the safety of his wife and family. He wondered whether people would find out where he lived and throw rocks at his home after the trial was over.[10]

Jury sequestration by its nature imposes burdens on almost everyone involved. It uproots people from home and work and places them in an artificial and controlled setting where conversations, reading, and television viewing are monitored. Local newspapers were censored, with any reference to the trial or the LAPD removed. Family separations tugged at the jurors. Almond, married for twenty-five years, missed his wife, with whom he was allowed a ten-minute conversation every day. He quickly tired of what he called the "gourmet meals" in the hotel and longed for burritos or fast food.

Tight security measures increased the pressure. The federal jurors were driven to court in unmarked vans from which they glimpsed barricades and other antiterrorist precautions around and under the Roybal Federal Building. The heavily armed U.S. marshals who escorted them wore bulletproof vests and were clearly on edge. On a relaxed weekend outing at Griffith Park, grim-faced marshals drew their guns when a rattlesnake was spotted slithering across a path.

The snake incident was amusing to some of the jurors and scary to others, but less natural dangers were unnerving to everyone. When jurors returned to their hotel each afternoon, marshals would block off the sidewalk on Wilshire Boulevard with a tent so they could enter without interference. Once a pedestrian who failed to heed a marshal's instructions to stop was pounced on and pinned to the ground. Another afternoon, marshals learned of a bomb scare at the hotel while transporting the jurors back from the courtroom. The vans returned to the Roybal Building while an excitable male juror screamed, "We're going to die, we're going to die."[11]

The chilling outburst in the van was a dramatic example of the strains imposed by a trial that jurors thought could ignite another riot. This fear was particularly palpable for the African American from Watts whom the defense had tried to remove from the case. Contrary to expectations of both sides, the Watts man gave the defense case a fair hearing. But he also told another member of the jury panel before deliberations began that he was afraid there would be new disorders if the defendants were acquitted.

Fear, in fact, was the thirteenth juror in U.S. v. Koon. The extent of this fear was inadequately recognized by reporters covering the trial, most of whom could escape the hothouse environment of downtown Los Angeles after work or on weekends. It was also insufficiently recognized by defense attorneys, who had talked themselves into deciding not to seek a change of venue by reasoning that the jury would be drawn from a seven-county area. What attorneys and reporters alike failed to understand was the pressures caused by the place in which the trial was conducted. Both the Roybal Building and the Hilton Hotel were on the edge of the area in which the nation's deadliest modern riot had recently occurred. No day went by without reminders of what had happened when another jury dared to free the officers who had beaten Rodney King.

The prosecutors were as unaware as the defense attorneys of the role fear played in influencing the jury. Clymer had endorsed the instruction calling upon jurors to disregard "external consequences" as soon as Davies proposed it. While prosecutors can be faulted for raising racial innuendos during the trial, they did not know the extent of anxieties among the jurors. Clymer told me he never heard of the bomb scare until I asked him about it three years after the trial.

The only participant in the trial who seemed to have recognized the importance of the jurors' emotional state was Almond, who told a fellow juror that a psychologist should visit to help them deal with their problems. Instead, the court and the marshals were focused on shielding jurors from outside influences. No one addressed the terrors that had accumulated in the minds and hearts of a jury whose least fearful member peered through the window of his hotel room each night to see if there were fires in South Central.

It was obvious to every juror that rioting was a more likely response to acquittals than to convictions. This put heavy pressure on those jurors who were inclined to believe in the innocence of the defendants. Almond was one of five such jurors. He believed throughout the trial that all the officers were innocent, later changing his mind about two of them. According to jurors on the other side, particularly Maria Escobel, Almond was the most determined of the proacquittal jurors. Almond insists he put external factors from his mind in reaching his decisions, and I have no doubt he conscientiously tried to do so. No fear of riots was discussed during deliberations. Most of the jurors seem to have struggled to reach honest decisions.

Still, the circumstances under which the deliberations were conducted are troubling. While jurors made a good-faith effort to rely on the evidence, it is humanly difficult for anyone to put aside fears and anxieties of the magnitude that existed in this trial.

Almond, forty-eight years old at the time of the trial and employed by a local government agency, was not a reluctant juror. He determined from the wording of the jury notice that he was being called to serve on what the jurors called "the Rodney King beating trial" and was fascinated by the prospect. Almond knew he had leadership abilities and believed he would be an effective foreman. When the jury met as a body for the first time on Easter Saturday, he nominated himself. An insurance executive who was Juror No. 8 and one of the four women on the panel also wanted the job. Almond took a sheet of paper and divided it into twelve parts, which he passed around to the other jurors. The vote divided largely on gender lines, with Almond winning 8–4 by some accounts and 7–5 by his own.[12]

As Paul DePasquale had observed before the trial, the jury candidates were volunteers. The twelve who were chosen considered themselves so fortunate that they rushed out to buy lottery tickets, juror Kathy Anderson later told her hometown newspaper. But some soon wondered if they had been as lucky as they had first believed. Some of the women thought Almond was rude to them and at least two of the male jurors agreed with them. Almond had a temper. While he prided himself in making decisions with the coolness of the engineer he was, he had been surprised to find himself weeping during King's testimony. But he was also impressed by Koon, considering him "an excellent police officer."

Almond believed the public expected the jury to reach verdicts. While he was willing to explore the idea that every defendant was innocent, he also said, "I think there might have been riots if we had not come up with a decision, if we had a hung jury."[13] This attitude made him an ideal foreman for the court, for Davies was so obsessed with avoiding a deadlock that he had rebuked Braun for attempting to ask prospective jurors if they would be willing to hold out for their opinion if they were in the minority. Braun saw the possibility of a mistrial as a useful middle ground. He was convinced that the government would not try the defendants a third time and thought a mistrial was more likely than acquittals to avert a riot.*

Not so Davies. Near the trial's end the judge told the attorneys he was willing to give jurors an instruction known as the Allen or "dynamite" charge calling on them to deliberate until they reached verdicts. Numerous rulings by higher courts have held that such instructions are improper until a jury reports a deadlock. Clymer, while also concerned about a mistrial, opposed the Allen instruction at the beginning of deliberations, saying it might constitute "reversible error" that would overturn convictions.

Absent such a charge, the court and the government were dependent on Almond's desire for consensus. When deliberations began, the jury leaned slightly toward acquittals. The nominal division is a bit misleading, however, as at least three members were irrevocably convinced that the police officers had used excessive force against King. This group was led by the perky Maria Escobel, Juror No. 7 and at twenty-nine the youngest member of the panel. She was joined by Juror No. 11 Eric Rasmussen, a welder and former Danish naval officer, and Juror No. 12 Martin De La Rosa, a grocery store checker who was a few months older than Escobel. De La Rosa was the last juror chosen and the only one who had never seen clips of the King

---

* During voir dire Braun tried to ask jury candidates if they would be willing to hold out for their point of view if it meant a mistrial. Davies cut him off, sending a clear message to the jurors that the court considered a mistrial unacceptable. Braun's view that a hung jury might be the preferable resolution of the socially explosive case was not shared by the other attorneys on either side.

beating on television. He thought Powell and Koon were "guilty from the first days" of the trial.[14] Rasmussen was certain of Powell's guilt "immediately" and said he had felt during the last week or ten days of the trial that Koon was guilty. "I kept waiting for the defense to put on something, and they never did," Rasmussen said.[15]

Studies of jury performance suggest that it is difficult for a juror to hold out for conviction or acquittal against a united majority. Escobel had an inner toughness that might have made her an exception, but she also had the advantage of knowing that she was not alone in believing that King had been brutalized. Rasmussen would "never, ever" have voted to acquit Koon and Powell, Escobel told me.[16]

While Almond was a diligent juror who would take persuading, he was not as passionate in his belief that all the officers were innocent as Escobel and Rasmussen were in their view that Powell and Koon at least should be found guilty. It was evident to Almond early on that the jury hard core would insist on convictions as the price of any consensus. Escobel agrees with this assessment. She told me after the trial that had the jury deadlocked on Powell, it would have been impossible even to consider the guilt or innocence of the other defendants.

On Sunday, after five jurors attended Easter services, deliberations began at 1:00 P.M. in the Roybal Building jury room. The jurors quickly caused a flurry of speculation by asking for a transcript of Melanie Singer's testimony, which Davies denied. Remembering how Singer had cried during her testimony, trial analysts incorrectly assumed the request was a bad sign for the defense. It was not. The jury was attempting to start at the beginning by assessing King's behavior and determining if the officers had reason to fear him. Everyone but Rasmussen agreed they had reasons for their fears. In the first of many angry confrontations among the jurors during deliberations, Juror No. 6 accused Rasmussen of having decided in advance that the officers were guilty.

The deliberations and confrontations continued on Monday and Tuesday, with jurors far apart. An early poll taken by Almond showed jurors leaning 7–5 to acquit, but no one believed this to be a hard count. The jurors took their work seriously, watching the videotape repeatedly at regular and slow speeds and reenacting the incident, with one juror playing Powell and another King. They found activity on the videotape that had been pointed out to them during the trial and activity that did not exist. Rasmussen believed Koon had used his Taser to torture King and said this was a common police treatment of young blacks. Other jurors thought they discerned Briseno blocking a blow by Wind, not Powell. This bizarre finding was not supported by any investigation of the incident or the recollection of any participant.

The early deliberations showed that these federal jurors had a broader range of life's experiences than their counterparts at Simi Valley. Two male jurors discussed personal experience with drug use. One had attended a rehabilitation program for marijuana users. The other acknowledged ingesting a panoply of drugs, including PCP, and questioned if this drug truly endowed users with superhuman strength, as experts had testified during the trial.

Had these men, both of whom supported the conviction of Powell and Koon, told any officer of the court of their history of drug use, they would not have been accepted as jurors.[17] And from a standpoint of fairness, they should not have been accepted, for their own experience with drugs led them to dismiss the issue of whether King's conduct on the night of his arrest was drug induced. The PCP user proved a particular boon to the government, for he minimized the negative effects of this drug in comments to other jurors. This was prejudicial to the defense contention that the officers had behaved as they did in part because of fear that King was crazed by PCP. While prosecutors contended that the defendants concocted the PCP defense, they never disputed the fact that PCP can cause those who use it to act dangerously. But one of the most outspoken members of this jury thought PCP use was not consequential.

In early deliberations some of the jurors discussed the defendants collectively. Almond prodded them to begin at the beginning and to break down the actions of each defendant. They started with Powell, who had inflicted most of the baton blows. Every juror more or less agreed that if there was no case against him, there could be no case against anyone.

But at first the jurors found it difficult to agree on anything except that King's facial injuries had been caused by Powell's baton swings. The evidence was so persuasive on this point that it showed the futility of Stone's attempts to prove King's injuries had been caused by falls to the ground. Almond observed that even Conta had said that head blows were permissible if not intentional. Almond felt so strongly about this that he later told me he would have "hung the jury up" rather than convict Powell on the basis of the head blows. But watching the enhanced videotape, jurors could not determine if Powell had swung wildly or cocked his arms and legs as Clymer insisted in his closing argument. Progress was slow. The jury quit early on Monday because Juror No. 1 complained of mental exhaustion, and again on Tuesday, when Juror No. 6 insisted that he could absorb no more.

Maria Escobel had no doubt that the officers had used excessive force, perhaps because King was black but probably because they were "pissed off" at his behavior.[18] Escobel was the daughter of Webster Moore, a former Black Panther with ties to radicals Huey Newton and Angela Davis. But raised in a middle-class family in Los Angeles, Escobel had, she said, "gone the other way" and avoided politics of any sort. Moore would later say that his daughter paid little attention to the Rodney King case until she served on the jury.[19] Escobel had attended California State University in Fullerton but dropped out because she could not afford the tuition. She had joined the postal service and married a Latino co-worker. Their son was three months old when her husband was killed in an automobile accident. At the time of the trial, Escobel was dividing her time among her son, who was now four, a night job operating a sorting machine at the post office, and a beauty shop she owned in Santa Ana with another woman.

Escobel impressed others as strong and intelligent. She had a gift for mimicry and the spunk to stand up to Almond. Like Almond, Escobel had realized from the wording of the jury notice that she was being asked to serve on a replay of the "Rodney King beating trial." She welcomed the opportunity. She told me she was "tired" of postal work and thought jury service would provide a respite. After the incident where the excused juror complained about her, the defendants and their attorneys decided that Escobel was an "agenda juror" who was out to get the officers who had beaten Rodney King. They would have been strengthened in this view had they known of the Black Panther background of Escobel's father, but they did not know this at the time. It was enough for the defense that Escobel was black and a mother who was willing to leave her four-year-old son with others during a long trial.

Almond realized that the court had forced the defense to accept the two black members of the jury. He decided on his own that Escobel was pursuing an agenda because she expressed a firm opinion early in deliberations that the defendants had used excessive force. But Escobel was not alone in having this opinion or in expressing it. Every juror was a volunteer; it could be said that all the jurors in this trial had agendas, if only to play a part in history.

The emotional intensity in the jury room during the climactic deliberations on Wednesday, April 14, suggests that Almond was right to believe the jurors needed psychological counseling. Indeed, Almond might have been able to use such counseling himself, for he called Juror No. 8 an "asshole" when she imperiously announced that she was going to write a letter to the judge complaining that the jury was quitting too early each day. Later Almond told another juror that he was willing to make peace with Juror No. 8 but was afraid he might hit her "in her fucking face" if she talked any more about writing a letter of complaint.[20]

It is a comment on the state of mind of the jurors that some of them considered Almond the calmest person in the room. In the recriminations that followed, one juror questioned the masculinity of another. Another ripped off his shirt to show hives he said had been caused by the strains of the deliberations. Another told a terrible family secret that caused other jurors to weep. Escobel suggested that some jurors would rather return to the hotel and "get fat" on rich food than stay in the jury room and make hard decisions.

Some of the most ferocious arguments occurred between Escobel and the Watts man, the other African American on the jury. The defense had fought to keep the Watts man off the jury, but he proved to be one of the most balanced jurors. Several of the other male jurors thought that Escobel unfairly baited him. But she felt put upon, too, and accused one of the white male jurors (not named in this book) of referring to blacks as "those people." Soon afterward, she broke down and ran crying from the room. Later, Escobel compared the Wednesday deliberations to an Alcoholics Anonymous session in which everyone needed to confess dependency before anything else could be accomplished. It was an apt analogy. When Escobel returned to the jury room, other jurors hugged and comforted her, and tensions eased.

This jury's emotional travails were later dramatized from Escobel's point of view by Anna Deavere Smith in *Twilight*, a powerful one-person play that mocked the police defendants and sympathized with the rioters. Smith's vibrant portrayal of "Maria," who was identified only by her first name, captured Escobel's charm and humor and credited her with bringing the jury to its senses.

Many jurors resented the attention focused on Escobel by this play and belittled her view that she played a decisive role in the jury's decisions. Some jurors even tried to exclude her from a jury reunion and would have done so except that Rasmussen refused to attend unless Escobel was invited. But Almond, who by all accounts was one of the most resistant to convictions and was fair-minded despite his temper, thinks Escobel played a significant role in the outcome of the trial.

By Wednesday afternoon, Almond had become weary of true confessions in the jury room. He still had a problem with the evidence, however. As much as he wanted consensus, he was unwilling to find Powell guilty on the basis of a generalized belief that he had used excessive force. Almond, very much the engineer as well as the good juror, needed to be shown a specific baton blow that violated policy. As he recalls it, Escobel found this blow—delivered by Powell to King's chest when he was on his back fifty-five seconds into the videotaped portion of the incident. While Clymer had not made much of this particular blow (he told me he thought it was horrible but did not know what to say about it), Sergeant Conta had called it a clear violation of policy. Escobel "loved Conta" and paid attention to his testimony.[21] Whether she or another juror could have found another blow that would have persuaded Almond is unclear, but it was this blow that brought the jury together. De La

Rosa, who had no doubt about Powell's guilt, agrees that the chest blow was decisive "for Bob and some of the others."*

There would be no more catharsis in the jury room. No formal vote was taken Wednesday, but Almond realized that the jury had reached a consensus. On Thursday, after a brief and unemotional review of the evidence against Powell, Almond asked: "Anybody here for not guilty?" No one raised a hand.

The jurors then turned to Tim Wind, with Almond taking a preliminary vote that produced an 8–4 margin for acquittal. Wind had been unfortunate to have Powell as a training officer, but he benefited from being compared to him by the jurors. Wind also may have benefited from the intensity of the Wednesday deliberations, for none of the jurors wanted to go through such an emotional session again. Some, notably Rasmussen, agreed with De La Rosa's opinion that some of Wind's kicks had been "vicious." But others in the proconviction faction, including Escobel, took a more charitable view.

The jury discussion about Wind showed that DePasquale had done his work well. The jurors agreed that defendants should be judged individually, as DePasquale (and Almond) had insisted, and many of them drew distinctions between the behavior of Wind and that of Powell. The most obvious difference was that Wind had stopped and stepped back between baton blows to evaluate their impact. (While this was not readily apparent to a layman at first viewing, it became obvious to everyone once it was pointed out.) Escobel also observed that Wind had used his baton on the legs and joints and shoulders, as dictated by policy and Koon's commands. He delivered no head blows and no blows to King's chest when he was on his back. In this, he benefited most from comparison with Powell.

Two other factors helped Wind. One was his conduct at Foothill Station where Powell went to tell his war stories. At least one juror was impressed that Wind had shooed away the officer who had shone his flashlight in King's eyes—a point first brought out by Clymer. The other factor stressed by jurors in posttrial interviews was Wind's rookie status, another emphasis of DePasquale. No juror advocated Conta's view that Wind could have disobeyed Koon or failed to back up Powell. By the end of the day, jurors voted unanimously to acquit Wind.

On Friday, April 16, the jury also acquitted Briseno. His fate was not in doubt before this jury, which unlike the state jury had heard no police

---

* Escobel believed that King cried and screamed as he was being beaten and that this could be heard on the audiotape. At her insistence, jurors listened quietly to the tape in an effort to hear these sounds. Some jurors agreed with her; some did not. All the jurors, however, were impressed with her point about the chest blow.

witnesses who depicted Briseno as a liar trying to save his skin at the expense of the other defendants. The federal jurors agreed that Briseno had tried to stop Powell from hitting King, and some shared Rasmussen's mistaken view that Briseno had tried to block Wind as well. Fred, Juror No. 9, was most convinced that Briseno had put his foot on King to keep him down and made this point forcefully. Neither Almond nor Escobel was certain about the stomp, which comes across on the videotape as an ambiguous action subject to varying interpretations. Almond and Escobel agreed that the videotape also showed Briseno running around aimlessly during much of the incident, but they didn't know what to make of this either. Almond was the more suspicious of the two, but he concluded that no evidence had been presented to show he meant to do King harm. Jurors examined Briseno's boot, which Braun had introduced as his sole evidence, and agreed that it was light. The vote to acquit was unanimous and swift.

That left only Koon, a hero to the state jurors but the principal villain of the King beating as far as the federal jurors were concerned. Even in this role, Koon earned grudging respect for his willingness to take responsibility for the actions of the officers under his command. Among the federal jurors, only Rasmussen totally bought the Clymer line that Koon was an outright liar. Escobel and a jury majority accepted a less extreme version of this argument, made forcefully by Kowalski as well as Clymer. These jurors recognized that Koon was telling the truth as he saw it but thought he interpreted every questionable action in the light most favorable to the defendants. De La Rosa realized that Koon had simply let events get away from him. "He wasn't trying to punish King," De La Rosa told me. "It just got out of hand."[22]

This was an accurate insight. Had Koon put on a defense that appealed to this view, explaining King's beating as a well-intentioned arrest gone wrong, it is conceivable he might have persuaded De La Rosa and other jurors that he lacked the intent required under the court's instructions for a finding of guilty. But the question of intent was never really debated by the federal jury because of the nature of the defense. Koon had conceded the issue of intent by insisting that every one of the more than fifty baton blows King received was a proper exercise of force. If that was not enough, he claimed responsibility for all of them.

Powell had been the first defendant named in the state indictment. Koon was named first in the federal indictment, suggesting the government's argument that he was, as the supervisor on the scene, most responsible for violating King's civil rights. The defense fought the case on the government's terms. Koon was the only defendant to testify, and defense lawyers rationalized that Powell would be acquitted if the jurors accepted Koon's explanation. In the actual deliberations, however, Powell had been convicted by the time Koon's fate was considered, and he took his sergeant down with him. If Koon was responsible for Powell's actions, as he claimed, it stood to reason that he was guilty, too.

The chest blow that persuaded Almond to vote for Powell's conviction also helped convict Koon. When Almond watched the tape in slow motion, he could see that Koon momentarily turned his head away at the precise moment Powell's baton blow landed on King's chest. This was an original and potentially useful observation. While nothing in the evidence explained it, Almond remembered Briseno's testimony that he had yelled at the sergeant in an unsuccessful attempt to get his attention. Had this diverted Koon? It was impossible to know, but Koon's action seemed to undermine his claim that he had carefully supervised the use of force.

The pressures weighing on the jurors in the hothouse of Los Angeles and the dynamics of the deliberations were against Koon. And in addition, he had been an unsympathetic witness in his own behalf. Almond and other jurors who might have been inclined to give him the benefit of the doubt had been put off by what they saw as his arrogance and absence of contrition. They liked Koon too little to put themselves in his shoes.

Even if he had been a more sympathetic witness, the best Koon could have hoped for was a deadlock, since at least four jurors were determined to convict him. If the jury had deadlocked on Koon, it is conceivable that it might have called it a day. A deadlock on Powell would have meant a deadlock on everyone, but the jury had completed its work on the other three defendants by the time it considered Koon, and it is unlikely the jurors would have revisited these verdicts.

At Simi Valley, under prodding from Darryl Mounger, Koon had revealed his softer side to the jury. Under Mounger's questioning, Koon's eyes had filled with tears at the memory of the morgue picture of the slain California Highway Patrol officers. In the federal trial, Koon had surprisingly connected with De La Rosa, who tended to dislike police officers and considered Koon "a smart-ass cocky cop." But during his testimony, Koon had made eye contact with De La Rosa, who abruptly changed his mind and decided that Koon "was just a person."[23] The juror never felt that way about Powell, who dropped his eyes whenever De La Rosa looked at him.

This connection with De La Rosa suggests that Koon might have made it difficult for jurors to agree on a verdict if he had aroused their sympathy. He did the opposite, almost daring them to convict him. Koon was too stiff-necked to seek the absolution of acquittal on anything except his own terms. When we talked in a corridor outside the courtroom after the defense rested its case, Koon said that acquittals would be a small victory for the defendants but "a giant verdict for policing." Asked why, he replied, "Use of force is what a policeman's life is all about. I don't mean that acquittals will be a license for police to go out and rain blows on suspects, but it does mean that they'll be able to do what they're taught."

If that meant police would do what the videotape showed the defendants doing to Rodney King, the jurors wanted none of it. By the time they considered the Koon verdict, what they wanted was to be done with the trial. No one held out for Koon's innocence, although one juror later said he was never convinced of Koon's guilt. But that juror did not raise his hand when Almond asked if anyone believed Koon was innocent. Koon was convicted. Fred, Juror No. 9, who had spoken out strongly for acquitting Briseno, led an exchange of high fives.

Controversial verdicts in high-profile cases are commonplace in Southern California. But the convictions of Koon and Powell were hailed as correcting a miscarriage of justice, with little consideration given to the question of whether the processes that produced these convictions were just.* Despite the acquittal of Briseno, the liberal Braun was disgusted at this lack of examination. As he saw it, praise for the federal jury had nothing to do with its competence and everything to do with the fact that convicting Koon and Powell was politically correct.

Braun had a point, as usual, but the acclaim that greeted the verdicts reflected the anxieties of Los Angeles more than a feeling that justice demanded convictions. Fear had been the thirteenth juror in the federal trial because fear was shaping public opinion in a city that had not yet assimilated the experience of the 1992 riots. While chances of a new round of disorders may have been remote in view of the extensive police preparations, fears of rioting ran deep. As the Los Angeles Times commented: "As a world media audience listened in to hear the judgment . . . one could almost hear a sigh of immense relief from a tense and troubled Los Angeles."

The jury concluded deliberations on Friday afternoon. By prearrangement, Davies kept the jurors sequestered for another night so that verdicts would be announced at the unusual time of 7:00 A.M. Saturday, April 17. "Fear set the schedule," observed Jim Newton.[24] Some 3,200 LAPD officers were on the streets, ten times normal patrol strength. The Los Angeles County Sheriff's Department deployed 1,400 officers, four times normal, and 600 National Guardsmen assembled on standby at local armories. Parking lots near the Roybal Building were cleared, and the area was ringed with police.

Koon was typically impassive when court clerk Jim Holmes read the guilty verdict, but Ira Salzman removed his glasses and rubbed his eyes. Michael

---

* Journalistic attention was diverted from trial analysis by the fiery catastrophe in Waco, Texas, on April 19, in which eighty men, women, and children died in the Branch Dividian compound. Some jurors told me that scheduled broadcast interviews in which they would have participated were canceled as a result of the Waco incident. With few exceptions, the journalistic spotlight never returned to the federal jurors.

Stone held Powell's arm and squeezed the hand of Powell's girlfriend. When the Koon verdict was read, Powell licked his lips and Stone whispered to him, "We're going down, bud." Wind bowed his head as he was found innocent, squeezing the pen with which he had taken notes during the trial. "Good luck, Mr. Wind," Clymer told him afterward.* Briseno clutched a tiny silver-and-black crucifix during the proceedings. He cried at the convictions of Koon and Powell, almost as if he had been found guilty himself.

In keeping with federal practice, Davies barred cameras and tape recorders in the courtroom throughout the trial. But the verdicts were carried over an open line to the press room in the Roybal Building and broadcast immediately to the waiting world. At First AME Church, the oldest black church in Los Angeles, a crowd of one hundred and fifty people roared with delight. As the news spread, motorists drove through Florence and Normandie, ground zero in the riots, honking car horns and playing rap music. Black teenagers danced in the streets. This Easter, Mayor Bradley said the following day, was "the first day of a new life for Los Angeles."

People of all races shared in the relief. Manuel Lozano, manager of the United Produce Market on Manchester Boulevard, greeted news of the convictions by rolling up a chain-link fence he had installed at the beginning of jury deliberations in front of his market, which had been cleaned out during the riots. "I think people should be feeling good about the verdicts," Lozano said. Jay Shin, who had participated in the armed defense of his Koreatown liquor store and the California Market, greeted customers happily, saying "It's a lot different from last year." Liz Blackman, a white gallery owner in West Hollywood, said, "It was like I was watching my home team win a football game."

The relief of Los Angeles was shared by national and state political leaders delighted to be spared the ordeal of responding to another riot. "Justice has been done, whether or not people agree or disagree with the verdict," said Governor Pete Wilson in Los Angeles. "Surely the lasting legacy of the Rodney King trial ought to be . . . a determination to reaffirm our common humanity and to make a strength of our diversity," President Clinton said in Pittsburgh.

Prosecutors and defense attorneys also perceived larger purposes in the verdicts. "A year ago the conscience of the community, the conscience of the nation cried out for justice," Kowalski said at a news conference of the prosecutors. "This verdict provides justice." Salzman, whose sadness at the verdicts was soon replaced by anger, deplored the proceedings as a circus.

---

* Wind remembers that Clymer shook his hand, which is also Salzman's recollection. Clymer says he did not shake Wind's hand. Reporters at the trial have conflicting recollections.

"Stacey Koon is not some sacrificial animal to be cast aside for peace in Los Angeles," he said.

But even the defense attorneys acknowledged that the convictions of Koon and Powell had bought this dubious but needed peace. The lawyers were not blameless, for they had failed to seek a change of venue that would have moved the trial out of riot-scarred Los Angeles. The jurors were responsible too, but it is hard to fault them for negligence, considering the context of fear and apprehension in which they deliberated. The greatest responsibility belonged to the government, which had pursued a prosecution that served the political purposes of embattled President Bush in an election year.

Hours after the trial, Harland Braun reflected on the competing verities of peace and justice. "Is it better that two innocent people get convicted, or that fifty people die tomorrow?" he mused. "I don't know."[25]

18

SECOND JUDGMENTS

"The sentences ordered by Judge Davies were severe indeed. Neither law nor justice requires that they be set aside or that any longer prison terms be imposed."

—Ninth Circuit Judge Stephen Reinhardt[1]

"Justice is in the eye of the beholder."

—Community activist Don Jackson[2]

NEAR THE END OF THE TRIAL THAT RESULTED IN HIS CONVICTION for violating Rodney King's civil rights, Stacey Koon wrote a one-sentence note to Judge John Davies. He put the note in an envelope and gave it to the court clerk with a request that it not be opened until the jury had completed its work. After the verdicts, Davies opened the envelope. The note read, "Your honor, out of deference to your penchant for precise and succinct language; thank you for a fair trial."

Koon's assessment is as open to question as were his tactics during the King arrest. Davies was certainly impartial, but it is hard to call the trial at which he presided "fair," when the impact on jurors of the fearful venue of Los Angeles is factored into the equation. It is also hard to call it fair using a common-sense definition of double jeopardy, rather than the legal fiction under which the Supreme Court has permitted acquitted defendants to be tried twice for the same conduct. And even if the issue of fairness is limited to what occurred in the federal courtroom, doubts remain.

The federal jury had been almost evenly divided when it began the emotional deliberations that could well have ended in a deadlock. In part the jurors' eventual unanimity was driven by a presumed imperative that consensus was necessary—a view encouraged by Davies, who abhorred the notion of a mistrial. Davies had proposed an exceptional instruction at the beginning of deliberations (the Allen, or "dynamite," charge) and might have given it to the jury had not the prosecution argued that it could lead to reversal of convictions on appeal. He also had made known his feelings about a mistrial early on, when he prevented defense attorney Harland Braun from questioning prospective jurors about their willingness to hold out against majority opinion.

The judge's message that a mistrial was undesirable proved a boon to the prosecution. Absent this message, it is conceivable that one of at least five jurors who began deliberations believing in Koon's innocence might have held out and produced a deadlock despite the fear of riots. Even though he has strongly defended the verdicts, the likeliest holdout was probably Bob Almond, who had the strength and courage to defy majority opinion but believed it a foreman's duty to reach consensus. Whether Almond would have been as adamant in his view if Davies had sent a message that a mistrial was acceptable cannot be known.

There were other fairness questions, notably Davies' ruling that allowed the government to introduce the damning state trial testimony of Theodore Briseno during rebuttal. Davies himself worried about the fairness of showing jurors the videotape of a defendant who had declined to testify and could not be cross-examined. After going back and forth on the issue, he decided to admit the videotape. His decision deprived Koon and Laurence Powell of a chance to confront a principal accuser.

But in his note to Davies, Koon was commenting on the judge's attitude, not his rulings. Koon had assumed at the beginning of his ordeal that he would be presumed innocent in fact, as well as legally. Remember that when Koon learned of the existence of the Holliday videotape, he thought it would make a splendid training film. Remember also that Koon had been shocked when Chief Daryl Gates jettisoned the officers involved in the King arrest in an attempt to save his job. The words "presumed guilty" that Koon used as his book title reflected his feelings of betrayal. These feelings were compounded at the state trial, where Koon sensed that Judge Weisberg assumed that the officers were in the wrong. That bothered Koon, even though Weisberg's conduct of the trial was impeccable and his decision to try the case in Simi Valley beneficial to the defense. Koon had an entirely different sense about Davies, who made no assumption about the guilt of the defendants.

As his evaluation of the judges suggests, Koon gave great weight to motivation. He resented President Bush for trying to gain political advantage by condemning the officers after the Simi Valley verdicts with comments that set a second trial in motion. As Koon saw it, both Gates and Bush had tried to save their jobs at the expense of justice, and both had failed. But Koon harbored no bitterness toward Rodney King or the prosecutors who succeeded in sending him to prison or toward most of the media. He realized that they all had jobs to do (King's "job," in Koon's view, was to avoid being sent back to prison for parole violation) and did them as best they could. Koon also understood why blacks might see him as a symbol of police brutality, although it bothered him that anyone would think him a racist. But he expected fairness from the judicial system. He respected Davies because he believed that the judge, in addition to conducting a fair trial under difficult circumstances, had made a genuine effort to understand why the defendants acted as they did.

If Koon was a magnanimous loser, the federal prosecutors were sore winners. What Koon saw as a sense of fairness on Davies' part was interpreted by the prosecutors as favoritism toward the police. They wanted the judge to throw the book at the two convicted officers, particularly Koon. With customary thoroughness, Steven Clymer set out to make a compelling case for the longest possible sentences.

The verdicts comforted LAPD leaders and disturbed the rank and file. Police Chief Willie Williams agreed with the verdicts and was pleased that supposedly improved procedures for responding to civil disorders had not been tested early on his watch. Mayor Tom Bradley, in his last months in office, proclaimed in a televised message that "Los Angeles has turned the corner" and expressed hope that the city could put the King case behind it and deal "with the real issues and the real problems that face us." But the legacy of the King case was one of those real problems, and both the city and the LAPD would have difficulty coming to terms with it.

Another real problem was the upcoming trial of the two young black men accused of attempting to kill truck driver Reginald Denny and assaulting others at the intersection of Florence and Normandie during the opening hours of the riots. In the public consciousness the Denny and King cases were inextricably linked, in large part because local television stations continued to juxtapose clips of the King beating and the assault on Denny. The comparison was also kept alive by Edi Faal, the attorney representing Damian Williams, the accused ringleader of the Denny assault. On April 7, as the federal trial drew to a close, Faal told Superior Court Judge John Ouderkirk that the officers had treated Rodney King in a fashion "very similar to the alleged conduct of the men accused of beating Mr. Denny." Ouderkirk rejected the argument, saying that the two cases were neither factually nor legally comparable, but he also did his best to see that the trials did not overlap. The judge did not begin screening jury applications until July 28. He set jury selection in *People of the State of California v. Damian Monroe Williams and Henry Keith Watson* for August 5, the day after the sentencing of Koon and Powell.

As with almost everything relating to the King case, that sentencing proved contentious. Prosecutors on July 9 filed a memorandum with the court asking that Koon receive a prison sentence of nine to ten years (ten was the maximum) and Powell a sentence of seven to nine years. They also asked that the two pay fines ranging from $15,000 to $150,000 and such "restitution to the victim as the court finds appropriate." Defense lawyers asked for probation or prison terms of less than a year. They pointed out that the lives of Koon and Powell had been destroyed and that they would never work again as police officers.

Davies was limited in his discretion. Federal sentences are governed by complex guidelines that rely on mathematical formulae to compute sentences. The guidelines were advocated by some conservatives as a way of curbing supposed leniency by liberal judges and favored by some liberals on the ground they would serve as a barrier to racial bias in sentencing. In theory the guidelines assure fairness because they require that criminals in different jurisdictions receive equivalent sentences for the same crimes.

But according to many legal scholars and trial judges, instead of eliminating sentencing discretion, the guidelines have effectively transferred it from judges who have a duty to be impartial to prosecutors who by definition are not. Prosecutors can influence sentences by adding or subtracting particular charges or "enhancements." For instance, the government sought longer sentences for Koon and Powell because of the seriousness of the injuries to King, even though the prosecution's key witness had testified that the officers were abiding by policy when these injuries were inflicted.

Even some who endorse uniform sentences in theory say that the complexity of the calculations required by the federal rules has proved confusing to judges and trial attorneys. And many critics of the guidelines argue that judicial discretion is an essential element of justice; trial judges, they say, are in a unique position to weigh the circumstances of each case. This point was made by Koon's attorney, Ira Salzman, who said, "Sentencing is not a Coke machine. You don't put in a quarter and get out a sentence."[3]

The guidelines do permit some leniency for criminals who accept responsibility for their actions. As Clymer saw it, Koon and Powell were disqualified from any sentence reduction on this ground because they continued to assert their innocence after they were convicted. In television appearances, Koon reiterated his belief that the force used against King was proper. Powell wrote an article for *The Thin Blue Line*, the publication of the Los Angeles police union, in which he said, "If I must go to prison, it is better to go there an innocent man." Citing these expressions of opinion in their sentencing memorandum, the government said, "Such attempts to excuse criminal conduct do not constitute an acceptance of responsibility."

In Koon's case, Clymer did not stop at what had been said outside of court. He claimed Koon committed "perjury" when he testified by providing "false justification" for the beating of King. "In this case, the jury's verdict necessarily constituted a finding that defendant Koon testified falsely," he said in the sentencing memorandum.

Put another way, the government wanted Koon to receive additional prison time for daring to present his honest version of events. Koon believed, as he declared in both criminal trials and his book, that he had supervised appropriate use of force against an unsearched felony suspect under the influence of PCP who failed to respond to verbal commands, a swarm, and two volleys from an electric stun gun. Deputy District Attorney Terry White, the prosecutor in the state trial, thought the force used against King was brutal and improper but did not doubt the sincerity of Koon's version of events. Neither did the Simi Valley jury, which deadlocked on the charge that Powell had used excessive force under color of authority. The four Simi Valley jurors who believed Powell was guilty were convinced that Koon was telling the truth. Clymer wanted Koon to spend additional years in prison for refusing to confess to a crime he was certain had not occurred.

Such behavior seemed vindictive to many of Koon's supporters. But Clymer was as much a true believer as Koon. Both men assumed that their motives were pure and their perceptions accurate and tended to discount opinions other than their own. What particularly galled Clymer, he told me in an interview after sentencing, was that Koon showed no "remorse," as if he should be remorseful for doing his job as he saw it.

When I pressed Clymer on the point of Koon's sincerity, the prosecutor compared the sergeant to a convicted marijuana dealer who denies wrongdoing because he does not believe that smoking marijuana should be illegal.[4] It was an absurd analogy. Koon never claimed that officers should be allowed to use excessive force and—as readers will recall—had turned in a fellow LAPD sergeant who struck two black transients with his baton. But to prosecute him effectively, Clymer needed to believe that Koon was a bad cop who had committed an evil act, not a good man who had made tactical misjudgments.

The community pressure that had weighed so heavily on the federal jurors now shifted to Davies, who was bombarded with letters and telephone calls. Black leaders urged the maximum sentence, while police officers advocated outright probation. Detective Roger Richards, a twenty-year veteran of the LAPD, hand-carried a letter to Davies that recounted his retraining in the use of the metal baton after the choke hold was banned. He wrote he had been taught to "power stroke the hell out of your opponent" and "break bones" to gain compliance, as the defense had contended during trial. Richards' letter made this historical point compellingly, but the jury had not accepted it as justification for the King beating, and Davies was not about to revisit it.

The judge was, however, receptive to information about the character of the defendants. Richards had worked with Koon in uniform patrol early in their careers and remembered him as a "no-nonsense cop" who played by the rules and treated suspects with respect and dignity. "Stacey did not tolerate any deviation from these principles, regardless of his partners' rank or seniority," Richards wrote. "His strength of character earned Stacey a quiet, unspoken respect among his contemporaries (as well as fear among those officers who were less than professional or had an inappropriate agenda)."[5]

Davies also received a plea for leniency from David Lombardero, former chief counsel for the commission that drafted the federal sentencing guidelines. Lombardero called the case "highly unusual" and wrote that "it clearly calls for departure from the guidelines." While acknowledging that he did not know all the facts of the case, Lombardero wrote: "Nonetheless, it is clear from the extensive media coverage that Mr. King's wrongful conduct in evading, resisting and even taunting police officers substantially provoked the defendants' conduct. Thus, the sentencing guidelines themselves explicitly sanction departure in this case."

Prosecutors responded by trying to discredit Lombardero. They filed a reply on August 3, the day before sentencing, saying that Lombardero had failed to mention he was a reserve police officer in the city of Monterey Park "and thus may have a bias in this case." They also claimed that Lombardero had overstated his influence on the sentencing guidelines.

Davies did not need outsiders to tell him that the sentencing posed exceptional problems. He knew that most members of the law enforcement community saw Koon and Powell as victims. Davies himself both respected the verdicts and sympathized with the convicted officers. He also faced a practical problem. Even the government acknowledged that the King arrest had begun lawfully and degenerated into an excessive use of force. The verdicts, however, did not say when the arrest became illegal. A rational sentencing determination required Davies to make his own analysis of what had happened at Foothill and Osborne.

The result of this analysis was a fifty-four-page memorandum that provided a cogent summary of the incident. Davies noted that Rodney King had consumed at least eighty ounces of malt liquor with two friends before embarking on his fateful drive on March 2, 1991. He described the police pursuit, King's refusal to comply with Melanie Singer's commands, and Koon's taking over the arrest. "Mr. King was a large, muscular man and a felony suspect," Davies wrote. "Sergeant Koon testified that he thought Mr. King may have been recently imprisoned because Mr. King appeared to have engaged in the body building common among prison inmates. The officers ordered Mr. King to lie in the felony-prone position. He refused to do so. Officers Powell, Wind, Briseno and Solano jointly attempted to place Mr. King in a felony-prone position. He resisted and became combative, forcing the officers to retreat."

It was at this point that "subsequent events were captured by Mr. George Holliday on videotape." Davies emphasized that the videotape had not captured the entire sequence of events and did not provide a conclusive record even of the events it had recorded. "Although the videotape creates a vivid impression of a violent encounter, careful analysis shows that it is sometimes an ambiguous record of the crucial events," Davies wrote. "A meaningful understanding of the events it depicts required the explanation of witnesses who are experts in law enforcement. At trial the government and the defendants agreed that much of the officers' conduct was justified and legal, yet vigorously disputed whether and when their behavior became illegal."

Davies said the "principal question for sentencing" of when the force became illegal was not answered by the verdicts and that this determination needed to be made separately for Koon and Powell. "Sergeant Koon's criminal liability is not derivative from Officer Powell's liability," wrote Davies, citing the legal case on which he relied for this assertion. "Sergeant Koon's conviction rests entirely upon the wrongfulness of his own conduct, that is, his willful refusal to prevent illegal use of force in his presence."

As the jury had done, Davies first examined Powell's conduct. To convict Powell, it was necessary to find he had "used objectively unreasonable force, and that he intended to use excessive force." Davies cited a 1989 case known as *Graham v. Connor* in which the Supreme Court held that the reasonableness of a use of force must be judged from the perspective of a reasonable officer on the scene "rather than with the 20/20 vision of hindsight." The court had cautioned that the "calculus of reasonableness must embody allowance for the fact that police officers are often forced to make split-second judgments—in circumstances that are tense, uncertain and rapidly evolving—about the amount of force that is necessary in a particular situation."

Davies then took into account "the totality of the circumstances, including facts not displayed on the tape." King was unsearched. He had not responded to the electrical charge of Koon's stun gun. He had been sweating profusely. "At least during the initial stages of the arrest process, Sergeant Koon may reasonably have suspected that Mr. King was under the influence of PCP because of Mr. King's erratic and recalcitrant behavior," Davies wrote.

Until this point the judge's analysis dovetailed with the contentions of the defense. Davies also had no doubt that the tape shows King charging toward Powell, as the defense said. But he dismissed out of hand the defense assertion that King had received at most a glancing blow on the head. As the judge described the action, "Powell took a step and struck Mr. King on the right side of his face and head with the side-handle baton. Mr. King fell to the ground. As Mr. King continued to attempt to rise, he was struck by Officer Powell and then by Officer Wind."

Davies observed that Powell struck King repeatedly on the lower extremities from the thirty-fifth second of the tape to the fifty-first second, also delivering "a blow to Mr. King's upper torso." Then, the judge took note of a chest blow 55:08 seconds into the videotape while King's hand was moving "in a downward direction across his chest and abdomen." Although Davies had no way of knowing it, this was the blow that juror Maria Escobel had used to persuade Jury Foreman Bob Almond that Powell had used excessive force. Davies did not find this blow illegal. After this blow "the application of force was suspended" and the officers watched King for ten seconds as he rolled over onto his abdomen. Then Powell reached for the handcuffs dangling from his right back trousers pocket. Davies saw that as evidence that Powell "perceived Mr. King to be no longer a threat and ready for cuffing."

At 1:05:20 on the tape, "Officer Briseno used his left foot to kick or stomp Mr. King in the upper thoracic area. Mr. King's body writhed in response. His feet rose, his head rose, and he raised his upper torso on his elbows. These movements by Mr. King were reflexive and nonvoluntary. He posed no threat." Davies observed that Powell struck King with his baton at 1:07:28 and then hit him another five or six times while Wind delivered four baton blows and kicked King six times. These blows and kicks continued until 1:26. Four seconds later, at 1:30:13, Powell handed his handcuffs to Briseno, who put them on King at 1:42. Davies said that "Officer Powell's conduct clearly crossed the line into illegality at 1:07:28 when he struck Mr. King despite his perception that Mr. King was no longer a threat." All the blows delivered in slightly less than nineteen seconds of the incident until force ceased at 1:26 were illegal.

Davies next dealt with Koon. The judge found he was not responsible for King's facial injuries or his broken leg because these had occurred when King was trying to resist or escape and force was being used legally. Davies also said Koon was not responsible for Briseno's stomp, which he could not have anticipated. The judge's discussion of Koon's conduct contained the germ of a legal defense superior to the one Koon had received. Davies suggested that Koon had reacted too slowly to the swiftly moving events before him, a conclusion similar to that reached by Detective Taky Tzimeas of Internal Affairs in an internal LAPD report the judge had never seen.

But Davies held Koon responsible for the conduct of Powell and Wind after 1:07:28, when Powell "crossed the line" and Wind's subsequent blows and kicks became "objectively unreasonable." Furthermore, Davies said that Koon was "liable for his failure to order the cuffing of Mr. King during the ten seconds immediately prior to the kick by Officer Briseno. . . ." Davies did not see the multitude of "golden opportunities" to take King into custody that prosecution witness Sergeant Mark Conta had described, but he thought Koon had missed at least this one chance.

On the whole, the judge's informed analysis of the incident was more perceptive and balanced than any presented during the trial. But as with every other evaluation, it required a bit of mind reading. The questionable point of the Davies findings is his statement that Powell struck King at 1:07:28 of the tape "despite his perception that Mr. King was no longer a threat." Powell had formed this perception three seconds earlier when he reached for his handcuffs. But Powell's perception changed once King started moving again. Powell never saw the Briseno stomp that caused this movement. He saw only that King was on the move again and hit him so he would not get up.

In fairness to Davies, who had studied the videotape attentively and reviewed the trial record, he did not have the benefit of Powell's perception. Powell had not testified in the federal trial, and his state trial testimony was not before the court. Briseno had not testified, either, except in the videotape of his state trial testimony that Davies allowed into evidence. Later, Powell and Briseno would tell a civil jury that they could not see each other at the crucial moment of the stomp. This racially diverse jury apparently believed the officers because it found them not liable for damages.

Davies had an additional handicap. His findings necessarily were governed by the premise that Powell had used illegal force and Koon permitted it, since these determinations were embodied in the verdicts. After reading the memorandum, the attorneys on both sides suspected that Davies might have found Powell and Koon innocent in a court trial if he had carried his analysis about King's responsibility for the incident to its logical conclusion. But Davies did not have this option. Instead, he took the common-sense view that the arresting officers had reason to use force but that the beating went on too long.

After completing his fact finding, Davies launched into a sentencing discussion that was far more controversial than his analysis of the incident. He began by deciding in favor of the government that the beating was an "aggravated" assault instead of the "minor" assault claimed by Powell's attorney. This was a critical issue that formed the basis of the mathematical calculation requiring a prison sentence. An aggravated assault, as defined by the guidelines, is a "felonious assault" that involves a "dangerous weapon" used with the intent of causing bodily harm. The dangerous weapon was Powell's police baton.

Deciding that the assault was aggravated gave the offense a score (or "base level," in the jargon of the guidelines) of fifteen. As he was required to do by law, Davies added points for the dangerous weapon and for King's injuries. He rejected a prosecution request for an additional increase in the score because of the magnitude of the injuries, pointing out that they "were attributable to a lawful use of force." The score now totaled twenty-seven, which meant a prison sentence of just under six to slightly more than seven years.

But to the dismay of a glum Clymer, Davies then proceeded to mitigate this sentence.

Variations from sentences, known as "departures," are permitted for various reasons. The sentences are nevertheless supposed to wind up in the range permitted by the numerical score. Davies, however, seized on a loophole that had been used by other judges who believed that mathematical calculations had led them to make unfair sentencing decisions. He pointed out that the federal sentencing commission had recognized the difficulties in prescribing "a single set of guidelines that encompasses the vast range of human conduct relevant to a sentencing decision." Davies then ticked off four factors that he said made the case atypical:

> First, Mr. King's wrongful conduct contributed significantly to provoking the offense behavior . . . .
>
> Second, defendants Koon and Powell have already sustained, and will continue to incur, punishment in addition to the sentence imposed by this court. The extraordinary notoriety and national media coverage of this case, coupled with the defendants' status as police officers, make Koon and Powell unusually susceptible to prison abuse. Moreover, Koon and Powell will be subjected to multiple adversarial proceedings and stripped of their positions and tenure by the LAPD.
>
> Third, while the offense of conviction involves a serious assault, there is no evidence, and the government does not argue, that Koon and Powell are dangerous or likely to commit crimes in the future.
>
> Fourth, defendants Koon and Powell were indicted for their respective roles in beating Mr. King only after a state court jury acquitted them of charges based on the same underlying conduct. Under these circumstances, the successive state and federal prosecutions, though legal, raise a specter of unfairness.

AFTER ELABORATING ON THESE POINTS, DAVIES SAID THAT "THE combined extraordinary circumstances of this case give rise to 'mitigating circumstances' that warrant a departure from the guidelines range." Citing a declaration of legislative intent when Congress was creating the guidelines, Davies said they were never intended to "be imposed in a mechanistic fashion." But he acknowledged that he could find "no helpful analogy" on which to base leniency because King's conduct had contributed to the offense. "In fact, very few guideline sections provide for downward adjustments at all," the judge added.

Davies concluded his calculations with an eight-level departure that reduced the score of the offense from twenty-seven to nineteen. He sentenced Koon and Powell to thirty months in prison and fined them nothing except a $50 mandatory assessment. Citing a presentence report by a federal probation officer who had recommended only a two-year sentence, Davies said Koon's assets were exhausted. "He has five dependent children who will be unduly burdened if a fine is imposed," Davies said. "Powell is likewise unable to pay a fine, and unlikely to become able to pay."

The sentences were a demonstration of judicial courage. Davies realized that such wide departure from the guidelines meant an appeal by the government and an outpouring of public criticism. "In a city struggling to heal itself, the sentencing of two Los Angeles police officers Wednesday was like the painful reopening of a wound," began a Los Angeles Times story on reaction to the sentences. It quoted James Thomas, a black man, as saying, "I'm disappointed, but it's deeper than that—I'd almost say grief. I just cannot believe that no matter what we do, no matter how we try to support the fabric of this country, that African Americans are still discounted as a people." Joseph Duff, president of the Los Angeles chapter of the NAACP, called the sentences a "travesty of justice." Juror Erik Rasmussen, who had claimed during deliberations that Koon had used his stun gun to "torture" King, said the officers should have received sentences of five to seven years.[6]

But police officers and their supporters were bothered that Koon and Powell were being required to do any time at all. Detective Bill Helm joked grimly that LAPD cars were being repainted with the motto: "To protect and to serve time." At Foothill Station, where Koon and Powell had worked, the reaction was bitter. "I think that we will have tears—if not in the eyes then in the hearts of officers throughout the department," said Captain Tim McBride. "It has been a long and difficult saga."[7] The Thin Blue Line, the voice of the Los Angeles police union, printed a special section brimming with outrage. It included a letter from Dr. Thomas Kando, a sociologist at California State University in Sacramento, who claimed that the national average of time served for murder was less than the sentences imposed on Koon and Powell.

The sentences increased the emotional stakes in the state trial of the Reginald Denny defendants, which began the next day. Noisy protests were held outside the Criminal Courts Building throughout jury selection and the trial. African-American demonstrators complained that the young black men who had yanked Denny from his cement truck and beaten and kicked him in the head until he was near death were the victims of a racist system. On the day Koon and Powell were sentenced, Reverend Cecil Murray of First AME Church warned that "anger will be intense" in the black community if Denny's assailants received longer sentences than the police officers.

Fear, once again, was a critical factor. The area from which the jury was chosen reached deep into South Central, Pico-Union, and Koreatown, embracing neighborhoods devastated by the riots. The venue that had damaged the defense in the King case now worked against the prosecution. Jury summonses had been mailed to 1,200 people, from whom Ouderkirk expected a turnout of 250. But only 153 people showed up when the jury screening process began on July 28, and most were unwilling to serve on this particular jury. Ouderkirk granted hardship excuses for almost any reason, including one prospective juror who said, "Does hardship include personal prejudice? I'm sick and tired of crime. I watch the news every night, and it would be difficult for me to be neutral."

The trial that would again test the patience and racial harmony of Los Angeles involved the two most prominent members of the original L.A. 4 defendants, Damian Monroe (Football) Williams and Henry Keith (Kiki) Watson. Gary Williams, who had stolen Denny's wallet as he lay unconscious beside his truck, had pleaded guilty to robbery and assaulting Fidel Lopez with a deadly weapon and had been sentenced to three years in state prison. A separate trial was pending for Antoine Miller, who had yanked open the door of Denny's truck. Lance Parker, who had fired a blast from his shotgun at the truck and narrowly missed the gas tank, was also being tried separately.

Attorneys began examining prospective jurors on August 5, the day after Koon and Powell were sentenced. These prospective jurors had answered a forty-five-page questionnaire that included an extensive section on the King case and a pointed question: "Are you concerned that your verdict in this case might incite a riot?" Any would-be juror who answered this question affirmatively was excused. Even so, it is unlikely that any candidate was unaware of the possibility of another riot. Everyone could see and hear the demonstrators as they came to court each day. The prospective jurors were also reminded of the tension by Ouderkirk, who warned them that they should not view the trial as an opportunity to "even the score" for the sentences given Powell and Koon.

Deputy District Attorney Janet Moore felt during jury selection much as Deputy District Attorney Terry White had felt in Simi Valley. White had been dismayed that most of the prospective jurors who were to pass judgment on the beating of a black man by white police officers were ardently pro-police and that no African Americans had any chance of making it onto the jury. Many of the jury candidates from whom Moore had to choose believed that the system was stacked in favor of the police and against blacks. On the one-to-five scale used by the prosecution to rate prospective jurors, with five the highest, few jury candidates rated above two. Several were rated minus one or minus two, meaning that they were unlikely to vote for conviction no matter how strong the evidence. While Ouderkirk had a reputation for favoring the prosecution, his willingness to excuse anyone who didn't want to serve removed many of the best jury candidates from a prosecution standpoint. "We had a tremendous flight of jurors in this case," Moore said afterward. "Just hordes of them refused to stay."[8]

Among those who fled were most of the middle-class jurors the prosecution wanted. Prosecutors took a small measure of comfort in Ouderkirk's willingness to excuse young black men, but the jury had nine women, which was too many for Moore's taste. "Culturally, mothers are brought up to forgive and to accept, and I just think they are a little more forgiving than men," she said after the trial.[9]

Moore and her cocounsel, Lawrence Morrison, comforted themselves, as prosecutors had in Simi Valley, by hoping that the videotape was powerful enough to convert jurors who sympathized with the defendants. Within a week the two sides had chosen a jury that reflected the ethnic diversity of Los Angeles: five non-Hispanic whites, three Latinos, three African Americans, and one Asian American. District Attorney Gil Garcetti, emphasizing the power of positive thinking, arrived in court less than an hour before completion of jury selection and proclaimed delight at the composition of the panel. He said he had "insisted" on a racially mixed jury so there would be community confidence in the verdicts.

But jury selection was not over, although Garcetti did not seem to realize it. Six alternates remained to be chosen, and defense attorney Edi Faal expected that some of them would become jurors. His perception was reinforced by jury consultant Jo-Ellan Dimitrius, who anticipated that the emotional strains of the case and the reluctance of some employers to accept prolonged absences would cause dropouts.

One of the alternates whom Faal and Dimitrius most wanted was Carolyn Walters, an assured African-American legal secretary and the very kind of juror who would have been anathema to Dimitrius when she was advising attorneys for the police officers in the Rodney King trials. Although Walters received a low rating from prosecutors, they made no effort to exclude her as an alternate. The prosecutors wanted to get the trial going after many delays. And they were reluctant to challenge any prospective juror out of valid concern that the replacement might be even more hostile to the prosecution. Walters became an alternate.

SO ONCE MORE, THE LOS ANGELES COUNTY DISTRICT ATTORNEY'S Office began a trial in which convictions were presumed certain because of a graphic videotape. The famous tape of the Denny assault had been shot for TV station KCOP from a helicopter by Bob Tur's wife, Marika, at an aerial distance of seventy feet. While this videotape had also recorded other assaults, several of them had been filmed in more detail from ground level by an amateur cameraman.* And once more there was a disconnect between the public statements by the district attorney and the private anxieties of his trial attorneys. Garcetti, elected because of public disenchantment with Ira Reiner after the Simi Valley verdicts and the riots, was always mindful of political considerations. Although Moore and Morrison knew they faced a skeptical jury, Garcetti compulsively praised the panel for its racial diversity. He had learned little from the King trials, which had shown that the biases and fears of jurors are as significant as videotaped evidence.

Damian Monroe Williams was twenty years old at the time of the trial. While not a celebrity or football hero, except in his own mind, he was a sweet-looking young man who aroused sympathy among many of the nine women, two of them African American, on the original jury. It was widely believed by blacks—and by some white legal experts as well—that Williams had been over-charged to satisfy the political needs of white authority. The most extravagant charges, notably the alleged torture of Denny, had been dismissed by the court, but Williams still faced ten felony counts that had the theoretical potential to keep him in prison for much of his life: Williams was charged with attempted murder and aggravated mayhem for his lead role in the Denny assault and with six counts of assault with a deadly weapon and two counts of robbery. Henry Keith Watson, who turned twenty-nine during the trial, faced one count of attempted murder, two counts of assault with a deadly weapon, and two counts of robbery.[10]

Rodney King was a symbol of supposed police brutality and of the mistreatment that African Americans believed they systematically received at the hands of police. Damian Williams was a symbol, too. To the defense and African-American activists, Williams symbolized justified black rage at the Simi Valley verdicts. To prosecutors he symbolized the impermissible lawlessness that had caused the riots and the deaths of fifty-four people. Deputy District Attorney Morrison used Williams as the emblem of the riots in his opening statement. "Certain days stand out in history," he said. "We, the citizens of Los Angeles, will not forget April 29, 1992. We saw vicious and horrible crimes broadcast into our living rooms." As he ticked off the crimes that occurred at Florence and Normandie, Morrison said, "While many of us have come to hear this case being referred to as the Reginald Denny case, it is not just about Reginald Denny. This is a case of those eight citizens who, like Mr. Denny, were victimized at that intersection."

---

* The ground-level video was taken by Timothy Allen Goldman with the assistance of two other people.

Morrison illustrated his opening statement with color slides that proved difficult for some jurors to watch. One juror winced and another juror's mouth opened wide as Morrison displayed a slide with a close up of a bloodied Denny. Other slides followed, also provoking obvious distaste among some jurors. The prosecution strategy was to rekindle the outrage that had gripped Los Angeles during the riots. But Morrison and Moore realized it would take more than outrage to obtain consensus from this jury, and they tried to appeal to black jurors by pointing out that the Florence and Normandie victims also had been rescued by African Americans. "The events of April 29, 1992, at Florence and Normandie brought out the best in human beings and also the worst in human beings," Morrison said. "Some of the victims you will be hearing from over the next few weeks are here only because of the selfless heroism of the good and decent citizens of this community of South Central who risked their lives."

Prosecutors clung to this theme from Morrison's opening statement through Moore's closing argument. Williams and Watson were portrayed as thugs who had injured and degraded helpless people whose lives were saved by the heroism of other African Americans. Particularly compelling was the testimony of Fidel Lopez, a contractor and Guatemalan immigrant who had been pulled from his truck, robbed of the $2,800 he was carrying to buy building supplies, and beaten severely. Williams had sprayed black paint on Lopez's genitals as he lay bloody and unconscious on the pavement. "Bennie Newton, African-America pastor, save my life after that," Lopez testified in halting English. Newton had died of cancer four months before the trial. Lopez remembered saying to him, "Please don't leave me here. Take me home."

Despite the efforts of the prosecution to balance the villainy of Williams and Watson with the heroism of Newton and Denny's black rescuers, racial feelings permeated the trial from beginning to end. It could hardly have been otherwise, for what had happened at Florence and Normandie was a race riot in which the assailants were African Americans and all the victims were Asian, Latino, or white. Alicia Maldonado Doby, one of the first prosecution witnesses, set a tone for the trial when she testified that the black youths at the intersection directed traffic "according to the color of your skin." As blacks stoned her car, she had heard a man prosecutors identified as Williams say, "Get her, she's not a sister." Maldonado had not anticipated the assault. "Ironically, my husband is African American," she said. "I never expected this from blacks."

The litany of racial accusations continued as Florence-and-Normandie victims described how they had been assaulted and degraded. Their stories were undergirded by the testimony of LAPD Officer Timothy McGrath, an African American, who testified that Damian Williams told him on the afternoon of the riots, "If you were any kind of nigger, you would be out here with us." The remark rankled. "It kind of hit me," McGrath said. "It was something I never heard in a situation like that." Like other officers in 77th Street Division who were then ordered out of the area, McGrath was cut off from television and didn't see the Denny assault when it occurred. After working thirty-six consecutive hours, he first saw the television clip of the attack on Denny at home two days later and instantly recognized Williams as Denny's assailant.

The prosecution needed the testimony of McGrath, helicopter observer Bob Tur, and other eyewitnesses because most of the victims had been too battered, scared, or confused to make a positive identification of their assailants. The videotapes showed Williams dressed in a white T-shirt, dark shorts, black-and-white tennis shoes and a blue bandana. Except for Gregory Alan-Williams, an African-American television actor and writer who rescued Takao Hirata from the mob, none of the witnesses accurately remembered Williams' attire, and Alan-Williams could not identify Williams. "Putting on a case like this is like assembling pieces of a jigsaw puzzle," Morrison said a week into the trial.[11]

For the most part, the prosecutors did an excellent job with this assembly. Even jurors who were disinclined to convict Williams and Watson of the most serious charges eventually agreed that they were the assailants shown on the videotape. But the effort required to put the puzzle together came at a price. Prosecutors were forced to spend too much time refuting defense challenges to divergent descriptions of Williams by his victims when they needed to establish the intent required for a verdict of attempted murder.

Tur, an observer in the news helicopter that shot the incriminating footage at Florence and Normandie, had provided a dramatic, live account of the Denny assault for radio station KNX and television station KCOP. He was an effective witness for identification purposes, vividly describing how Williams hit Denny in the head with a brick and then "did a pirouette, a turn and made a victory sign with his hands and fingers." Tur also identified Watson as the man who had kicked truck driver Larry Tarvin in the head and afterward pinned Denny to the pavement with his foot as others beat him.

But Tur's testimony harmed as well as helped the prosecution. His credibility was challenged on cross-examination by Faal and Watson's attorney, Earl Broady Jr. Faal tried to impugn Tur's reputation for veracity, at which he failed, and to show that he was biased against the defendants, at which he succeeded. "I do have a bias in this case," Tur acknowledged. "I'm a witness. I saw something terrible out there. Mr. Williams beat a lot of people up."

The reaction to Tur in the courtroom demonstrated an ugly aspect of the trial that was downplayed by the media. Prosecution witnesses were subjected to threats and sometimes jostling from onlookers who had come to court in support of the defendants. One spectator was detained for three hours after trying to intimidate Tur during a recess. This community hostility to the prosecution was not lost on the jurors.

One prosecution witness who was not biased against the defendants was their most famous victim. Reginald Denny had suffered ninety-seven broken bones and permanent facial damage when he was pulled from the cab of his truck and beaten with a claw hammer and the brick hurled by Williams. The televised pictures of the assault had horrified the world, perhaps even more than the King beating, and had made Denny the defining symbol of the riots. In the aftermath of the riots, this soft-spoken truck driver who loved country music and drag races seemed a throwback to the flower children of the 1960s who preached peace and love. When he came to court to testify on August 25, Denny was accorded the media fanfare and public deference Los Angeles reserves for its celebrity victims.

Like King in the federal trial, Denny presented both an opportunity and an obstacle to the prosecutors who had called him as a witness. His appearance allowed them to play again the gruesome videotape of the assault, during which one juror shook his head repeatedly. But Denny remembered even less about his ordeal than King had remembered about his. When Moore showed Denny a close-up photo of him lying bloodied in the intersection and asked if it depicted his condition after the attack, Denny replied, "I couldn't tell you. Probably. I don't remember."

Denny did remember the "very shocking" scene that had confronted him as he drove toward the Florence-Normandie intersection. He had seen cars going the wrong way and heard "clutter sounds" of things being broken. "It was totally wild," Denny said. "I couldn't quite figure out what was going on. It was like a moment of shock, mainly disbelief. It was total madness."

Ahead of him in the intersection, Denny could see Tarvin's white medical-supply truck being looted. As he delicately tried to maneuver his eighteen-wheeler around Tarvin's smaller truck, Denny worried that the driver would be held accountable for loss of the goods. Denny drove slowly because he was preoccupied with avoiding people who he said "would have been just spots on the road" if he had struck them with his 80,000-pound truck. Then he heard the "incredible sound" of the passenger window in his cab shattering and looked to his right. He said he was "really startled, like gasping my last breath" when he heard the window smash. It was the last thing he remembered.

The jurors were in awe of Denny, whose gentleness and forgiving spirit seemed almost incomprehensible to them. At one point, Moore brought him over to the jury box so jurors could see the permanent depression on the right side of his head, which looked as if a divot had been taken out of it with a golf club. To Moore's surprise, Denny took the hand of an interested female juror and placed it in the depression caused by the brick. From then on, other members of the jury called her "The Hand." She had actually touched Reginald Denny.[12]

Defense attorneys were brief and wisely gentle in their cross-examination. Denny told Broady that he had suffered no injuries to his neck. This helped Broady's client; the videotape showed Watson putting his foot on Denny's neck after he was dragged from the cab. The exchange echoed another aspect of the King incident, in which Officer Briseno had benefited because he caused no lasting injury when he put his foot on King's neck or upper back.

But the overall impact of Denny's performance was the opposite of Rodney King's effect in the civil rights trial. Denny's lack of any desire for retribution from the men who had nearly killed him dazzled Faal and won over even Williams' combative mother, Georgiana, who waved to Denny as he left the courtroom during a recess. Denny leaned over a row of spectators, shook her hand, and embraced her. He then hugged Joyce Watson and shook the hand of Henry Watson, the parents of Kiki Watson. "God bless you," Joyce Watson said. "I have prayed for us all to come together, and it happened today," she told reporters afterward. "I feel so much better. I have prayed for that man."[13]

Janet Moore kept her emotions under control, but she was angry with Denny for legitimizing the impulses of leniency on this defense-friendly jury. "He took a lot of guilt off their shoulders and basically said to them, Hey, it's okay if you let [the defendants] go," Moore said after the trial.[14]

DENNY'S FORGIVING ATTITUDE ALSO PLAYED SQUARELY INTO THE hands of Edirissa Mohammed Omar Faal, the courtly and elegantly tailored lawyer from the West African nation of Gambia who took over the Damian Williams defense after his first lawyer was fired. Faal, who stood six feet tall and weighed 205 pounds, had an engaging courtroom presence but seemed somewhat out of place in a California criminal courtroom. He was primarily a civil litigator in Orange County, where he often represented impoverished clients against big corporations, and he taught a comparative course on world legal systems at USC. Faal, who had trained for the law in London at Middle Temple, Inns of Court, spoke in a heavily accented, lilting voice and often referred to one or other of the prosecutors as "my learned friend." Moore found his manner charming but thought his knowledge of criminal law deficient and his legal theories bizarre. Her attitude seems to have been shared by Ouderkirk, who found fault with the form of many of Faal's motions and quickly denied them.

But Faal often made up in creativity whatever he may have lacked in his grasp of legal fine points. In a civil suit against a naval laboratory brought by a man who had lost a hand in an explosion, Faal contended that the victim was working off a previous debt to the government and was therefore not an employee who was ineligible for damages but an indentured servant entitled to recompense. This novel theory amused the judge, but the attorney representing the laboratory said it helped Faal win a $750,000 arbitration award for his client.

In the Denny case, Faal believed from his study of the videotape that the assault was "a thoughtless and random act of violence" rather than a planned or premeditated crime.[15] This was a crucial perception because in order to convict Watson and Williams of attempted murder, the jury had to find a specific intent to kill Denny. If that had been the defendants' intention, Faal argued, Denny would have been killed because he was completely within their power. This was a mainstream legal argument. Defense lawyers often assert that a killing is not murder as defined by the law because the killer lacked specific intent. Faal's more inventive contention was that Williams had not attempted to disable or disfigure Denny as alleged in the charge of aggravated mayhem, which also carried a life term. As Faal saw it, aggravated mayhem required a "refined thinking" that had not been present in the Florence-Normandie intersection.

In defending Williams against the brutal evidence of the Tur videotape, Faal resembled the apocryphal lawyer who contends that his client wasn't at the scene, didn't commit the crime, and was mentally unbalanced if he was found to have committed it. For good measure, Faal also exploited racial antagonisms, and he was more straightforward about it than federal prosecutors had been in the Rodney King civil rights trial. Williams had been arrested by Chief Daryl Gates, the embodiment of white police authority. He was being tried by white prosecutors before a white judge who jurors thought favored the prosecution. "I never lost sight of the racial division in the courtroom," Faal said later. He and the other defense attorneys would make as many as twenty-five objections in a row. When Ouderkirk overruled all of them, Faal would look knowingly at the jury. Then he would lean back and make no more objections, trying to communicate to the jury that this was "their" courtroom—the white folks' courtroom—in which they could do as they pleased. "Many of the jurors told me afterwards that they got the point," Faal said.[16]

Whatever one thinks of these tactics, it is hard to fault Faal for his everything-but-the-kitchen-sink defense. While Faal faced a sympathetic jury, he had a weak case that tempted him to try anything that might raise doubts. As it turned out, most of his approaches bore fruit, even the unconvincing suggestion that police had arrested the wrong man. In addition to forcing prosecutors to devote too much time to proving that Williams was the assailant shown in the two videotapes, the mistaken-identity defense gave Faal opportunities to humanize a client he dared not put on the witness stand.

Faal took advantage of these opportunities, with some unintended help from the prosecution. When prosecutors asked Williams to approach the jury box and display a rose-colored tattoo on his forearm that was a critical identifying mark, Williams allowed jurors to see the tattoo and touch his arm. Faal said this "human touch" made it harder for jurors to view Williams as a monster.[17] At another point, while contending that the videotape showed a gap in the front teeth of Denny's assailant, Faal had Williams smile to show he had no such gap. The jurors laughed. There was no doubt that Williams was the man shown in the two videotapes, and even the jurors most supportive of the defense accepted this fact. But in the process of disputing the prosecution's identification, Faal succeeded in humanizing Damian Williams, as the defense had failed to do for Stacey Koon in the civil rights trial.

Denny also served defense purposes. "Denny could have hurt us," Faal said afterward. "When he came to court, he could have made statements relating to how his life has been ruined forever. . . . He could have made statements that would incite someone to feel very strongly against the defendants." Denny did not do this, but Faal was more uncomfortable during his testimony than at any other time during the trial. "I couldn't wait for him to leave that courtroom because the more you see him, the more you listen to him, the more you will not be able to understand how someone could do what they did to him," Faal said. "Reginald Denny was the last person that deserved that type of treatment."[18]

The treatment of "this fine man," as Faal called him, had been so vicious that the defense attorney tried to spread the blame. He sought to persuade jurors that Denny had been injured by a rock or brick hurled through the window of his cab before he was dragged out into the street. The principal evidence for this was that Denny remembered turning his head to the right just before he was assaulted. Faal also called an Orange County plastic surgeon in an attempt to show that the brick thrown by Williams had landed above Denny's ear behind the area where his skull had been caved in. The argument and Faal's technique of using still frames from the videotape were reminiscent of the contention of defense attorneys that Rodney King had been injured by falls to the ground instead of baton blows—and similarly unpersuasive.

But Faal was not finished. For the majority of jurors who did not doubt Williams' principal role in injuring Denny, Faal offered a defense that his client was part of a mass outrage that consumed South Central after the verdicts. The historical evidence for this proposition is scant. Riots did not erupt in most black neighborhoods after the verdicts, and despite the emotions of the crowd, most of the gang members in the area of Florence and Normandie rationally refrained from serious violence when the police were present, at least until fueled by liquor and success later in the evening. At one point Williams apparently returned home and calmly changed shirts, adding to the problem of identifying him. When he returned to the streets, Williams shared the surprise of his peers that the LAPD had not returned to take control of the intersection. As Maldonado and others testified, Williams and other gang members then took control themselves, directing traffic and conducting assaults according to skin color.

Faal, however, believed that the young man who seemed so docile in court had been swept up in "group contagion" that prompted "random" violence. Prosecutors thought this contention was baseless but realized it could give sympathetic jurors an excuse to acquit the defendants. They fought to prevent Faal from calling a final witness whom he presented as an expert on mob violence.

The witness was Armando Torres Morales, a professor of clinical social work at the UCLA School of Medicine and a former probation officer. With the jury out of the courtroom, he discussed theories of mass hysteria and claimed that rioters at Florence and Normandie had acted out of frustration with the verdicts and not by conscious choice.* Moore said it was absurd to use such sociological factors to explain the conduct of Williams and Watson, particularly since Morales had not made studies of the riots or the defendants. Ouderkirk compromised. He allowed Morales to testify in general about his group contagion theory without relating it to the conduct of the defendants or without mentioning "riots." Jurors, however, made their own connections. When Morales described "impulsive, thoughtless action" that can be triggered by "sudden information [of] a major disappointment," jurors knew he was talking about the supposed reaction of the defendants to the verdicts.

Moore countered with a witness who took a dim view of group contagion. Lewis Yablonsky, a sociologist at California State University Northridge, said the theory had been discredited because it failed to explain why individuals behave differently in such stressful situations. "Most people see it as quite out of date," he said.

Returning to the theme of individual responsibility in her closing argument, Moore said Williams and Watson had "no one else to blame than

* Morales compared the actions of the Los Angeles rioters to the "group contagion" of police officers at the 1968 Democratic National Convention in Chicago who he said lost control because white, middle-class demonstrators threw urine and feces at them. It was a counterproductive example (based on my opinion as a reporter at that convention) because the conduct of individual officers varied widely. Ouderkirk did not permit Morales to make this comparison to the jury.

themselves" for what they had done. "They are here because they acted in a violent and unconscionable way," she said. "They are not here because we are holding them responsible for the Los Angeles riot."

Nevertheless, the verdicts in *People v. Williams,* even more than those in *U.S. v. Koon,* were a judgment on the riots. The power of the community to influence the trial's outcome had been recognized in advance by African-American activists led by Williams family spokesman Don Jackson, a key witness in an earlier high-profile trial involving alleged police brutality in Long Beach. Jackson, a sophisticated activist, helped organize demonstrations outside the courthouse and attended the trial dressed in African garb. "We stepped in with an African presence in the courtroom," he told Jim Newton after the trial. "We were attentive and vigilant. We showed up every day, and the jury could see that we were there . . . . We had an impact, and if people don't like that, too bad."[19]

The impact of the activists was devastating. In the King civil rights trial, the jurors' anxieties about the violence their verdicts might cause were mostly in the background. In the Denny case, fear was a constant presence. Carolyn Walters, the African American who started the trial as an alternate and ultimately became the forewoman, would remember the trial as "forty days of hell"—and Walters was the most unflappable person on a jury continually aware of the "African presence" of which Jackson boasted. As they deliberated, jurors could hear shouts of "no justice, no peace" from demonstrators who paraded outside the courthouse with a sign that said, "The rebellion was justified."*

The jury was sequestered during deliberations on the eighth floor at the downtown Hilton Hotel, two floors down from where the jurors in the King civil rights case had spent the entire trial. Unlike the King jurors, however, jurors in the Denny case did not experience an emotional epiphany that resolved divisions and led to speedy verdicts. There was too much pressure. Five original jurors were replaced by alternates as Ouderkirk struggled to avoid a mistrial. The judge excused two women jurors during the trial for health reasons and dismissed an elderly black man just before deliberations after finding that he had talked about the case to friends and relatives. Another woman juror was excused for personal reasons after deliberations started. Still another, a black woman in her mid-fifties who was known to other jurors as "Been There, Done That," was dismissed after Walters submitted a note to the judge on behalf of the eleven other jurors saying that the woman "cannot comprehend anything we've been trying to accomplish."

---

* As in the trials of the police officers, the names of the jurors in the Williams-Watson trial were kept secret. In contrast to the other two trials, most jurors in this case maintained their anonymity after the trial. Walters, however, identified herself and freely discussed the proceedings.

Only a single alternate was left, and at least three of the surviving jurors were shaky. One of them, unsettled by sequestration, ran down a hotel corridor screaming, "I can't take it any more." When Ouderkirk refused to remove her, Faal accused the judge of "manipulating the jury." Ouderkirk also retained a female juror who became ill but said she could continue and, more questionably, an Asian woman who told the court through Walters that she feared for her life and her family's safety. The Asian woman had replaced the juror who had been dismissed for failing to comprehend. Ouderkirk, who had twice urged the jury to continue deliberating, responded to the Asian woman's expression of fearfulness by re-reading to the entire jury portions of his instructions that said, "You must not be influenced by public opinion or public feeling" and "Apply the law regardless of consequences."

The changes in the composition of the jury justified the effort Faal and his jury consultants had made in selecting favorable alternates. Four of the five alternates who became jurors were sympathetic to the defense. They included Walters, who replaced a white woman who was believed by both sides to be pro-prosecution. Among those who were excused, only the man dismissed for talking about the case was considered favorable to the defense.

Luck is often a handmaiden of hard work, and the defense was fortunate as well as dedicated. Faal had opposed the dismissal of Been There, Done That, but jurors agreed after the verdicts that keeping her on the jury would surely have caused a deadlock. Faal had wanted Ouderkirk to dismiss the woman who ran screaming down the corridor, but she stayed on the jury and caused no problem for the defense. Faal had also wanted Ouderkirk to dismiss the fearful Asian woman, as the judge probably should have done. While Faal accurately perceived that this juror was proprosecution, he was unaware that the white woman who would have replaced her held similar opinions and might have clung to them longer because she was less fearful. In retaining the Asian juror, Ouderkirk kept off the panel the one alternate who might have held out and deadlocked the jury.

In its final version, the jury consisted of four African Americans, four Latinos, two Asian Americans, and two whites. Except for one black and one Latino, all were women. The popular and outgoing Walters, known to other jurors as "Socksy" because of her habit of wearing bright, flashy socks to court, volunteered to serve as forewoman and was elected without opposition. She was a former keyboard player for the band Jade and felt at ease among people of different races and ethnic groups. Walters grew up in the tiny northern California town of Herlong, where blacks are few, and had worked six years as a legal secretary for a prominent Los Angeles entertainment law firm. At the time of the trial she was on disability leave after a partial hysterectomy.

The forewoman was intelligent, opinionated, and focused. She believed that young black males were often treated harshly by the police and had been outraged, along with many other African Americans, when Daryl Gates made his grandstanding arrest of Williams. Walters thought that some of the original charges lodged against Williams were "ridiculous" and thought he remained overcharged despite the considerable paring down of the counts against him before the trial began.[20]

Prosecutors later complained that Walters was an "agenda juror," echoing the opinions of prosecutors about forewoman Dorothy Bailey in Simi Valley and the defense view of juror Maria Escobel in the federal trial. Walters, like Bailey and Escobel, denied having an agenda.[21] While her low opinions of the police and her feelings that Williams had been overcharged made her receptive to defense arguments, she did not condone the beating of Denny. If Walters (or Bailey or Escobel) had an agenda, it was one drawn from life's experiences rather than ideology. Walters' value as a forewoman, which may have been useful to the prosecution as well as to the defense, was that she pulled together a conflicted jury.

The jurors' confusion was evident in a series of handwritten notes passed to Ouderkirk during the deliberations. The first hinted at an obsession with legal details. In an unusual blunder, defense attorney Earl Broady had conceded in his closing argument that the videotape showed Watson assaulting Larry Tarvin, a fact Broady had disputed during trial. The juror's note asked if this admission could be considered as evidence. Later notes asked if "or" meant "and" or if the word "likely" meant "it did occur." Some jurors combed the instructions to see if the word "feet" was mentioned. It wasn't, and jurors concluded that Watson could not be convicted of using a deadly weapon for kicking Denny or Tarvin. Robert Pugsley, a criminal-law professor at Southwestern University School of Law who had observed the trial, thought jurors had become entangled in minutiae. "They probably made more of legal jargon and terminology in the form of the jury instructions than they needed to or was useful for ultimate decision making," he said.[22]

What may be most remarkable about this jury is that it reached verdicts at all. This was largely the doing of Walters, who had a knack for compromise and a determination to produce as many verdicts as possible. Most Denny jurors shared Walters' opinion that the defendants had been overcharged.* They agreed with Faal that Williams and Watson could have killed Denny if they had wanted to do so and therefore had not intended to

---

* Prosecutor Janet Moore, who was not involved in the case when the original charges were filed, agrees in retrospect that it was a mistake to charge the defendants with robbery since they took nothing from their victims. But she believes that the attempted murder and mayhem charges were "absolutely appropriate."[23]

commit murder. Several jurors accepted the defense argument that Denny had been injured by a brick before he was dragged from the cab. Janet Moore concluded from her interviews of jurors that some of them were desensitized by the continued showing of the videotape, which had been Ira Reiner's concern at Simi Valley with the Holliday videotape. And several jurors liked the defendants. "They seemed just like anyone, just like you and I," one woman juror told *The New York Times*. "I see them just as two human beings. They just got caught up in the riot. I guess maybe they were in the wrong place at the wrong time."

In an interview after the trial, Walters said that Williams should have been convicted of assault with a deadly weapon for his attack on Denny. This is what is known in California as a "lesser included offense" to the crime of attempted murder and would normally have been a permissible verdict. But Faal had exercised the defense option of permitting no lesser verdict on the attempted murder charge, giving the jury an all-or-nothing-choice. It was, said Walters, a "brilliant gamble." She said jurors agreed that Williams had assaulted Denny with a deadly weapon and believes there would have been a conviction on this charge.[24]

The verdicts, most of them delivered on October 18, 1993, and the rest two days later, provided another jolt to trial-weary Los Angeles. Taken in their totality, they were an immense victory for the defense. Watson was acquitted of all felony charges except the assault on Tarvin, on which the jury deadlocked 9–3 for acquittal. He was convicted of misdemeanor assault against Denny, a crime carrying a penalty of only six months in jail. Since Watson already had spent a year and a half in jail waiting for trial, Ouderkirk ordered him released.

Particularly revealing in terms of the jury's sympathies was the fact that nine jurors rejected the charge that the muscular Watson had assaulted Tarvin, the frail driver who was dragged from his medical-supply truck and beaten savagely while an onlooker said, "No pity for the white man." Tarvin, who was six inches shorter and weighed 85 pounds less than Watson, had suffered permanent facial scars and other injuries. Realizing that any jury was likely to be horrified by this assault, attorney Broady had tried to cast doubts upon the identification of Watson. Given Broady's startling admission in his closing argument that Watson was indeed the man shown brutalizing Tarvin on the videotape, it seems likely that a more neutral jury would have found Watson guilty on this charge.

Williams was acquitted of attempted murder, aggravated mayhem, and causing "great bodily injury" to Denny. He was convicted of simple mayhem for his role in the Denny beating, the lightest felony possible. Williams was acquitted of felony assault against his other victims but convicted of misdemeanor assault against Fidel Lopez, Jorge Gonzalez, Takao Hirata, and

Alicia Maldonado. He was acquitted of assaulting firefighters Terrance Manning and Fred Mathis. Williams' mother Georgiana was jubilant. "I said it wasn't over until the fat lady sang," she said after delivering a religious hymn in the courtroom corridor. "I just sang."

Referring to the pressures on jurors in the King and Denny trials, Jim Newton wrote after the verdicts that "the threat of riots is a hard fear to ignore, either consciously or subconsciously."[25] Law professor Pugsley said, "I just can't for the life of me imagine any twelve normal human beings who have been living in this metropolitan area for the last two and a half years going into the task [of being jurors] without a background consciousness of danger and volatility."[26] And the remaining alternate in *People v. Williams*, a white woman in her thirties who termed the verdicts "a sad day for America," agreed that fear had been a factor. "The message the jury sent out basically is that if you don't believe or agree with a verdict it's okay to go into the streets, to choose certain fellow human beings, throw rocks at their cars, beat them up, and take their property," she said.[27]

This accusation angered the jurors, who through Walters issued a statement denying that their verdicts had been influenced by "intimidation [or] fear of another riot" or racial factors. But there is little doubt that fear was part of the process. The Asian woman who said she feared for her life held out for two days in favor of convicting Williams of attempted murder before changing her vote. And most of the jurors, with the notable exception of the self-assured Walters, were so afraid of being identified even after the light verdicts that they went to unusual lengths to preserve their anonymity. One Denny juror who was indignant at the notion that fear of riots had been a factor in the jury's decision expressed her views for a fee on KCAL, a local television station. She insisted that her voice be electronically altered to prevent identification and wore a baseball cap. With her face in shadows, she then declared that she and her colleagues had not been swayed by fear.

The special target of this disguised juror's wrath was District Attorney Garcetti, who when the jury was impaneled had hailed its diversity but now described its verdicts as "incomprehensible." Referring to the "no justice, no peace" battle cry of the activists, Garcetti said that the jurors had opted for peace at the expense of justice. But Garcetti's surprise at the trial's outcome was considerably more incomprehensible than the verdicts. The district attorney knew that most prospective jurors had been too fearful to respond to the summonses. He also knew that most of those who had responded had asked to be excused. The prosecution had faced an uphill battle from the start—as the analysis of jury questionnaires by Moore and Morrison had shown. Ignoring these realities and the Simi Valley lesson that a violent videotape does not guarantee conviction, Garcetti had raised high and unrealistic expectations, as he would do again three years later in the O. J. Simpson trial. This exacerbated public anger and disappointment at the outcome.

A LOS ANGELES TIMES POLL TAKEN SOON AFTER THE VERDICTS found that 75 percent of Latinos, 66 percent of whites, and 53 percent of blacks believed the jurors were "motivated more by fear for their own safety and of civil unrest" than by "fair and sensible consideration of the evidence." The poll found that two-thirds of whites and Latinos disagreed with the verdicts and that only a bare majority of African Americans approved of them. Confidence in the justice system, low when the trial began, had declined among all groups. The poll's "ray of hope," as the *Times* put it, was that levels of anger were considerably less than after the verdicts in Simi Valley.

Still, there was anger enough to go around. California Attorney General Dan Lungren, in touch with the public mood, called the verdicts "a body blow to the justice system" and said the justifications for the jury's leniency resembled the excuses used in the old South when white juries refused to punish white lynchers.[28] Using similar imagery to make a different point, Harland Braun said, "The jury is there because we value the idea of bringing the community into a criminal trial. But when the community becomes a lynch mob, we ask the jury to shut that out. I don't see how they can."[29]

Talk radio stations in Los Angeles were flooded with calls from angry listeners who denounced the verdicts. While African-American leaders praised the jury's decisions, KFI talk show host John Kobylt said that "a silent majority" of black callers disagreed with the verdicts and disapproved of the media focus on militant blacks who lauded them.[30] Vaughn Reid, an African American, told a reporter that the verdicts had sent a wrong message that it was okay "for young, outraged, disenfranchised gang members to assault."[31] While many blacks saw the King and Denny beatings as equivalent, most did not see Damian Williams as a hero or a victim.

Reginald Denny saw the verdicts as providing Williams and Watson the kind of opportunity he had been given by his black rescuers and the doctors at Daniel Freeman Memorial Hospital. "The next step for me would have been death," Denny said in a television interview. "I've been given a chance, and so I'm going to extend that courtesy toward some guys who obviously were a little bit confused. [I] hope that they see the light now and don't follow in those footsteps again . . ."[32] Takao Hirata, so badly beaten he could not remember the attack, was nearly as forgiving. "I don't hold any grudges," he told the *Rafu Shimpo*, a Japanese-American newspaper in Los Angeles. "If they do some jail time, that is all I care about."[33]

But victims Larry Tarvin and Fidel Lopez, who remained deaf in one ear from the assault, were disturbed by the verdicts. "They deserved to get a much harsher punishment for inflicting so much harm to people," Tarvin said on the television program, *American Journal*. And Alicia Maldonado, who had been physically uninjured but—in Janet Moore's phrase—"emotionally traumatized" by the assault in which she lost her purse and her rosy illusions about Los Angeles,[34] was dismayed. She denounced the jury for cowardice, quit her job, and moved away. "The message this sends out is that hoodlums run the city and everyone is too scared to do anything about it," she said.[35]

Moore, while disappointed, realized that the verdicts reflected more than what had happened in the courtroom. From experience in prosecuting gang murders, she knew that juries were not immune to community pressures. "We really were up against . . . a community perception that the justice system is not fair to the African American," Moore said.[36] She had shared the dismay of blacks when the killer of Latasha Harlins received probation. And she realized that most blacks regarded the thirty-month sentences given Koon and Powell as too lenient. The timing of these sentences just before jury selection had been devastating. "We had two or three African-American [prospective jurors] say to us, I thought I could be fair, I came in here wanting to be fair, but after that sentence, there is no way I can be fair," Moore said.[37]

Los Angeles police officers found it hard to be philosophical about the verdicts. As many officers saw it, they sent a message that Los Angeles juries were hard on cops and easy on criminals. The prevailing LAPD view was that Koon and Powell were doing time for doing their jobs while Watson walked and Williams faced only a few years in prison for his brutal crimes. Officers joked grimly that Powell would have been acquitted if he had used a brick instead of a baton on Rodney King.

The verdicts also reinforced reactionary attitudes among the LAPD rank and file. Some officers believe that the justice system too often gives blacks a break at the expense of others, particularly the police. The sentence in the Latasha Harlins case had ratified a widespread belief among African Americans that the justice system discriminated against them; the verdicts in the Denny case confirmed a mirror-image perception among the police.

Even officers who understood that the verdicts were more a product of fear than of prejudice were dismayed. "It drives me crazy when people compare the King beating to this," said Fred Ochoa, a twenty-seven-year-old juvenile gang officer at Van Nuys Station. "Most officers feel the same. In the King trial it could have been any officer in a situation trying to subdue someone. In the Denny trial we've arrested guys for similar stuff and gotten convictions. In King, the intent was to subdue, not kill. When you throw a rock at someone's head, it's got to enter your mind this might kill them." Ochoa thought that the verdicts in the Denny case signified a continuing "downward trend of respect for law enforcement, the justice system or any kind of authority."[38]

Damian Williams was a beneficiary of this trend. But his greater fortune was to be represented by the compassionate Faal, who sought to save him from a life of crime. Faal had five sisters and four brothers. By the time of the trial he had developed a familial feeling for Williams, whom he thought of "more like a younger brother than a client." Faal did not think his work was finished because he had helped save Williams from spending his life in prison. He made it a point to keep in touch with him and encourage him to read and study. "If I could guide him in any modest way to become a constructive member of society, that would be a big accomplishment for me," Faal said.[39]

Williams, who had older brothers but did not know the identity of his father, seems to have regarded Faal as the father figure of whom he was much in need. During interrogation after his arrest on May 12, 1992, Williams sobbed when asked about the assaults at Florence and Normandie. "I never seen my daddy," he said. "I bet if I had a father, I wouldn't be in this predicament that I'm in right now."[40]

After Williams was convicted, Faal urged him to take responsibility for his actions as the beginning of rehabilitation. He made some steps in this direction, even while leaning on the group contagion theory Faal had offered in his defense. "People were just out of control like a pack of rats running around after cheese," Williams told the *Wave* community newspapers. "I was just caught up in the rapture." But Williams acknowledged that this had not made it right. "What we did was wrong," he said. "It was unjustified, even though it was in the heat of the moment. Being in jail has caused me to mature a lot, and I see that."

The court was skeptical that Williams had seen the light. In an emotional hearing on December 7, 1993, Judge Ouderkirk said Williams' "statement of remorse did not ring true" and before passing sentence ordered the playing of the videotapes showing each of his attacks. This provided grist for the mill of activist Don Jackson, who complained afterward that "they didn't show Soon Ja Du shooting Latasha Harlins in the back of the head" when she was granted probation or the videotape of the King beating at the sentencing of Powell and Koon.

Ouderkirk, however, was determined to make it as clear as he could that the behavior of Williams was unacceptable. The judge recalled that Williams had done a "victory dance in the intersection" within a few feet of Mr. Denny's bloody body and concluded his remarks by saying, "Mr. Williams, it isn't tolerable in this society to attack and maim people because of their race." Ouderkirk then sentenced Williams to ten years in prison, the maximum possible. This sounded longer than it was, for with credit for his time in jail while awaiting trial, Williams would be eligible for release in three years and eight months.

The sentencing rekindled smoldering passions. Denise Harlins, who had kept alive the flame of memory for her niece Latasha, compared Ouderkirk's sentence of Williams to the probation that Judge Karlin gave Soon Ja Du after a jury convicted her of the Harlins killing. "This really kind of stones the heart," she said.[41] Carolyn Walters, who attended the sentencing, said she found Ouderkirk's sentence "a little harsh" and had hoped that he would add only two years to the time Williams had already served. Janet Moore responded that Walters had possessed "a hidden agenda from the very beginning" of the trial.[42]

The trial had been a victory for the defense, and no one knew this better than Williams, who smiled and raised his arms at his supporters as he left the courtroom. This enraged Garcetti, who was critical that the law would permit Williams to be released so soon. "Mr. Williams . . . will serve only about four years and will come out the same way you saw him," Garcetti said.[43]

Damian Williams stood virtually alone as a symbol of unwarranted racial violence to the majority of Angelenos and as a symbol of justified black rage to his supporters. The other criminal cases arising from the Florence-Normandie assaults didn't arouse nearly as much passion, and their disposition went almost unremarked. Henry Watson, who was sentenced the same day as Williams, did not serve any additional time. Prosecutors were realistic about the difficulty of convicting him of the Tarvin assault in another trial and had agreed to a plea bargain. Watson pleaded guilty to the felony of assaulting Tarvin with a deadly weapon (a charge on which Williams had been convicted of a misdemeanor) and admitted he had personally injured Tarvin. "I'd just like to apologize to Mr. Tarvin and Mr. Denny, Mr. Lopez and all the other victims that were there at the intersection on April 29, 1992," Watson said. He received four years' probation from Ouderkirk, who accepted as genuine Watson's declaration of remorse.

Antoine Miller, who had yanked opened the door of Denny's truck, also gained his freedom through a plea bargain. Three weeks after Williams and Watson were sentenced, he pleaded guilty to assault with a deadly weapon for throwing a metal-encased telephone book into the car driven by Marisa Bejar. The book had opened a gash on her head and showered her seven-month-old baby with glass from the car window. Miller also pleaded guilty to the misdemeanors of stealing a bag containing Denny's papers from his truck and receiving Alicia Maldonado's stolen purse. He had been released on bail after the trial of Williams and Watson after spending seventeen months in jail and was placed on probation.

Lance Jerome Parker, the last Denny defendant, insisted on a jury trial. It was held in May 1994, when the media spotlight had moved to other matters and community activists were no longer campaigning in court and on the streets. Free of the outside pressures that had influenced other riot-related trials, a racially diverse jury convicted Parker of the felony of firing a shotgun into Denny's truck and misdemeanor vandalism while acquitting him of two other charges and deadlocking on a fifth count. Defense attorney La Chelle Woodert delivered an emotional plea for mercy, and Superior Court Judge Florence-Marie Cooper put Parker on probation. The Reginald Denny case, as it was known, vanished into history.

BUT THE RODNEY KING CASE DID NOT. KING POPPED INTO THE news periodically, usually because of brushes with the law but also because of his protracted lawsuit to win civil damages. Then there was the government's effort to extend the sentences of Koon and Powell, who had begun serving their time in the Federal Prison Camp in Dublin, California. Two days after Judge Davies issued his sentencing report, outspoken Congresswoman Maxine Waters of Los Angeles launched a campaign for longer terms. She collected the signatures of the twenty-five members of the Congressional Black Caucus on an August 6 letter to Attorney General Janet Reno urging the Department of Justice to appeal.[44] Reno promised and delivered a high-level review.

Appeals of sentences are unusual except when the government has clear evidence of judicial impropriety. But the Clinton administration at the time had numerous differences with the Black Caucus, most notably on a pending crime bill, and was anxious to avoid additional conflicts with representatives of the Democratic Party's most loyal constituency. Considering the symbolic significance of the issue to blacks, appealing the sentences was an easy political call. But even without this pressure, the Justice Department had an interest in preserving federal sentencing guidelines because of the enormous leverage they provide to prosecutors. And Steven Clymer believed strongly that an appeal was justified on the merits and so recommended. The Justice Department quickly authorized an appeal.

It was heard by the Ninth Circuit, the westernmost division of the federal appellate court system, which simultaneously considered the appeals of the convictions. Powell and Koon were now represented by appellate specialists William Kopeny and Joel Levine, while Clymer and Irv Gornstein of the Justice Department's Civil Rights Division represented the government. The attorneys filed their briefs, replied to each other in another set of briefs, and argued their cases before a three-judge panel drawn randomly from the more than twenty judges on the Ninth Circuit. And once again, the luck of the draw was against the officers.

The three-judge panel was headed by Betty Binns Fletcher of Seattle, described by a fellow federal judge as "one of the true pioneers among women in our profession."[45] Fletcher, seventy-one years old when she wrote the court's decision in *U.S. v. Koon*, had been the first woman partner of her prestigious law firm, first woman president of her local bar association, and first woman board member of the Washington state bar association. Appointed to the Ninth Circuit Court in 1979 by President Carter, she quickly forged a reputation as a liberal, especially on civil rights and civil liberties issues. In 1982, Fletcher wrote a significant opinion restricting body searches to cases in which there is clear indication that a suspect has contraband concealed on his body. In 1992, she overturned the tax conviction of a man who refused to take the traditional oath in his tax-evasion trial.

Judges, no less than jurors, have opinions. Fletcher had shared the public revulsion at the beating of Rodney King and believed that a miscarriage of justice had occurred at Simi Valley. Her decision in *U.S. v. Koon* can be best understood if read as a document that expresses her feelings about the case as well as her legal assessment of the trial. The opinion was written by Fletcher and also signed by Judge James Browning, a 1961 appointee of President Kennedy, and Judge James Fitzgerald, a senior district judge from Alaska and 1974 appointee of President Ford who was temporarily serving on the court.

Fletcher's feelings were especially evident in her account of the "background" of the case. She seemed as unaware as a casual viewer of the television-edited clip of the Holliday videotape that Rodney King had charged toward Officer Powell before he was hit. "As the videotape begins, it shows that King got to his feet in an attempt to escape. Powell and Wind began to strike King with their batons," she wrote, as if Powell and Wind had set upon King as he tried to stroll away.

After describing the subduing of King in terms used by Davies in his sentencing report, Fletcher referred to the messages sent by Powell and Koon on their radios and in-car computers and emphasized the supposed taunting of King by Powell in Pacifica Hospital. The background statement devoted nearly as much space to these matters as to the beating itself. The alleged taunting, although a major issue in the state trial, was a minor aspect of the federal trial because the government had determined that a crucial witness to the conversation was unreliable and had not called him to testify. Fletcher nonetheless regarded the taunting as self-evident and significant.

The issue raised by Koon and Powell to which Fletcher gave most attention was the question of whether the videotape of Officer Briseno's state trial testimony should have been admitted in the federal trial. After observing that this testimony was "highly damaging to Koon and Powell," she accurately summarized its major points, then brushed aside defense contentions that Davies was wrong to have allowed the government to use the videotape during rebuttal. Fletcher accepted at face value the government's claim that it had not known whether Briseno would testify. For the government to have used the videotape during its case-in-chief could have been "unnecessarily duplicative," Fletcher wrote, as if this were of greater concern than whether it was fair to the defendants.

Fletcher also decided that the government's use of the Briseno videotape had not prevented defense attorneys from cross-examining Briseno. She found it sufficient that he had been cross-examined at the state trial and that portions of the cross-examination were shown to the federal jurors on videotape. The defense attorneys in the federal trial had objected that they had no chance to cross-examine Briseno about observations based on the FBI-enhanced videotape because this version of the tape did not exist at the time of the state trial. Fletcher was unimpressed. "The failure of a defendant to discover potentially useful evidence at the time of the former proceeding does not constitute a lack of opportunity to cross-examine," she wrote. Fletcher cited as her legal basis for this ruling the case of *Thomas v. Cardwell*, in which a prosecution witness from a first trial was unavailable at a second trial because he had been found to be schizophrenic.

After quoting from this case, Fletcher wrote:

> Much the same applies here. Appellants did not lack the opportunity to cross-examine Briseno; they lacked only some of the tools which were later developed by the government or by appellants themselves, and which appellants argue would have allowed them to cross-examine Briseno to better effect. Appellants' failure to take full advantage of their opportunity to cross-examine in the first trial—by developing those tools earlier—cannot alter the fact that they *had* the opportunity.

What "opportunity" could she have had in mind? Most of the "tools" to which Fletcher refers were created by the government with its extensive resources after the state trial and were beyond the technological capability of the defense. But even if the defense had been able at Simi Valley to develop the superenhanced video that the FBI produced for the federal trial, it would not have substantially changed the cross-examination unless Briseno also changed his mind on the basis of it—as he claimed to have done. While Fletcher did not have before her the record of the LAPD Board of Rights hearing or the civil trial in which Briseno related his changed opinion of the facts based on the enhanced videotape, the issue had been raised by Stone in the federal trial when he asked for exclusion of the videotape.

To conduct the kind of cross-examination that Fletcher claimed the defense had an opportunity to make at Simi Valley, the defense attorneys would have needed to know (a) that their clients would be tried again for the same conduct in federal court if acquitted, (b) that the FBI would develop a better videotape, and (c) that Briseno would see the videotape and change his testimony because of it. If all this had been known at Simi Valley, Briseno might not have testified and there would have been neither need nor opportunity to cross-examine him. And if Briseno had testified that he understood why Powell and Koon had viewed King as a threat, the entire dynamics of the cross-examination would have changed. To maintain, as Fletcher did, that attorneys for Koon and Powell in the federal trial had an "opportunity" to cross-examine Briseno about a perception he had formed on the basis of new evidence after the state trial is inaccurate and unfair.

Fletcher reviewed a series of other issues involving alleged errors in the trial, agreeing with the government position in every case. The defense briefs had weakly argued the issue of double jeopardy, and Fletcher swiftly decided (as most other judges would have) that the trial was permissible under the definition accepted by the Supreme Court. She carefully reviewed the court's refusal to allow peremptory challenges against the two black members of the jury, finding that Davies acted properly in each case. The defense briefs made a spirited argument that the man from Watts, Juror No. 263, should have been excused for cause because he said on his questionnaire that the Simi Valley verdicts were "unfair," then changed his mind about them during voir dire. Davies had refused to excuse him or to allow a peremptory challenge. Fletcher reviewed the arguments and decided that "the evidence points in both directions."

The legal question that seemed to bother Fletcher most was whether the government had inflamed the jury in its closing argument. Defense briefs had contended that Barry Kowalski acted improperly when he said that the videotape had caused "horror and outrage" throughout the world, "from Paris to Tokyo," because it had shown the officers beating a man who was on the ground. The government had dealt honestly with this issue on appeal, with Clymer conceding in his rebuttal brief and his oral argument before the court panel headed by Fletcher that this statement was improper.

Fletcher called the statement "troubling" and reprinted the paragraph from Kowalski's closing argument in full in her decision. She said it could have "easily incited the passions, fears, and prejudices of the jurors, remind them of the social ramifications of their verdict, and persuade them to convict the defendants for reasons irrelevant to appellants' guilt."

After saying this, however, Fletcher dismissed Kowalski's comments as unimportant. It was [she said] "a few sentences from a trial that lasted more than a month and from detailed closing arguments that lasted many hours" in a trial in which there was "substantial independent evidence" that the defendants were guilty. The defense had made a similar statement in attacking King's credibility. The court had admonished the jury to base its verdicts on the evidence (as if courts did not do so in every trial) and "to ignore what they knew about the first trial or what the possible ramifications of any verdict might be." And "finally, the verdicts acquitting two police officers and finding two guilty is indicative of the jury's ability to weigh the evidence without prejudice," she wrote. ". . . In light of these factors, we conclude that the jury's ability to weigh the evidence impartially was not materially affected by the prosecutor's improper remarks."

This determination adopted as fact assertions by the government that were at best a guess. Neither Fletcher nor the prosecutors knew why the jury had reached its decisions, and the U.S. attorney in Los Angeles made a policy of not finding out.* But it was naive of Fletcher to assume that the jury ignored "possible ramifications" of its verdicts because of court instructions that also served as a reminder of the possible destructive consequences of acquittals.

In dismissing the import of Kowalski's comments, Fletcher ignored the context in which the jury deliberated. Although she had no way of knowing that the jury foreman had scanned South Central from his hotel room to look for fires or that a bomb threat had panicked jurors en route to their hotel, Fletcher might have given weight to the probable emotional impact of the deadly Los Angeles riots. Ira Salzman had raised the point early in the trial when he sought a postponement because of a CBS poll showing that 75 percent of Los Angeles residents believed new riots were likely if the defendants were acquitted. Harland Braun had appealed to jurors in his closing argument not to be swayed by fears of a "riot in the city." Fletcher took no notice of these fears, and her contention that the acquittal of Wind and Briseno shows that jurors weighed the evidence without prejudice is a non sequitur. For all she (or anyone else) knew, the jury might have acquitted all the defendants if the trial had been conducted in a less fearful atmosphere. No one contended that jurors made a conscious decision to ignore the evidence and sacrifice Powell and Koon to appease the passions of the community. Rather, the defense concern about Kowalski's "Paris to Tokyo"

---

* Clymer told me that the policy in the U.S. Attorney's Office was not to talk to jurors after a trial in which there were convictions. But juror interviews would not have resolved the issue, since jurors insisted (as did jurors in the Denny trial) that fear of riots played no role in their verdicts. None of the jurors I interviewed mentioned the controversial remark by Kowalski, although most expressed awareness of the community outrage to which he referred. These interviews were conducted before the appellate court's ruling.

comments was that fears of new riots created a context in which a fair trial was impossible.

Still, it is unlikely that very many judges, no matter what their view of the case, would have set aside the convictions on any of the grounds raised in the appeal. "No trial is error-free," said Fletcher nearly two years later. "We look at the paper record to see if egregious errors have prevented a fair trial."[46] Her overall assessment of Davies' performance was in accord with Stacey Koon's. "He conducted the trial with impeccable fairness and careful and thoughtful attention to its every aspect," Fletcher wrote about Davies in upholding the convictions.

But Fletcher seemed to have had a judge other than Davies in mind when she reviewed his sentences. This may have been the arena in which Fletcher's opinion of the case most guided her. In most cases, defendants would be fortunate to have Fletcher review a sentence appealed by the government as too lenient. "I have felt that sentencing discretion and the guidelines that spawned them have moved too much discretion into the prosecutor's office and away from the judges who know most about the case," Fletcher told me.[47]

When Fletcher reviewed the sentences in *Koon*, however, she showed little tolerance for judicial discretion. Except for finding that Davies had acted appropriately in refusing to impose an additional sentence because of the extent of King's injuries, Fletcher agreed with the government on every point. She disallowed the sentencing reduction made by Davies because of King's contribution to the incident and a further reduction for a combination of factors that included the susceptibility of police officers to prison abuse, the fact that Koon and Powell were unlikely to commit other crimes, and the "spectre of unfairness" raised by the second prosecution. Fletcher also found that the "personal and professional consequences" suffered by Koon and Powell because of their convictions could not be considered as a basis for sentence reduction. Davies was told to resentence the officers to longer terms. ". . . The sentences imposed by the district court are inconsistent with the structure and policies of the sentencing guidelines and the federal sentencing statutes," Fletcher wrote in her decision for the three-judge panel.

This decision was taken stoically by Koon and hard by Powell. "He's shaky and upset," said Michael Stone after talking to his client. African-American leaders hailed the ruling, as did Edi Faal and Rodney King's lawyer, Steven Lerman. Daryl Gates called the rejection of Davies' sentences "disgusting" and said the officers had been "put through absolute hell" without taking note of his own contribution to the process. "I'm sort of knocked over," said Harland Braun, who said the decision was "neither intellectually courageous nor politically astute."[48]

Fletcher's decision also disappointed Judge Stephen Reinhardt, the best-known liberal on the Ninth Circuit. Reinhardt, too, was a Carter appointee and a fierce critic of the sentencing guidelines. A Democratic activist and ranking member of the Los Angeles Police Commission that had selected Gates as chief, Reinhardt took complaints about police misconduct seriously and had helped modify the LAPD's shooting policy. Gates viewed him as the department's bete noire.

But in another of the ironies of the Rodney King affair, Reinhardt emerged as a defender of Davies' sentences. This was a tribute to the consistency of Reinhardt's liberalism. He believed that federal penalties for many crimes were too harsh and were made harsher still by the rigid sentencing guidelines. "I tend to be sympathetic with any judge who departs downward on sentencing because the defendant is having some problem," Reinhardt said. "The sentences are so severe for almost every crime that they tend to be long even with downward departures."[49]

Reinhardt knew that everyone is influenced by his life's experiences. His experience on the Police Commission had made him aware of incidents where suspects were shot or beaten with much less provocation than Rodney King had presented. While Reinhardt believed Powell had acted brutally, he knew that the King case was not the "aberration" that Gates claimed it to be. The officers involved, said Reinhardt, "had the bad luck to be caught on videotape, but they weren't rogue cops."[50]

In addition to favoring judicial discretion, Reinhardt was convinced that the sentences meted out to Koon and Powell were appropriate. "I thought the punishment meted out by Davies was quite severe," Reinhardt said. "Putting a cop in prison for three years is different than just putting anyone in prison for three years."[51]

Reinhardt tried to prod the full court into reviewing the decision of the Fletcher panel. He needed the votes of a majority of active judges on a court where there were several vacancies and one judge who had recused himself. He lost by either one or two votes, with the precise tally kept secret under court rules. Reinhardt then sought a review of the decision by the Supreme Court, writing a stinging dissent that took issue with virtually every sentencing conclusion of Judge Fletcher.

"In stretching to reach its result, the panel casts aside the basic principles that should underlie judicial sentencing, even in the age of the guidelines," Reinhardt wrote. "It is only by exalting the rigid calculations of charts and tables over the judgment of human beings that the panel reaches its conclusion that Judge Davies was too lenient." Without naming Fletcher he criticized her by saying that the opinion endorsed "the mechanical and inflexible approach to sentencing" she had often decried. He criticized the full court for passing up a chance to clarify prior rulings and give trial judges "clear guidance" on sentencing.*

Reinhardt's dissent suggested that Fletcher's sentencing opinion was swayed by her feelings about the case. The panel's rejection of the sentencing reduction, he wrote, "is dictated less by the language or spirit of the guidelines than by hostility to Judge Davies' decision to depart." When asked about this comment nearly two years later, Reinhardt said of Fletcher, "I think her views of the sentence clearly were influenced by her views of the case."[52] But he added that this was not peculiar to Fletcher. Reinhardt's dissent was signed by eight other judges, some of them conservatives who rarely approved of sentencing reduction. When it came to sentencing, the King case cut across the usual ideological lines.[53]

Fletcher's opinion and Reinhardt's dissent stoked the embers of the fires ignited by the Rodney King incident. Her ruling was another blow to the morale of the LAPD, where officers were disgusted that King had been awarded millions of dollars in damages while Koon and Powell were serving time. Forcing a judge to add to their prison sentences seemed monstrous to rank-and-file officers, and they showed their feelings by making fewer arrests. But the larger impact of the opinion and the dissent was that they prodded the Supreme Court into reviewing the sentencing aspect of Fletcher's opinion. More was at stake in this review than the freedom of Koon and Powell. As Ira Salzman put it, "What this case is about is whether judges can look at people as individuals or whether they have to look at them as numbers."[54]

Although black leaders applauded Fletcher's decision that Koon and Powell should serve longer terms, African-American defendants stood to benefit most from relaxing the Draconian federal sentencing guidelines. The number of blacks in prison in the United States is vastly disproportionate to the black population and is growing at a rapid rate. Much of the increase is due to federal laws that impose longer sentences for possession of a small amount of crack cocaine, the drug of choice in black communities, than for possession of the same amount of powdered cocaine, which is preferred by white drug users.

As Fletcher observed, the severe sentencing guidelines have strengthened the power of federal prosecutors who decide whether a case shall be charged under federal statutes or under state laws which are usually more lenient. The

---

* Reinhart said the Fletcher panel had examined the factors used by Davies in sentence reduction out of context, and decided they were not "appropriate" without determining if the guidelines prohibited them. He said this enhanced the rigidity of the sentencing process by creating a new category of "inappropriate" factors. Reinhardt was particularly critical of Fletcher's rejection of the vulnerability of Powell and Koon to prison abuse as a factor in sentencing.

year before the Rodney King case, every white accused of cocaine possession in Los Angeles was charged in state court. Every defendant in federal court charged with crack cocaine possession was black. With few exceptions, this continues to be the pattern. Some federal judges in Los Angeles have objected to the sentences they are required to impose in relatively minor drug cases, but their hands have been tied by a combination of mandatory minimum sentences and the sentencing guidelines.

The irony that blacks would benefit the most from a broad-gauged Supreme Court decision that used *U.S. v. Koon* to restore a measure of sentencing discretion was not lost on Stacey Koon. While he had accepted imprisonment and career loss with remarkable equanimity, it always bothered him if someone accused him of racism or said that King had been beaten because he was black. Koon was delighted when it was suggested to him that black criminal defendants could be the principal beneficiaries of his sentencing appeal. "That's fine with me," he said.[55]

19

BACK TO THE FUTURE

"He's tough enough to turn L.A. around."

—Richard Riordan 1993 campaign slogan

"I am not a liar."

—Police Chief Willie Williams[1]

A S THE CRIMINAL AND CIVIL CASES SPAWNED BY THE RODNEY King
incident dragged on through the courts, change came slowly to Los Angeles. The 1992 riots had discredited high-profile officials, speeding the retirement of Chief Daryl Gates and Mayor Tom Bradley and prompting
District Attorney Ira Reiner to drop his reelection campaign. By the summer of 1993, when Willie Williams had been police chief for a year, Los Angeles had a new mayor and Los Angeles County a new district attorney.
Despite the turnover, however, municipal politics remained democratic in
form but exclusionary in substance, with the city's largest ethnic group and
third largest racial group isolated from its political life.

During Bradley's twenty years as mayor, Los Angeles had advanced from
the era when it was ruled by an oligarchy and celebrated by its boosters as
the "white spot" of America. African Americans had obtained access to
power and developed a sophisticated political leadership. Homeowner asso-
ciations and other voluntary groups had learned to lobby and otherwise influence the city council. Now boosters celebrated the diversity reflected in
the 1990 census, which found that 40 percent of the city's population was
Latino, 37 percent Anglo (non-Hispanic white), 13 percent African American and 9 percent Asian. Since the census, the proportions of Latinos and
Asians have steadily increased, while the proportions of Anglos and African
Americans have declined.

But the political demography of Los Angeles in the early 1990s sharply
conflicted with the census. Anglos held most elected offices and African
Americans a higher proportion of offices than their percentage of the

population. Latinos were vastly under-represented in the government and Asians barely represented at all. Indeed, Los Angeles was two cities. One city, overwhelmingly Latino and increasingly Asian, provided the huge, dependable workforce required by small businesses, service industries, and an expanding garment industry. But few Latinos or Asians voted, and most were cut off from political life by language and cultural barriers or by lack of citizenship, information, or interest.

The other city was the electorate, two-thirds white and with a median age much older than the population. This city resisted spending tax revenues on a school system in which so many students came from homes where Spanish was the first language—even though most of these children learned to speak English proficiently. The electorate wanted more police but resisted raising taxes to pay for them, a principal reason that Los Angeles had so few police officers in relation to its population. "The people don't vote who need the services, and the people who vote decide what little services they shall have," observed political analyst Sherry Bebitch Jeffe.[2]

One cause of the subordination of Latinos and Asians in the city's politics was that many of them were newcomers, even though Southern California had been settled by Spaniards and Mexicans, and Asians have lived in the region for more than a century. The Latino population nearly doubled between 1970 and 1980 and increased by 50 percent more from 1980 to 1990, when the census counted 1,400,000 Latinos in the city of Los Angeles and 3,350,000 in Los Angeles County. The Asian population increased similarly from a smaller base to 321,000 in the city and 925,000 in the county. But an estimated 40 percent of Latino adults and more than half the Asians were not citizens, and a disproportionate number of Latino and Asian newcomers were too young to vote.

Latinos were also excluded from power by deliberate decisions of the whites in power. Los Angeles is home to more people of Mexican descent than any city in the world except Mexico City, yet after the pioneering Edward Roybal left for Congress in 1962 no Latino served on the fifteen-member Los Angeles City Council until Richard Alatorre was elected in 1985. The following year the Justice Department used the Voting Rights Act, which had been amended in 1975 to include "persons of Spanish heritage" and Asians as well as blacks, to challenge the 1981 redistricting of the city council as biased against Latinos. The federal lawsuit produced a redistricting, and Gloria Molina was elected to the city council in 1987.

The Justice Department next assaulted an Anglo redoubt on which no Latino had served since 1875—the Los Angeles County Board of Supervisors, which controls a budget of $12 billion and serves a population of 9 million. Roybal had run for supervisor in 1958 and lost to an Anglo rival by 393 votes after four recounts and some mysterious vote shifting.

Working with the Mexican American Legal Defense and Education Fund (MALDEF), the Justice Department in 1987 filed a lawsuit to secure Latino representation on this board.[3] A federal judge found that Latino voters had deliberately been dispersed among several districts to prevent them from electing a Latino and ordered a redistricting. The adept demographer Leo Estrada was commissioned to draw boundaries for a new district so far-flung that it embraced every contiguous census tract in the county with a Latino majority, concentrating Latinos instead of dispersing them. The hard-driving Molina mobilized grass-roots support, defeated a male Latino in a runoff election, and dedicated her triumph to Roybal. "This victory should have been celebrated thirty years ago," she said.[4]

But the election that gave Latinos an overdue voice on the Board of Supervisors also advertised their political weakness. Barely 88,000 of the 1,800,000 residents in the new district voted, a turnout of only 5 percent. The election confirmed that Latinos were a political force only when they were an overwhelming majority. Well aware of this, Molina declined to run for mayor.

On its face, the 1993 Los Angeles mayoral election was an advertisement of diversity, with twenty-four candidates of varied racial and ethnic backgrounds competing in the first round of voting on April 20. But few had the money to wage a citywide campaign and none came close to matching the resources of Richard Riordan, a white Republican entrepreneurial lawyer who was one of the wealthiest men in Los Angeles. Riordan, seeking elective office for the first time and known to only 3 percent of the electorate when the campaign began, obtained 33 percent of the vote. He faced City Councilman Michael Woo, who finished second with 24 percent, in a June 8 runoff. The leading Latino candidate in the first-round election ran fifth, with only 7 percent of the vote, and the two top African-American candidates finished sixth and seventh, amassing 8 percent of the vote between them.

A sophisticated exit-poll analysis by the *Los Angeles Times* dispelled the illusion of diversity. Riordan had received 45 percent of the votes of Anglos, who comprised two-thirds of the electorate. He won only 4 percent of the votes of blacks (18 percent of the voters), ran a distant second to Woo among Latinos, and finished an even more distant second among Asians. Although together they accounted for half the population, Latinos made up only 8 percent and Asians just 4 percent of the voters.

Riordan, then sixty-three years old, did best among high-income white males over fifty. This was an enormous advantage, for fully half of all voters in the April election were over fifty and half of these were over sixty-five. Nearly 60 percent of the voters had annual incomes of more than $40,000 and more than 33 percent made more than $60,000. As John Brennan, then director of the *Los Angeles Times* Poll saw it, this electorate was a "voter aris-tocracy" that was "dangerous" to democracy.[5]

Nonetheless, the voters had produced a runoff between candidates of con-trasting visions who seemed fairly evenly matched. Woo was a Democrat in a city in which Democrats held a 2–1 registration edge. Although municipal elections are non-partisan, no Republican had been elected mayor since 1957. While Woo received only 13 percent of the dominant Anglo vote in the April election, a majority of the Anglos were Democrats who had previously voted for Bradley.

Woo, the first Chinese-American member of the Los Angeles city coun-cil and its only Asian, shared with Riordan the advantages of family wealth. He had been educated as an urban planner at the University of California at Santa Cruz, where he became politically active in opposition to the Vietnam War, and was elected to the city council in 1985 at the age of thirty-two. An unabashed liberal, Woo was the first council member to call for the resigna-tion of Chief Gates after the Rodney King incident. He saw himself as heir ap-parent to the leadership of Tom Bradley's political coalition.

The coalition Woo sought to lead had been built on the votes of blacks, Jews, and white liberal Democrats and the financial support of downtown business interests which shared the profits and dreams of Bradley's world city. But the loose ties that bound this coalition had been frayed by recession and demographic change, then severed by the racial conflicts of 1992. By 1993, with the rebuilding of South Central stalled and tourism rebounding slowly, business leaders had become disconsolate. As they saw it, Los Angeles was governed by a deadweight bureaucracy in which cumbersome procedures, reg-ulations, and fees discouraged growth. Obtaining even a simple building per-mit became such a protracted adventure that some businesses gave up and moved out. Riordan's promise to turn around a city that was neither safe nor efficient struck a responsive chord.

As for the rest of the coalition, Woo could count with certainty only on African Americans, who loyally backed any Democrat against any Repub-lican. But black voting strength in Los Angeles had declined as middle-class African Americans fled South Central for communities with less crime, better schools, and affordable homes. The black population increased by more than 50 percent in sixty Los Angeles County communities between 1980 and 1990 but declined 17 percent in South Central.

Jews, who vote in high numbers and more consistently for Democrats than any group except blacks, were targets of the Woo and Riordan campaigns in the runoff. Woo needed Jewish support to offset Riordan's advantage among Anglo conservatives, especially in the San Fernando Valley. But many Jews were critical of the city's response to the riots and unenthusiastic about any alliance with African Americans.

The runoff went unheeded in voter-scarce Westlake and Pico-Union, where the population density was 50,000 a square mile, the highest in Los Angeles. These squalid midcity neighborhoods were home to recent immigrants from Central America who lived in high-rise buildings in which several families were jammed together in tiny rental apartments in violation of city codes. On May 3, an arson-caused fire in a Westlake apartment building killed ten people and injured forty, most of them mothers and young children. The building had been the scene of two previous arson incidents that had revealed defective smoke detectors and other violations of city ordinances. Firefighters said the landlords should have been cited after these incidents but that bureaucratic delays had blocked action. When a reporter asked how this could have happened, Fire Department Battalion Chief Dean Cathey responded, "That is not an acceptable answer, but that's life in Los Angeles."[6]

The tragedy caused not a ripple in the runoff campaign. Violation of fire codes almost certainly would have become an issue if those affected by this lawlessness had been eligible to vote. But city government winked at such violations, while businessmen profited from the cheap labor supplied by the ill-housed immigrants. Woo identified with government and Riordan with business. Although both candidates deplored the loss of life, neither engaged an issue that to this day remains a neglected scandal of Los Angeles.

The issue that preoccupied voters and the mayoral candidates was not fire safety but police protection. Los Angeles voters fear crime, and their fears were fed by local television, which ignored government and politics and featured "action news" of murders, catastrophes, or police chases. In 1993, Angelenos also worried about the possibility of another civil disorder. At the time of the runoff, Stacey Koon and Laurence Powell were awaiting sentencing, and Damian Williams had yet to be tried. Fear was a factor in the election, as in the jury deliberations in these trials.

For white voters the avuncular Riordan was more reassuring than the boyish-looking Woo. Riordan's message was also more reassuring. Woo said he would heal racial discord and bring Los Angeles together. Riordan said he was "tough enough to turn L.A. around." He promised to add 3,000 new officers to the 7,700-member police force within four years. It was an effective theme, for the riots had made a persuasive case that the thin blue line was much too thin.

Wanting more police officers was one thing, however, and paying for them another. Gates often lamented that politicians were too "cheap" to pay for the police they said the city needed. Riordan was no exception. His promise would have been extravagant in prosperous times, and Los Angeles in 1993 was suffering its worst economic downturn since the Depression. Although there was no money in the municipal coffers to pay for a significant police department expansion, Riordan promised to accomplish it without raising taxes.

Riordan's smoke-and-mirrors approach was encouraged by Proposition 13, which requires a two-thirds vote to raise taxes. Even in November 1992, when riot memories were fresh, the city ballot measure known as Proposition N, which would have modestly raised property taxes to hire 1,000 new police officers failed to win a two-thirds margin. It was put back on the April 1993 ballot as Proposition 1. Belatedly its supporters realized that trying to meet the two-thirds requirement was a waste of time and money. Without any organized campaign on its behalf, the measure nonetheless won 59 percent of the vote.

John Brennan's exit polling on Proposition 1 revealed the contradictory attitudes of the Los Angeles electorate. Conservative Anglos who tended to be most outspoken about the need for more police were least willing to raise taxes to pay for them. But the measure was favored by 70 percent of Jews and 68 percent of blacks. Although African-American political leaders often described the LAPD as an army of occupation in South Central, ordinary blacks wanted more police soldiers on the streets.*

The defeat of Proposition 1 hurt Woo, who had pinned his hopes for LAPD expansion on voter approval of a tax increase. He was also damaged because he was part of a city government that was unpopular after the riots. Riordan won the runoff by eight percentage points in an election that ratified the Anglo political domination of Los Angeles. Non-Hispanic whites comprised 72 percent of the electorate, an even larger proportion than in the April election, when African-American and Latino candidates were in the running. Two of three Anglo voters voted for Riordan in the runoff. Woo was favored by 94 percent of blacks, nearly 70 percent of Asians and 57 percent of Latinos.[7] Had Latinos and Asians voted in proportion to their numbers, Woo would have won.

As the city's first venture-capitalist mayor, Riordan was a variant of a recurrent political type: the businessman who promises to rescue government through good management. Riordan was a variant because he was also an intellectual with a library of more than 40,000 books. And although he did not seem to realize it, he was also a variant of a recognizable Los Angeles type: the reformer who seeks to resolve social conflicts by process. In espousing nonpartisan managerial principles of "good government," he followed in the footsteps of the Progressives who had sought to remake Los Angeles early in the century.

---

* The support of South Central for Proposition 1 reflected the dependence of its residents on the police. Well-off whites in more prosperous areas could protect their homes with private security services, which became a booming business in Los Angeles after the riots.

The Progressives were Protestants in a white Protestant city with a small-town flavor. Riordan is a Roman Catholic in a vibrant multi-ethnic metropolis in which the largest immigrant groups are also Catholic. He had close ties to Cardinal Roger Mahony, the city's most influential white cleric and a leader of the church's progressive wing. He developed relationships with Latino community leaders and maintained a strong alliance with Councilman Alatorre, the city's most influential Latino politician, who had backed Riordan in the mayoral runoff. While sometimes naive, Riordan was no yahoo. He realized he was an anomaly as a white mayor of a rainbow city and told me frankly that he was probably a transitional figure who would be succeeded by a woman or a Latino.[8]

Born May 1, 1930, in Flushing, New York, Richard Joseph Riordan was the youngest of eight children. He was raised in affluent surroundings in New Rochelle, New York, and attended Jesuit schools and Santa Clara University before transferring to Princeton, where he earned a degree in philosophy and was attracted to the teachings of Jacques Maritain, an influential French Catholic philosopher who encouraged an awareness of personal responsibility to the community that he called "true humanism." Riordan then attended University of Michigan Law School, graduating first in the class of 1956. He was recruited by O'Melveny and Myers, the prestigious Los Angeles law firm in which Warren Christopher was then a young lawyer on the fast track.

Riordan had a Midas touch. He became an expert in stock market and tax law and a multimillionaire through investment in high-tech firms and mastery of leveraged buyouts. He parlayed an $80,000 inheritance from his businessman father into a $100-million fortune, $6 million of which he spent to become elected mayor. In 1975, he founded his own law firm, which specialized in restructuring financially troubled businesses. Riordan's most noted success was the rescue of debt-ridden Mattel Toys, which had closed a Los Angeles factory with 250 employees and moved its manufacturing operation to Mexico.

But Riordan's life was also tragedy ridden. He lost a five-year-old sister to a brain tumor, a thirty-five-year-old sister to a fire, and a forty-one-year-old brother to a mudslide. His only son drowned while diving in the ocean. One of his four daughters died of bulimia. Riordan's first marriage ended in an annulment after twenty-three years, and his second in separation. At the time of his election he lived in a $6-million French colonial mansion in Brentwood that the Los Angeles Times found "bears the marks of a somewhat distracted owner," including droppings on the floor deposited by Riordan's three Yorkshire terriers.[9]

Riordan's friends knew him as a soft touch who rarely kept his wallet in his pocket when confronted with a hard-luck story. He donated $3 million a year to charities, focusing on those that benefited children. "He couldn't save his own, so he is trying to save all the rest," wrote Faye Fiore.[10] Riordan gave "Read to Write" computer laboratories to thousands of schools across the country. In East Los Angeles, he financed purchase of the La Puente Learning Center, which teaches English to Latinos, and gave the center $1.5 million and 27 computers. Friend and campaign manager William Wardlaw, also wealthy, said this generosity partly reflected "Irish guilt or Catholic guilt," and Riordan did not dispute him. But more than guilt was involved. "It's obvious that it is wrong in society to have young children who are doomed to a life of poverty and disaster when I can do something about it," Riordan said.[11]

As mayor, Riordan drew a dollar-a-year salary and struggled to adapt his gadfly style to government. He was a quick study—perhaps too quick—and impatient with the glacial maneuverings of an entrenched bureaucracy. Jean Merl wrote that Riordan appeared "uncomfortable with the demands of democracy and the cumbersome give-and-take it requires." He was particularly uncomfortable with a parochial city council that was skeptical of his political abilities. Riordan compared dealing with the council "to climbing the last five hundred feet of Mount Everest."[12] He preferred dealing with the public but resented the time it required. "I was hoping I could spend most of my time as a problem solver, and I found that I have to spend about half my time getting out to the public, being a popular figure," he said.[13]

But Riordan knew what he believed and was determined to make an impact. Sherry Bebitch Jeffe found him "an odd combination of Ronald Reagan and Bill Clinton." Like Reagan he was a "big picture" optimist who was "at ease with himself and his values" and enunciated broad policy goals whose implementation was left to subordinates. But Riordan had Clinton's proclivity for becoming "sidetracked by damage control" and personnel issues. He was also a Clinton-style centrist. In 1994, Riordan endorsed Senator Dianne Feinstein, a respected Democrat who had been responsive to the city's needs, against Republican Michael Huffington, a multimillionaire oil scion in a rush for high office. The mayor's apostasy disgusted conservative delegates to the 1994 California Republican convention who wore buttons describing Riordan as RINO, short for "Republican in Name Only."

Riordan's pragmatism, however, failed to land Los Angeles an anticipated award from the Clinton administration that would have designated the city a "federal empowerment zone" and would have provided $600 million in social-service grants and tax breaks for poor neighborhoods, including many in South Central. Because the program had been created in response to the 1992 riots, city officials assumed their application would be accepted. But federal officials found the application vague and unfocused and rejected it in December 1994. Riordan was furious. He claimed the guidelines were rigged to favor Eastern cities and refused to take a mollifying call from Clinton.

By this time, "empowerment" had become a central Riordan theme. He defined the word for Jeffe as "giving people the power to make decisions, the power to make mistakes and the power to correct mistakes—all with confidence." Riordan tried to correct his own mistakes. Putting aside his anger at the empowerment zone rejection, he plunged into negotiations with the Clinton administration and obtained a secondary award of more than $400 million in tax grants and loan guarantees, which he used to start a Community Development Bank to finance projects in poor neighborhoods.

Political leaders are often defined by crisis. Riordan's defining moment occurred at 4:31 A.M. on January 17, 1994, when he and millions of other Southern Californians were shaken awake by the Northridge earthquake. This devastating temblor (6.7 magnitude on the Richter scale) claimed seventy-two lives, eighteen more than the 1992 riots, and inflicted $25 billion in property damage. The Santa Monica Freeway, the world's busiest, was severed for months, tangling traffic on the city's nearby streets. The earthquake largely spared South Central, which had borne the brunt of the riots. It was most destructive in the San Fernando Valley, where sixteen people were killed in the collapse of a single apartment building. Riordan visited scenes of destruction and vowed that the city would rebuild. "I think people care about L.A., and they're not going to give up on it," he said on radio the day after the quake. "I believe in making decisions. It's easier to get forgiveness later than to get permission now."[14]

Make decisions Riordan did. With a steady hand and resonant voice he pushed government and business to assist victims and put the city back on its feet. The Los Angeles Emergency Operations Board, dysfunctional during the riots, became recovery central. Police Chief Williams presided over the meetings with Riordan at his side.* Their cooperation prompted Bill Boyarsky in his popular column in the Los Angeles Times to contrast the Riordan-Williams performance with the way Bradley and Gates, "two burned-out feuding men," had neglected the board during the riots. "Running meetings, cheering up the homeless, talking to President Clinton, working with Gov. Pete Wilson, snapping out orders, persuading enemies to sit down together, Riordan has given Los Angeles far more energetic and

---

* What wasn't publicly known at the time was that Riordan, who had arrived at the Emergency Operations Center before 5:30 A.M., was exasperated at Williams, who didn't show up until six hours later. Despite the entreaties of the mayor and members of the LAPD command, Williams spent most of the morning at home. "Williams' excuse was that his wife was upset and he didn't want to leave her alone—not thinking of the hundreds of officers who had left their frightened families and damaged houses to get to work," wrote Diane K. Shah in the July 1997 issue of Los Angeles Magazine.

aggressive leadership than we had during the bleak and confusing days of the 1992 riots," Boyarsky wrote.[15]

Still, the mayor's budget—nearly $4 billion by 1996—reflected the priorities of the business community and the well-off Anglos who were his core constituents rather than the concerns of the non-voting majority. Riordan's backers wanted a more streamlined government, and the mayor tried to oblige by cutting business taxes and reducing the payrolls of agencies except the police department. Constrained by a "weak mayor" system that Bradley had used as an excuse for inaction, Riordan campaigned for city-charter amendments to give him power to hire and fire managers of departments who had long operated with virtual autonomy. With editorial backing from the Los Angeles Times, the charter amendments passed in the 1995 municipal elections with 62 percent of the vote.

But Los Angeles remained two cities, and Riordan, for all his generosity and charisma, rarely connected with the second. He was distanced from newer Latino and Asian immigrants, who did not vote, and distanced even further from African Americans, who did. Blacks held three of the fifteen Los Angeles City Council seats, representing districts in which Latinos were a majority or plurality of the population. African-American members of the council disdainfully viewed Riordan (in Councilman Nate Holden's words) as a "white aristocrat" who did not understand the problems of the poor.

Riordan disputed the accuracy of Holden's perception but on occasion reinforced it. Before the opening of the Century Freeway, he visited El Santa Niño, a Catholic Charities center, and invited excited youngsters to bring their bicycles to the freeway and join him in a celebratory ride. Councilwoman Rita Walters, an African American, overheard the conversation and told Riordan that the children's parents were too poor to afford bikes. On his car phone riding back to City Hall, Riordan obtained a donation of twenty-six rebuilt bicycles, helmets, and a training course for the center. When he later discovered that more bicycles were needed, he paid for them out of his own pocket. Walters acknowledged that Riordan came through for the children but criticized his "noblesse oblige attitude." Riordan was frustrated by this criticism. "Let no good deed go unpunished," he said.[16]

African-American politicians were frustrated, too, in ways Riordan did not understand. During the twenty years of Bradley's reign they had enjoyed easy access to City Hall, and even black politicians who had criticized Bradley during his declining years as mayor remembered him nostalgically. Riordan was judged by the standards of this sentimental memory as well as by his performance, a comparison he had no hope of winning. Less than a year after Riordan's election, Councilman Mark Ridley-Thomas said that

Bradley had done more for South Central on his worst day than Riordan would do on his best.[17] Riordan assumed that all such statements were politically motivated. He never realized that much of what the black council members said about him had less to do with his actions than with the fact that they genuinely missed Tom Bradley.

FEW AFRICAN AMERICANS AT ANY LEVEL MISSED DARYL GATES. Most black politicians had clamored for Gates' removal after the King beating and the Christopher Commission report. Now, with Willie Williams at the LAPD helm, blacks who felt frozen out of City Hall found a welcome mat at Parker Center. Williams had a strong base in the African-American community and meant to build on it. He realized that in time this base might help him hold his job.

But it was not the support of blacks alone that Williams courted. He saw his mission as restoring public confidence in the LAPD and plunged into this task with verve and conviction. He promised a revitalized department that would emphasize community policing and implement the recommendations of the Christopher Commission. He attended hundreds of meetings with an array of community, religious, homeowner, and business groups of every racial and ethnic background. He won support from the gay community by changing an objectionable question on the LAPD application form. He called upon the Crips and the Bloods to extend their truce to the innocent people who were their victims.

In his role as LAPD ambassador, Williams was a huge success. Gates had received an 81 percent disapproval rating in a *Los Angeles Times* poll taken after the riots. Williams received a 52 percent approval rating in October 1992, when many people were still withholding judgment. By February 1993, his approval rating had soared to 67 percent. It continued to climb, peaking at 73 percent in June 1994. In person and on television, Williams came across as stolid and reassuring to a city weary of police controversy and racial conflict. Public confidence in the LAPD rose in tandem with the chief's approval ratings, although a bit more slowly.

The LAPD deals with the voteless majority of Latinos and Asians as often as it does with the electorate. Williams was popular in this second city, too. A survey by Sergio Bendixen for Spanish-language television station KVEA and *La Opinion* on the first anniversary of the riots showed that Williams had nearly as much support from Latinos as from blacks, which had never been true for Mayor Bradley. The survey measured attitudes of African Americans in South Central, most of whom were registered voters, and Latinos in Pico-Union, most of whom were ineligible to vote. Slightly more than two-thirds of each group approved of Williams and, by lesser majorities, of the LAPD.*

Williams was impressed with the public response—too much so, critics later said. Soon after he became chief, he took his wife, Evelina, to a restaurant for dinner and was surprised when other diners stood and applauded. But Williams soon learned that it was not easy to translate his popularity into support from the city council for the LAPD's neglected material needs.

The new chief had been appalled at the dilapidated condition of LAPD equipment and had campaigned vigorously for the new communications system that voters approved in November 1992. But he was discouraged that a companion initiative to raise taxes to pay for police expansion failed to win the required two-thirds vote and then lost again the following April. As Williams saw it, Los Angeles was close to the bare minimum of police resources. "Think about the supermarket," Williams said early in 1993. "You've got the Grade-A supermarket. Then you've got the supermarket where everything's in boxes with generic labels." The LAPD was a cut below even this no-frills market. "We're not able to do generic, cardboard-box policing anymore because of the [lack of] resources," Williams said.[18]

Williams' frame of reference was Philadelphia, which proportionally spends much more on its police department. The LAPD had been starved for two decades by declining revenues, the restrictions on taxation imposed by Proposition 13, and Bradley's stinginess toward a department that had demeaned him and supported his political opponents.[19] This dubious legacy weighed heavily on Williams. His task was made more difficult by his commitment to community policing, which requires extra personnel.

And Williams made things difficult for himself by refusing to rely on members of the LAPD high command who could have helped him. The best of these was Assistant Chief Bernard C. Parks, an African American and hard-boiled officer of the old school who had risen through the ranks and been a candidate for chief of police when Williams was selected. Although Williams appointed Parks his top assistant and put him in charge of LAPD operations, he never really trusted him. Parks found the new chief impervious to advice, and Williams came to believe that Parks was trying to undermine him. When Mayor Riordan pressed Williams for improvements in LAPD managerial procedures, the chief made Parks the scapegoat. Riordan wanted action, not excuses, and told Williams that he should make changes

---

* Blacks approved of the LAPD by a 54–32 percent margin and Latinos by a 64–25 percent margin, with the balance undecided. But there was a significant difference in attitude within these groups among those who had a negative view of the LAPD. The principal complaint among African Americans with a negative view was that the LAPD harrassed minorities or was racist. More than half the Latino critics of the LAPD said the police were not doing enough to reduce crime or responded too slowly to emergency calls.

in his team if he was dissatisfied with its performance. On September 12, 1994, in an ill-advised shakeup, Williams demoted Parks to deputy chief, making an enduring foe of one of the LAPD's most respected police officers.

Williams' demotion of Parks demonstrated that his recognition of the LAPD's material deficiencies was not matched by understanding of its human needs. As an outsider in a department that trusted insiders, Williams needed to cultivate the loyalty of the men and women under his command as urgently as he needed public approval. Even skeptical old-timers recognized that Gates had stayed too long, and many of them realized that Williams was likely to be more successful than his predecessor at obtaining the patrol cars and equipment that the department sorely needed. But dispirited Los Angeles cops wanted more than new cars. They hungered for leadership and were prepared to rally behind a chief, even an outsider, who made it a top priority to restore the pride and elan of the once-great LAPD.

Williams did not provide this leadership. Nor did he recognize that his every move and utterance was receiving attention from a gossipy department that soon decided it didn't like what it saw and heard. Part of Williams' problem was his physical appearance. Gates had kept himself trim and athletic. He looked like a police chief—or at least the way LAPD officers thought a chief should look. Williams was so portly that he kept his weight a secret and could not fit into a regular LAPD uniform. Worse, he flunked the Peace Officers Standards and Training (POST) test, required of all California peace officers, and was able to carry a service revolver only because the Police Commission issued him a special permit.

When some of the chief's supporters gently suggested that he could improve his image by reducing, Williams agreed. He also promised to pass the POST test and learn Spanish, the second language of Los Angeles. But he lost only a few pounds and learned only a few words. And he never passed the POST test, which a change in California law spared him from having to retake. He never made the rank and file feel proud that he was their chief.

Two incidents crystallized rank-and-file disapproval of Williams. The first occurred on a Friday night in October 1994 when Charles Heim of Metro Division, a popular officer, was shot and killed during a narcotics raid. Williams and his wife were in Las Vegas, an hour's flight away, celebrating their twenty-eighth wedding anniversary. Tradition required the chief to return immediately and offer condolences to the family. But Williams did not come back until Sunday, and word of this perceived affront spread through the ranks. Williams said he had telephoned after he learned of the shooting and been told that family members were too grief stricken to see him. But officers resented Williams for using Heim's family as an alibi. After more than two years on the job, he was expected to know that an LAPD chief returns to town when an officer dies in the line of duty.

The public was unaware of the Heim incident. But it was a prelude to the most damaging public controversy of Williams' career. In December 1994, a onetime LAPD deputy chief named Stephen Downing wrote the Police Commission, calling for an investigation of reports that Williams had solicited various perquisites and accepted free rooms and meals from Las Vegas casinos. The recipient of Downing's letter was not the Williams-friendly Police Commission that had hired the chief. Following the usual practice, Riordan had appointed his own commission, filling it with people who shared a commitment to strong management.* The commission president in 1993 and 1994 was Rabbi Gary Greenebaum, an executive of the American Jewish Committee who had been active in the successful 1992 campaign to pass Charter Amendment F, the key reform recommendation of the Christopher Commission.

This amendment had given the Police Commission broad new authority over the LAPD, and Riordan's commissioners attempted to exercise it. In the year-and-a-half between their appointment and the receipt of the Downing letter, the commissioners had begun to wonder about Williams. All agreed that the chief (in Greenebaum's words) had done a "miraculous job" in restoring public confidence in the LAPD. But they found Williams a hesitant manager lacking the interest or capacity for the nuts-and-bolts work needed to carry out the Christopher Commission recommendations. They did not question his integrity. "None of us believed the charges were true," Greenebaum recalled afterward.[20] But the commissioners felt they had to investigate the allegations. The chief did not oppose the inquiry; he told the commission that he had done nothing inappropriate.

But the investigation soon became a nightmare for Williams, who was slow to produce the records he claimed would exonerate him. Against the advice of aides, he withdrew into a shell and stopped giving interviews. As his personal attorney, he hired Melanie Lomax, a sharp-tongued civil rights lawyer who as a police commissioner in 1991 had led the abortive effort to fire Chief Gates after the videotaped beating of Rodney King.

Williams believed that his problem was Riordan and LAPD officers whom he suspected of leaking damaging material to the Police Commission and the media because they did not accept him as chief. But Williams' real problem was Williams—and the tactics he and Lomax used to fight the accusations. In a letter to the commission on January 5, 1995, at the onset of the investigation, Williams denied all the charges. Of the accusation that he

---

* Riordan's first Police Commission was dedicated and hard-working but lacked the police expertise that Jesse Brewer had provided the previous commission and on which Stanley Sheinbaum often had relied. Riordan had intended to appoint former police chief Thomas Reddin but had been dissuaded by Williams, who hadn't wanted the old LAPD looking over his shoulder.

had accepted "comps" in Las Vegas, the chief wrote, "I have never accepted without cost lodging, meals or show tickets at any Las Vegas Hotel. Whenever I stayed in Las Vegas I paid all bills due from my personal expenses."

This was not literally true. Williams had stayed at Caesars Palace five times between 1992 and 1994. Records obtained from Williams and the hotel after he reluctantly agreed to make them available showed that the chief had received free lodging, meals, and phone calls from Caesars worth $1,545.37. The commissioners were stunned and angry. Williams had told them repeatedly that he had not accepted anything. "Twenty-four hours after the last time he lied to us, he finally turned over the records," Greenebaum said.[21]

Commissioners knew they could not walk away from their findings, but they did not want a public confrontation with a popular chief. On April 16, they sent Williams a letter indicating an intention to reprimand him, the lightest penalty possible. Williams was outraged. Although a reprimand carried no punishment, it would go into his personnel file and damage his chances of being reappointed for a second five-year term.

Williams rationalized that he had not taken anything from Caesars because "comps" and discounts of various sorts to gamblers are common practice in Las Vegas. The chief said that he and his wife played slot machines. "No one will ever convince me or anyone who is reasonable and fair that hotel discounts are considered free and without cost if they are wholly dependent upon play and spending at any casino hotel in the United States," Williams said months later when the Los Angeles Times published an account of the discounts he had received from Caesars. "The pay is through your play."[22] Williams did not explain why he had not offered this defense in his original letter to the commission. He said it was a question of "semantics."

Still, the commission wanted to avoid a showdown. When Williams met with Greenebaum early in May, the rabbi told him there was "still time to recant" and avoid a reprimand. Williams said he had nothing to recant and wanted Greenebaum to tell him to his face that he had lied. Greenebaum did. Williams held similar dialogues with Enrique Hernandez, Jr., who had replaced Greenebaum as commission president, and the three other commissioners. In a closed-door meeting on May 16, the Police Commission voted unanimously to reprimand Williams on the basis of the written charge sent to him in April:

> During the course of our recent investigations, you orally and in writing knowingly made false statements to the Board as to whether you and/or your wife had ever accepted without cost, lodging or meals, at any Las Vegas hotel, contending that you always paid all such charges from your personal funds. Your responses to the Board in this regard were neither accurate nor forthright, and were misleading.[23]

The commission's action put the ball in Riordan's court. Williams asked the mayor to reject the reprimand and stiffly delivered a formal statement to reporters on May 24 in which he declared, "I am not a liar." But on June 12, Riordan upheld the Police Commission's action. He issued a written statement that the commissioners "merit the gratitude of our city" and had conducted their investigation "independently, judiciously, responsibly, thoroughly and fairly."

This did not end the controversy. In the June 1991 election, voters had approved Proposition 5, giving the city council the power to override decisions made by various boards and commissions appointed by the mayor.[24] Using this measure as its basis, the council asserted authority over the reprimand of Chief Williams. On June 20, 1995, the council debated the issue behind closed doors for three-and-a-half hours. Then, without even looking at the Police Commission record of its inquiry or at Williams' personnel files, the city council voted 12–1 to overturn the reprimand. The override effort was led by Mark Ridley-Thomas, the chief's principal ally on the council. Williams had threatened to sue the city for "improper release of personnel information," and Ridley-Thomas claimed a lawsuit could bring municipal government to "a screeching halt." The dissenter was Richard Alatorre, who said the council was embarrassing itself by taking such action in the dark.

Nine days later, Police Commission President Hernandez and Commissioner Greenebaum resigned in protest. Hernandez said the city council's action mocked Charter Amendment F and the Christopher Commission's effort to establish the Police Commission as the civilian authority over the LAPD. "If you truly believe in those reforms, this is a death blow," Hernandez said.[25] Greenebaum said that to overturn the reprimand without looking at the files was "a cowardly act."[26]

The city council lacked a sense of history as well as courage. Reformers in Los Angeles had waged a long and difficult struggle to gain civilian authority over the LAPD. Chief Parker and his successors had held off the reformers for nearly half a century by insisting that the LAPD could be kept free of corruption only if it remained totally independent. It took the King case, the Christopher Commission, and the riots to persuade voters to pass Charter Amendment F and supposedly bring the LAPD under civilian control. With a single shameful vote, the city council had tossed away this hard-won reform.

In shrinking from their responsibility, council members displayed both a desire to tweak Riordan and a familiar fear of confronting a police chief who was more popular than they were. Four years earlier a similarly timid calculation had led the City Council to block a Police Commission attempt to fire Daryl Gates after the Rodney King incident. Shortly before the council voted to override the reprimand of Williams, a *Los Angeles Times* poll gave the chief a 64 percent public approval rating.[27] Council members may also have feared that a reprimand would stir racial discord—which was close to the surface in Los Angeles, where the O. J. Simpson murder trial was under way. Williams had support from most black leaders, and Greenebaum said some council members told him they feared a reprimand of the chief would produce another civil disorder.

Missing from this political calculus was an assessment of the damage caused to LAPD morale by giving the chief a break that rank-and-file officers rarely received. Detective Cliff Ruff, then president of the Los Angeles Police Protective League complained: "There is a double standard for discipline of police management. The men and women who risk their lives daily are subjected to more severe punishment for false and misleading statements than the reprimand the chief received."[28]

LAPD disciplinary records support Ruff's contention. Thirty-three LAPD officers had been disciplined for lying in the twelve months before the attempt to reprimand Williams, most of them suspended for several days without pay. A detective told Carla Hall of the *Los Angeles Times* that an officer who used the chief's "semantics" defense in an LAPD Board of Rights hearing would be told he was making a self-serving statement and failing to accept responsibility. Officer Joseph Walker, an African American with twenty-five years of LAPD service, had been suspended for thirty days without pay for falsely reporting his location to a superior and not working that day—charges he denied. "If I had done the same thing [as Williams], I would probably be fired," Walker said.[29]

The LAPD manual forbids officers from placing themselves "in a position of compromise by soliciting or accepting gratuities." Department tradition is even stricter than LAPD policy. When Chief Parker was rooting out corruption from what had been a notoriously dishonest department, he made any acceptance of favors or gratuities a firing offense. Parker's attitude became embedded in LAPD culture. Similar attitudes prevailed among police professionals in much of the West, where local governments are usually nonpartisan and patronage is banned in police hiring. "East Coast chiefs are used to taking much more liberties and gratuities, being given much more favors in the community," said Joe Gunn, a decorated LAPD veteran of the *Dragnet* days who became Riordan's liaison to the Police Commission. The few officers who defended Williams said he simply failed to understand the LAPD culture.

Williams foolishly hailed the council's decision to reject the reprimand as vindication, but he never recovered from the controversy. Until then he had been lionized in the local media. Afterward the coverage became more critical of both the council and the chief—and also of the Police Commission for not proposing a harsher penalty. Former Assistant Chief David Dotson, whose testimony to the Christopher Commission had undermined Gates, wrote in the *Los Angeles Times*, "The public, let alone the criminal-justice system, must have confidence in the honesty of its officers. Liars are valueless. Seen in this light, the Police Commission's punishment for what it considered to be Williams' untruthfulness seems surprisingly weak."[30]

The *Times* itself was reluctant to attack Williams editorially despite disappointment with his performance. The newspaper had long been a voice for police reform; now it ducked the issues raised by the chief's conduct and the council's vote with a quizzical hands-in-the-air editorial headed: "Well, Let's Hope It Works." The editorial drew an acerbic letter from Gates, who remained committed to the lost cause of total independence for the LAPD. Gates said Charter Amendment F had produced the city's first "political-police corruption" in forty-eight years. "As for Chief Williams, he will never again be able to sign a disciplinary action against a police officer in good conscience," Gates wrote.[31]

Gates was mistaken. Williams had rationalized his statements to the Police Commission as fully as Gates had rationalized the LAPD's unpreparedness for a race riot. Despite their differences, Williams and Gates were alike in their pattern of holding others responsible for self-inflicted troubles. Both blamed the mayor, the Police Commission, the media, or disgruntled members of the LAPD for their problems. They rarely blamed themselves for anything, and there is no evidence to suggest that Williams was bothered by pangs of conscience in signing disciplinary orders.

If anything, Williams was even less willing than his predecessor to face reality. Gates in his memoirs gave self-serving interpretations of controversies in which he had been involved; Williams' memoirs ignored all controversies in which he did not appear in a good light.[32] In his book Williams relates a searing account of meeting with the father of a woman LAPD officer who had been shot and killed during an arrest. But he does not mention his decision to remain in Las Vegas after the similar death of Officer Heim, the controversy over his trips to Las Vegas, or any of the many disputes over his management of the department. He told Jim Newton that reports of staff conflict and rank-and-file dissatisfaction were all "B.S."

Newton's interview with Williams in June 1995 ended six months of isolation in which the chief had holed up in his Parker Center office. Williams did not persuade Newton, who reported in a page-one story on June 18 that the LAPD was "drifting toward paralysis, some of its top leaders frozen by uncertainty, divided loyalties and fading confidence in their boss, according to sources in and around the LAPD." This authoritative article set the tone for much subsequent coverage.

With Williams reeling, the Los Angeles Police Protective League joined the attack. Ted Hunt, the progressive Police Academy instructor who had earlier skeptically analyzed the LAPD's "military paradigm," was now a director of the league. Hunt, a fierce critic of Gates, had welcomed the selection of Williams, and his column in the August 1995 issue of the league newspaper, *The Thin Blue Line*, reflected a sense of betrayal. "LAPD used to be a ship afloat with no one at the helm," Hunt wrote. "Today there is a 'captain.' He's not lost. He's at the helm steering us for the rocks. . . . The cloud of suspicion that hangs over his head, his failure to communicate and his counterproductive policies have put his administration on a pattern of self-destruct."

Cliff Ruff wrote a column in the same issue calling upon Williams to make public the record of the Police Commission investigation. "If you're innocent, we want to support you," Ruff said. But the newspaper's most potent commentary was a cartoon depicting Williams as Pinocchio, his nose growing longer as he declared: "I am not a liar."*

EVEN A CHIEF WHO WAS COMMUNICATIVE, TRUSTED, AND STEEPED in the LAPD culture would have found the transitional years of the early 1990s challenging. The department had suffered as many blows as Rodney King, beginning with the videotape of that incident and continuing through the Christopher Commission report, the riots and the long goodbye of Chief Gates. When William Violante, a twenty-three year LAPD veteran, left the Los Angeles Police Protective League to join the Riordan administration in mid-1993, he claimed that department morale was at "an all-time low."[33]

Morale had been on a downward slope even before the King incident. The rate of LAPD resignations and retirements began increasing in the mid-1980s as salaries fell below those of suburban departments where the stress was less. Attrition spurted in 1992, the year of the riots. In 1994, a record 479 officers left the LAPD, including 147 with less than ten years' experience. Low pay was the largest single reason cited by the departing officers, but nearly half mentioned a combination of factors, including lack of command support or leadership, poor morale, and inadequate equipment.

In the post-Rodney King LAPD, officers tended to avoid confrontations that had the potential to cost them their job—or worse. "An officer can go

---

* Williams typically dismissed such criticism. He claimed in a television interview that he was supported by 90 percent of LAPD officers. However, a Police Protective League poll of its membership said that 84 percent of officers believed that the chief's refusal to release his records of the Las Vegas controversy had damaged his ability to lead the department.

down an alley where the gangsters hang out or he can go down a main street where nothing is happening," said Sergeant Tim Day of the Van Nuys Division. "Why would you choose to go down the alley when the public doesn't seem to support you for your efforts?"[34] The captain of Foothill Division told officers he would prefer to have them suffer minor injuries rather than be charged with unnecessarily shooting a suspect. Proactive policing gave way to what officers called "drive and wave," which meant driving around in a police car until someone made a 911 call. Arrests within the department plummeted from 289,000 in the fiscal year 1990–91 to 189,000 in fiscal 1994–95.

While it was less publicized, the quality of LAPD arrests also declined. A July 22, 1993, memorandum to District Attorney Gil Garcetti from Donald Eastman, head deputy in the office's Complaint Division, found that the quality of felony arrests filed in LAPD territory had "substantially decreased" and usually involved suspects who had been "caught in the act" or named by another suspect. A "surprisingly high" percentage of suspects had been arrested by private security officers, other police agencies, or civilians. The decrease in filings was most notable in cases of homicides, robberies, burglaries, or other crimes requiring "investigative legwork." Cases frequently were dismissed in preliminary hearings because of the absence of police or civilian witnesses. When deputies in the district attorney's office attempted to refile the stronger cases, detectives did not return phone calls. "Dozens of perfectly good felony prosecutions are allowed to die . . ." Eastman wrote.

Eastman blamed the "deplorable lack of investigative work" mostly on personnel shortages caused by tight budgets. But he said that low morale was a significant factor at the patrol level, where officers "have figured out ways to fill their shifts with arrests which are easy to make." Eastman cited an officer who said civilians are protected from double jeopardy while police faced four levels of review for split-second actions: inquiries by the department, the district attorney, and the U.S. attorney plus the threat of civil lawsuits. "An experienced LAPD detective recently told me that a community gets the kind of police work it asks for," Eastman wrote. "His opinion is that the city does not want its police officers to be involved in violent activity, so police are not putting themselves in situations where violence may occur. He analogized the situation to a person who buys a guard dog and is then shocked when the dog bites a burglar."

The new LAPD defensiveness led to virtual abandonment of the controversial side-handled metal baton that had been used to subdue Rodney King. Officers so often left their batons in their cars or at the station that an alarmed Deputy Chief Lawrence Fetters on February 16, 1994, sent an urgent memorandum to LAPD commanding officers. "This notice is to remind Department personnel of Department policy in carrying a baton while on duty," the Fetters memo said. "Recent field incidents indicate there may be a perception among officers that carrying the baton is discretionary."

The necessity for such a notice horrified officers of the old school. Joe Gunn said the memo demonstrated how little accountability existed within the police system. "What are the sergeants doing out there?" he asked. "No commanding officer had to write a memo to my officers and tell them to carry a baton. [If] they didn't have their baton with them, I damn well took them aside and said, 'Where's your baton?'"[35]

Officers continued to leave their batons behind, however. The punishments given the officers in the King case sent a far louder message than any memo from a deputy chief. Criminal suspects watch television, too, and they were aware that officers who used their batons were now more likely to be required to justify their conduct than before the King case. As a result, claims of excessive force against the LAPD vastly increased even as the number of sustained complaints was declining. But even unfounded complaints deterred proactive policing. Many an LAPD officer in the post-King era preferred facing a chewing out for not having a baton to becoming the target of a complaint that required hours of paperwork, interrogation by superiors, and an inevitable notation in the personnel file. Small wonder that few officers bothered to drive down the alleys where the gangsters were. In the post-King LAPD, such aggressiveness was not worth the risk.

While LAPD officers were less willing to make difficult arrests, they had a practical alternative to use against combative suspects for the first time since the choke hold was restricted to deadly-force situations in 1982. The alternative, endorsed by Williams and approved by the city council in 1993, was a cayenne-pepper gas that causes severe inflammation of eyes and nose, breathing difficulties, and a burning sensation on the skin. Chemically, the pepper spray is known as oleoresin capsicum and called "OC" within the LAPD. Issued to officers in hand-held aerosol canisters, OC soon replaced the baton as the LAPD's intermediate weapon of choice. In 1994, its first full year of department-wide use, pepper spray was used 823 times. Batons were used in only 41 arrests, a 92 percent drop from the pre-King year 1990, when batons were used 501 times.

The electric stun gun known as the Taser—the weapon Stacey Koon fired twice in attempting to subdue Rodney King—also fell into disuse. The Taser had been used 233 times in 1990, usually by sergeants. After the King incident, use of the stun gun dropped precipitously despite its proven effectiveness in felling suspects without hurting them. No officer wanted to use a side-handled baton and risk becoming another Laurence Powell. No sergeant wanted to use a Taser and become another Stacey Koon.

In fact, few LAPD officers wanted to use force of any kind. This was the most enduring legacy of the King case. "It's probably better to let a suspect get away than use a baton on someone, because you're going to be second-guessed," said Cliff Ruff.[36] The new LAPD attitude also resulted in expansion of the department's nonlethal arsenal to include foam-rubber projectiles and beanbags. These were issued to the elite Metro Division, one of the few remaining bastions of proactive policing within the LAPD. Higher-ups had rejected Metro's requests for these weapons before the riots, where they might have made a difference at Florence and Normandie. As Metro Lieutenant Michael Hillmann had predicted, the nonlethal projectiles soon proved their worth in quelling hostile gatherings. One of the by-products was a decline in officer-involved shootings.

Some new equipment was less successful. Beginning in October 1994, the LAPD obtained through donations five high-tech "night vision scopes" similar to those used by the military in Operation Desert Storm. The scopes convert dim light such as starlight into electrical energy and then into greenish-white images to spot suspects in the dark. But when Raymond Fisher, who had replaced Greenebaum on the Police Commission, observed a pursuit from an LAPD helicopter a year later, the scope was broken. Police cars were tied up for hours on the perimeter of the chase before a single suspect could be captured.

Equipment malfunctions and shortages were frequent in these transitional years. Much basic equipment was worn out or antiquated. Handcuffs jammed and car brakes failed during felony pursuits. Narcotics investigations were postponed until officers could borrow sophisticated cameras from the Drug Enforcement Administration. Williams complained that LAPD officers spent 40 percent of their time on paperwork because they lacked a computerized system. City Councilwoman Laura Chick said the LAPD was in a "dangerously pitiful position" in terms of equipment and technology, "back in the days of Wyatt Earp."[37]

On this issue, at least, Riordan and Williams were on the same wavelength. In the summer of 1994, the mayor launched a drive to obtain $15 million in private donations to computerize the LAPD and joined the chief at Newton Station to call attention to the department's plight. "Take a minute and look around this [roll-call] room," Riordan said during a tour of the decrepit station, built in 1925. "This equipment is not like a good wine which improves with age. Just ask yourself if you could run your business with these tools."[38]

Such exhortations attracted contributions but failed to overcome the obstacles of bureaucracy and recession-tightened budgets. In 1993, the budget approved by the city council included money for 327 new patrol cars while eliminating the jobs of 70 persons who installed radios in these vehicles. Since patrol cars without radios were worthless, a compromise was worked out to restore some of the eliminated positions. Still, it took a year before the first new cars were on the streets.

DESPITE ALL ITS TROUBLES, THE LAPD WAS SLOWLY RECOVERING its institutional morale and capability when the O. J. Simpson murder trial began. This televised media event was of no benefit to race relations anywhere, but it was particularly harmful to Los Angeles and its embattled police department. The defense managed to turn this case into a trial of the LAPD as much as of the icon-athlete Simpson. And unlike the defendant, the LAPD was convicted.

It is not unusual for defense lawyers to challenge the credibility of the police. Questioning the legality of a search, in this case of Simpson's home and grounds, is a familiar tactic in many jurisdictions. Many defense lawyers in Los Angeles had questioned the practices of the troubled LAPD laboratory, as Simpson's attorneys did in claiming that blood samples were contaminated.[39] While the LAPD was hypersensitive to criticism after the King case and the riots, it could have weathered such traditional attacks.

But Detective Mark Fuhrman transformed the trial into a morale-shattering ordeal. As the world remembers, Fuhrman was the LAPD detective who testified that he found Simpson's bloody glove outside his Brentwood mansion several hours after Nicole Brown Simpson and Ronald Goldman were stabbed to death on June 12, 1994. In answer to a defense question, he testified early in the trial that he had not used the derogatory word "nigger" in ten years. This statement was a lie. Between April 1985 and July 1994, aspiring screenwriter Laura Hart McKinny, a North Carolina professor, had taped nearly fourteen hours of interviews with Fuhrman. On these tapes, Fuhrman repeatedly demeaned African Americans, Mexican Americans, and women, and boasted of brutalizing suspects. Recalled to the stand for questioning, he invoked the Fifth Amendment and refused to answer questions on the ground of possible self-incrimination. Fuhrman was the LAPD's worst nightmare, live on national television.

In a tape excerpt that Judge Lance Ito allowed to be read to the Simpson jury, Fuhrman told McKinny, "We have no niggers where I grew up." This, too, was a lie. Fuhrman was born and raised in the small Washington State timber town of Eatonville. According to Fox Butterfield of *The New York Times*, Fuhrman and his younger brother as children had "run-ins" with two African-American boys who lived in town. One of them remembered as an adult that the Fuhrman boys would see them on the street and say, "Here come the niggers."[40]

Fuhrman's parents were divorced when he was seven, and he became "very mistrustful and paranoid." Fuhrman enlisted in the Marines in 1970 when he was eighteen years old and later told doctors that he had "fond memories" of becoming a "trained killer" in Vietnam.[41] This was another lie. Fuhrman was never in combat. His Vietnam service consisted of duty aboard the *USS New Orleans,* an amphibious ship stationed off the coast. Fuhrman rose to the rank of sergeant but left the Marines after five years. Accepted into the Los Angeles Police Academy, he graduated second in his class in 1975 and became an LAPD officer.

As a patrol officer, Fuhrman impressed his superiors by showing up for work early, immaculately dressed. He impressed his peers with his militancy. Sergeant Roberto Alaniz, who worked alongside Fuhrman for five years, thought he was an outstanding cop. "He had excellent tactics," said Alaniz. "He didn't show any fear. If you were a criminal and you knew Officer Mark Fuhrman was going to be in Westwood, you wouldn't go there. If you resisted arrest, he'd put you down right there. He had no problem with using force [to counter] force. But as long as you followed the rules and did everything right, nothing happened to you."[42]

Latinos were disparaged in several of the sixty-one excerpts of McKinny's taped interviews with Fuhrman that were played outside the presence of the Simpson jury. Fuhrman claimed to have slapped members of "Mexican gangs" who wouldn't or couldn't speak English and slurred "all your Mexicans that can't even write the name of the car they drive." Alaniz never saw this side of Fuhrman. "He asked me to work with him," said Alaniz. "I'm Hispanic. If he's a racist, why would he have asked me to work with him?" Alaniz thought he was hearing someone other than Mark Fuhrman on the McKinny tapes. "I never heard him use racial slurs," he said.[43]

But the tapes were a compendium of slurs, many directed at blacks. Fuhrman also made numerous derogatory comments about women officers. Again, however, black and female officers who worked with Fuhrman had a different impression. Sergeant Toish Ellerson, a black woman, told Greg Krikorian of the *Los Angeles Times* that she "never had any problems" with him. "I knew he was aggressive," said Sergeant Ed Palmer, an African American. "I knew he was a little arrogant. But I never got racism at all."[44]

Fuhrman also befriended Deputy District Attorney Danette Meyers, an African American, after she received a death threat from a defendant he had investigated. He took it upon himself to guard Meyers on his own time. "They became good friends and on several occasions he had her over for dinner with his wife and two children," wrote Vincent Bugliosi of Charles Manson prosecuting fame.[45] On the McKinny tapes, Fuhrman gives no hint that he had social relationships with blacks, on or off the LAPD.

On the tapes, Fuhrman boasts of arresting suspects on pretexts and mistreating them. One story was based on an October 18, 1978, incident that occurred in Boyle Heights after two LAPD officers were shot. Police swarmed over this Mexican-American community, rounding up suspects. Fuhrman told McKinny how officers had beaten up four of them. "We broke 'em, their faces were just mush," he said. "They had pictures of the walls with blood all the way to the ceiling, and finger marks from trying to crawl out of the room."

This case produced sixteen citizen complaints against twelve officers and a request from civil rights leaders for an investigation, which was conducted by Internal Affairs. All the officers were cleared. The complaints were reviewed by the Special Investigations Division of the district attorney's office, at the time headed by Gil Garcetti under the oversight of Johnnie Cochran Jr., the number-three man in the district attorney's office. Cochran, who as Simpson's attorney would accuse the LAPD of ignoring Fuhrman's racism and penchant for violence, decided there were no grounds for prosecuting the officers.

It is not unusual for police officers to react violently when one of their own is shot. (Both officers survived but the prognosis of one was uncertain when police swarmed into Boyle Heights.) The "code of silence" has special relevance on such occasions. "Oh, they knew damn well I did it," Fuhrman told McKinny. "But there was nothing they could do about it. Most of the guys worked 77th together. We were tight. I mean, we could have murdered people."

But there is no evidence that Fuhrman was the rogue cop of his self-portrayal—and there is substantial evidence that he lied to McKinny. After the Simpson trial the public defender's office reviewed thirty-five major cases in which Fuhrman was involved and found no misconduct. "I was surprised," said Deputy Public Defender Michael Clark, who conducted the review.[46] Significantly, blacks who had been convicted after being arrested by Fuhrman and had incentive to emphasize any misconduct in order to win new trials had no complaints. Later, an investigation ordered by Chief Williams, which was conducted by Internal Affairs officers and members of the Police Commission, called most of Fuhrman's statements "unfounded" and "ludicrous." The panel found Fuhrman had been reasonably truthful only when he claimed to have participated in efforts to create a hostile work environment for female officers at the West Los Angeles Station, where he belonged to an informal group known as "Men Against Women." Otherwise, the report concluded, "just about everything Fuhrman told McKinny which could be connected to an actual event was bigger, bloodier, and more violent than the facts."[47]

The consensus is that Fuhrman was striving to impress McKinny, either to earn his $10,000 fee or because he was attracted to her. Fuhrman gave credence to the latter view when he told ABC's Diane Sawyer, "I was also trying to impress somebody very much. I can shoot a pretty good line of bull . . . There's a gap in my personality. I was looking for something to be more than I was."[48]

Fuhrman's search for "something" led him to Joseph Wambaugh's police novels, familiar ground to other LAPD officers, and Wambaugh himself considered Fuhrman a character he had created. But Fuhrman reminded Sergeant Alaniz of Harry Callahan, the fictional Clint Eastwood detective known as "Dirty Harry." Alaniz believed that Fuhrman had copied the behavior of Callahan during an incident in which a police station parking lot came under fire from a sniper. While other officers took cover, Fuhrman strolled casually to his car after telling Alaniz, "If there is someone out there who tries to shoot me, I will shoot him back."[49]

Whoever his role model may have been, it seems clear that Fuhrman was driven by demons that his outward confidence concealed. Divorced twice during his early years in the LAPD, Fuhrman was so moody and depressed when off duty that he sometimes did not talk or smile for days. In 1981, he went to the department's behavioral-science section and confessed his depression and feelings of violence. A psychologist recommended Fuhrman's removal from the force, and he was placed on paid leave. For more than a year he drew workers' compensation and attended art classes at Long Beach City College while the Los Angeles Board of Pension Commissioners considered his request for a stress-disability pension that would have given him 50 percent of his salary for life.

Such "psycho" pensions were granted to 175 LAPD officers in the early 1980s. So many officers sought them that both the LAPD and the pension board became suspicious of such claims. Nonetheless, Fuhrman's application was unusual. According to psychiatrist Ronald Koegler, who evaluated Fuhrman, stress claims typically involved complaints of mistreatment by superior officers. Fuhrman had nothing bad to say about others, only about himself. "I answer everything with violence," he told the pension board. Fuhrman told John Hochman, an assistant professor of clinical psychiatry at UCLA Medical Center, that he had quit the Marines because he was "tired of having a bunch of Mexicans and niggers that should be in prison" refuse to carry out orders. As a police officer, Fuhrman said he had beaten, choked and kicked a man after he was unconscious and "was afraid that he would kill someone if he continued to work the streets."

Stress-disability applicants are given a standard psychological test, and the results of Fuhrman's examination suggested he was faking. So, too, did Fuhrman's personnel records, which contained no citizen complaints of excessive force. Even Fuhrman's claim that he left the Marines because of his racial attitudes may have worked against him. The pension board grants disability pensions only for conditions originating during municipal service, and Fuhrman acknowledged that he harbored racist feelings when he joined the LAPD. While it might be risky to put such an officer back on the streets, the LAPD assured the board it had other alternatives. Sergeant Larry Palmer testified that the "department had a variety of light duty, low-stress jobs available for Officer Fuhrman. Gun, uniform, and public contact would not be required." In light of this testimony and the absence of evidence to support Fuhrman's assertions, the board voted unanimously to deny the stress disability claim.

The board's decision was defensible, but the LAPD's subsequent handling of Fuhrman was remiss. Either Fuhrman was an avowed racist with violent impulses or he was willing to tell outrageous lies to obtain a lifetime public pension to which he was not entitled. Either should have disqualified him from further service as a police officer, and the LAPD should also have been concerned about the danger he posed as a witness if the statements he made in seeking the pension were revealed in court. According to Ira Reiner, who was then city attorney, "The department should have initiated proceedings to remove Fuhrman without granting him a pension."[50] Instead, the LAPD assigned Fuhrman to a desk job in its Personnel Division. Eight months later he was given back his gun and returned to the streets as a patrol officer in West Los Angeles.

The LAPD's slipshod disposition of the Fuhrman affair was not unusual. The department under Gates lacked a dependable mechanism for keeping problem officers off the streets. But this deficiency was not necessarily because the LAPD (or Gates) condoned excessive force or racism, as critics often charged. Part of the problem was that the LAPD had an awareness of the stress of police work. It was the first police department in the nation to establish formal counseling for officers who complained of stress or behavioral problems, and it attempted to retrain such officers, sometimes with success.

This was a progressive approach, but the LAPD was excessively bureaucratic and compartmentalized. The compartment for dealing with stress disability claimants was different from the compartment for dealing with officers who broke department rules. Since the LAPD considered lying a serious offense, Fuhrman would have been suspended for telling lesser lies to a superior in the normal course of his police duties. But telling whoppers to the pension board did not count. The LAPD treated stress claims almost as a game in which winners received lifetime bonuses and left the force, while losers, as in Monopoly, went back to Go and were reassigned. Fuhrman's case should have been different, for he had confessed attitudes that were more destructive than the statements normally made in such proceedings. But the LAPD took no advantage of the opportunity Fuhrman had provided for getting rid of him. In this respect the damage the LAPD sustained because of Fuhrman was entirely self-inflicted.

In the decade between Fuhrman's return to the streets and his involvement in the Simpson case, his personnel record was dotted with citizen complaints, mostly for minor roughness or obscenities. Most of these complaints were dismissed for lack of evidence, as they usually are when the suspect is the only witness, but Fuhrman received a one-day suspension in 1984 for improperly seizing a pedestrian's wrist and another one-day suspension in 1986 for leaving an "improper remark" on a windshield. The racial attitudes Fuhrman expresses on the McKinny tapes were reflected on the job in blunt denunciations of the affirmative action programs that were increasing the numbers of African Americans and women in the LAPD. When Fuhrman's superiors reproached him, he replied that he had a right as an American citizen to say what he thought.

Nonetheless, Fuhrman was promoted to detective in 1989 and assigned to West Los Angeles Division, which includes the affluent area where O. J. Simpson lived. Detective Cliff Ruff, who does not condone excessive force or racism, considered Fuhrman "a fine detective."[51] So did Fuhrman's supervisor, Gary Fullerton, who said that in terms of "merit and ability, Mark was right up there at the top."[52] After he became a detective, Fuhrman seems to have become less strident in denouncing affirmative action and women officers. He also toned down his statements in later tape recordings with McKinny.

But Fuhrman's record of racism caught up with him. Except for this record, he would not even have been a detective in West Division at the time of the Nicole Brown Simpson and Ronald Goldman murders. Four months earlier, Fuhrman had been scheduled to be transferred to the prestigious LAPD unit that investigated officer-involved shootings, an assignment he coveted. Then, Assistant Police Chief Parks learned about the pending transfer. Parks had felt the bitter sting of racism in his long LAPD career, and he wanted no racists in such sensitive positions. He read the records of the pension board findings and blocked Fuhrman's transfer. Fuhrman went to see Parks in an effort to reverse the decision, but he was unyielding. "I told him he wasn't the best candidate," Parks said.[53]

Had it not been for this action, Fuhrman would not have been available for duty on the night he was sent to Simpson's home. But Parks' decision not to give Fuhrman an assignment in the officer-involved shootings unit speaks well of him. Parks took a harsh view of misconduct and almost certainly would have fired Fuhrman after his stress claim had the decision been his. "The LAPD disciplines too many and fires too few," he sometimes said. The officer-involved shootings unit had been a focus of controversy, and Parks knew that assigning a racially biased officer to such a sensitive job after the King case and the riots was the equivalent of setting a time bomb and waiting for it to explode. He had no way of knowing that the bomb would go off anyway in the murder trial of Simpson.

District Attorney Garcetti did not know what Parks had done, but he knew more than a year before the McKinny tapes were played that it was risky to use Fuhrman as a prosecution witness. Fuhrman himself gave the warning after testifying in the Simpson preliminary hearing on July 6, 1994. According to Garcetti, Fuhrman told prosecutor Marcia Clark about his rejected disability application. Although Garcetti said he considered the information a "bombshell," he did little about it. After Simpson's acquittal he told reporters from the Los Angeles *Daily News* that he had been "legally prohibited" from seeing Fuhrman's personnel file.* Garcetti said his office had "checked with the people [Fuhrman] worked with" and received "nothing but positive comments."[54]

Another warning about Fuhrman arrived in the July 25, 1994, issue of *The New Yorker*. Writer Jeffrey Toobin quoted from the pension board hearings and disclosed the defense strategy of portraying Fuhrman as a racist cop who had planted the bloody glove as evidence. This was an "incendiary" defense, as the Toobin article called it, and far-fetched, but it is mystifying that Garcetti ignored it.

Bugliosi later contended, in his book *Outrage*, that Fuhrman was a victim in the Simpson trial. He was a detective who had been awakened in the middle of the night and sent to a crime scene where he did "absolutely nothing wrong at all." As usual, Bugliosi has a point. The defense offered no evidence to show that Fuhrman planted Simpson's bloody glove, and the detective certainly did not deserve Cochran's description of him as "a genocidal racist, a perjurer, America's worst nightmare, [and] the personification of evil," let alone his absurd comparison of Fuhrman to Adolf Hitler. But the greater victims were the men and women of the Los Angeles Police Department. A veteran officer who listened to the Fuhrman tapes told me that he felt as if the LAPD were drowning and its life flashing before his eyes on national television.

The tapes inspired the LAPD's critics to recall the Rodney King incident and depict it as a racial beating. Syndicated cartoonist Jim Borgman showed four LAPD officers whaling away at a fallen King and saying: "Actually, Mr.

---

* This was disingenuous at best. The personnel files of Fuhrman's stress-disability application were a matter of public record because he had filed a lawsuit after the board denied his claim. The court had upheld the board's decision, and the public record of the lawsuit was stored in a building a short walk from Garcetti's downtown office.

King, you're lucky. Mark Fuhrman's off duty tonight." A detective told the *Los Angeles Times,* "I have to come to work and have these citizens hate me. I see they hate me because I'm a white police officer, and I might as well be a Mark Fuhrman." Sergeant Susan Yocum pleaded on the *Times* op-ed page for public understanding that Fuhrman did not epitomize the LAPD. "The vile statements on those tape recordings have absolutely no bearing on how LAPD officers should be seen today," she wrote. "How dare anyone compare me to Mark Fuhrman. How dare anyone compare the officers I work with to Mark Fuhrman."

But Yocum, a well-regarded officer who had made a similar plea after the King incident, acknowledged the inevitability of such comparisons. "The King case, the delayed response to the riots, now the Fuhrman tapes and all the unfortunate incidents in between have caused morale to plummet," Yocum wrote. "Every time I think that we have hit bottom, things get worse."[55]

Fuhrman retired with a pension earned from twenty years of service. The question of whether he committed perjury was investigated by prosecutors from the office of California Attorney General Dan Lungren, who entered into a plea agreement with Fuhrman's lawyer, Darryl Mounger. On October 2, 1996, Fuhrman pleaded no contest to a single charge of perjury before Judge John Ouderkirk, who had presided over the trial of Reginald Denny's assailants. Ouderkirk noted that the plea was equivalent to an admission of guilt, and Fuhrman acknowledged he had lied under oath when he testified that he had not used the word "nigger" in ten years. Fuhrman was placed on three years' probation and allowed to serve it in Idaho.*

Reflecting on the damage done by Fuhrman, Chief Williams said, "it will take years for this department to overcome." Deputy Chief Parks thought Fuhrman had antagonized the "silent majority of people in the middle" who were neither critics nor fans but usually gave police the benefit of the doubt.[56] "Fuhrman hurt all of us," Cliff Ruff said. "He hurt the credibility of every working man and woman on this department. We don't know how the trial would have come out without him, but we know that police are now asked at voir dires whether they have used the N-word."[57]

---

* Although the plea agreement was criticized by black leaders and some legal scholars, the deal had, as Jim Newton observed, "distinct advantages" for both sides. Conviction of Fuhrman was no sure thing; the prosecution would have had to show that the lie was "material," which is not easy to prove. Fuhrman probably would have contended that he was not thinking about the McKinny tapes when he testified that he had not used the word "nigger" in a decade. But the deal was a good one for Fuhrman, too. It spared him mounting legal bills as well as the possibility of a prison term.

WILLIAMS' REPUTATION ALSO SUFFERED DURING THE SIMPSON trial, which coincided with the controversy over his Las Vegas trips. Early in the trial, Bill Boyarsky compared the chief's inept defense of his casino visits with the LAPD laboratory's shaky handling of blood samples. Later, after Fuhrman became the issue, comedy writer Tony Peyser quipped, "Chief Willie L. Williams was so upset by what Fuhrman reportedly said on the tapes that he dropped a roll of quarters at the slot machine he was playing in Las Vegas."[58]

The recurrent police complaint throughout the Simpson trial was that Williams failed to stand up for the LAPD when its integrity or professionalism was questioned. As the defense systematically put the LAPD in the dock, officers expected their chief to function as their advocate. This was unrealistic. Williams could not have won a war of words with Cochran and the defense "dream team." What went on in the courtroom overshadowed anything said at Parker Center.

But the barrage of publicity arising from the Fuhrman tapes prompted Williams to abandon his sensible low-profile strategy. The chief first promised a "biopsy" of Fuhrman's career, setting in motion the investigation that later showed Fuhrman had invented most of his stories. But Williams then announced that he possessed a list of a hundred potential "problem officers." The list was an invention. After Jim Newton asked to see it and a surprised Police Commission President Deirdre Hill said she didn't know what Williams was talking about, the chief admitted that no such list existed. By now Williams had become desperate to show vigilance against police misconduct. On September 1, three days after Fuhrman tape excerpts were played in court, Williams held a news conference in another effort to send a message that misconduct would not be tolerated on his watch.

The message was delivered at the expense of Andrew Teague and Charles Markel, eighteen-year LAPD veterans. Markel was a valued detective with an excellent record. Teague had made the Christopher Commission's problem-officer list because of eighteen citizen complaints against him. Williams accused Teague, a detective-in-training, of forging signatures on reports identifying two murder suspects and of lying in court about what he had done. The murder charges had been dismissed. Williams said Markel had used the "code of silence" to cover up for Teague. The chief said he had suspended both detectives and relieved them of their guns and badges, and that as many as a hundred other cases the detectives had investigated would be reexamined. "We will not tolerate this type of action from any employee, new or veteran, inside the Los Angeles Police Department," Williams declared.

Williams hoped to display enlightened leadership and take the spotlight off Fuhrman. What he demonstrated instead was an unfair rush to judgment as precipitous as that which Gates had made in the Rodney King case.

Teague, an inexperienced detective working a complex gang-murder case, had prepared a bogus photocopied report and affixed the signatures of two murder suspects in an attempt to induce a confession from a supposed witness. Prosecutors agreed this was a legal ruse and acceptable investigative practice. As it turned out, Teague never showed the bogus documents to the witness, but they found their way into the case files. Under cross-examination by a defense attorney at a preliminary hearing for the first two suspects, Teague had testified that the signatures were genuine.

When confronted afterward, Teague said he had forgotten about the ruse. An LAPD Board of Rights concluded that he had no motive to lie— "Teague's lapse of memory concerning the ruse documents had an opposite effect of actually weakening the case against [the two murder suspects]."[59] The board blamed Teague's "foggy recollection" on a heavy workload, a lapse of nearly five months between the filing of the charges and the preliminary hearing, and rushed preparation of his testimony under the supervision of a deputy district attorney involved in another murder case. District attorney's investigators decided there was no basis for filing criminal charges against Teague (there had never been even the suggestion of a prosecution of Markel) and said they knew of no other cases that had been tainted by either detective.

That left discipline to the LAPD Board of Rights, to which the two detectives appealed their suspension. On April 9, 1996, the board cleared Teague and Markel of serious misconduct and found only that they had failed to prepare properly for court. Teague received a one-day suspension and Markel a reprimand. The LAPD captain who headed the board took note of the many citizen complaints lodged against Teague but observed there had been none since 1988. The board's action was reported in the newspapers but received notably less broadcast coverage than the original accusations. Markel and Teague complained that their reputations had been ruined by a chief who was more interested in scoring political points than in determining the truth—and later sued Williams for defamation. "He's the top police officer in the city of Los Angeles, and his handling of this was disgraceful," Markel said.[60]

Williams was unyielding. He believed he had been right to suspend the detectives and the Board of Rights wrong to give them a slap on the wrist. The chief found Teague's explanation "incredible." Williams remembered using "ploys" as a detective in Philadelphia, "but I can tell you [even] as a rookie detective, I didn't forget what I did when I went to court."[61]

The Teague and Markel incident illustrated how difficult it was for a chief with a reputation as a grandstander to impose his disciplinary will on a department that resisted it. Stanley Sheinbaum had said during the Gates controversy that the greatest obstacle to LAPD reform was not the chief but the elaborate system of legal, contractual, and civil service protections acquired over the years by the LAPD rank and file. Sheinbaum believed that officers who were most frequently the targets of citizen complaints became adept at exploiting this system to preserve their careers.

Williams felt hamstrung by the LAPD's disciplinary procedures. He had wondered why Gates had not dealt more severely with the problem officers on the Christopher Commission list and was now learning that it was not as easy as he had thought. A Los Angeles police chief can uphold or reduce a penalty imposed by a Board of Rights, but he cannot increase it. Teague was not an isolated case. Jaxon Van Derbeken of the *Daily News* reported in the late summer of 1996 that Williams had regularly instructed a subordinate to write letters to heads of LAPD Boards of Rights complaining that they had been too lenient.

By now Williams was fighting a rear-guard action to persuade anyone who would listen that he deserved a second five-year term. More questions were raised about the LAPD's leadership in the back-to-back findings of the Blue Marble and Merrick Bobb reports. Blue Marble, commissioned by the city at Riordan's behest, was a voluminous study of the LAPD by two consulting firms, Blue Marble Partners and Decision Making Associates. Much of the report was technical, but it contained the damaging morsel that one of every four emergency calls was abandoned in progress and delivered an assessment of LAPD training that Jim Newton termed "a shocking indictment."[62] The report found the Police Academy understaffed and training officers in the field overwhelmed. It also said that thirty-one patrol officers (soon known as the "Chronic 31") had repeatedly failed their shooting tests. And this was apparently only the tip of the iceberg. Senior firearms instructor Lawrence Mudgett told Newton that the LAPD had two hundred officers "who are extremely weak shooters."[63]

Following Blue Marble came Merrick Bobb, a report for the Police Commission. Known by the name of its principal author, its purpose was expressed in its title: "In the Course of Change: The Los Angeles Police Department Five Years After the Christopher Commission." Attorneys Bobb and Mark Epstein found the pace of reform slow and were unimpressed even with the dramatic drop in injuries to suspects following the virtual abandonment of the baton. They said the ratio of injuries to arrests was unchanged, suggesting that there were many fewer injuries because there were many fewer arrests.

Merrick Bobb delivered a mixed assessment of the LAPD record in recruiting and promoting minorities and women, another Christopher Commission priority. The LAPD had a higher percentage of women (14.4) than any other police department in California, and a percentage of African-American officers (14.3), comparable to that of blacks in the population.

But Latinos and Asians remained significantly underrepresented. Overall, the report gave the LAPD fairly high marks for diversity in hiring and low ones for failing to promote Latinos, Asians, and women. No woman in the LAPD had risen above captain, a rank that once was the ceiling for blacks. While Merrick Bobb diplomatically avoided naming Williams, the report suggested that he was at best a transitional chief. "The LAPD does not currently have an overarching vision and plan that is adequate to perpetuate the LAPD's reputation as the nation's finest," the report said.

The accumulation of such criticisms and Jim Newton's probing stories gradually eroded Williams' popularity, his principal currency in his bid for a second term. A Los Angeles Times poll in June 1996 gave Williams a 56 percent approval rating, down eight points from 1995, when he had been enmeshed in the Las Vegas controversy and seventeen points from his 1994 high. Slightly less than a majority wanted his contract renewed. Most ominously for Williams, he had lost the confidence of Anglos and Latinos who in previous surveys had backed him nearly as strongly as African Americans. Now the racial lines were drawn. While 72 percent of blacks thought Williams deserved a second term, majorities of Anglos and Latinos wanted him replaced.

The chief's declining popularity was noticed by his erstwhile allies on the city council, whose support Williams needed to survive. Not even President Clinton was more attentive to polls than this council, and some members privately regretted their in-the-dark 1995 decision to overturn the reprimand of the chief. Williams felt unappreciated and a bit sorry for himself. As he saw it, he had taken command of a badly damaged department in which people had lost confidence and through hard work and hundreds of public appearances quickly restored its image. Williams thought his critics took this for granted. "People seem to feel, oh that was nice, that was worth two sentences and carry on," he told me in the summer of 1996.[64]

In fact, Mayor Riordan gave Williams considerable credit for this accomplishment. The mayor knew that Williams had been a reassuring presence in the dark days. The two had worked well in the campaign to expand the LAPD and upgrade its equipment. But Riordan was convinced that Williams had rested on his early laurels. He found Williams "tremendously charismatic" and expected him to display this charisma within the department, as well as in his public speeches.[65]

What frustrated Riordan most was that the chief talked such a good game. In private meetings, Williams often agreed with the mayor's blunt pleas for managerial changes and wrote down what Riordan said on a yellow legal pad, which Joe Gunn, the mayor's Police Commission liaison, called the "black hole" from which nothing emerged. "Williams never argued," Jim Newton observed later. "He just didn't deliver. That stifled both debate and progress, and it drove Riordan nuts."[66]

The lack of trust between Riordan and Williams was sadly reminiscent of the troubled relationship between Mayor Bradley and Chief Gates. Then a black mayor and a white police chief had nursed grievances against each other and left Los Angeles unprepared for the 1992 riots. Five years later the city was led by a white mayor and a black police chief who were as unsympathetic to each other as Bradley and Gates had ever been. Riordan and Williams at least talked to each other, but neither proved much of a listener. The conflict with Williams hampered Riordan's aspiration to be seen as a mayor for all Los Angeles. Williams' deficient leadership mocked the naive hope of police reformers that the LAPD's problems could be solved by bringing in an outsider.

ULTIMATELY, WILLIAMS WAS SENT PACKING FOR MUCH THE SAME reasons Gates had been forced to retire: He was damaged by criticism from within his department and outmaneuvered by an able lawyer who was skilled at forging political consensus. Gates' downfall, engineered by Warren Christopher, was based largely on the testimony of the chief's high-ranking subordinates before the Christopher Commission. Williams' nemesis was the Police Commission, whose authority over the LAPD had been strengthened by Charter Amendment F, the Christopher Commission's capstone achievement.

In 1997, the Police Commission was chaired by Raymond C. Fisher, who had served as a deputy counsel of the Christopher Commission. He resembled Christopher in style and background; both were low-key lawyers and lifelong Democrats who were much in demand as political advisers. Christopher had worked for Governor Pat Brown in the 1960s; Fisher for his son, Governor Jerry Brown, a decade later. And Fisher shared Christopher's view that the key to reform of the LAPD was a chief who would be accountable for the lapses or misconduct of his officers.

Police reform hung in the balance when Riordan appointed Fisher to the commission after Rabbi Greenebaum's resignation. Under the provisions of Charter Amendment F, the decision of whether Williams should be given a second five-year term was up to the Police Commission. But the city council could overturn the commission by a two-thirds vote, as it had done with the Williams reprimand. As police reformers saw it, another such action would undermine the commission's authority and make Charter Amendment F truly a dead letter. Riordan wanted a Police Commission that would be seen as independent of the mayor and would do its work so carefully that even a hostile city council would find it hard to challenge the result. Fisher fit the bill. He had backed Riordan's opponent, Michael Woo, in the 1993 mayoral election. Edith R. Perez, another lawyer and the only woman on the five-member commission, was also a Democrat who had supported Woo.

Fisher joined the commission in July 1995 and became its president a year later. He initially hoped to rescue Williams, not fire him, but he soon became as frustrated as everyone else with the chief's proclivity for promising changes that he never made. Perez was particularly critical of what she saw as the chief's failure to implement Christopher Commission recommendations cracking down on sexual harrassment within the department. "You will never root out all the bad apples, but we have not made the progress that we should have given all the time that has passed," she said.[67]

Williams was frustrated, too. He could not understand why he was the target of so much criticism when the crime rate was declining and public approval of the LAPD was on the rise. He was tempted to walk away but did not want to be labeled a quitter, and he did not feel that he could afford to step down without a financial settlement. After weeks of indecision, Williams applied on January 2, 1997, for a second term.

The commission plunged into hours of meetings on the application with community groups, public officials, LAPD officers, and members of the chief's staff. It met twelve hours with Williams. African-American members of the city council called for the chief's retention, as did State Senator Tom Hayden, the onetime radical activist who was Mayor Riordan's opponent for a second term in the April 1997 election. Fisher tried to ignore the clamor, but he was bothered by the racial overtones of the political debate. The man most on the spot was T. Warren Jackson, the only African American among the police commissioners. His vote was key, since neither Fisher nor any of the other commissioners wanted a decision along racial lines. But Jackson, a soft-spoken corporate executive, was also disillusioned with Williams' seeming inability to manage his troubled department.

It soon became evident to Fisher that the commissioners were unanimous in believing that the LAPD needed a new chief. They were especially impressed by the strength of feeling against the chief among the LAPD rank and file and by the critical findings of the Blue Marble and Merrick Bobb reports. When Williams realized that the tide was running against him, he and his lawyers asserted that the commission had made up its mind in advance at Riordan's behest. This tactic angered Fisher, who issued a statement in which he said that he was "extremely disturbed" that the chief "would make such an accusation without adequate factual or legal basis and before any decision has been made regarding his reappointment." The *Los Angeles Times* weighed in with a March 3 editorial that accurately summarized the state of affairs: "Williams and LAPD: This Bad Marriage Needs to End."

And end it did a week later. On March 10, at a news conference at Parker Center, Fisher announced that the commission had voted unanimously to deny Williams' request for a second term. He tried to soften the blow by saying that Williams had been a "welcome, calming presence" after Gates and had improved the LAPD's public image. But a twenty-two-page report issued by the commission documented numerous managerial failures and pointedly noted the chief's unpopularity within the department. "The commission is also troubled by Chief Williams' tendency to personally claim most of the credit for all of the positive changes in the department, while accepting very little responsibility for its shortcomings," the report said.[68]

Fisher and the commission were kind. Williams had taken office during a crisis with backing from nearly all segments of the community and the opportunity to make the most fundamental changes in the LAPD since Bill Parker. He had blown his opportunity. As Jim Newton put it later, the well-meaning chief had failed because he was not a leader: "He failed because he never grasped Los Angeles politics, because he felt threatened by talented subordinates, because he didn't care about winning the loyalty of his staff, because he didn't seek or take good advice, because he mishandled a key set of 1994 staff changes, because he twice hired bumbling lawyers and because . . . the job simply overwhelmed him. He also failed because he lied."[69]

Warren Christopher had returned to his Los Angeles law practice after four years as Secretary of State, still keenly interested in municipal public affairs. As the controversy over reappointing Williams neared a climax, people on both sides had urged Christopher to express his opinion. He refused, believing that anything he said might be interpreted as interference with the Police Commission. But Christopher was secretly delighted by the commission's decision—and even more so when the city council did not attempt to override it.[70] What mattered to Christopher was not the fate of a particular chief but the principle of establishing civilian control over the LAPD. He found it "ironic" that Williams, a black outsider in a department that preferred white insiders, was the first casualty of this principle, but thought it appropriate nonetheless. "Proposition F worked as it was intended, which is healthy," Christopher said. "Under the old system, Chief Williams would have been there permanently. You can commend the process whether or not you agree with the outcome."[71]

20

JUDGMENTS AND LEGACIES

"Rodney King was a defining incident. I used to wish we could take back those five minutes, but more good than harm has come from them for the LAPD."

—LAPD Lieutenant John Dunkin[1]

"Most people of a certain age remember what they were doing when John F. Kennedy was shot. Many remember what they were doing when the Challenger exploded. If you live in Los Angeles, anyone can tell you where they were when the riots occurred and how they felt. Most of them felt fear and an overwhelming sense of loss."

—Los Angeles Deputy Mayor Robin Kramer[2]

RODNEY GLEN KING'S LIFE WAS DOGGED WITH DIFFICULTIES IN the five years after the March 3, 1991, incident that made him an international symbol of police abuse. The videotape that aroused "horror and outrage . . . from Paris to Tokyo" also made King an enduring celebrity who attracted the media spotlight, especially when he ran afoul of the law while behind the wheel. These incidents were part of a recurring pattern. King suffered from alcoholism, which had killed his father, and he had not learned to take responsibility for his actions. Although usually gentle when sober, King became wild and temperamental when drinking. But despite everything that had happened, King continued to drink and drive.

King's next brush with the law after March 3 was trivial. He was driving in the suburb of Santa Fe Springs on May 11, 1991, when Los Angeles County sheriff's deputies pulled him over because the windows of his car were excessively tinted, which is against the law in California. The windows were so dark that the deputies did not recognize King until he had stopped. When they saw who it was, they wanted no part of him. Although he was driving without a license and the registration on the car had expired, King was not even cited.

Seventeen days later, King was arrested in a bizarre incident that began when he picked up a transvestite prostitute whom he later said "looked like a nice lady" on a Hollywood street corner.[3] The prostitute happened to be under surveillance by two undercover LAPD vice officers, who followed King's car to a carport in a back alley where they observed what one of the officers said was "all the signs of lewd conduct." Then the prostitute spotted the vice officers. King panicked and drove away, nearly running over one of the officers. After dropping the prostitute off on a street corner, he drove a few blocks and flagged down a police car. King urged the two uniformed LAPD officers to follow him back to the scene in their patrol car, which they did. King was clearly frightened. He said he thought the vice officers were robbers who intended to kill him. Because the Los Angeles County district attorney was prosecuting the King beating, the case was investigated by the California attorney general's office, which filed no charges.

King was back in the news on June 26, 1992, after a fight with his wife, Crystal Lynette Waters, who called police from their Studio City apartment in midafternoon. She complained that King had hit her and said she feared for her life. This incident occured two months after the Simi Valley verdicts and the riots, and the LAPD was effectively between police chiefs. Officers consulted Deputy Chief Mark Kroeker, then the division chief in the San Fernando Valley and one of the LAPD's most respected commanding officers. Kroeker went to the apartment and talked with King, who had calmed down and was cooperative. He was handcuffed, led out of the apartment through a back alley, and taken to the North Hollywood Station. But Waters declined to press charges, and King was released four hours later. Kroeker said he had seen "minor cuts" on Water's hands and arms.[4] King's attorney, Steven Lerman, said the cuts occurred while King and Waters were struggling over a tape recorder and that King had not struck his wife.[5]

Less than a month later, on July 16, King was arrested in Orange County at 1:40 A.M. by officers who noticed him backing out of a restaurant parking lot erratically and hitting a concrete block. He was given a sobriety test, which he failed, and booked into the Orange County Jail. Five hours later King was released on his own recognizance. Lerman's explanation was that King had been drinking excessively because of stress from the beating. The attorney also suggested that King had been targeted because of his race. Again no charges were filed.

King had been a sympathetic figure after the beating and an appealing one when he pleaded for racial peace during the riots. But to the public, the accumulation of incidents in which he was arrested but not prosecuted made him seem more victimizer than victim. Letters to the editor and calls to radio talk shows complained that ordinary people arrested for driving under the influence spent the night in jail and were required to post bond. Police critics and King's lawyers said in response that King was being singled out by police, even though the LAPD, in particular, was reluctant to touch him with the proverbial ten-foot pole. King's supposed untouchable status may have encouraged his drinking and driving. On August 21, 1993, in another 1:40 A.M. incident, he crashed his car into a concrete wall near a downtown Los Angeles nightclub. King and two passengers were not injured, but King's blood alcohol tested 0.19, nearly two-and-a-half times the legal limit. He was again released on his own recognizance. This time, however, he was finally charged with violating his parole.

Parole violators in California have been returned to prison for less, but authorities recognized that King's core problem was alcoholism. Drinking alcoholic beverages (even if he had not been driving) violated King's terms of parole, and he was sent for 60 days to an alcoholism-treatment center. This was potentially a useful punishment, and King promised to make the most of it. In 1994, as a result of the same incident, King was convicted for driving under the influence, fined $1,438, and ordered to perform twenty days of community service. Mandatory jail terms are imposed for second drunk-driving convictions in California, but King had never been prosecuted for driving while intoxicated on March 3, 1991, and that charge was dismissed by District Attorney Garcetti after the statute of limitations lapsed.

On May 21, 1995, King was again arrested for driving under the influence, this time near New Castle, Pennsylvania, where he had traveled to attend his father-in-law's funeral. He was driving with two male friends in a rental car when it veered off the road and became stuck in the mud. A twenty-year-old rookie police officer responded to the emergency call. King identified himself as the driver, and the officer gave him three field sobriety tests, all of which he flunked. King refused to submit to a blood-alcohol test and was placed under arrest, the first ever made by the novice officer.

Ten months later King was tried and acquitted in New Castle by an all-white jury that deliberated for more than six hours. The jury forewoman said the jurors had decided in King's favor after learning that the arresting officer had received help from a judge in preparing a "crib sheet" to guide his testimony in court. The officer acknowledged under oath that he had lied when he said he had prepared the crib sheet himself. King thanked his attorney and the people of Pennsylvania for the verdict, said New Castle was a nice place to visit, and told reporters he might come back to do some fishing.

Late in 1995 when this trial was pending, King told me he had enrolled in a twelve-step program to treat his alcoholism and no longer drank and drove. At the time of the interview King also faced a trial in Alhambra,

California, on misdemeanor charges of spousal abuse, assault with a deadly weapon, reckless driving that caused injury, and hit-and-run. His attorney in this proceeding was Edi Faal, Damian Williams' capable attorney in the Reginald Denny beating trial. Impressed with what Faal had done for Williams, King had sought him out.

The "deadly weapon" King was accused of using against his wife was his automobile. He had been arrested on July 14, 1995, on the way to the Altadena home he and Crystal Waters shared with their two-year-old daughter and Waters' two sons. In the midst of an argument, King pulled off the freeway and told Waters to get out of the car. She started to get out, reached back to get her wallet, and either jumped or fell into the roadway. King sped away, leaving her with a bruised arm and a head wound that required stitches. Waters filed for divorce. She told police that King had tried to run her over.

In most of his driving escapades after March 3, 1991, King had benefited from his celebrity status. Columnist Patt Morrison suggested at one point that for "every cop who may long to claim the bragging rights to . . . King's scalp" there were dozens who would rather ticket Mother Teresa than King, "the most famous driver since Ben-Hur steered a chariot."[6] But allegations of spousal abuse were another matter. One of the issues raised during the O. J. Simpson murder trial was whether police had ignored earlier complaints of abuse by Nicole Brown Simpson. This claim and Simpson's subsequent acquittal had raised public consciousness about spousal abuse, especially when celebrities were involved. Faal thought the charges against King were flimsy, but he could not avert a trial.

As Faal saw it, the charges had more to do with money than with King's conduct. During cross-examination, Faal suggested to Waters that she had implicitly tried to blackmail his client by offering to drop the charges if King gave her $300,000. Waters denied this. The jury acquitted King of the charges of spousal abuse, assault, and reckless driving but found him guilty of misdemeanor hit-and-run driving. "I feel good, and I'm going to Disneyland," King smilingly told reporters.[7] He hoped for no more than a fine, but Municipal Court Judge Michael Kanner on August 21, 1996 sentenced him to ninety days in jail. Faal appealed the conviction.[8] While the appeal was pending, Municipal Court Judge Barbara Johnson on September 13 sentenced King to thirty days of work on a highway cleanup crew for violating probation on his 1994 drunk driving conviction. He later served this sentence, showing up late a few times but otherwise causing no problems.

As his legal scrapes suggest, King was a troubled man. His biggest problem was his drinking, but he was also afflicted by the prospect of good fortune. From the moment the edited videotape of the beating aired on television, it was obvious that King had a potent lawsuit against a city accustomed to shelling out awards for injuries inflicted by LAPD officers. King, although dirt-poor, was perceived as potentially wealthy. Lawyers competed to represent him, and friends and family members vied for his favor. King's intelligence was limited, and he lacked the sophistication to deal with the competing claims. Except for trusting his mother, Odessa, he did not know where to turn. King was as confused and easily used as the simpleminded boxer in Budd Schulberg's novel, *The Harder They Fall*, who is beaten up in the ring and exploited outside it—and winds up penniless.

This analogy may not be entirely fair to the two lawyers who represented King in his protracted civil proceedings. The first was Lerman, who became King's lawyer because Johnnie Cochran Jr., the city's best-known African-American attorney, failed to return a call from King's mother. (Cochran told me he never got the message because of a mistake in his office.) With her battered son behind bars, Odessa King was desperate for help. A friend gave her Lerman's name.

Lerman, a Beverly Hills attorney, had never handled a case of such magnitude and wanted to keep it. "I thought another lawyer was going to snatch him away, lure him away with a promise of a large amount of cash," Lerman said.[9] Because he feared he would lose his star client and was concerned for King's physical safety, Lerman kept him hidden and guarded by his investigator, former LAPD officer Tom Owens. As recounted earlier, Deputy District Attorney Terry White, the lead prosecutor in Simi Valley, believed Lerman was overprotective and that the criminal case suffered because of it.

Whatever the validity of this criticism, Lerman realized that King had a "hell of a case" against the city.[10] But it was not a case that aged well. Had Lerman pressed for a quick resolution, he would have been dealing with a city government that was sympathetic to King and concerned that a jury might give him a gigantic award. But Lerman was in no hurry to settle. Instead, he upped the ante. After saying he would ask $56 million ("$1 million for each blow"), he filed a lawsuit seeking damages of $83 million.

Nearly fourteen months elapsed between the time Lerman became King's lawyer and the Simi Valley verdicts. He cannot be faulted for failing to anticipate an outcome that was also unforeseen by the city's political leadership, the LAPD high command, and most of the media, but he should have realized that time was not on King's side no matter what the jury decided. The public wanted justice for Rodney King, which to many people meant punishing the officers responsible. Once that happened, even sympathetic jurors became skeptical about the need for punitive damages.

Johnnie Cochran later said that King's "best day" came during the riots, when he uttered his cry from the heart, "Can we all get along?"[11] But his best day for winning a favorable settlement was any day before the 1992 riots, which hardened racial attitudes throughout Los Angeles and made the city council resistant to any award to King that would be perceived as overly generous. This political reality undermined the negotiations Lerman undertook after the riots with council members and representatives of City Attorney James Hahn. By late June, Lerman believed he had an agreement. He and King cruised the city in an automobile for ninety minutes while the council debated, expecting to respond to a settlement offer on his car phone. But the council delayed action. Negotiations continued, and in September, Lerman and Hahn's deputies crafted a $5.9-million agreement that was presented to the City Council.

The council member who took the lead in evaluating the proposed settlement was Zev Yaroslavsky, a prominent politician and LAPD critic who in the early 1980s had been in the forefront of the effort to restrict LAPD use of the choke hold after blacks died from it while in police custody. After the King beating, he called for citywide hearings to determine if there was "a pattern of excessive use of force by LAPD officers."[12]

But Yaroslavsky had been radicalized by the riots that lapped the edges of his Fairfax neighborhood, the most heavily Jewish area of Los Angeles. Yaroslavsky had tried to play a peacemaker's role. As he described his experience, "My car was totally destroyed . . . I was shot at while trying to retrieve my clothing. The camera shop around the corner was torched. My daughter went to a magnet school that had a race riot."[13] Yaroslavsky believed the riots had fostered a lawless attitude that continued after the disorders ended. In the months afterward his new car was burglarized and neighbors, including a rabbi, were mugged. Yaroslavsky considered the proposed settlement a "raid on the treasury."[14] He knew that an award of nearly $6 million would not sit well with the West Los Angeles voters whom Yaroslavsky would soon ask to elect him county supervisor. (He won easily.) Furthermore, legal experts assured Yaroslavsky that a jury would be unlikely to give King that much money.

Yaroslavsky proposed an award of $1.25 million, which he called "a generous and fair offer—generous to Mr. King and fair to the taxpayers." It would have been awarded as a lump sum of $250,000 plus annual payments of $75,000 for twenty years, a considerable amount considering the tax-free nature of such awards. Lerman's fees and expenses would have been determined by a court. The council approved this proposal on a 9–3 vote that reflected the racial divisions of the city. Two of the three African-American members voted against the Yaroslavsky proposal; the other was among the three absentees. The $1.25-million offer was rejected by Lerman, who accused the city of negotiating in bad faith. A few days later King rejected Lerman and replaced him with Milton Grimes, an Orange County criminal attorney and an African American.

There had not been a day during the year and a half he represented King that Lerman had not feared losing his client.[15] He particularly worried that members of Crystal Waters' family, whom Lerman called "the enemy within," would insist on steering King to an African-American lawyer.[16] Grimes was an obvious choice. But Lerman did not take defeat graciously. He claimed to have spent at least $150,000 on the case, including the cost of bodyguards to protect King, and filed charges with the California Bar Association that Grimes was "a shyster that ripped off this case from my office."[17] Grimes in turn accused Lerman of "unethical and unprofessional conduct" for withholding some of King's records and lobbying with family members to win King back as a client.[18]

Grimes, then forty-seven, had been raised in the rural South where he recalled harsh police treatment of blacks and remembered his sharecropper grandfather warning him not to look at white women. He said he had become a lawyer to help blacks wrongly accused of crimes, and he often injected allegations of racism into the simplest cases. Grimes made no apology for doing this. "Let my critics live the life of a black man and then talk about being sensitive to race," he said.[19]

After King became his client, Grimes tried to raise his "black consciousness." He created the Justice for King Committee, an all-black group that exposed King to African-American professionals and black history. King had no interest in becoming a racial symbol and remained disengaged. But Grimes did what others had failed to do by hiring Judy Sampson, an Orange County educator, to tutor King in reading. She taught King three times a week and became his friend.

King's progress was slow but no more so than the progress of his lawsuit. It finally came to trial in March 1994 before a jury of seven women and three men in the Los Angeles courtroom in which Stacey Koon and Laurence Powell had been convicted. United States District Judge John Davies once more presided.

"Welcome to the third annual spring Rodney King trial," quipped reporter Linda Deutsch of the Associated Press in the press room. By now, three years after the beating, the Rodney King case was old hat. No longer did curious spectators line up in the hallway of the Roybal Federal Building for scarce courtroom seats. Nor did demonstrators compete for noontime attention while the attorneys held news conferences. Deutsch, an award-winning trial reporter, filed her customary balanced and informed stories, but media interest was much diminished except when King or the convicted officers testified. Not even Daryl Gates drew much of a crowd. The national media paid little attention to the civil trial, and coverage in the Los Angeles Times and the Daily News was more abbreviated than in either of the criminal trials.

This atmosphere of normality did not help Grimes and his legal team. "Justice" had been politically pre-defined in the federal criminal trial of the officers as requiring some convictions. No similar pre-determination influenced the civil trial. Two officers had been punished, as jurors were reminded when a gaunt Koon testified in jail clothes. Jurors were not sequestered, and they had no reason to fear that any decision they reached would cause another riot.

If a presumption of any sort existed during the civil trial, it was probably that the amount of the damage award should be held down. Two weeks into the trial a man told jurors in a restaurant that they were "wasting taxpayers' money." Grimes asked for a mistrial, which Davies denied, instead ordering extra security for the jurors at lunch breaks. It was a telltale incident. The riots and King's repeated brushes with the law had changed public perceptions. It was not uncommon to hear people say that Koon and Powell deserved to be in prison but that King should be there with them.

King, however, had one important advantage in the civil trial. Before it began, the city council had agreed that the city was liable for the damages suffered by King, with the amount to be determined by the jury. This action was a concession of the council majority, led by Yaroslavsky, to the three African-American members and Councilman Mike Hernandez, who wanted the city to offer King more than $1.25 million. It steered a middle course between granting an award that might be seen as exorbitant and defending the King beating.

But as Judge Davies noted in an exchange with Assistant City Attorney Don Vincent early in the trial, this concession meant that the city assumed responsibility for injuries that were "constitutionally inflicted" as well as for those that were not. It was a key point. There had been considerable debate in both criminal trials about the early seconds of the videotape. It shows King charging toward Powell, who responds by striking him, apparently on the head, with his baton. Prosecutors had conceded the legality of this initial swing, the probable cause of King's most severe injuries. But the council's concession of liability meant the city was as liable for injuries from this blow as for later blows that had been found excessive.

Grimes did not make the most of this concession. He was a criminal attorney who lacked experience trying civil cases, and he was determined to present the March 3, 1991, incident as a racial beating. King obliged. Although he had testified in the federal criminal trial that he did not know if officers had called him "nigger" or "killer," he was now certain they had used the racial epithet.

The evidence did not support this accusation. The city introduced a German sound expert, Angelika Braun, who said she did not hear racial epithets on the audiotape, and the defense responded with George Papcun, the New Mexico audiologist who said he heard the words, "Nigger, put your hands behind your back." But this phrase supposedly had been uttered by Officer Theodore Briseno during handcuffing and did not support the extravagant claim that Koon had called King a "nigger" and told him to run for his life. Although the jury did not know it, the FBI analysis of the tape had found no evidence of a racial slur, by Briseno or anyone else. Furthermore, David Love, the sole black among the police bystanders, testified, as he had at Simi Valley, that he heard no racial epithet. He said he would have remembered if any such word had been used because "as an Afro-American it would have offended me."

This sort of argument was beside the point to Federico Sayre, a skilled Orange County civil litigator whom Grimes had asked to make the case for damages. Since the city had conceded responsibility, Sayre saw nothing to gain from retrying the criminal case. Instead, he set out to show that King had suffered permanent injuries that entitled him to a substantial award. His medical witnesses included F. David Rudnick, then director of the UCLA Neuralbehavior Clinic and a physicist as well as a psychiatrist. On the basis of interviews, an examination of King, and talks with family members, Rudnick had found what he considered persuasive evidence of residual but permanent brain damage. Its manifestations included loss of memory and concentration as well as headaches, heightened anxiety, and sleep loss. His testimony undergirded much of what King had said on the witness stand.

Rudnick's testimony seems to have impressed the jurors. But it was virtually ignored in the closing argument by Grimes. Sayre thinks King might have received more money if Grimes had emphasized Rudnick's testimony about brain damage instead of his own theories about the racist motives of the officers.[20] And Vincent is convinced King's award would have been lower without the efforts of Sayre and Rudnick.[21] As it was, the jury awarded King $3.8 million in compensatory damages—more than a third of the $9.6 million sought by Grimes and well below the $5.9 million Lerman and the city attorney had agreed on before the City Council rejected it. Sayre, recognizing that the award satisfied no one, thought it "about right."[22] Vincent, with little leverage after the council conceded liability, was also satisfied. But the verdict was only the first part of a two-phase trial. In the second phase the jury was asked to assess Grimes' claim for $15 million in punitive damages against fifteen defendants, including former LAPD Chief Gates.

Grimes apparently believed he could obtain a large punitive award if he could show that what happened to King was the product of LAPD policy. To this end, Grimes and Oakland civil rights attorney John Burris, another member of King's legal team, cited Christopher Commission findings of excessive force and racism within the LAPD. Grimes, who said Daryl Gates "knew or should have known" about such practices, displayed an open hostility toward Gates that startled other lawyers. "A lawyer shouldn't show personal animosity," said Laurie Levenson. "I've prosecuted murderers to whom I've acted in a friendlier fashion than Grimes does to Gates."[23]

Levenson, the Loyola Law School professor and former federal prosecutor who monitored both the criminal and civil trials, believed that Grimes' examination of the former chief was counter-productive. Gates was hard of hearing, a disability he traced to time spent on the firing range with inadequate protection for his ears, and he needed to have many questions repeated. But he coolly deflected every accusation that he condoned racism or excessive force, and he took advantage of several openings to explain police work. At one point he managed a little lecture about the LAPD's racial sensitivity training and noted that only a tiny percentage of the in-car computer transmissions monitored by the Christopher Commission contained racist comments. "I don't think you would find any organization in the world" with such a low percentage of racial remarks, he said. Nonetheless, any officer who had made an offensive remark was disciplined, Gates added. Grimes, who was rebuked by Davies for arguing, displayed a superficial grasp of the Christopher Commission report. He gave Gates an opportunity to make a speech about due process by asking him why he hadn't immediately fired the officers involved in the King beating. When asked the question again, Gates said, "That was the politic thing to do. You do what is right."

In fact, Gates had condemned the beating and jettisoned the officers accused of it, much to the disgust of Stacey Koon. He had shown less concern about due process for the officers involved in the King affair than about saving his own job, although he seems in retrospect to have had qualms about his conduct. Testifying by telephone at a Board of Rights hearing for Briseno, Gates later indirectly expressed regret for yielding to political pressure. In the civil trial, Grimes gave Gates a chance to rewrite history. The former police chief was such an impressive witness that he helped other defendants as well as himself. Defense attorneys recognized this and stopped objecting to questions by Grimes. They wanted to keep Gates on the stand as long as possible.

Soon after Gates finished, Judge Davies dismissed him as a defendant. Davies was skeptical from the outset that Gates had legal responsibility for the abuse of King, but he gave the defense the chance to prove it. In his view, the defense had not come close to doing so. "Bad management is not enough," Davies said in dropping Gates from the lawsuit. "Allowing racism is not enough. Poor supervision is not enough. There is no evidence of causation." The judge also dropped most of the bystander officers as defendants, saying that they had played too minor a role to be considered liable for punitive damages. Six individual defendants remained: Koon, Powell, Briseno, and Tim Wind, plus Briseno's partner, Rolando Solano, and Louis Turriaga, who had drawn a forty-four-day suspension for putting his foot in King's face during the handcuffing and dragging him improperly to the side of the road.

Most of these officers gave a good account of themselves. Wind, who had not testified in the criminal trials, was especially effective. Although there was no way for the jury or Grimes to know it, Wind's account had not changed materially since he first gave it to Internal Affairs. Wind's wife, Lorna, broke down on the witness stand as she described the personal hardships the family had endured since the King incident, even though her husband had twice been found not guilty.

Koon, who was questioned by Burris, was more relaxed and effective than at the federal criminal trial. So was his attorney, Ira Salzman, who was experienced in civil work. Koon bridled only when Burris sought to demonstrate misconduct by playing small fragments of the videotape. "You're playing this in snippets," Koon said. "It happened in real time." Koon said he had not called King a racial name and once more shouldered blame for what the other officers had done. "I take responsibility for this incident from the very beginning," he said.

The jury, reduced to six women and three men after one juror was excused, deliberated eleven days. It found that Koon and Powell had acted with malice but decided that King did not deserve punitive damages. This was a considerable victory for the defendants, who Salzman said "have been victimized just like Rodney King." Briseno had filed an unusual counterclaim alleging that he was injured when King struck him in the chest during the handcuffing attempt before the videotape began. The jury found in Briseno's favor but again assessed no damages.

All the trials arising from the King beating produced jury surprises, and the big surprise of the civil trial was the forewoman, Ester Soriano-Hewitt, a Filipino American and the widow of onetime Black Panther Raymond (Masai) Hewitt, who had been targeted by FBI Director J. Edgar Hoover for his radical activities.[24] Several years later, she was working in a gang prevention program when she met Hewitt. They fell in love, married, and had three sons. He died of a heart attack in 1988.

Soriano-Hewitt told the other jurors that she had been married to an African American but told no one of his background. Had he known, Vincent told me, he would have challenged her for cause and if necessary used a peremptory challenge to keep her off the jury.[25] Had this happened, the civil trial might have ended in deadlock. "She's the one who kept the jury together," said juror Gail Sanders, a psychiatric technician. "We were very lucky to have her."[26] Soriano-Hewitt, who worked for Los Angeles County in the financial and planning section of a dispute-resolution program, was skilled at mediation. In the first phase of the trial, she persuaded white jurors to give King higher compensatory damages than they thought he deserved. In the second phase she persuaded the jury's sole African-American member, a South Pasadena seamstress who wanted the jury to award punitive damages, to go along with the majority. "The jurors had a hard time dealing with King," Soriano-Hewitt told a reporter after the trial. "They had a difficult time just seeing him as a person. If Rodney King was Denzel Washington, everyone would have awarded him millions of dollars. But he's not. He is who he is."[27]

King was disappointed with an award he had been led to believe would be higher. His disappointment was heightened because Grimes had rejected an offer from the city at the end of the first phase of the trial that would have paid $1 million of King's legal fees in return for abandoning claims to any punitive damages. Grimes was unapologetic. "Just because the outcome was zero punitives did not make the offer reasonable," he said. He had a point. The city's lawyers no less than Grimes had expected punitive damages and wanted to cut potential losses. Grimes did not have the advantage of hindsight when he rejected the offer.

But Grimes can be faulted for mindless insistence that the King beating was an act of deliberate racism. He was inclined to cry racism even when the claim was unsupported by the evidence. In this case his one-note strategy was not recommended by the jury composition, as Grimes might have recognized had he been less blinded by ideology. The claim of racism seems to have repelled white jurors without bolstering King's case for higher damages. Even had the African-American juror held out for a punitive award, the most Grimes would have achieved was a deadlock requiring yet another trial.

Grimes, however, was not self-critical. He blamed others for the results of his poor judgment, railing against the jury and excoriating Judge Davies for undermining his case by dismissing Gates as a defendant. It was a weak excuse, for Davies had followed a basic rule of law. King, however, blamed Grimes. Soon after the trial he went back to Lerman.

THE CIVIL JURY HAD DEMONSTRATED UNCOMMON COMMON SENSE in the balanced verdicts that made King a millionaire and spared the officers financial liability. But its care went largely unnoticed in a city that had been racially polarized by the riots and wanted the Rodney King case to go away. Most quoted reactions in newspaper articles differed along racial lines, with whites critical of the size of the award and blacks believing that King deserved more. Few persons of any race praised the jury.

After the Simi Valley trial and again after the Los Angeles trial of the defendants who battered Reginald Denny, it was frequently said that juries are incapable of fairly evaluating the evidence in racially charged trials, a view later ratified for millions of Americans in the Simpson murder trial. But that media circus, with its celebrity defendant and powerhouse defense attorneys, was unique. Juries return guilty verdicts in the vast majority of criminal cases in Southern California, as elsewhere. In the racially divisive trials examined in this book, juries of untrained citizens often performed as well or better than judges with professional training and long experience.

The shooting death of Latasha Harlins by Soon Ja Du was a crime born of racial hostility and cultural misunderstanding that foreshadowed the assaults by African Americans on Asians, whites, and Latinos during the riots. A mixed-race jury found that Du had shot Harlins intentionally in the back of the head and reached a sensible verdict of voluntary manslaughter that normally would have sent Du to prison for several years. That this trial ended in the devastating injustice of Du's being freed was the fault not of jurors but of judges. The blame is shared by Judge Joyce Karlin, who was presiding over her first criminal trial, and senior colleagues who ducked the case because they wanted to avoid controversy.

The state trial of the officers accused of assaulting Rodney King would normally have been conducted in Los Angeles, where the incident occurred. Instead, it was moved out of the city by an appellate court that had steadfastly refused to grant similar changes of venue for nearly two decades. This precedent-shattering change of venue was principally the work of Justice Joan Dempsey Klein, a distinguished jurist who was concerned that controversies arising from the King case were disrupting Los Angeles. Had Klein left well enough alone and followed precedents, the officers would have been tried in Los Angeles, and Powell probably would have been convicted.

Klein's mischief making was compounded by Judge Stanley Weisberg. Any plain reading of Klein's ruling shows that she wanted the trial held outside the Los Angeles media market, but Weisberg ignored her wishes. Instead, he kept the trial within the Los Angeles media market, placing it in Simi Valley, a community with one of the nation's highest concentrations of police officers and few blacks. These decisions produced a jury that was conscientious but lacking in diversity. When the trial ended in acquittals and triggered the Los Angeles riots, blame was heaped on the jurors instead of the judges responsible for moving the trial.

Among the jury's critics was George Bush, then an embattled incumbent president whose political fortunes were sinking in California. Bush had been shocked when he saw the edited videotape of the King beating. He knew little about the case and assumed that the Simi Valley verdicts were a miscarriage of justice. Desperate in an election year to gain support among African Americans, Bush set in motion the process that led to retrial of the officers.

The most persistent criticisms of the Simi Valley verdicts came from liberals who assumed the officers were acquitted because they were white and King was black. But after Koon and Powell were convicted of violating

King's civil rights and after Damian Williams was acquitted of the more serious felonies arising from his brutalization of Reginald Denny and others, conservatives joined the antijury chorus. The conservative assumption was that a jury with an African-American forewoman and several black members had gone easy on Williams because he was black and Denny was white. The result of the civil rights trial of the officers was widely seen—and not exclusively by conservatives—as an exercise in political correctness that redressed the Simi Valley verdicts.

In fact, the odds were against the jurors in these two trials, largely due to the climate of fear that pervaded post-riot Los Angeles. The jurors knew when they were impaneled that unpopular verdicts might ignite more riots. They were reminded during deliberations of the volatility of the city—the federal jurors by a terrifying bomb scare and the Williams jurors by the chants of demonstrators. To expect impartiality under such circumstances is to ask more of any jury system than it can possibly deliver.

The civil jurors who sifted competing claims for damages in "the third annual spring Rodney King trial," were spared these riot-born pressures. The diminished media attention in a city grown weary of the King case and the knowledge that the threat of riots had vanished with the convictions of Koon and Powell freed the civil jurors to decide the issues on their merits, as they did. What the jurors demonstrated in the process, perhaps unknowingly, was that the legality of the King arrest was a close question rather than the open-and-shut case of police brutality that it was popularly assumed to be.

The mythology of the King incident derives almost entirely from the edited version of the Holliday videotape. That version begins more than halfway through an incident in which Stacey Koon tried to take King into custody without hurting him. This fact in itself sets the incident apart from numerous proven cases of police brutality in which victims were hit, choked, or shot without provocation. It also sets the incident apart from classic police pursuits in which excited or angry officers, adrenaline pumping, reflexively beat a suspect once they catch him. Several minutes elapsed between the end of the King pursuit and the first baton blows, an interim in which officers tried to take King into custody—first with verbal commands, then by gang-tackling him and trying to handcuff him, then with Koon's two bursts from his powerful electric stun gun. King was not struck with a baton until he climbed to his feet after being hit by the second burst from the Taser, then charged toward Laurence Powell.

That these facts are not known or remembered by the public even after three trials is primarily the fault of television. KTLA won the prestigious

Peabody Award for showing the Holliday videotape, but when editors at that Los Angeles station deleted the frames of King's charge in their effort to remove subsequent blurry footage, they removed the explanation for Powell's first and most damaging baton blow.* Had television not stacked the deck against the officers with its shameless editing of the videotape (done, it seems, in the interests of improving picture quality, rather than out of editorial bias), the Simi Valley trial might have ended differently. What the editing did for the defense in that trial was establish that the media had not told the whole truth. From that premise it was a small leap for jurors who were suspicious of the media to conclude that King was a bogus victim. The jurors were visibly surprised when the complete tape was played the first time—and not by the defense but by the prosecutor during his opening statement. At that moment the prosecution's burden of proof became heavier.

Repeated viewings of the videotape reveal that it is chock-full of information not apparent to the untrained eye. Although the tape cannot explain motivation—the purpose of Briseno's stomp, for instance—it does resolve issues in which the action itself is self-explanatory. Officer Tim Wind especially benefits from an informed viewing. To casual viewers he seems as unrestrained as Powell. But when it is known that LAPD officers are taught to step back and evaluate the impact of baton blows and when Wind is isolated in slow-motion viewings, it is obvious that he follows this policy throughout the incident—as the jurors decided in the two criminal trials.

Even after learning that the videotape shows more than is apparent to the untrained eye, I found it ugly to watch in any version. So, it turned out, did many police officers, although often as much for the incompetence it reveals as for the violence. Experienced police officers can see that Powell is incompetent in his use of the side-handled baton. Several officers have told me that Koon should have intervened to stop the beating before he did, and relatively few of them share Koon's view that the incident reflects textbook use of force. Koon himself acknowledges that the action shown on the video is ugly: He testified in Simi Valley that the "brutal" force used against King was more violent than any other he had witnessed during fourteen-and-a-half years on the LAPD.

Where police perceptions part company with the public's perception is in recognizing that the incident looks vastly different on video than it did to the officers at the time. Fear ruled the field where King was beaten. The arresting officers had reason to suspect that King was on drugs, probably

---

* Newspapers are not blameless in their coverage. Most reporters (including me) relied initially on the edited footage and were not aware of the deleted footage until much later. The LAPD also shares the blame. Although KTLA had given the department an unedited copy of the tape, Gates was trying to distance himself from the officers and made no effort to call the editing to the attention of the public or the media.

PCP, when he behaved so strangely after leaving his car. Their suspicions were heightened when he flung them off his back as they tried to handcuff him, which also made them aware of King's strength. King's amazing ability to shake off the effects of the two 50,000-volt volleys from Koon's stun gun was the clincher. None of the officers who made contact with King—Powell, Wind, Briseno, and Roland Solano—had ever seen anything like that. Later speculation that the stun gun's electric darts had not made proper contact did not occur to any officer at the time.

It was Koon's misfortune that he was at this point dependent upon a marginal police officer who panicked when King charged toward him. But anyone who seeks to understand this incident needs to put himself in Powell's shoes at this critical moment. Perhaps King was trying to escape, assuming he was sober enough to formulate a plan, but Powell could not know that. What Powell saw was a huge and uncontrollable man who could not be stopped by a stun gun bearing down on him at point-blank range. Perhaps Powell was even more afraid because King is black, but there is no doubt he also would have been terrified and swinging away if King were white.

Training is supposed to overcome fear, but Powell was ill trained. Less than two hours earlier, in a coincidence too improbable for fiction, he had flunked a baton test at roll call and was then embarrassed when Wind, the rookie he was responsible for training, demonstrated its proper use. In the opinion of Sergeant Charles Duke, the defense use-of-force expert in both criminal trials, Powell should have been reassigned to desk duty pending remedial training.

Instead, Powell was sent out into the night and history to do one-sided battle with King, armed with a metal club that he did not know how to use. This barbaric weapon by its nature causes more injuries than the modified choke hold still used by most police forces. It is not the baton's injurious force, however, but its wild and clumsy use that makes the videotape so distasteful. Powell hits King over and over again not because Powell is vicious but because he is inept. A baton blow is so painful that a single well-delivered power stroke can stop even a powerful man. A properly trained officer would have flattened King, breaking his collarbone but not splitting his face with no more than two or three strokes—before the videotape really had time to roll. Although King would have been injured, there would have been no dramatic footage to outrage public opinion. What the videotape shows is not street justice but the horrendous violence that occurs when training and tactics fail.

Koon did not have the luxury of analysis by hindsight. He barely knew Powell and was unaware that the officer he had picked as his point man to control King had just failed a baton test at the beginning of his shift. Koon made a split-second decision to take command because he saw California

Highway Patrol Officer Melanie Singer advancing on King with gun drawn, a dangerous tactic that could have resulted in a shooting. Koon's command to officers to holster their weapons before he tried the swarm or used the Taser may have been a life-saving order. Had King been shot, it is unlikely any officer would have been prosecuted, for the videotape was not yet rolling.

The action that occurred before the videotape began is the fundamental reason that the video cannot be relied upon for an understanding of what happened to Rodney King. The events that were not videotaped after King stopped his car took at least five or six minutes. Eighty-one seconds elapse on the video between Powell's first baton blow and the handcuffing.

The other problem with the videotape is its perspective. To viewers of the video, the beating of King seems callous as well as brutal because officers can be seen watching with folded arms, as if they have no cares in the world. But Koon could not see those officers. He stood within a cone of light that shone downward from the police helicopter, his gaze fixed on King and Powell. If Briseno's testimony can be believed—and it was crucial to the conviction of Koon and Powell—Koon was so focused on the activity in front of him that he did not respond to shouted questions. Koon has no recollection that anyone said anything to him. Such behavior is common in crisis situations, where officers often "tunnel in" on a perceived danger and ignore everything else. Koon denied to Internal Affairs detectives (against his own interests) that he experienced tunnel vision, but they did not believe him.

Various investigators who examined the videotape—among them Taky Tzimeas of Internal Affairs, Detective Cliff Ruff, and Jack White, the district attorney's investigator—concluded that Koon became so involved in the action that he was a participant rather than a supervisor. As a result, he failed to recognize when King ceased to be a threat and allowed the beating to go on too long. When the stun gun failed to stop King, Koon went into a funk, or so Tzimeas believes. He then committed tactical misjudgments, not criminal acts.

Whether Powell engaged in criminal conduct is a closer question. Reasonable jurors in any jurisdiction, left free to decide without the external pressure that existed in the federal civil rights case, might reach one decision or another on the charge on which the Simi Valley jury deadlocked: assault under color of authority. Powell was an immature braggart and a borderline cop. Even Sergeant Duke, who had no doubt that all of Powell's blows were justified, questions whether he should ever have been a police officer.

But Powell was in no way an instigator of this incident. He first used his baton when King charged toward him, and the evidence strongly suggests that it was this initial blow that struck King in the face. Even Powell's prosecutors conceded that the action was within LAPD policy, which prohibits intentional head blows but makes an exception for self-defense. Powell *was* defending himself. While he subsequently persuaded himself that he had not hit King in the head, his statement to Internal Affairs reveals that he had no real idea where his first blows landed. This statement was self-incriminating and thus unavailable to prosecutors, but Powell had told the truth to some of the officers questioned by the FBI. In fact, he told it on national television while awaiting the verdicts in the federal trial. The first time he saw the tape, Powell recalled, he said, "Is that even me?"[28]

The prosecution was not interested in this recollection, which reflected the fear and confusion that was Powell's true defense, because it undermined the false contention that the officers were administering street justice. But the defense wasn't particularly interested either. Powell's lawyer did him no favor by insisting, in defiance of Wind's observation to the contrary, that King was not hit in the head. As we have seen, this foolish insistence allowed prosecutors to make an effective issue of the head blows and depict Powell as a brute.

Koon, who had not seen or did not remember the head blow, contributed to this damaging defense. He had yelled at the officers not to hit King in the head and wanted to believe they had obeyed his commands. The head blows should have been irrelevant to Powell's guilt or innocence, but the defense's blind pursuit of its insupportable theory that the pavement caused King's head injuries made it relevant in the second trial and in the court of public opinion.

Prosecutors were as relentless as the defense in excluding facts that conflicted with their theories. They contended, for instance, that the officers had invented the notion that King was on PCP after the fact even though it was clear from comments made at the scene that the officers who confronted King thought he was "dusted." Impartial investigators, notably Tzimeas, had no doubt that the officers believed King was on PCP and suspected it themselves. But this useful and probably factual perception was dismissed by prosecutors because it undermined their theory that King was beaten into submission because the defendants wanted to punish him for being a wise guy and trying to escape.

The prosecution's claim that the King beating exemplified street justice was a preposterous caricature of the incident that occurred on March 3, 1991. But so was Koon's contention that the incident was a well-conceived exercise of proper police tactics that deserved to be incorporated into a training film. One important, ignored fact established by the Internal Affairs investigation was that Powell could not hear the commands barked out by Koon, probably because of the roar of the helicopter. The defense ignored this information because it contradicted Koon's claim that the incident was a controlled use of force in which Powell was responding to his orders. Prosecutors ignored it because it undermined their theory that Koon was directing a controlled punishment of King. The conflicting theories of control were powerfully presented in the trials, but neither reflected the reality of an incident that really was not controlled at all.

The King beating and arrest cannot be understood without trying to see them from Powell's perspective. While Koon was unaware of the presence of officers beyond the cone of light, Powell did not even know what the officers within this cone were doing. He was so afraid and exhausted that he also did not know that his partner Wind was beside him, swinging and kicking at King. As difficult as it may be for viewers of the video to realize, Powell imagined that he faced King alone. His mental state was revealed in his use of the personal pronoun when, glassy-eyed and panting, he told Officer Susan Clemmer immediately after the incident, "I was scared. The guy threw me off his back. I thought I was going to have to shoot him." These words have the ring of truth—at least as Powell perceived it. Although his conduct was incompetent and appalling, there is definitely reasonable doubt that he possessed criminal intent. His guilt in the first trial was a close call.

As for the second trial, there was no fair basis for charging Powell or anyone else with violating King's civil rights. Koon, Powell, Wind, and Briseno were scapegoats for the Los Angeles riots. Catastrophes require scapegoats, and the riots have been variously called the Pearl Harbor or the Vietnam of the LAPD. But no attempt was made to punish the leaders whose negligence had produced the disaster in the field. Instead, a sergeant and three rank-and-file officers took the blame for riots that occurred principally because the city's leadership failed at almost every level.

President Bush and Attorney General William Barr did not set out to make scapegoats of innocent men. They were truly shocked by what they saw on the Holliday videotape and by the ferocity of the riots. They hoped to discourage further rioting and limit political damage when they set in motion the federal prosecutions. William Kristol, a Barr confidant who was then Vice President Quayle's chief of staff, had succinctly captured the political reality: "Legally it was a questionable thing, but they felt they had to do it for obvious reasons." Once the trials were set in motion, the natural inclinations of dedicated prosecutors with access to unlimited resources did the rest.

The federal trial of the officers was as political in origin as any trial of radicals during the Cold War. And like many of those trials, it was also driven by fear—fear of more riots if the officers who had beaten King were not punished. While these fears were not groundless, it is unfortunate that Bush allowed himself to be stampeded by them. It is also unfortunate that the influential Southern California chapter of the American Civil Liberties Union, with its proud tradition of opposing double jeopardy, allowed distaste for the LAPD to lead it to endorse a dubious prosecution.

IF THE CIVIL RIGHTS TRIAL OF THE OFFICERS WAS POLITICAL, SO IN A broader sense was the King case itself. Political decisions had kept the LAPD small and limited its weaponry to guns and clubs; too much was expected of too few officers, who were inadequately equipped. But the police were popular, and politicians had looked the other way when suspects were shot or beaten. It took the videotape of the King beating to force a reassessment. For those doing the reassessing, it was easier to blame Koon and Powell than themselves.

The reassessment was inhibited by the political structures of Los Angeles. The structures were devised by Progressive reformers who distrusted politics and feared the people. They created a system that diffused civilian power and enabled the LAPD to become an unaccountable central authority. Politicians could starve the department financially, as Mayor Tom Bradley had done, but they could not control it. The astute Ed Davis recognized this in the 1970s, when he declined to run for mayor on the ground that he had more power as police chief. But times had changed. In the early days the white majority had regarded the LAPD as a unifying force. No police department could play that role once Los Angeles became the diverse rainbow city that it is today.

There is no question that the LAPD built by Chief Parker was an excellent force. Parker inculcated an abiding sense of professionalism that was valued after him by Tom Reddin, Ed Davis, and Daryl Gates. As the Christopher Commission noted, the LAPD maintained high standards of integrity and punished corruption. LAPD tactical innovations and drug education programs were widely copied, and police officers throughout the land admired the LAPD's gung-ho, proactive style.

But the society the LAPD served was changing rapidly. The courts started restricting arbitrary police mistreatment of criminal suspects, and civil rights advocates (and later opponents of the Vietnam War) challenged police resistance to social change. These developments had a profound impact in Los Angeles, where authoritarian elements had long believed that the police had the right to harass radicals, spy on politicians, keep minorities in their place, and use force against any suspect who dared to flee. Former LAPD Assistant Chief David Dotson, knowledgeable and enlightened on these issues and no fan of Gates, believes such questionable conduct became rare during the Gates years. Still, it took the King case, the Christopher Commission report, and the Mark Fuhrman tapes for the LAPD to confront the darker side of its legacy.

Many blacks believe, with Milton Grimes, that there was nothing un-usual about the Rodney King case except that the videotape caught police in the act of abusing a black man. Basing their assumptions on the edited videotape, many assumed that the evidence was powerful enough to over-come the prejudice of those who would never take a black man's word against a white officer. When it did not turn out that way, it seemed to blacks as if justice were unobtainable. This feeling fueled black rage, and not only at Florence and Normandie.

But the riots, like the videotaped beating of King, did not occur in a so-cial vacuum. They occurred in an area of Los Angeles where an enormous pool of unemployed and underemployed black youths was available to riot. Watts was a classic race riot ignited by a drunk driving arrest in a commu-nity distrustful of the police after days of unusually hot weather had driven residents out of homes that lacked air conditioning. Although that riot trag-ically destroyed one of the region's most intact and flourishing black com-munities, it was mostly confined to Watts. The savage 1992 riots, beginning as a protest to the verdicts in a relatively well off black neighborhood, spread through South Central and beyond, spurred by revenge, liquor, greed, and the contingent impulses of the mob. The riots might have been stopped or contained by quick and decisive police action. But after the police break-down the riots rapidly gained momentum because a small army of jobless youths were available to participate. Decades of decline had brought this jobless army into being.

ON APRIL 29, 1997, THE FIFTH ANNIVERSARY OF THE RIOTS, LOS Angeles took stock of the impact of the disorders. Many assessments were gloomy. "The big lesson that has been learned is that no one really cares," said Celes King III, chairman of the Congress of Racial Equality.[29] Angela Oh said of the Korean community, "There is a tremendous amount of bit-terness, but it's held in silence."[30] Bayan Lewis, a sensitive police officer who became LAPD interim chief after Willie Williams departed, said the de-partment was now listening to the people of South Central, "but that does not address the socio-economic conditions prevailing there—the poverty and the lack of jobs and rebuilding. What I see are lots of promises made after the riots, an initial burst of effort, and some inflow of money and im-provement of skills. Now, five years later, it's gone."[31]

When compared to the promises, the inflow never amounted to much. The Small Business Administration approved 5,500 disaster-loan applica-tions and disbursed $334 million in Los Angeles County. But while most businesses in Hollywood and on the fringes of the riot area were rebuilt, business owners in South Central found it hard to get financing to rebuild burned-out stores. In 1995, Vice President Al Gore and Mayor Riordan presided at a gala opening of the Los Angeles Community Development Bank—the consolation prize awarded by the Clinton administration after it declined to designate Los Angeles a federal empowerment zone. The bank had $740 million in assets, $430 million from the government and another $310 million kicked in by private banks at Riordan's behest. But by the fifth anniversary of the riots, it had made only two loans totaling $2.7 million.[32]

There was another side to this story. What the federal government and corporate America failed to do in a grand way was done bit by bit by the new immigrants from Mexico, Central America, and Asia—the voteless people demonized by Governor Pete Wilson and others for supposedly driving up welfare costs and otherwise being a burden on American citizens. The economic evidence contradicted this political view.[33] What salvaged Los Angeles in the mid-1990s was a burst of economic activity led by Latino immigrants. Because of it South Central is one of the nation's few inner cities where purchasing power increased during the 1990s.

Many of these immigrants were part of an extended family that included second- and third-generation citizens and legal residents. Their combined contribution was part of a growing pattern of Latino influence that in the late 1990s has transformed Southern California. The Latino population, 42 percent of Los Angeles County in 1995, has grown steadily, en route to a projected majority in the first decade of the twenty-first century. Latinos are already a majority in South Central, from which the exodus of African Americans accelerated. Southern Californians eat Mexican food, listen to mariachi and ranchera music and attend museums featuring Mexican muralists David Siqueiros and Rodolfo Morales. Univision, the leading Spanish-language television network, boasts larger audiences for its news programs than any English-language network. Young Latino families pooled their resources to buy houses and help ignite a real estate boom.[34] "We are redefining what it means to be an American in Southern California," said scholar Gregory Rodriguez, who called the new culture "Latino-American."[35]

Los Angeles County has a small-business economy in which 94 percent of firms employ fewer than fifty people. As a prominent Latino put it, these small businesses became "the engine of the revived economy" that pulled Southern California out of its post-Cold War recession.[36] In South Central, observed economist Jack Kyser, this Latino-led revival began during the "gut-wrenching economic downturn, when the media was focusing on the flight of business and the white middle class from Southern California."[37] Grocery chains had promised thirty-one new supermarkets in the riot area. They built only sixteen, but Latino and Asian entrepreneurs opened scores of small new markets. Cheap labor contributed to an explosion of light manufacturing in the toy, furniture, biochemical, garment, and food-processing industries. A

1996 study found that 700 of Los Angeles County's 1,100 food processing firms were located in poor neighborhoods, employing 30,000 people and serving diverse tastes for tortillas, pastas, noodles, and other ethnic staples.[38]

This study was conducted by RLA (formerly Rebuild Los Angeles), which under entrepreneur Peter Ueberroth had sought a $500 million corporate investment to make South Central an inner-city showcase. After that grandiose dream faded, RLA became a tiny nonprofit agency that linked businesses in self-help networks and performed such unassuming tasks as teaching export regulations to furniture manufacturers. RLA was mandated to shut down five years after its creation. Its last president was Linda Griego, a Latino who worked as a baker while earning her history degree at UCLA, and served as deputy mayor under Tom Bradley. Griego, now a restaurant owner, understood the economic realities. "Corporate America opens plants to make money," she said. "Believing that General Motors would open a plant in South Central when it was closing plants throughout the United States didn't make sense."[39]

Instead, reconstruction of South Central proceeded brick by brick, following the path of Latino migration from east to west. Huntington Park, just east of South Central, resembled a prosperous Mexican town, with more Spanish-language signs than English ones. By the fifth anniversary of the riots, Spanish-language signs were prevalent even in Florence-Normandie and Hyde Park, where some neighborhoods still had more African Americans than Latinos.

Ultimately, Latinos also began to have political impact. Latinos had been described for decades as the "sleeping giant" of Southern California politics, but the giant began to stir in 1994 after voters approved Proposition 187 to deny medical and educational benefits to illegal immigrants.* The proportion of Latino voters in the 1997 Los Angeles municipal election doubled from four years earlier. Latinos were still only 15 percent of the electorate, but they provided the margin of victory for a $2 billion bond issue to rebuild a neglected public school system in which two-thirds of the students spoke Spanish as their native language. The increased turnout also helped Mayor Riordan, who had cultivated the Latino community. He won reelection by 2–1 against Tom Hayden, a lone wolf Democratic state senator who is disliked by his party's establishment. In 1993, Riordan had been elected solely because of overwhelming Anglo support. In 1997, he also won substantial

---

* Proposition 187 was favored by every category of voters except Latinos. Some Latino analysts worried that passage of this initiative would trigger a campaign to reduce benefits for legal immigrants—as soon happened with the 1996 welfare bill. Taken together, Proposition 187 and the welfare legislation alarmed and to some degree radicalized Latinos. Pollster Sergio Bendixen found that the surge in Latino turnout in the 1997 Los Angeles election came largely from younger and more liberal voters among whom the turnout has traditionally been low.

majorities among Latinos and Asians. But he remained unpopular with blacks, a majority of whom voted for Hayden.

The 1997 elections were a troubling reminder to African Americans of their diminished importance. "At the low end, blacks complain they can't get entry-level service jobs because immigrants work for less," said Jarrette Fellows Jr., managing editor of the weekly *LA Watts Times.* "Middle-class blacks complain about loss of power; they have a feeling of helplessness and think their votes don't count."[40] The newspaper is published in the Crenshaw district instead of the once black bastion of Watts, now 60 percent Latino. Fellows and other analysts could read the handwriting on the wall: If Latinos fielded candidates and voted, African Americans stood to lose two of their three city council seats and representatives at every level of government.[41]

So as they counted gains and losses on the fifth anniversary of the riots, Latinos tended toward optimism and blacks to pessimism. "The riots may have been the birth of L.A., as well as the death of its innocence," said writer Richard Rodriguez.[42] But Julian Dixon, a black congressman who represented a multicultural Los Angeles district and had backed Riordan for reelection, thought the city's bright economic future would be imperiled unless it came to terms "with the cultural clash and different cultural identities."[43] This was difficult, for Latinos, Asians, and Anglos remained distrustful of African Americans five years after the riots. Sociologist and writer Earl Ofari Hutchinson, one of the city's most thoughtful African-American voices, observed that a principal legacy of the riots was that "individuals have stopped talking to one another and retreated from collective action."[44]

Joe Hicks, a veteran community analyst who had battled in vain to keep the Black-Korean Alliance alive, continued the struggle. He founded the Multi-Cultural Collaborative, a nonprofit group that seeks to unite poor people in South Central across racial and ethnic lines. "The Rodney King question—Can we all get along?—can't be answered in the abstract," Hicks said. "You have to build alliances. The economic realities of South L.A. have erected barriers among racial and ethnic groups. The future of this city is bound up on its ability to find common ground."[45]

THE LOS ANGELES POLICE DEPARTMENT AND THE POLICE Commission also struggled to find answers to the "Rodney King question." Diversity training for recruits was intensified. Deputy Chief Mark Kroeker initiated a program that sent selected LAPD officers to live in Guadalajara, Mexico, to improve their Spanish-language skills and learn the customs of the people.[46] At the urging of Raymond Fisher, the Police Commission chose Katherine Mader, an experienced prosecutor, as the

LAPD's first inspector general. She tackled sensitive issues of sexual harassment and domestic violence by officers against their spouses. She was backed by Deputy Chief Bernard Parks and especially by interim Chief Bayan Lewis, who created a specialized unit within the Internal Affairs Division to deal with domestic violence. The LAPD had long ignored these issues; by 1997, it was in the forefront of the nation's police departments in addressing them.

The banner of the new LAPD became "community policing," a principal theme of the Christopher Commission. Community policing replaced the *Dragnet* model of gung-ho policing that had been the LAPD way since the days of Chief Bill Parker except for a brief period in the 1970s when Chief Ed Davis introduced the basic car plan. Davis had been partly motivated by recognition that the LAPD had been isolated and lacked reliable information about the black community during the 1965 Watts riot. A similar impulse stirred revival of community policing after the 1992 disorders.

Willie Williams had needed no convincing about the wisdom of community policing. He came from Philadelphia, where police respond to every call and therefore have day-to-day contact with citizens in non-emergency situations. But the LAPD, with its history of manpower shortages, responded only to serious crimes and had fewer friendly or routine contacts with city residents. Williams thought this was a mistake. He held the view enunciated by Sir Robert Peel when he organized the London Metropolitan Police in 1829: that crime prevention is the principal duty of the police and requires citizen participation. On occasion Williams had quoted Peel's classic definition of community policing: "The police are the public, and the public are the police."

Under Williams, community advisory boards were established in each of the city's eighteen police divisions, co-chaired by an LAPD captain and a civilian. While these boards supposedly established community priorities for police attention, the members were selected by the LAPD and lacked accountability to the communities they represented. They exercised no oversight but may have marginally increased police awareness of community attitudes.

The LAPD rank and file had never been enthusiastic about community policing. When Chief Davis introduced the basic car plan a quarter century before, it was greeted with disdain by officers, who scoffed at serving cookies at neighborhood meetings and becoming, in Ted Hunt's useful phrase, "social workers with guns." But some veteran officers remembered the Davis era as a golden one for the LAPD and recognized that the basic car plan had won support for the police in minority neighborhoods. Considering the latent support that existed for community policing among

these old-timers, Williams might have sold the idea had he been more popular within the LAPD.

But Williams wasn't respected, and skepticism about community policing prevailed. A committee of thirty-four experienced officers told the chief
late in 1994 that community policing was hampered by rank-and-file resistance, lack of officers, and insufficient support from other city agencies.[47]
In 1995, Williams put a high-level commander in charge of community
policing and gave him broad authority. The commander, Garrett Zimmon,
believed too much had been expected too quickly; he said there was a "perception that community policing was a light bulb—you reach up and pull
it and it turns on overnight."[48] Zimmon meant well, but progress was slow.
In 1996, Williams conceded that community policing "is happening much
slower that I would have liked, and I'm sure slower than the community
would like, too."[49]

What Williams meant by this is not precisely clear. His notion of community policing lacked the specificity of the basic car plan, and he had no
yardstick for measuring success. He credited community policing for improving the image of the LAPD, which it did, and for reducing crime, which
was questionable. Although crime rates declined in Los Angeles in the mid-
1990s, they dropped even more rapidly in cities such as New York and Houston that adopted some of the aggressive tactics for which the LAPD had
been famous. Whether community advisory boards changed any LAPD priorities is also unclear. Zimmon cited marginal successes: more foot patrols
in a high-crime corridor of Reseda, identification of two crack houses in
77th Street Division, formation of a soccer league, and distribution of gifts
to needy children in Pacific Division. But no one knew whether such activity was the result of policy or the dedication of individual officers.

As a slogan, however, community policing was politically irresistible. It
had been advocated by the Christopher Commission and embraced by two
mayors, their police commissions, and most of the city council. The division
captains who headed the community advisory boards and the police brass
at Parker Center muffled their doubts and went along. But as Jim Newton
observed, "they still had no real idea of what community policing meant or
how to implement it."[50]

Joe Gunn, the cop-turned-screenwriter who was Mayor Riordan's liaison
to the Police Commission, saw the LAPD commitment to community policing as an overdue "attitudinal change."[51] Officer Ted Hunt, the longtime Police Academy instructor who became a director of the Police Protective
League, was also cautiously optimistic, seeing community policing as a stepping stone to a new era in which officers would "redefine the nature of police work" through "social triage." Hunt believes that the police officer of the
future will still "get the bad guys" but will also become a first line of defense

in helping battered women and abused children reach the agencies that are supposed to help them. He would be the first to say that many dedicated police officers already perform this role.

It was as a bridge to this new era of police work that community policing was welcomed by the people of Los Angeles. Los Angeles learned from the King case and the deadly riots that a police department in a democracy cannot succeed apart from the community it is supposed to protect and serve. Community policing, however ill defined, responded to a yearning for a police force that would be a servant of the people rather than their master.

The city council, sensing the public mood, demonstrated in the summer of 1996 that the tide had turned against warp-speed expansion of the LAPD. Riordan had promised when he ran for mayor in 1993 that he would not seek a second term unless he added 3,000 new police officers, a nearly 30 percent increase over four years. The promise would have been difficult to carry out even if Riordan had not attached to it a feckless pledge to accomplish the expansion without raising taxes. He squeezed various city agencies and tried to divert airport revenues to police expansion but came up short. In 1996, however, election-year competition between a Democratic president and a Republican Congress produced a federal bill that offered money for police forces throughout the nation, including $53 million for the LAPD.

But the city council balked at accepting this largess. Councilwoman Laura Chick, also elected in 1993 on a platform of police expansion, pointed out that the federal gift required matching funds and was "one-time money." She said Los Angeles would be stuck with paying the accumulated costs of a larger police force when it was no longer receiving federal funds and would be forced to starve other programs to do it. Richard Alatorre, the mayor's staunchest council ally, offered an amendment to the 1996 budget to slow the LAPD buildup and broaden the definition of "public safety" to include parks, libraries, streets, and lighting. "The city has got to be about more than how we patrol our streets," Alatorre said. "It's got to be about the quality of life on those streets."[52] The council passed the amendment and overrode Riordan's veto of it despite the mayor's lament that rejecting federal funds was "inconceivable."

Even if the city council had fully cooperated, Riordan could not have carried out his campaign promise. The LAPD recruited nearly enough officers to meet his goal, but the mayor underestimated the impact of attrition on the dispirited department. The LAPD had 7,700 officers when Riordan promised to add 3,000. By the time he took office in July 1993, the number had dropped to 7,400, a number the mayor later adopted as his baseline. When he was reelected in 1997, the LAPD had 9,500 officers and hundreds more in the Police Academy pipeline. Riordan had fallen short of his promise by 900 to 1,200 officers, depending on which baseline is used.

In terms of quantity, Riordan's accomplishment was still significant. The LAPD had never before had 9,000 officers, and every hire above this mark set a new record. What's more, Riordan and Chief Williams had worked with the Police Commission and the council to replace worn-out equipment and begin bringing the LAPD into the computer age. Given the realities of tight budgets and decades of neglect, it is hard to see how more could have been done in four years to expand police capabilities. Chiefs from Parker through Gates had prided themselves on doing more with less than other cities. The "thin blue line" reflected doctrine as well as fiscal reality, and neither would change overnight.

But Riordan's promise led him to emphasize numbers at the expense of training. There had been no shortage of officers when Rodney King was stopped. The most enduring lesson to be drawn from Powell's confrontation with King is the danger of deploying a badly trained officer. As police expansion accelerated, veteran officers complained that there were not enough experienced trainers. Others did not like the fact that the Police Academy had modified physical-training standards as more women were recruited. Sergeant Duke believed that the twin goals of expansion and gender diversity unwisely encouraged the Police Academy to graduate recruits who lacked the skills to become good officers.[53]

What the Police Academy lacked in the rigor of its training it may partly have made up for in new methods of arresting resistant suspects. Sergeant Greg Dossey, a twenty-four-year veteran of the LAPD, was at USC obtaining his doctorate at the time of the King incident. He replaced Sergeant Mark Conta, the prosecution hero and defense villain of the federal civil rights trial of the King officers, as lead instructor at the Police Academy in what the LAPD then called physical-training and self-defense tactics. Dossey consulted with twenty-five martial arts experts and devised a new program for teaching police recruits how to arrest resistant suspects without using unnecessary force. In 1995, the LAPD began teaching the new curriculum at the Police Academy, under the nomenclature "arrest and control skills." As Dossey put it, "The idea was to develop techniques that were humane and effective, which we did." These techniques emphasize "grappling" or "multiple officer takedowns," another aspect of the legacy of the Rodney King case.[54]

The new curriculum was expanded to the field in 1996, with a goal of training every officer in the revised techniques by the end of 1997. The field training included a day of classroom work and four days of practice on exercise mats. As Dossey saw it, borrowing a phrase from earthquake reconstruction, his mission was "to retrofit the entire department."

Even so, training could not keep pace with department expansion. "My gut feeling is that we're running a terrible risk," said Lieutenant John Dunkin, a onetime paratrooper and a twenty-seven-year LAPD veteran in charge of homicide detectives in South Bureau. Dunkin thought the new training regimen was excellent but believed that the "nuances and social skills of police work" are learned on the street with experienced officers as teachers.[55] He uneasily remembered trying to juggle duty rosters and pair rookies with veterans when he had been watch commander at the Rampart Division during an earlier LAPD expansion. That was 1990, when a shortage of experienced officers prompted then-Captain Tim McBride to accept Laurence Powell as a training officer at Foothill Division—a decision McBride later regretted.

Division captains throughout the city made similar decisions during the much greater expansion launched by Riordan four years later. This posed an obvious risk that the mayor preferred not to contemplate, even though it was a frequent topic in LAPD ranks. Veteran officers disagreed about whether the inexperience of the trainers was offset by the improvement in the training. Cliff Ruff and Ted Hunt in 1996 thought that the combination of improved training and officer reluctance to use force after what had happened to Powell and Koon had reduced the risk of another Rodney King incident. Duke, echoing the words spoken by Officer David Zeigler three years earlier, said, "We could have a Rodney King case tonight."[56]

Whether or not there is such a case, the Rodney King affair has benefited the LAPD. As a result of it, the LAPD obtained permission to use pepper spray and other non-lethal weapons and virtually abandoned the side-handled metal baton that Ted Hunt called "the caveman's weapon of choice." The Police Academy expanded cultural-awareness and language training. And the LAPD reexamined the way officers behaved on the streets. Lieutenant Dunkin said it best: "The Rodney King case forced us to examine ourselves and make changes we needed to make, changes we wouldn't have made on our own. You can't do police work independent of everybody else in the city. We did what we thought was right, but the Rodney King case taught us that this isn't enough. You don't get to do things in secret. You have to be accountable to the people."[57]

The new accountability sacrificed the four officers who had tried to follow LAPD policy in violently subduing Rodney King after their nonviolent attempts to take him into custody failed. Few people remember, if they ever knew, that these officers had attempted for several minutes to take King into custody by nonviolent means before the videotape began. From the moment the edited video aired on television, the incident was reduced to "white LAPD officers beating a black motorist," as if King were out for a

Sunday-afternoon drive and the officers had decided to beat him because he is an African American.

In fact, the King beating was a product of official negligence, and the officers became scapegoats for a system that allowed resistant suspects to be beaten into submission with metal batons. What distinguished the incident from other arrests in which suspects suffered even more serious injuries was less its brutality than the fact that portions of it were videotaped and shown on television. Had the incident been seen as the inevitable result of a flawed policy for which Mayor Bradley and the city council shared responsibility instead of as an isolated incident of police brutality with probable racial motivation, the chain of events that culminated in the riots might have unfolded differently. Perhaps public opinion might still have demanded indictments, but the defense of the officers would have seemed more reasonable if LAPD policy had also have been on trial. Instead, with awful consequences, civilian and police authorities treated the King beating as the aberration Gates claimed it to be.

The assumption that criminal convictions were inevitable made possible the mayhem of 1992. Although the unrest was stoked by accumulated discontents, the evidence suggests that the riots could have been averted, or quickly contained, had the LAPD prepared for acquittals and the protests that were certain to follow.

As with the policies that produced the King beating, the police breakdown during the riots was not entirely the fault of the police. Chief Gates was most responsible, but blame for the breakdown is shared by his slow-moving subordinates and by Mayor Bradley, who assumed with Gates that the officers would be convicted and did not use his emergency powers to mobilize the city. Some of the responsibility also rests with Councilman Mark Ridley-Thomas and other African-American politicians who wanted police kept out of South Central during jury deliberations in Simi Valley so their presence would not provoke a riot. When the riot came because the police were not present, these same politicians accused the LAPD of abandoning South Central.

The new leaders of Los Angeles did not dwell on past errors as the city resumed its march into its multicultural future. Los Angeles is not an introspective city. Gates and Bradley disappeared from public view once out of office, although Gates briefly reemerged into the spotlight in 1996 as a defender of Riverside County sheriff's deputies who were videotaped beating illegal immigrants after a high-speed freeway chase. Too late, he warned against a rush to judgment. As for Rodney King, his driving mishaps and legal scrapes became so routine that the Los Angeles Times brushed them off with tiny stories, often in a roundup of the day's events.

BUT THE 1991 DRIVING ESCAPADE THAT ENDED IN THE VIDEOTAPED beating of Rodney King cast a long shadow over the LAPD. Out of it came the Christopher Commission and the recommendations for reform by which the LAPD was judged and found wanting. The Christopher Commission wanted a police chief who would be accountable to the public for the actions of his officers—a standard that forced Chief Gates into retirement, cost Chief Williams a second term, and was uppermost in the minds of Police Commission President Raymond Fisher and his colleagues as they sought a new leader for the LAPD in the summer of 1997.

By then, the LAPD was a transitional department haunted by conflicting legacies. "The LAPD has changed drastically in the last five years, but it's not clear what it's become," observed Lieutenant Dunkin. "We're struggling to find an identity as a kinder, gentler police force that still does aggressive police work." The two leading candidates for chief—Deputy Chief Bernard C. Parks and Deputy Chief Mark A. Kroeker—believed these goals were compatible. Both men were fifty-three-year-old officers with a capacity for hard work, reputations for competence and integrity, and similar backgrounds. Both had joined the LAPD in 1965, the year of the Watts riot, and served in a variety of demanding posts. Both had continued their studies after becoming officers and earned master's degrees in public administration from the University of Southern California. Although many wanted to be chief, the choice came down to Parks or Kroeker.*

Kroeker, a personable son of Mennonite missionaries, was raised in the Belgian Congo and Europe. He speaks French fluently and Spanish passably and is attuned to the city's multi-culturalism. He was an enthusiast for community policing before it was fashionable; as deputy chief in the San Fernando Valley, he had organized meetings after the King beating to allow citizens to express their views. As deputy chief in crime-ridden South Bureau during the Williams years, he reached out to the community. Officers who worked for Kroeker found him dedicated and often inspirational. A poll taken by the Los Angeles Police Protective League showed that three-fourths of rank-and-file officers wanted Kroeker as their chief. He had cultivated union support by favoring one of the league's pet proposals—a change in the work week to three days of twelve-hour shifts.

---

* The Police Commission screened thirty-two candidates, twenty of them from outside the department. Under procedures prescribed by Charter Amendment F, the list was narrowed to three—Parks, Kroeker, and Sacramento Police Chief Arturo Venegas Jr.—and given to Riordan for his selection. But it was evident from the beginning of this process that the commission did not want to go outside the LAPD. This was recognized by former New York city police comissioner William Bratton, the only outsider who might have stood a chance. "My instinct tells me the job's going to go to an insider," Bratton said in explaining why he did not apply.

But the Police Commission thought a three-day work week contained too many pitfalls, and the proposal was scotched by the capable interim Chief Bayan Lewis.[58] Kroeker's support for the plan did not help his campaign for chief; it seemed to his critics that he too readily told his audiences what he thought they wanted to hear. Kroeker was also considered relatively lenient in dealing with officers accused of misconduct, another mark against him.

Parks was at the other extreme. He showed zeal in punishing officers who used excessive force or engaged in other serious misconduct, but sometimes penalized officers harshly for minor violations. Parks was set in his ways, strong in his opinions, and renowned as a detail man. His backers said he was firm and principled, while his detractors complained that he was rigid and uncompromising.

Parks, who was born in Texas and raised in South Central, was the LAPD's highest-ranking black officer after Williams departed. Slender and six-feet-two-inches tall, he matched the LAPD image of a chief as Williams never had. Parks was also steeped in the intricacies of police work. Early in his career he had come under the tutelage of Ed Davis, the most creative of the LAPD chiefs after Bill Parker. Parks admired Davis but realized that there were many others in the LAPD who were less progressive in their racial attitudes. Whenever possible, he blocked the advancement of officers he considered racist—as he did in refusing to put Detective Mark Fuhrman in charge of the unit that investigated officer-involved shootings. The Police Commission and the mayor respected Parks and had no doubt that he was the best manager in the LAPD. But they also knew he had never been keen about community policing and worried that he would not reach out enough to be an effective chief.

As career disappointments piled up in the 1990s, Parks had often been on the verge of retiring. He nearly quit when he lost out to Williams for the chief's job in 1992, mostly because the Police Commission was determined to hire an outsider. He almost left again in 1994 after Williams humiliated him by demoting him from assistant chief to deputy. What kept Parks from retiring this time was the city council's decision, prompted by Richard Alatorre, to continue paying him the assistant chief's salary—an action less important to Parks for the money than for his reputation. In the summer of 1997, the Police Commission realized Parks probably could bring order out of the managerial chaos that prevailed. Still, the commissioners hesitated. In at least one meeting they talked wistfully about finding someone who would combine Kroeker's public presence with Parks' managerial ability. But no such candidate existed. Ultimately, Parks was ranked first and Kroeker second on the list that Fisher gave Riordan in his last act as Police Commission president.

It pained the mayor to reject either man. During the Williams years he had separately urged Parks and Kroeker not to retire, an act that each took as a hint that he would become chief if he stayed. Riordan felt more comfortable with Kroeker, but he wanted a tough-minded manager, which argued for Parks. Racial politics also favored Parks; choosing him would allay the concerns of African Americans that Williams had been pushed out because he was black.[59] But Riordan probably would have opted for Parks in any case because the two men were mirror images in management style. They shared the view, most famously expressed in Harry Truman's saying "The buck stops here," that the number-one man is always responsible for what happens. At City Hall on August 6, Riordan announced that Parks was his choice, then watched approvingly as Parks answered a question from Jim Newton about whether he would take the responsibility if crime increased on his watch. Parks said that a decrease in crime would be "a positive" for Los Angeles, then added pointedly: "If it increases, the chief of police hasn't done his job."

This set the tone for a news conference that Parks turned into a bravura performance. Promising to maintain "community-oriented policing," he said the LAPD would be tough on crime, treat citizens properly, and make Los Angeles "the safest big city in the United States." Later, Parks said he would pay attention to the "mental health" of his police officers.[60] When a reporter asked how anyone who had worked so long in the LAPD could change it, Parks said he was "the best person to change it" because he knew the department's strengths and weaknesses. Councilwoman Laura Chick was charmed. "What a lovely beginning," she said. "We've all longed for a chief like that." And Councilman Alatorre called the appointment "a great day for Los Angeles."[61] His only regret, he said, was that it came five years too late.

THE "RODNEY KING POLICE OFFICERS," AS THEY WERE SOMETIMES known, remained pariahs. Tim Wind and Ted Briseno had been acquitted by twenty-four jurors in two criminal trials and found not liable for King's injuries by ten other jurors in a civil trial. It made no difference. Their police careers were over, and they experienced long periods of joblessness and despair. It was the misfortune of both officers to be involved in a social calamity that destroyed the innocent and the guilty with as much impartiality as any natural disaster. Latasha Harlins was dead, and her killer was free. Damian Williams would emerge from prison in the late 1990s, still a young man while Reginald Denny and his fellow victims at Florence and Normandie would suffer from their injuries for the rest of their lives. The officers acquitted of abusing Rodney King would face many of the same obstacles as those who were convicted.

Sergeant Duke calls Tim Wind the "real victim" of the incident. Even prosecutors found him a sympathetic figure. Gates tried to fire him nonetheless, in keeping with his practice of discarding anyone who might be a political liability. The LAPD, in fact, announced that Wind had been fired; it was what Gates wanted people to believe. Without announcement, however, Gates had yielded to the entreaty of Wind's attorney that Wind was entitled to a hearing, and he had rescinded the dismissal. In March 1994, at a proceeding known as a Liberty Interest Hearing, Wind's conduct during the King incident was reviewed by Captain Robert Gale, who found that Wind was "honest and sincere" and had conducted himself in a "professional and dignified" manner during the hearing and his three trials. At the three-day hearing, Gale determined that Wind had used his baton properly but that his six kicks violated policy. He recommended a six-month suspension and reinstatement, but Chief Williams fired Wind instead.[62]

Wind struggled for three years to find work between each of the three spring trials. He was a political target for militant blacks, and the rap singer Ice Cube wrote a song urging that Wind be sent back to Kansas in a casket. Other officers and Koon's lawyer, Ira Salzman, tried to help Wind find a job. In October 1994, over protests from African Americans, Wind was hired as a part-time community service officer in Culver City, a small city in western Los Angeles County. He was paid $9.32 an hour to process subpoenas, run errands, and wash Police Chief Ted Cooke's car once a week. Wind did not wear a badge or carry a gun. Cooke braved continuing criticism for hiring Wind and keeping him on the payroll.

Lorna Wind continued to work, recovered from a miscarriage, and held their family together. The baby boy they had brought with them from Kansas was now in grade school and didn't understand what had happened to his father. Tim Wind, who acknowledged that he too often felt sorry for himself, persevered. He attended community college, earned straight As, and discovered that he no longer wanted to be a policeman. During his trials, he had analyzed the strategies and tactics of lawyers on both sides and decided he could do as well as some of them. But he couldn't afford law school. Then, in 1996, he won a workers' compensation award for severe gastrointestinal and psychological disorders. But the city council appealed the decision, and the Winds continued to struggle.[63]

Briseno also struggled to support himself and his family—with the added handicap of unremitting hostility from the police community. Officers could forgive Briseno's stomp of King, whatever its motivation, but not his testimony against Powell and Koon at Simi Valley. An unsympathetic police Board of Rights—one of whose members in a Freudian slip called the board "the department"—recommended in mid-1994 that Briseno be fired. Williams, who needed no urging, complied. Briseno appealed to a state court but lost.

Briseno's economic ruin was not enough for the LAPD. The department wanted to make an example of him and found willing accomplices in the

Ventura County District Attorney's Office. At the LAPD's behest that office conducted a ten-month investigation and late in 1994 issued a report contending that Briseno lied under oath at Simi Valley. This assertion was described by Harland Braun as a "slander." It was at least gratuitous, for the Ventura district attorney had no intention of prosecuting Briseno. Indeed, the report acknowledged that proving perjury "would be exceedingly difficult." But in a disgraceful postscript to the official negligence that marked the King case, the Ventura County prosecutors had delivered the LAPD's message that an officer who dared to testify against his comrades would never be forgiven.

As for Briseno, he was in Braun's words "psychologically disabled." With the help of his brother and Braun, he finally found night work as a private security guard at much reduced pay and with no pension. Briseno was in debt, worried about providing for his family, and bothered by the belated realization that he would never again work as a police officer. Police work had been his life, and he missed it.

Koon and Powell went to prison, usually a perilous place for police officers. Family members and friends believed they were in particular danger because of the notoriety of the King case, and Judge John Davies had cited this concern as one of his reasons for reducing their sentences. Officials of the Federal Bureau of Prisons insisted that Koon and Powell could be protected. When they entered prison in October 1993, they were assigned to the Federal Prison Camp in Dublin, California, in the southeastern San Francisco Bay area, a prison without walls or gun towers that was reserved for non-violent offenders. There, 65 percent of the inmates were drug offenders and another 25 percent had been convicted of white-collar crimes. It was one of the safest federal prisons, but in 1995 it was converted to a women's prison, and Powell and Koon were transferred.

Powell was sent to the Boron Correctional Work Camp near Edwards Air Force Base, north of Los Angeles, where the prison population was more varied and not exclusively non-violent. The compensation was that he was now only a hundred miles away from his family and girl friend, to whom he became engaged while in prison. They visited him frequently and raised money for his legal appeals by selling copper bracelets patterned after the ones used to remember prisoners of war and T-shirts that said, "To Protect and To Serve—Time."

In October 1995, Powell was sent to My Break Transitional Center in Garden Grove, a halfway house in Orange County, where he spent the final two months of his sentence. He was released on December 13, after two years in prison plus the two months in the halfway house, a standard good-behavior reduction for a federal prisoner with a thirty-month sentence. Powell had long since sold his home to pay his legal expenses, and his appellate attorney had filed a pauper's declaration. But his financial plight had gained the attention of conservatives, led by Los Angeles County Supervisor Mike Antonovich, who planned a "welcome home" fund-raising dinner at the Los Angeles Police Academy on December 14. The sponsors hoped to raise $50,000 of the more than $150,000 owed by Powell in legal fees. Mike Stone announced that he would forgive the rest of the bill.

But African Americans considered the dinner an affront, and Councilman Mark Ridley-Thomas moved to stop it. The Police Academy dining hall is operated by a private, nonprofit group of active and retired LAPD officers who call themselves the Los Angeles Police Revolver and Athletic Club. After Ridley-Thomas warned that the city council would review the city's leasing agreement with the club if the Powell dinner were held, the club canceled the event. A make-up dinner sponsored by the Legal Affairs Council was held on February 22, 1996, at a hotel in Washington, D.C.[64]

Koon's path to freedom proved more eventful and perilous. He balked at being transferred to Boron, even though he would have been nearer his family, because the work camp had a general prison population. Federal inmates cannot choose where they will be incarcerated, but prison officials were mindful of their promises to protect the officers and reluctant to send Koon to a facility he believed was dangerous. So Koon was held for eleven days in the hospital ward of the Kern County Jail in Bakersfield while prison officials considered alternatives. Then he was driven to the Federal Correctional Work Camp in Sheridan, Oregon, where he remained for ten months.

Sheridan, a former military base, was isolated and safe. The Re-Entry Community Corrections Center in Rubidoux, California, was neither. Koon was transferred to this thirty-bed, halfway house in Riverside County, sixty miles east of Los Angeles, on October 16, 1995, two months before his scheduled release. He was pleased to be back in Southern California. But Koon received an unsigned death threat after he arrived and soon became aware that Rubidoux was the center of a high-crime area with a majority African-American population. The little town reminded Koon of 77th Street Division in South Central.

The assignment of Koon to Rubidoux, for reasons never explained, was a blunder by the Bureau of Prisons. It was a final act of negligence in the King case that would have lethal consequences. The bureau had many halfway homes available, such as the one to which Powell went in Garden Grove, where Koon's presence would have caused no problem. But after Koon objected to Boron, where prison officials thought he could have been protected, they sent him to an unguarded halfway house operated by a private agency in a crime-ridden neighborhood. Furthermore, news of the transfer was made public, and Koon's presence in Rubidoux was known and resented.

Koon celebrated his forty-fifth birthday on Thanksgiving, November 23. He was given a furlough for the holiday, left Rubidoux early in the morning, and was home in Castaic, north of Los Angeles, when an angry thirty-five-year-old African American named Randall Tolbert burst into the halfway house shortly after noon and demanded to see Koon. Tolbert, a gang member with a long prison and arrest record for violent offenses, including attempted murder, carried a plastic garbage bag that contained liquor, drugs, and a sawed-off shotgun. Family members said afterward he had been using PCP for three days. Tolbert became enraged when told that Koon wasn't at the halfway house and brandished the shotgun at a staff member, insisting that he give him Koon's telephone number. Tolbert then dialed the number, identified himself as a member of the Westside Project Crips and shouted into the phone, "Get back down here, motherfucker, you fucking cop faggot, get your ass back here. I'm going to blow you away."[65]

This was the first of three phone conversations Koon had during the afternoon with Tolbert, who also called his own family members and various TV stations from the halfway house. Koon reported his conversations to a nearby sheriff's office. He functioned as a hostage negotiator, trying to calm Tolbert and obtain information about his whereabouts in the halfway house. Between calls, Tolbert pistol-whipped a woman visitor in the dining hall and shot a resident in the chest from a distance, not injuring him seriously. Both escaped. Tolbert then moved to another part of the house, taking with him as hostages a staff member, a woman who serviced vending machines, and Karl Milam, sixty-seven, a friend who was visiting her from Phoenix.

The standoff continued until 3:30 P.M., when Tolbert killed Milam with a shotgun blast to the head. A Riverside County sheriff's SWAT team rushed into the house at the sound of the shot and a deputy stumbled over Milam's body, possibly saving himself from being shot as well. As the SWAT team knew from what Tolbert had told Koon, the gunman was in a room at the back of the house. Tolbert fired as the SWAT team entered, and the four sheriff's deputies shot him dead. The Los Angeles Times quoted Tolbert's brother as saying that Koon's presence in Rubidoux "was eating at all of us," and it quoted his mother as recalling that her son "loved baking cakes" and had promised to return and bake one for Thanksgiving.[66]

Koon never went back to Rubidoux. He was allowed to spend the last weeks of his incarceration in a form of house arrest, from which he was released on December 14. While he had missed his family, prison had not damaged him. Laurence Powell was bitter about the way the system had treated him, but Koon told me he had tried to make prison a "positive experience" and improve himself "physically, mentally, and spiritually."[67]

Koon knew that dieting, exercising, and weight-lifting would make him healthier and "burn up time" in prison. He lost forty-five pounds and returned home weighing 175—too slim to fit into his old clothes.[68] During his two years in prison, he also made it a point of reading two or three books a week instead of watching movies or television. As Koon saw it, prison gave him an opportunity for educational improvement similar to military service, when he had completed a year of correspondence courses at the University of Southern California. Mental and spiritual improvement overlapped; Koon completed two correspondence courses in a program of study to become a Roman Catholic lay teacher.

Koon said he was motivated in these studies by the religious involvement of his wife, Mary, and by his own need to deal "with the anger of the case." This anger had been directed at the federal government for prosecuting him a second time and at Daryl Gates, Mark Conta, and Ted Briseno. Unlike Powell, Koon bore no malice toward Rodney King. He worried that his anger would fester and turn him into a perpetual complainer. "I hate people like that, and I don't think other people like them, and I sure as hell didn't want to be that way," he said. So he tried to dampen his anger through prayer and meditation, about which he talked hesitantly because he didn't want to be labeled a "religious fanatic." The process seemed to work. "No good comes out of holding [a] grudge," he said. "The good comes out of being a forgiving person."[69]

Koon was able to focus on self-improvement in large part because of the largess and fund-raising skills of Alfred Regnery, the publisher of Koon's book, *Presumed Guilty*. Koon was destitute when he went to prison. He worried about providing for his five children, the oldest of whom was then fifteen. When Koon's father died in the summer of 1994, he did not attend the funeral because he could not afford to pay the costs of the guards who would have been sent to supervise him. Regnery, a well-known sponsor of conservative causes, launched a defense fund to pay Koon's legal bills and support his family. A fund-raising letter sent over Koon's name said: "I am the political scapegoat of radicals and self-serving liberal politicians who know that I am innocent." This letter and other appeals, one by Mary Koon, raised millions and caused some resentment among Koon's co-defendants.*

But the Rubidoux incident was a frightening reminder to Koon's family that he could never expect a normal life. Stacey Koon and Rodney King were marked men, false symbols of the racial animus that permeates American life.

---

* Records of the Koon Defense Fund filed with the Virginia Office of Consumer Affairs show that $9,181,622 was raised in 1994 and 1995. All but $2,414,400 of this money was consumed by fundraising and other expenses. Of the latter amount, $1,187,757 was used for legal expenses and family support while $474,511 went into a trust fund for the Koon children and $167,086 into a trust fund for Mary Koon. Another $400,067 was placed in trust for Stacey Koon and the balance used for unspecified contributions. I have rounded the numbers and combined figures from the two years. Briseno told me he would gladly have spent three years in prison for this kind of money.

They were linked forever by the incident that had made them famous and notorious.

King was for many whites an embodiment of black lawlessness. While no paragon, he was an easygoing man with a minor criminal record who was a menace only when behind the wheel of an automobile after he had been drinking. His multimillion dollar damage award aside, he had paid a high price for his alcoholism. King told me he still dreams about the beating and is fearful when he sees a police officer. When an officer approached him and shook his hand as he was eating in a fast-food restaurant in Orange County, King was overjoyed.[70]

Koon was to blacks a symbol of white police brutality. This was even more unfair than the stereotype of King. As the FBI learned when it investigated him, Koon had a hard-earned reputation as a good cop and a family man. Black officers who had worked with him liked him and considered him enlightened on racial issues. Koon had rarely felt in danger in the black neighborhoods of 77th Street Division, but he had learned from Rubidoux that he was no longer safe on the streets.

Along with their acquitted colleagues, Koon and Powell had lost their police careers. Chief Williams could not wait to fire them and did so as soon as their convictions had been affirmed and their dismissals recommended by LAPD boards of rights. Koon, in a show of defiance, refused to accept the paperwork served him by his board or appear at what he regarded as a sham procedure. But his dismissal was automatic, for California law prohibits felons from serving as police officers. Koon worked part-time at home analyzing alleged cases of police brutality for a conservative legal foundation or assisting his attorney, Ira Salzman. Most of the time, as Koon put it, he was a "house husband" who took care of the children while his wife worked. After two years in prison he enjoyed this role.[71]

Powell went back to school, where he excelled in math and physics and displayed the affinity for computers that had already been apparent in his police work. But he could not find full-time work. Powell said prospective employers were sympathetic but didn't want to "hire controversy."[72] His father, however, remained confident that his son would get his chance.

The first six months of 1996 were an anxious period for Koon and Powell, who faced the prospect of additional years in prison if the Supreme Court upheld the Ninth Circuit Court of Appeals and found that Judge Davies had violated federal sentencing guidelines when he gave them thirty-month terms. Although Judge Stephen Reinhardt, the liberal conscience of the Ninth Circuit, had characterized these sentences as "severe indeed," the government contended that the sentences were too lenient. More was at stake than the freedom of the two former LAPD officers. Advocates of judicial discretion hoped that the high court would use *U.S. v.*

Koon to restore judicial powers that had been weakened by the rigid and complex guidelines.

On June 13, 1996, the Supreme Court cautiously seized its opportunity. While failing to issue as sweeping a decision as advocates of judicial discretion wanted, the high court overturned the Ninth Circuit by a unanimous 9–0 vote and found that Davies had used mostly valid factors in rejecting the lengthy sentences sought by the government. "It has been uniform and constant in the federal judicial tradition for the sentencing judge to consider every convicted person as an individual and every case as a unique study in the human failings that sometimes mitigate, sometimes magnify, the crime and punishment to ensue," Justice Anthony Kennedy wrote. "We do not understand it to have been the congressional purpose to withdraw all sentencing discretion from the United States District Judge."

The court unanimously agreed that Davies had the authority to find that King's "wrongful conduct contributed significantly to provoking" Koon and Powell. This was the single most important factor in the judge's decision reducing the sentences to thirty months from the seventy- to eighty-seven-month sentences that the guidelines required in the absence of mitigating circumstances. Six of the nine justices agreed that Davies also had acted properly on two other grounds he had used for reducing the sentences: the "spectre of unfairness" raised by the second prosecution and the susceptibility of Koon and Powell to abuse in prison. The court ruled against the trial judge on two other points. Eight justices agreed that Davies had erred in reducing the sentences on the grounds that Koon and Powell had lost their careers and were unlikely to commit further crimes. With that the court unanimously ordered that the case be sent back to Davies for resentencing.*

The decision was welcomed in the ranks of the federal judiciary, where judges increasingly chafed at the restraints of the sentencing guidelines. And it was hailed by Edi Faal, the Orange County lawyer from Africa who proved as thoughtful in behalf of Rodney King as he had been in defense of Damian Williams in the Reginald Denny case. "Mr. King's position is that we should close the books and move on," Faal said. "They already have served their time in prison, and Mr. King does not believe they need to serve more."[73]

But the prosecutors were not ready to throw in the towel. In briefs submitted for the resentencing hearing, they went through the motions of seeking more prison time without bothering to recommend a specific sentence. The government's new focus was on monetary punishment. Davies

---

* Three justices—David Souter, Ruth Bader Ginsburg, and Stephen Breyer—disagreed with the majority on two sentencing factors. They would not have allowed Davies to consider that the second prosecution had created an appearance of unfairness or that Koon and Powell were susceptible to prison abuse. Justice John Paul Stevens wrote a separate opinion saying that he would have upheld Davies on all sentencing factors, including the two found invalid by the court majority.

originally had declined to fine Koon and Powell on the ground that they couldn't pay. Knowing that this was true, the government had not pressed the issue on appeal. Now, however, the government asked Davies to impose substantial fines, especially on Koon, because of money raised by the defense funds.

On September 26, 1996, Koon and Powell were resentenced in Davies' eighth-floor courtroom in the Roybal Federal Building in downtown Los Angeles. The standing-room-only days of the King case were long gone. Only forty persons attended, mostly lawyers, family members, and others with a connection to the case. Most of the media were preoccupied with jury selection in the second O. J. Simpson trial across town in Santa Monica. The people in the courtroom seemed almost happy to see one another. Powell was unusually relaxed and chatty. Barry Kowalski, who had flown in from Washington to represent the Justice Department, was also in a good mood. He reminisced with a marshal about their Marine days in Vietnam and told me he felt as if he were attending a college reunion. It was an apt metaphor. Jim Newton wrote in his next-day story in the *Los Angeles Times* that the "once-bitter disputes that gripped Davies' courtroom through the winter and spring of 1993 gave way to a reunion air . . ." But it was an odd reunion, like a ceremony in which soldiers from opposing sides who had once tried to kill each other met to talk nostalgically about the war.

Lawrence Middleton, the only African-American member of the federal trial team, dispelled the festive mood with a final passionate appeal to extend Koon's punishment. Middleton observed that neither Koon nor Powell had expressed remorse. He recalled that Davies had reduced their sentences in part because their notoriety had increased the likelihood of prison abuse. Referring to Koon, Middleton said, "The defendant has used the same notoriety to profit. He's profited to the tune of $10 million"—slightly exaggerating the amount raised by the Koon Defense Fund, of which less than one-fourth had gone to Koon and his family. Outside the courtroom, Ira Salzman said bitingly that Koon hadn't asked to lose his career and become a convicted felon.

Davies was courteous but unimpressed with the government's argument. He told Middleton that the case had been remanded only for reconsidering prison terms and that imposing a fine at this late date would be a form of additional jeopardy. Davies also made short work of Middleton's contention that he should give Koon and Powell longer terms because the Supreme Court had struck down the two mitigating factors he had originally applied. "I'm certain in this case even if I had not used two erroneous factors . . . I still would have imposed exactly the same sentences," Davies said. Powell and Koon declined the judge's offer to address the court, and the defense attorneys made no oral arguments.[74] Davies reimposed the thirty-month sentences. Koon shook hands with his lawyers, and Powell hugged his sister. Protected by armed guards, the two men slipped out a side door.

Mike Stone, who had fought a good fight for Powell and won and lost (and won again in the civil trial), thought the Rodney King case was finally over. "It's done," he said as he left the courtroom. "It's finally done." Newton, whose informed coverage had impressed both sides and the judge, shared this view. He wrote the next day in the *Los Angeles Times* that the hearing had "effectively closed out the episode that reshaped the city's legal and political landscape."[75]

Stacey Koon wasn't so sure. He had been delighted when the Supreme Court upheld most of what Davies had done, saying that he was "proud" to have played a part in changing the law.[76] "It was a privilege to be a defendant in a case that helped restore sentencing discretion," he told me after he was resentenced. But Koon had heard the edge in Middleton's voice when he appealed for further punishment. Perhaps because Koon himself is so indomitable, he did not expect the prosecutors to give up. He predicted that the government would appeal the court's decision.[77]

Despite his pessimistic assessment, Koon was eager for what he called "closure on this case." It bothered him that he had become a symbol of police brutality and especially that he was a symbol of racism, which he abhors. Koon had a family to help raise, and he did not want to brood about prison or dwell on the past. He had gone over the events of March 3, 1991, again and again in his mind and was convinced that he had done his best to carry out LAPD policy with the weapons at his disposal and the officers at hand. At times he seemed almost to regret this analysis. "If I thought I had done wrong, I would have pled guilty," he said. "I wouldn't have put the city and my family through this."[78]

But Koon did not think what he had done was wrong, and he did not second-guess Rodney King or Laurence Powell or the photographer George Holliday for taking the videotape. Faith and fatalism led Koon to believe that everything that had happened the night of the King arrest had been for a purpose and that good would come out of it for Los Angeles and the LAPD. "I wouldn't change what happened one iota," Koon said.[79]

As far as the appeal was concerned, Stone and Newton were right, and Koon was wrong. The government realized that an appeal was fruitless and did not ask a higher court to impose fines. Koon learned about the government's decision from a lawyer's message on his answering machine when he came home one afternoon after taking his children to Magic Mountain, a popular amusement park. He called me with the news, saying that the case was indeed over. The mask of stoicism dropped away, and for the first time since the nightmare began, he seemed happy.

But Koon was right in a larger sense when he said that the King case would never be over. The incident had changed the way Los Angeles thought about its police force, and in time it had changed the police force itself. People would remember the Holliday videotape and the videotapes of the assaults at Florence and Normandie. They would remember Rodney King and Reginald Denny. They would remember Laurence Powell and Stacey Koon.

The Struggles of the Survivors— an Epilogue

EIGHT YEARS TO THE DAY AFTER THE VIDEOTAPED BEATING that, as federal prosecutor Barry Kowalski put it, caused "horror and outrage" from "Paris to Tokyo," Rodney Glen King faced yet another criminal prosecution, the third since the incident. This time he was charged in San Bernardino County, California, of misdemeanor counts of injuring a child, causing corporal injury to her parent, and vandalizing property. The aggrieved parent was Carmen Simpson and the child her sixteen-year-old daughter, Candace, whom King had fathered out of wedlock when he was seventeen. The arrest warrant was issued on March 3, 1999, the anniversary of the televised beating that led to many of the events described in this book.

King pleaded innocent to the charges, which have not been adjudicated at this writing, calling them a "family misunderstanding." Whatever their legal merit, they were symptomatic of long-standing problems. Despite his $3.8 million civil damage award for the injuries inflicted in the beating, King is still struggling to find himself. The effort has led him ever farther from the central city—most recently to Fontana, in the San Gabriel Mountains, an outer ring among the endless suburbs of Los Angeles.

King has been unable to flee the problems that beset him long before March 3, 1991, as his detractors are quick to point out. After King's latest arrest, former LAPD Chief Daryl Gates said King would be "in trouble the rest of his life" because he was "in denial about his substance-abuse problems." A well-informed friend of King, speaking anonymously, offered a more sympathetic but also disheartening assessment: "Rodney has developmental problems that have not been addressed," the friend said. "He's basically a nice man with limited intellect who becomes easily frustrated [and] doesn't know how to deal with his problems when this happens and lashes out at others, sometimes violently. . . . He has had psychological assistance that helped him deal with the impact of the beating, but no one has really addressed his inability to deal with frustration."

Still, Rodney King has tried, often under conditions that would frustrate anyone. Two dozen lawyers laid claim to $1.5 million in statutory legal fees that had been added to King's civil damages. Subsequently, an arbitration judge awarded lawyer Milton Grimes $1.192 million of King's $3.8 million civil judgment and part of the fees claimed by other attorneys. King could not make sense of this tangle. At this writing, he has sued to recover money from his first attorney, Steven Lerman, who has prepared a counterclaim.

Away from the courtroom, King has learned to have fun. He enjoys surfing, which he says gives him "good vibrations." The cover of the March 28, 1999, edition of *Los Angeles Times Magazine* showed King cradling a blue surfboard along the Pacific shoreline. The accompanying story, by freelance writer Ed Leibowitz, describes King's life as "a series of trials" but adds that "some of his money problems are the kind that many people might envy." Leibowitz credits three people with helping King—tutor Judy Sampson, Cal Poly–Pomona political science professor Renford Reese, and King's cousin, Terese Avarette, who shares King's condo and looks after his business interests. So far, the most significant of these is a hip-hop record label, Straight Al-Ta-Paz Records, that features a band known as Stranded. King has written a song, "Can We All Get Along." A website promoting his record company uses the motto "something good out of something bad."

LIFE HAS ALSO BEEN A SERIES OF PERSONAL AND PROFESSIONAL struggles for the former LAPD officers who were twice tried on criminal charges in the King affair. Innocent people died in the Los Angeles riots, and defendants who are found innocent sometimes suffer as much as those who are found guilty. The two officers acquitted in both of these trials have found the going as difficult as the two who were convicted. This is especially true for Ted Briseno, whose taped testimony played a crucial role in the convictions. "It's particularly hard on Ted because he's not accepted by either side," said his lawyer, Harland Braun. "But it's hard on all of them because they have lost their earning power and can never work as police officers again. That's all Briseno knew or wanted to do." Briseno holds a security job in the Los Angeles area.

Tim Wind, the probationary officer who also was twice acquitted, has courageously battled depression and other medical problems with worthwhile results. While continuing as a low-paid community service officer in Culver City, he graduated with honors from Loyola Marymount University with a bachelor of arts degree in urban studies; he hopes to become a lawyer.

Laurence Powell, who was convicted on federal charges of violating King's civil rights, married and moved to the San Diego area after release from federal prison. A friend describes his life as extremely difficult. Powell, who has computer aptitudes, is currently working in a computer store.

Stacey Koon, the former sergeant who also was convicted in the federal trial, is financially and emotionally secure. He completed but never published a novel about crime and cops in Los Angeles that he began in prison. After his release, he did some consulting and investing but spends most of his time as a self-described "Mr. Mom" who tends the house while his wife, a nurse with a master's degree, works. "I take care of the kids, cook the meals, go to the ballgames," Koon told me. "I don't look back."

REGINALD DENNY SHARES WITH RODNEY KING THE DISTINCTION of being a famous videotaped victim, but he lacks the financial cushion that King obtained from his damage award or that Koon received from benefactors. The near-fatal beating that Denny suffered when he was dragged from his cement truck early in the Los Angeles riots left him susceptible to seizures, unable to drive a truck, and destitute. Although he graduated at the top of a marine-mechanics class in 1997, he has been unable to find regular work and subsists on $120 a week in disability. A *People* profile on March 15, 1999, reported that Denny sleeps at the homes of friends because he can't afford rent. Denny is "withdrawn," avoids crowds, and still suffers from emotional problems but remains forgiving of his attackers. A $40 million lawsuit filed on behalf of Denny and other riot victims by Johnnie L. Cochran Jr. on grounds that police had failed to provide adequate protection was dismissed by a federal court in May 1998.

Damian Williams, the former gang member who hurled a slab of concrete that crushed Denny's skull and left a permanent indentation on his right temple, was released from prison in 1997. He worked for a time as a peer-pressure counselor for Congresswoman Maxine Waters, whose district includes the intersection of Florence and Normandie Avenues, the epicenter of the 1992 riots where Denny was beaten. Williams is now a full-time student at Los Angeles Southwest College, majoring in psychology. His attorney, Edi Faal, told me that Williams hopes to become a counselor to young people in South Central Los Angeles and help them avoid the pitfalls of gangs.

Faal, the soft-spoken lawyer who impressed jurors with his defense of Williams, provides a link between the trials known by the names of the victims—King and Denny. He is currently representing King in the pending criminal charges and in his civil lawsuit against former attorney Lerman. He has also written an as yet unpublished mystery novel. Most of Faal's clients come from what he calls "the lower stratum of society," and he takes an interest in many of them, including Williams, that extends beyond the courtroom. He is not alone in this among the defense attorneys. Harland Braun continues to show concern for Briseno, as does Ira Salzman for Koon. Both are sympathetic to Wind.

THE STATE PROSECUTORS IN THE PRINCIPAL TRIALS EXAMINED in this book still work for the Los Angeles County district attorney. Roxane Carvajal, who prosecuted Soon Ja Du in the killing of Latasha Harlins, supervises the Los Angeles Huntington Park office and is president of the Women Lawyers of Long Beach. Janet Moore, prosecutor of Damian Williams, is the assistant head deputy in the Torrance office. Alan Yochelson, the number-two prosecutor in the trial of the "Rodney King officers," participated in the O. J. Simpson case and then headed a new unit in Van Nuys where he successfully prosecuted sex crimes, child abuse, and domestic violence. He is now supervisor of the Sylmar office. Terry White, the lead prosecutor at Simi Valley, served as legal adviser to the grand jury for two years and is now supervisor of the El Monte office. In a 1999 television documentary by Manifold Productions shown on The Learning Channel, White discussed the issues of the King case with quiet dignity and reiterated his belief that King was not beaten because of his race.

Federal prosecutors of the King officers have taken new and interesting assignments. Barry Kowalski, who once prosecuted the Ku Klux Klan, now heads the Justice Department's investigation into new allegations in the assassination of Martin Luther King Jr.—an essentially thankless task but one that could produce a report of historical importance. Alan Tieger went to The Hague and successfully prosecuted the first Serb accused of war crimes in Bosnia. He has since been detailed to the inspector general's office in the U.S. Justice Department as part of an inquiry into whether the Clinton administration accelerated amnesty procedures for Latino immigrants so they could vote in the 1996 elections. Lawrence Middleton served on the Justice Department's church-arson task force and obtained a conviction in Macon, Georgia. He returned to the U.S. attorney's office in

Los Angeles to head the Public Corruption and Fraud Unit and successfully prosecuted a defense subcontractor who had improperly produced aircraft parts and made false statements.

Only Steven Clymer, a top prosecutor in the U.S. attorney's office in Los Angeles, left government service—and he did not stay away for long. After the trial of the King officers, Clymer became an associate law professor at Cornell Law School. He is currently on leave, serving with a task force investigating health-care fraud and working out of the U.S. attorney's office in Syracuse, New York.

Stanley Weisberg, the Los Angeles County Superior Court judge who moved the state trial of the King officers to Simi Valley, remains on the bench. He became familiar to viewers of Court TV as the trial judge in successive prosecutions of the Menendez brothers, convicted of murdering their parents and sentenced to life terms. John Ouderkirk, the trial judge in the Damian Williams prosecution, also remains a Superior Court judge. But U.S. District Judge John Davies, who presided over the federal civil rights trial in the King case and resisted the clamor for longer sentences of the two convicted officers, retired from the bench and now mediates civil disputes in Los Angeles. The U.S. Supreme Court ruling upholding Davies' sentence has been cited in several decisions on judicial discretion under federal sentencing guidelines.

Joyce Karlin, reassigned from Superior Court after she placed Soon Ja Du on probation, became a highly regarded Juvenile Court judge. But she retired in 1997 after six years on the bench to care for her young daughter. "I never became comfortable with anyone else raising her," she said. Soon Ja Du completed her five years of probation without incident and slipped from sight.

MANY OF THE POLITICAL AND POLICE FIGURES WHO PLAYED leading parts in the events described in this book have left the stage, and some have returned in other roles. Warren Christopher, who served as U.S. secretary of state from 1993 to 1997, returned to his law firm in Los Angeles and became an advocate for city charter reform. The proposals of the Christopher Commission that he headed in the wake of the King beating remain an enduring blueprint for police reform.

Daryl Gates, who stepped down as LAPD chief in 1992, has been active in retirement. He hosted a radio talk show for a year and a half, and he has developed three interactive video games related to police work. He and his brother, Steve, operate an investigative agency known as Chief.

Willie Williams, who succeeded Gates as police chief and was in 1997 denied a second five-year term by the Police Commission, in 1999 became chief operating officer of Argus Services Company, a Dallas-based medical-records firm owned by family members.

Raymond Fisher, who chaired the Police Commission that denied Williams a second term, in 1997 became associate attorney general, the number-three position in the U.S. Justice Department. In March 1999, President Clinton nominated Fisher as a federal appellate judge on the Ninth Circuit.

Former District Attorney Ira Reiner, who withdrew from his 1992 reelection campaign after trailing in the primary, is in private practice in Los Angeles. He was an NBC commentator on legal issues during the O. J. Simpson trial.

LOS ANGELES, UNDER MAYOR RICHARD RIORDAN, AND THE LAPD, under Chief Bernard Parks, have made fitful progress. Riordan has made education a priority and in 1999 backed reform candidates who won significant victories in school board elections. Spurred by global trade, immigrant entrepreneurs, and a renaissance in the entertainment industry, Los Angeles at the end of the twentieth century shared in the national prosperity and progressed in human relations. Latinos and Asians increasingly participate in local politics. Riordan named Joe Hicks, who had tried vainly to preserve the Black-Korean Alliance after the 1992 riots, as executive director of the Los Angeles Human Relations Commission and increased its funding. Hicks' Korean counterpart in the Alliance, Bong-Hwan Kim, became acting director of the Multi-Cultural Collaborative that Hicks had founded. Hicks, a former black nationalist and former Communist, is, with Riordan, an apostle of the multicultural "world city" that Tom Bradley had envisioned.

Los Angeles crime rates fell steadily during the late 1990s, as did legal complaints against its police department. Riordan in his 1999–2000 budget belatedly made good on his 1993 pledge to increase the LAPD by 3,000 officers to a total of 10,000. A Los Angeles Times poll in March 1999 found that 64 percent of Angelenos approved of the job the LAPD was doing but that Parks remained unknown to 43 percent of the city's residents. Unlike his predecessors, Parks has not sought the limelight. It is worth noting, however, that during the first two years of his leadership the LAPD has been spared the high-profile incidents of alleged police brutality that have plagued New York City and other jurisdictions.

But the LAPD is hardly problem-free. Parks was limited by restrictive civil-service rules and a city council jealous of its prerogatives in choosing his deputy chiefs, which may have hampered his efforts to make the LAPD more responsive. Perhaps because he is a strict disciplinarian, Parks is unpopular with the LAPD rank-and-file, and he has clashed frequently with the police union. Moreover, no less than Gates and Williams, Parks does not want a civilian Police Commission looking over his shoulder. Attorney Merrick Bobb, whose trenchant studies of the LAPD had provided a basis for replacing Williams, said in March 1999: "The LAPD resists civilian oversight, and the Police Commission has been reluctant to prod too hard. The LAPD still wants to exercise control over all information that comes out of the department."

The LAPD's determination to control the flow of information contributed on November 10, 1998, to the resignation of Inspector General Katherine Mader, who reported to the Police Commission and had displeased its executive director and Parks with her independent investigations of the LAPD. Mader landed on her feet as head of a new unit in the district attorney's office that investigates money laundering, but Bobb thought it a bad sign that the first inspector general in the city's history had been forced out. The commission left the post vacant until May 28, 1999, when Mader was replaced by Assistant U.S. Attorney Jeffrey C. Eglash, a prosecutor specializing in public corruption and government fraud cases. After the riots, voters approved changes in the city charter proposed by the Christopher Commission that were supposed to establish effective civilian oversight of the LAPD. Mader's departure suggests that the long struggle to achieve this accountability is far from over.

TOM BRADLEY, THE TOWERING POLITICAL FIGURE IN LOS Angeles during the second half of the twentieth century, died on September 29, 1998, of a heart attack at the age of eighty. The stories after his death focused not on the problems of his later years but on his many achievements. In a column in *The Washington Post*, I called him a Texas sharecropper's son who had transformed Los Angeles into the shining metropolis of the West. Riordan recalled that Bradley had "united a city that was divided" after the 1965 Watts riot. "He has left a great legacy for all Angelenos, from the Olympics, to the skyline, to diversity," Riordan said.

Jesse Brewer, whom Bradley in 1952 had brought into the then-segregated LAPD where he served for thirty-nine years as an outstanding police officer and then was a force for reform as a Bradley-appointed member of the Police Commission, died on November 19, 1995, also of a heart attack. The headline on a *Los Angeles Times* editorial summed up his contribution: "LAPD and L.A. Lose a Hero."

Los Angeles County Sheriff Sherman Block, who had wanted to send in deputies to quell the 1992 riots before the LAPD allowed him to do so, died on October 29, 1998, of a massive brain hemorrhage five days before the election in which he was seeking a fifth term.

Richard Rhee, who organized an effective armed defense of the California Market in Koreatown during the 1992 riots, died of lung cancer on June 15, 1997. He said after the riots that the "light had gone out of Los Angeles." Rhee was a brave man, but he was mistaken about that.

—Lou Cannon
Summerland, California
May 1999

Cast of Key Characters

VICTIMS

Rodney King – beaten by LAPD officers on March 3, 1991.

Latasha Harlins – shot and killed by Soon Ja Du on March 16, 1991.

Reginald Denny – beaten by Damian Williams and accomplices on April 29, 1992.

Fidel Lopez – beaten on April 29, 1992.

Sai-Choi Choi – beaten on April 29, 1992.

Raul Aguilar – beaten and his legs run over by car on April 29, 1992.

Takao Hirata – beaten by Damian Williams and accomplices on April 29, 1992.

Larry Tarvin – beaten by Henry Watson and accomplices April 29, 1992.

Scott Miller – fireman shot in face by unknown assailant on April 29, 1992.

And the **fifty-four people** who died in the Los Angeles riots from April 29–May 4, 1992.

DEFENDANTS

Soon Ja Du – accused of murdering Latasha Harlins.

Stacey Koon – LAPD sergeant accused of permitting unlawful force while supervising the arrest of Rodney King.

Laurence Powell – LAPD officer accused of using unlawful force against Rodney King.

Theodore Briseno – LAPD officer accused of using unlawful force against Rodney King.

Timothy Wind – LAPD probationary officer accused of using unlawful force against Rodney King.

Damian Williams – accused of attempted murder of Reginald Denny and various assaults.

Henry Watson – accused of attempted murder of Reginald Denny and assaulting Larry Tarvin.

PROSECUTORS

People v. Soon Ja Du – **Roxane Carvajal**, Los Angeles County deputy district attorney.

People v. Laurence Powell et al. – **Terry White** and **Alan Yochelson**, Los Angeles County deputy district attorneys in state trial of the officers accused of assaulting Rodney King.

U.S. v. Stacey Koon et al. – **Steven Clymer** and **Lawrence Middleton**, Assistant U.S. attorneys in Los Angeles. **Barry Kowalski** and **Alan Tieger**, Justice Department attorneys, Civil Rights Division. Lead members of prosecution team in federal civil rights trial of the officers accused of assaulting Rodney King.

People v. Damian Williams and Henry Watson – **Janet Moore** and **Lawrence Morrison**, Los Angeles County deputy district attorneys.

DEFENSE ATTORNEYS

For Soon Ja Du – **Charles Lloyd** and **Richard Leonard.**

For Stacey Koon – **Darryl Mounger** in state trial, **Ira Salzman** in federal trial.

For Laurence Powell – **Michael Stone** in both trials.

For Timothy Wind – **Paul DePasquale** in both trials.

For Theodore Briseno – **John Barnett** in state trial, **Harland Braun** in federal trial.

For Damian Williams – **Edi Faal**.

For Henry Watson – **Earl Broady Jr.**

JUDGES AND JURORS

Joyce Karlin – Superior Court trial judge in *People v. Du*.

Stanley Weisberg – Superior Court trial judge in *People v. Powell*.

Dorothy Bailey – jury forewoman in *People v. Powell*.

Anna Charmaine Whiting – a member of this jury.

John Davies – U.S. District judge in *U.S. v. Koon* and Rodney King's federal civil lawsuit for damages.

Robert Almond – jury foreman in *U.S. v. Koon*.

Maria Escobel – a member of this jury.

John Ouderkirk – Superior Court trial judge in *People v. Damian Williams and Henry Watson*.

Carolyn Walters – jury forewoman in this trial.

Joan Dempsey Klein – Justice of the Second District of the California Court of Appeal.

Stephen Reinhardt – Judge of the U.S. Court of Appeal for the Ninth Circuit.

Betty Fletcher – Judge of the U.S. Court of Appeal for the Ninth Circuit.

Anthony Kennedy – Justice of the U.S. Supreme Court.

THE LAPD

William Parker – chief 1950–1966.

Edward Davis – chief 1969–1978.

Daryl Gates – chief 1978–1992.

Willie Williams – chief 1992–97.

Bayan Lewis – interim chief 1997.

Bernard C. Parks – chief 1997—

Greg Baltad – an officer in Metro Division.

Ricky Banks – 77th Street Division officer and rescuer of civilians during riots.

Ron Banks – commander during riots.

Michael Bostic – commander and prosecution use-of-force expert witness in state trial of the Rodney King officers.

Jesse Brewer – assistant chief under Gates, later member of the Police Commission.

Susan Clemmer – backup officer at Rodney King pursuit, defense witness.

Mark Conta – a sergeant, prosecution use-of-force expert witness in the federal criminal trial of the Rodney King officers.

David Dotson – assistant chief under Gates.

Charles Duke – sergeant with SWAT team, witness for defense in both trials.

John Dunkin – homicide detective and a spokesman for Chiefs Gates and Williams.

Mark Fuhrman – a detective.

Ronald Frankle – deputy chief under Gates.

Michael Hillmann – lieutenant in Metro Division.

Matthew Hunt – deputy chief in South Bureau during riots.

Ted Hunt – LAPD officer, Police Academy instructor, and board member of Los Angeles Police Protective League.

Paul Jefferson – captain of 77th Street Division during riots.

Mark Kroeker – deputy chief under Gates and Williams.

Scott Landsman – sergeant, Police Academy instructor, and martial arts expert.

James Lumpkin – 77th Street Division officer and rescuer of civilians during riots.

Katherine Mader – inspector general of the LAPD.

Tim McBride – captain of Foothill Station at time of Rodney King beating; later LAPD commander and spokesman for Chief Williams.

Greg Meyer – sergeant, later lieutenant, and use-of-force expert.

Michael Moulin – lieutenant in 77th Street Division during riots.

Danny Nee – 77th Street Division officer and rescuer of civilians during riots.

Lisa Phillips – partner of Nee and rescuer of civilians.

Cliff Ruff – detective and former president of Los Angeles Police Protective League.

Corina Smith – police officer and friend of Laurence Powell.

Charles Strong – sergeant in 77th Street Division during riots.

Theresa Tatreau – assistant watch commander at 77th during riots.

Nick Titiriga – sergeant in 77th Street Division during riots.

Taky Tzimeas – Internal Affairs Division detective in charge of Rodney King beating inquiry.

Robert Vernon – deputy chief under Gates.

PUBLIC OFFICIALS

Tom Bradley – mayor of Los Angeles 1973–93.

Richard Riordan – mayor of Los Angeles 1993–

William Barr – attorney general under President Bush.

Sherman Block – sheriff of Los Angeles County.

Laura Chick – member of the Los Angeles city council, chair of the Public Safety Committee.

Warren Christopher – head of the Independent Commission on the Los Angeles Police Department.

Raymond Fisher – president of Los Angeles Police Commission, 1996–97, deputy counsel, Christopher Commission.

Gil Garcetti – district attorney, Los Angeles County, 1992—

Rabbi Gary Greenebaum – member of the Los Angeles Police Commission, 1993–95.

Roger Gunson – deputy district attorney, Los Angeles County.

Joe Gunn – liaison of Mayor Riordan to Police Commission.

Edith Perez – president of the Police Commission, 1997—

Ira Reiner – district attorney, Los Angeles County, 1984–1992.

Mark Ridley-Thomas – member of the Los Angeles city council.

Stanley Sheinbaum – Police Commission president under Bradley.

William Webster – former FBI and CIA director, chair of commission that investigated Los Angeles riots.

Hubert Williams – former Newark Police chief and co-chair of this commission.

Pete Wilson – governor of California 1991—

Michael Woo – former member of City Council, defeated by Riordan in 1993 mayor's race.

Zev Yaroslavsky – member of City Council, later Board of Supervisors.

OTHERS

Warren Cereghino – news director of KTLA at time of King beating.

Johnnie L. Cochran Jr. – civil attorney for Reginald Denny.

Jo-Ellan Dimitrius – defense jury consultant in Rodney King and Reginald Denny trials.

Leo Estrada – demographer and member of Christopher Commission.

Milton Grimes – civil attorney for Rodney King.

Linda Griego – last director of Rebuild Los Angeles (RLA).

George Holliday – amateur cameraman who videotaped Rodney King beating.

Donald Jones – Los Angeles fireman who rescued Sai-Choi Choi.

Steven Lerman – civil attorney for Rodney King.

Timothy Manning – battalion chief with Los Angeles Fire Department.

Terry Manning – his brother, also a battalion chief with the Fire Department.

Bennie Newton – minister who rescued Fidel Lopez.

Jim Newton – reporter for the *Los Angeles Times.*

Tom Owens – private investigator for Rodney King.

Richard Rhee – owner of California Market and organizer of Koreatown defense during riots.

Melanie Singer – California Highway Patrol officer who pursued Rodney King, witness in both trials.

Peter Ueberroth – first director of Rebuild Los Angeles (RLA).

Jaxon Van Derbeken – reporter for the Los Angeles *Daily News.*

Notes

This book is based on more than two hundred interviews conducted by me and Jaxon Van Derbeken; hundreds of documents, news articles, and books consulted by me and Mary Cannon; and my observations as a reporter for *The Washington Post* during the criminal trials of the so-called Rodney King officers and the Los Angeles riots of 1992. Most of the sources are identified in the text or in the following notes, and the published material is listed in the bibliography.

There are some exceptions to this practice. A handful of interviews, mostly of jurors and jurists, were conducted under conditions of anonymity. I subjected anonymous comments to a higher standard than on-the-record remarks, using them only if they could be verified by a second source. But I did rely on some important documents that are not public records, notably the transcripts of interviews conducted by the LAPD Internal Affairs Division of officers involved in the Rodney King incident. I also used other internal reports and memoranda, mostly from the LAPD, particularly a report that analyzed police response during the first thirty-six hours of the riots.

For the sake of brevity, testimony or other statements made in open court during the trials discussed in this book have not been cited in the notes. References to the *Daily News* are to the Los Angeles newspaper published in the San Fernando Valley.

All of the interviews listed in these notes were conducted by me unless otherwise indicated.

PROLOGUE

1. Different figures have been used for the death toll because of conflicting opinions about whether some of the deaths were a consequence of the riots or simply coincided with them. The Los Angeles County Coroner's Office determined that fifty-four deaths were attributable to the riots, and that is the number I have used throughout this book.

1. DREAM CITY

1. Malcolm Jones, Jr., "Kick Back with Crime," *Newsweek,* July 4, 1994.
2. J. Gregory Payne and Scott C. Ratzan, *Tom Bradley: The Impossible Dream,* p. 8.
3. For an account of how Bradley lobbied Councilman Marvin Braude to change his vote and approve the contract that made the Olympics possible, see ibid., p. 224.
4. Juan Antonio Samaranch, president of the International Olympic Committee, was warmly applauded when he thanked Los Angeles for "sixteen wonderful days of sports, peace, and friendship" but greeted by shouts of "no, no" when he proclaimed the games closed.
5. Interview with Jane Pisano, June 22, 1994.
6. Not quite "every economist" was bullish on California. One notable exception was David Hensley of the UCLA Business Forecasting Project, whose gloomy assessments of California's economic prospects in the late 1980s and early 1990s were dismissed as too pessimistic. In most cases they proved entirely accurate; occasionally, they were not quite pessimistic enough. Richard W. Stevenson, "California Goes From Economic Leader to Laggard," *The New York Times,* October 17, 1991.
7. James Rainey and Marc Lacey, "Riordan's First Year at the Helm," *Los Angeles Times,* July 3, 1994.
8. Interview with Kevin Starr, July 20, 1993.
9. The figure for aerospace job losses from 1988 to 1993 was provided to me in July 1993 by Brad Williams, an economist and executive director of the California Commission on State Finance. Williams estimated that 200,000 of the 800,000 jobs lost by California from 1990 to 1993 were directly or indirectly attributable to aerospace layoffs. The estimate of 300,000 jobs lost in California from all defense spending reductions was made by economist David Friedman in 1994.
10. According to 1990 state census data cited in the "Apparel Industry Profile," 65 percent of the dressmakers and 70 percent of the tailors were of Latino or Asian origin.
11. Raphael J. Sonenshein, *Politics in Black and White* pp. 151–55. Non-Hispanic whites made up 64 percent of the city workforce when Bradley became mayor and 46 percent of the workforce in 1991. The percentage of Latino city workers more than doubled, from 9.3 to 19.9 percent, and that of Asians nearly doubled from 4 to 7.5 percent. The percentage of blacks changed only slightly, from 21.9 to 22.4 percent, but blacks had declined from 17 to 13 percent of the city's population during this time. In the Bradley years, blacks benefited most from promotions. The percentages of blacks in professional jobs increased from 5 to 12 percent; the percentage in top-level administrative jobs increased from 1.3 to 10.5 percent. Women also made gains, from 16 to 25 percent of the total workforce and from 3 to 15 percent of the top administrative jobs.

12. Allen J. Scott and E. Richard Brown, editors, "South-Central Los Angeles: Anatomy of an Urban Crisis," Working Paper Series, The Lewis Center for Regional Policy Studies, University of California, Los Angeles, June 1993. Useful data on the economic situation of Latinos is provided in "Latinos and the Los Angeles Uprising: The Economic Context," a report issued by the Tomas Rivera Center and prepared by Manuel Pastor Jr. of Occidental College in 1993.

13. Interview with Felicia Bragg, February 16, 1994. Bragg said she benefited from the 1965 riot because the white community afterward was trying to reach out to Watts. Since she was a bright student and an "unthreatening" figure, she was often called upon to speak at churches and received a scholarship to the University of California at Santa Barbara, where she majored in history and received a degree. Bragg's mother continues to live in Watts, and Felicia Bragg has maintained her ties with the community.

14. Interview with Pete Wilson, May 21, 1993.

15. Southern California executives and owners of small businesses were particularly incensed about the costs of complying with air pollution restrictions imposed by the South Coast Air Quality Management District, known by its initials as "AQMD," which required such things as afterburners for bakery bread ovens, low-pressure spraying equipment for paint shops, and combination washer-dryers for cleaners. While such regulations increased costs and probably contributed to business flight, they also succeeded slowly in reducing the smog that is the bane of Southern California.

16. Dean Takahashi, "Ueberroth Asks High-Tech Crowd for Hand," Los Angeles Times, May 7, 1992.

17. Jesse Katz, "Crips, Bloods Look Back—and Ahead—with Anger," Los Angeles Times, March 21, 1993.

18. Interview with Alicia Aguilar by Jessica Crosby, July 22, 1993, in the garment district of downtown Los Angeles with translation by Nanette Vernengo.

19. Interview with Jay Mathews, July 17, 1994.

20. The Santa Monica Freeway (Interstate 10), the world's busiest, skims the northern border of South Central in an east-west direction. The Harbor Freeway (Interstate 110) bisects South Central on a north-south line. The San Diego Freeway (Interstate 405) runs on a north-south line to the west, buffered from South Central by Hawthorne, Inglewood, Ladera Heights, and Culver City. On the east the buffer between South Central and the Long Beach Freeway (Interstate 710) is the mainly black city of Compton and the increasingly Latino cities of South Gate, Cudahy, and Bell. The new Century Freeway (Interstate 105) slices along the southern border. This is of necessity a rough description of South Central. Scholars disagree as to its precise boundaries.

21. In the early 1990s the population was both growing and changing in composition. More non-Hispanic whites were leaving Los Angeles and California than were arriving, but the loss was more than offset by the high birth rates of the young Latino and Asian populations. According to estimates of the

California Department of Finance, widely accepted as reliable, Los Angeles County had a population of 9,158,400 at the end of 1992. The populations of the city and South Central were presumed to have grown accordingly.

22. The observations about the surprising increase in crime were made by James Q. Wilson of UCLA in a May 17, 1994, interview. The data on violent crime is taken from the FBI's *Uniform Crime Reports.* While nearly all cities recorded an upturn in violent crime in the late 1980s, it is worth noting that the increase was greater in Los Angeles than in any of the nation's other major cities except New York.

23. A poll by Bendixen & Associates, commissioned by the Los Angeles Spanish newspaper *La Opinion* and a Spanish-language television channel, showed early in 1993 that 54 percent of blacks and 64 percent of Latinos had a positive opinion of the LAPD. This was a year after the riots and was roughly equivalent to levels of support for the LAPD among these groups before the Rodney King incident of March 3, 1991. "Public Opinion Survey of Residents of South Central Los Angeles and Pico Union," Bendixen & Associates, Survey dates: April 22–25, 1993.

24. The best example of this is Proposition 1 on the Los Angeles city ballot in the April 1993 election that would have raised local property taxes to hire more police officers. It received 57 percent of the vote. *Los Angeles Times* exit polls showed that 68 percent of blacks had supported the measure, while a slight majority of white Protestant conservatives opposed it. "There is an interesting contradiction because white home owners who are scared to death of crime were the least inclined to vote for Proposition 1," John Brennan, then director of the *Times* Poll, told me.

25. The 1993 poll by Bendixen & Associates found that among blacks with negative opinions of the LAPD, 52 percent said police harassed them or were racist, while 33 percent said police did not do enough to reduce crime and 7 percent cited a slow response by police. Among Latinos with negative views of the LAPD, 28 percent cited harassment or racism, 31 percent a failure to reduce crime, and 26 percent slow response. Sergio Bendixen is a pollster and analyst of Latino affairs in Miami, New York, and Los Angeles. This poll on attitudes toward the LAPD was conducted among blacks in South Central and Latinos in Pico-Union.

2. TRIAL BY VIDEOTAPE

1. Stacey C. Koon, *Presumed Guilty*, p. 22.

2. Rodney King's comment about feeling like a "crushed can" was made to a federal grand jury on July 23, 1992. Laurence Powell told LAPD Internal Affairs investigators on March 23, 1991, that he had feared for his life while trying to take King into custody. His "scared to death" comment is from his March 31, 1992, testimony in the state trial of Koon, Powell, Wind, and Briseno where the four officers were accused of feloniously beating King and other charges. The Timothy Wind quotation about the size of King's arms is

from an interview with me on July 26, 1994, and is virtually identical with his statements to LAPD Internal Affairs investigators on March 4, 1991, testimony in the 1994 trial of King's lawsuit for civil damages and his testimony before an LAPD administrative hearing on March 16, 1994. Wind's account of events never changed on any significant point. Ted Briseno's recollections are from his April 3, 1992, testimony in the state trial, an interview with me on February 9, 1993, and his testimony before an LAPD hearing. Stacey Koon told me on March 17, 1993, during the federal trial, that he believed King was in danger of being shot. Koon's comment about the violence of the King beating is from his testimony on cross-examination during the state trial on March 20, 1992.

I had access to the transcripts, none of which are public records, of the interrogations of Koon, Powell, and Wind conducted by the LAPD's Internal Affairs investigators. Briseno did not give a statement to Internal Affairs.

3. Beth Laski, "Man Who Shot Video Says He Did Right Thing," *Daily News* (Los Angeles), March 7, 1991.

4. Interview with Ed Turner, August 3, 1994.

5. "U" was used as a reference to "you" or "unit." Koon contended in both trials and his book that he intended it as "you" and that the message was an effort to alert the watch commander, Lieutenant Patrick Conmay, that a major incident had occurred. Koon, *Presumed Guilty*, p. 47.

6. Holliday's unrequited telephone calls proved embarrassing to the LAPD and CNN. At Foothill Station police investigators attempted to find out who had discouraged Holliday from bringing in his videotape, but no officer ever acknowledged taking the call. The day after the beating Rodney King's brother Paul went to Foothill to file a brutality complaint. He told Sergeant Steven Flores, who took the complaint, that there might be a videotape of the incident. Flores told Paul King that if he obtained a tape he should call him back and release it to the LAPD. Flores then wrote in his report that the force used against King was "justified" and recommended no further action unless a videotape or eyewitness statement was obtained.

The disclosure that Holliday had received no answer when he telephoned CNN in Los Angeles led to installation of an answering machine at the Los Angeles bureau that provides afterhours callers with an Atlanta phone number.

7. Interview with Warren Cereghino, November 17, 1993.

8. Interview with Tim McBride by Jaxon Van Derbeken, August 1, 1994.

9. A compilation of network usage by the First Amendment Center in Nashville provided to me by John Siegenthaler found that in these eighty-seven network evening news stories the tape was played forty-seven times. The presumption (of Siegenthaler and me) is that the tape was used approximately the same number of times on the network morning news shows. The Center for Media and Public Affairs in Washington, D.C., counted two hundred evening news clips of the Holliday videotape broadcast between March 5, 1991, and the April 29, 1992, verdict. Researcher Daniel Amundson said this count

included every clip of the King beating that was shown, including multiple clips shown during any one news report. As far as I have been able to determine, no similar compilation of usage was made in the Los Angeles media market, where the tape was shown recurrently on local news channels in the weeks after the beating and during every development in the political controversy that rocked the city in the following months.

10. Interview with Warren Cereghino, November 17, 1993.
11. Interview with David Farmer, August 1, 1994.
12. Interview with Paul Jefferson, May 11, 1994.
13. Daryl F. Gates, *Chief*, p. 4.
14. Testimony by Tim Wind on March 16, 1994, at a Liberty Interest Hearing conducted by Captain Robert Gale of the LAPD, an administrative proceeding at which Wind was attempting to win reinstatement.
15. Ibid.
16. The study, *Nonlethal Weapons vs. Conventional Police Tactics: The Los Angeles Police Department Experience* was the master's thesis at California State University, Los Angeles, of Greg Meyer, an LAPD officer and a police tactics consultant.
17. Associated Press, "Acquitted Sergeant Writes of Beatings," *Los Angeles Times,* May 17, 1992.
18. Interview with Greg Baltad, March 10, 1994.
19. Interview with Ted Briseno, February 9, 1993.
20. At the scene were the two Highway Patrol officers, the two Los Angeles Unified School District officers, and twenty-one LAPD officers. The LAPD officers included, on the ground, five directly involved in the King arrest—Koon, Powell, Wind, Briseno, and Rolando Solano—plus the fourteen "bystander officers" and, in the air, an LAPD helicopter pilot and an observer. One reason for the presence of so many LAPD officers, according to Diane Marchant, an attorney who represented many of the bystander officers in subsequent disciplinary proceedings, was the policy of taking probationary (rookie) officers to the scenes of arrests for instructional purposes. Four officers at the scene, including Wind and Solano, were probationers.
21. Interview with Ted Briseno, February 9, 1993.
22. Tim Wind interview with LAPD Internal Affairs investigators, March 4, 1991.
23. Interview with Tim McBride by Jaxon Van Derbeken, August 1, 1994.
24. Interview with Tim Wind, July 26, 1994.
25. Interview with Ted Briseno, February 9, 1993.
26. Tim Wind testimony at Liberty Interest Hearing, March 16, 1994.
27. Melanie Singer testimony at federal trial, March 26 and 29, 1993.
28. Laurence Powell testimony at state trial, March 31, 1992.
29. Tim Wind interview with LAPD Internal Affairs investigators, March 4, 1991.
30. Stacey Koon interview with LAPD Internal Affairs investigators, March 14, 1991.

31. Briseno told me in the 1993 interview that he was surprised to see in the videotape that he had put up one hand. His recollection was that he had raised two hands to block Powell's baton blow.
32. LAPD Board of Rights hearing, August 25, 1987.
33. Interview with Michael Stone, October 4, 1993.
34. Interview with Taky Tzimeas, January 10, 1995.
35. Ibid.
36. Interview with Tim Fowler, December 21, 1993.
37. Interview with Angela King, April 5, 1994.
38. Conversation with Stacey Koon, March 29, 1993.
39. Peter J. Boyer, "The Selling of Rodney King," *Vanity Fair*, July 1992.
40. Interview with Rodney King, December 18, 1995.
41. Ibid.
42. Ibid.
43. Janet Gilmore, "Life Remains Full of Legal Problems for Multimillionaire Rodney King," *Daily News,* July 8, 1996.
44. Ashley Dunn and Andrea Ford, "The Man Swept Up in the Furor," *Los Angeles Times,* March 17, 1991.
45. Rodney King testimony at federal trial, March 9, 1993. Parole Officer Tim Fowler said that King made a similar statement to him when he visited him in his jail cell after the beating.
46. Richard A. Serrano, "King Tells of Beating, Racial Taunts by Police," *Los Angeles Times,* January 16, 1992.
47. Analysis of the Holliday videotape by the National Audio Forensic Lab quoted in Koon, *Presumed Guilty,* p. 248.
48. Rodney King testimony at federal grand jury hearing, July 23, 1992.
49. Interview with Scott Landsman, July 15, 1994.
50. Interview with Charles Duke, October 5, 1993.
51. Greg Meyer thesis. In a section titled "Myths About the Taser," Meyer wrote that the Taser had a "high degree of success against violent drug suspects" and that the "oft-repeated assertion" that the stun gun was ineffective against drug users was "simply misinformation."
52. Interview with Taky Tzimeas, January 10, 1995.
53. Interview with Cliff Ruff, February 3, 1994.
54. Interview with Nick Titiriga, March 13, 1994.
55. Interview with Cliff Ruff, February 3, 1994.
56. Interview with Taky Tzimeas, January 10, 1995.

3. THE DRAGNET LEGACY

1. W.H. Parker, "The California Crime Rise," *Journal of Criminal Law, Criminology and Police Science,* 1957, pp. 721–729.
2. From recommendation of Captain Robert Gale summarizing the proceedings in Wind's appeal for reinstatement in Liberty Interest Hearing, LAPD record, June 22, 1994.

3. Ibid.

4. Interview with Tim Wind, July 26, 1994.

5. Carey McWilliams, *Southern California: An Island on the Land*, p. 60. For a discussion of the relations between Mexicans and Anglos in California at this time, see the section, "Californios and Mexicanos" pp. 49–70.

6. Joseph G. Woods, "The Progressives and the Police: Urban Reform and the Professionalization of the American Police," UCLA doctoral thesis in history, 1973, p. 15. (Hereafter Woods)

7. Ibid., p. 21.

8. Ibid., pp. 162–63.

9. Interview with Ted Hunt, August 30, 1994.

10. Jack Webb, *The Badge*, p. 247.

11. Woods, p. 425.

12. Parker was delighted when the academy was described in press accounts as "the West Point of police training."

13. Center for the Study of Democratic Institutions. *The Police: One of a Series of Interviews on the American Character.* An Interview by Donald McDonald with William H. Parker, Chief of Police of Los Angeles, 1962, p. 12. (Hereafter Parker interview with McDonald)

14. Daryl F. Gates, *Chief*, p. 31.

15. Dick West, "Chief Parker Collapses, Dies at Award Banquet," *Los Angeles Times*, July 17, 1966.

16. Woods, p. 443.

17. Parker interview with McDonald, p. 14.

18. Webb, *The Badge*, p. 243.

19. Woods, p. 454, and see the discussion by Parker in interview with McDonald, pp. 24–25.

20. Gates, *Chief*, p. 32.

21. The 1854 court decision extended to the Chinese the provisions of an 1850 law passed by the first California Legislature which prohibited any "Black or Mulatto person, or Indian," from testifying against a white person in court. During the Civil War, the provision applying to blacks or mulattos was repealed while Chinese continued to be barred from testifying against whites. After the 1871 lynching of the Chinese, eight whites were convicted and sentenced to prison terms of two to six years. But the convictions were overturned, and all were freed in 1873.

22. Raphael J. Sonenshein, *Politics in Black and White*, p. 22.

23. Ibid., p. 23.

24. Interview with Tom Bradley, January 19, 1994.

25. Interview with Jesse Brewer, December 15, 1993. Another example of racism was described by Joseph T. Rouzan Jr., who joined the LAPD in 1955 and was later a police chief in Compton and Inglewood. When he complained early in his LAPD career about the attitude of a white fellow foot-beat officer, he was promised by a supervisor that the situation would be remedied. The next night Rouzan walked the beat by himself while the

offending officer was assigned to a radio patrol car with a white partner. Interview with Joseph Rouzan by Jaxon Van Derbeken, August 18, 1994.

26. Gates discusses this incident in his book (p. 107) without naming Deadwyler. The incident received enormous public attention because it occurred within nine months of the Watts riot, and the coroner's inquest was televised for the first time in the city's history. Gates said that Parker "was reacting to the cries of racism that he knew would be hurled at him. And because he had been ill he just wasn't up to it." Like several of Gates' references to Parker, the explanation is patronizing. Parker was vigorous and outspoken until his death. The more probable reason that Parker called the action "murder" is because that is what he believed it to be.

27. The commissioner was Herbert A. Greenwood, the third black to serve on the Police Commission and the first to use the post as a sounding board for criticism of racial discrimination by the LAPD. Greenwood resigned in 1959 after failing to make headway in his disputes with Parker and being consistently outvoted on the commission.

28. This was a recurrent theme of Parker during the violent summer of 1964. See the *Los Angeles Times* of April 19, April 28, May 7, June 26, and July 21, 1964.

29. Gates, *Chief*, p. 34.

30. Homer F. Broome Jr., *LAPD's Black History: 1886–1976*, p. 117.

31. Interview with Jesse Brewer, September 7, 1994. Gates omits any mention of the Yorty campaign promise in his book, giving Parker full credit for desegregation of the LAPD.

32. Ibid., Brewer interview.

33. Broome, *LAPD's Black History: 1886–1976*, p. 116.

34. Interview with Jesse Brewer, September 7, 1994.

35. Ibid.

36. Interview with Hubert Williams, March 4, 1994. Williams was fascinated by the LAPD policy of responding only to calls involving crimes. As a result of this policy, almost every encounter between civilians and LAPD officers was in a situation which involved crime or violence. Williams believes that police officers in departments that also respond to non-emergency calls often develop good relations with civilians. That rarely happened in Los Angeles.

37. Interview with Tom Bradley, January 19, 1994.

38. Parker interview with McDonald, p. 8.

39. Ibid., pp. 3–4.

40. Stacey C. Koon, *Presumed Guilty*, p. 63.

41. Woods, pp. 493–494. Bruce Smith, the police expert who ranked the LAPD fifth, was an admirer of Parker and his department, which he placed well above the police departments of New York, Philadelphia, and Chicago. But it wasn't good enough for Parker, who delivered a scathing attack on Smith's rankings.

42. Parker interview with McDonald, p. 10.

43. Interview with Hubert Williams, March 4, 1994.

4. OFFICIAL NEGLIGENCE

1. Interview with Scott Landsman, July 18, 1994.

2. Interview with Johnnie Cochran, November 11, 1993.

3. Interview with Terry White, October 5, 1993.

4. This phrase was used by Los Angeles police officers interviewed by Jaxon Van Derbeken, Jessica Crosby, and me. David Dotson, who joined the LAPD in 1958 and retired as assistant chief in June 1992, said in a December 21, 1993, interview with me that in his early years as an officer "If you ran you got beat, period." Subsequently, under Ed Davis and then Gates, the LAPD laid down strict rules to avoid such actions, "at least in vehicular pursuits," Dotson said.

5. Gates relates in *Chief* that he became alarmed after one of his officers recalled a scene from *Gorillas in the Mist* where African natives butchered a native gorilla. But despite his relief at learning that Powell and Wind had handled the disturbance-of-the-peace incident correctly, Gates nonetheless concluded that the MDT message sent by Powell was "clearly racist" and suggested a "possible bias," p. 320.

6. Gates contends the MDT transmissions were leaked to the press soon after he told Bradley and police commissioners about them. He bases this opinion on questions he promptly received from reporters asking if the audiotapes of the incident contained comments that displayed racial bias. Gates said no biased comments existed on the audiotapes, an answer that was at once technically truthful and deliberately misleading. The incriminating transcript was based on digital, not audio, transmissions. Gates and Bradley said separately that they advocated immediate release of the transcripts, but District Attorney Ira Reiner advised against their release until the grand jury completed its work and returned indictments on March 14, 1991. Gates, *Chief*, pp. 320–321.

7. Interview with Tim Wind, July 26, 1994.

8. Ibid.

9. Interview with John Sheriff by Jaxon Van Derbeken, September 27, 1994.

10. Karen Nikos, "Ex-LAPD Officer Gets Three Years' Probation In Beating Incidents," *Daily News*, October 26, 1991. In sentencing Lance Braun, Superior Court Judge John H. Reid said that "a reasonable person would have to conclude" that the timing of the case had something to do with the King incident. "But, that's just a side issue and not an issue that's before me," he added.

11. Interview with Jerry Guzzetta, April 6, 1994.

12. Interview with Jo-Ellan Dimitrius, September 16, 1993. She told me: "Had Larry been given his own opportunity to do what he wanted to do, I don't think he would have become a cop."

13. Jaxon Van Derbeken, "In the Eye of the King Storm," *Daily News*, February 2, 1992.

14. Ibid.

15. John Hurst and Leslie Berger, "Crisis in the LAPD—The Rodney G. King Beating; Four Officers—Their Paths To Trial," *Los Angeles Times*, February 3, 1992.

16. The investigation of this incident, which occurred on October 3, 1990, dragged on for more than a year, largely because Powell could not be interviewed once he became the target of a criminal inquiry in the King case. By the time the investigation of the earlier incident was completed, the trial in Simi Valley was about to begin and no action was taken. Not until July 16, 1992, did the newly installed police chief, Willie Williams, formally reprimand Powell for "serious misconduct" in hitting Ramos. Williams noted in his reprimand that he would also have imposed a "substantial penalty" for this offense had not the one-year statute of limitations on punishment expired.

17. Hector Gonzalez and Courtenay Edelhart, "Charge Surfaces: Black Students Claim Officers Attacked Them," *The Wave*, March 13, 1991.

18. Interview with Jack White, January 31, 1994.

19. Lynne Duke, "Black in LAPD Blue; Officers Voice Shock at Beating," *The Washington Post*, March 31, 1991.

20. Arnold Steinberg, "Los Angeles County Voters–Change of Venue Study," April 20, 1991. Because voter rolls are used (along with driver's licenses) as the source of jury lists in Los Angeles County, Steinberg polled a random sample of 1,000 registered voters. He found an "overwhelming" level of public awareness of the King incident. "In more than a decade of survey research work throughout California, especially in Los Angeles County, I cannot recall an event which comes even close to this incident in terms of its penetration of public consciousness. . . . " he concluded.

21. Van Derbeken, "In the Eye of the King Storm," Hurst and Berger, "Crisis in the LAPD—The Rodney G. King Beating; Four Officers—Their Paths to Trial."

22. Rick Orlov and Jaxon Van Derbeken, "Mayor Wants Racism Probe: 21 of Its Officers, Not 15, Were at Beating, Department Says," *Daily News*, March 20, 1991.

23. Interview with Terry White, October 5, 1993.

24. Interview with Tom Owens, October 8, 1993. Owens also wrote a similar account in *Lying Eyes*, a book about his involvement in the King incident, pp. 60 and 99.

25. This anecdote is from a confidential interview.

26. The LAPD distributed surveys to 960 officers and received responses from 650. To the question of whether racial bias by officers contributed to "a negative interaction between police and community," 24.5 percent answered affirmatively, 55.4 percent disagreed and 20.1 percent had no opinion. *Los Angeles Police Department Opinion Survey*, 1991.

27. Interview with Joseph T. Rouzan Jr. by Jaxon Van Derbeken, August 18, 1994.

28. Interview with John Sheriff by Jaxon Van Derbeken, September 27, 1994.

29. Ibid.

30. Interview with Daryl Gates, February 4, 1994.

31. Cliff Ruff comment to author, February 3, 1994.

32. Beth Barrett and David Parrish, "The Record Against LAPD: 254 Officers Named in 3 or More Excessive-Force Cases" and "Juries, Attorneys Find Fault Where Department Finds None," *Daily News*, June 9, 1991. Officer Henry's story was reported as part of an examination of police abuses involving 254 LAPD officers named in three or more cases of excessive force. This story was one of the best media examinations of LAPD practices in the wake of the King beating.

33. Joseph G. Woods, *The Progressives and the Police: Urban Reform and the Professionalization of the American Police*, UCLA doctoral thesis in history, 1973, p. 502.

34. Jerry Cohen, "Lore and Legend of Ed Davis," *Los Angeles Times*, December 18, 1977.

35. Ibid.

36. Interview with Jesse Brewer, December 15, 1993.

37. James Q. Wilson, *Thinking About Crime*, p. 69.

38. Ed Davis, *Staff One*, p. 136.

39. Jerry Cohen, "Lore and Legend of Ed Davis."

40. Bradley told me that he was "absolutely" convinced that the community-relations officers were the foundation of a political machine to back Davis. Interview with Tom Bradley, January 19, 1994.

41. Ibid.

42. Interview with Ed Davis, January 11, 1994.

43. Reinhardt said, "Gates decided that team policing wasn't needed and that we couldn't afford it." Interview with Stephen Reinhardt, January 27, 1994.

44. Ibid.

45. Interview with Ted Hunt, August 30, 1994.

46. Interview with Ed Davis, January 11, 1994.

47. Interview with Stephen Reinhardt, January 27, 1994.

48. Daryl Gates, *Chief*, p. 9.

49. Bill Boyarsky, "A Cowboy Cop With A Thoughtful Side Confronts the L.A. of the '80s," *Governing*, December 1988.

50. Interview with Bill Boyarsky, September 27, 1994.

51. Bill Boyarsky, "Gates Discusses Police Issues—Past, Present, Future," *Los Angeles Times*, March 27, 1978.

52. Gates, *Chief*, p. 197.

53. Three LAPD officers, two of them white, who were interviewed for this book, told me of this practice, which was much resented in minority communities.

54. Letter from Police Chief Daryl Gates to the Police Commission, May 7, 1982.

55. Greg Meyer, "Brutal by Default," *Daily Journal*, August 19, 1993, quoting then-city councilman Farrell as saying this in an article in the *Los Angeles Times*, October 7, 1981.

56. Interview with Robert Simpach by Jaxon Van Derbeken, October 27, 1994.
57. Ibid.
58. The accounts of the police witnesses, except for Simpach, and of the neighbor witnesses is taken from an August 10, 1984, report on the Mincey death submitted to the Police Commission by the Special Investigations Division of the Los Angeles County District Attorney's Office. See also "Death Sparks Furor over LAPD Choke-Hold Policy," by Deborah Cawthon, *Daily News*, April 11, 1982.
59. Deborah Cawthon, "Family of Police Choke Hold Victim Express Anger, Grief," *Daily News*, May 23, 1982.
60. Gates, *Chief*, p. 215.
61. MacNeil–Lehrer NewsHour, March 28, 1991.
62. Charles P. Wallace, "Bar-Arm Choke Hold Banned," *Los Angeles Times*, May 7, 1982.
63. Boyarsky, "A Cowboy Cop with a Thoughtful Side Confronts the L.A. of the '80s."
64. Interview with Greg Meyer by Jaxon Van Derbeken, on August 26, 1994. Also, Yaroslavsky is quoted in a *Los Angeles Herald-Examiner* story, August 22, 1981.
65. Interview with David Zeigler, November 16, 1993.
66. Interview with Greg Meyer, September 6, 1994. Meyer has also expressed this view in articles in police professional journals and in an op-ed piece in the *Los Angeles Times*, June 14, 1994, "Finding a Safe Way to Subdue Violent Suspects."
67. James Rainey, "Final Suit Over LAPD's Use of Chokehold Settled," *Los Angeles Times*, September 29, 1993. The city paid $1,550,000 to five Mincey relatives in lawsuits arising from his death.
68. Charles P. Wallace, "City Considers Policy Change on Chokeholds," *Los Angeles Times*, May 12, 1982.
69. Deborah Cawthon, "Chief Gates Defends His Enforcement of Ban on Choke Hold," *Daily News*, June 16, 1982.
70. Interview with Scott Landsman, October 26, 1994.
71. Interview with Greg Meyer, September 6, 1994.
72. Whether the LAPD vigorously pursued attempts to find medium-force alternatives to the metal baton remains an open question. Gates and other police experts have told much the same story as Hunt, essentially that such efforts were hindered by lack of funds. But the LAPD did purchase some capture nets on an experimental basis. Officer Simpach told Jaxon Van Derbeken in a September 8, 1994, interview that one such net was assigned to Foothill Division and that he and two other officers used it to arrest a PCP user who was taken into custody without injury. The nets were effective only in certain situations. "You couldn't use it inside, you couldn't use it up against something," Simpach said. "It would have worked perfectly against Rodney King. He was right out in the open."
73. Interview with Charles Duke, October 5, 1993.

74. From "A Training Analysis of the Los Angeles Police Department," October 21, 1991. Prepared by the Training Review Committee of the LAPD.

75. Interview with Scott Landsman, October 26, 1994.

76. Interview with Charles Duke, October 5, 1993.

77. Ibid.

78. Lou Cannon and Jessica Crosby, "Buffeted Los Angeles Police Department Is Described as Demoralized," *The Washington Post*, July 24, 1993.

5. LATASHA'S SHIELD

Unless otherwise specified, the dialogue in this chapter at the scene of the shooting is drawn from police records and the trial transcript.

1. Much as it is difficult to determine from the Holliday videotape how many times Rodney King was struck by police officers, so is it impossible to know with certainty from the in-store videotape how many times Harlins hit Du with her fists. Statements and legal motions by the district attorney refer to "two to four blows" on some occasions and to "more than two blows" in others. Soon Ja Du testified that she was struck twice by Harlins, but she also said she was dazed after the first blow. I have based the number of three blows on my own viewing of the videotape. Others who have watched the tape believe Harlins hit Du four times.

2. Survey by the National Institute of Justice. See "The Crime Funnel," by David C. Anderson, *The New York Times Magazine*, June 12, 1994.

3. Probation Officer's Report to the Superior Court of California, County of Los Angeles, submitted November 8, 1991.

4. Interview with Richard Rhee by Lou Cannon and Jessica Crosby, February 16, 1994.

5. Edward Taehan Chang, "Perspective on Korean Americans," *Los Angeles Times*, May 31, 1994.

6. Interview with Angela Oh, June 10, 1994. Oh's tabulation from Korean-language newspapers showed forty-six assaults and nineteen deaths, of Korean business owners or their customers in 1993.

7. Interview with Gina Rae, May 18, 1994.

8. Andrea Ford and John H. Lee, "Racial Tensions Blamed in Girl's Death," *Los Angeles Times*, March 20, 1991.

9. Jesse Katz and John H. Lee, "Conflict Brings Tragic End to Similar Dreams of Life," *Los Angeles Times*, April 8, 1991.

10. Ibid.

11. Probation Officer's Report, November 8, 1991.

12. Ibid.

13. Ford and Lee, "Racial Tensions Blamed in Girl's Death."

14. Interview with Glenn Britton, April 19, 1994.

15. Interview with Charles Lloyd, February 15, 1994.

16. Lloyd told me in the interview that he "had to" pass the bar on the first try. He said he was insecure and driven to succeed and related his desire for material success to his boyhood poverty during the Depression. "When you start at a younger age, enough is never enough," he said. "Rolls Royces, brand-new suits, Rolex watches. Enough is just never enough."
17. Interview with Charles Lloyd, February 15, 1994.
18. The Dus had financial support from the Korean community, but legal expenses nonetheless seem to have taken most of their savings. According to probation records, the Dus were drawing $15,000 a month from their two markets at the time of the Harlins shooting. The report said that Sandy Du had dropped out of nursing school to work and help pay the family's legal expenses.
19. Interview with Richard Leonard, June 8, 1994.
20. Interview with Charles Lloyd, February 15, 1994.

6. CHRISTOPHER'S COURSE

1. Unless otherwise identified, the quotations in this chapter attributed to the Christopher Commission are from the Independent Commission on the Los Angeles Police Department report, or from a separate report released simultaneously, "Selected Messages From The LAPD Mobile Digital Terminal System: November 1, 1989–March 4, 1991." The Commission also released the testimony of Daryl Gates, Jesse Brewer, David Dotson, and Robert Vernon. I have used the terms "Independent Commission" and "Christopher Commission," as the panel was usually called, interchangeably.
2. Among the misinformation provided to the media by the mayor's aides and widely reprinted and broadcast was the accusation that Gates was to blame for withholding the racist computer messages sent by Officer Laurence Powell just before the King affair. As we have seen, Bradley knew about these messages only because Gates had promptly informed him after they were found by LAPD investigators. At the request of the district attorney, they were kept secret until the officers had been indicted.
3. John Rofe and Patrick McGreevy, "Gates Lashes Out at Critics," *Daily News*, March 14, 1991.
4. Bradley and Gates have given nearly identical accounts of this meeting in interviews with me and others, and Gates has repeated it in his book.
5. Interview with Warren Christopher, June 1992.
6. Transcript of the first public hearing of the Independent Commission, May 1, 1991. The record of this meeting—from which the testimony of George Aliano and Ramona Ripston is also quoted—is stored in the commission archives at the University of Southern California.
7. Bill Boyarsky, "Echoes of the McCone Commission," *Los Angeles Times*, May 3, 1991.

8. Bradley squeaked through with 51.9 percent of the vote. His principal opponents were Nate Holden, a city councilman and African American who cut into Bradley's support among blacks, and Baxter Ward, a frequent candidate who made it a practice not to accept campaign contributions. Bradley raised $2.6 million, outspending Holden by a 11–1 margin and narrowly averting a runoff. Raphael Sonenshein said that the election showed "definite signs of softness in Bradley's base" and that it was not certain he would have won a runoff election. For a more detailed analysis, see Sonenshein, *Politics in Black and White*, pp. 198–202.

9. Ted Rohrlich, "Majority Says Police Brutality Is Common," *Los Angeles Times*, March 10, 1991.

10. Gates was temporarily reinstated on April 8, 1991, by an order from Judge Ronald Sohigian. The chief's status remained uncertain for several weeks, however, as the city council and the Police Commission tried unsuccessfully to negotiate a settlement. On May 7, Police Commission President Dan Garcia resigned, saying the council had undercut the commission's authority. On May 13, Sohigian ruled that the council had acted within its authority in reinstating Gates. See "Gates Reinstatement Upheld" by Rick Orlov in the *Daily News*, May 15, 1991.

11. Jaxon Van Derbeken, "Jovial Chief Jokes with Supporters," *Daily News*, April 6, 1991.

12. Daryl Gates, *Chief*, p. 338.

13. In *The Virginian: A Horseman of the Plains*, an influential novel published in 1902, Owen Wister provided the first successful fictional description of the American cowboy. The book was on the national best-seller list for six years and became a popular play and, much later, a movie. The developers of Southern California could say, as Wister's Virginian does on page 128 of this novel: " . . . True democracy and true aristocracy are one and the same thing. If anybody cannot see this, so much the worse for his eyesight."

14. Interview with John Spiegel, November 29, 1993. Spiegel said he told lawyers he recruited to serve on the commission: "Look, this is a special time. We need you to take three months. It's going to be miserable, but we will get it done in three months." The commission almost made this deadline. It asked for and was given an extra week to complete its work.

15. Ibid.

16. One of these lunches was with Jay Mathews, then the Los Angeles bureau chief of *The Washington Post*, and me. Christopher asked us as least as many questions as we asked him. No notes were taken, but I was impressed with Christopher's determination to produce a report that would be considered widely credible, not just to critics of the LAPD.

17. Interview with Leo Estrada, February 1, 1994.

18. The commission maintained its financial independence by not using public funds for any of its work. The Weingart Foundation provided a grant to the commission, and various firms provided office space, copying, or printing as-

sistance. The Claremont University Center served as fiscal agent. But by far the largest contribution came in the form of donated legal and accounting services: attorneys contributed 16,000 hours; accountants and statistical consultants, 9,000 hours.

19. John Brooks Slaughter, "'I Was Stunned' by the Frequency and Bravado of Scurrilous Comments," *Los Angeles Times,* July 14, 1991.

20. Interview with Leo Estrada, February 1, 1994.

21. Gates told me, in a February 4, 1994 interview, that he was uncertain whether the assistant chiefs were a necessary layer of police management. This view may have influenced him to keep the Brewer post vacant, although it is likely he would have filled it eventually except for the distractions of the Rodney King case. The offer to give Brewer the job held by Vernon appears to have been genuine and suggests that Gates was not fully happy with Vernon's performance.

22. Brewer had made this complaint before, about division commanders in general and McBride in particular. It was Brewer's belief that holding division commanders responsible for excessive force, a recurrent problem in Foothill, would give them an incentive for discipline that was otherwise lacking.

23. Jaxon Van Derbeken, "Foothill Division Head to Stay," *Daily News,* April 17, 1991.

24. Coroner's inquests were held into thirty-two of the thirty-four deaths in the Watts riot. Of these, twenty-six were held to be justifiable, one accidental, one homicidal without determination, and four criminal. None of the four criminal deaths was attributed to police officers. For a detailed examination of these inquests, see Robert Conot, *Rivers of Blood, Years of Darkness,* pp. 396–409.

25. Interview with Leo Estrada, February 1, 1994.

26. Patrick McGreevy and John Polich, "Mayor Says Public Good Is At Stake," *Daily News,* April 3, 1991. The day Bradley had tried to force him out, Gates had said, "If the blue-ribbon committee, after intensive examination, comes to the conclusion that I have been derelict somehow in my duty, then that would be the time that people would say, 'Chief, maybe you ought to go.' I'm not stupid. . . . Then I would say, 'Hey, I must have failed somewhere,' and I suppose that would be the time to retire."

27. Lisa Pope, "Vernon Defends Job Conduct," *Daily News,* June 12, 1991.

28. Robert Vernon, *L.A. Justice,* p. 128.

29. Diane K. Shah, "Playboy interview: Daryl Gates; Los Angeles, California Chief of Police" *Playboy,* August, 1991.

30. Interview with Bryce Nelson, October 4, 1994.

31. Interview with Andrea Ordin, November 28, 1994.

32. Ibid.

33. Tracy Wilkinson, Andrea Ford, and Tracy Wood, "Panel Urges Gates to Retire; Report on Police Cites Racism, Excess Force," *Los Angeles Times,* July 10, 1991.

34. Several officers who used racial humor in reference to members of the same racial (or ethnic) group were disciplined, but Gates did not consider these to be examples of the "racism" of which the Christopher Commission complained.

35. Interview with Andrea Ordin, November 28, 1994.

36. Interview with Leo Estrada, Februry 1, 1994.

37. An example of Christopher's methods of obtaining agreement was provided by Estrada, who clashed with Mosk during several of the commission's twenty-six closed meetings. Typically, Christopher would let them debate a few minutes before saying, "I think we should bracket this discussion." He would then summarize the opposing views and the next day send each person a letter suggesting a compromise. In this way he steadily narrowed differences with a view toward obtaining a consensus. Interview with Leo Estrada, February 1, 1994.

38. Richard A. Serrano, "'They Hit Me, So I Hit Back'," *Los Angeles Times*, October 4, 1992.

39. Gates, *Chief*, p. 350.

40. Ibid., p. 351.

41. Interview with Daryl Gates, February 4, 1994.

42. Ibid.

43. Ibid.

44. Interview with Gregory Dust, November 28, 1994.

45. Kerbrat was killed on February 11, 1991. The killer was Jose Amaya, thirty-two, an illegal immigrant from El Salvador whom Gates subsequently referred to as a "drunken Salvadoran." Valladares fired ten shots at Amaya, killing him. His companion, who was arrested and charged with drinking in public, was not harmed. Leslie Berger and Eric Malnic, "Death of First LAPD Woman Officer Killed in Line of Duty Came During Routine Stop," *Los Angeles Times*, February 23, 1994.

46. Stacey C. Koon, "'It's Time for Gates to Step Down'," *Los Angeles Times*, May 12, 1991.

7. KARLIN'S WAY

1. Jesse Katz and Stephanie Chavez, "Blacks Seek to Channel Anger Over Sentence," *Los Angeles Times*, November 17, 1991.

2. Interview with Joyce Karlin, January 6, 1994.

3. Ibid.

4. Bettina Boxall, "Self-Assured Judge Doesn't Avoid Unpopular Stands," *Los Angeles Times*, November 16, 1991.

5. Shawn Hubler, "New Site Ok'd for Grocer's Murder Trial," *Los Angeles Times*, August 28, 1991.

6. Ibid.

7. As an example of the disparity between Asians in the population and in the electorate, the April 1993 mayoral election is instructive. Councilman

Michael Woo, a Chinese American, was the first major Asian candidate to run for mayor of Los Angeles. Asians at the time were 10 percent of the population but only 3 percent of the electorate, according to a *Los Angeles Times* exit poll. Woo finished second in a large field and lost to Richard Riordan in a runoff election.

8. Interview with Richard Leonard, June 8, 1994.
9. Charisse Jones, "Deliberations in Trial of Grocer Interrupted for Ruling on Dispute," *Los Angeles Times,* October 10, 1991.
10. Andrea Ford and Tracy Wilkinson, "Grocer is Convicted in Teen Killing," *Los Angeles Times,* October 12, 1991.
11. Jesse Katz and Frank Clifford, "Many Find Verdict Fair, But There Is Still Outrage," *Los Angeles Times,* October 12, 1991.
12. Probation Officer's Report to the Superior Court of California, County of Los Angeles, submitted November 8, 1991. The report quotes Du as saying about blacks, "Didn't understand at first. Later paid less attention . . . [to] their way of living."
13. Interview with Charles Lloyd, February 15, 1994.
14. Probation Officer's Report, November 8, 1991.
15. Karlin told me that she thought the Los Angeles police had been negligent in returning the gun without checking its condition or test-firing the weapon. But the LAPD has no policy for checking the condition of stolen weapons before returning them to their legal owners. Richard Leonard said that he thought the department had acted appropriately in returning the weapon to the Dus.
16. There are three versions of Karlin's statement, which differ in minor details. Karlin wrote out what she intended to say. She slightly altered her comments in delivering her sentence. They were further altered, for editing reasons and to delete references to Roxane Carvajal, when published as an op-ed article in the *Los Angeles Times.* The version I have used is what Karlin said in court, with minor deletions and the correction of what appear to be two typographical errors in the transcript. Additionally, her remark that a .38 revolver "cannot go off accidentally" was added from her op-ed piece.
17. Tracy Wilkinson and Frank Clifford, "Korean Grocer Who Killed Black Teen Gets Probation," *Los Angeles Times,* November 16, 1991.
18. Interview with Richard Leonard, June 8, 1994.
19. Interview with Leon Jenkins, April 15, 1994.
20. Interview with Andrea Ford, June 8, 1994.
21. Interview with Tim Fowler, December 21, 1993. Fowler said that while King was "the straw that broke the camel's back, the riots were not just about Rodney King."
22. Interview with Angela Oh, June 10, 1994.
23. Interview with Ira Reiner, October 13, 1993.
24. Interview with Lawrence Middleton, September 14, 1993.

8. JUDICIAL NEGLIGENCE

1. Interview with Roger Gunson, October 19, 1993.
2. Interview with Ira Reiner, July 12, 1994.
3. Interview with Roger Gunson, October 19, 1993.
4. Henry Unger, "Profile: Judge Bernard J. Kamins, Los Angeles Superior Court," *Daily Journal,* March 6, 1987.
5. The survey was conducted by Arnold Steinberg, a well-known conservative political pollster in Los Angeles County.
6. Interview with Patrick Thistle, December 19, 1994.
7. Interview with Joan Dempsey Klein, July 1, 1994.
8. This is from a confidential interview with a judge who is a friend of Klein.
9. Klein decision, July 23, 1991. (232Cal.App.3rd 785; 283 Cal.Rptr.777) The quotations in this chapter attributed to Klein are from this decision unless otherwise identified.
10. The "totality of the circumstances" also involved the LAPD. Klein's ruling observed that the difficulty of obtaining a fair trial "is excacerbated by the the fact the defendants are police officers. . . . The fact that the videotape depicts local officers in such conduct threatens the community's ability to rely on its police and has caused a high level of indignation, outrage and anxiety."
11. Staff Reports, "Profile: Judge Stanley Martin Weisberg, Los Angeles Superior Court," *Daily Journal,* June 1, 1989.
12. Weisberg gave no interviews to the media after the June 1, 1989, *Daily Journal* profile referred to above. He nonetheless received glowing press coverage when he was appointed to replace Kamins and again at the beginning of the trial in Simi Valley. A March 6, 1992, profile in *The New York Times* credited him for rescuing a case that had been "mired in confusion" before he was named the trial judge. "Judge in Police Beating Trial Sets Aside Confusion," the headline said; the article is by Richard Perez-Pena.
13. Interview with Joan Dempsey Klein, July 1, 1994.
14. Interview with Patrick Thistle, December 19, 1994.
15. Simi Valley and neighboring Thousand Oaks have consistently ranked among the nation's safest cities with populations of more than 100,000, according to FBI statistics. Thousand Oaks was the nation's safest city from 1989 through 1991, and Simi Valley the safest city in 1993. Daryl Kelley, "Simi Valley Tops List of Safest U.S. Cities," *Los Angeles Times,* May 2, 1994.
16. Richard A. Serrano, "King Case Shifts to Courtroom in Simi Valley," *Los Angeles Times,* February 4, 1992.
17. According to 1990 Census Bureau figures, Orange County had a black population of 42,681 compared to 15,629 for Ventura County although the percentage of blacks in Orange (1.8) was lower than in Ventura. But black participation in politics is greater in Orange County than in Ventura County, and both counties draw jurors from voter registration rolls.

18. Alameda County has a black population of 18 percent, the highest of any county in California. The black population of Los Angeles County is 11.2 percent and of Sacramento, 9.3 percent. Riverside County, which was briefly considered by Weisberg and discarded for reasons that are not clear, has a black percentage of 5.4 and Fresno, which Thistle thought a likely site for the trial, a black percentage of 5. There would have been a likelihood of a racially diverse jury in any of these counties and a strong probability of such a jury in Alameda or Sacramento.

19. Letter from Stanley Weisberg to me, dated May 9, 1994.

20. Andrea Ford and Daryl Kelley, "King Case To Be Tried In Ventura County," *Los Angeles Times,* November 27, 1991.

21. These comments came in a confidential interview with a judge who has known Weisberg for many years.

22. Interview with Ira Reiner, July 12, 1994.

23. Reiner relied heavily on a 1970 case, *Jackson v. Superior Court,* involving the murder of a prison guard by three inmates. The defendants asked for a change of venue to San Francisco on grounds they could not obtain a fair trial in Monterey County, where the prison was located. The change of venue was granted and the prosecution then asked that the case be transferred to San Diego instead. The trial judge agreed, but his decision was overturned by the appeals court, which held that the prosecution had no right to ask for a change of venue in a criminal action "on the ground that a fair and impartial trial cannot be held in the county."

24. Weisberg letter, May 9, 1994.

25. Interview with Joan Dempsey Klein, July 1, 1994.

26. Ibid.

27. Interview with Roger Gunson, October 13, 1993.

28. Ford and Kelley, "King Case to be Tried in Ventura County." King's attorney Steven Lerman is quoted in this story as saying that he had "every confidence in the great citizens of Ventura County that they will get justice done."

29. Interview with Darryl Mounger, October 24, 1993.

30. Interview with Johnnie Cochran, November 11, 1993.

31. Ventura County is culturally and geographically divided by a mountain range that separates the cities in the eastern part of the county from the west. Thousand Oaks and Simi Valley, in the east, are more centered on Los Angeles, while Ventura and Oxnard, in the west, have a more distinct and independent identity. My impression from the demographics and the voir dire is that the Simi Valley location of the trial probably produced a more conservative jury than would have been seated in the downtown Ventura courthouse. Judge Weisberg was sensitive to personal hardships and excused prospective jurors who said it would be difficult for them to commute to Simi Valley.

32. Only 3 of the 260 prospective jurors claimed never to have seen the videotape.

33. Interview with Terry White, October 5, 1993.

34. Ibid.

35. Interview with Jo-Ellan Dimitrius, September 16, 1993.

36. Ibid.

37. Interview with Terry White, October 5, 1993.

38. Dawn Webber, "No Blacks Chosen for King Case Jury," *Daily News*, March 3, 1992.

39. Rene Lynch, "Minority Leaders Say Verdict Seen as Racist Could Blow Lid off Powder Keg," *Daily News*, April 5, 1992.

40. Ibid.

41. Richard A. Serrano and Carlos V. Lozano, "Jury Picked for King Trial; No Blacks Chosen," *Los Angeles Times*, March 3, 1992.

42. Henry Weinstein, "White Says the Jury Was the Worst Possible," *Los Angeles Times*, May 8, 1992.

43. D. M. Osborne, "Reaching for Doubt," *The American Lawyer*, September 1992.

44. I discussed my observation about this juror, which was also noticed by a member of the prosecution team, with an editor at *The Washington Post*. Since there was no way for me to discuss it with the juror, my editor and I thought the observation too subjective to put in a story without knowing more about the reason for it.

9. BEYOND THE VIDEOTAPE

1. Koon's testimony during the *The People of the State of California vs. Laurence Powell, Timothy E. Wind, Theodore Briseno and Stacey Koon*, hereinafter *People v. Powell*. Direct quotations from the trial have not been noted except for a few exceptional instances. I have noted significant statements made by the participants in interviews or statements outside of court.

2. Andrea Ford and Jim Newton, "Victim's Sister Ends Emotional Testimony," *Los Angeles Times*, February 7, 1995. Cochran made this remark outside court after a video was played showing O. J. Simpson attending his daughter's recital a few hours before Nicole Brown Simpson and Ronald Goldman were murdered.

3. For instance, one witness had seen police confront an armed assailant; another had seen police beating a handcuffed man. Such discrepancies are not unusual in criminal cases, but they were compounded in this one because most witnesses were across the street and behind a fence that partially impeded their view. The recollections of witnesses were further confused after they watched the videotape and tried to reconcile what they thought they remembered with what they saw on the screen.

4. Interview with John Barnett, October 18, 1993.

5. Ibid. The prosecution was aware of the problem but didn't know what to do about it. After the trial, without mentioning Barnett, I asked prosecutor Alan Yochelson about Barnett's theory that the videotape had enabled the defense to obtain a favorable jury. Yochelson asked me if I had been talking to Deputy District Attorney Roger Gunson—who held a similar theory. At the time, I had not yet interviewed Gunson.

6. Ibid., Barnett interview.
7. Jaxon Van Derbeken, "In the Eye of the King Storm," *Daily News*, February 2, 1992.
8. *People v. Powell*.
9. Interview with Dorothy Bailey, January 4, 1995.
10. Ibid.
11. Interview with Ira Reiner, September 17, 1993.
12. Interview with Dorothy Bailey, January 4, 1995.
13. Interview with Anna Charmaine Whiting, January 13, 1995.
14. Lou Cannon, "New King Trial Unfolds in the Same Troubled City," *Santa Barbara News-Press*, March 9, 1993.
15. Interview with Mike Stone, October 4, 1993.
16. Interview with John Barnett, October 18, 1993.
17. Barbara Murphy, "Satellite Dish Helps L.A. County Prosecutors Follow Trial," *Daily News*, March 6, 1992.
18. Interview with Alan Yochelson, October 19, 1993.
19. Ibid.
20. Ibid.
21. Dawn Webber, "CHP Officer Says King Hit in Head," *Daily News*, March 7, 1992.
22. Richard A. Serrano, "CHP Officer Describes Chase, Beating of King," *Los Angeles Times*, March 7, 1992.
23. Interview with Ira Reiner, September 17, 1993.
24. Judge Weisberg had kept information about King's robbery conviction out of the record but had allowed defense attorneys to say in opening statements that King was on parole at the time of the incident. In ruling that the reference to King's parole (and hence acknowledgement that he was an ex-convict) was admissible, Weisberg said it "could reflect upon his state of mind during the particular incident . . . and could explain to some extent the conduct that was perceived."
25. Interview with Terry White, October 5, 1993.
26. Interview with Alan Yochelson, October 19, 1993.
27. Interview with Ira Reiner, September 17, 1993.
28. Ibid.
29. Interview with Alan Yochelson, October 19, 1993.
30. Peter J. Boyer, "The Selling of Rodney King," *Vanity Fair*, July 1992.
31. Interview with Anna Charmaine Whiting, January 13, 1995.
32. *People v. Powell*.
33. Richard A. Serrano, "Key Witness Not on List for King Case," *Los Angeles Times*, February 23, 1993.
34. Henry Weinstein, "Keeping King Off Stand Was a Wise Move, Experts Say," *Los Angeles Times*, March 19, 1992.
35. Interview with Darryl Mounger, October 24, 1993.
36. Interview with Mike Stone, October 4, 1993.
37. Interview with Darryl Mounger, October 24, 1993.

38. Interview with Mike Stone, October 4, 1993.
39. *People v. Powell.* Clemmer described King's words only as "an obscenity" until she was directed by Weisberg to relate his exact words.
40. There is general agreement among officers I interviewed that this was a common practice of Koon, who usually showed up for his shift ahead of time.
41. Van Derbeken, "In the Eye of the King Storm."
42. Interview with Anna Charmaine Whiting, January 13, 1995.
43. Interview with Terry White, October 5, 1993.
44. Ibid.
45. Ibid.
46. Koon was referring to a notorious incident of April 6, 1970, in Newhall, California, when two CHP officers responded to a radio alert concerning a car in which a man had been seen brandishing a weapon. They stopped the vehicle and were shot to death by the driver and his passenger. Two more CHP officers who arrived at the scene moments later were also killed in an exchange of fire with the two men. The picture of the slain officers, all of them twenty-three or twenty-four years old, was shown to LAPD recruits when Koon was in the Police Academy for its shock value to warn of the danger of approaching a vehicle in which the occupants might be armed. The LAPD (and after the Newhall incident, the CHP) taught that the occupants in such circumstances should be ordered to leave the car and show their hands before an officer approached.

10. JUDGMENT AT SIMI

1. This is from the transcript of *People v. Powell.* Unless otherwise noted, quotations in this chapter attributed to the defendants, witnesses, and attorneys are taken directly from trial testimony.
2. Ibid.
3. On December 10, 1992, an LAPD Board of Rights recommended a forty-four day suspension for Louis Turriaga for putting his foot on King's head during the handcuffing, dragging King in a manner that caused further injury, and failing to report the incident. He was exonerated of a fourth charge that he had failed to intercede in King's behalf. The recommendation was accepted by Chief Willie Williams. Jaxon Van Derbeken, "LAPD Finds 1st Officer Guilty in King Beating," *Daily News*, December 11, 1992. John L. Mitchell, "LAPD Discipline Urged for Officer in King Case," *Los Angeles Times*, December 11, 1992.
4. Interview with Anna Charmaine Whiting, January 13, 1995.
5. Tim Wind interview with LAPD Internal Affairs investigators, March 4, 1991. He gave similar accounts to Captain Gale in his Libery Interest Hearing and in the King civil trial.
6. Interview with Mike Stone, October 4, 1993.
7. Stone's final witness was Sergeant Roman Vondriska of the California Highway Patrol, the Singers' supervisor at the time of the King pursuit and arrest.

He inflicted additional damage on Melanie Singer's credibility by saying that he had asked her at the end of her shift, five and a half hours after the incident, if Powell's head blows to King had been intentional. "She was not sure if they were intentional strikes to the head," Vondriska said.

8. Interview with Paul DePasquale, October 6, 1993.

9. Wind suffered from severe gastro-intestinal disorders which his doctors said were caused by stress. He twice underwent surgery after the trial.

10. I received several calls at the Los Angeles office of *The Washington Post* from LAPD officers offering to provide me with material casting Briseno in a derogatory light. With one exception, none of these callers had anything negative to say about the other officers involved in the incident.

11. Interview with Terry White, October 5, 1993.

12. This was not an unusual concern. LAPD Sergeant Greg Dossey told me in an October 11, 1996, interview that he had studied injuries received by LAPD officers during arrest of resistant suspects and found that 55 percent of them resulted from baton blows by other officers. Dossey used 1988 as the year of his case study.

13. This presumes that the jury, which was not sequestered until deliberations, followed the instructions of Weisberg not to read accounts of the case. Briseno's prior record had been reported in stories in the *Los Angeles Times* and *Daily News*.

14. Conversation with Cliff Ruff, July 2, 1996.

15. Interview with Roger Gunson, October 19, 1993.

16. Ibid. Sergeant Conta declined requests to be interviewed.

17. Interview with Roger Gunson, October 19, 1993.

18. Interview with Alan Yochelson, October 19, 1993.

19. Interview with Terry White, October 5, 1993.

20. Interview with Alan Yochelson, October 19, 1993.

21. Interview with Roger Gunson, October 19, 1993.

22. Daryl Gates, *Chief,* paperback edition, p. 416.

23. Ibid., p. 413.

24. Michael Connelly and Jim Newton, "Gates, Special Unit Found Liable for Robbers' Deaths, *Los Angeles Times,* March 31, 1992.

25. Interview with Terry White, October 5, 1993.

26. Interview with Ira Reiner. October 13, 1993.

27. White quote, interview with Terry White, October 5, 1993. Reiner quote, interview with Ira Reiner, September 17, 1993.

28. Gates, *Chief,* p. 4.

29. Sheryl Stolberg, "Karlin Upheld in Sentencing of Grocer," *Los Angeles Times,* April 22, 1992.

30. A *Los Angeles Times* telephone poll of 591 Ventura County residents taken on May 5, the last day of the riots, found that 69 percent disagreed with the verdicts. Carlos V. Lozano, "The Times Poll: Verdicts Anger Ventura County," May 7, 1992.

31. Interview with John Barnett, October 18, 1993.

32. Gates, *Chief,* paperback edition, p. 417.
33. Interview with Paul Jefferson, May 11, 1994.
34. Ibid.
35. Nina J. Easton, "Power to the Pastor," *Los Angeles Times Magazine,* August 16, 1992.
36. Lou Cannon, "Bradley, Black Leaders Try to Head Off Violence," *The Washington Post,* April 28, 1992.
37. Shawn Hubler, "Black Leaders Accuse Gates of Inflaming Racial Tensions," *Los Angeles Times,* April 29, 1992.
38. D. M. Osborne, "Reaching For Doubt," *The American Lawyer,* September 1992. Osborne used pseudonyms for the jurors in her account. Because the jurors have been identified in various news accounts, I have used their real names.
39. Ibid.
40. Ibid.
41. Ibid.
42. Ibid.
43. Ibid.
44. Interview with Dorothy Bailey, January 4, 1995.
45. Ibid.
46. Osborne, "Reaching For Doubt."
47. Interview with Dorothy Bailey, January 4, 1995.
48. Interview with Anna Charmaine Whiting, January 13, 1995.
49. Ibid.
50. Osborne, "Reaching For Doubt."
51. Ibid.
52. Interview with Anna Charmaine Whiting, January 13, 1995.
53. ABC News *Nightline,* "First King Trial Jury Foreman Speaks," March 8, 1993.
54. Interview with Terry White, October 5, 1993.
55. Linda Deutsch, "Jurors Deliberate for Sixth Day, Officer Calls King 'Political Puppet'," Associated Press, April 28, 1992. Richard A. Serrano and Tracy Wilkinson, "All 4 in King Beating Acquitted," *Los Angeles Times,* April 30, 1992.
56. Interview with Paul DePasquale, October 6, 1993.
57. Interview with Steven Lerman, October 20, 1993.
58. Ibid.
59. Amy Wallace and David Ferrell, "Verdicts Greeted With Outrage and Disbelief," *Los Angeles Times,* April 30, 1992.
60. Keith Stone and Rick Orlov, "Protesters Shoot, Beat, Loot, Burn," *Daily News,* April 30, 1992.
61. Interview with Tom Owens, October 12, 1993.
62. Ibid.
63. Hector Tobar and Leslie Berger, "Verdict Greeted With Relief and Elation Among LAPD Officers," *Los Angeles Times,* April 30, 1992.

64. Interview with Michael Moulin, April 20, 1994.
65. Interview with Anna Charmaine Whiting, January 13, 1995.
66. Ibid.

11. ANATOMY OF A BREAKDOWN

1. Lou Cannon, "When Thin Blue Line Retreated, L.A. Riot Went Out of Control," *The Washington Post*, May 10, 1992.
2. Interview with Charles Duke by Jaxon Van Derbeken, August 22, 1994.
3. Ellis E. Conklin and Aurelio Rojas, "Watts: 20 Years After the Madness; Little Change Noted Since the Days of 'Burn, Baby Burn'," UPI, July 30, 1985.
4. Intra-Department Correspondence dated September 2, 1965 from Inspector D. F. Gates to Deputy Chief R. E. Murdock, re: Riot Control Activity—August 11 through August 23, 1965.
5. Daryl Gates, *Chief*, p. 92.
6. Comment of Clyde Kronkhite, a former high-ranking LAPD officer. Cannon, "When Thin Blue Line Retreated, L.A. Riot Went Out of Control."
7. Interview with LAPD Lt. Greg Meyer by Jaxon Van Derbeken, August 26, 1994.
8. Interview with Michael Hillmann, August 19, 1994.
9. Interview with Bayan Lewis by Jaxon Van Derbeken, August 29, 1994.
10. "Analysis of the Los Angeles Police Department's Planning, Preparedness and Response to the 1992 Riot (The First Six Hours)," prepared by Lt. Gary Williams of LAPD, July 8, 1992.
11. "The City in Crisis: A Report by the Special Advisor to the Board of Police Commissioners on the Civil Disorder in Los Angeles," October 21, 1992. This document is commonly known as the Webster report and is so referred to in this chapter. I separately interviewed Mr. Webster and Mr. Williams, and any references to these interviews are cited in the notes.
12. The italics used here are used by the authors of the Webster report.
13. Interview with Hubert Williams, March 4, 1994.
14. Ibid.
15. Robert Vernon, *L.A. Justice*, p. 160. Vernon said he told Gates on April 10, 1992: "It's my opinion we'll have some disturbances regardless of how the verdict goes."
16. Ibid., p. 156.
17. Interview with Pete Durham by Jaxon Van Derbeken, September 14, 1994.
18. Ibid.
19. Interview with Thomas Lorenzen by Jaxon Van Derbeken, August 15, 1994.
20. Interview with John Sheriff by Jaxon Van Derbeken, September 27, 1994.
21. Gates, *Chief*, paperback edition, p. 426.
22. Vernon, *L.A. Justice*, p. 160.
23. Interview with Tim McBride by Jaxon Van Derbeken, August 8, 1994.
24. Interview with Michael Hillmann, August 19, 1994.
25. Ibid.

26. Ibid.
27. Ibid.
28. Interview with Pete Durham by Jaxon Van Derbeken, September 14, 1994.
29. Interview with Michael Hillmann, August 19, 1994.
30. Ibid.
31. Ibid.
32. Interview with Dan Koenig by Jaxon Van Derbeken, September 27, 1994.
33. Dr. Bert Useem and Commander David J. Gascon, "Riot Control and the Los Angeles Riot of 1992."
34. Vernon, *L.A. Justice*, p. 160.
35. Interview with Daryl Gates, February 4, 1994.
36. Ibid.
37. Interview with Paul Pesqueira by Jaxon Van Derbeken, October 31, 1994. Hunt, whom I interviewed on use-of-force issues pertaining to his experience at the Police Academy, declined comment on whether he had warned Gates about the possibility of riots.
38. Interview with Ira Reiner, September 17, 1993.
39. Gates wanted to promote McKinley to the rank of captain, which would have been commensurate with his position as head of Valley Bureau. But the promotion was subsequently blocked after the riots.
40. Interview with Paul Jefferson, May 11, 1994.
41. Interview with Greg Meyer by Jaxon Van Derbeken, August 26, 1994.
42. Interview with Charlie Strong by Jaxon Van Derbeken, November 2, 1994.
43. Ibid.
44. David Ferrell, "Taps for a Police Legend on 77th Street," *Los Angeles Times*, March 3, 1995.
45. Gates, *Chief*, paperback edition, p. 443.
46. Interview with Paul Jefferson, May 11, 1994.
47. Ibid.
48. This is Moulin's recollection, and officers recall that he left the roll-call room and then returned to it. Jefferson, however, remembers that he and Moulin watched the verdicts together in his office.
49. Interview with Michael Moulin, April 20, 1994.
50. Interview with John Edwards by Jaxon Van Derbeken, October 13, 1994.
51. Interview with Michael Moulin, April 20, 1994.
52. Stephen Braun and Leslie Berger, "Chaos and Frustration at Florence and Normandie," *Los Angeles Times*, May 15, 1992.
53. Interview with Charlie Strong by Jaxon Van Derbeken, November 2, 1994.
54. Interview with John Ayala by Jaxon Van Derbeken, November 3, 1994.
55. Interview with Don Schwartzer by Jaxon Van Derbeken, November 1, 1994.
56. Interview with Tom Bradley, January 19, 1994.
57. Interview with Tim McGrath by Jaxon Van Derbeken, November 3, 1994.
58. Whitman, "The Untold Story of the LA Riot," *U.S. News & World Report*, May 31, 1993.
59. Interview with Sam Arase by Jaxon Van Derbeken, October 12, 1994.

60. Interview with Bart Bartholomew, June 3, 1995.
61. Whitman, "The Untold Story of the LA Riot."
62. Interview with Terry Keenan, October 13, 1994.
63. Interview with Perry Alvarez by Jaxon Van Derbeken, October 31, 1994.
64. Police crowd estimates fluctuated wildly. The LAPD internal review used a range (50 to 500) so broad as to be virtually meaningless. Part of the difficulty in determining the size is that the crowd was never static. It seems to have grown considerably in the period immediately after the pursuit of Seandel Daniels and the three arrests and almost certainly numbered in the hundreds by the time the police withdrew.
65. Interview with Tom Tavares by Jaxon Van Derbeken, October 26, 1994.
66. Interview with Bart Bartholomew, June 3, 1995. Whitman, "The Untold Story of the LA Riot."
67. Interview with Michael Moulin, April 20, 1994.
68. Ibid.
69. Marc Lacey and Shawn Hubler, "Rioters Set Fires, Loot Store; 4 Reported Dead," Los Angeles Times, April 30, 1992.
70. Interview with Charlie Strong by Jaxon Van Derbeken, November 2, 1994.
71. Interview with Danny Calderon by Jaxon Van Derbeken, November 2, 1994.
72. ABC News Nightline, "Moment of Crisis: Anatomy of a Riot," May 28, 1992.
73. Interview with Bart Bartholomew, June 3, 1995.
74. Ibid.
75. Ibid.
76. Whitman, "The Untold Story of the LA Riot."
77. Peter J. Boyer, "Looking for Justice in L.A.," The New Yorker, March 15, 1993.
78. Whitman, "The Untold Story of the LA Riot."
79. Interview with Jim Lumpkin by Jaxon Van Derbeken, October 28, 1994.
80. Ibid.
81. Ibid.
82. Cannon, "When Thin Blue Line Retreated, L.A. Riot Went Out of Control."
83. Interview with Charlie Strong by Jaxon Van Derbeken, November 2, 1994.
84. Interview with Bart Bartholomew, June 3, 1995.
85. Interview with Tom Tavares by Jaxon Van Derbeken, October 26, 1994.
86. Interview with Michael Moulin, April 20, 1994.
87. Interview with Paul Jefferson, May 11, 1994.
88. Gates, Chief, paperback edition, page 442.
89. Interview with Michael Moulin, April 20, 1994.
90. Interview with Daryl Gates, February 4, 1994.
91. Interview with Hubert Williams, March 4, 1994.
92. After Action Report prepared by Stan Brittsan, cited by Jaxon Van Derbeken.
93. Interview with Bruce Hagerty by Jaxon Van Derbeken, October 5, 1994.
94. Interview with Theresa Tatreau by Jaxon Van Derbeken, February 10, 1995.
95. Interview with Michael Hillmann, August 19, 1994.
96. Interview with J. J. May by Jaxon Van Derbeken, September 27, 1994.

97. Interview with Lisa Phillips by Jaxon Van Derbeken, October 6, 1994.
98. Ibid.
99. Ibid.
100. Ibid.
101. According to Phillips, she and Nee decided that it would be too alarming to Oh's family to tell her that she had been attacked by a mob and said instead that she had been injured in a minor car accident.
102. Useem and Gascon, "Riot Control and the Los Angeles Riot of 1992."
103. Interview with Michael Moulin, April 20, 1994.
104. Interview with J. J. May by Jaxon Van Derbeken, September 27, 1994.
105. Interview with Andy Lamprey by Jaxon Van Derbeken, August 17, 1994.
106. Interview of George Morrison by Jaxon Van Derbeken, June 7, 1995.
107. David Freed and Ted Rohrlich, "LAPD Slow in Coping with Wave of Unrest," *Los Angeles Times*, May 1, 1992.
108. Gates, *Chief*, paperback edition, p. 426.
109. Ibid.
110. Interview with Ron Frankle, October 10, 1995.
111. Interview with George Morrison by Jaxon Van Derbeken, June 7, 1995.
112. Interview with Daryl Gates, February 4, 1994. Also see Daryl Gates, *Chief*, paperback edition, p. 428.
113. Ibid., p. 427.
114. Interview with Daryl Gates, February 4, 1994.
115. Interview with Tom Tavares by Jaxon Van Derbeken, October 26, 1994.

12. NIGHTMARE CITY

1. This comment was made by Chief Gates at a Brentwood political event on the first night of the riots. A transcript was made by one of the guests and furnished to me. It is referred to hereafter as "Gates at Brentwood."
2. Interview with Greg Baltad, March 10, 1994.
3. The commentator was Bob Tur of KCOP, channel 13, in Los Angeles, who later testified at the trial of Damian Williams. Tur is often referred to as pilot of the helicopter; he is a pilot but on this day was the observer in a five-person helicopter crew, providing commentary for radio station KNX and for KCOP. The videotape footage was shot by Tur's wife, Marika, and is the most comprehensive record of events at Florence and Normandie in the early hours of the riots.
4. Television interview with Larry Tarvin broadcast on May 4, 1992 on KABC, channel 7, in Los Angeles.
5. David Whitman, "The Untold Story of the LA Riot," *U.S. News & World Report*, May 31, 1993.
6. Ibid.
7. Prosecutor Moore thought this was "almost as sick" as the assault on Denny. Interview with Janet Moore, March 16, 1994.
8. ABC News *Nightline* program, "Moment of Crisis: Anatomy of a Riot," May 28, 1992.

9. Interview with Donald Jones by Jaxon Van Derbeken, October 17, 1994.

10. Laurie Becklund and Stephanie Chavez, "Beaten Driver a Searing Image of Mob Cruelty," *Los Angeles Times*, May 1, 1992.

11. Whitman, "The Untold Story of the LA Riot."

12. Interview with Theresa Tatreau by Jaxon Van Derbeken, February 10, 1995.

13. Interview with Bruce Hagerty by Jaxon Van Derbeken, October 5, 1994. This dialogue is based on the accounts of Tatreau and Hagerty.

14. Interview with Paul Jefferson by Jaxon Van Derbeken, May 5, 1992.

15. Ted Rohrlich and Leslie Berger, "Lack of Materiel Slowed Police Response to Riots," *Los Angeles Times*, May 24, 1992.

16. Interview with Paul Jefferson, May 11, 1994.

17. Ibid.

18. Interview with Andy Lamprey by Jaxon Van Derbeken, August 17, 1994.

19. Interview with Thomas Lorenzen, August 15, 1994. Lamprey and Lorenzen agree that this was the instruction. Lorenzen said, "Ultimately I had them come back. . . . In order for them to drive into Florence and Normandie and get in, intact, with their vehicles, they would have had to engage significant crowds of looters. And I didn't want them tied up doing that. I told them look for victims and to quickly reconnoiter the area and to return to the command post if they didn't have any victims or violent crimes occurring in their presence."

20. Ibid.

21. Interview with Ron Banks by Jaxon Van Derbeken, February 15, 1995.

22. Interview with Mike Albanese by Jaxon Van Derbeken, August 22, 1994.

23. Gates at Brentwood.

24. Ibid.

25. Cited in the Webster report and in an LAPD internal report.

26. Hillmann, in an August 19, 1994, interview with Jaxon Van Derbeken and me, was self-critical of his decision to send C Platoon to Parker Center. Given the information he possessed at the time, however, it is difficult to see how he could have made any other decision.

27. The LAPD internal report said that Metro "was deployed and had roll calls in too many different locations at too many times outside the South Central area."

28. Hillmann was implicitly critical of the pilot's performance. In calling for more helicopters he said he complained: "I want some combat pilots that know how to fly these goddamn things and are willing to take rounds through the fuselage and keep these sonofabitches airborne."

29. The other sergeant was Charles Duke, to whom Lamprey repeated his conversation with Banks. Subsequently, Lamprey told Jaxon Van Derbeken that what Banks said to him did "Banks no credit," but declined to repeat his words. Banks said in a February 15, 1995 interview with Van Derbeken that he "hoped" he hadn't said that the riots would burn themselves out.

30. Interview with Andy Lamprey by Jaxon Van Derbeken, August 17, 1994.

31. Interview with Michael Hillmann, August 19, 1994.

32. Interview with Terrance Manning by Jaxon Van Derbeken, October 10, 1994.

33. Timothy V. Manning, Terrance J. Manning, and Christopher S. Kawai, "Los Angeles City Fire Department 'Historical Overview Report' of the Los Angeles Civil Disturbance, April 29, 1992," October 1992; Category II, Chapter 5, p. 104, hereafter referred to as Fire Department Report.

34. Interview with Terrance Manning by Jaxon Van Derbeken, October 10, 1994.

35. The size of the convoy is uncertain. Manning remembers four police and four fire vehicles, including his car. Six police cars and two fire trucks were sent to the scene of the first fire, but it is not known if all of the police cars participated in the convoy.

36. Interview with Greg Baltad, March 10, 1994.

37. Interview with Terrance Manning, by Jaxon Van Derbeken, October 10, 1994.

38. Interview with Greg Baltad, March 10, 1994.

39. Interview with Julio Nunez by Jaxon Van Derbeken, November 2, 1994.

40. Interview with Terrance Manning by Jaxon Van Derbeken, October 10, 1994.

41. Post-riot accounts contain discrepancies about the number of officers and firefighters present at the command post at any given time. According to the Fire Department Report, "200 to 300 LAPD officers [were] awaiting direction" at the command post when Parsons made his plea to Jefferson for escorts. The Webster report said there were 480 officers at the command post as early as 7 P.M. and that the number had grown to 1,790 by midnight. Whether some officers who left the command post and then returned to it were counted twice is unclear. But there is no doubt that hundreds of unassigned officers were in the command post when the Fire Department was pleading for escorts.

42. Michele L. Norris, Avis Thomas-Lester, and David Von Drehle, "In L.A., Death Drew Few Distinctions," *The Washington Post*, May 11, 1992.

43. Daryl Gates, *Chief*, paperback edition, p. 431.

44. Interview with Daryl Gates, February 4, 1994.

45. Interview with William Webster, September 23, 1993.

46. Interview with Terrance Manning by Jaxon Van Derbeken, October 10, 1994.

47. Interview with William Webster, September 23, 1993.

48. Interview with Daryl Gates, February 4, 1994.

49. Interview with Hubert Williams, March 4, 1994.

50. Interview with Daryl Gates, February 4, 1994.

51. Interview with Hubert Williams, March 4, 1994.

52. This is Wilson's recollection, as recounted by an aide. It is supported by the Webster report and, in a more general way, by accounts given by Gates.

53. Interview with Daryl Gates, February 4, 1994.

54. Interview with Sergeant Tom Tavares by Jaxon Van Derbeken, October 26, 1994.

55. Interview with Paul Jefferson, May 11, 1994. As the story of what Gates had done circulated through the LAPD, it was said that the chief had thrown the contents of his cup at Jefferson. But both Gates and Jefferson remember the chief slamming down the cup, not throwing it. The coffee cup apparently was filled with soda.

56. Interview with Daryl Gates, February 4, 1994.

57. Ibid.

58. Williams believes the LAPD could have contained the riots by quickly establishing a perimeter south of the Santa Monica Freeway and west of the Harbor Freeway and by then obtaining assistance from neighboring police forces in Culver City, Inglewood, and Hawthorne. He concluded from an analysis of incident reports that such an approach would have worked until about 7:00 P.M., when the riots were still confined to a relatively small area.

59. Interview with Scott Landsman, July 15, 1994.

60. Interview with Daryl Gates, January 25, 1993.

61. Interview with Scott Landsman, July 15, 1994.

62. Interview with Daniel Nee by Jaxon Van Derbeken, September 23, 1994.

63. Interview with Lisa Phillips by Jaxon Van Derbeken, October 6, 1994.

64. Interview with Kelly Kilmartin by Jaxon Van Derbeken, March 19, 1995.

65. Ibid.

66. Interview with Carl Butler by Jaxon Van Derbeken, November 3, 1994.

67. Ibid.

68. Interview with Terrance Manning by Jaxon Van Derbeken, October 10, 1994.

69. The Webster report criticized the decision to use Metro on grounds that the twelve-hour shifts of the Metro officers did not match the twenty-four hour shifts of the firefighters. The LAPD internal report expressed concern that Metro was diverted from its mission by the escort duty. At the time, however, harassed commanders at the command post believed that the quickest way to provide firefighters with escorts was to turn to the LAPD's most battle-tested division, which unquestionably was Metro.

70. Interview with Henry (Grady) Dublin by Jaxon Van Derbeken, August 25, 1994.

71. Interview with Roger Blackwell by Jaxon Van Derbeken, September 19, 1994.

72. Interview with Mike Albanese by Jaxon Van Derbeken, August 22, 1994.

73. Patt Morrison, "After the Riots: The Search for Answers; Symbol of Pain Survives Flames; Neighbors Rescue Market where Latasha Harlins Was Killed," Los Angeles Times, May 7, 1992. It was also reported that some of the blacks who protected the store did not want the store burned because the Dus would then have been able to collect fire insurance. But the Dus no longer owned Empire Liquor at the time of the riots. Leon Jenkins, attorney for the Harlins family, told me in an April 15, 1994, interview that preventing the collection of insurance was not the motive. "It's a symbol," Jenkins said. "We wanted it to stand. It had nothing to do with insurance. . . . It's the only way that Latasha will be remembered."

74. Dunn, "Looters, Merchants Put Koreatown Under the Gun," *Los Angeles Times*, May 2, 1992.

75. Interview with Richard Rhee by Lou Cannon and Jessica Crosby, February 16, 1994.

76. Dunn, "Looters, Merchants Put Koreatown Under the Gun."

77. Interview with David Joo by Lou Cannon and Jessica Crosby, December 23, 1993.

78. Interview with Soon S. Cho by Jessica Crosby, August 11, 1993.

79. A comment by Joan Petersilla, director of the Criminal Justice Research Program for RAND in Santa Monica. "Latinos and the Los Angeles Uprising: The Economic Context," prepared by Manuel Pastor Jr., The Tomas Rivera Center, 1993, p. 9.

80. Lynne Duke and Gabriel Escobar, "A Looting Binge Born of Necessity, Opportunity," *The Washington Post*, May 10, 1992.

81. Daryl Gates, *Chief*, paperback edition, p. 439. During a discussion after my interview with him, he brought up the subject and again expressed his gratitude to Bradley.

82. The Webster report used bookings in Newton Division to arrive at this finding. In some divisions bookings apparently took even longer.

83. Gates said he initiated the call. Block said he did.

84. Wilson news conference, May 1, 1992 in Los Angeles.

85. Norris, Thomas-Lester and Von Drehle, "In L.A., Death Drew Few Distinctions."

86. Interview with Brian Liddy by Jaxon Van Derbeken, October 14, 1994.

87. Norris, Thomas-Lester and Von Drehle, "In L.A., Death Drew Few Distinctions."

88. Interview with Ricky Banks by Jaxon Van Derbeken, October 31, 1994.

89. Interview with Richard Rhee by Lou Cannon and Jessica Crosby, February 16, 1994.

13. AFTER THE FALL

1. George Ramos, "When Loving L.A. Turns to Heartache," *Los Angeles Times*, May 4, 1992.

2. Lou Cannon, "New Chief Takes the Helm of L.A. Police Department," *The Washington Post*, July 1, 1992.

3. The reader is reminded that I am using the death toll of the Los Angeles coroner's office, which excluded fatalities not directly attributable to the riots. I also relied on the coroner's data on the race and ethnicity of the victims.

4. Irene Wielawski and Scott Harris, "Hospitals Practice Battlefield Medicine in Caring for Stream of Violence Victims," *Los Angeles Times*, May 2, 1992.

5. The job-loss figure is a composite based on several contemporary estimates and employment data. Some authorities use higher figures. It is impossible

to establish job loss with any precision because many people in South Central are employed outside the area, some of them in domestic work or part-time jobs that are part of a vigorous underground economy that exists in Southern California.

6. Jean Merl, "Born From the Ashes of Watts, Center Dies in Flames of Riot," *Los Angeles Times*, May 2, 1992.

7. Ruben Castaneda and Paul Taylor, "L.A. Residents Face Grim Reality of Devastation, *The Washington Post*, May 3, 1992.

8. Ibid.

9. Robert Vernon, *L.A. Justice*, page 227.

10. Peter A. Morrison and Ira S. Lowry, "A Riot of Color: The Demographic Setting of Civil Disturbance in Los Angeles," RAND 1993.

11. Paul Taylor, "L.A. Police Paralysis During Riot Evident," *The Washington Post*, May 7, 1992.

12. Carla Rivera, "Riot Still Taking Its Toll," *Los Angeles Times*, March 28, 1993.

13. Sheryl Stolberg, "Karlin to Remain on Criminal Bench," *Los Angeles Times*, November 28, 1991.

14. Laurie L. Levenson, "Reiner Is Out of Bounds," *Los Angeles Times*, November 22, 1991.

15. On June 20, 1996, the California Supreme Court ruled unanimously that judges could reduce sentences by overlooking prior convictions. The court said the three-strikes measure violated the constitutional doctrine of separation of powers by allowing prosecutors, who are part of the executive branch, to ignore prior convictions without giving judges this authority. The case, known as *People v. Romero*, upheld a San Diego judge's six-year sentence of a man convicted of possessing thirteen grams of cocaine. Had prior convictions of burglary and attempted burglary been taken into account, he would have received twenty-five years to life.

16. The riots had been a fearful time for Karlin, who lived within range of the disorders. Daryl Gates knew that the Harlins case as well as the Simi Valley verdicts were on the minds of the rioters and graciously offered his secure and distant home to Karlin and her husband during William Fahey during the riots. They thanked him but stayed elsewhere.

17. Louis Sahagun and John Schwada, "Measure to Reform LAPD Wins Decisively," *Los Angeles Times*, June 3, 1992.

18. Sheinbaum once told me wryly that he had been a "premature" advocate of peace between Israel and the Palestinians, a comparison to the "premature anti-Fascists" of the left who had been early opponents of the Nazis.

19. Lee Linder, "Philly Commissioner Ready to Assume Police Chief Job in Los Angeles," Associated Press, May 15, 1992.

20. Interview with Ken Reich, September 20, 1995.

21. Robert Scheer, "Los Angeles Times Interview: Peter Ueberroth," *Los Angeles Times*, May 17, 1992.

22. Peter V. Ueberroth, "What Will *You* Do for Your City?" *Los Angeles Times*, January 6, 1993.

23. Ibid.
24. Interview with Ken Reich, September 20, 1995.
25. Ibid.
26. E. Scott Reckard, "L.A. Rebuild Chief Admits Frustration," Associated Press, September 30, 1992.
27. Bill Boyarsky, "Dead-End Realities and Recovery," *Los Angeles Times*, April 14, 1993.
28. Gary Lee, "On a Crusade To Improve Stricken Area," *The Washington Post*, April 17, 1993.
29. Patrick J. McDonnell, "Latino Merchants Stage Protest Over Lack of Riot Recovery Aid," *Los Angeles Times*, March 18, 1993.
30. Robert Scheer, "Los Angeles Times Interview: Maxine Waters; Veteran Legislator Makes People Angry—But She's Never Ignored," *Los Angeles Times*, May 16, 1993.
31. Journalistic and academic estimates of the number of Korean-owned businesses destroyed or damaged beyond repair during the riots vary widely. Published accounts have put the figure as low as 1,000 and as high as 2,500. The most generally used figure is 2,000, about two-thirds of the businesses lost in the riots. See Bill Boyarsky, "Korean-Americans Ask Why Recovery is Black and White," *Los Angeles Times*, March 14, 1993.
32. Penelope McMillan, "Korean-American Protesters Pelted from City Hall Windows," *Los Angeles Times*, July 8, 1992.
33. K. Connie Kang and Marc Lacey, "Court Rejects Appeal of Rules for Liquor Stores," *Los Angeles Times*, July 15, 1994.
34. Interview with Karen Bass, September 21, 1995.
35. The prominent official was Joe Hicks, executive director of the Los Angeles chapter of the Southern Christian Leadership Conference. See "Black-Korean Alliance Says Talk Not Enough, Disbands," by Jake Doherty, *Los Angeles Times*, December 24, 1992.
36. Interview with Felicia Bragg, February 16, 1994.
37. Joseph Nocera, "City of Hype," GQ, April 1993.
38. Lou Cannon, "A Year After Riots, 'Lotus Land' Seeks to Shed Badlands Image," *The Washington Post*, April 30, 1993.
39. Peter Rainer, "'Falling Down' Trips Over Its Own Hate," *Los Angeles Times*, March 15, 1993.
40. Amy Wallace and K. Connie Kang, "One Year Later, Hope and Anger Remain" *Los Angeles Times*, April 30, 1993.
41. Carla Rivera and Dean E. Murphy, "Ueberroth Quits Rebuild L.A. Post," *Los Angeles Times*, May 22, 1993.

14. PRESUMED GUILTY

1. Telephone interview with Steven Clymer, November 20, 1995.
2. Jim Newton, "Officers' Indictment Called Political," *Los Angeles Times*, August 7, 1992.

3. Interview with William Kristol, October 17, 1995. This point was also confirmed by Bush Press Secretary Marlin Fitzwater.

4. Earl Ofari Hutchinson, "The Political Victimization of Laurence Powell and Stacey Koon," *Ofari's Bi-Monthly*, September/October 1993.

5. Interview with William Kristol, October 17, 1995.

6. Interview with William Barr, September 24, 1993.

7. Ibid.

8. Telephone interview with Steven Clymer, November 20, 1995.

9. Interview with William Barr, September 24, 1993.

10. Typical of the comment in California newspapers was an August 7, 1992, *San Francisco Examiner* editorial that began: "Federal indictments of four Los Angeles police officers in the Rodney King beating case ought to be a first step toward getting the assurance of real justice that the cop-friendly jury in Simi Valley couldn't supply."

11. Paul Hoffman, "Double Jeopardy Wars: The Case for a Civil Rights 'Exception'," *UCLA Law Review*, Volume 41, Number 3, February 1994.

12. The committee often used the name "Free the L.A. 4+" to include three other defendants charged with crimes arising from the incidents at Florence and Normandie. The others were Anthony Lamar Brown, accused of spitting on Reginald Denny as he lay helpless on the ground and another assault; Lance Jerome Parker, accused of shooting at the gas tank of Denny's truck and assault with a deadly weapon; and Lewis Curl Foster, who pleaded no contest to three counts of assault with a deadly weapon and was sentenced to a three-year prison term. After the trial of Gary Williams was severed from the trial of the principal defendants, activists on occasion referred to the others as the "L.A. 3." For the sake of simplicity, I have used "Free the L.A. 4" throughout this book.

13. Interview with Ira Reiner, September 17, 1993.

14. Jim Newton, "3 Plead Not Guilty in Denny Case; Black Trial Judge Removed," *Los Angeles Times*, August 26, 1992.

15. Jim Newton, "Spotlight Stolen in Denny Drama," *Los Angeles Times*, September 9, 1992.

16. Peter J. Boyer, "Looking for Justice in L.A." *The New Yorker*, March 15, 1993.

17. Nancy Hill-Holtzman and Jim Newton, "Lawyer Adds Bizarre Note to Denny Case," *Los Angeles Times*, August 13, 1992.

18. Seth Mydans, "Beating Case Prosecutors: 2 Styles Focus as One," *The New York Times*, March 5, 1993.

19. Ibid.

20. Telephone interview with Darryl Mounger, October 24, 1993. In the interview, Mounger told me that he had been a lawyer only fifteen months before he took on this case, which consumed a year. It made him well known but he didn't have time to try other cases.

21. Interview with Cliff Ruff, February 3, 1994.

22. Telephone interview with Harland Braun, November 30, 1995.

23. Ibid.

24. Four persons were charged with manslaughter after a helicopter explosion during the filming of the movie killed actor Vic Morrow and two Vietnamese children. Braun told me that he tried during this trial to minimize conflicts among the defendants, a situation similar to the one he faced in the King civil rights trial. All of the defendants in the "Twilight Zone" case were acquitted.

25. Telephone interview with Harland Braun, November 30, 1995.

26. Cliff Ruff, then a director and subsequently president of the Los Angeles Police Protective League, told me in a February 3, 1994, interview that the league had consulted with "a well-known criminal attorney" who said the $80,000 fee was reasonable for the federal trial because the lawyers would be "going over much of the same ground." But Ruff acknowledged that the league may not have fully appreciated the high quality of the federal prosecution and the willingness of the government to spend whatever it took to obtain convictions.

27. Telephone interview with Harland Braun, November 30, 1995.

28. Interview with Diane Marchant, August 15, 1994.

29. Traditionally, California prosecutors presented their cases at preliminary hearings in open court rather than seeking indictments from a grand jury. This practice was changed by a 1990 initiative, and Clymer contends that state prosecutors at the time of the King incident were unaccustomed to using grand juries. This is accurate, but California criminal attorneys with whom I have discussed the issue believe it is a small point. No matter what their experience, state prosecutors could not have used a California grand jury as Clymer and Kowalski used the federal grand jury because of the significant difference in the rules of procedure.

30. Michael L. Piccarreta and Jefferson Keenan, "Dual Sovereigns: Successive Prosecutions and Politically Correct Verdicts," *The Champions*, September/ October 1995.

31. Interview with Ed Nowicki, October 17, 1995.

32. Ibid.

33. Hunt declined to be interviewed on the subject. This account was provided by three LAPD officers who were at the scene.

34. Station executives denied they were reacting to the tense situation and blandly insisted that they were showing "news judgment," as they said they had during the riots. See "TV Stations Tread Easily on Coverage of Unrest," by Rick Du Brow and Greg Braxton, *Los Angeles Times*, December 16, 1992.

35. According to Jaxon Van Derbeken, police list this murder as "cleared" or solved because investigating detectives believe they know the identity of Delcomber's killers although they lack the evidence to charge them.

36. Ted Rohrlich and John L. Mitchell, "LAPD Widely Saluted for Swiftly Quelling Incident, *Los Angeles Times*, December 16, 1992.

37. Interview with Vivienne Swanigan, November 18, 1995.

38. Ibid. Swanigan said she wears her hair straight and isn't certain if the people who ran at her car knew she was an African American. "I don't think they cared," she said. "They certainly didn't stop to look."

39. Interview with Vivienne Swanigan by Jaxon Van Derbeken, February 15, 1995.

15. PLAYING THE RACE CARD

1. Rodney King testimony in *United States of America v. Stacey C. Koon*, March 9, 1993.

2. Telephone interview with Steven Clymer, October 24, 1995.

3. Robert Reinhold, "Justice Dept. Is Left Shaken By Disclosure in King Case," *The New York Times*, November 21, 1992.

4. Interview with Harland Braun, February 8, 1993.

5. Secretary of State Stimson said this in 1929.

6. Interview with Steven Clymer, September 14, 1993.

7. Courtroom Television Network, "The 'Rodney King' Case: What the Jury Saw in *California v. Powell*," VHS videocassette, 1992.

8. Interview with Lawrence Middleton, September 14, 1993.

9. Carla Rivera, "2nd King Trial Revives L.A.'s Fears and Hopes," *Los Angeles Times*, February 3, 1993.

10. Ibid.

11. Jim Newton, "Riots' Shadow Hangs Over King Jury Selection," *Los Angeles Times*, January 31, 1993.

12. Jim Newton, "Prospective King Jurors Get Bias Questionnaire," *Los Angeles Times*, February 4, 1993.

13. The black population of the seven counties in the 1990 census was 1,245,938 or 8.24 percent of the total. Blacks were 2.34 percent of the population in Ventura County, where the state trial was held, and 11.20 percent of the population in Los Angeles County, where it would have been held except for the change of venue. The percentage of blacks on the jury pool was a visual estimate made by reporters on the scene, including me. Ten percent was the figure used by Jim Newton of the *Los Angeles Times*, whose coverage of the trial was reliable and comprehensive.

14. Interview with Ira Salzman, September 27, 1993.

15. Telephone interview with Steven Clymer, October 24, 1995.

16. Interview with Harland Braun, February 8, 1993.

17. Telephone interview with Steven Clymer, October 24, 1995.

18. Ibid.

19. Paul Lieberman, "King Jury Reflects Growing Impact of Racial Diversity," *Los Angeles Times*, February 28, 1993.

20. Seth Mydans, "Sudden Detours in Los Angeles Trial," *The New York Times*, February 24, 1993.

21. Interview with Jo-Ellan Dimitrius, June 9, 1994.

22. Interview with Maria Escobel, December 13, 1993.

23. Clymer said afterward that some media accounts sensationalized this aspect of his opening statement, pointing out that he never used the words "shown off." The words were used in quotation marks in a page-one *Los Angeles Times* headline which said, "Beaten King Was 'Shown Off' by 2 Officers, Jury Told." The story by Jim Newton under this headline quoted Clymer accurately and did not make the headline's additional mistake of blaming Wind for an action that was entirely Powell's initiative. I think it unlikely, however, that public perceptions would have differed if the headline had been more precise. Clymer sought to give jurors the impression that Powell had treated King as a trophy, and this was the only element of his statement that was new, since the Powell detour to Foothill had not been revealed in the state trial.

24. Telephone interview with Steven Clymer, October 24, 1995.

25. Ibid.

26. Interview with Laurie Levenson, November 27, 1995.

27. Jim Newton, "King Case Prosecutors Gamble on Eyewitnesses," *Los Angeles Times*, March 7, 1993.

28. Conta was the only police witness in any of the King trials who declined to be interviewed for this book. Other officers and members of the prosecution told me he was under psychological strain because he had been ostracized by rank-and-file LAPD officers because of his testimony.

29. Interview with Jim Newton, April 19, 1994.

30. Telephone interview with Harland Braun, November 30, 1995.

31. Ibid.

32. Interview with Barry Kowalski, January 2, 1996.

33. Telephone interview with Harland Braun, November 30, 1995.

34. Jim Newton, "'I Was Just Trying to Stay Alive,' King Tells Federal Jury," *Los Angeles Times*, March 10, 1993.

35. Interview with Maria Escobel, December 13, 1993.

36. Jim Tranquada, "King says officers used racial slurs," *Daily News*, March 10, 1993.

16. THE OTHER VIDEOTAPE

1. Interview with Stacey Koon, December 4, 1995.

2. Lou Cannon, "King Arrest Said to Follow Guidelines," *The Washington Post*, March 18, 1993.

3. Jim Newton, "Final Prosecution Witnesses Criticize Report on King," *Los Angeles Times*, March 16, 1993.

4. Interview with Stacey Koon, December 4, 1995.

5. Interview with Steven Clymer, September 14, 1993.

6. Ibid.

7. The transcript of the federal trial was replete with inaccuracies. This was frustrating for the competing attorneys, especially during the preparation of appellate briefs, and sometimes for reporters covering the trial. Where conflicts between my notes and the transcript exist on any significant point, I have

consulted versions used in other news accounts, especially the *Los Angeles Times* and the Associated Press. When these conflicts involved opening statements or closing arguments, I have also checked with the attorneys involved. On the few matters where the accounts were still in conflict, I have relied on the version used by Jim Newton in the *Los Angeles Times,* whose reportage provided the most complete account of the trial.

8. Interview with Ed Nowicki, October 17, 1995.
9. Interview with Stacey Koon, December 4, 1995.
10. Interview with Maria Escobel, December 16, 1993.
11. Interview with Steven Clymer, September 14, 1993.
12. Interview with Taky Tzimeas, January 10, 1995.
13. Interview with Mike Stone, October 4, 1993.
14. Lou Cannon and Jessica Crosby, "Defense Rests in King Beating Case To Avoid Grilling of Officer Powell," *The Washington Post,* April 1, 1993.
15. Jim Newton, "CHP Officer Weeps as She Recounts Beating," *Los Angeles Times,* March 27, 1993.
16. Interview with Harland Braun, July 20, 1993.
17. Jim Newton, "King Jury Sees Key Videotape; Prosecutors Rest," *Los Angeles Times,* April 7, 1993.
18. Ibid.

17. THE THIRTEENTH JUROR

1. Linda Tontini, "Juror Says Tape Key to Decision," *North County Blade-Citizen,* April 18, 1993.
2. Interview with Tim Wind, August 11, 1994.
3. Interview with Harland Braun, July 20, 1993.
4. Ibid.
5. From this trial, wrote historian S.G.F. Brandon in *The Trial of Jesus of Nazareth,* "has flowed terrible consequences for the Jewish people, held guilty by generations of Christians of the murder of Christ." This book, a critical examination by a British professor of comparative religion, was sent to Braun after the trial of the officers by someone who had read an account of Braun's analogy in the newspapers. Braun told me that it convinced him that Jesus had been tried by the Romans for sedition.
6. Interview with Bob Almond, January 5, 1994.
7. The phrase "even if they saw it for five or ten seconds" was omitted from the transcript of the trial used on appeal, another example of the deficiency of this transcript.
8. Jim Newton, "King Case Is Handed to Jury, Deliberations Resume Today," *Los Angeles Times,* April 12, 1993.
9. Interview with Bob Almond, January 5, 1994.
10. Ibid. In "For Juries, High Anxiety," by Patricia Edmonds, *USA Today,* October 14, 1993, Almond said, "No one discussed it openly, but the idea of rioting wasn't ever out of my mind."

11. Confidential interview with a juror.

12. Interview with Bob Almond, January 5, 1994.

13. Ibid.

14. Interview with Martin De La Rosa, January 6, 1994.

15. Interview with Eric Rasmussen, January 8, 1994.

16. Interview with Maria Escobel, December 16, 1993.

17. The questionnaires handed out to prospective jurors did not ask if they had used drugs. They did ask if they "or any close relative or friend" had been charged with a crime. As far as I can determine, both jurors answered this question in the negative, although at least one of them had been charged with a drug offense. I have never seen the questionnaires, which were sealed by Judge Davies. Had any juror acknowledged that he was a drug user, he would have been excused for cause under the practice of the court.

18. Interview with Maria Escobel, December 16, 1993.

19. Gregg Zoroya, "For Juror No. 7, Fame Is the Game," *The Orange County Register*, August 1, 1993.

20. Interview with Martin De La Rosa, January 6, 1994.

21. Interview with Maria Escobel, December 16, 1993.

22. Interview with Martin De La Rosa, January 6, 1994.

23. Ibid.

24. Jim Newton, "How the Case Was Won," *Los Angeles Times Magazine*, June 27, 1993.

25. Lou Cannon, "In the Two King Beating Trials, Almost Everything Was Different," *The Washington Post*, April 18, 1993.

18. SECOND JUDGMENTS

1. Dissent by Judge Stephen Reinhardt of the U.S. Court of Appeal for the Ninth Circuit to a decision of a three-member panel of the court denying rehearing of an appeal in *U.S. v. Koon* by the full court. Filed January 12, 1995.

2. Jim Newton, "L.A. Trials Show 'Blind Justice' Is Hard to Achieve," *Los Angeles Times*, October 24, 1993.

3. Jim Newton, "Long Prison Terms for Powell and Koon Urged," *Los Angeles Times*, May 29, 1993.

4. Conversation with Steven Clymer, December 20, 1994.

5. *The Thin Blue Line*, September 1993.

6. Jim Newton, "Koon, Powell Get 2½ Years in Prison," *Los Angeles Times*, August 5, 1993. Anthony Duignan-Cabrera and Michael Connelly, "Sentencings Reopen L.A.'s Painful Wounds," *Los Angeles Times*, August 5, 1993.

7. Ibid., Newton story.

8. Interview with Janet Moore, March 16, 1994.

9. Ibid.

10. The crime of aggravated mayhem was the byproduct of a notorious 1978 California case in which a man raped a young runaway, chopped off her

forearms with an ax, and left her in a drainage culvert to die. She survived, and her assailant was convicted, sentenced to fourteen years in prison, and released on parole after eight years. A public outcry ensued, and the state legislature created the crime of aggravated mayhem, which was punishable by a maximum sentence of life imprisonment.

11. Edward J. Boyer, "Motorist Beaten in Riots Cannot Identify Attackers," *Los Angeles Times*, August 25, 1993.

12. Interview with Carolyn Walters, April 8, 1994.

13. Edward J. Boyer, "Denny Testified, Hugs Mothers of Defendants," *Los Angeles Times*, August 26, 1993.

14. Interview with Janet Moore, March 16, 1994.

15. Interview with Edi Faal, March 17, 1994.

16. Ibid.

17. Ibid.

18. Ibid.

19. Newton, "L.A. Trials Show 'Blind Justice' Is Hard to Achieve."

20. Interview with Carolyn Walters, April 8, 1994.

21. Ibid. "I didn't have any agenda except to make sure the right decisions were made," Walters told me. "If I had had a hidden agenda, I wouldn't have become the forewoman but would have stayed in the background and made it difficult for the jury to reach a decision."

22. Seth Mydans, "Juror in Denny Case Recounts Stress and an Obsession With Legal Detail," *The New York Times*, October 27, 1993.

23. Interview with Janet Moore, March 16, 1994.

24. Conversation with Carolyn Walters, April 6, 1994, prior to a panel discussion before an Arizona Bar Association symposium.

25. Newton, "L.A. Trials Show 'Blind Justice' Is Hard to Achieve."

26. Mydans, "Juror in Denny Case Recounts Stress and an Obsession With Legal Detail."

27. Edward J. Boyer, "Denny Juror Says Riot Fears Did Not Influence Verdicts," *Los Angeles Times*, October 26, 1993.

28. Dan Morain and Edward J. Boyer, "Lungren Calls Verdicts 'Body Blow' to Justice," *Los Angeles Times*, October 27, 1993.

29. Newton, "L.A. Trials Show 'Blind Justice' Is Hard to Achieve."

30. Edward J. Boyer and John L. Mitchell, "Attempted Murder Acquittal, Deadlock Wind Up Denny Trial," *Los Angeles Times*, October 21, 1993.

31. Interview with Vaughn Reid by Jessica Crosby, October 20, 1993.

32. Amy Wallace and John Hurst, "'Let's Get on with Life,' Denny Says After Jury Verdicts," *Los Angeles Times*, October 19, 1993.

33. Peter Larsen, "Reaction Ranges from Jubilation to Indignation," *Daily News*, October 19, 1993.

34. Interview with Janet Moore, March 16, 1994.

35. Morain and Boyer, "Lungren Calls Verdicts 'Body Blow' to Justice."

36. Interview with Janet Moore, March 16, 1994.

37. Ibid.

38. Interview with Fred Ochoa by Jessica Crosby, October 20, 1993.

39. Interview with Edi Faal, March 17, 1994.

40. Jim Newton, "Denny Defendant Admits to Attack on Tape," *Los Angeles Times*, August 8, 1992.

41. Edward J. Boyer and Andrea Ford, "Williams Given Maximum 10 Years in Denny Beating," *Los Angeles Times*, December 8, 1993.

42. Ibid.

43. Ibid.

44. Many members of the Black Caucus, including Waters, had criticized the long sentences meted out to black defendants under a combination of the federal sentencing guidelines and the maximum minimum sentences. The August 6 letter was carefully worded to endorse judicial discretion. It said that Davies had the "authority" to give the sentences he did, which the government disputed, but said, "Most experts agreed that the minimum four to seven years sentence should have been followed in this case."

45. Carol Angel, "Profile: Judge Betty B. Fletcher," *Daily Journal*, October 21, 1992.

46. Interview with Betty Fletcher, May 24, 1996.

47. Ibid.

48. Jim Newton and Henry Weinstein, "Court Orders Longer Sentences for Koon, Powell," *Los Angeles Times*, August 20, 1994.

49. Interview with Judge Stephen Reinhardt, May 16, 1996.

50. Ibid.

51. Ibid.

52. Ibid.

53. All nine dissenters disagreed with the Fletcher panel's overruling of Davies' sentences and urged reconsideration by the full court. Three of these judges declined to sign the fourth part of Reinhardt's dissenting opinion, which assailed the court for its policy of withholding from the public the tallies by which it votes to hear cases en banc (by the full court) and the positions taken by individual judges. Reinhardt has long opposed such secrecy, which he said in his dissent immunizes "our individual actions from public scrutiny."

54. Jim Newton, "Supreme Court to Write Next Chapter in King Case," *Los Angeles Times*, January 7, 1996.

55. Interview with Stacey Koon, June 13, 1996.

19. BACK TO THE FUTURE

1. Jim Newton, "Chief Sees Riordan as Force in Controversy, Sources Say," *Los Angeles Times*, May 26, 1995.

2. Lou Cannon, "For Many in L.A., No Vote and No Say," *The Washington Post*, May 17, 1993.

3. Peter Skerry in *Mexican Americans* contends that this lawsuit was "widely regarded" as an attempt by the Reagan administration to embarrass Mayor Bradley, who was running for a second time for governor, p. 332.

4. Ibid., p. 334.

5. Cannon, "For Many in L.A., No Vote and No Say."

6. Ibid.

7. Riordan did well by historical standards for a Republican in obtaining 43 percent of the Latino vote.

8. During his 1993 campaign, Riordan commented on the emergence of women as political leaders in California, mentioning San Diego Mayor Susan Golding and Senator Dianne Feinstein, who had been mayor of San Francisco. Riordan told me he would not be surprised if a woman succeeded him as mayor of Los Angeles. A year later (March 11, 1994) he speculated that a Latino would be mayor within eight to twelve years.

9. Faye Fiore and Frank Clifford, "Mystery Mayor," *Los Angeles Times Magazine,* July 11, 1993.

10. Ibid.

11. Ibid.

12. Interview with Richard Riordan, March 11, 1994.

13. Ibid.

14. This was a frequent Riordan formulation when he tried to skirt regulations or bureaucratic obstacles.

15. Bill Boyarsky, "Riordan Shows a Steady Hand in Leading a Rattled City," *Los Angeles Times,* January 23, 1994.

16. Jean Merl, "The Mayor's Midterm Exam," *Los Angeles Times Magazine,* June 11, 1995.

17. Interview with Mark Ridley-Thomas, March 24, 1994.

18. Interview with Willie Williams, January 27, 1993.

19. The population of Los Angeles increased by 670,000 during Bradley's twenty years as mayor, but the size of the LAPD did not change.

20. Interview with Gary Greenebaum, July 6, 1996.

21. Ibid.

22. The *Los Angeles Times* obtained Police Commission documents relating to the investigation after the controversy had been resolved and published portions of them in its lead story on September 15, 1995, written by Jim Newton. Williams was furious and threatened a lawsuit against those who had "leaked" the information.

23. Some commissioners also wanted to reprimand Williams for taking free tickets from Universal Studios in Los Angeles. LAPD Officer Jerry Hallinger, a Williams aide, told the commission that Williams had asked him to obtain Universal tickets two days before he was sworn in as chief and had done so about twice a year since. Williams denied the charges. Lacking any documentation, the commission found that the allegation was "not resolved."

24. Mayor Bradley often complained of being hamstrung by the city's "weak mayor" system. Since giving the council override authority reduced the mayor's power, Bradley had vetoed the measure a year earlier and meant to veto it again. But in a lapse that was strange even by the bizarre standards of Los Angeles politics, he signed the measure and put it on the ballot. When

Bradley learned from news accounts what he had done, he tried and failed to have a court rescind his action. The mayor then wrote the ballot argument against the measure, calling it a "naked power grab" by the council. But Proposition 5 passed with 60 percent of the vote.

25. Jim Newton, "2 Quit Police Panel, Saying Council Has Stymied Reforms," *Los Angeles Times*, June 30, 1995.

26. Interview with Gary Greenebaum, July 6, 1996.

27. Williams' support was broadly based. The *Times* survey found that the chief was backed by 69 percent of Latinos, 67 percent of Anglos, and 59 percent of African Americans. The survey also found that nearly two-thirds of those polled thought Williams was the victim of a smear, even though a near majority also believed he had shown poor judgment in taking the Las Vegas gratuities.

28. Stephanie Simon, "Penalties More Severe in LAPD Ranks, Cases Show," *Los Angeles Times*, June 23, 1995.

29. Carla Hall, "Boss Got Break They Wouldn't Get, Officers Say," *Los Angeles Times*, June 22, 1995.

30. David Dotson, "Council's Action Ensures a One-Term Police Chief," *Los Angeles Times*, June 25, 1995.

31. Daryl F. Gates, "Discipline in the LAPD," Letter to the Editor, *Los Angeles Times*, July 2, 1995.

32. Willie L. Williams with Bruce B. Henderson, *Taking Back Our Streets*, 1996.

33. Interview with William Violante, June 23, 1993.

34. Julie Tamaki, "Use of Force a Gray Area for Men in Blue," *Los Angeles Times*, June 26, 1993.

35. Interview with Joe Gunn, June 24, 1996.

36. Jim Tranquada, "Police Shy Away from Using Force," *Daily News*, March 5, 1995.

37. Jim Newton, "L.A. Police Hampered by Woeful State of Equipment," *Los Angeles Times*, October 31, 1994.

38. Marc Lacey, "Riordan Leads Drive to Computerize LAPD," *Los Angeles Times*, August 17, 1994.

39. The overworked LAPD laboratory had been a focus of contention in other famous trials. It failed to preserve fingerprints and blood samples in the trial of Marvin Pancoast, accused of killing Alfred Bloomingdale's mistress Vicky Morgan, with a baseball bat, although prosecutor Stanley Weisberg obtained a conviction without this evidence. Many LAPD investigators had so little confidence in the department lab that they tried to avoid using it on sensitive matters; this is why Detective Taky Tzimeas of Internal Affairs had gone to an outside lab to establish that Rodney King had ingested an analogue of marijuana.

40. Fox Butterfield, "Behind the Badge," *The New York Times*, March 2, 1996.

41. All the information in this paragraph is from Butterfield, "Behind the Badge."

42. Jan Golab, "The Friends of Fuhrman," *Los Angeles Magazine*, October 1995.
43. Ibid.
44. Greg Krikorian, "Co-Workers Paint Different Portrait of Mark Fuhrman," *Los Angeles Times*, November 8, 1995.
45. Vincent Bugliosi, *Outrage: The Five Reasons Why O. J. Simpson Got Away With Murder*, p. 133.
46. Greg Krikorian, "Review of 35 Fuhrman Cases Reveals No Racism," *Los Angeles Times*, January 19, 1996.
47. Los Angeles Police Department Report of the Mark Fuhrman Task Force, Executive Summary, May 5, 1997, pp. 59–60. In his book *Murder in Brentwood*, Fuhrman acknowledged that he had made up his recollections to McKinny and "let my imagination run wild," p. 270.
48. *PrimeTime Live*, ABC-TV, October 8, 1996.
49. Krikorian, "Co-Workers Paint Different Portrait of Mark Fuhrman."
50. Conversation with Ira Reiner, July 15, 1996.
51. Interview with Cliff Ruff, July 2, 1996.
52. Fox Butterfield, "Behind the Badge," *The New York Times*, March 2, 1996.
53. This was what Parks recalled saying when I interviewed him on August 3, 1996. Lieutenant William Hall, who headed the unit that investigated officer-involved shootings, had arranged on a Friday for Fuhrman to be given a car and start work on Monday before Parks got wind of the pending transfer. In an interview with Jaxon Van Derbeken for this book, Hall recalled that Parks made a similar statement to him at the time. "He said he was going to stop it because [Fuhrman] wasn't the best choice," Hall said.
54. *Daily News* interview with Gil Garcetti, October 25, 1995.
55. Susan F. Yocum, "Don't Tar Us All With the Fuhrman Brush," *Los Angeles Times*, September 1, 1995.
56. Interview with Bernard Parks, August 3, 1996.
57. Interview with Cliff Ruff, July 2, 1996.
58. "Punchlines," *Los Angeles Times*, August 17, 1995.
59. Board of Rights Rationale on Findings of Detective Charles Markel, #21866 and Detective Andrew Teague, #21972. April 8, 1996.
60. Alan Abrahamson, "Police Cleared of Tainting Evidence," *Los Angeles Times*, April 10, 1996.
61. Interview with Willie Williams, July 29, 1996.
62. Jim Newton, "LAPD Training Practices Are Slipping, Report Says," *Los Angeles Times*, April 18, 1996.
63. Jim Newton, "When LAPD Officers Can't Shoot Straight," *Los Angeles Times*, May 4, 1996.
64. Interview with Willie Williams, July 29, 1996.
65. Interview with Richard Riordan, June 24, 1996.
66. Jim Newton, "Help Wanted," *Los Angeles Times Magazine*, July 27, 1997.
67. Interview with Edith Perez, February 11, 1997.

68. Decision of The Board of Police Commissioners On the Application of Chief Willie L. Williams for Reappointment To A Second Term as Chief of Police of The City of Los Angeles, March 10, 1997.

69. Newton, "Help Wanted."

70. By this time, Williams had so few supporters on the City Council that they did not even try to override the Police Commission. Instead, the debate focused on whether Williams was entitled to a financial settlement, which Riordan favored but several council members thought would set an undesirable precedent. Williams originally sought $3 million. He agreed to a settlement of $375,000, with the condition that he would not file any lawsuit against the city.

71. Interview with Warren Christopher, April 23, 1997.

20. JUDGMENTS AND LEGACIES

1. Interview with John Dunkin, September 13, 1996.

2. Interview with Robin Kramer, July 2, 1996.

3. *The Michael Jackson Show,* KABC radio, June 23, 1997.

4. Jennifer Bowles, "Rodney King Arrested in Domestic Dispute," Associated Press, June 26, 1992. See also "King Arrested, Then Freed, After Wife Is Injured During Argument," by Josh Meyer and Eric Malnic, *Los Angeles Times,* June 27, 1992.

5. Interview with Steven Lerman, October 20, 1993.

6. Patt Morrison, "The Undying Echo of Fate," *Los Angeles Times,* July 31, 1996.

7. "King Guilty of Hit-Run, Acquitted of Battery," Associated Press, July 12, 1996. See also "After Mixed Verdict, King Looks to the Future," by Mayrav Saar, *Los Angeles Times,* July 12, 1996.

8. The appeal lost. King served thirty days in the Los Angeles County Jail and was released in mid-September 1997. He was not treated specially. Because of jail overcrowding, most inmates convicted of similar crimes serve a third or less of their actual sentences.

9. Interview with Steven Lerman, October 20, 1993.

10. Ibid.

11. Interview with Johnnie Cochran, November 11, 1993.

12. Letter to constituents who wrote Councilman Yaroslavsky about the King beating, dated March 19, 1991.

13. Interview with Zev Yaroslavsky, June 23, 1993

14. Interview with Zev Yaroslavsky, February 3, 1994.

15. Interview with Steven Lerman, October 20, 1993.

16. Ibid.

17. Richard A. Serrano, "Attorneys at War Over Representation of King," *Los Angeles Times,* May 26, 1993.

18. Ibid.

19. Rene Lynch, "King's New Attorney Known for Testing Limits of the Law," *Los Angeles Times,* October 20, 1992.

20. Interview with Frederico Sayre, August 20, 1996.

21. Interview with Don Vincent, August 18, 1996.

22. Interview with Frederico Sayre, August 20, 1996.

23. Interview with Laurie Levenson, May 6, 1994.

24. John L. Mitchell and Tina Daunt, "King Jury's Voice of Reason Carried a Private Burden," *Los Angeles Times*, June 3, 1994.

25. Interview with Don Vincent, August 18, 1996.

26. Mitchell and Daunt, "King Jury's Voice of Reason Carried a Private Burden."

27. Ibid.

28. *Day One*, ABC-TV News, April 11, 1993. Powell made a similar statement to LAPD Internal Affairs investigators when he was interviewed soon after the King incident.

29. "Has L.A. Healed Since the Riots?," *Daily News*, April 27, 1997.

30. Lou Cannon, "Scars Remain Five Years After Los Angeles Riots," *The Washington Post*, April 28, 1997.

31. Ibid.

32. Douglas Young, "Inner City Can't Get the Money," *Los Angeles Business Journal*, April 14–20, 1997.

33. Many studies have shown that Mexican-American immigrants, by far the largest component of California's immigrant population, use welfare programs proportionally less than non-Hispanic whites or African Americans. For instance, a 1997 study by Professor David E. Hayes-Bautista at the University of California at Los Angeles, based on a 1996 Census Bureau survey, found that 43 percent of Mexican Americans living in poverty used Medicaid compared with 88 percent of all Americans in poverty. Only 6 percent of Mexican Americans in poverty used Supplemental Social Security (SSI) income compared to 13 percent of the nation's poor as a whole. See "Latino Newcomers May Rely Less on Aid," by Yvette Cabrera, *Daily News*, July 30, 1997.

34. Nine of the ten surnames on a 1996 list of most-frequent homebuyers in Los Angeles County were Latino. Dennis Macheski of the Concord Group, a real estate consulting firm, found that Latinos formed 26,000 households in Los Angeles and neighboring Ventura County in 1996. Asians formed 13,000 new households and African Americans 3,000 new households, while the households of non-Hispanic whites decreased by 15,000.

35. Lou Cannon, "Southern California's Boom Is Latino-Led," *The Washington Post*, July 12, 1997.

36. The businessman is Frank Moran, president of the Latin Business Association and a leader in the drive to promote Latino small business in Los Angeles. Moran, whose parents are from Mexico and who grew up in the public-housing projects of East Los Angeles, owns a temporary placement service. He was interviewed on June 20, 1997.

37. Cannon, "Southern California's Boom Is Latino-Led."

38. RLA (Rebuild LA), "Rebuilding's LA's Neglected Communities," May 1996, p. 11.

39. Interview with Linda Griego, September 3, 1996.

40. Cannon, "Scars Remain Five Years After Los Angeles Riots."

41. Two of the three Los Angeles city council districts represented by blacks have Latino population majorities and the other has a Latino plurality, as does the only Los Angeles County supervisorial district represented by an African American.

42. Shawn Hubler and John L. Mitchell, "A Legacy as Complex as the '92 Riots," *Los Angeles Times*, April 20, 1997.

43. Cannon, "Scars Remain Five Years After Los Angeles Riots."

44. Ibid.

45. Ibid.

46. "LAPD Officers to Study Spanish, Travel to Mexico," *Los Angeles Times*, July 15, 1994.

47. Jaxon Van Derbeken, "Community Policing Needs Cited in Report," *Daily News*, November 27, 1994.

48. Jaxon Van Derbeken, "Community-policing Director Named in LAPD Revamp," *Daily News*, April 20, 1995.

49. Willie L. Williams with Bruce B. Henderson, *Taking Back Our Streets*, p. 225.

50. Jim Newton, "Help Wanted," *Los Angeles Times Magazine*, July 27, 1997.

51. Interview with Joe Gunn, June 24, 1996.

52. Jodi Wilgoren, "City Council Wants to Slow Police Buildup," *Los Angeles Times*, May 20, 1996.

53. Interview with Charles Duke, August 14, 1996.

54. Interview with Greg Dossey, October 11, 1996.

55. Interview with John Dunkin, September 13, 1996.

56. Interview with Charles Duke, August 14, 1996.

57. Interview with John Dunkin, September 13, 1996.

58. Riordan favored Parks as interim chief, but the decision was up to the Police Commission. Fisher thought it unfair to give anyone an advantage by making him the interim chief and held out for someone who was not an applicant to replace Williams. The commission appointed Lewis on a 3–2 vote. Lewis was a decisive interim chief who made it easier for his successor by tackling sensitive issues and making key personnel changes, some of them unpopular. In the process he earned the gratitude of Riordan.

59. While running for reelection, Riordan had met with four influential black leaders who were supporting him—Congressman Julian Dixon, County Supervisor Yvonne Brathwaite Burke, Reverend Cecil Murray, and John Mack of the Urban League—and gave them the impression he backed Parks. Riordan told me that his commitment to Parks was only for the job of interim chief, but he would have disappointed his African-American supporters if he had chosen Kroeker.

60. Parks made this comment in the mayor's office after his appointment. He told me that the department needed to pay more attention to the behavioral problems of officers who suffered job stress.

61. Chick and Alatorre made these comments to me after the appointment of Parks.

62. Letter from Captain Robert Gale to the Chief of Police dated June 22, 1994. See "Dismissal of Officer Upheld," by Jaxon Van Derbeken, *Daily News,* June 29, 1994.

63. Wind originally was awarded $86,000 by a judge. The city council, led by Mark Ridley-Thomas, wanted him to receive no compensation. In 1997, a court awarded Wind $20,000.

64. The *Los Angeles Times* reported on February 23, 1996, that a hundred people attended this dinner and that half as many, led by Jesse Jackson, marched outside in protest. Edwin Powell told me that four hundred people attended the dinner.

65. Robert Deitz, *Willful Injustice,* p. 11.

66. This is based on the *Los Angeles Times* accounts in "2 Die as Gunman Seeks Koon at Halfway House," by Ralph Frammolino, November 24, 1995, and "Family Tells of Slain Gunman's Anger at Koon," by Tom Gorman and Bettina Boxall, November 25, 1995, and Koon's account to me of the incident.

67. Interview with Stacey Koon, December 4, 1995.

68. Koon told me that the reason he had worn jail fatigues when he testified at Rodney King's civil trial was that his civilian clothes no longer fit him.

69. Interview with Stacey Koon, December 4, 1995.

70. Interview with Rodney King, December 18, 1995.

71. Interview with Stacey Koon, December 4, 1995.

72. Powell told me this in a conversation in Judge Davies' courtroom while he was awaiting resentencing on September 26, 1996.

73. David Savage and Jim Newton, "Justices Uphold Lenient Sentences in King Beating," *Los Angeles Times,* June 14, 1996.

74. Under federal court rules in Los Angeles, the briefs filed by both sides in the sentencing hearing are not a public record.

75. Jim Newton, "Judge Refuses to Return Koon, Powell to Prison," *Los Angeles Times,* September 27, 1996.

76. Interview with Stacey Koon, June 13, 1996.

77. Interview with Stacey Koon, September 26, 1996.

78. Ibid.

79. Ibid.

Bibliography

BOOKS AND MANUSCRIPTS

Abelman, Nancy and John Lie. *Blue Dreams: Korean Americans and the Los Angeles Riots.* Cambridge, MA: Harvard University Press, 1995.

Brandon, S.G.F. *The Trial of Jesus of Nazareth.* New York: A Scarborough Book, Stein and Day, 1979.

Broome Jr., Homer F. *LAPD's Black History: 1886–1976.* Norwalk, CA: Stockton Trade Press, Inc., 1978.

Bugliosi, Vincent. *Outrage: The Five Reasons Why O. J. Simpson Got Away with Murder.* New York: W. W. Norton & Company, 1996.

Bullock, Paul, editor. *Watts: The Aftermath by the People of Watts.* New York: Grove Press, Inc., 1969.

Center for the Study of Democratic Institutions. *The Police: One of a Series of Interviews on the American Character.* An Interview by Donald McDonald with William H. Parker, Chief of Police of Los Angeles with a Comment by William C. Baggs. The Fund for the Republic, 1962.

Cohen, Jerry and William S. Murphy. *Burn, Baby, Burn! The Los Angeles Race Riot, August 1965.* New York: E. P. Dutton & Co., Inc., 1966.

Conot, Robert. *Rivers of Blood, Years of Darkness.* New York: Bantam Books, 1967.

Cose, Ellis. *The Rage of a Privileged Class.* New York: HarperCollins, 1993.

Darden, Christopher with Jess Walter. *In Contempt.* New York: Regan Books, 1996.

Davis, Edward M. *Staff One: A Perspective on Effective Police Management.* Englewood Cliffs, NJ: Prentice-Hall, Inc., 1978.

Davis, Mike. *City of Quartz.* New York: Vintage Books, 1992.

Dear, Michael J., H. Eric Schockman and Greg Hise, editors. *Rethinking Los Angeles.* Thousand Oaks, CA: Sage Publications, 1996.

Deitz, Robert. *Willful Injustice: A Post-O. J. Look at Rodney King, American Justice, and Trial by Race.* Washington, D.C.: Regnery Publishing, Inc., 1996.

Dimitrius, Jo-Ellan Huebner. Abstract of the Dissertation: *The Representative Jury: Fact or Fallacy?* Claremont Graduate School, 1984.

Domanick, Joe. *To Protect and To Serve: The LAPD's Century of War in the City of Dreams.* New York: Pocket Books, 1994.

Fletcher, George P. *With Justice for Some: Protecting Victims' Rights in Criminal Trials.* New York: Addison-Wesley Publishing Company, 1996.

Fogelson, Robert M. *The Fragmented Metropolis: Los Angeles, 1850–1930.* Berkeley: University of California Press, 1993.

Fuhrman, Mark. *Murder in Brentwood.* Washington, D.C.: Regnery Publishing, Inc., 1997.

Garcia, Mario T. *Memories of Chicano History: The Life and Narrative of Bert Corona.* Berkeley: University of California Press, 1994.

Gates, Daryl F. with Diane K. Shah. *Chief: My Life in the LAPD.* New York: Bantam Books, 1992.

Gates, Daryl F. with Diane K. Shah. *Chief: My Life in the LAPD.* New York: Bantam Books, 1993. (Paperback edition)

Goldstein, Fred and Stan Goldstein. *Prime-Time Television: A Pictorial History from Milton Berle to "Falcon Crest".* New York: An Opus Book, Crown Publishers, Inc., 1983.

Gooding-Williams, Robert, editor. *Reading Rodney King, Reading Urban Uprising.* New York: Routledge, Inc., 1993.

Grier, William H. M.D. and Price M. Cobbs, M.D. *Black Rage.* New York: Bantam Books, 1969.

Hazen, Don, editor. *Inside the L.A. Riots: What really happened—and why it will happen again.* New York: Institute for Alternative Journalism, 1992.

Koon, Stacey C. *The Public Guardians: The Lives, Times and Ideas of the Great Law Enforcers Who Contributed to the Theory and Concepts of American Policing.* Master thesis at California State University, Los Angeles, April 1978.

Koon, Sgt. Stacey C., LAPD with Robert Deitz. *Presumed Guilty: The Tragedy of the Rodney King Affair.* Washington, D.C.: Regnery Gateway, 1992.

Los Angeles 2000 Committee. *LA 2000: a city for the future.* Los Angeles: The 2000 Partnership, 1988.

Los Angeles Times Staff. *Understanding The Riots: Los Angeles Before and After the Rodney King Case.* Los Angeles: Los Angeles Times, 1992.

Marc, David and Robert J. Thompson. *Prime Time, Prime Movers.* Boston: Little, Brown and Co., 1992.

McDonald, Donald. Interview with LAPD Chief William Parker, 1962. See Center for the Study of Democratic Institutions.

McWilliams, Carey. *Southern California: An Island on the Land.* Santa Barbara and Salt Lake City: Peregrine Smith, Inc., 1946, 1973.

Meyer, Greg. *Nonlethal Weapons vs. Conventional Police Tactics: The Los Angeles Police Department Experience.* Master thesis at California State University, Los Angeles, March 1991.

Owens, Tom with Rod Browning. *Lying Eyes: The Truth Behind the Corruption and Brutality of the LAPD and the Beating of Rodney King.* New York: Thunder's Mouth Press, 1994.

Pate, Antony and Edwin E. Hamilton. *The Big Six: Policing America's Largest Cities.* Washington, D.C.: Police Foundation, 1991.

Payne, J. Gregory and Scott C. Ratzan. *Tom Bradley: The Impossible Dream.* Santa Monica, CA: Roundtable Publishing Inc., 1986.

Reich, Kenneth. *Making It Happen: Peter Ueberroth and the 1984 Olympics.* Santa Barbara: Capra Press, 1986.

Rieff, David. *Los Angeles: Capital of the Third World.* New York: Simon & Schuster, 1991.

Rothmiller, Mike and Ivan G. Goldman. *L.A. Secret Police: Inside the LAPD Elite Spy Network.* New York: Pocket Books, 1992.

Skerry, Peter. *Mexican Americans: The Ambivalent Minority.* Cambridge, MA: Harvard University Press, 1993.

Skolnick, Jerome H. and James J. Fyfe. *Above the Law: Police and the Excessive Use of Force.* New York: The Free Press, 1993.

Smith, Anna Deavere. *Twilight: Los Angeles, 1992.* New York: Anchor Books, 1994.

Sonenshein, Raphael J. *Politics in Black and White: Race and Power in Los Angeles.* Princeton, NJ: Princeton University Press, 1993.

Sparrow, Malcolm K., Mark H Moore and David M. Kennedy. *Beyond 911: A New Era For Policing.* New York: Basic Books, Inc., 1990.

Steinberg, James B., David W. Lyon, Mary E. Vaiana, editors. *Urban America: Policy Choices for Los Angeles and the Nation.* Santa Monica, CA: RAND, 1992.

Ueberroth, Peter with Richard Levin and Amy Quinn. *Made in America: His Own Story.* New York: William Morrow and Company, Inc., 1985.

Vernon, Robert. *L.A. Justice: Lessons from the Firestorm.* Colorado Springs, CO: Focus on the Family, 1993.

Walters, Dan. *The New California: Facing the 21st Century.* 2nd Ed. Sacramento: California Journal Press, 1992.

Webb, Jack. *The Badge.* Englewood Cliffs, NJ: Prentice-Hall, Inc., 1958.

West, Cornel. *Race Matters.* Boston: Beacon Press, 1993.

Williams, Chief Willie L. LAPD with Bruce B. Henderson. *Taking Back our Streets: Fighting Crime in America.* New York: A Lisa Drew Book/Scribner, 1996.

Wilson, James Q. *Thinking About Crime,* Rev. Ed. New York: Basic Books, Inc., 1983.

Wister, Owen. *The Virginian: A Horseman of the Plains.* New York: The Heritage Press, 1902.

Woods, Joseph G. *The Progressives and the Police: Urban Reform and the Professionalization of the American Police.* Doctoral thesis in history, University of California, Los Angeles, 1973.

Wright, Richard. *Black Boy: A Record of Childhood and Youth.* New York: Harper & Row, 1937.

ARTICLES AND DOCUMENTS

ABC News. *Day One,* April 11, 1993.

_____ . *Nightline,* "First King Trial Jury Foreman Speaks," March 8, 1993.

_____ . *Nightline,* "Moment of Crisis: Anatomy of a Riot," May 28, 1992.

Abrahamson, Alan. "Police Cleared of Tainting Evidence," *Los Angeles Times,* April 10, 1996.

Anderson, David C. "The Crime Funnel," *The New York Times Magazine,* June 12, 1994.

Angel, Carol. "Profile: Judge Betty B. Fletcher," *Daily Journal,* October 21, 1992.

Assembly Special Committee on the Los Angeles Crisis. "To Rebuild Is Not Enough: Final Report and Recommendations," September 28, 1992.

Associated Press. "Acquitted Sergeant Writes of Beatings," *Los Angeles Times,* May 17, 1992.

_____ . "King Guilty of Hit-Run, Acquitted of Battery," July 12, 1996.

Barrett, Beth and David Parrish. "The Record Against LAPD: 254 Officers Named in 3 or More Excessive-Force Cases," *Daily News,* June 9, 1991.

_____ . "Juries, Attorneys Find Fault Where Department Finds None," *Daily News,* June 9, 1991.

Bendixen & Associates. "Public Opinion Survey of Residents of South Central Los Angeles and Pico Union," April 1993.

Berger, Leslie and Eric Malnic. "Death of First LAPD Woman Officer Killed in Line of Duty Came During Routine Stop," *Los Angeles Times,* February 23, 1994.

Bowles, Jennifer. "Rodney King Arrested in Domestic Dispute," Associated Press, June 26, 1992.

Boxall, Bettina. "Self-Assured Judge Doesn't Avoid Unpopular Stands," *Los Angeles Times,* November 16, 1991.

Boyarsky, Bill. "A Cowboy Cop with a Thoughtful Side Confronts the L.A. of the '80s," *Governing,* December 1988.

_____ . "Dead-End Realities and Recovery," *Los Angeles Times,* April 14, 1993.

_____ . "Echoes of the McCone Commission," *Los Angeles Times,* May 3, 1991.

_____ . "Gates Discusses Police Issues—Past, Present, Future," *Los Angeles Times,* March 27, 1978.

_____ . "Riordan Shows a Steady Hand in Leading a Rattled City," *Los Angeles Times,* January 23, 1994.

Boyer, Edward J. "Denny Juror Says Riot Fears Did Not Influence Verdicts," *Los Angeles Times,* October 26, 1993.

_____ . "Denny Testified, Hugs Mothers of Defendants," *Los Angeles Times,* August 26, 1993.

_____ . "Motorist Beaten in Riots Cannot Identify Attackers," *Los Angeles Times,* August 25, 1993.

Boyer, Edward J. and Andrea Ford. "Williams Given Maximum 10 Years in Denny Beating," *Los Angeles Times,* December 8, 1993.

Boyer, Edward J. and John L. Mitchell. "Attempted Murder Acquittal, Deadlock Wind Up Denny Trial," *Los Angeles Times,* October 21, 1993.

Boyer, Peter J. "Looking for Justice in L.A.," *The New Yorker,* March 15, 1993.

_____ . "The Selling of Rodney King," *Vanity Fair,* July 1992.

Braun, Stephen and Leslie Berger. "Chaos and Frustration at Florence and Normandie," *Los Angeles Times*, May 15, 1992.

Butterfield, Fox. "Behind the Badge," *The New York Times*, March 2, 1996.

Cabrera, Yvette. "Latino Newcomers May Rely Less on Aid," *Daily News*, July 30, 1997.

Cannon, Lou. "A Year After Riots, 'Lotus Land' Seeks to Shed Badlands Image," *The Washington Post*, April 30, 1993.

_____ . "Bradley, Black Leaders Try to Head Off Violence," *The Washington Post*, April 28, 1992.

_____ . "For Many in L.A., No Vote and No Say," *The Washington Post*, May 17, 1993.

_____ . "In the Two King Beating Trials, Almost Everything Was Different," *The Washington Post*, April 18, 1993.

_____ . "King Arrest Said to Follow Guidelines," *The Washington Post*, March 18, 1993.

_____ . "New Chief Takes the Helm of L.A. Police Department," *The Washington Post*, July 1, 1992.

_____ . "New King Trial Unfolds in the Same Troubled City," *Santa Barbara News-Press*, March 9, 1993.

_____ . "Riordan Names Black Officer to Head LAPD," *The Washington Post*, August 7, 1997.

_____ . "Scars Remain Five Years After Los Angeles Riots," *The Washington Post*, April 28, 1997.

_____ . "Southern California's Boom Is Latino-Led," *The Washington Post*, July 12, 1997.

_____ . "The New Blue Line: A Police Force in Transition Searches for Leadership," *California Journal*, July 1997.

_____ . "When Thin Blue Line Retreated, L.A. Riot Went Out of Control," *The Washington Post*, May 10, 1992.

Cannon, Lou and Jessica Crosby. "Buffeted Los Angeles Police Department is Described as Demoralized," *The Washington Post*, July 24, 1993.

_____ . "Defense Rests in King Beating Case to Avoid Grilling of Officer Powell," *The Washington Post*, April 1, 1993.

Castaneda, Ruben and Paul Taylor. "L.A. Residents Face Grim Reality of Devastation," *The Washington Post*, May 3, 1992.

Cawthon, Deborah. "Chief Gates Defends his Enforcement of Ban on Choke Hold," *Daily News*, June 16, 1982.

_____ . "Death Sparks Furor over LAPD Choke-Hold Policy," *Daily News*, April 11, 1982.

_____ . "Family of Police Choke Hold Victim Express Anger," *Daily News*, May 23, 1982.

Chang, Edward Taehan. "Perspective on Korean Americans," *Los Angeles Times*, May 31, 1994.

Christopher Commission, see Independent Commission on the Los Angeles Police Department.

Cohen, Jerry. "Lore and Legend of Ed Davis," *Los Angeles Times*, December 18, 1977.

Conklin, Ellis E. and Aurelio Rojas. "Watts: 20 Years After the Madness; Little Change Noted Since the Days of 'burn, baby burn'," UPI, July 30, 1985.

Connelly, Michael and Jim Newton. "Gates, Special Unit Found Liable for Robbers' Deaths," *Los Angeles Times*, March 31, 1992.

Courtroom Television Network. "The 'Rodney King' Case: What the Jury Saw in *California v. Powell*," VHS videocassette, 1992.

Deutsch, Linda. "Jurors Deliberate for Sixth Day, Officer Calls King 'Political Puppet'," Associated Press, April 28, 1992.

Doherty, Jake. "Black-Korean Alliance Says Talk Not Enough, Disbands," *Los Angeles Times*, December 24, 1992.

Dotson, David. "Council's Action Ensures a One-Term Police Chief," *Los Angeles Times*, June 25, 1995.

Du Brow, Rick and Greg Braxton. "TV Stations Tread Easily on Coverage of Unrest," *Los Angeles Times*, December 16, 1992.

Duignan-Cabrera, Anthony and Michael Connelly. "Sentencings Reopen L.A.'s Painful Wounds," *Los Angeles Times*, August 5, 1993.

Duke, Lynne. "Black in LAPD Blue; Officers Voice Shock at Beating," *The Washington Post*, March 31, 1991.

Duke, Lynne and Gabriel Escobar. "A Looting Binge Born of Necessity, Opportunity," *The Washington Post*, May 10, 1992.

Dunn, Ashley. "Looters, Merchants Put Koreatown Under the Gun," *Los Angeles Times*, May 2, 1992.

Dunn, Ashley and Andrea Ford. "The Man Swept Up in the Furor," *Los Angeles Times*, March 17, 1991.

Easton, Nina J. "Power to the Pastor," *Los Angeles Times Magazine*, August 16, 1992.

Edmonds, Patricia. "For Juries, High Anxiety," *USA Today*, October 14, 1993.

Ferrell, David. "Taps for a Police Legend on 77th Street," *Los Angeles Times*, March 3, 1995.

Fiore, Faye and Frank Clifford. "Mystery Mayor," *Los Angeles Times Magazine*, July 11, 1993.

Ford, Andrea and Daryl Kelley. "King Case To Be Tried In Ventura County," *Los Angeles Times*, November 27, 1991.

Ford, Andrea and Jim Newton. "Victim's Sister Ends Emotional Testimony," *Los Angeles Times*, February 7, 1995.

Ford, Andrea and John H. Lee. "Racial Tensions Blamed in Girl's Death," *Los Angeles Times*, March 20, 1991.

Ford, Andrea and Tracy Wilkinson. "Grocer is Convicted in Teen Killing," *Los Angeles Times*, October 12, 1991.

Frammolino, Ralph. "2 Die as Gunman Seeks Koon at Halfway House," *Los Angeles Times*, November 24, 1995.

Freed, David and Ted Rohrlich. "LAPD Slow in Coping with Wave of Unrest," *Los Angeles Times*, May 1, 1992.

Gates, Daryl F. "Discipline in the LAPD," Letter to the Editor, *Los Angeles Times*, July 2, 1995.

Gilmore, Janet. "Life Remains Full of Legal Problems for Multimillionaire Rodney King," *Daily News*, July 8, 1996.

Golab, Jan. "The Friends of Fuhrman," *Los Angeles Magazine*, October 1995.

Gonzalez, Hector and Courtenay Edelhart. "Charge Surfaces: Black Students Claim Officers Attacked Them," *The Wave*, March 13, 1991.

Gorman, Tom and Bettina Boxall. "Family Tells of Slain Gunman's Anger at Koon," *Los Angeles Times*, November 25, 1995.

Governor's Commission on the Los Angeles Riots. "Violence in the City—An End or a Beginning?," December 2, 1965.

Granger, David. "The Unforgiven," *GQ*, March 1996.

Grigsby, J. Eugene. "Rebuilding Los Angeles: One Year Later," *National Civic Review*, Fall 1993.

_____ . "The Aftermath of Los Angeles: What Next?," October 4, 1992.

Hall, Carla. "Boss Got Break They Wouldn't Get, Officers Say," *Los Angeles Times*, June 22, 1995.

Harrison, Lt. Gen. William H. (U.S. Army Ret.). "Assessment of the Performance of the California National Guard During the Civil Disturbances in Los Angeles, April & May 1992," Report to the Honorable Pete Wilson, Governor, State of California, October 2, 1992.

Hayes-Bautista, David E. "Demographic Changes and Implications for Health: U.S.A. 1997–2020."

Hill-Holtzman, Nancy and Jim Newton. "Lawyer Adds Bizarre Note to Denny Case," *Los Angeles Times*, August 13, 1992.

Hoffman, Paul. "Double Jeopardy Wars: The Case for a Civil Rights 'Exception'," *UCLA Law Review*, February 1994.

Hubler, Shawn. "Black Leaders Accuse Gates of Inflaming Racial Tensions," *Los Angeles Times*, April 29, 1992.

_____ . "New Site Ok'd for Grocer's Murder Trial," *Los Angeles Times*, August 28, 1991.

Hubler, Shawn and John L. Mitchell. "A Legacy as Complex as the '92 Riots," *Los Angeles Times*, April 20, 1997.

Hurst, John and Leslie Berger. "Crisis in the LAPD/The Rodney G. King Beating; Four Officers—Their Paths to Trial," *Los Angeles Times*, February 3, 1992.

Hutchinson, Earl Ofari. "The Political Victimization of Laurence Powell and Stacey Koon," *Ofari's Bi-Monthly*, September–October 1993.

Independent Commission on the Los Angeles Police Department. "Report," July 9, 1991.

_____ . "Executive Session: Testimony of Chief Daryl Gates, June 14, 1991."

_____ . "Selected Messages from the LAPD Mobile Digital Terminal System, November 1, 1989–March 4, 1991."

_____ . "Testimony of Assistant Chief David D. Dotson, June 14, 1991."

_____ . "Testimony of Assistant Chief Robert L. Vernon, June 14, 1991."

_____ . "Testimony of Former Assistant Chief Jesse Brewer, June 19, 1991."

Jones, Charisse. "Deliberations in Trial of Grocer Interrupted for Ruling on Dispute," *Los Angeles Times*, October 10, 1991.

Jones Jr., Malcolm. "Kick Back with Crime," *Newsweek*, July 4, 1994.

Kang, K. Connie and Marc Lacey. "Court Rejects Appeal of Rules for Liquor Stores," *Los Angeles Times*, July 15, 1994.

Katz, Jesse. "Crips, Bloods Look Back—and Ahead—With Anger," *Los Angeles Times*, March 21, 1993.

Katz, Jesse and Frank Clifford. "Many Find Verdict Fair, But There Is Still Outrage," *Los Angeles Times*, October 12, 1991.

Katz, Jesse and John H. Lee. "Conflict Brings Tragic End to Similar Dreams of Life," *Los Angeles Times*, April 8, 1991.

Katz, Jesse and Stephanie Chavez. "Blacks Seek to Channel Anger Over Sentence," *Los Angeles Times*, November 17, 1991.

Kelley, Daryl. "Simi Valley Tops List of Safest U.S. Cities," *Los Angeles Times*, May 2, 1994.

Koon, Stacey C. "'It's Time for Gates to Step Down'," *Los Angeles Times*, May 12, 1991.

Krikorian, Greg. "Co-Workers Paint Different Portrait of Mark Fuhrman," *Los Angeles Times*, November 8, 1995.

_____ . "Review of 35 Fuhrman Cases Reveals No Racism," *Los Angeles Times*, January 19, 1996.

Lacey, Marc. "Riordan Leads Drive to Computerize LAPD," *Los Angeles Times*, August 17, 1994.

Larsen, Peter. "Reaction Ranges from Jubilation to Indignation," *Daily News*, October 19, 1993.

Laski, Beth. "Man Who Shot Video Says He Did Right Thing," *Daily News*, March 7, 1991.

Lee, Gary. "On a Crusade To Improve Stricken Area," *The Washington Post*, April 17, 1993.

Levenson, Laurie L. "Reiner Is Out of Bounds," *Los Angeles Times*, November 22, 1991.

_____ . "The Future of State and Federal Civil Rights Prosecutions: The Lessons of the Rodney King Trial," *UCLA Law Review*, February 1994.

Lieberman, Paul. "King Jury Reflects Growing Impact of Racial Diversity," *Los Angeles Times*, February 28, 1993.

Linder, Lee. "Philly Commissioner Ready to Assume Police Chief Job in Los Angeles," Associated Press, May 15, 1992.

Los Angeles County and City commissions on human relations. "McCone Revisited: A Focus on Solutions to Continuing Problems in South Central Los Angeles," January 1985.

Los Angeles Police Department. *Los Angeles Police Department Opinion Survey*, 1991.

Lozano, Carlos V. "The Times Poll: Verdicts Anger Ventura County," *Los Angeles Times*, May 7, 1992.

Lynch, Rene. "King's New Attorney Known for Testing Limits of the Law," *Los Angeles Times*, October 20, 1992.

_____ . "Minority Leaders Say Verdict Seen As Racist Could Blow Lid Off Powder Keg," *Daily News*, April 5, 1992.

Mader, Katherine. "Domestic Violence in the Los Angeles Police Department: How Well Does the Los Angeles Police Department Police Its Own?," Report of the Domestic Violence Task Force, July 22, 1997.

Mann, Eric. "The Poverty of Corporatism," *The Nation*, March 29, 1993.

Manning, Timothy V., Terrance J. Manning, and Christopher S. Kawai. "Los Angeles City Fire Department 'Historical Overview Report' of the Los Angeles Civil Disturbance, April 29, 1992," October 1992.

McCone Commission, see Governor's Commission on the Los Angeles Riots.

McCone Revisited, see Los Angeles County and City commissions on human relations.

McDonnell, Patrick J. "Latino Merchants Stage Protest Over Lack of Riot Recovery Aid," *Los Angeles Times*, March 18, 1993.

McGreevy, Patrick and John Polich. "Mayor Says Public Good Is At Stake," *Daily News*, April 3, 1991.

McMillan, Penelope. "Korean-American Protesters Pelted from City Hall Windows," *Los Angeles Times*, July 8, 1992.

Merl, Jean. "Born From the Ashes of Watts, Center Dies in Flames of Riot," *Los Angeles Times*, May 2, 1992.

_____ . "The Mayor's Midterm Exam," *Los Angeles Times Magazine*, June 11, 1995.

Meyer, Greg. "Brutal by Default," *Los Angeles Daily Journal*, August 19, 1993.

_____ . "Finding a Safe Way to Subdue Violent Suspects," *Los Angeles Times*, June 14, 1994.

Meyer, Josh and Eric Malnic. "King Arrested, Then Freed, After Wife Is Injured During Argument," *Los Angeles Times*, June 27, 1992.

Mitchell, John L. "LAPD Discipline Urged for Officer in King Case," *Los Angeles Times*, December 11, 1992.

Mitchell, John L. and Tina Daunt. "King Jury's Voice of Reason Carried a Private Burden," *Los Angeles Times*, June 3, 1994.

Morain, Dan and Edward J. Boyer. "Lungren Calls Verdicts 'Body Blow' to Justice," *Los Angeles Times*, October 27, 1993.

Morrison, Patt. "After the Riots: The Search for Answers; Symbol of Pain Survives Flames; Neighbors Rescue Market where Latasha Harlins Was Killed," *Los Angeles Times*, May 7, 1992.

_____ . "The Undying Echo of Fate," *Los Angeles Times*, July 31, 1996.

Morrison, Peter A. and Ira S. Lowry. "A Riot of Color: The Demographic Setting of Civil Disturbance in Los Angeles," RAND, 1993.

Murphy, Barbara. "Koon Insists Every Blow Was Justified," *Daily News*, March 23, 1992.

_____ . "Satellite Dish Helps L.A. County Prosecutors Follow Trial," *Daily News*, March 6, 1992.

_____ . "Schism Grows Among Officers in Beating Trial," *Daily News*, April 3, 1992.

Murphy, Barbara and Dawn Webber. "Videotape Expected to Be Star Witness," *Daily News*, January 26, 1992.

Mydans, Seth. "Beating Case Prosecutors: 2 Styles Focus as One," *The New York Times*, March 5, 1993.

_____ . "Juror in Denny Case Recounts Stress And an Obsession With Legal Detail," *The New York Times*, October 27, 1993.

_____ . "Sudden Detours in Los Angeles Trial," *The New York Times*, February 24, 1993.

Newton, Jim. "2 Quit Police Panel, Saying Council Has Stymied Reforms," *Los Angeles Times*, June 30, 1995.

_____ . "3 Plead Not Guilty in Denny Case; Black Trial Judge Removed," *Los Angeles Times*, August 26, 1992.

_____ . "Beaten King Was 'Shown Off' by 2 Officers, Jury Told," *Los Angeles Times*, February 26, 1993.

_____ . "Chief Sees Riordan as Force in Controversy, Sources Say," *Los Angeles Times*, May 26, 1995.

_____ . "CHP Officer Weeps as She Recounts Beating," *Los Angeles Times*, March 27, 1993.

_____ . "Community-Based Policing Slowly Takes Root at LAPD," *Los Angeles Times*, June 21, 1996.

_____ . "Denny Defendant Admits to Attack on Tape," *Los Angeles Times*, August 8, 1992.

_____ . "Final Prosecution Witnesses Criticize Report on King," *Los Angeles Times*, March 16, 1993.

_____ . "Help Wanted," *Los Angeles Times Magazine*, July 27, 1997.

_____ . "How the Case Was Won," *Los Angeles Times Magazine*, June 27, 1993.

_____ . "Judge Refuses to Return Koon, Powell to Prison," *Los Angeles Times*, September 27, 1996.

_____ . "King Case Is Handed to Jury, Deliberations Resume Today," *Los Angeles Times*, April 12, 1993.

_____ . "King Case Prosecutors Gamble on Eyewitnesses," *Los Angeles Times*, March 7, 1993.

_____ . "King Jury Sees Key Videotape; Prosecutors Rest," *Los Angeles Times*, April 7, 1993.

_____ . "Koon, Powell Get 2½ Years in Prison," *Los Angeles Times*, August 5, 1993.

_____ . "L.A. Police Hampered by Woeful State of Equipment," *Los Angeles Times*, October 31, 1994.

_____ . "L.A. Trials Show 'Blind Justice' Is Hard to Achieve," *Los Angeles Times*, October 24, 1993.

_____ . "LAPD Training Practices Are Slipping, Report Says," *Los Angeles Times*, April 18, 1996.

_____ . "Long Prison Terms for Powell and Koon Urged," *Los Angeles Times*, May 29, 1993.

_____ . "Number of Arrests by LAPD Plunges Since '91," *Los Angeles Times*, March 13, 1996.

_____ . "Officers' Indictment Called Political," *Los Angeles Times*, August 7, 1992.

_____ . "Parks Calls Cutting Crime Key Test of Success as Chief," *Los Angeles Times*, August 7, 1997.

_____ . "Prospective King Jurors Get Bias Questionnaire," *Los Angeles Times*, February 4, 1993.

_____ . "Riordan Picks Parks as New Chief of Police," *Los Angeles Times*, August 6, 1997.

_____ . "Riots' Shadow Hangs Over King Jury Selection," *Los Angeles Times*, January 31, 1993.

_____ . "Spotlight Stolen in Denny Drama," *Los Angeles Times*, September 9, 1992.

_____ . "Supreme Court to Write Next Chapter in King Case," *Los Angeles Times*, January 7, 1996.

_____ . "When LAPD Officers Can't Shoot Straight," *Los Angeles Times*, May 4, 1996.

_____ . "'I Was Just Trying to Stay Alive,' King Tells Federal Jury," *Los Angeles Times*, March 10, 1993.

Newton, Jim and Henry Weinstein. "Court Orders Longer Sentences for Koon, Powell," *Los Angeles Times*, August 20, 1994.

Nikos, Karen. "Ex-LAPD Officer Gets Three Years' Probation in Beating Incidents," *Daily News*, October 26, 1991.

Nocera, Joseph. "City of Hype," *GQ*, April 1993.

Norris, Michele L., Avis Thomas-Lester and David Von Drehle. "In L.A., Death Drew Few Distinctions," *The Washington Post*, May 11, 1992.

Novak, C.A. "The Years of Controversy: The Los Angeles Police Commission, 1991–1993," Police Foundation, 1995.

Olivo, Antonio. "Cultivating Understanding," *Los Angeles Times*, March 27, 1996.

Orlov, Rick. "Gates Reinstatement Upheld," *Daily News*, May 15, 1991.

Orlov, Rick and Jaxon Van Derbeken. "Mayor Wants Racism Probe: 21 of Its Officers, Not 15, Were at Beating, Department Says," *Daily News*, March 20, 1991.

Osborne, D. M. "Reaching for Doubt," *The American Lawyer*, September 1992.

Parker, W. H. "The California Crime Rise," *Journal of Criminal Law, Criminology and Police Science*, 1957.

Pastor Jr., Manuel, Ph.D. "Latinos and the Los Angeles Uprising: The Economic Context," *The Tomas Rivera Center*, 1993.

Perez-Pena, Richard. "Judge in Police Beating Trial Sets Aside Confusion," *The New York Times*, March 6, 1992.

Piccarreta, Michael L. and Jefferson Keenan. "Dual Sovereigns: Successive Prosecutions and Politically Correct Verdicts," *The Champions*, September/October 1995.

Pope, Lisa. "Vernon Defends Job Conduct," *Daily News*, June 12, 1991.

Rainer, Peter. "'Falling Down' Trips Over Its Own Hate," *Los Angeles Times*, March 15, 1993.

Rainey, James. "A Man of Conflicting Images," *Los Angeles Times*, August 3, 1995.

_____ . "Final Suit Over LAPD's Use of Chokehold Settled," *Los Angeles Times*, September 29, 1993.

Rainey, James and Marc Lacey. "Riordan's First Year at the Helm," *Los Angeles Times*, July 3, 1994.

Ramos, George. "When Loving L.A. Turns to Heartache," *Los Angeles Times*, May 4, 1992.

Reckard, E. Scott. "L.A. Rebuild Chief Admits Frustration," Associated Press, September 30, 1992.

Reinhold, Robert. "Justice Dept. Is Left Shaken by Disclosure in King Case," *The New York Times*, November 21, 1992.

Rivera, Carla. "2nd King Trial Revives L.A.'s Fears and Hopes," *Los Angeles Times*, February 3, 1993.

_____ . "Riot Still Taking Its Toll," *Los Angeles Times*, March 28, 1993.

Rivera, Carla and Dean E. Murphy. "Ueberroth Quits Rebuild L.A. Post," *Los Angeles Times*, May 22, 1993.

Rofe, John and Patrick McGreevy. "Gates Lashes Out at Critics," *Daily News*, March 14, 1991.

Rohrlich, Ted. "Majority Says Police Brutality Is Common," *Los Angeles Times*, March 10, 1991.

Rohrlich, Ted and John L. Mitchell. "LAPD Widely Saluted for Swiftly Quelling Incident," *Los Angeles Times*, December 16, 1992.

Rohrlich, Ted and Leslie Berger. "Lack of Materiel Slowed Police Response to Riots," *Los Angeles Times*, May 24, 1992.

Saar, Mayrav. "After Mixed Verdict, King Looks to the Future," *Los Angeles Times*, July 12, 1996.

Sahagun, Louis and John Schwada. "Measure to Reform LAPD Wins Decisively," *Los Angeles Times*, June 3, 1992.

Savage, David and Jim Newton. "Justices Uphold Lenient Sentences in King Beating," *Los Angeles Times*, June 14, 1996.

Scheer, Robert. "Los Angeles Times Interview: Maxine Waters; Veteran Legislator Makes People Angry—But She's Never Ignored," *Los Angeles Times*, May 16, 1993.

_____ . "Los Angeles Times Interview: Peter Ueberroth," *Los Angeles Times*, May 17, 1992.

Scott, Allen J. and E. Richard Brown, editors. "South-Central Los Angeles: Anatomy of an Urban Crisis," Working Paper Series, The Lewis Center for Regional Policy Studies, University of California, Los Angeles, June 1993.

Senate Special Task Force on a New Los Angeles. "New Initiatives for a New Los Angeles, Final Report and Recommendations," December 9, 1992.

Serrano, Richard A. "Attorneys at War Over Representation of King," *Los Angeles Times*, May 26, 1993.

_____ . "CHP Officer Describes Chase, Beating of King," *Los Angeles Times*, March 7, 1992.

_____ . "Key Witness Not on List for King Case," *Los Angeles Times*, February 23, 1993.

_____. "King Case Shifts to Courtroom in Simi Valley," *Los Angeles Times*, February 4, 1992.

_____. "King Tells of Beating, Racial Taunts by Police," *Los Angeles Times*, January 16, 1992.

_____. "'They Hit Me, So I Hit Back'," *Los Angeles Times*, October 4, 1992.

Serrano, Richard A. and Carlos V. Lozano. "Jury Picked for King Trial; No Blacks Chosen," *Los Angeles Times*, March 3, 1992.

Serrano, Richard A. and Tracy Wilkinson. "All 4 in King Beating Acquitted," *Los Angeles Times*, April 30, 1992.

Shah, Diane K. "Playboy interview: Daryl Gates; Los Angeles, California Chief of Police," *Playboy*, August 1991.

_____. "Who Killed Willie?" *Los Angeles Magazine*, July 1997.

Shaw, David. "Media Failed to Examine Alleged LAPD Abuses," *Los Angeles Times*, May 26, 1992.

Simon, Stephanie. "Penalties More Severe in LAPD Ranks, Cases Show," *Los Angeles Times*, June 23, 1995.

Slaughter, John Brooks. "'I Was Stunned' by the Frequency and Bravado of Scurrilous Comments," *Los Angeles Times*, July 14, 1991.

Staff Reports. "Profile: Judge Stanley Martin Weisberg, Los Angeles Superior Court," *Daily Journal*, June 1, 1989.

State Bar of Arizona, Continuing Legal Education. "Spin Doctors Jury Consultants: Effective Use & Ethical Responsibilities," April 1994.

Steinberg, Arnold. "Los Angeles County Voters–Change of Venue Study," April 20, 1991.

Stevenson, Richard W. "California Goes From Economic Leader to Laggard," *The New York Times*, October 17, 1991.

Stolberg, Sheryl. "Karlin to Remain on Criminal Bench," *Los Angeles Times*, November 28, 1991.

_____. "Karlin Upheld in Sentencing of Grocer," *Los Angeles Times*, April 22, 1992.

Stone, Keith and Rick Orlov. "Protesters Shoot, Beat, Loot, Burn," *Daily News*, April 30, 1992.

Takahashi, Dean. "Ueberroth Asks High-Tech Crowd for Hand," *Los Angeles Times*, May 7, 1992.

Tamaki, Julie. "Use of Force a Gray Area for Men in Blue," *Los Angeles Times*, June 26, 1993.

Taylor, Paul. "L.A. Police Paralysis During Riot Evident," *The Washington Post*, May 7, 1992.

Tobar, Hector and Leslie Berger. "Verdict Greeted With Relief and Elation Among LAPD Officers," *Los Angeles Times*, April 30, 1992.

Tontini, Linda. "Juror Says Tape Key to Decision," *North County Blade-Citizen*, April 18, 1993.

Tranquada, Jim. "King Says Officers Used Racial Slurs," *Daily News*, March 10, 1993.

_____. "Police Shy Away from Using Force," *Daily News*, March 5, 1995.

Ueberroth, Peter V. "What Will You Do for Your City?," Los Angeles Times, January 6, 1993.

Unger, Henry. "Profile: Judge Bernard J. Kamins, Los Angeles Superior Court," Daily Journal, March 6, 1987.

Useem, Dr. Bert and Commander David J. Gascon. "Riot Control and the Los Angeles Riot of 1992."

Van Derbeken, Jaxon. "Community Policing Needs Cited in Report," Daily News, November 27, 1994.

_____ . "Community-Policing Director Named in LAPD Revamp," Daily News, April 20, 1995.

_____ . "Foothill Division Head to Stay," Daily News, April 17, 1991.

_____ . "In the Eye of the King Storm," Daily News, February 2, 1992.

_____ . "Jovial Chief Jokes with Supporters," Daily News, April 6, 1991.

_____ . "LAPD Finds 1st Officer Guilty in King Beating," Daily News, December 11, 1992.

Wallace, Amy and David Ferrell. "Verdicts Greeted With Outrage and Disbelief," Los Angeles Times, April 30, 1992.

Wallace, Amy and John Hurst. "'Let's Get On With Life,' Denny Says After Jury Verdicts," Los Angeles Times, October 19, 1993.

Wallace, Amy and K. Connie Kang. "One Year Later, Hope and Anger Remain," Los Angeles Times, April 30, 1993.

Wallace, Charles P. "Bar-Arm Choke Hold Banned," Los Angeles Times, May 7, 1982.

_____ . "City Considers Policy Change on Chokeholds," Los Angeles Times, May 12, 1982.

Webber, Dawn. "CHP Officer Says King Hit in Head," Daily News, March 7, 1992.

_____ . "King Prosecutors Lack Expert on Use of Force," Daily News, April 3, 1992.

_____ . "King Trial Raises Fears Over Policy," Daily News, March 30, 1992.

_____ . "No Blacks Chosen for King Case Jury," Daily News, March 3, 1992.

Webster, William H. and Hubert Williams. "The City in Crisis," A Report by the Special Advisor to the Board of Police Commissioners on the Civil Disorder in Los Angeles, October 21, 1992.

Weinstein, Henry. "Keeping King Off Stand Was a Wise Move, Experts Say," Los Angeles Times, March 19, 1992.

_____ . "White Says the Jury Was the Worst Possible," Los Angeles Times, May 8, 1992.

West, Dick. "Chief Parker Collapses, Dies at Award Banquet," Los Angeles Times, July 17, 1966.

Whitman, David. "The Untold Story of the LA Riot," U.S. News & World Report, May 31, 1993.

Wielawski, Irene and Scott Harris. "Hospitals Practice Battlefield Medicine in Caring for Stream of Violence Victims," Los Angeles Times, May 2, 1992.

Wilgoren, Jodi. "City Council Wants to Slow Police Buildup," *Los Angeles Times*, May 20, 1996.

Wilkinson, Tracy and Frank Clifford. "Korean Grocer Who Killed Black Teen Gets Probation," *Los Angeles Times*, November 16, 1991.

Wilkinson, Tracy, Andrea Ford, and Tracy Wood. "Panel Urges Gates to Retire; Report on Police Cites Racism, Excess Force," *Los Angeles Times*, July 10, 1991.

Wilson, James Q. and George L. Kelling. "Broken Windows," *The Atlantic Monthly*, March 1982.

Yocum, Susan F. "Don't Tar Us All With the Fuhrman Brush," *Los Angeles Times*, September 1, 1995.

Young, Douglas. "Inner City Can't Get the Money," *Los Angeles Business Journal*, April 14–20, 1997.

Zoroya, Gregg. "For Juror No. 7, Fame Is the Game," *The Orange County Register*, August 1, 1993.

Index